The Aging Experience

The Aging Experience

An Introduction to Social Gerontology

Second Edition

RUSSELL A. WARD
State University of New York at Albany

1817

HARPER & ROW, PUBLISHERS, New York
Cambridge, Philadelphia, San Francisco,
London, Mexico City, São Paulo, Sydney

Sponsoring Editor: Alan McClare
Project Editor: Pamela Landau
Production Manager: Jeanie Berke
Compositor: ComCom Division of Haddon Craftsmen, Inc.
Printer and Binder: R. R. Donnelley & Sons Company
Art Studio: Fineline Illustrations, Inc.

The Aging Experience: An Introduction to Social Gerontology,
Second Edition

Library of Congress Cataloging in Publication Data

Ward, Russell A.
    The aging experience.

    Includes bibliographical references and index.
    1.   Gerontology--United States.   I.   Title.
HQ1064.U5W36   1984   305.2'6   83-22727
ISBN 0-06-046901-3

For My Moms:
Carol Jessop and Win Morgan

Contents

Preface *xi*

1 Introduction to the Study of Aging   **1**

Aging Themes in Literature *2*
The Development of a Science of Aging *2*
The Field of Social Gerontology *4*
Why Study Aging? *6*
The Definition of Old Age *7*
The Nature of Age Differences *9*
Methodological Issues *14*
Conceptual Frameworks in the Study of Aging *17*
Summary *19*

2 Characteristics of the Older Population   **21**

Demographic Characteristics *21*
Health *29*
Psychological Functioning *35*
Psychological Disorders and Related Problems *38*
Social and Economic Characteristics *42*
Some Cautionary Notes *48*
Summary *51*

3 Aging in Sociocultural and Historical Context   **53**

Aging in Preindustrial Societies *53*
Aging and Modernization *59*

The Aged in America   *63*
A Model of Age Stratification   *66*
Minority Aging   *75*
Summary   *80*

4 **The Psychological Experience of Aging**   82

Activity and Disengagement   *82*
A Life Course Perspective on Aging   *85*
Developmental Issues and Aging   *92*
Stress and Aging   *97*
Aging and the Self   *100*
Role Change and Socialization   *103*
Aging, Growth, and Age Stratification   *105*
Sex Differences and the Aging Experience   *106*
Successful Aging   *109*
Summary   *111*

5 **Images of Aging: Personal and Social**   113

Aging and the Social Self   *113*
Subjective Age Identity   *115*
Attitudes Toward Old People   *118*
Sources of Old-Age Attitudes   *124*
Consequences of Old-Age Stereotypes   *126*
Summary   *130*

6 **Work and Retirement**   132

Work and Aging   *133*
Retirement Issues   *138*
The Emergence of Retirement   *139*
The Decision to Retire   *142*
The Consequences of Retirement   *146*
Retirement Income   *159*
Preparation for Retirement   *169*
Summary   *173*

7 **The Use of Time: Opportunities and Constraints**   176

Leisure   *178*
Voluntary Associations   *186*
Education and Aging   *190*
Religion and Aging   *192*
The Volunteer Role   *195*
Social Change and the Use of Time   *197*
Summary   *198*

8 The Family Life of Older People   201

The Aging Couple   *202*
Divorce and Singlehood   *206*
Sexuality in Later Life   *207*
Widowhood   *209*
Aging and the Extended Family   *218*
The Grandparent Role   *225*
Aging and the Family: Some Conclusions   *228*
Summary   *229*

9 Older People in the Community   231

Social Networks   *232*
The Age Mix of Housing for the Aged   *238*
The Impact of Housing   *248*
Neighborhood and Community Contexts   *249*
Crime and the Elderly   *252*
Summary   *257*

10 The Politics of Age   259

Age Stratification and Age Conflict   *260*
Age and Political Participation   *261*
Age and Political Attitudes   *263*
Generations and Social Change   *267*
The Senior Movement: Past, Present, and Future   *269*
The Consequences of Aging Group Consciousness   *279*
Summary   *281*

11 Services for Older People   283

Institutionalization of the Aged   *285*
The Political Economy of Old-Age Institutions   *287*
The Impact of Institutionalization   *292*
Quality of Institutional Care   *298*
Community-Based Services for the Aged   *301*
Factors Affecting Delivery and Use of Services   *304*
The Government and Services for the Aged   *309*
Summary   *316*

12 Death and Dying   319

Death and Social Structure   *320*
Orientations Toward Death   *322*
Reactions to the Dying   *332*
Reactions of the Dying   *336*
Caring for the Dying   *340*

Bereavement   *343*
Euthanasia and the Right to Die   *348*
Summary   355

13 The Future of the Aging Experience   **358**

The Nature of Age Differences   *358*
Conceptual Frameworks   *359*
Aging in the Future   *360*
Policy and Planning for the Aged   *368*
The Future of Social Gerontology   *371*
Some Final Comments   *374*

REFERENCES   **375**

INDEX   **437**

Preface

The study of aging is a tremendously varied field. It is, of necessity, multidisciplinary, and this is its strength and its weakness. The blending of many disciplines—sociology, psychology, economics, biology, and so on—reminds us that human behavior is multifaceted. No single approach can lay claim to possession of "truth." Gerontology has long benefited from recognition of this fact. Yet the multiple "truths" of aging also make it an exceedingly complex topic, not easily grasped in its entirety.

This complexity makes writing a book about aging a difficult task best accomplished by narrowing the field to some degree. Although this book is intended as an introduction to knowledge and issues in gerontology, its focus is clearly sociological—*social* gerontology. The emphasis is on the nature of the aging experience as it is shaped by the social context within which it occurs.

I have attempted to make this book as comprehensive an overview of sociological aspects of aging as possible without overburdening the reader. In particular, a very lengthy list of references is cited. These references obviously include work that is clearly gerontological, but a conscious effort has also been made to include more general sociological references. This allows the reader an opportunity to understand the position of gerontological issues within broader sociological frameworks. Although material is included on aging in other cultures and societies, the focus is on aging and gerontology in the United States.

Chapter 1 is an introduction to the study of aging, its issues, and concerns. Chapter 2 is intended to be a resource chapter, providing the "facts and figures" that can inform later discussions. Chapters 3, 4, and 5 present the major theoretical themes that should be referred to throughout the book. Chapter 3 discusses cross-cultural differences in aging, integrating them into a general model of age stratification. Chapters 4 and 5 consider the social-psychological consequences of aging: developmental changes over the life course, personality, and the impact of aging on the self. These chapters lay the foundation for the remainder of the book.

Chapters 6 through 12 deal with particular substantive areas. Retirement and leisure are discussed in Chapters 6 and 7. Chapter 8 presents material on aging and the family, including marriage, widowhood, and extended family relationships. The community context of aging, encompassing problems of social integration and housing, is considered in Chapter 9. This is followed in Chapter 10 by a discussion of the politics of age and the potential for "senior power." Chapter 11 deals with service issues and Chapter 12 with the sociology of death and dying. Finally, Chapter 13 presents an overview and a look to the future of aging and of social gerontology.

Whereas the basic structure of this second edition is the same as in the first edition, the two editions are substantially different in other respects. Indeed, revision represented a significantly greater task than was originally envisioned. Much of this involves bringing the statistics and research citations up to date.

Other revisions represent changes in emphasis or focus. Recognizing the linkages between aging and the rest of the life cycle, a "life course" perspective is given greater emphasis throughout this edition. Material on minority aging has been substantially expanded (in Chapter 3), and some introduction to the biology of aging has been added to Chapter 2. Chapter 9 is now organized more generally around the effects of environment and social networks. These changes represent just some of the many incorporated into this second edition. Gerontology is a very "busy" field.

This is not a "how to" book on aging or a road map to "golden aging." There is, after all, only so much that can be learned from books. Malcolm Cowley, in *The View from 80,* notes:

> To enter the country of age is a new experience, different from what you supposed it to be. Nobody, man or woman, knows the country until he has lived in it and has taken out his citizenship papers.[1]

There are many ways to be "old." It is hoped, however, that this book will inform readers about the factors that shape the nature and quality of later life. This information can then perhaps be used to shape the reader's own aging experience, or that of others.

Inevitably, in a work of this scope there are too many people who have contributed to adequately acknowledge each individually. Whereas this book is not actually *for* older people, it is certainly *about* them, and a debt is owed to their willingness to be "studied." A debt is also owed to those researchers and thinkers who have contributed to the knowledge presented in this book.

Other more direct contributions need acknowledgment. This book has profited from suggestions and comments offered by Susan Sherman, Art Richardson,

[1]Malcom Cowley, *The View from 80.* New York: Penguin Books, 1982, pp. 2–3.

Mark LaGory, Vivian Wood, and Gordon Streib. Valuable suggestions were also made by the reviewers, Vern Bengtson, University of Southern California/Los Angeles; Robert Kastenbaum, Arizona State University; Nancy J. Osgood, Ph.D., Virginia Commonwealth University; and Vivian Wood, Ph.D., University of Wisconsin/Madison. I am more generally indebted to Vern Bengtson and Powell Lawton for their personal encouragement and scholarly inspiration. Students in my classes have also stimulated my thinking through their comments and questions. Carol Jessop and Billie Albrecht provided excellent typing assistance. My editors, Dick Heffron for the first edition and Alan McClare for the second edition, have assisted in many ways. Portions of the work for the second edition were completed while on sabbatical leave, for which I thank the State University of New York at Albany. Finally, I would like to thank Marjorie and Matthew for making everything so worthwhile.

Russell A. Ward

The Aging Experience

chapter *1*

Introduction to the Study of Aging

Aging and the aged have been subjects of interest throughout history. The sources of this interest are varied: Fascination with longevity and the dream of immortality, fear of the presumed "pathologies" of aging and the finality of death itself, conflict over the intergenerational transfer of power, humanitarian concern over the circumstances of the aged. Concern with the aging experience is heightened by the aging of the population in modern societies. The population aged 65 and older in the United States has grown from 3 million, or 4 percent, of the total population in 1900, to 25 million, or 11 percent, of the population in 1980; life expectancy has increased from the midforties to the midseventies. This aging presents individuals and societies with important challenges and opportunities.

For the individual there is the challenge of a greatly expanded life cycle, for most of us a span of 70 or 80 years. Today's elderly are pioneers in a world where old age is no longer unusual. But how well will they and we use this additional time? Will we simply live out patterns established in adolescence and young adulthood, or will greater longevity cause us to reexamine the patterning of our lives? Because these and many other questions confront all whose old age lies ahead, the subject of aging is attracting increased interest among young people.

The growing number of older people also presents challenges to the larger society. On the one hand, the aged have greater need for many types of services. As we shall see, many older persons are faced with poor health, poverty, inadequate housing, and related problems. On the other hand, older people increasingly belie negative stereotypes about their problems and capabilities. This raises ques-

1

tions about the place of the aged in modern society because the elderly have a right to meaningful roles and activities.

Scientific interest in aging has grown along with the aging of the population. This interest is still quite new, however, and knowledge in many areas remains limited. The study of aging is in a state of ferment as old ideas are displaced by new ones, a process repeated over and over. The future of the aging experience is itself a source of controversy. We will have ample opportunity as we proceed to see the extent to which the study of aging offers frontiers for new ideas.

AGING THEMES IN LITERATURE

Long before aging aroused scientific interest, old age was a theme in the stories, myths, and cultures of societies. In her extensive review Simone de Beauvoir (1972) notes that this theme occurs throughout history, and much of the treatment of aging is negative. For example, the Egyptian philosopher and poet Ptahhotep wrote in 2600 B.C. that "old age is the worst of misfortunes that can afflict a man." Greek literature frequently reflected the conflict among generations, even among the gods; Zeus attacked his father and unseated the Titans, who were the "old" gods.

Plato and Aristotle both touched on the subject of age, although they came to rather different conclusions. Plato argued that the wisest men should serve as guardians of society, which implied a gerontocracy because education would not bring its "full harvest" until the age of 50. Aristotle, however, emphasized declines of competency with old age and spoke much more positively about youth. This argument about the politics of age is still very much with us, of course.

Old age is also a theme in Shakespeare's sonnets and in his play *King Lear,* one of the few great works in which the hero is an old man. It is not coincidental that *King Lear* is one of Shakespeare's tragedies, inasmuch as the common treatment of old age through much of the literature reviewed by de Beauvoir depicts it as a time of misfortune and decline.

The myths and literature concerning aging present three prominent themes, all involving a search for prolonged life: the *antediluvian* theme, the *hyperborean* theme, and the *rejuvenation* theme (Birren & Clayton, 1975). The antediluvian theme involves belief in the greater longevity of earlier peoples. Birren and Clayton note, for example, that according to the book of Genesis, Adam lived for 930 years and Noah for 950 years. The hyperborean theme "arises from the belief that in some distant place there is a culture or society whose people enjoy a remarkably long life" (Birren & Clayton, 1975:15). An interest in those who live beyond normal life spans remains strong, as evidenced by our fascination with such reputedly long-living people as the Abkhazians in the Soviet Union (see Chapter 3). Finally, the rejuvenation theme is found in many legends, such as the search for the Fountain of Youth by Juan Ponce de León, which resulted in the discovery of Florida. It is perhaps ironic that Florida still represents in many ways this search for eternal youth. Certainly this theme is still prominent in American culture, as even a casual look at current ads for skin cream and hair coloring suggests.

THE DEVELOPMENT OF A SCIENCE OF AGING

The scientific study of aging also has a long history (see Birren & Clayton, 1975). For example, Benjamin Franklin was interested in the aging process and the possibility that, in Frankensteinian fashion, lightning could resurrect the dead. However, Quételet, a Belgian statistician of the 1800s, is considered to be the first gerontologist because of his statistical description of the distribution of traits by age. In the first large-scale survey related to aging, Sir Francis Galton demonstrated age differences in 17 different human abilities, such as visual accuracy and reaction time, through data collected from over 9000 visitors to the International Health Exhibit in London in 1884.

Despite these early interests in old age, the scientific study of aging is a twentieth-century phenomenon. A number of studies in the early part of this century concerned biological and psychological aspects of aging (Birren & Clayton, 1975). G. Stanley Hall's *Senescence, the Second Half of Life* (1922) was an early classic, emphasizing old age as a period of life with its own unique aspects. The perception of old age as a "social problem" had emerged by the 1930s, and there was growing recognition of the need for collective action on behalf of the aged (Maddox & Wiley, 1976). This was reflected in the passage of the Social Security Act of 1935.

It was during the post-World War II era, however, that gerontological research began to accelerate. By that time it was becoming apparent that old age was an expectable experience and the population as a whole was aging. This, combined with such trends as widespread retirement, stimulated scientific and policy interest in aging. The Gerontological Society of America was established in 1945, and began publishing the *Journal of Gerontology* in 1946. The International Association of Gerontology was founded in 1950, and similar associations developed in the countries of Denmark, Switzerland, Mexico, and Israel during the 1950s.

Early work in gerontology dealt largely with problems rather than with the aging process as a phenomenon. Psychology was the first discipline to approach aging as a process (Maddox & Wiley, 1976). Consideration of the social implications of the changing demographic structure of modern societies was stimulated by a Social Science Research Council research planning report (Pollak, 1948), and the late 1950s and early 1960s witnessed growing interest in the social processes associated with aging. The literature published on aging between 1950 and 1960 equaled that of the previous 115 years (Birren & Clayton, 1975). Handbooks on aging published around 1960 by James Birren, Clark Tibbitts, and Ernest Burgess gave further impetus to this work, as did White House Conferences on Aging in 1961 and 1971. Government sponsorship of research grew during the 1960s through federal agencies such as the National Institute of Child Health and Human Development and the National Institute of Mental Health. These efforts were further stimulated by the creation of the Administration on Aging (1965), the National Institute on Aging (1975), and the Center for Studies of the Mental Health of the Aging (1976).

These developments have been accompanied by the emergence of gerontological curricula as colleges and universities have responded to growing intellectual interest in aging and to expanding opportunities for employment in programs and services for older people (Peterson & Bolton, 1980). Early strength in gerontology emerged at the University of Chicago, the University of Michigan, Duke University in Durham, N.C., and the University of Southern California. The federal government played an important role in financing training programs and centers on aging at universities during the 1970s. In 1975 the Leonard Davis School at the University of Southern California became the first school of gerontology in the United States.

The last 30 years have clearly seen an explosion of gerontological interest. Publications in the psychology of aging increased by 270 percent between 1968 and 1979 (Poon & Welford, 1980), and an attempt to create a bibliography of biomedical and social research for 1954–1974 yielded 50,000 titles (Woodruff, 1975). The Gerontological Society of America has grown from very modest beginnings to over 4000 members. By 1976 approximately 1300 colleges and universities had gerontological course content. This knowledge explosion, typical of all scientific areas, has certain implications for a text such as this.

A comprehensive review of all the work in the field is not possible. The pace of knowledge growth suggests that this work is already obsolescent as this passage is being read. Even when the focus is narrowed to the sociology of aging, only very selective attention can be given to the tremendous wealth of information available. The intention of this book is to introduce the "state of the art" in social gerontology, reviewing important theoretical debates and empirical findings, and highlighting what seem to be the critical sociological issues posed by aging.

The reader (and future gerontologist?) need not feel "left at sea" by the flood of research and information. Gerontology, perhaps more than most fields, has been characterized by attempts to bring order to the research explosion through the publication of bibliographies and literature reviews. For example, Riley and Foner (1968) published an "encyclopedia" of research findings through the mid-1960s, and "The Handbooks of Aging Series" (Binstock & Shanas, 1976; Birren & Schaie, 1977; Finch & Hayflick, 1977) provides valuable reviews of the field. It remains true, however, that there is much we do not know about aging and the aged. Debates and uncertainties lend an air of excitement and intellectual ferment to the study of aging, and one task of this book is to point to gaps and needed directions.

THE FIELD OF SOCIAL GERONTOLOGY

Before proceeding further, we should define the field and scope of this book. *Gerontology* is the study of aging. It includes all of the processes that are part of the aging experience as well as those that intrude upon, and affect, that experience. Thus, gerontology is truly a multidisciplinary field that includes the medical researcher studying the causes of arteriosclerosis, the experimental psychologist studying the effect of the age of rats on learning, the sociologist studying the impact of modernization on the position of the aged, the economist studying social security systems, and the social worker studying the need for services. Indeed, college faculty teaching courses with gerontological content may be found under more than 20 different departmental designations (Peterson & Bolton, 1980).

There has been some debate about whether gerontology itself represents a discipline, or is instead a topical area cutting across disciplines. Although various certificates and degrees are offered in gerontology, the more typical pattern involves gerontological emphasis within more traditional disciplines and professional programs (such as psychology, sociology, economics, social work, or nursing). It is also true that whereas gerontologists appear to agree that a common body of knowledge is necessary for effective work in gerontology, there is only very general agreement about the content of this "core" (Johnson et al., 1980). Such disagreements are indicative of the relative youth of gerontology as a field of study.

In general terms the subject matter of gerontology involves three major elements: biological, psychological, and social. The biological element concerns the impact of aging on physiology, cellular biology, and bodily systems. Senescence, the deteriorative nature of biological aging, has been a major focus. There have been a number of theories about the nature of this process, and considerable research is being done on the impact of aging on the organism.

The psychology of aging concerns relations between age and sensory processes (such as vision and hearing), perception, psychomotor performance, mental functioning (such as memory, learning, and intelligence), and so on.

The biology and psychology of aging will not be emphasized here, but neither can they be ignored when discussing the social aspects of aging. The health of older people, for example, is an important factor in the impact of aging on individual personality and behavior, and on the society as a whole. Similarly, changes in sensation and perception affect the viability of housing environments for older people.

The focus of this book is on the social aspects of aging, the study of which is termed *social gerontology.* Individuals do not age in a vacuum—they age within a social context, which to a large extent determines their experience of aging. This social context encompasses the family or friends at one level and the society or culture at another level. The social framework determines the meaning of aging for the individual and whether aging will be primarily a positive or negative experience. This means that aging is a complex, varied, and changing experience because the social context within which it occurs differs across individuals and over time.

> There is no pure process of aging—the ways in which children enter kindergarten, or adolescents move into adulthood, or older people retire are not preordained. In this view the life course is not fixed, but widely flexible (Riley, 1978:41).

The aging of individuals also affects the social context in a variety of ways, whether one is concerned with a small family or a large society. For example, older individuals may have unique qualities that a society may or may not use to its advantage. Alternatively, the aged have certain handicaps that may or may not prove detrimental to a society.

Social gerontologists have a threefold task. First, we need to understand aging as an individual experience. What is it like to "be old"? How do people manage the possible accompaniments of aging—health problems, retirement, widowhood? We are still groping for answers to such questions. Social gerontology has been very useful in dispelling many of the myths about old age, but we are still trying to find the realities.

The second task is to understand the position of the aged in the political, economic, and social realms of each society. We know that older people encounter widely differing circumstances in different cultures. We can go back to Herodotus, the Greek historian, for accounts of this diversity.

> Herodotus tells us of some tribes who worshipped their elders as gods and of others who ate them. At one extreme were the Issedones, who gilded the heads of their aged parents and offered sacrifices before them. At the other were the people of Bactria, who disposed of their old folk by feeding them to flesh-eating dogs; or the ancient Sardinians, who hurled their elders from a high cliff and shouted with laughter as they fell on the rocks below. (Fischer, 1977:6)

Even in America, we have apparently changed from a cult of old age among the Puritans to a cult of youth in contemporary society (Fischer, 1977). But we are only now beginning to appreciate fully the complex reasons for such differences.

The third task is to understand the societal consequences of aging. Aging of the population raises many new policy issues, as exemplified in retirement. Earlier in this century, population aging contributed to the emergence of retirement as a mechanism for opening positions in the labor force to young workers. More recently the costs of systems of retirement income have been rising dramatically, and the emphasis may be shifting to encourage older workers to remain in the labor force. Other consequences of population aging may be reflected in political change and conflict, cultural values, or familial patterns.

There are many significant issues to be addressed by social gerontology. What is the place of older people in society, and how well are they integrated into modern cultures? How do we define and accordingly react to old age? What consequences does rising life expectancy have for individuals and society? How is successful adaptation to aging achieved? How much conflict is there among different generations? What happens to people who retire or are widowed? How do the aged react to the prospect of death? What services do the elderly need and how are they best provided? These and many other questions form the subject matter of this book.

WHY STUDY AGING?

The question—Why study aging?—may seem an odd one. But the reasons occasionally given for the need to study social gerontology can be misleading. First, old age as a developmental period of life is not completely distinct from other developmental periods, such as adolescence or middle age. Similar processes of socialization and adaptation are evident throughout the life cycle. Aging truly begins at birth, and it is unfortunate that old age is viewed as a separate period of an individual's life. There is increasing recognition that old age must be incorporated into an integrated understanding of the life cycle.

Second, many people are drawn to the study of aging by a desire to help "all those poor old people." Although this is certainly laudable, too heavy emphasis on the problems of the aged may only contribute to stereotypes of old age as a period of unmitigated misfortune and unhappiness. Such stereotypes may generate negative attitudes toward aging and the aged, resulting in denial of aging and withdrawal from the aged. It is true that older people may encounter many problems—ill health, poverty, depression, feelings of uselessness—however, society itself often causes or exacerbates these conditions.

These problems must be recognized and dealt with, but it must also be noted that our often irrational fear of aging and negative stereotypes about the aged are not based on a realistic picture of the "typical" older person (if there is such a thing). Most older people are *not* isolated from their families, are *not* in ill health or senile, and are *not* preoccupied with feelings of boredom and loneliness. We need to discard the stereotypes of old age as either gloom and misfortune or the serene "golden years." Both are true, and yet neither is true.

Finally, it must be recognized that people are not suddenly "reborn" on their sixty-fifth birthday. Older persons are not really so different from younger persons, and their difference may have very little to do with age itself. The best predictor of what a person will be like at age 65 is what he or she was like at age 45 or any other earlier age. The cheerful grandmother was probably a cheerful mother. The cranky retiree was probably a cranky worker. We are all prisoners of our pasts. And there is as much variety among older people as in other age groups.

Aging represents more than simple individual continuity, of course, or there would be no point to studying it. What makes aging interesting sociologically is that the individual ages *within a context*—a context that constrains the ability to maintain continuity. It is the existence of these constraints, and their more or less unique configuration, that allows one to treat old age as a distinct developmental period. The constraints are many, the most obvious, perhaps, being the biological decrements that accompany aging—increases in chronic illness and declining biological and psychological functioning. The social context of aging also creates constraints on personal continuity through policies and institutional arrangements that affect the employment, health, housing, and other situations of the aged, and through social attitudes toward aging reflected in those policies. Individuals encounter change as they age, such as retirement and widowhood, and the meaning and impact of those changes are products of the social environment. Thus, aging is not a straight-line extrapolation from earlier patterns of living, but must be seen in the following light:

> . . . to a great extent his last years depend upon those of his middle life. . . . Yet there is no inherent justice: Far from it. Illness and the social context may wreck the end of an active and open-hearted life. Earlier choice and present chance step in to give each old age its particular aspect. (Beauvoir, 1972:505)

THE DEFINITION OF OLD AGE

How do we determine whether someone is young, middle-aged, or old? Chronological age is certainly a basis for judgments about an individual's "stage of life." In some situations, society may define age in formal chronological terms, as with policies concerning eligibility for Social Security and compulsory retirement. Chronological age is at best a very rough indicator of what an individual is like, however, because it only partially reflects the biological, psychological, and sociological processes that truly define life stages. Indeed, it is unfortunate that we stereotype people according to age as much as we do.

Such categories as middle age and old age are social constructions, based on a wide variety of cues and standards that are socially defined. Just as male and female or black and white refer to more than biological attributes, so too is age a "social fact" endowed with social meaning. To say that someone is adolescent or old is to locate him or her in the social structure, implying different roles, expectations, opportunities, and constraints that are sequenced over the life cycle. The meanings of these social ages themselves vary across cultures and over time. Calhoun (1978), for example, analyzes the meanings attached to old age in the United States from 1945 to 1970 and the emergence of a new, more positive concept of aging—the "senior citizen." Whereas early concern with aging in this period focused on the needs and adjustment problems of older people, researchers, the media, and public interest groups have promoted more flexible and valued definitions of aging. Retirement, for example, is increasingly viewed as a positive transition to be favorably anticipated with leisure as a prized commodity.

This is not to say that the life cycle is a simple or universal sequence from one clearly defined set of roles to another. Individuals encounter many changes linked to chronological age, reflecting their passage through stages of work career, family development, or other involvements (Clausen, 1972). The family cycle alone is comprised of a series of transitions: dating, young married couple, new parents, parents of adolescents, the "empty nest" when children leave, retirement of either or both spouses, widowhood, and possibly remarriage. Even this sequence of events is oversimplified. The study of the life cycle is complicated by the fact that different life dimensions, such as work and family, may be synchronized in a variety of ways as individuals experience transitions at different ages (if, indeed, they experience them at all). Some persons marry at 18 and have three children by the time they are 23; others marry at 30 and have only one child; still others never marry at all. Some persons begin work careers at 18, others at 25 or 30, and others never embark on any meaningful work career. Career changes, divorce and remarriage, and other transitions further complicate the life course.

All is not chaos, however. Roles and statuses, and their sequences of occurrence, are *age-graded* (linked to age) in all societies and cultures. In this way, chronological time is transformed into *social time*.

> . . . there exists what might be called a prescriptive time-table for the ordering of major life events: a time in the life span when men and women are expected to marry, a time to raise children, a time to retire. . . . Men and women are aware not only of the social clocks that operated in various areas of their lives, but they are aware also of their own timing and readily describe themselves as "early," "late," or "on time" with regard to family and occupational events. (Neugarten et al., 1968:23–24)

Thus there are social expectations about age-appropriate behavior and the timing of events and transitions throughout the life cycle. The life course is an orderly sequence to the extent that these social definitions of age are explicit and adhered to. Social time results in an *age-stratification system,* according to which different age groups occupy different positions in the social structure, with associated rights, duties, rewards, and costs (Riley et al., 1972).

The social definitions of age vary among societies and constitute a major way in which the social context shapes the aging experience. It appears that age has become increasingly loaded with social meaning in modern societies, resulting in more clearly differentiated "stages" in the life cycle. Hareven (1980) notes that childhood was "discovered" as a unique stage by the urban middle class of the early nineteenth century, and adolescence emerged as a separate stage in the late nineteenth century. A "preschool" stage seems an even more recent addition to discussions of childhood development. During this century, especially since World War II, transitions into adulthood (completion of schooling, entrance into full-time work, and marriage) have become more closely linked to a narrower age range (Hogan, 1981); for example, persons born around 1910 typically completed these transitions in 18 years, whereas those born around 1940 typically completed them in only 10 years (Winsborough, 1979). Evidence of such trends in the age-grading of role transitions "strongly suggests that there now exist sharper and more uniform life-course transitions and more clearly demarcated periods of 'stages' of life" (Smelser & Halpern, 1978:310). The increased intellectual and political attention to aging stimulated by the growth of the older population and the emergence of retirement as a widespread phenomenon also indicate that old age has become an increasingly distinct stage in the socially defined life cycle.

To summarize, age itself is an ambiguous dimension. Chronological age tells us little about the social and social-psychological circumstances of individuals. Age is a social construct with social meanings and social implications. In this regard, age appears to have grown in importance in differentiating the positions and experiences of individuals in modern societies. Indeed, the common saying that "you're only as old as you feel" recognizes that age is more than a matter of years.

THE NATURE OF AGE DIFFERENCES

It is absurd to think that one can accurately predict social and psychological characteristics simply from an individual's age; it is equally absurd to deny the existence of age differences. One would certainly expect age variations in political orientations and affiliations, religious involvement, leisure activities, attitudes toward death, and so on. A primary task of social gerontology is to account for such differences and to specify the conditions under which they occur. It must be stressed, however, that age *differences* are not the same as age *changes* or age *effects.* This is a point that complicates both theory and research in aging and creates the potential for very misleading interpretations. This complication arises from the fact that age differences may be the product of either "developmental time" or "historical time" (Bengtson, 1973).

Aging Effects

Developmental time refers to the changes in people as they grow older—they become more or less religious, more or less conservative, and so on. Thus, the person who is now 65 is in certain respects different from the same person 30 years earlier. These maturational or developmental changes may be termed *aging effects,* of which there are two types: *intrinsic* and *reactive.*

Intrinsic aging effects are changes that naturally accompany the aging process, regardless of social context. Reactive aging effects, on the other hand, are shaped by the social context within which aging takes place so that aging represents a varied experience. People in different societies, or different subgroups within a society, or different historical periods, will age within different social contexts. It is often difficult, or even impossible, to clearly distinguish intrinsic and reactive aging effects. Increasing religiosity, for example, may be viewed as an inevitable accompaniment of approaching death or as a consequence of the social conditions of aging and social definitions of death (as something to look forward to or avoid). There is a danger of ethnocentrism in social gerontology—of seeing the aging process in American society, for example, as being the same as in all societies. Purported intrinsic age changes must withstand the test of both cross-cultural and cross-time comparisons, which are still relatively infrequent. Although many biological and physiological changes associated with age seem to be universal and inevitable, it is best to assume that social and psychological age changes are reactive—until proven otherwise. Certainly, the essence of the approach taken in this book is that aging is a socially shaped experience.

One reason individuals change with age, of course, is that they experience changes in roles and expected behaviors as they move through the life cycle (Clausen, 1972). The need to adjust to new experiences and life conditions, particularly at points of status and role transition, provides an impetus for personal change, even in identity. It is not surprising that those who are retired differ from those who work, or that those with children differ from those with none. These experiences and transitions are themselves shaped by social context. Aging coexists with other social locations that differentiate individuals. The meanings and experiences of aging differ for men and women, blacks and whites, upper class and lower class, and "aging thus must be examined in the context of events which . . . gain meaning by reference to the individual's location within the broader social structure" (Bengtson et al., 1977:327).

The nature of the life cycle is also affected by the larger society and patterns of social change. Retirement, for example, is a relatively new social institution, as is widespread college attendance. Additionally, the timing of events in the life cycle changes. Industrialization has affected the timing of life events in the family and economic spheres (Neugarten & Moore, 1968). This is recognized in the important role of historical time.

> The biographies of men and women, the kinds of individuals they have become, cannot be understood without reference to the historical structure in which the milieux of their everyday life are organized. (Mills, 1959:175).

The implications of historical time are reflected in two other potential sources of age differences or age changes that do not represent aging effects: *cohort effects* and *period effects*.

Cohort Effects

Historical time refers to the succession of generations. This implies that differences in age groups may be related to differences between generations rather than to the aging process. The term *cohort* refers to individuals born at the same time. Members of a cohort experience similar events at similar times in the life cycle. This similarity of experience creates the potential for a "generational consciousness" (Mannheim, 1952). Thus age groups differ in ways not attributable to aging, and social change becomes likely when there is marked discontinuity between the experiences of a cohort and those of its predecessor (Ryder, 1965).

Society can be thought of as composed of a succession of cohorts flowing through time, each of which is shaped by a unique configuration of events. For example, persons born in 1890 grew up when frontier expansion was still a reality, encountered two world wars, went through the Great Depression during their middle (or working) years, and experienced the "future shock" of the 1970s at the end of their lives. Comparisons across generations indicate two major points about cohort analysis. First, events experienced by one cohort may not be encountered by another. Cohorts from 1890 and 1910 lived through a depression and global war; the 1950 cohort has not. Second, events may be experienced by different cohorts at different stages of the life cycle. What are the different consequences of the Depression for wage earners (the 1890 cohort) and for children (the 1920 cohort)? How does the 1890 cohort react to the rush of the 1970s compared with the cohort born in 1950?

The shared experience of a cohort will shape the norms, values, attitudes, and behaviors of its members. This includes different socialization experiences, such as child-rearing practices. Older people today may be more religious than younger people because they were brought up in a more religious environment, not because they have become more religious with age. Other age differences may simply reflect the fact that current older persons have less education than younger cohorts. Readers might reflect on the implications of the events shaping their own cohorts for their own old age.

Some cohorts experience events of such magnitude, and so early in their lives, that they are felt to carry an indelible generational stamp. Many older people now living grew up during the Depression of the 1930s, and it is generally believed that this permanently affected their values and life-styles.

Elder (1974) has published one of the few empirical studies of the long-term impact of the Depression on individuals. His book, which follows a group of Oakland schoolchildren born in 1920–1921, is an excellent example of the benefits to be gained from a cohort analysis and the dangers of oversimplifying or exaggerating cohort effects. Elder begins by cautioning us against a monolithic view of the Depression years. He notes that the conditions of life varied according to age, sex, race, and place of residence, and it was not a time of great economic deprivation for at least half of the population. It was most likely to be the "worst of times" for the foreign-born, the working class, and self-employed members of the middle class. For those who were deprived, this study provides evidence of drastic alterations in patterns of living, as families adapted to hardship. Most relevant for these children were changes in the division of labor and authority patterns within the family, resulting in the extension of adult responsibilities. This meant greater involvement in household affairs for girls, particularly because mothers often worked outside the home; and greater social independence and freedom from traditional parental restraints for boys, who were more likely to work. In effect, childhood was cut short.

Deprivation during the Depression seems to have made a lasting impression on individuals' perspectives on the world: greater preference for the Democratic party, greater preoccupation with domestic economic problems, and a more optimistic outlook on economic opportunities for contemporary youth. Deprivation and memories of the humiliation and shame of doing without continue to color evaluations of later life.

> Through memories and actual experiences in the 30s, hardships in the Depression made a substantial difference in the way the Oakland adults have charted their life gratification. The observed variations are consistent with the theory that Depression experiences established a frame of reference for defining life periods as relatively good or bad times. From a relative perspective, adults who remember what it was like to have very little in the 30s appear to be more appreciative of their life situation in the more affluent, secure years of the 40s and 50s. (Elder, 1974:262)

Elder finds little support, however, for the ideas that deprivation during the Depression made these people more committed to work or more preoccupied with job security and material success. Interestingly, deprivation as a child had little impact on adult status. Among the males, deprivation seems to have spurred ambition, resulting in greater clarity of career goals and greater concentration of effort and energy to achieve those goals. In fact, Elder finds that in the middle class those who were deprived as children were psychologically healthier as adults. The protected lives of their more privileged peers left them with reduced capacities to cope with adult problems.

Elder's findings underline the variability and complexity of cohort effects. The concept of general cohort effects involves two underlying assumptions: that similar experiences produce similar effects, and that historical events, particularly those encountered relatively early in life, continue to affect behavior throughout life (McQuaide & Sauer, 1979). Yet Elder's study shows that any event is likely to be experienced in many different ways because cohorts are composed of many different subgroups defined by social class, sex, and other factors. Even when events have similar initial effects, the subsequent uniqueness of individual biographies will weaken cohort similarities.

This points out another reason not to stereotype all "old people." There is tremendous variability among older people, a fact that cannot be overemphasized. Bear in mind that the older population is itself composed of different co-horts. We all recognize the differences between 50-year-old persons and 30-year-olds, yet we often overlook the 20-year difference between those who are 90 and those who are 70. Neugarten (1974) distinguishes between the "young-old" (55 to 75) and the "old-old." The young-old are characterized by better health, more education, relative affluence, and greater political activism. Thus they run counter to the negative stereotypes about aging. Neugarten suggests that the young-old have an increasing concern with the meaningful use of time and will operate as agents of change in creating more positive images of aging and opportunities for older people. Recent cohorts entering old age have a quite different composition from earlier cohorts—better education, fewer foreign-born, fewer with a rural background (Cain, 1967; Uhlenberg, 1979).

Social gerontology must be sensitive to the fact that the nature of aging is partly determined by the characteristics of persons undergoing the aging process so that the capabilities and needs of the aging in the future may be quite different from those now evident.

Period Effects

Period effects represent an additional source of age differences or age changes that may be misinterpreted as cohort or aging effects. Certain processes and events occurring in the larger society may stimulate general patterns of change in behavior patterns or attitudes. It appears, for example, that attitudes about women's roles have become more egalitarian in American society over the past few decades. If one were to look at members of a particular cohort, there would likely be evident changes with age in such attitudes. These changes might be interpreted as aging effects, or perhaps cohort effects, when in fact they are period effects—events and trends affecting the attitudes of all ages and cohorts.

Research indicates that the relative position of older people in American society has improved over the past 30 years (Pampel, 1981). Pampel indicates that this is partly due to compositional changes in successive cohorts of older people—improved education and occupational status, for example. But the patterns of improvement are only partly accounted for by such cohort effects. Period effects appear to be the more important source of these changes. Recent cohorts entering old age have encountered a more favorable social context for aging in terms of norms and expectations, benefits and supports, lobbying groups, and the like.

The possibilities of aging, cohort, and period effects introduce tremendous complexity to the task of understanding aging and the characteristics of older people: aging effects may vary by cohort or period, period effects may vary by age or cohort. An example is offered by the typical finding that older people are more conservative than younger people. Glenn (1974) has noted that there are several possible explanations for this age difference. It may be that aspects of biological aging, such as energy decline and loss of brain tissue, result in cautiousness and resistance to change. This could be viewed as an intrinsic aging effect. Alternatively, passage through the life cycle results in the accumulation of family responsibilities, occupational mobility, and so on. This may lead to a shift away from egalitarian ideals and toward self-interest. To the extent that social age-grading creates such differences over the life cycle, this can be interpreted as a reactive aging effect. Finally, older people may be more conservative because they grew up in a more conservative society or because they have less education. This would be a cohort effect.

To further complicate matters, Glenn combines these three explanations of age differences. He suggests that as people accumulate experience, they become less susceptible to change—each new experience has a smaller "marginal" impact—and their personal characteristics stabilize after young adulthood as a natural, or intrinsic, accompaniment of aging. Whether this means that older people are more conservative or more liberal than other age groups depends on the nature of societal change (period effects) and cohort change (cohort effects). Current older people grew up in a conservative environment, followed by societal changes toward liberalism and more liberal cohorts. Although older people have followed the general trend toward liberalism, they have changed more slowly than other cohorts, and thus appear more conservative. There is general support for this thesis of increased stability with age, as early "formative" years of higher changeability are followed by relative stability in behaviors and attitudes later in life (Glenn, 1980).

METHODOLOGICAL ISSUES

The distinctions between age differences and age changes, intrinsic and reactive aging effects, and aging, cohort, and period effects imply that particular care needs to be taken in the design and interpretation of research. Most gerontological research has been *cross-sectional*—studying one sample of people at one point in time. Although the sample may include a number of age groups, cross-sectional research can only show age differences. It cannot distinguish between age differences and age changes or between aging, cohort, and period effects. Such research is valuable, if only in a suggestive way, but there is a danger of overinterpreting the results.

Because the concern in much gerontological research is with the nature of age changes, a *longitudinal* design is an appropriate approach. Longitudinal research involves the study of samples at more than one time, as when a national sample of individuals in 1960 is compared with a similar sample in 1970. The best longitudinal approach for studying individual change is the *panel* study, which follows a group of individuals through time. This allows the researcher to look at the actual change shown by each individual.

If a researcher wished to study the impact of retirement on individuals, a cross-sectional design would compare workers and retirees at a single point in time. Such a study might find differences between current workers and retirees, but would not indicate whether the retirees had changed because of retirement or had always been different from this sample of workers. A panel study would gather data about the same individuals as workers and following retirement. Thus the researcher would know whether individuals had actually changed.

Panel studies, however, are typically limited to members of a single cohort and relatively limited periods of time. A more general design is needed to begin to separate aging, cohort, and period effects. Norval Glenn's book, *Cohort Analysis* (1977), provides an excellent introduction to the nature and problems of such research. Glenn defines *cohort analysis* as the study of one or more cohorts at two or more points in time. Table 1.1 presents an example of a *standard cohort table* used in research where cross-sectional surveys are done of different age groups at different times.

Such data can be analyzed in many ways. Comparisons within a data-gathering period indicate cross-sectional age differences (comparing A-E-I-M-Q-U for 1950). Change in these age differences can be studied across time (for 1950, 1960, 1970, and 1980). Age changes can be investigated for each cohort (comparing A-F-K-P follows a single 10-year cohort over time), and these age changes can be compared across cohorts (comparing A-F-K-P with E-J-O-T). Finally, different cohorts can be compared at the same age (M-N-O-P gives a comparison at age 50–59). These comparisons allow one to begin separating aging, cohort, and period effects by asking various questions of the data. Do cohorts display patterns of age changes, and are these patterns similar or different across cohorts? Do age groups and cohorts display similar or different patterns of change across the time periods? Are persons of the same age similar or different across cohorts and time periods?

Obviously, gathering the type of data represented in Table 1.1 could be exhausting, time-consuming, and costly for any single researcher. It is no accident that most gerontological research is cross-sectional. Happily, researchers increasingly have access to data gathered by others. Cross-sectional studies conducted in different time periods may be combined for use in a format like Table 1.1. For example, Gallup polls have been conducted since 1937, the National Opinion Research Center conducts many national surveys covering a variety of topics, the Michigan Survey Research Center has conducted National Election Surveys since 1952, and the federal government conducts many surveys and censuses, including the Annual Housing Survey, the National Nursing Home Survey, and the Health Interview Survey. Data from various panel studies are also available. For example, the Social Security Administration's Retirement History Study interviewed a sample of men and women aged 58–63 in 1969 and continued studying them

Table 1.1 AN EXAMPLE OF A STANDARD COHORT TABLE

Age at time of study	Time of measurement			
	1950	1960	1970	1980
20–29	A	B	C	D
30–39	E	F	G	H
40–49	I	J	K	L
50–59	M	N	O	P
60–69	Q	R	S	T
70–79	U	V	W	X

until 1979, and the National Longitudinal Surveys of Labor Market Experience followed national samples of men and women of different ages from 1966 through 1981.

The availability of such data should not be considered a panacea, however. Topics of interest to any particular researcher may or may not be available. Specific questions may not be comparable across surveys—even very minor changes in the wording of questions can affect the comparability of responses. Sampling issues are also raised by such analyses. Different surveys may use different sampling techniques so that they may not be representative of the same population. A major methodological concern in panel studies is the loss of part of the sample over time (sample "mortality"). Individuals may refuse to be interviewed again, move, or die. This can be a problem particularly in studies of older panels. For example, in a major study of retirement (Streib & Schneider, 1972), an original group of workers was followed for a period of 7 years. At the end of those 7 years, only 1969 of the original 3793 respondents were still in the study. The danger is that the final sample is no longer representative of the original sample—dropouts may be older, in poorer health, and so forth. Thus knowledge about the impact of retirement may be restricted to those who "survive" such panel studies. A similar concern arises more generally with cohort analysis. Because of selective mortality (by sex, race, or social class), cohorts may change in their composition as they age. What appears to be age-related change in average behaviors and attitudes of a cohort may instead be attributable to such compositional changes.

Even in the absence of such problems, analysis of data such as that in Table 1.1 presents the researcher with tremendous complexities. Whereas there is some debate on this matter, there appears to be no definitive statistical method for separating aging, cohort, and period effects (Glenn, 1977; Palmore, 1978). To infer whether one or more of these effects is reflected in empirical trends and differences, the researcher must usually rely on assumptions based on theory or other knowledge.

It is clear, then, that the study of aging presents particular conceptual and methodological complexities. Research in social gerontology also requires the same decisions and encounters the same problems as other kinds of social research. The researcher must be concerned with the appropriateness of different research techniques, such as interviewing, observation, and experiments: methods that have all been used fruitfully in the study of aging. Measures that are used must be *valid*—they must accurately reflect the concepts they are intended to measure—and be *reliable,* so that the same results can be achieved from repeated measurements of the same phenomenon.

Accurate sampling is always critical to good research. If the sample is not representative, the results are of questionable validity. This has been a particular problem in the study of aging, since comprehensive lists of older people are not available. Those that approach completeness, such as Social Security and Internal Revenue lists, are not available to the researcher. The telephone book omits persons without telephones, and is therefore biased against the poor and institutionalized. Organizational membership lists overrepresent those who are healthy and middle class, whereas studies in institutions, such as nursing homes, overrepresent the chronically ill and senile. In addition, sampling designs too often fail to incorporate racial and ethnic subgroups in the older population.

If interviewing is used, certain difficulties may arise with older respondents. The aged may be skeptical of social research because they are likely to be wary of strangers or may see the interviewer as a government "snoop." Hearing and vision difficulties, often coupled with mental confusion, can be particular problems with institutionalized populations. Various response biases may occur. For example, older people may have more difficulty understanding questionnaire forms and are more likely to state "no opinion" (Riley et al., 1972). Even age may be inaccurately reported. This has led to skepticism concerning claims of unusual longevity in certain cultures (Medvedev, 1974). It is a common observation that older people give more favorable evaluations of their life circumstances than seems warranted by objective conditions, and such denial or defense may depend upon question format (Carp & Carp, 1981).

Finally, certain ethical questions are particularly salient with older populations (Reich, 1978). Easily accessible groups of older people may be vulnerable to overselection and exploitation. Reduced competence and freedom may hinder truly voluntary informed consent to be studied. Such issues are of particular concern with institutionalized older people.

CONCEPTUAL FRAMEWORKS IN THE STUDY OF AGING

Clearly, the study of aging is a very complex field. The older population is characterized by great variability in ages, cohorts, ethnicities, personalities, health, and so on. Social gerontology also encompasses many substantive areas of study—retirement, widowhood, political behavior, personality. Because it is difficult to generate an orderly understanding of this complexity, there is some danger that social gerontology could become a series of discrete, unrelated subject areas, lacking any sense of the integrated nature of the aging experience, its relationship to the larger society, and its overall impact on the aging individual. Maddox and Wiley (1976) have noted that:

> The social scientific study of aging needs but currently lacks widely shared paradigms which would provide common conceptualization of issues, standard measurements, and clearly defined agendas for the systematic testing of hypotheses derived from theory. Applied, problem-oriented studies of the societal consequences of aging predominate. (p. 4)

They also note that systematic theory development has been "strikingly absent" in gerontology.

This is not to say that social gerontology is unrelated to, or has ignored, such broader sociological paradigms as structural functionalism, conflict theory, social exchange theory, or symbolic interactionism. But students of gerontology will find no single overarching framework, no "grand theory" of aging, to guide their understanding. There are theories in social gerontology, of course. Chapter

4, for example, discusses disengagement theory and activity theory, and Chapter 9 discusses frameworks emphasizing social integration. But none of these approaches adequately captures the complex social nature and consequences of aging. This is perhaps as it should be, given the relative newness of the field and the complexities of aging. But integrating frameworks are needed to facilitate an understanding of those complexities. Three such frameworks seem particularly helpful in that regard, and can serve as frames of reference for the chapters that follow.

Age Stratification

The first framework recognizes the "macro" nature of aging: the fact that society and the social structure affect the nature of aging in a variety of ways. This means that all societies have an *age stratification system* (Riley, 1971; Riley et al., 1972). Age is one of the criteria for determining the position of individuals in the social structure, thereby placing different age groups in different statuses. Individuals are socialized—more or less—to accept these age-related positions. All age groups in a society can be analyzed on this basis, although the focus here will be on older age "strata."

Whereas all societies can be characterized according to age stratification, the nature of the particular age stratification system will differ from society to society. Because of this, aging will be a different experience in different societies and in the same society at different times. By examining the age stratification system, we can understand the ways in which social structure affects the relative position and evaluation of older people. As societies change, the nature of age stratification changes, and with it the position of the aged. In American society, for example, urbanization and industrialization have been accompanied by the development of retirement as an institution, changes in family structure, and alterations of sex roles. The impact of such changes on the aging experience, and the nature and meaning of age-related transitions for individuals, can be understood within a model of age stratification (see Chapter 3).

Symbolic Interactionism

The second broad perspective, *symbolic interactionism,*[1] assists with a more "micro" approach to aging: a recognition that the nature and impact of aging must also be understood at the *individual* level. There are as many different aging experiences as there are aging individuals. Each person approaches old age from a unique background of experience, personality, and life-style and experiences a different configuration of age-related changes. An understanding of the individual impact of aging requires an appreciation of the interpretation and meanings of the events that may accompany aging. Some persons dread retirement as an end to usefulness, others look forward to a deserved reward for a lifetime of hard work. The meaning of aging and its concomitants evolve from "symbolic interac-

[1]For a more complete introduction to symbolic interactionism, see Stryker (1981).

tions" between the individual and other individuals, groups, and the society (Marshall, 1978). Marshall indicates the need for a dynamic perspective on the ways in which individuals fashion their *own* lives through negotiation and socially constructed realities. Aging is a social experience, and its meanings are socially defined. But it is the individual who ultimately translates those meanings and definitions and makes sense of aging as a *personal* experience.

A Life Course Perspective

The final framework, broadly termed the *life course* perspective, is one that recognizes the complex processes and causal factors we have discussed in this chapter (Hareven, 1978; Elder, 1981). Aging is recognized as a lifelong process involving the interaction of biological, psychological, and social processes. Individuals pursue many different pathways in work, family, and other arenas, and the patterns of age-linked change associated with this "interacting bundle of career timetables" (Roth, 1963:114) are reflected in the tremendous variability of the aging experience. The life course is partly a result of the idiosyncratic events of individual biographies, and partly a result of the more structured norms, social timetables, and age hierarchies associated with age stratification. This all takes place within the larger context of history and social change, affecting the timing, order, and meaning of events. Thus, as Elder (1981) points out, development across the life span must be understood as contextual and multidimensional as individuals follow multiple, changing pathways from birth to death. These patterns of development are not only consequences of the larger context and the events experienced over the life cycle. As recognized by symbolic interactionism, human beings are also purposeful negotiators of their own lives so that "individuals are both products and producers of their history" (Elder, 1981:78). Indeed, new cohorts and new patterns of aging can themselves cause social change.

Society and history (both personal and social) structure people's lives in various ways, determining the broad parameters of the situations in which they find themselves, creating constraints, potentialities, and problems. Because of this, we can speak of patterns or trends that differentiate age groups. But it must be kept in mind that people are not totally determined by rigid effects of social structure and history. Although we often talk generally about "the aged," we should not ignore the uniqueness of individuals. The life course perspective reminds us of the complexity, variability, and flexibility of the aging experience, and of the *process* by which lives are lived.

SUMMARY

There is a long history of interest in aging, as reflected in cultural themes and early scientific inquiry. The major thrust of gerontological research has come within the last 30 years, however. Gerontology has become a truly interdisciplinary field, encompassing biological, psychological, and social concerns, although there has been debate about whether gerontology itself constitutes a discipline. The primary focus of this book will be on the social aspects of aging.

Aging and the aged are not separate from the rest of the human experience, and old age is neither entirely gloomy nor completely serene. There is considerable personal continuity. Nonetheless, personal change and the social context place age-related constraints on individuals that make old age a sociologically interesting period.

Age is itself a social construction. We have conceptions of distinct age periods such as middle age and old age because societies assign social positions partly on the basis of age. Societies differ in the way in which this is done, resulting in cross-cultural differences in the aging experience.

The existence of age differences may reflect a number of different phenomena: aging effects, period effects, or cohort effects. This points to the need for more complex research designs which incorporate longitudinal as well as cross-sectional studies. There are additional methodological issues in the study of aging, including sampling and response biases.

No single theory adequately captures the social complexity of aging, but three conceptual frameworks are particularly useful to a coherent understanding of the aging experience. First, all societies can be characterized by their age stratification systems, which result in age-differentiated expectations, sanctions, and rewards. Second, the meaning of aging must be sought at the individual level, as each aging person interprets the experience according to the symbolic meanings available to him or her. Third, a life course perspective recognizes the complex interplay of individual, social, and historical processes in shaping aging as a lifelong process.

chapter 2

Characteristics of the Older Population

In assessing the sociological position and problems of any group, it is important to have an understanding of who comprises that group. There are many stereotypes and claims made about the aged, many of them patently false and perhaps most of them in some way exaggerated. This chapter may confuse as much as it clarifies if its presentation of "facts and figures" is taken to mean that "the old" are a homogeneous group and that their diversity can be captured in a series of tables. With this disclaimer in mind, let us look at the *general* characteristics of older people.

DEMOGRAPHIC CHARACTERISTICS

The Population of Older People

The most striking statistical fact about the older population is the great increase during this century in the number of people over 65 in the United States. Table 2.1 indicates that the number of persons over 65 has increased from 3 million in 1900 to over 25 million in 1980. This older population has increased more rapidly than the general population, rising from 4.1 percent of the population in 1900 to over 11 percent in 1980. Projections indicate that 32 million people will be over 65 by the year 2000 and that by that time they may comprise over 12 percent of the population. The aging of the general population is further indicated by the rising median age shown in Table 2.1. The rate of growth is highest in the oldest segments of the older population. Between 1970 and 1980 the number of persons

21

Table 2.1   POPULATION 65 AND OVER AND MEDIAN AGE OF TOTAL POPULATION IN THE UNITED STATES, 1900–2030

Year	Population age 60 and over		Median age of total population
	Number (in thousands)	Percent of total population	
1900	3,099	4.1	22.9
1920	4,929	4.7	25.3
1940	9,031	6.9	29.0
1960	16,675	9.3	29.5
1980	25,544	11.3	30.2
Projections:[a]			
2000	32,000	12.2	35.5
2030	55,000	18.3	38.0

[a]Assuming replacement-level fertility (2.1 children per woman).

Sources: Beth J. Soldo, "America's Elderly in the 1980s," *Population Bulletin,* vol. 35, no. 4 (Population Reference Bureau, Inc., Washington, D.C., 1980), pp. 7, 9; U.S. Bureau of the Census, 1981a.

Table 2.2   PROJECTED TOTAL DEPENDENCY RATIO, AGED DEPENDENCY RATIO, AND YOUNG DEPENDENCY RATIO: 1980–2030

Type	Number of persons per 100 aged 18–64		
	1980	2000	2030
Total dependency ratio (under 18 and 65 and over)	64.3	63.2	73.8
Aged dependency ratio (65 and over)	18.4	19.9	31.8
Young dependency ratio (under 18)	45.8	43.2	42.0

Source: Beth J. Soldo, "America's Elderly in the 1980s," *Population Bulletin,* vol. 35, no. 4 (Population Reference Bureau, Inc., Washington, D.C., 1980), p. 39.

aged 65 and over increased by 23 percent, whereas persons 85 and over increased by 60 percent (increasing from 7.1 percent of the older population to 9.2 percent) (Soldo, 1980).

Even if our total knowledge of aging were restricted to this growth in the size and proportion of the older population, we should expect some important consequences. The aged generate a disproportionate demand for certain services, including health care and financial assistance, and therefore represent an increasing "burden" on society, particularly the younger, working population who support societal programs.

Demographers use the *dependency ratio* to measure the degree of demand placed on society. Table 2.2 indicates projected trends in this ratio and its "young" and "aged" components. The aged dependency ratio has been rising, and will continue to do so, perhaps leading to conflict over scarce resources and a decline in willingness to support special programs such as Medicare and Social Security (see Chapter 11). At a more individual level, it is expected that by 2000 four out of five persons aged 60 and over will have a living parent so that older people themselves will be called on to assist their aged parents.

That changing age structure affects the whole society can be seen in the effects of the post-World War II "baby boom" cohort. When this cohort was young, schools had to be built to accommodate them; now there are too many schools and too few students. Tables 2.1 and 2.2 indicate substantial increases in the older population and the aged dependency ratio by 2030, when this cohort will have entered old age. This will bring a major crunch to the financing of Social Security and other pension plans. The impact will also be felt in such areas as the need for more nursing-home beds as the proportion of the "old-old" (75+) increases. Even by the year 2000 the nursing-home population is expected to increase by nearly 50 percent.

This picture is itself too simplified. Although there will be more aged in the future, they are likely to be healthier and in better financial condition than today's aged. In addition, the rising old-age dependency ratio will be counteracted by a declining proportion of children. But aging clearly presents modern societies with important issues to be addressed.

Life Expectancy and the Demographic Transition

The general aging of the population is a relatively recent phenomenon. Figure 2.1 presents *survival curves* indicating the percentage who survive to certain ages,

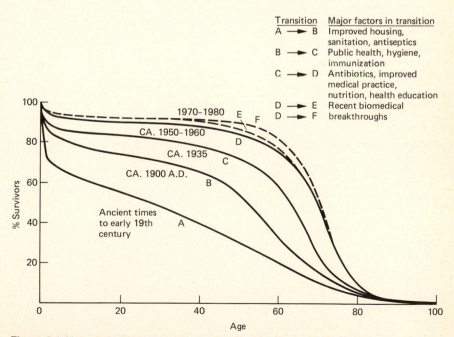

Figure 2.1 Human survivorship trends to the present. (*Source:* Bernard Strehler, "Implications of Aging Research for Society," *Federation Proceedings* 34 (1975), p. 6, © by the Federation of American Societies for Experimental Biology. Reprinted by permission.)

from ancient times to the present. There was little change prior to the nineteenth century, with life expectancies ranging from approximately 18 years in prehistoric times, to 22 in ancient Rome, to 35 in the American colonies (Schulz, 1978). The most dramatic changes have occurred during this century, as accompaniments of modernization and the *demographic transition* (Cowgill, 1974). Two aspects of this transition contribute to an older population. First, the fertility (birth) rate tends to decline. Fertility sets the limit on the size of any particular birth cohort. When the fertility rate declines, already existing cohorts will be a comparatively larger part of the population. Second, public health measures (particularly in sanitation and the control of communicable diseases) result in lower mortality (death) rates. Because the greatest effect is on infant and child mortality, there will be an initial increase in younger age groups, but over time, as fertility declines, the proportion of older people rises. This pattern is well illustrated by the effects of high postwar fertility. The aging of this baby-boom cohort, combined with subsequent reduced fertility, will result in a significant aging of the overall population. Indeed, the future aged dependency ratio is highly sensitive to changes in fertility, making it difficult to make projections. Whereas fertility has been at or below replacement levels in a number of highly developed countries—such as the United States, England, and Sweden—there are indications of a recent rise in the birthrate that may slow population aging.

That aging of the population is associated with modernization can be seen from international comparisons (Siegel, 1981). The proportion of the population

Table 2.3 LIFE EXPECTANCY AT BIRTH AND AT AGE 65, BY RACE AND SEX: 1900, 1950, AND 1978

Age, sex, and race	1900	1950	1978
		Life expectancy at birth	
Total	47.3	68.2	73.3
Men	46.3	65.6	69.5
Women	48.3	71.1	77.2
White	47.6	69.1	74.0
Men	46.6	66.5	70.2
Women	48.7	72.2	77.8
Nonwhite	33.0	60.8	69.2
Men	32.5	59.1	65.0
Women	33.5	62.9	73.6
		Life expectancy at age 65	
Total	11.9	13.9	16.1
Men	11.5	12.8	14.1
Women	12.2	15.0	18.0
White	—	—	16.4
Men	11.5	12.8	14.0
Women	12.2	15.1	18.4
Nonwhite	—	—	16.1
Men	10.4	12.5	14.0
Women	11.4	14.5	16.1

Source: Beth J. Soldo, "America's Elderly in the 1980s," *Population Bulletin,* vol. 35, no. 4 (Population Reference Bureau, Inc., Washington, D.C., 1980), p. 16.

aged 65 and over ranges from 2.9 percent in Africa to 11.2 percent in Western countries and Japan. Life expectancy exhibits similar variation: 46.2 years in Africa, 54.4 in Asia and Oceania, 63.1 in Latin America, 69.0 in Eastern Europe and the U.S.S.R., and 72.6 in Western countries and Japan. The United States is not the "oldest" country, as most Western European nations have older age structures; in Austria, East and West Germany, and Sweden the proportion aged 65 and over exceeds 15 percent (Soldo, 1980).

Table 2.3 presents more detailed statistics on trends in life expectancy in the United States during this century. There has been a marked increase in life expectancy, with the greatest increases occurring in the first half of the century. Note, however, that although life expectancy at birth has increased substantially, there have been much smaller increases in life expectancy at age 65. Declines in *infant* mortality have contributed most to the aging of the population. Whereas death cannot be avoided, it has been postponed, as more people survive childhood to live until old age. In fact, the rate of infant mortality in 1900 was equivalent to the current mortality rate for persons 85 and over. Older persons now account for approximately two thirds of all deaths (Soldo, 1980).

These trends are reflected in changes in the leading causes of death (Table 2.4), with *infectious communicable diseases* (tuberculosis, pneumonia, scarlet fever) being replaced by *chronic degenerative diseases* (cancer, cirrhosis of the liver, heart diseases) as the major causes of death. The percentage of deaths caused by heart diseases and cancer, for example, has risen from 11.7 in 1900 to 58.2 in 1977. Older people are more likely than younger people to die from these chronic illnesses, and more people are living to an age that makes them "eligible" for such diseases. Heart diseases, cancer, and cerebrovascular diseases (mainly stroke) account for over 75 percent of all deaths at ages 65 and over.

Although reduced mortality in later life has not been a major cause of increased life expectancy, such reductions have occurred and have even been accelerating in recent years in many modern societies (Myers, 1978). For example, the mortality rate for persons aged 85 and over decreased by 25 percent from 1968 to 1977. Whereas deaths due to cancer have been increasing in the older population during the past decade, deaths due to heart diseases and strokes have been declining. Thus, the aging of the population will continue, a trend that must be addressed by social policy.

The patterns in Table 2.3 indicate that life expectancy is higher for females than for males, and for whites than for nonwhites (primarily blacks). Combining these, it is interesting that nonwhite females have a higher life expectancy than white males. The lowest life expectancy is for nonwhite males, although for those who reach 65, racial differences in life expectancy are very slight. Indeed, there is a racial "crossover" in mortality rates at about age 75, with mortality becoming lower for blacks. This may reflect differential susceptibility to diseases or a "survival of the fittest" among minority groups (Manton et al., 1979). Nonetheless, higher infant mortality and less adequate health care result in "younger" minority populations: 7.9 percent of blacks are aged 65 and over, with a median age of only 24.6 in the black population (Soldo, 1980).

Table 2.4 TEN LEADING CAUSES OF DEATH IN THE UNITED STATES, 1900 AND 1977: RATE (DEATHS PER 1,000 POPULATION) AND PERCENT OF ALL DEATHS

1900	Rate	Percent of all deaths	1977	Rate	Percent of all deaths
1. Influenza and pneumonia	202.2	11.8	1. Heart diseases	332.3	37.8
2. Tuberculosis	194.4	11.3	2. Cancer and other malignant neoplasms	178.7	20.4
3. Gastritis and related (stomach inflammations)	142.7	8.3	3. Cerebrovascular diseases	84.1	9.6
4. Heart diseases	137.4	8.0	4. Accidents	47.7	5.4
5. Cerebrovascular diseases	106.9	6.2	5. Influenza and pneumonia	23.7	2.7
6. Infections of the kidney	81.0	4.7	6. Diabetes mellitus	15.2	1.7
7. Accidents	72.3	4.2	7. Cirrhosis of the liver	14.3	1.6
8. Cancer and other malignant neoplasms	64.0	3.7	8. Arteriosclerosis	13.3	1.5
9. Early infancy diseases	62.6	3.6	9. Suicide	13.3	1.5
10. Diphtheria	40.3	2.3	10. Early infancy diseases	10.8	1.2

Sources: U.S. Public Health Service, 1981a, p. 1; U.S. Bureau of the Census, 1975, p. 58.

Sex Ratio

Because the average woman lives longer than the average man, a substantial majority of older persons are women (more than 59 percent of those over 65 in 1980). This is largely a product of changes in the past 40 years and is especially true at older levels (Figure 2.2). Currently, the average woman can expect to outlive the average man by about 8 years. This difference results partly from sex differences in causes of death. Medical advances in treating infectious diseases, such as influenza and tuberculosis, have been greater than for degenerative diseases, such as cancer and heart disease, and men are more likely than women to die of degenerative diseases. Whether these mortality differences are linked to traditional sex roles or to inherent susceptibility to certain diseases can only be speculated upon at this point. However, older women, particularly widows living alone, should be high-priority targets of social policies, given their vulnerability to low income, poor health, and isolation.

Place of Residence

As with other age groups, of course, older people can be found in any number of residential settings. Older people are most numerous in the largest states—nearly one third of all persons over 65 reside in New York, California, Pennsylvania, and Illinois. In some states the proportions of population 65 and over is low: Alaska (2.6 percent), Utah and Hawaii (7.7 percent), and Wyoming (8.1 percent) (Soldo, 1980). Other states have relatively high proportions, including Florida (18.1 percent), Arkansas (12.8 percent), and Iowa (13.1 percent).

The fact that some states are relatively "older," however, tells us very little

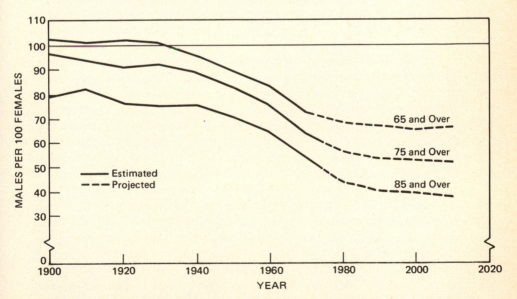

Figure 2.2 Sex ratios in the older ages: 1900 to 2010. (*Source:* U.S. Bureau of the Census, 1976, p. 12.)

about who those older people are, why they are there, and what the aging experience may be like for them. Younger people migrate out of some states including
many midwestern states, such as Iowa, Kansas, and Nebraska, as well as other
states such as Maine and Arkansas. Older people migrate to other states, especially Sunbelt states. From 1970 to 1979 the number of persons 65 and over increased by more than 60 percent in Nevada, Arizona, and Florida.

Older people who "move in" are likely to be very different from those who
are "left behind," particularly because older migrants often have better health
and higher incomes. In the short run such migrants may boost local economies
without increasing service demand, whereas outmigration of the old may concen-
trate rather than reduce service demand (Longino & Biggar, 1982). Each state
has its own pattern of recruitment and retention of older people and must develop
policies to meet the needs of its own particular older population.

The United States is an urban society, and 62 percent of older people live
in metropolitan areas. Older people are more likely than the general population
to be concentrated in central cities (and over half of older blacks are central-city
residents). This largely reflects "aging in place" of city residents, rather than migration of older persons into cities (Lichter et al., 1981). Although the elderly
are underrepresented in suburban areas, the proportion residing there has increased over the past 20 years. This reflects the aging of those who moved to the
suburbs in the 1940s and 1950s as well as recent migration of older people to
suburbs and small metropolitan areas (Lichter et al., 1981).

Although most older people reside in metropolitan areas, they represent
a greater proportion of the total population in nonmetropolitan areas, particularly
in small rural towns that function as farm retirement centers. This partly reflects
migration out of rural areas by the young as they seek educational and employment opportunities. But older people have also displayed a net migration from
metropolitan to nonmetropolitan areas since the 1960s, a "turnaround" that has
also been evident in the general population since the 1970s (Lichter et al., 1981).

Older people are also unevenly distributed within metropolitan areas. There
is evidence of substantial and growing residential age segregation, reflecting a
number of ecological processes (Cowgill, 1978; LaGory et al., 1980; Chevan,
1982). Older people have relatively low residential mobility, so they "age in place"
within older neighborhoods. When they do move, older persons are economically
disadvantaged in the competition for space and are therefore more likely to be
confined to areas with older, cheaper housing. Residential age segregation also
results from changing housing needs over the life cycle. Single and young married
people are often attracted to the central city by the excitement and diversity of
urban life and the accessibility to employment and city services. Families with
children, however, are attracted to suburbs, which offer more living space, clean
environments, better schools, and so on. In middle age and beyond there is less
need for space and a tendency to move to smaller, more economical houses or
apartments nearer the center of the city. Accessibility to city services, particularly
public transportation, may again become important. These ecological processes
of choice and stability combine to produce a clustering of older persons in more
centrally located areas of smaller, cheaper, multiunit housing.

Although housing needs do change through the life cycle, older people constitute the least mobile age group in the society. Among noninstitutionalized older persons, only 18 percent of those aged 65 to 74 and 16 percent of those 75 and over changed residence between 1975 and 1979, compared with 40 percent of the total population (Soldo, 1980).

Long-distance migration by relatively affluent older persons, such as to retirement communities in Florida or Arizona, has become more prevalent in the past 20 years, but still accounts for only a very small minority. Of those who moved between 1975 and 1979, more than half remained in the same county and less than one quarter moved to a different state (Soldo, 1980).

Residential mobility by older people represents a number of patterns (Biggar, 1980a; Longino & Jackson, 1980). Local moves, such as within the same county, typically represent a desire for smaller, cheaper housing or a need for assistance. Such movers tend to be in poorer health, have lower socioeconomic status, and are more likely to be widowed. Indeed, within-county moves peak in the over-85 age group. Longer-distance migration more often involves persons in their 60s who have better health and higher socioeconomic status and are still married. Interstate migration, for example, often represents a desire for the leisure and recreational amenities of a retirement life-style. Such migrants disproportionately choose Sunbelt destinations: Florida for those residing East of the Mississippi and California or Arizona for those West of the Mississippi (Biggar, 1980b). However, approximately one fifth of interstate migration represents *return migration* to the state of one's birth (Longino, 1979). Such persons tend to be less well off than other long-distance movers, and perhaps they are seeking to bolster the resources (especially family) available to meet their increasing needs.

It is clear that older people reside in many different settings. This diversity must be taken into account in developing services as well as theories about aging. The "graying of the suburbs," for example, represents growing service burdens on local government combined with a shrinking tax base. Rural and small-town older persons may have more intact social networks, but they are likely to be more isolated from health care and transportation, whereas the reverse is true of the aged in cities. Although states, such as Florida, may benefit in the short run from inmigration of relatively healthy and economically independent older persons, the service needs of these persons are likely to grow as they age.

HEALTH

Health is basic to any discussion of the aging experience because health, particularly *self-rating* of health, is one of the most consistent predictors of life satisfaction among the aged (George & Bearon, 1980).

Before discussing "objective" indicators of health in the older population, it should be recognized that people do assess their own health, which is perhaps more important in determining satisfaction than "actual" health. Many older people come to accept certain pains and disabilities as inevitable or unimportant. Their self-ratings, based only in part on objective health, decline less with age than objective ratings, as the definition of *good health* changes during the life cycle. Arthritis, for example, may be viewed as normal by an older person but be intolerable for a younger person. Cockerham and associates (1983) asked persons aged 18 to 93 to rate their health "compared to others your age." Age was associated with better perceived health; 40 percent of persons older than 60 considered their health "much better" compared to 25 percent for those aged 18 to 60. In another study comparing "young-old" (65–74) and "old-old" (75 +) persons with comparable objective health, Ferraro (1980) found higher personal health ratings by the old-old. Approximately 7 out of 10 older persons in the community evaluated their health as good or excellent (Soldo, 1980). Subjective ratings represent only one measure of health, however (others will be discussed later), and subjective adaptations may become a barrier to seeking needed assistance.

Aging and Biological Change

The most basic and intriguing biological question associated with aging concerns why organisms age and die. Each animal species has a set, limited life span: 3 years for rats, 40 years for horses, and 50 years for apes (Fries & Crapo, 1981). The limit of the human life span appears to be approximately 115 years. There have been claims of much longer life spans, particularly in certain cultures (see Chapter 3), but these appear to be quite exaggerated. Kurtzman and Gordon (1976) indicate that the longest confirmed life span is 113 years, although it was reported in 1982 that Arthur Reed, of Oakland, Calif., had celebrated his 122nd birthday (an age verified by the Social Security Administration, from which he had been receiving benefits since 1944). Of those who reach 85, however, only one in 10,000 will reach 110.

The sources of this "biological clock" are not well understood, although it has long been a subject of interest. Hippocrates, for example, attributed it to a decline in "body heat," and Sir Francis Bacon conjectured about the existence of a "vital spirit." More recently, a number of theories have emerged that, singly or in combination, may account for the limited life span (Kurtzman & Gordon, 1976; Fries & Crapo, 1981). Some argue that the limit is genetically induced, representing preprogrammed genes or an accumulation of genetic errors in cell reproduction. The *autoimmunity* approach asserts that there is a reduced capacity to recognize and destroy foreign substances (such as mutated cells) and incorrect destruction of normal cells. Other theories attribute the biological limit to the production of certain chemicals, inability of aged cells to coordinate their functions, wear-and-tear and the accumulation of cellular malfunctions, and other processes.

Such processes can be studied in many ways. Cultures of cells can be subjected to varying conditions to see how long they reproduce. Animals with short life spans, such as rats, serve as more natural sources of information. Certain human conditions also offer unique opportunities. *Hutchinson-Gilford syndrome,* for example, represents a "caricature" of aging in young children, as biological aging usually begins around age 2, with "death of old age" typically occurring by age 13.

Interest in the causes of limits to the life span is, of course, partly stimulated by a desire to extend the life span. Earlier "prescriptions" for long life have included taking garlic or vitamins in massive quantities, precise doses of gold or mercury, and using sex hormones from monkeys (Kurtzman & Gordon, 1976). More scientific research indicates that many factors are related to longevity, including diet, body weight and blood pressure, smoking and alcohol consumption, heredity, exercise and sleep, morale and hopefulness, marital status and social support, and intelligence (Schulz, 1978; Markides & Pappas, 1982). Some have questioned whether the life span should be extended because this might put too great a population strain on societies. But Fries and Crapo (1981) note that greater understanding of biological aging may also reduce the incidence of "premature death" and result in greater health and vigor in the later stages of the normal life span.

The patterns of survivorship that were presented in Figure 2.1 indicate that there has been no change in the apparent limit of the human life span. Rather, increased life expectancy represents a "rectangularization of the survival curve" as more people approach the limit because of the elimination and reduction of diseases (Fries & Crapo, 1981). Some increases in life expectancy are still possible through such processes. Kurtzman and Gordon (1976) estimate that life expectancy could be increased by nearly 11 years by the elimination of major cardiovascular and renal diseases, and nearly 6 years by the elimination of heart diseases.

The biology of aging involves more than just a determination of the limits of life, of course. The process of *senescence,* involving the deterioration of functioning of cells and organs, begins early in adulthood and continues throughout life (Kart et al., 1978; Hickey, 1980; Fries & Crapo, 1981). This process is reflected in many physical changes: wrinkled skin, reduced muscular strength, stiff joints, increased vulnerability to infection.

Human organs gradually diminish in function over time. As Alexander Leaf (1973:52) describes it, on the average a person of 75 compared to himself at 30 will have 92% of his/her former brain weight, 84% of his/her basal metabolism rate, 70% of his/her kidney filtration rate, and 43% of his/her maximum breathing capacity. (Kart et al., 1978:9–10)

These changes sound frightening, but for the most part are relatively benign. Fries and Crapo (1981) note that normal, healthy organisms maintain an excess *organ reserve* that is needed only when under exceptional stress, so this reserve can diminish without affecting normal functioning. But the ability to maintain *homeostasis*—to regulate bodily functions within precise limits—declines as organ reserve is diminished, and the average person at age 85 has less than half of original reserve capacity. Thus, older persons are less able to adapt to physiological stress and are more vulnerable to infections.

Senescence is a normal, natural process, but there is also considerable variability. Different parts of the body are affected in different ways and at different rates. Individual variability is associated with such factors as diet, exercise, and life-style. A distinction should also be made between *intrinsic* changes linked to biological aging and *extrinsic* changes associated with disease and environmental factors. Aging and senescence are *not* diseases, and people do not die of "old age," except to the degree that senescence makes them susceptible to disease.

Nutrition is one factor that is associated with the biology of aging. General theories of biological aging contain nutritional components, and diet plays an important part in the course of diseases which may accompany aging (Kart et al., 1978). The nutritional needs of older people are both lesser and greater than those of younger people. Caloric requirements decline with age, as physical activity typically declines. It has been estimated that caloric needs decline by 5 percent per decade between 55 and 75 and by 7 percent after 75 (Kart et al., 1978). But dietary balance remains important, and nutrients are absorbed less efficiently because of age-related physiological changes. Poor nutrition can lead to other problems. Iron deficiency can lead to anemia, for example, and calcium deficiency over a period of time is associated with osteoporosis, a weakening of the bone structure.

Unfortunately, a significant portion of the older population is below recommended nutritional levels, with the most common deficiencies including calcium, iron, and vitamins C, A, and B (Barrows and Roeder, 1977). Indeed, it has been estimated that "at least 8 million older people are in desperate need (of a good diet) and that most nutrition programs reach only a tiny proportion of that number and serve those participants an average of only 7 meals every 10 weeks" (Fernandes, 1981:79). The nutritional deficiencies of older people reflect a variety of factors. Loss of teeth, denture problems, and reduced smell and taste may make eating more difficult or less enjoyable. Social factors are also involved, including social isolation and lack of money or transportation for shopping. Finally, nutritional problems in later life may reflect long-standing dietary habits.

Health Conditions

To simply state that older people suffer more health problems is misleading. *Acute* (temporary) conditions, such as injuries, pneumonia, and influenza, tend to decline with age (Table 2.5). In fact, the highest rate of acute conditions occurs among children under 5 (as any parent could tell you).

Chronic conditions are longer-term conditions that are generally progres-

Table 2.5 INCIDENCE OF ACUTE CONDITIONS (NUMBER PER 100 PERSONS PER YEAR), BY AGE, 1980

	Age				
Condition	All ages	Under 6	6–16	17–44	45 and over
All acute conditions	222.2	399.8	293.0	222.6	130.6
Infectious and parasitic	24.6	56.3	42.5	21.3	9.8
Respiratory	116.2	201.1	159.5	113.3	71.2
Digestive	11.4	18.6	13.4	13.0	6.0
Injuries	33.4	35.2	40.4	38.6	21.6
All other acute conditions	36.6	88.6	37.3	36.3	22.0

Source: U.S. Public Health Service, 1981b, pp. 12, 15.

sive and irreversible. The prevalence of chronic conditions increases with age, and only 14 percent of noninstitutionalized older persons are free of them. The most common chronic illnesses are arthritis, heart problems, hypertension, and diabetes, with each of the first three affecting at least 20 percent of the older population.

These chronic conditions result in the need for greater health spending by older people. They spend more on drugs, are more likely to see a physician, and have more and longer hospital stays. Older persons account for over one third of all health-care costs in the United States (Hickey, 1980). By 1980, average annual medical expenses for persons 65 and over was more than $2000, nearly three times that for the total population.

Disability

The critical question concerning chronic conditions is the extent to which these conditions handicap the aged in their daily routines, or how age affects *functional* health. Older people do have more health restrictions on their activities. Table 2.6 indicates that in 1980 39 percent of all older people had limitations on major activities, and another 6 percent had less severe limitations. The aged also suffer more days of disability (Table 2.7). In 1980 the average older person was bedridden for 2 weeks, compared with half that amount for the total population. The major causes of limitations are arthritis and rheumatism, heart conditions, visual impairments, hypertension, and impairments of lower extremities and hips. However, *most* older persons do *not* suffer activity limitations due to health problems, an important fact to keep in mind in discussing their capabilities.

Whereas institutionalization represents the most complete form of disability, stereotypes about the aged tend to exaggerate the extent to which they are institutionalized. Only 6 percent of all persons aged 65 and over are in long-term care institutions (96 percent of these in nursing homes) (U.S. Bureau of the Census, 1979). This figure is misleading, however, because it refers to nursing-home populations at any particular moment. There is a greater possibility that any older individual will reside in a nursing home *at some time.* Studies of death certificates indicate that from 20 to 30 percent of all deaths to persons 65 and over occur in nursing homes or other extended-care facilities (Lesnoff-Caravaglia, 1978). Institutionalization does increase with age, but even for persons over 85, approximately 80 percent reside in the community at any one time. Females are more likely to be institutionalized than males, and nonwhite rates are lower in nursing and personal-care homes but higher in mental institutions (Hickey, 1980).

Implications of Chronic Illness

One cannot overemphasize the importance of chronic illnesses, both in shaping the aging experience and creating critical social policy needs, because chronic illnesses are an increasing part of the total illness load on society. Chronic illnesses require therapeutic approaches quite different from acute illnesses because they must often be managed rather than cured, and their long-term nature makes them extremely expensive.

Chronic illnesses also have a much greater impact on the individual and

Table 2.6 LIMITATION OF ACTIVITY DUE TO CHRONIC CONDITIONS, BY AGE AND SEX, 1980

	Percent with no activity limitation	Percent with limitation, but not in major activity[a]	Percent with limitation in major activity[a]
Both sexes:			
All ages	85.6	3.5	10.9
Age 17–44	91.4	3.1	5.5
Age 45–64	76.1	5.1	18.8
Age 65 and over	54.8	6.2	39.0
Males:			
All ages	85.3	3.5	11.2
Age 17–44	90.8	3.4	5.8
Age 45–64	74.7	5.1	20.2
Age 65 and over	51.2	4.6	44.2
Females:			
All ages	85.9	3.5	10.6
Age 17–44	91.9	2.8	5.3
Age 45–64	77.4	5.2	17.4
Age 65 and over	57.3	7.4	35.3

[a]"Major activity" refers to ability to work, keep house, or engage in school or preschool activities.
Source: U.S. Public Health Service, 1981b, p. 24.

Table 2.7 DAYS OF DISABILITY PER PERSON PER YEAR, BY AGE, 1980

	Restricted activity days	Bed-disability days
All persons	19.1	7.0
Age 17–24	12.5	4.7
Age 25–44	16.5	6.1
Age 45–64	26.5	8.4
Age 65 and over	39.2	13.8

Source: U.S. Public Health Service, 1981b, p. 22.

his or her patterns of living (Strauss, 1975). There are the psychological burdens of alternating remission and relapse as the person is torn between hopefulness and hopelessness. The chronically ill often face prolonged regimens to control symptoms, which may be complicated, time-consuming, uncomfortable, and expensive. Persons with multiple chronic conditions face multiple and sometimes competing regimens.

> Mr. Smith has both chronic bronchitis and a stomach hernia. For the first, he is supposed to do several minutes of daily postural drainage. But this enhances the probability that he will get heartburn from his hernia. Furthermore, if he attempts to reduce the probability of his hernial heartburn by using a high pillow while sleeping, that sometimes brings on pains, ordinarily quiescent, from a pinched neck nerve. (Strauss, 1975:32)

The presence of chronic illness may require partial or complete redesigning of one's life-style, partly because of the physical requirements associated with the disease. The following illustrates the problems faced by a person who has emphysema:

> The degree of planning for an ordinary activity (shopping for groceries) becomes long and complicated. A patient lives on the second floor. He must "recoup" oxygen after walking a single block even if on flat terrain. The grocery store is uphill, so after half a block he needs to rest in order to get his breath back. If he chats with the grocer then he needs to rest for the trip back home. If he carries a bag of groceries that means still more oxygen expenditure; so, even though the route home is downhill, he can only go 3/4 of the block before becoming winded. Then at home he has a flight of stairs with which to contend. Twelve steps is his usual oxygen supply. With the extra grocery weight he requires "getting his wind back" every six to eight steps. What normals can do in twenty minutes is stretched out to one hour or more. (Strauss, 1975:104)

Other chronic ailments—poor hearing, high blood pressure, arthritis—will have their own effects on activities and normal routines. One consequence of these limitations may be social isolation, compounded by feelings of embarrassment over visible handicaps or "distasteful" symptoms.

Public policy has not adequately addressed the growing prevalence of chronic illnesses in modern society (Strauss, 1975). The person with multiple ailments may need widely scattered sources of care, and money can become a preoccupation. The mobility needs of the chronically ill are neglected—curbstones are too high, entry doors too heavy, benches, ramps, and railings too infrequent. Although they deal with large numbers of chronic problems at one stage or another, hospitals are often poorly organized to meet the multiple needs of the chronically ill. Instead, each disease is treated in isolation. Attention is too seldom paid to the social and psychological needs of chronic patients, particularly their pain and anxiety. Strauss suggests the need for a much wider range of services for those with chronic diseases, including counseling and education, redesign of physical and social environments, managerial assistance (referral and coordination, money management), and daily maintenance services (cooking, cleaning, transportation).

Because older persons often have multiple chronic conditions, particularly careful assessment is needed to uncover remediable conditions and to better match services to their needs. Rubenstein and associates (1982) describe the use of "geriatric assessment units," which are interdisciplinary approaches to medical and psychosocial assessment. Preliminary evidence indicates that such approaches result in increased diagnostic accuracy, improved rehabilitation outcomes, and more appropriate service placement (including reduced institutionalization).

PSYCHOLOGICAL FUNCTIONING

We tend to have an image of psychological decline in old age, whether considering perception, learning, intelligence, or some other aspect. The question of this stereotype's accuracy is complex and undoubtedly needs a book by itself, but some of the more basic trends should be noted here.

A variety of studies do indicate declines with age in sensation and perception. There are age-related declines in vision, hearing, and taste (Botwinick, 1978). Visual acuity peaks at about 20 and remains relatively constant until the forties, when decline typically occurs. Few people over 60 do not need vision correction. The most common problem involves focusing on nearby objects, which hinders reading. Similarly, hearing decline begins after 20 and there is typically less sensitivity to taste after 50. In general, older people have higher *sensory thresholds,* requiring higher levels of stimulation which limits their performance (Botwinick, 1978). Older people also respond more slowly to environmental stimuli, apparently due to changes in the central nervous system. Such impairments represent important barriers to interacting fully with the world and can restrict activities in important ways.

The importance of sensory impairments is too easily underestimated by younger persons. As taste or smell declines, there may be less interest in eating, resulting in malnutrition. Poor hearing and eyesight may be embarrassing and lead to avoidance of social interaction. Poor eyesight or a disturbed sense of balance make even such simple movements as climbing stairs or crossing streets dangerous and confusing. Some training programs for staff who work with the aged are employing simulation of these impairments—nose clips, ear plugs, goggles that make the floor appear unstable—to give them an appreciation of the world as it is experienced by their clients (Shore, 1976).

Intellectual Abilities

Probably the greatest research attention has been paid to age differences in intellectual capacity: intelligence, learning, memory, problem solving. In general, the evidence suggests that intellectual ability does decline, but the decline may be smaller, start later, and involve fewer functions than was once thought (Botwinick, 1977). There is certainly ample evidence that older people can and do learn.

Cross-sectional studies of intelligence have yielded what Botwinick (1977) terms a "classical aging pattern": a peak in intelligence in the late teens and early twenties, followed by a decline with age. Decline is greatest for psychomotor performance skills involving speed and perceptual integration, and less in verbal skills involving stored information. The greatest decline occurs after age 70. Longitudinal studies of aging and intelligence show the same pattern, although decline is less and starts later (Botwinick, 1977). These studies do indicate, however, that people with high intelligence when they are young tend to retain it as they age.

Some forms of intelligence are more age-sensitive than others. A distinction is often made between *fluid* and *crystallized* intelligence (Horn & Donaldson, 1980). Fluid intelligence involves nonverbal skills that are relatively independent of education and experience, being more directly related to the functioning of the nervous system. Crystallized intelligence involves the use of habits of judgment based on experience to solve problems. There appears to be some decline with age in fluid intelligence, although this is not progressive throughout adult life, whereas the "cultural knowledge" reflected in crystallized intelligence appears to increase with age.

Age-related declines in intellectual abilities reflect a number of processes. There appears to be a slowing of perceptual processing and age-related reduction in the amount of material that can be attended to (Hoyer & Plude, 1980). Such deficits are quite minimal with familiar, well-practiced skills, however. More novel and complex tasks result in greater performance deficits for older persons (Cerella et al., 1980). Some aspects of memory display age-related declines, but not all. There are rather pronounced decrements in the capacity and time required to remember newly learned information, perhaps reflecting inefficiency in entering and retrieving information rather than in actual memory storage capacity. But there seem to be no age-related difficulties in retrieving older, basic information (Botwinick, 1978; Fozard, 1980).

The entire area of research on intellectual functioning is plagued with tremendous complexities. Some age differences may reflect differences in level or type of education across age cohorts. Schaie (1975) suggests that intelligence itself does not decline with age; rather, the information and skills of older people become obsolete in a changing society. It has also been suggested that declines in memory, learning, or intelligence with age do not reflect a general aging effect. The theory of *terminal drop* states that "many human functions are not primarily related to chronological age as such but tend to show marked decline prior to death during a period ranging from a few weeks to a few years" (Palmore & Cleveland, 1976:76). According to this concept, the normal aged maintain stable functioning until they enter the "drop" period preceding death. Because death becomes increasingly likely with age, terminal drop will show up as a gradual decline with age in cross-sectional designs.

It is also possible that although older people do not *perform* tasks which measure learning as well, their *capacity* to learn may not be impaired. Older people perform more cautiously and desire greater certainty before committing themselves to a response, sacrificing speed for accuracy (Botwinick, 1978). This may reflect feelings of inadequacy, and Botwinick notes that older people may be inappropriately and overly aroused in experimental situations. Age decrements tend to be less when time pressures are reduced. Older people may also be less motivated to perform well on laboratory tasks they find meaningless and irrelevant. Perhaps college sophomores are more easily impressed by the chance to participate in "science" (no offense intended to sophomore readers). Finally, many of these studies indicate that older people may remember or learn less than younger people because they are unskilled at using techniques—"mediational strategies"—that organize and retrieve information more efficiently. This might be because younger people are typically better or more recently educated, rather than any innate decline in intellectual capacity with age.

These are important points to remember in developing retraining programs for older workers or adult education programs. The aged may "fail" in such programs because they lack interest or study skills, not because they cannot learn. In such cases, the fault lies as much with the program for failing to gear itself to the population being served. The learning and performance of older people can be improved through training or practice if the context is appropriately structured (Botwinick, 1978). Baltes and Baltes (1982), for example, report on ADEPT (Adult Development and Enrichment Program), a program involving community residents aged 60 to 85. One of the findings of this project was that training in the types of thinking and problem-solving skills required by items on intelligence tests resulted in significantly improved performance on each of seven types of intelligence tests. Older people learn best when the pace is not too fast and material or tasks are meaningful to them. They can benefit from being taught "how to learn" through strategies for organizing and mediating information.

It is clear that aging does not bring major general declines in mental ability. Baltes and Baltes (1982) note that early gerontological work focused on "normative" aging, emphasizing decline and deterioration. But it has become clear that there are large individual differences as some show sharp declines with age, others improve, and most show considerable stability. There is also much more individual "plasticity" than is often acknowledged, as it has been demonstrated that intervention can yield individual improvement in learning and problem solving. The degree to which the intellectual functioning of older individuals varies is uncertain, as are the factors that shape such variability, but Willis and Baltes (1980) conclude that chronological age accounts for much less variability in intellectual ability, at least until the 70s, than does cohort, education, or health. Even when intellectual declines do appear, it is not at all clear that they affect the ability of the vast majority of older people to function in their everyday lives.

Contrary to stereotypes of intellectual stagnation and decline in old age, creativity and personal growth *can* continue to the very end of life. Many of our greatest statesmen, scientists, educators, and scholars have functioned into old age: John XXIII was chosen Pope at 77, Golda Meir became prime minister of Israel at 71, Pablo Picasso executed three series of drawings between 85 and 90, and Frank Lloyd Wright completed New York's Guggenheim Museum at 89. Even apparent declines in productivity may have little to do with age. In a study of scientific productivity, Cole (1979) found an increase in the 30s and a decrease after age 50. He attributed this to a reward system that discourages scientists whose work is not favorably received so that those who continue publishing represent the "elite" members of their cohort. Dennis (1966) found that some scholars (historians, philosophers, and novelists) were most productive in their 50s and 60s, probably requiring and benefiting from longer periods of preparation and the accumulation of experience in their work.

PSYCHOLOGICAL DISORDERS AND RELATED PROBLEMS

In the discussion in the previous section on the normal range of psychological functioning, the relatively slight age differences that occur seem to have little effect on everyday living. As with any age group, however, older people may also suffer from more severe psychological impairment. Indeed, the incidence of mental illness increases with age, due primarily to increases in depression and organic brain disorders. Butler and Lewis (1982) offer a "conservative" estimate that 15 percent of the older population need mental health services. The rate of hospitalization for psychiatric disorders rises with age. In 1976, older persons represented 28.7 percent of the patients in state and county mental hospitals (Butler & Lewis, 1982); from one-third to one-half of these were admitted earlier in life and grew old in the institution, while the remainder were hospitalized in later life.

Psychological disorders are most prevalent among those with advanced age (75+) and in poor physical health (Pfeiffer, 1977). Rates are higher for widowed than for married persons, and highest for those who are separated or divorced.

Changes and problems that may accompany aging are associated with psychological disorders. Butler and Lewis (1982) state that "loss is a predominant theme in characterizing the emotional experiences of older people" (p. 43). Adaptation to such losses as widowhood, physical illness, low income, and reduced activity and status requires the expenditure of considerable physical and emotional energy. This can lead to a variety of emotional reactions, including grief, guilt, depression, anxiety, rage, and feelings of helplessness, as well as to a variety of adaptive techniques, including denial, suspicion and fear, regression, and rigidity (Butler & Lewis, 1982). Losses can accumulate and trigger disruption or destruction of the social supports that aid in coping, and mental disorder may itself lead to social isolation (Lowenthal, 1964).

Although much remains to be learned, progress has been made in understanding the effects of psychological treatment for older people. As with cognitive skills, psychological impairments of the elderly are responsive to intervention, and older people can benefit from the full range of treatments, from individual psychotherapy to drug therapy (Eisdorfer & Stotsky, 1977; Butler & Lewis, 1982). Unfortunately, older people may confront expectations that treatment is ineffective and hopeless. Butler and Lewis suggest that ageism has become "professionalized" in the mental health field in the form of pessimism about the treatability of older patients. Whereas older people are overrepresented in institutional settings, they represent only 2 to 3 percent of outpatients in psychiatric clinics, community mental health centers, and private therapy. Even the movement away from institutional treatment of psychiatric disorders in mental hospitals has not benefitted older persons, because they have instead been admitted to psychiatric facilities in general hospitals and to nursing homes (Gatz et al., 1980). We will return to such service-related problems in Chapter 11. There is a particularly critical need for treatment in nursing homes, where as many as three fourths of the residents may have moderately severe or severe mental disorders (Pfeiffer, 1977).

There are two basic types of psychological disorders. *Functional* disorders do not have a physical basis; their origins appear to be emotional, though they are not entirely separable from organic functioning. *Organic* disorders do have a physical basis; they occur because of impaired functioning of the brain.[1]

---

[1]Much of the material in the next two sections has been drawn from Butler and Lewis (1982) and Pfeiffer (1977). For a more complete discussion, the reader is referred to these two excellent sources.

Functional Psychological Disorders

The most common psychological disorder among older people is *depression.* Typical symptoms are psychological—sadness, apathy, pessimism, feelings of helplessness and worthlessness—and physical—fatigue, loss of appetite, sleeplessness. Alcoholism and suicide may be manifestations of depression, and depression may also be reflected in physical complaints. Depression may be triggered by psychosocial stress, such as role loss, social isolation, or poverty (see Chapter 4).

A variety of other functional disorders are also found in the older population. *Paranoid* disorders involve delusion and associated disturbances in mood, behavior, and thinking. These are typically less serious than in younger people, and usually represent short-term reactions to stress. Paranoid disorders are quite responsive to treatment. *Hypochondriasis,* involving overconcern with health and bodily complaints for which there is no physical basis, is a functional disorder commonly associated with depression. *Anxiety* disorders may be generalized or represent a response to specific problems and threats.

Although some functional disorders may begin late in life in response to age-related changes and threats, or first appear then after an accumulation of factors throughout life, others are carried into old age. *Manic-depressive* and *schizophrenic* disorders, for example, generally begin relatively early in life, and it is rare to see their onset in old age. The classic age of onset for schizophrenia is adolescence, and manic-depressive disorders usually begin before 30. *Personality disorders,* involving maladaptive and inflexible personality traits such as obsessive compulsiveness, are also generally deeply ingrained throughout life.

Organic Psychological Disorders

Organic psychological disorders, or *organic brain syndromes* (OBS), account for about half the significant mental impairment of the aged, but the proportion increases with age. Approximately 4 to 6 percent of the older population suffer from OBS, including approximately one in five of those over 80 (Soldo, 1980). OBS is probably the most feared psychological disorder of old age. Organic brain syndromes may involve disturbance of a variety of functions, including memory, learning, speech, and orientation to the world, and may be associated with anxiety, depression, euphoria, delusions, and other symptoms.

Organic psychological disorders are often referred to by the inaccurate and emotion-laden term *senility,* which implies progressive and irreversible deterioration felt to be caused by general aging processes. But organic brain syndromes represent disease processes, not normal aging. Butler and Lewis (1982) stress that we must look for reversibility in *all* disorders, as prompt and accurate diagnosis and treatment are essential. An estimated 10 to 20 percent of organic disorders are treatable and reversible, involving temporary impairment caused by such factors as alcoholism, anemia and malnutrition, drug reactions, and head injuries. The most common causes of OBS, Alzheimer's disease and cerebral arteriosclerosis, are not considered reversible, however. Such cases involve progressive brain-cell deterioration and degeneration. This is the most disabling and tragic handicap facing the aged, involving progressive intellectual and cognitive impairment and personality disorganization. Unfortunately, we have much to learn about organic brain syndromes, and we have not yet developed adequate programs to identify and serve older people with OBS (Gatz et al., 1980).

Alcoholism and Drug Abuse

Although many older people are able to drink in moderation and derive pleasure from it, alcoholism has been identified as the most serious drug abuse problem among the aged (Snyder & Way, 1979). Although recorded rates of alcoholism are lower among the elderly, theirs is more likely to be a hidden condition because most are retired and therefore less visible to the community. Atkinson and Schuckit (1981) estimate the rate of alcoholism to be from 2 to 10 percent in the general elderly population, and perhaps 20 percent in the nursing home population. About half of these are persons who began alcohol abuse at a younger age, whereas the remainder represent late-life alcoholics responding to age-related losses. The highest incidence is among elderly widowers. Compared with younger alcoholics, older alcoholics exhibit lower drinking levels and less personality disorder (Atkinson & Schuckit, 1981). The limited literature on treatment suggests that elderly alcoholics are amenable to treatment.

Persons aged 55 and over exhibit the largest consumption of legal drugs, including tranquilizers and sedatives (Petersen et al., 1979; Atkinson & Schuckit, 1981). Whereas it appears that relatively few older people take a large number of these drugs, the drugs can lead to emotional and physical dependence (Butler & Lewis, 1982). Adverse drug reactions may also be associated with mixing prescription drugs with over-the-counter drugs or alcohol, or with the number and complexity of drugs taken by a particular individual. Addiction to opiates (e.g., heroin) among the aged is likely to be hidden by the family and ignored by police, but Schuckit (1977) has estimated that at least 1 percent of all opiate addicts are older people. This figure may rise in the future if the current heavier use of opiates among younger cohorts persists through the life cycle, although there is some evidence that addicts may "mature out" or "burn out" with age (Petersen et al., 1979).

Suicide

Suicide rates raise particular doubts about stereotypes of the placid "golden years." An estimated 10,000 persons aged 60 and over commit suicide each year, representing approximately one-fourth of all suicides by persons aged 10 and over (Miller, 1979). Age patterns vary by race and sex (Table 2.8). Nonwhite rates peak around 30, whereas white females peak around 50. White males exhibit a steady increase in suicide rates in later life, however, so that the highest rate of reported suicides occurs among white males in their eighties.

It is not clear why suicides continue to increase into old age only for white males. One possibility is that the status loss of retirement and reduced income are particularly demoralizing for white males (Miller, 1979; Seiden, 1981). Mar-

**Table 2.8   SUICIDE RATES IN THE UNITED STATES, BY AGE, SEX,
             AND RACE, 1977 (PER 100,000 POPULATION)**

Age	White males	White females	Nonwhite males	Nonwhite females
15–24	22.9	5.5	15.5	4.0
25–34	26.7	9.3	25.7	6.8
35–44	24.7	11.2	16.0	5.1
45–54	27.3	13.6	11.7	5.2
55–64	30.9	11.2	13.3	4.4
65–74	37.5	9.4	11.8	1.9
75–84	48.4	7.5	13.2	3.4
85 +	49.9	4.4	12.5	2.3

Source: U.S. Public Health Service, 1981a, pp. 1–43.

shall (1978) notes that there has been some decline in suicide rates for aged white males in the last 30 years and that this is highly related to improvement in their income status.

It is noteworthy that older people are less likely than younger groups to attempt suicide, but are more likely to be successful (Miller, 1979). Older people less frequently communicate their suicidal intentions, and use more lethal weapons. It appears that geriatric suicides are less often used as a call for help or a way to manipulate others. Butler and Lewis (1982) note that "a rational or philosophical decision to kill oneself is undoubtedly more common in old age as people perceive themselves to be failing" (p. 80).

Suicide in old age may be triggered by such stressful events as poor health, widowhood, and retirement. Sociological theories also relate suicide to loss of social integration (Liska, 1981), and age-linked changes may disrupt the social networks of older people. Widowhood can lead to social isolation, and there is a well-documented relationship between widowhood and suicide (Bock, 1972). Bock also notes that low income and poor health can affect networks of social relationships. The highest elderly suicide rate occurs in the lowest classes, who are less likely to be married, have fewer social ties in the community, and are least likely to belong to community organizations.

SOCIAL AND ECONOMIC CHARACTERISTICS

Education

In discussing differences between age groups, education is a critical factor. Figure 2.3 reflects the sizable gap in education. In 1980 40 percent of people 65 and over had at least a high school education compared with 86 percent of those aged 25 to 34, and about one tenth of the older population are "functionally illiterate" (Soldo, 1980). Many characteristics of the aged, such as greater fatalism and conservatism and less political activism, may really reflect educational differences between *cohorts.* Low education also represents a barrier to needed services. Walmsley and Allington (1982) compared the reading ability of a sample of older persons with the readability levels of forms pertaining to health insurance, Social Security, food stamps, and the like. Most of their sample had reading abilities at or below an eighth-grade level, whereas 98 percent of the forms were written at or above a ninth-grade level and 42 percent were above a twelfth-grade level. Only 16.5 percent of the sample had reading levels that matched all the forms.

The educational gap has been narrowing, however. The average educational level of older persons has increased from about 8 years in 1940 to about 10 years in 1980, and should reach 12 years by 1990. Better-educated cohorts of older people may behave quite differently from older people today. Associated with higher education will be higher socioeconomic status, and future older people may be more involved in community roles, more politically active, more liberal, and so on.

Marital Status

The marriage relationship is an important source of both socioemotional and economic support for many people, which makes the increase in the likelihood of widowhood with age significant. This is one area, however, in which men and women experience aging very differently. Put simply, most older males are married and most older females are widowed (Table 2.9). This is true of whites and nonwhites, although nonwhites of both sexes are more likely than whites to be widowed. Even among persons aged 75 and over, two thirds of men are married whereas two thirds of women are widowed. Indeed, the average age at widowhood for women is only 56 (Soldo, 1980). This striking sex difference in widowhood is reflected in a number of disadvantages for older women, including living alone and poverty.

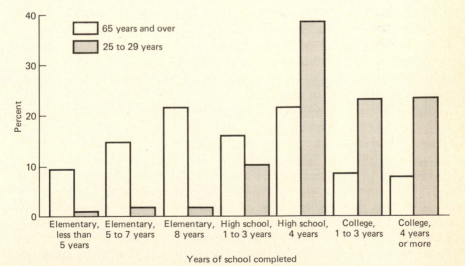

Figure 2.3 Percent of persons aged 65 and over and 25–29, by years of school completed: 1978. (*Source:* U.S. Bureau of the Census, 1979, p. 15.)

Table 2.9 MARITAL STATUS OF PERSONS 65 AND OVER, BY SEX, 1980
(PERCENTAGE OF POPULATION)

	Male			Female		
	All	65–74	75 +	All	65–74	75 +
Never married	5.1	5.4	4.4	5.9	5.6	6.4
Married						
Spouse present	75.5	79.4	67.7	38.1	48.1	22.1
Spouse absent	2.0	2.2	1.7	1.7	2.0	1.2
Widowed	13.6	8.5	24.0	51.0	40.3	68.0
Divorced	3.7	4.4	2.2	3.4	4.0	2.3

Source: U.S. Bureau of the Census, 1981b, p. 7.

Table 2.10 LIVING ARRANGEMENTS OF NONINSTITUTIONALIZED PERSONS
65 AND OVER, BY SEX, 1980 (PERCENTAGE OF POPULATION)

	Male		Female	
	65–74	75 +	65–74	75 +
In families	85.9	77.0	62.6	48.2
Head of household	78.9	67.0	10.0	11.2
Spouse of head	2.6	3.2	45.8	20.7
Other relative	4.4	6.9	6.9	16.4
Living alone	12.5	21.6	36.3	50.6
Living with unrelated individuals	1.6	1.3	1.0	1.1

Source: U.S. Bureau of the Census, 1981b, p. 21.

Living Arrangements and Housing Quality

Table 2.10 indicates the living arrangements of noninstitutionalized older persons. Older women are much more likely than older men to live alone. Although older women are less likely to live in families, they are more likely to live with other relatives, such as their adult offspring. The proportion of men and women living in such families has been declining, and the proportion of them living alone is increasing, indicating greater residential independence of the aged from their families. As we shall see in Chapter 7, however, families continue to be important sources of assistance for older people.

In some respects, most older people appear to be reasonably well-housed. Nearly three fourths of the older population own their homes, with paid-up mortgages for 80 percent of these (Soldo, 1980). The housing of older people has generally improved in quality over the past 30 years, and Struyk and Soldo (1980) indicate that over 80 percent of renters and over 90 percent of owners reside in housing with no major deficiencies. Struyk and Soldo also note high housing satisfaction, as some 80 percent rate their housing as "excellent" or "good." Such statistics are somewhat misleading, however, as they partly reflect the psychological importance of "home" and strong attachment to a place in which one has lived for 20 years or more; the median length of occupancy by older persons was 22 years in 1976 (Struyk & Soldo, 1980). Housing satisfaction may also reflect a perceived lack of options.

Although most older people own their own homes, compared with other age groups their houses tend to be smaller, older, and to have less adequate physical facilities, such as central heating, insulation, and complete plumbing (Struyk & Soldo, 1980). One survey of elderly homeowners found that 22 percent had a serious problem needing repair, and 50 percent had a "critical deficit," having a safety hazard or lacking some needed facility (Rabushka & Jacobs, 1980). Housing deficiencies are more prevalent among renters, blacks, and rural residents (Lawton, 1980; Struyk & Soldo, 1980). Struyk and Soldo also indicate that housing costs are "excessive" for two fifths of older renters and one third of homeowners, and resources may be inadequate for necessary repairs and maintenance.

A number of programs have been directed at the housing needs of the older population, but many gaps remain (Struyk & Soldo, 1980). Availability of low-cost housing is limited, and Carp (1976) has estimated that for every older person in public housing there are another 40 in need of such housing. Older people are also overrepresented in lower-quality neighborhoods with inferior housing, trash and litter, high crime, and inadequate services. Struyk and Soldo (1980) note that older people are likely to be owners in neighborhoods dominated by rental property, so supporting their housing maintenance represents a key to preserving the housing stock of aging neighborhoods.

Labor Force Participation

Our society, and most people in it, have come to expect retirement as a "natural" accompaniment of the aging process. But retirement as a widespread occurrence is a product of the twentieth century. The proportion of men aged 65 and over working has declined from over two thirds in 1900 to less than one fifth now (Table 2.11). Retirement by men aged 55 to 64 has also been increasing in the past 30 years. There are many reasons for these trends—the emergence of pension systems and compulsory retirement, changes in the occupational structure, changing attitudes toward work and leisure, to name a few (see Chapter 6). It should be recognized, however, that about one fifth of all males over 65 *do* work, so retirement is not inevitable.

Labor force participation by women has shown a very different pattern. There has been little change during this century in the proportion of women over 65 who work, but the proportion of women between 55 and 64 who work has increased from 14.1 percent in 1900 to 41.5 percent in 1980. Thus, as women have returned in greater numbers to the work force following child rearing (and, indeed, many never left it), their aging experience is altered by the need to adjust to retirement.

Labor force participation by older blacks is, for the most part, quite similar to that of whites, although black females of all ages have been more likely to work than white females. The gap at the older age ranges (55 and above) has narrowed over the past 30 years, however, so that there are currently only slight differences.

Economic Status

One major concern has been the extent to which the aged are financially handicapped, whether this means poverty or some higher but still inadequate income.

Table 2.11 **LABOR FORCE PARTICIPATION (PERCENT OF NONINSTITUTIONALIZED POPULATION IN LABOR FORCE) BY AGE AND SEX, 1900–1980**

	1900	1947	1980
Males			
55–64	93.3	90.0	72.3
65 and over	68.3	48.0	19.1
Females			
55–64	14.1	24.0	41.5
65 and over	9.1	8.0	8.1

Sources: Beth J. Soldo, "America's Elderly in the 1980s," *Population Bulletin,* vol. 35, no. 4 (Population Reference Bureau, Inc., Washington, D.C., 1980); U.S. Bureau of the Census, 1940, p. 93, and 1981a, p. 33.

Table 2.12 **POVERTY STATUS (PERCENT BELOW LOW-INCOME LEVEL) FOR ALL PERSONS, AND FOR 65 AND OVER POPULATION, BY RACE, 1959–1979**

	1959	1970	1979
All persons	22.4	12.6	11.6
All persons 65 and over	35.2	24.5	15.1
Whites	33.1	22.5	13.2
Blacks	62.5	48.0	35.5

Source: U.S. Bureau of the Census, 1981c, p. 13.

Not all older people are in financial difficulty. In 1978, for example, 18 percent of families headed by someone aged 65 and over had incomes greater than $20,000 (Soldo, 1980). But income is clearly lower for older persons. In 1978 the median annual income for families headed by someone 65 or over was only $10,140, compared with $19,310 for all families (Soldo, 1980).

The most frequently used measure of poverty is an index developed by the Social Security Administration. The index is set at different levels for different types of families. In 1979, for example, the nonfarm low-income level was $3515 for unrelated individuals 65 and over and $4392 for a family of two with a head 65 or over. Using this index, Table 2.12 indicates that poverty has been declining among older people over the past 20 years. Although the gap has narrowed, older people continue to have higher rates of poverty than the general population, with nearly one of every six older persons still living in "official" poverty. It is also clear that poverty continues to be quite high among older blacks, one third of whom are below the low-income level.

Poverty varies across subgroups of the older population, as indicated in Table 2.13. Poverty is much higher for unrelated individuals (living alone or with nonrelatives) than for older persons residing in families. Women also have higher rates of poverty, and older widows living alone are particularly vulnerable. Finally, poverty is two to three times as likely among older blacks as among older whites. More than one third of all older blacks and more than a half of unrelated individuals are below the poverty level.

Table 2.13 POVERTY STATUS (PERCENT BELOW LOW-INCOME
LEVEL) OF PERSONS 65 AND OVER BY FAMILY
STATUS, RACE, AND SEX, 1979

	Whites	Blacks
All persons	13.2	35.5
Males	9.5	26.9
Females	15.8	41.7
All persons in families	6.9	24.0
Male head	7.3	21.4
Female head	8.1	34.7
Unrelated individuals	26.5	58.5
Males	22.3	44.8
Females	27.6	64.8

Source: U.S. Bureau of the Census, 1981c, pp. 19–20.

Ironically, these statistics both overestimate and underestimate the degree of financial hardship in the older population. They overestimate hardship by overlooking benefits and supports apart from income (Schulz, 1980). Older people receive a variety of tax benefits, including nontaxation of Social Security benefits, double personal exemptions on income taxes, and reduced property taxes. Older people may also receive income *in kind,* such as subsidized housing, food stamps, and Medicare health benefits, which soften the impact of low income. Schulz (1980) indicates that transfers (such as public assistance) and in-kind income reduced the level of poverty from 13.1 percent to 4.0 percent of the 65-and-over population in 1976, resulting in less poverty than in the under-65 population.

The aged may also possess assets that are not included in the income statistics: *liquid* assets, such as cash and bank deposits, which are easily converted to goods and services or money, and *nonliquid* assets, such as ownership of a house or business, which require more time to convert. The Retirement History Study of the Social Security Administration has found that nearly 90 percent of the older persons studied had some assets, but these were often quite small (Friedman & Sjogren, 1981). The median value of total liquid assets in 1975 was only $1909, and one fifth had none at all. Although nearly two thirds owned their own homes, these typically represented quite modest assets—the median value was $14,000, and half the sample had either no housing equity or less than $10,000.

The statistics cited earlier also underestimate financial hardship, as the low-income index is itself very low, and arbitrarily so. Inclusion of the "near-poor" (those with incomes no greater than 25 percent above the poverty level) yields a more realistic picture because such persons are also in a very marginal financial situation. In 1979 nearly one fourth (24.7 percent) of the older population were either poor or near-poor, compared with one sixth of the total population (U.S. Bureau of the Census, 1981c). Nearly half (49.2 percent) of older blacks and 41.1 percent of older female household heads (with no husband present) were poor or near-poor.

It is clear that low income is a substantial problem for older persons, many of whom become "poor" for the first time in their lives. Whereas some older people are quite comfortable financially, most are not, and there is no evidence that reduced income is accompanied by reduced need or desire to consume goods and services. Older families spend a greater share of their income than younger families on food, housing, and health care (Soldo, 1980). These areas are particularly likely to be affected by inflation. Despite Medicare the average older person had out-of-pocket health expenses of $1745 in 1977, and the median fuel bill for households headed by an older person increased by 64 percent between 1975 and 1979 (Soldo, 1980).

What low income in old age often means is poor nutrition, inadequate housing, neglect of medical needs, and failure to fulfill psychological needs. Money cannot buy happiness, but how many of us would want to give up restaurants, travel, movies, and visits with family because we are old?

Figure 2.4 indicates the major sources of income for older persons. Earnings and assets make important contributions, but Schulz (1980) notes that these sources are unevenly distributed—earnings to the nonretired and assets primarily to relatively few high-income older persons. Social Security benefits represent the single most important source of income. Indeed, about one fourth of all older people receive at least 90 percent of their income, and two thirds at least half, from Social Security (Marsh, 1981). (Social Security and other pension programs are discussed in Chapter 6.) Eleven percent of the older population receive some form of public assistance, including 37 percent of black females and 22 percent of black males (Marsh, 1981).

SOME CAUTIONARY NOTES

There is always a danger in using statistics to describe the position of any group. There are a variety of potential "social meanings" to be derived from any seemingly objective statistic. For example, although older people are more likely to live in poverty than the general population, most older people do not live in poverty.

One question that inevitably arises from the statistics reviewed here is: How well off are the aged in American society? There are two ways of answering this question. First, it is clear that older people are deprived (in health, housing, income, and so forth) compared to the general population. This chapter has outlined many needs of older people that have not been adequately met by existing social policies. However, in a more "objective" sense, older people have probably

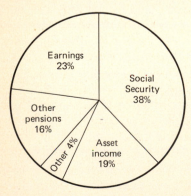

Figure 2.4 Sources of money income for the population 65 and over, 1978. (*Source:* Adapted from Robert Marsh, "The Income and Resources of the Elderly in 1978," *Social Security Bulletin* 44, no. 12 (1981))

never been better off than they are currently in American society. People are living longer, their health is better, and their average standard of living (physical shelter, food, and so on) has certainly risen since preindustrial times. Even in the last 20 years the proportion of older people living in poverty has been more than halved. Thus, older people are *relatively* deprived but in better *absolute* condition.

This objective standard of evaluation, however, can also be misleading. Human beings have a variety of needs beyond the simply physical. Abraham Maslow (1954) has suggested the existence of a set of "basic" needs, organized into a hierarchy, with higher-level needs becoming more important as lower-level needs are satisfied. His hierarchy of needs includes:

1. physiological needs (food, health)
2. safety
3. belongingness and love needs
4. esteem needs (achievement, appreciation)
5. self-actualization ("what a man can be, he must be")
6. preconditions for basic need satisfaction, which are defended because of their necessity, not as ends in themselves (freedom to speak and act)
7. desire to know and understand
8. aesthetic needs

What Maslow suggests is that once one's needs for food, good health, shelter, and so forth are satisfied, concern moves to belonging, esteem, or self-actualization. Modern societies may satisfy lower-level needs but leave the aged deprived in other ways. A sufficient retirement income, for example, does not mean that one belongs, is accorded prestige and appreciation, or can continue to grow as a person. For older people, the question becomes whether the system of age stratification makes available the kinds of roles and options that allow them to meet the needs outlined by Maslow. Without such roles, the aged will continue to be deprived in a very real sense and can experience social and psychological "starvation" in the midst of physical "comfort."

Maslow's higher-order needs may be of particular concern to older people of the future, who can be expected to be healthier, better educated, and in more favorable economic situations. Even the diversity among succeeding cohorts of the aged has been declining, as fewer elderly are foreign-born or rural-born. Uhlenberg (1977) suggests that growing stability in the nature of the older population lessens the cultural and social dislocations associated with aging. As the aged are increasingly similar to the rest of society, old age itself may be a less distinct part of the life cycle, and much of our current thinking in gerontology may require revision.

A discussion of needs and deprivations requires a balance between recognizing problems of the aged and avoiding an exaggeration of their difficulties. A 1975 survey (National Council on the Aging, 1975) suggests that the public does exaggerate the problems experienced by older people, and this may contribute to negative stereotypes and avoidance. The general public was asked to indicate "very serious" problems experienced by "most people over 65." Table 2.14 compares these responses to the "very serious" and "somewhat serious" problems actually expressed by older persons. For example, 62 percent of the public felt that not having enough money to live on would be a very serious problem for most persons over 65, but only 15 percent of older respondents said this was actually a very serious problem for them. When one includes "somewhat serious" problems, the differences are smaller, but there does seem to be overstatement of the problems of the aged, particularly of such problems as loneliness, not feeling needed, and not having enough job opportunities.

This chapter itself perhaps emphasizes the problems of aging to the relative exclusion of its joys and benefits. Take retirement as an example. Does it really sound so bad to not have to set an alarm clock when you go to bed, not have a "boss," travel and visit with family and friends? The National Council on the Aging study found that the most frequently expressed "rewards" of aging were leisure time, independence, and freedom from responsibility. Such rewards were more likely to be stressed by those with greater education and higher income, however, which indicates that one's ability to enjoy old age can be hindered by low income, poor health, or other decrements that may accompany aging.

Table 2.14 **PERSONAL EXPERIENCE VERSUS PUBLIC EXPECTATION OF PROBLEMS EXPERIENCED BY OLDER PEOPLE (PERCENTAGE OF POPULATION INTERVIEWED)**

	Personal experience (65+)		Public expectation
	"Very serious"	"Very serious" or "Somewhat serious"	"Very serious" problems attributed to "Most people over 65"
Fear of crime	23	47	50
Poor health	21	50	51
Not enough money to live on	15	40	62
Loneliness	12	29	60
Not enough medical care	10	23	44
Not enough education	8	25	20
Not feeling needed	7	19	54
Not enough to do to keep busy	6	17	37
Not enough friends	5	16	28
Not enough job opportunities	5	12	45
Poor housing	4	11	35
Not enough clothing	3	8	16

Source: Myth and Reality of Aging in America, 1975, published by The National Council on the Aging, Inc., a study prepared by Louis Harris and Associates, Inc., pp. 31–32. Reprinted by permission.

All of this suggests that a "cost-benefit" analysis of old age is a very complex matter. There is tremendous variability from one person to another, even in what they perceive as costs or benefits. One person's boredom is another's leisure time. The results in Table 2.14, however, do suggest that a wide range of problems are experienced by at least a substantial minority of older people, and though exaggerated, there are very real difficulties and deprivations experienced by many of them, particularly among certain subgroups.

SUMMARY

The population and proportion of older people has risen substantially in the United States during this century. Life expectancy has expanded to over 70 years for the average person. This aging of the population, related to declines in fertility and mortality (especially infant mortality) that accompany the demographic transition, presents critical issues to modern societies as reflected in the rising aged dependency ratio.

Because females tend to live longer than males, they constitute the majority of the older population. The aged are likely to reside in urban settings and are differentially distributed among the states. As a proportion of the population, the aged are most heavily concentrated in small towns. The older population is also unevenly distributed within metropolitan areas, as ecological processes and personal choice create patterns of residential age segregation.

Residential mobility is quite low in the older population, although it has been increasing. Long-distance migrants tend to be well off physically and economically, whereas local movers are generally less well off. Such migration streams affect service needs in states and localities.

There is an apparently unchanged limit to the human life span of about 115 years. A number of theories are being pursued to explain and perhaps alter this "biological clock." The deteriorative process of senescence occurs throughout adulthood, although at varying rates for different bodily systems and different individuals. These deteriorative changes, however, generally have little effect on normal functioning. Poor nutrition, stemming from both physiological and social factors, is a substantial problem in the older population.

Older people are less likely to suffer from acute health conditions, but chronic conditions increase with age and nearly half of all older persons have activity limitations due to chronic conditions. Older people may also have several chronic conditions, creating particular problems in diagnosis and treatment. Approximately 6 percent of the aged reside in institutions, but this understates the proportion who enter nursing homes at some time in their lives.

Sensation and perception tend to decline with age, but age patterns are less straightforward for intelligence, learning, and memory. Some intellectual abilities tend to decline with age, but the decline is smaller, starts later, and may involve fewer functions than was once thought. Decrements may reflect cautiousness, lack of motivation, or inefficient skills, rather than declining capacity, and may also reflect a "terminal drop" prior to death, rather than gradual loss caused by age per se. The older population displays tremendous variability in mental capacities, and creativity and growth are not inevitably stifled by old age. There is also evidence that intervention can be successful in improving intellectual functioning.

Approximately one in six older persons and perhaps 80 percent of nursing-home residents suffer from at least moderate psychopathology. Functional disorders, lacking a physical basis, include depression, paranoid reactions, hypochondriasis, and anxiety reactions. Organic disorders may be either reversible or irreversible. Contrary to many stereotypes, older persons with psychological disorders can benefit from therapeutic intervention. Alcoholism and drug abuse constitute other problems in the older population. Suicide peaks in middle age for females, but continues to rise in old age for white males. Suicide may be related to the social marginality experienced by some older persons.

Older people have less education, although the gap with other age groups is narrowing, and future cohorts of the aged may behave quite differently because of this. Most older males are married, whereas most older females are widowed. This is reflected in living arrangements—older women are much more likely to live alone. Most older people own their homes, although their houses tend to be older and in worse condition than those of younger persons. Housing is a particular problem for widows and rural and minority aged.

Retirement has come to be expected, although one fifth of all males over 65 do work. Women have become increasingly likely to work prior to age 65 so that retirement is becoming an issue for them as well as for men.

Although the extent of poverty among the aged has declined, they are more likely to have a low income than younger persons, and it is still true that nearly one in six is below the low-income level. Poverty is particularly prevalent among blacks and women who live alone. These statistics underestimate financial hardship, as one in four older persons is poor or near-poor. Whereas other sources of financial support may soften such statistics, it is nevertheless true that the aged suffer economic hardships.

It is not entirely clear how these statistics should be interpreted. Although the aged are deprived in relation to the rest of the population, their living conditions have improved in modern societies. This may mean, however, that the aged now feel handicapped regarding other needs, both social and psychological. Additionally, we may exaggerate the problems of aging, thus contributing to negative stereotypes and avoidance.

chapter *3*

Aging in Sociocultural and Historical Context

Aging is not the same experience in different societies or even in the same society at different times. The aged may be better or worse off, depending upon the structure of the society, the conditions of life (including the environment), attitudes toward aging, services provided to older people, family structure, and so on. One must look at the system of age stratification for a particular society to understand the position of the aged in that society. Before looking at an age stratification model in greater depth, however, it would be helpful to first have some appreciation of the position of the aged in various specific societies.

AGING IN PREINDUSTRIAL SOCIETIES

The impression is sometimes given that the aged were treated reverentially in primitive, preindustrial societies—that there existed a "golden age of aging"—and that older people are much worse off in modern societies—neglected by their families, forced into boring and meaningless retirement, and derogated by the "youth culture." But we must be wary of simplistic "before and after" statements. It may be thought that the aged were held in awe because of their rarity in preindustrial societies, but there were often reasonable prospects of reaching old age if one survived the first few years of life. In seventeenth-century New England, for example, two thirds of those who survived to age 20 could expect to live to 60 (Demos, 1978). Persons aged 60 and over constituted about 10–15 percent of the over-20 population—only about half the percentage now, but not an overwhelming difference. The reality of aging in preindustrial societies was also often far from idyllic. Stearns (1976) notes that traditional culture in France has not venerated old age; rather, "old age was a horror and old people a great nuisance."

There are severe limitations on our knowledge of aging in preindustrial societies. The historical study of aging, at least before 1800, derives largely from scattered literary and artistic sources and available demographic records (births, marriages, and deaths) (Laslett, 1976). Even more recent accounts of aging in preindustrial societies are often based on occasional references to the elderly in ethnological accounts by anthropologists. Nevertheless, there is ample evidence that the status of old people varied considerably among such societies.

The natural environment certainly affects the position of the aged. The aged will be worse off when the climate is severe, the environment harsh, and resources inadequate. Life under such conditions becomes a daily fight for survival, and culture, religion, and sentiment are luxuries that can ill be afforded. Holmberg comments on the Bolivian Siriono tribe:

> Since status is determined largely by immediate utility to the group, the inability of the aged to compete with the younger members of the society places them somewhat in the category of excess baggage. Having outlived their usefulness they are relegated to a position of obscurity. Actually the aged are quite a burden. They eat but are unable to hunt, fish, or collect food; they sometimes hoard a young spouse, but are unable to beget children; they move at a snail's pace and hinder the mobility of the group. . . . When a person becomes too ill or infirm to follow the fortunes of the band, he is abandoned to shift for himself. (1969:224–225)

Neglect and abandonment of the aged were apparently rather common occurrences. Simmons (1945) found it to be customary in 18 out of 39 tribes he studied. The Yakuts of Siberia, for example, expelled their aged from the family and forced them to become beggars and slaves (de Beauvoir, 1972). The Chukchee tribe of Siberia engaged in ceremonial killing of the aged in front of the entire community:

> A great feast was given in their honour, a feast in which they took part: the assembly ate seal-meat, drank whiskey, sang, and beat upon a drum. The condemned man's son or his younger brother slipped behind him and strangled him with a seal-bone. (de Beauvoir, 1972:51)

The social rights and roles of the aged are more developed in farming and handicraft economies, characterized by permanent residence, stable food supply, herding and cultivation, closely knit family relations, and the growth of magical and religious beliefs (Simmons, 1960). These more wealthy, settled societies enjoy a margin of security that allows them to be kinder to those who become dependent. Indeed, it is in the adults' own interest to look after the aged because they may (and hope to) reach that state themselves. Many societies, including ancient Israel and China and the Incas of Peru, developed rules for food sharing that involved special treatment of the old and feeble (Goody, 1976).

Such societies may also utilize the skills of older people for light economic tasks. Simmons (1960) notes that auxiliary tasks for the aged are less prevalent in simple collecting, hunting, and fishing societies, but there are more opportunities for secondary economic functions in herding, farming, and handicraft economics. For example, older people unfit for work served as scarecrows under Inca law, and Chippewa old women winowed rice, made fishnets, tanned hides, and supervised both the storing of fish and the work of young girls. The aged can better preserve their economic functions in low-productivity economies, in which any labor is of value (Rosow, 1965; 1974). Stable farming economies may also enable the aged to attain directive roles because of their experience or familiarity with special skills. Simmons (1960) notes that the aged often work as craftsmen, priests, midwives, or "beauty experts." They may also be involved in entertainment: games, songs, or storytelling.

This points out that the security of the aged was not based solely on charity, but on positions of social significance because of useful abilities or control over valued resources. The position of the aged is particularly related to their possession of *strategic knowledge* that is of use to the society in a number of forms (Rosow, 1974). The aged often use their accumulated wisdom, skill, and tact in the conduct of political, civil, and judicial affairs (Simmons, 1960). Simmons (1945) has noted that 56 out of 71 tribes he studied had "old chiefs" (almost universally male), and older persons are frequently used as arbitrators. Confucianism linked aging with wisdom and possession of a sense of the "golden mean" (Piovesana, 1974), and the heroes of ancient China were literati and officials whose qualifications increased with age. Age alone rarely qualifies an individual for responsibility, however. Such positions almost always go to older *males* who have demonstrated personal ability. Leadership by the aged is more likely in stable societies with advanced economies and complex social organization (Simmons, 1960).

Older people will also be respected if they are seen as the guardians of cultural knowledge, the recollected past, and memories, thus insuring cultural continuity through time (de Beauvoir, 1972; Rosow, 1974). This gives them the strategic function of bearers and interpreters of culture—a living "storehouse" of the culture—as among the Aleuts in the northern Pacific:

> Before the advent of Russian priests, every village had one or two old men at least, who considered it their especial business to educate the children; thereupon, in the morning or the evening, when all were at home, these aged teachers would seat themselves in the center of one of the largest village courts or "oolagmuh": the young folks surrounded them, and listened attentively to what they said—sometimes failing memory would cause the old preceptors to repeat over and over again the same advice or legend in the course of a lecture. The respect of the children, however, never allowed or occasioned an interruption of such a senile oration. (Elliott, 1886:170–171)

This role is less important when traditions and knowledge are transmitted in written rather than oral form or when daily life is so hard that it prevents consideration of culture.

The aged will also be more significant when they are seen as links to the past and the supernatural in tradition-oriented societies (de Beauvoir, 1972; Simmons, 1960; Rosow, 1974). Older people often function as seers and priests, keepers of shrines, and leaders of rites. As such, they mediate between man and the unknown, relying upon subtle and esoteric methods rather than physical strength.

> The very weakness of the aged makes their blessings and curses more powerful. The ability to change the world by words alone is often seen as characteristic of those who cannot change it by other means; hence, the curse of the beggar, the gypsy, the outsider, and the weak has much greater force than that of the soldier, the chief, or the politician; it is equally so with the young and the old. (Goody, 1976:128)

Among the Polar Eskimos the aged were reputedly able to raise storms and produce calms (Simmons, 1960), and they were important in the complex Navajo culture because of their magical incantations (de Beauvoir, 1972).

Older persons are better off in societies that allow for the acquisition and exercise of property rights and in which property is institutionalized and guaranteed by law (Simmons, 1960; de Beauvoir, 1972; Rosow, 1965, 1974). Property is based on right rather than strength or abilities that can decline with age. Property also gives the aged power over other age groups and, therefore, a reason to expect or demand deference. In agricultural societies, younger generations are dependent upon their elders for the transmission of scarce resources, such as farmland. This dependence is less in hunting societies where individuals must rely on their own abilities rather than the accumulation of others, and in societies with open frontiers where the young can make their own fortunes ("Go west, young man!").

Related to the importance of property in settled societies is the tendency for strongly organized, relatively unchanging societies to look to the aged for support, whereas youth is ascendant in changing or more revolutionary societies (de Beauvoir, 1972). Respect, authority, and power were accorded to the elders of ancient China, India, and Greece, as they upheld tradition in static, strongly hierarchical societies. This is also reflected in the gerontocratic leadership of the Roman Senate (from *senex,* aged) and the Spartan Gerusia (from *gera,* old) (Fischer, 1977).

Finally, the position of older people depends on the extent to which they are embedded in an extended family structure that provides them with positions of respect and authority as well as economic and social security (Simmons, 1960; Rosow, 1974). It was fairly common for older persons in preindustrial societies to marry younger persons and to be left in charge of the children. Older *men* often achieved power and authority from family position, as the patriarchs of Rome, China, and Japan. Deference to the aged within the family may be linked to their religious importance, as links to the past. Ancestor worship in China was centered in the family and reinforced by the teaching of filial piety in Confucianism (Piovesana, 1974).

One reason for the importance of the extended family is that it ties older people into a system of mutual dependence (Rosow, 1974). This may involve repayment for services rendered to the family earlier in life or continued opportunity to give and receive various kinds of support. To the extent that mutual obligation within the family is weakened, older people must look elsewhere to meet their needs. As we shall see later, there has been continuing debate about the effects of modernization on family structure, and there has been a tendency to overemphasize the amount of family support received by the aged in preindustrial societies. But where a stable extended family system did exist, the aged acquired greater security.

The bases of older people's position can be condensed into four basic prestige-generating components (Press & McKool, 1972):

1. *advisory component:* the experience of older people generates expertise that is useful to others;
2. *contributory component:* older people can make valued contributions to cultural, familial, or economic activities;
3. *control component:* older people have direct control over the behavior or welfare of others because of their monopoly over necessary objects, property, ritual process, or knowledge;
4. *residual component:* older people retain prestige associated with previous statuses from which they have "retired."

Age itself is not the source of prestige, but rather societal *perception* that age-linked characteristics are worthy or useful. As societies change, the perceived value of old age may also change, regardless of the actual characteristics of older people. We shall see this when discussing the consequences of modernization. Lozier (1975), for example, has suggested that the residual component is most likely to be found in small, stable, rural communities where the aged can "retire to the porch" and live off social credit they have accumulated in the community. The aged are likely to lack this accumulated credit and social integration in the more mobile, anonymous cities of modern societies.

It is also true, as de Beauvoir (1972) has noted, that most societies have mixed feelings about the aged—love, disgust, respect, fear. Older people may be mocked in private but treated with public deference, or honored in words but neglected in practice. Respect accorded to the aged in general does not assure the position of any particular older person. Finally, it appears that older men are more likely to be accorded positions of respect and authority than older women, and prestige for aged men offers no assurance for women (Simmons, 1960).

Some Hyperborean Examples

There has been recent interest in some current preindustrial societies that reflect the hyperborean theme, combining extreme longevity with high status for the aged, such as groups in the Ecuadorian Valley of Vilcabamba, in the province of Hunza in Pakistan, and in Abkhasia of the Georgian Soviet Socialist Republic (Leaf, 1973). The claims of long life coming from these areas are striking. Nine persons out of 819 residents of a Vilcabamba village claimed to be over 100 years of age. Benet (1974) indicates that 2.6 percent of the Abkhasians were over 90, compared with only 0.1 percent in the Soviet Union as a whole, and some residents claim to be 120 or 130 years old. There are certain commonalities among these cultures: diets low in calories and animal fats, a high level of physical activity into old age, moderation in consumption of alcohol and tobacco, lack of retirement, and high status for the aged. One can begin to outline possible reasons for longevity in the Abkhasian culture, which has received the most attention of the three (Benet, 1974).

The Abkhasians live in rural villages in the Caucasus Mountains. The health of aged Abkhasians seems better than that of similarly aged people in other cultures, and physical processes of aging seem to be delayed—wrinkles and gray hair occur only in extreme age, baldness is rare, posture is erect, and the aged retain good vision and hearing, and their own teeth. Benet notes that

> The extraordinary ability of the aged to recover from stress or illness has also been recorded on many occasions. One example is Akhutsa Kunach, one hundred fourteen years old. . . . During the previous winter, while cutting timber in the woods, he had been injured by a falling tree. Three ribs were broken. Two months later the doctors diagnosed him as fit to work, and he resumed all his former duties. He still felt responsible for his family, and directed the proper reception for his guests. (1974:12)

The elaborate folk medicine practiced in the region may partly account for this good health as well as the dietary practices of the Abkhasians. Moderation is highly valued and being fat is viewed as an illness. The diet consists primarily of milk and vegetables, with little meat or animal fat and few spices. The average food intake is less than 2000 calories. Arteriosclerosis is virtually unknown, apparently because of the low cholesterol content of the diet.

Other possible reasons for longevity relate to the social position of the aged and the outlook on aging it implies. The life cycle is uniform, with no sharp, stressful discontinuities among age groups. Retirement is unknown. The aged remain active up to their capacity with few feelings of uselessness. This results in a consistent, unbroken life pattern, with little need for wrenching adjustments to role transitions. The Abkhasian culture is also characterized by stress-avoiding mechanisms, notably a lack of competition and a stoic life-style. A placid state of mind, free from worry and strain, is emphasized. There is also a culturally reinforced expectation of long life and good health.

Older people among the Abkhasians assume considerable responsibility for village decision making. They are viewed as the keepers of tradition and cultural continuity, presiding over ceremonies, mediating disputes, and utilizing their knowledge of medicinal herbs. The aged also retain considerable authority in the family, remaining integrated into the extended family and community.

Although such cultural characteristics may indeed contribute to longevity, we must nonetheless be somewhat skeptical about the claims of extreme ages in these societies. Even in modern societies the very old (90 or 100) are objects of attention and awe, contributing to the possibility of age exaggeration. A recent attempt to verify age claims in Vilcabamba found evidence of systematic age exaggeration after age 70 (Mazess & Forman, 1979). All 23 persons claiming to be centenarians were found to be younger than 100 (ranging in age from 75 to 96); one man who claimed to be 127 was probably 91—his mother was born at least five years before his own claimed date of birth. Whereas extreme longevity seems to be questionable, Mazess and Forman note, however, that there is a high proportion aged 60 and over in Vilcabamba, nearly twice the national and regional averages. Therefore the factors discussed above may contribute to longevity, even if the hyperborean dream has not been achieved.

AGING AND MODERNIZATION

It has been common in social gerontology to note the detrimental effects of modernization and industrialization on the relative status of the aged and describe their respect and authority in more traditional preindustrial societies. Although the position of older people varied in preindustrial societies, there are processes of modernization that could be expected to undermine their status. The trend from home-based to factory production may undermine the extended family. In rapidly changing modern societies the experience of the aged becomes obsolete, they do not command new skills, tradition is less important because of future orientation, and local group life is attenuated. These arguments imply that the prestige-generating capacities and characteristics of the aged are devalued in modern societies.

Donald Cowgill (1974a, 1974b) has organized a coherent framework for understanding the effects of modernization. Cowgill's model traces the effects of what he sees as the four most salient defining aspects of modernization: (1) the application of modern health technology, (2) the application of scientific technology to the economy, (3) urbanization, and (4) mass education and the increase of literacy. The key features of the model are diagramed in Figure 3.1.

One consequence of modern health technology is the "aging" of the population, a distinctly modern phenomenon that began in Western Europe as a by-product of the demographic transition. As life is prolonged, death is less effective in creating openings in the labor force. Intergenerational competition arises over jobs, and retirement emerges as a social institution for opening up the labor force to younger workers. Unfortunately for the aged, modernizing societies are also typically characterized by a work ethic and strong feelings against dependency, and older people must relinquish the work role, the primary definer of their usefulness and worthiness, to take on the lower status (both financially and socially) of the retirement role.

Cowgill's model also points out that new technology creates new occupations and the young are most likely to become the occupational pioneers of developing societies. Cohn (1982) has found that economic development is associated with reduced representation of older people in high-status occupations. The aged remain in more traditional occupations, which are less in demand and may become obsolete. This creates additional pressure for retirement and the lowered status that may accompany it.

The third aspect of modernization is urbanization. Young people are attracted to the city by the promise of exciting changes and new career opportunities. Once there, they marry and establish permanent residence. This presumably

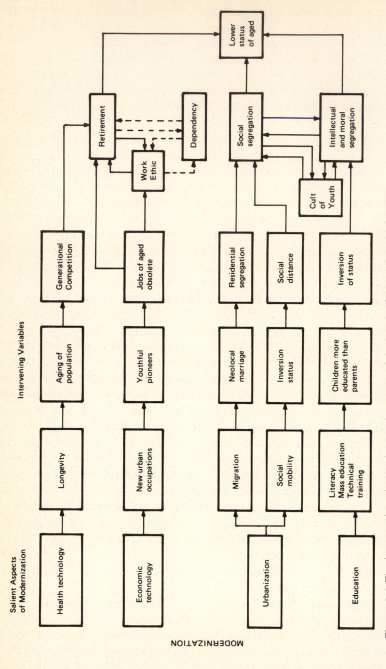

Figure 3.1 The impact of modernization on the status of the aged. (*Source:* Donald Cowgill, "Aging and Modernization: A Revision of the Theory," in Jaber Gubrium (ed.), *Late Life: Communities and Environmental Policies,* 1974 p. 141. Reprinted courtesy of Charles C. Thomas, Publisher, Springfield, Illinois.)

breaks up the extended family, at least early in the modernization process when the society is still relatively rural. This results in residential segregation of the generations and accentuation of social differences between them.

Increasing urbanization in modern and modernizing societies, accompanied by the new occupations for the young, results in social mobility. Status is inverted, with younger people occupying more prestigious positions than their parents and grandparents. This serves to increase the social distance between generations. Cowgill notes that

> . . . the young move into the new, more glamorous, better-paying urban jobs, leaving behind—both physically and psychologically—the grubby, archaic, rural way of life. The young are in the stream of progress; the old are left behind. The young have improved their station; the old stand still and suffer by comparison. (1974a:13)

Finally, modernization is accompanied by a drive to promote literacy. The primary recipients of mass education efforts are the young, who thus acquire more education than their parents. Again, there is an inversion of status and, because of these educational changes, an increasing moral and intellectual difference between generations.

Cowgill suggests that this social, moral, and intellectual separation combines with other characteristics of developing countries to produce lower status for the aged. Modernizing societies have a tendency to glorify youth as the embodiment of progress and achievement, and youth is viewed as the very means for attaining that progress. The rapidity of change in such societies also means that the young are socialized for a very uncertain future. The traditions and accumulated experiences of older generations are increasingly seen as irrelevant because they no longer apply to the emerging order of things. This is perhaps the core meaning of a "generation gap."

The model argues that the major aspects of modernization combine to lower the status of the aged as the four prestige-generating components discussed earlier are undermined. The advice, contributions, and control of older people are reduced or devalued, and the reduced resources for power and prestige place older people at a disadvantage in social exchange (Dowd, 1980). Residual status becomes less available in a highly mobile, impersonal urban society. This is a telling indictment of the view that modernization brings a more civilized culture. Certainly we do not abandon our aged on ice floes or force them to beg in the streets. But Cowgill's model suggests that the elderly are abandoned socially and psychologically, making them unnecessary, marginal, and alien to their own society. Indeed, the culture is no longer their own but belongs to the young.

This model of modernization receives at least partial support from some recent studies. Palmore and Whittington (1971), investigating the economic, social, residential, and health status of older people, found that the status of the aged compared to the nonaged population had generally declined from 1940 to 1969. Palmore and Manton (1974), in a cross-cultural study of 31 countries, found the relative status of the aged lower in more modernized societies. But cautions have also been raised about oversimplifying the nature and impact of modernization (Achenbaum & Stearns, 1978). The model tends to truncate what is in reality a very slow, incremental pattern of societal changes that is neither unidirectional nor uniform. The actual modernization experienced by the elderly may proceed slowly and somewhat eccentrically, as they are often clustered in more traditional craft occupations and rural areas. Also, just as there are great variations in preindustrial societies and traditional culture, which were far from uniformly benign toward the aged, there are variations in the position of older people in modern societies. Some recent studies point this out.

Japan is a modern, industrialized, urban society, yet the status of the aged has apparently remained quite high (Palmore, 1975a, 1975b). Their integration into the family appears higher than in Western societies because the aged are much more likely to share their children's residences and fulfill important functions within the family. They operate as caretakers, perpetuators of religious affairs, and senior advisers on family problems, and provide affectional support for grandchildren. The aged of Japan are also more likely to continue working, with greater opportunities (traditions of seniority, high rates of self-employment) and a strong work ethic. Cohn (1982) indicates that the practice of "permanent employment" in Japan, whereby workers remain with the same employer until retirement, has protected older workers from occupational status loss.

The respect for the aged in Japan is reflected in the honorific language used about them, the preference given them in family matters, and the content and language of legislation pertaining to them. For example, Respect for Elders Day has been a national holiday since 1963. Palmore argues that this respect for older people has two main roots. First, Japan is a *vertical society* that emphasizes hierarchical relationships and the deference due persons in superior positions, stressing deference and respect rather than independence and equality. Second, Japanese society stresses *filial piety*. Respect and obligations to parents and grandparents are learned and observed within the family, and this is connected to the importance of ancestor worship.

This description of aging in Japan may be exaggerated. Chadwick (1976) suggests that Palmore presents a somewhat romanticized view, ignoring the gap between government ideology and practice, the necessity of work at very low wages by the elderly because of early mandatory retirement from principal occupations combined with low pensions, and an apparent worsening of the position of older people. Despite the fact that social services for the elderly are less developed in Japan, however, traditions of filial duty have continued (Maeda, 1980), and Japan reminds us that the nature and consequences of modernization depend upon the cultural context within which it occurs.

Observations on the People's Republic of China offer a similar reminder (Treas, 1979; Cherry & Magnuson-Martinson, 1981). The authority of age has been part of the basic fabric in traditional Chinese society, but the combination of industrialization and the youthful Communist revolution might be expected to undermine the status of older people. Instead, these studies indicate that the long-standing cultural values are reinforced by contemporary realities. Economic necessity binds generations together, especially in rural areas where the pensions of housing of older people are valuable to the younger generation. Responsible social roles are available after retirement, including housekeeping and child care when both parents work, and voluntary community service.

Modernization is clearly not a monolithic process. It proceeds at different rates, under different conditions in each society, and need not result in marginality and alienation for the aged. Shanas and associates (1968), comparing the position of older people in the United States, Great Britain, and Denmark, suggest that the aged are more strongly integrated into industrial society than our theories indicate. They also note, however, that the aged are "kept at arm's length from the social structure" (p. 425) and that such societies tend formally to *accommodate* to older people rather than *integrate* them. Although there were considerable similarities among the three countries, a number of differences were evident even among these Western cultures. For example, income inequality by age was less in Denmark and greater in the United States, and home-help services, such as visiting nurses, were less developed in the United States. Family relationships were more loosely knit in Denmark than in the United States and Great Britain.

There are also variations in the position of older people within any particular society. Because of its unusual immigration history, for example, Israel is composed of four older populations: local or imported, Western or Oriental (Bergman, 1980). Bergman notes that many current older people are from the founding generation of the state of Israel, and they may view retirement as a more unwelcome and traumatic event than future cohorts. The United States is also comprised of many ethnic and racial subcultures that have not been fully homogenized by the "melting pot" (Greer, 1974). These variations will be discussed later in this chapter.

THE AGED IN AMERICA

The complexity of historical change in the position of older people can be further understood by looking at their position in America. Historical research suggests that although modernization has indeed accelerated the decline in status of the aged, this decline was evident even before such modern phenomena as mandatory retirement, urbanization, and mass education of the young, and there is no simple relationship between modernization and the status of older people.

In his study tracing the status of the aged from colonial times to the present, Fischer (1977) indicates that the Puritans viewed old age as a sign of the Elect, and Puritan writers made a cult of age. A large body of literature, such as the sermons of Cotton Mather, instructed people how to behave toward their elders. The respect accorded to old age was not simply a sign of affection or deference, but rather of *veneration* interwoven with religious overtones. Elders ran the churches and occupied places of honor in meetinghouses. There was no concept of retirement because of age per se; for example, clergy and schoolmasters were more likely to die in office than retire. The aged occupied positions of community leadership, and "grey champions" (to use Fischer's phrase) were particularly likely to be turned to in times of crisis.

The position of the colonial elderly was mixed. Whereas elites were venerated, the destitute aged were often scorned and mistreated, and old age for all was often a time of physical suffering, because medical knowledge was not advanced. The cultural convention was to honor old age, but attention was also given to mental and physical infirmities.

> Consider, for example, the opinion of William Bridge, sometime fellow of Harvard College and author of the earliest treatise on this subject anywhere in the colonies. "Old age is a dry and barren ground," he begins. "The state of old age is a state of weakness and of much infirmity." Bridge proceeds to spell this out in great detail, separating the natural from the moral infirmities. The moral ones make an especially long list. Older people are likely to be "too drowsy and remiss in the things of God . . . too touchy, peevish, angry, and forward . . . very unteachable . . . [because] they think they know more than others . . . full of complaints of the present times." (Demos, 1978:251).

Thus there were distinctly negative undertones in the attitudes toward the aged even in colonial times, despite the honor and respect prescribed as their due. The aged also carried a heavy responsibility to keep active; serene, carefree retirement was denied them. Fischer and Demos both indicate that veneration was a cold emotion, engendering little affection or sympathetic understanding.

Granting these other characteristics, the overall picture is one of respect and authority accorded to the aged. Partly this was based on economic coercion, as control of land was retained until advanced age, guaranteeing that the elders would be surrounded by "seeking" children. Veneration of the aged was also an instrument of conservatism in a tradition-bound society, insuring continuity, stability, and permanence. In this sense, veneration of the aged in colonial America can be likened to that of ancient China and Greece.

According to Fischer, this cult of old age was undermined in the late eighteenth and early nineteenth centuries. Wealth supplanted age as the basis of meetinghouse seating. Legislatures began to require retirement from office at age 60 or 70. Fashions that had previously been designed to accentuate age (such as powdered wigs) now flattered youth (hair dyes, hairpieces). Terms that had previously indicated respect were now used to derogate *(gaffer, fogy, superannuated)* and new pejoratives for the aged *(codger, fuddy-duddy, geezer)* emerged during this period. One indication from Fischer's work that old women may have always been held in lower esteem than old men is the fact that insulting references for them have a much longer history; such terms as *hag, crone,* and *old maid* date to the fourteenth and fifteenth centuries.

Fischer attributes these changes to fundamental changes in world culture, exemplified in the American and French Revolutions, ushered in by demographic, political, economic, and ethical change. The earlier closed, authoritarian societies were being broken down, supplanted by expanding ideals of equality and liberty. Growing inequality of wealth displaced other inequalities, such as age, and the cultural homogeneity upon which veneration of the aged was based was lost. Rather than modernization and a cult of youth that derogates the aged, the cult of old age was overthrown by an emerging ideal of age *equality*.

However, Fischer's study does support Cowgill's model in that the modern era in American society seems to have ushered in a cult of youth through which earlier veneration of the aged, initially supplanted by age equality, is finally replaced with derogation of the old and celebration of youth. With the institution of retirement, mass education, growing age inequality in income, and residential separation of the generations, the old came to be seen as alien and useless. The nation itself developed a youthful self-image, and its heroes and legends shifted from elders and Founding Fathers to young men, from Daniel Boone to Charles Lindbergh. Literature increasingly cast old age as pathetic and empty. As early as the nineteenth century, Henry David Thoreau stated that: "Practically, the old have no very important advice to give the young" (Fischer, 1977:115). Fischer notes that this cult of youth reached its peak in the 1960s.

Achenbaum (1978) indicates similar trends. Prior to the midnineteenth century the usefulness of old age was emphasized. Longevity was viewed as evidence of the superiority of American life, the elderly exemplifying the values of moderation and industry. The aged were venerable because of their experience and continued to actively serve in many capacities. The problems of older people were viewed as "peculiar sorrows" that helped them understand the meaning of life.

Achenbaum suggests that changes in the position of older people became apparent after the Civil War. An emphasis on values of efficiency and impersonality in large organizations, coupled with increased attention to "senile pathology," contributed to a perception of old age as obsolescence rather than culmination. The problems of old age became a focus of national attention between World War I and World War II, contributing further to images of physical and mental decline and economic uselessness.

These studies indicate that Americans have always viewed old age with some ambivalence, and that there has not been a neat relationship between modernization and the status of older people. Although structural changes associated with modernization are implicated in changing beliefs and values about old age, Fischer and Achenbaum emphasize the independent role played by ideas and values. Achenbaum suggests that both approaches contain some truth, thus there is a need to go beyond simplified unicausal theories; indeed, shifts in the status of the aged have not always coincided with shifts in their actual situations and capabilities.

There is also evidence that modernization may lower the status of older people only in its earlier stages. Palmore and Manton (1974) found some improvement in the relative position of older people in the most modernized societies they studied. Similarly, Pampel (1981) has found improvement in the relative financial status of older people in the United States since World War II. This is partly due to cohort succession; recent cohorts entering old age have a better education, higher occupational status, are fewer foreign- or rural-born, and so on. But he argues that "processual changes" have been more important—normative support for leisure, institutionalization of retirement-income programs, efforts of public interest groups in support of the aged, and so on. Calhoun (1978) has described the efforts of various interest groups since World War II to establish more positive images of old age. Gerontological research, combined with educational and media interest in aging, has helped dispel some of the myths about aging, and a "retirement ethic" has begun to emerge with leisure as a prized commodity. Thus societies in advanced stages of modernization appear to become aware of the devalued status of the aged and begin to create more positive images and opportunities for older people.

There is clearly great variation across and within societies in the meaning and significance of old age with no simple "before and after" relationship between preindustrial and modern societies. Aging is a complex social phenomenon; its meaning and consequences depend on the context in which aging occurs. One helpful approach to understanding this complexity is available in a model of age stratification.

A MODEL OF AGE STRATIFICATION

The principle that the nature of the aging experience is dependent upon the characteristics of its social context is recognized in a recent attempt to develop a model of *age stratification* as a framework for organizing and understanding research on aging (Riley et al., 1972). Every society divides people into age strata. This stratification reflects and causes age-related differences in capacities, expected roles, and rights and privileges. We all have some awareness of social-class stratification and sex-role stratification. We know that being in the working class or upper class affects educational and occupational opportunities, political power, health, and many other things. We also know that men and women are expected to play "appropriate" roles. The recognition that age is also important in the same ways, with equally important consequences, is relatively new, however. This model can be used to study all age groups, but the focus in this book will be on its usefulness in understanding the position of the aged. The basic characteristics of the age stratification model are shown in Figure 3.2.

Models such as this are sometimes deceptively simple because they frequently formalize what is "common sense" or "accepted knowledge." The virtue of a theoretical model, however, is that it combines these common-sense understandings of the world into a more coherent statement, thereby helping us to understand the implications of what we "know" and suggesting the questions that need to be addressed. More specifically, the model of age stratification relates to two basic issues: (1) the meaning of age and the position of age groups in a particular social context, and (2) transitions individuals encounter over the life cycle because of these social definitions of age.

The *life course* perspective also recognizes that age stratification is a dynamic process (Elder, 1981). The meanings of age vary across cultures, cohorts, and historical periods. The life course is also transactional as individuals make choices and negotiate transitions within the broader context of age stratification. There is an interplay between the individual and the social structure.

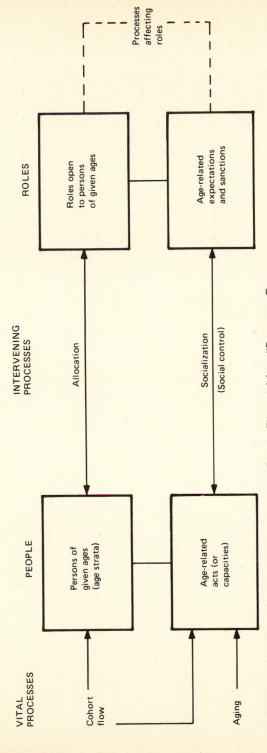

Figure 3.2 Elements in a model of age stratification. (*Source:* Figure 1.2 from "Processes Related to Structural Elements," in Chapter 1, "Elements in a Model of Age Stratification," in *Aging and Society,* Volume three: *A Sociology of Age Stratification,* by Matilda White Riley, Marilyn Johnson, and Anne Foner, p. 9, © 1972 by Russell Sage Foundation. Reprinted by permission of Basic Books, Inc.)

Age Strata and Age-Related Capacities

The model begins with the seemingly simple recognition that people are distributed into various age strata. These age strata may be defined in various ways. Chronological age is certainly one criterion, or the life cycle could be divided into developmental stages: infancy, early childhood, adolescence, young adulthood, mature adulthood, middle age, and old age. One might also define different age strata within the spheres of family or work. Depending upon how strata are defined, they may be complex or simple and the boundaries between them sharp or indistinct. Chronological age gives very clear differentiation, whereas the border between mature adulthood and middle age is more difficult to pin down.

Speaking literally, these age strata arise because of *cohort flow.* As new earth forms new layers over old layers of earth in a canyon, new cohorts are born to succeed earlier cohorts. The process of aging results in individual mobility across age strata. Social-class stratification and age stratification are similar in that both order people and roles in society, but one clear difference is that age mobility is universal, inevitable, and irreversible. You cannot become younger or stop the flow of time.

Linked to this demographic age stratification is the fact that there are age-related acts or capacities. People of different ages behave differently, have different abilities, and may be motivated by different attitudes and values. These age differences may be attributable to either aging effects or cohort effects, as discussed in Chapter 1.

The model to this point seems quite simplistic. Its importance, however, lies in the implications for individuals being in an *age stratification system.* To understand these implications, we need to look at the rest of the model: structural elements (roles and age-related expectations and sanctions) and processes (allocation and socialization) that link people and roles.

Age-Grading of Roles

The model of age stratification emphasizes that age is one criterion for determining what roles an individual will play in the society. Allocation refers to "a set of mechanisms for the continual assignment and reassignment of individuals of given ages to the appropriate roles" (Riley et al., 1972:11). There are a number of such allocating mechanisms, including the spreading of information about roles, screening of qualifications, and certification. It is sufficient here to simply note that one's age is likely to determine the roles that will be played. This is true to a greater or lesser degree in all societies.

Age operates in a number of ways as a criterion for entering and leaving roles. Age may be a *direct* criterion. There are formal rules that prescribe an age range for school attendance, minimum age for entering the work force or voting, or a maximum age for working (mandatory retirement policies). Additionally, there are informal norms and beliefs about the kinds of roles "appropriate" for people at various ages, which reflect the values and perceived needs of a particular society. Age norms may also be factual regularities—the average or usual age for entering or leaving certain roles—translated into normative standards. People may perceive the 18-year-old college professor as "too young" or the 45-year-old newlywed as "too old," and such norms may serve as a barrier to behavior. Results from a study by Neugarten and associates (1965) suggest that there is some consensus about such age expectations, as indicated in Table 3.1.

Age may also be an *indirect* criterion for allocating people into roles by reflecting social, psychological, or biological characteristics. Certainly there are biological limits on the ability to enter the mother role. Most college professors are at least 25 by the time they acquire the necessary specialized training. The careers of professional athletes are circumscribed by age-related physical capabilities.

The existence of age norms that guide allocation into roles is universal, but the content of those norms reflects the history, structure, and values of particular societies and cohorts within them. In this century there has been a quickening of some aspects of the family cycle and a lengthening of other periods (Neugarten & Moore, 1968). Individuals typically marry earlier, have children earlier, and have their last child leave the house earlier now than in 1900. Thus, they are likely to be an older couple without children in the home longer, and are also likely to be widowed for a longer time. People also begin working later and end working earlier than they used to. Such changes alter the nature and rhythm of the individual life course.

The size, composition, and experiences of particular cohorts affect both the timing and order of events. The "normative" order of events comprising the transition into adulthood for males, for example, is to complete education, enter the labor force, and then get married (Hogan, 1978). The ability to do so, however, depends upon the unique history of a particular cohort, including such factors as military service, economic depression, and farm origin. Figure 3.3 indicates that there has been cohort variation in the extent to which male cohorts have followed the normative pattern for transitions into adulthood. There has increasingly been normative ordering in cohorts born since 1940, which have had greater discretion in the timing of college education and military service.

Failure to follow norms of timing and order may have negative consequences for individuals. Hogan (1978, 1980) has found that young males who follow a "disorderly" sequence of transitions earn less later in life and are more likely to be divorced. He suggests that nonnormative patterns disrupt the harmony between one's own life-style and the institutional structures that provide the context for one's life.

Whatever the source of age norms—tradition, negotiation, factual regularities—they are all based on assumptions about age-related capacities and limitations (Atchley, 1975). These norms are often flexible or ambiguous, however, and specific age norms may differ by social class, sex, or ethnicity. Thus, age norms must be "translated into reality at various social levels by particular people in particular situations" (Atchley, 1975:268). Nevertheless, age is a universal criterion for allocating roles, which creates what Atchley calls "decision demands": points in the life cycle at which individuals must choose from a field of alternative

Table 3.1 CONSENSUS IN A MIDDLE-CLASS MIDDLE-AGED SAMPLE REGARDING VARIOUS AGE-RELATED CHARACTERISTICS

	Age range designated as appropriate or expected	Percent who concur	
		Men (N = 50)	Women (N = 43)
Best age for a man to marry	20–25	80	90
Best age for a woman to marry	19–24	85	90
When most people should become grandparents	45–50	84	79
Best age for most people to finish school and go to work	20–22	86	82
When most men should be settled on a career	24–26	74	64
When most men hold their top jobs	45–50	71	58
When most people should be ready to retire	60–65	83	86
A young man	18–22	84	83
A middle-aged man	40–50	86	75
An old man	65–75	75	57
A young woman	18–24	89	88
A middle-aged woman	40–50	87	77
An old woman	60–75	83	87
When a man has the most responsibilities	35–50	79	75
When a man accomplishes most	40–50	82	71
The prime of life for a man	35–50	86	80
When a woman has the most responsibilities	25–40	93	91
When a woman accomplishes most	30–45	94	92
A good-looking woman	20–35	92	82

Source: Reprinted from "Age Norms, Age Constraints, and Adult Socialization," *American Journal of Sociology* 70, p. 712, by Bernice Neugarten, Joan Moore, and John Lowe by permission of The University of Chicago Press. © 1965 The University of Chicago Press.

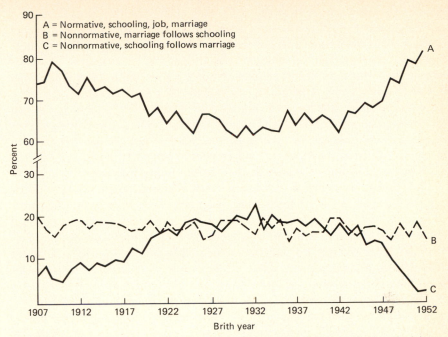

Figure 3.3 Percent of birth cohort in each of three temporal ordering categories of adult transitions, U.S. males born 1907–1952. (*Source:* Dennis Hogan, "The Variable Order of Events in the Life Course," *American Sociological Review* 43 (1978), p. 579. Reprinted by permission.)

age-linked positions in the social structure. In order to understand the implications of this for the aging individual, one must understand the characteristics of the roles available to people of different ages.

There are a multitude of roles people can play: student, spouse, worker, politician, retiree. These roles differ in a variety of ways. First, roles will emphasize different qualities. Some roles, such as the worker role, are *instrumental*— defined in terms of task orientation or their productive content. Other *expressive* roles, such as husband or wife, have more of an emotional content. Second, roles provide different types of rewards: money, a sense of fulfillment, relaxation, friendships, prestige, and so on. For example, teachers may derive more prestige and fulfillment from their work, but truck drivers may be paid better. Finally, roles themselves are socially evaluated according to the values and needs of the social group, so that some roles are highly valued and others are derogated. We tend, for example, to have different feelings about the student, worker, and retiree roles.

The fact that roles are age-graded within an age stratification system and possess different characteristics creates age differences and, perhaps more importantly, structured age inequalities. *The combination of normative age expectations and social values influences the relative social positions of age strata because age stratification affects the role qualities, rewards, and identities available to people of different ages.* Each age group will be evaluated, by others and by themselves, according to the roles its members typically play and the evaluation of those roles according to the dominant values and needs of the society. When societies respect the cultural knowledge and accumulated experience of the aged and allow them to play roles that capitalize on these qualities, the aged will be respected. Cowgill's model of modernization suggests that such roles are less valued and available in modern societies, being replaced by less valued roles, such as retiree.

This recognizes the hierarchical nature of age-stratification systems, as age relations are also power relations (Foner & Kertzer, 1978; Dowd, 1980). Power and prestige resources are distributed unequally across age groups, and age conflict may result from the desire to gain or retain such rewards. Such conflict is itself a potential source of change in the nature of age stratification.

It is the age stratification of roles that both frees and limits the aged in modern societies. They are freed from many obligatory adult roles to use their time as they wish, and potentially to change and grow. Yet values, institutional structures, and norms about "age-appropriate behavior" also limit their options. Leisure pursuits, for example, are not always freely chosen, as we shall see in Chapter 7. The opportunities made available to older people will determine whether old age is a time of status or stigma, growth or stagnation, self-expression or anxiety.

Modern societies have made age a more important status variable than in the past. We have seen the emergence of "adolescence" as a distinct life period with prolonged education, and retirement has played a major role in separating "old age" from the adult life cycle. In some respects, however, we may now be moving toward a more "age-irrelevant" society (Neugarten & Hagestad, 1976). Educational opportunities are growing for the aged. Career change is increasingly prevalent during middle age, and leisure options and values are expanding throughout the life cycle. The achievement of age-irrelevance requires a loosening up of the constraints that limit the options for all age groups.

Age Norms and Socialization

There is some debate about the nature of "age-appropriate" behavior norms for older people. There do appear to be some age-related expectations in the results cited in Table 3.1; the same study also found that older people were even more likely than younger people to subscribe to age constraints—to feel that people should "act their age" (Neugarten et al., 1965). Wood (1971) also suggests that certain age norms have emerged: a widow's grief should not be so prolonged as to make others uncomfortable or hinder adjustment, grandparents should not interfere in the socialization of children, older people should keep up their club memberships. We will see in Chapter 9 that specific norms may also emerge in specialized settings, such as retirement communities.

Others have argued, however, that old age is really a "nonrole" characterized by normlessness in that most norms for older people are really "middle-aged" norms—primarily related to maintaining independence, social activity, and religiosity (Bengtson, 1973; Rosow, 1974). Norms for older people tend to be quite limited and ambiguous, offering few real guidelines for behavior.

More research into the nature of age-related expectations is clearly needed. How do they arise? Norms are best viewed as emerging within specific interaction situations. The fact that there are very broad expectations about older people tells us very little about the norms encountered by particular older people within their specific social groups and situations. To what extent do age norms really constrain behavior? For example, is a 65-year-old woman really less likely to get married because it would be "age-inappropriate"? If there are age norms, how are they enforced? Norms imply sanctions—people are rewarded for following them and punished for disregarding them. More research on the operation and effects of sanctions, such as social disapproval, is needed.

The role transitions occurring over the life course pattern our lives, creating important changes in our social and personal worlds; and age stratification means these transitions and their timing are not necessarily chosen by us because they are shaped by various age norms and allocation processes. Thus, to understand the nature of any stage of the life cycle requires an understanding of the role transitions of that stage and the pressures and strains that accompany them. Uncertain timing and discontinuities associated with transitions represent inherent sources of tension and conflict in age-stratification systems as role allocation may be inadequately linked to individual readiness (Foner & Kertzer, 1978). Let us take adolescence as an example. Modern societies have prolonged childhood by postponing entrance into adult family, work, and community roles. Yet these "children" feel physically, intellectually, and emotionally capable of participating in the larger community. The age stratification of roles prevents this participation, thereby contributing to such diverse youth phenomena as alienation, the generation gap, and juvenile delinquency. Gang delinquency, for example, has been seen by some as a striving for "manhood" in modern societies that provide few transitional rituals or adultlike roles for adolescents.

> When a society does not make adequate preparation, formal or otherwise, for the induction of its adolescents to the adult status, equivalent forms of behavior arise spontaneously among adolescents themselves, reinforced by their own group structure, which seemingly provide the same psychological content and function as the more formalized rituals found in other societies. This the gang structure appears to do in American society, apparently satisfying deep-seated needs experienced by adolescents in all cultures. (Bloch & Niederhoffer, 1958:17)

This means that the second intervening process in the age stratification model, *socialization,* is a key to an understanding of any life stage. Socialization "serves to teach individuals at each stage of the life course how to perform new roles, how to adjust to changing roles, and how to relinquish old ones" (Riley et al., 1972:11). Socialization thereby contributes to both the maintenance of society and the well-being of individuals. Age stratification makes socialization a life-long process because people move into and out of a succession of roles as they age. Age-linked transitions will be easier if there is continuity between old and new roles and preparation for the new status (Riley, 1976). Retirement, for example, will be less stressful if it is gradual and if individuals are prepared with knowledge about pension benefits, likely housing and health needs, and the general nature of the retiree role.

One problem associated with being "off-time" for certain transitions (early retirement, late marriage) may be faulty or incomplete socialization. Lennon (1982), for example, investigated the psychological consequences of the timing of menopause, which generally occurs to women between 45 and 54. She found that women do not experience psychological distress when menopause occurs "on time," but menopause is likely to be a source of distress when it occurs early or late. Lennon concludes that "on-time individuals are likely to receive concrete assistance in the form of advice, information, and emotional support, since they will tend to know others undergoing similar experiences" (p.362).

In a sense, socialization teaches people to desire what is available to them. Problems develop when individuals are not socialized for the roles they occupy, are not allocated to the roles for which they are prepared, or are prepared incorrectly for their roles. All of these situations may occur with older people. Indeed, Rosow (1974) suggests that a critical problem of aging is the lack of socialization for an old-age role. Older people are unwilling to take on the diminished status and "uselessness" of the retirement role, and there are no institutions or situations that really help older people prepare for old age. This means that age-related capacities, attitudes, and values, reflecting cohort and aging effects, are not adequately matched by socialization to the roles available to the aged.

Margaret Clark (1967) has suggested that older people in American society face a very basic cultural discontinuity. Although certain value orientations are stressed in adulthood—status and achievement, acquisition, competitiveness, high levels of aspiration, agressiveness, and so on—she found that virtually opposite value orientations characterized those who had adapted well to old age—congeniality, conservation, resilience, harmoniousness, cooperation, "reasonable" aspiration. This suggests a potential imbalance between allocation and socialization. As adults, we are socialized into a set of values that cannot be achieved in old age because of the positions older people occupy.

This should not be taken to mean that older people necessarily *ought* to be socialized to accept the roles currently open to them. Those roles may not be meaningful or rewarding, and a lack of socialization for them may constitute a pressure for needed change in the nature of age stratification. Similarly, we should not assume that *no* socialization occurs for old age, even if there is no universal old-age role.

Even with the loss of *formal* roles for older people and the absence of general socialization for an old-age role, older people encounter *informal* expectations and roles in their interactions with family and friends. The very ambiguity of old age offers possibilities for "role making," as individuals define their own old age in creative ways. A symbolic interactionist perspective on aging recognizes the negotiated quality of transitions (Marshall, 1978).

> . . . the opportunities, expectations, and demands that social structures pose for individuals are communicated and maintained through a complex interpersonal process in which individuals are active agents. Thus, people not only choose among social positions or roles, they attempt, in varying degrees, to make the social expectations and opportunities confronting them in any given

role or position as compatible as possible with their needs, values, and abilities. (House, 1981:555)

Just as individuals negotiate and shape the life course, cohorts may collectively exert influence on age stratification. Waring (1975) notes that although "cohort flow" is generally uneventful, lack of fit between cohorts and the roles available to them may lead them to challenge existing patterns of age stratification. Cohorts entering old age are increasingly well educated, native- and urban-born, financially secure, and have access to greater resources for income, medical care, and recreational possibilities. Uhlenberg (1979) suggests that this has produced a widening gap between the abilities of older people and their opportunities to use their abilities constructively, creating a pressure for societal provision of more adequate social roles for the elderly.

The age stratification system in any society is complex and dynamic. Age locates individuals in the social structure through processes of allocation and socialization, but age stratification is also fluid. Cohort succession and structural changes, such as modernization, alter the nature of age stratification. Individuals are active agents in creating their own life course. The choices they make are facilitated or thwarted by changing external conditions: wars, economic opportunities, demographic changes in mortality and fertility, norms about the expected timing and order of events, and institutional changes affecting different age groups (such as retirement).

Age stratification also coexists with other systems of stratification. Neugarten and Moore (1968) point out that the timing of events in the family cycle differs according to social class, and those of higher classes tend to marry and have children later. In a sense, this means that lower- and working-class people "age" earlier than those from the middle and upper classes. Societies are also stratified according to sex. To the extent that males and females play different roles throughout the life cycle, the nature of their aging experience will also differ.

The task of understanding the aging experience is clearly complicated by the interactions of age stratification and other stratification systems. There is no simple relationship between age and status. Individuals of the same age may differ greatly in their social class and status, depending upon the roles they play or have played in the past. Older people who play valued roles, as in politics for example, are accorded prestige despite a general devaluation of their age group, and middle-aged persons in devalued roles may have very low status.

MINORITY AGING

Recognizing this complexity in the aging experience, it is important to keep in mind the existence of ethnic subgroups in the older population. Ethnicity refers to the variety of groups that have a distinctive sense of "peoplehood" on the basis of race, religion, or national identity (Gelfand, 1982). Such ethnic identity is an important feature of American life, as the "melting pot" is in many respects more a wish than a reality. White ethnic groups constitute important segments of the older population. In 1970 immigrants represented 14 percent of the older population, although this should decline to only 5 percent by the end of the 1980s due to more restrictive immigration laws (Gelfand, 1982). Elderly immigrants tend to be clustered around East Coast and midwestern cities that offered work opportunities for immigrants in the 1800s. For example, Italian-Americans are concentrated around New York City, and concentrations of Poles can be found in such cities as Chicago, Gary, and Buffalo (Gelfand, 1982).

Older blacks number 2 million and constitute 8 percent of the aged population. There are numerous other minority groups represented among the elderly: Mexican-Americans, Chinese, American Indians, and so on. Minority populations in the United States are relatively young compared with the white population; 8 percent of blacks, 6 percent of Chinese, and 4 percent of Hispanics are aged 65 and over, compared with over 11 percent of the white population. Such relative youth is attributable to several factors, including higher fertility, lower life expectancy, and recent immigration by younger persons in certain groups. The minority older population is growing, however. It is estimated, for example, that black aged will increase by 46 percent by the year 2000, compared to a 25 percent increase in white aged (Soldo, 1980). Our knowledge about minority aged is somewhat sparse, although there has been increased attention in recent years.

There is great variability within this minority population. There are cohort differences within each group, as will be noted, for example, in discussing Asian-American aged. Each racial and ethnic minority has also had its own collective experience. This ethnic history is important to an understanding of these elderly groups; blacks have experienced the effects of slavery and racial discrimination, Jews have experienced the Holocaust of World War II, and Japanese-Americans have undergone World War II internment camps.

The diverse subcultures arising from these experiences may provide important coping structures (religion, family, ethnic organizations) for minority aged in which ethnicity represents an important resource in dealing with problems of aging (Bengtson, 1979; Holzberg, 1982). There is evidence of family proximity and mutual assistance among ethnic aged, as well as other "natural" support networks. Valle and Mendoza (1978) have described an informal *servidor* system among older Latinos in San Diego that referred older persons to appropriate agencies for assistance. Informal support networks can be especially valuable for those who live in cohesive ethnic communities characterized by intensive interaction patterns. For example, Myerhoff (1978) found that consciousness of special culture and collective self-definition gave important meaning to the lives of a group of aging Jewish immigrants. Ethnically based mutual-aid societies have been an important source of community support for the aged since colonial times (Kutzik, 1979).

Particular attention has also been paid to the disadvantages faced by minority aged, many of which were apparent in the statistics presented in Chapter 2: poverty, substandard housing, worse health, and so on. Such disadvantages may accelerate the process of aging for minority persons. There is a danger, however, of exaggerating the racial or ethnic basis of either the coping structures or disadvantages found among minority aged. Jackson (1980) argues that the unique strength sometimes attributed to minority family support is largely a myth. When such support does exist, it is necessitated by the fact that minority aged have historically been excluded or served poorly by most social programs. Jackson also indicates great similarity between aged blacks and whites when appropriate socioeconomic controls are introduced. More generally, it appears that the "distress" associated with minority status is largely attributable to low income rather than to minority status itself (Mirowsky & Ross, 1980).

The importance of ethnicity also tends to decline across generations, as social and geographic mobility increasingly remove succeeding generations from their ethnic origins. Krause (1978), for example, reports on a study of three generations of Italian, Polish, and Slavic women. Each succeeding generation was less likely to report that "being (Italian/Jewish/Slavic) is very important to me," declining from 93 percent among grandmothers, to 81 percent among mothers, to 62 percent among daughters.

Nonetheless, attention needs to be paid to the diversity of circumstances among minority aged. And aged minorities, especially poorer ones, clearly need assistance in gaining access to community resources that frequently exclude them. Let us look more closely at segments of the minority older population that have received the most attention.

Black Aged

Blacks aged 65 and over constitute about 8 percent of the black population, whose median age of 24 is about six years younger than that of the white population. The black aged population has grown substantially, increasing by 28 percent from 1970 to 1978 (Gelfand, 1982). Although most older blacks reside in the South, it is an increasingly urban group: 55 percent of older blacks lived in central cities in 1977, compared with 29 percent of older whites. Reflecting patterns of segregation, older blacks reside disproportionately in central-city poverty areas. Lower education and occupational status coupled with higher rates of unemployment during adulthood contribute to lower retirement income and high rates of poverty among older blacks. There has been only slight progress in narrowing the racial income gap; the median income of older blacks was 65 percent of that of older whites in 1969, and 73 percent in 1976. Older blacks are also more likely to live in substandard housing, have their activities limited by chronic illness, and so on. These disadvantages reflect a lifetime of reduced opportunities and access to services.

It has also been suggested that certain elements of the black experience contribute to the well-being of older blacks, reflecting adaptation over the life course to a hostile environment. Blacks are highly segregated, and this ghettoization presents barriers to involvement in the surrounding community.

Many aged black people live on tenaciously, in urban ghettos and the recesses of rural areas all over America. They learned years ago to live within prescribed areas—physical, social, economic—that limited their full participation in the American social scene. (Davis, 1971:53)

But the ghetto may also represent a source of subcultural integration and protection. Wylie (1971) suggests that aged blacks receive support and respect within the black extended family because of African cultural traditions and the importance of the extended family arising in response to slavery. Churches and voluntary associations have also been cited as important supports for black aged (Clemente et al., 1975).

As suggested earlier, however, there is little evidence that blacks grow old within a uniquely supportive social environment. In control groups for socioeconomic status, Jackson and Walls (1978) indicate little racial difference in support from family and friends, respect from the young, religiosity, or involvement in voluntary associations. It does not appear that low-income older blacks are better off than comparable older whites, nor do they appear to be worse off in most respects; but there are proportionately more of them.

Hispanic Aged

Hispanic aged represent the second largest group of minority aged, accounting for 2.5 percent of the older population. This is a very heterogeneous group. One half are Mexican-American, residing primarily in the Southwest and California, 10 percent are Puerto Rican clustered in New York and New Jersey, and 8 percent are Cuban, mostly in Florida; the remainder come from Central or South America and Europe. Except for the Cuban population, 13 percent of which was aged 65 and over in 1978, these are relatively young populations (approximately 4 percent aged 65 and over). With the exception of a large rural population among Mexican-Americans, Hispanic aged are heavily urban.

Similar to black aged, Hispanic aged are disadvantaged in health, income, and housing. Both black and Hispanic aged, for example, have a median education of only 5 to 7 years, and their income is only half that of older whites (Gelfand, 1982). They face additional disadvantages in seeking services because of language and cultural barriers, including a highly individualistic orientation that resists turning to outside agencies (Trinidad, 1977). Because of their recent immigration, Hispanic aged are less likely than black aged to be receiving Social Security.

The Hispanic extended family appears to be particularly supportive of its older members. Compared with black and white aged, Hispanic aged interact more with children, receive greater assistance, and play more direct roles in family life through advice and child rearing (Cantor, 1979; Bengtson et al., 1981). This, however, reflects both necessity and desire. Bengtson and associates indicate that all three groups view the government as the primary resource for older people in need. Maldonado (1975) suggests that the assumption that Mexican-American aged are cared for within extended families has been used to justify inadequate services. He also indicates that their position in the extended family has been weakened in the transition from rural to urban living; minorities are not immune to the processes reflected in Cowgill's model.

Asian-American Aged

In 1970 there were approximately 27,000 Chinese aged 65 and over in the United States (6 percent of the Chinese population) and 47,000 Japanese (8 percent of the population). They reside principally in urban areas in Western states, although there are also sizable concentrations in such cities as Boston and New York. Both groups are predominantly first-generation immigrants, and their current position reflects a unique cohort/historical position of growing old in a foreign land, having faced cultural barriers and an often hostile white community during their early adult years (Kalish & Moriwaki, 1973). Years of discrimination and fears of deportation may make them reluctant to seek aid from service bureaucracies. Indeed, aged Chinese-Americans have lived very insulated lives within Chinatowns and may know little of the services "out there" (Carp & Kataoka, 1976).

Some disadvantages are similar to those of other minorities. Low-paying jobs and employment not covered by Social Security result in low income; 50 percent of aged Chinese in San Francisco's Chinatown have incomes below the poverty level (Carp & Kataoka, 1976). But other aspects of their situation reflect their historical position. Because of restrictive immigration laws, for example, most aged Chinese are males, many of them lacking family ties.

Aged Chinese and Japanese face a cultural discontinuity. They were socialized and are still oriented to a traditional culture emphasizing interdependence and filial piety. They are growing old in a very different milieu, their children socialized in a culture emphasizing individualism and self-reliance, which gives less status to the experience and wisdom of the aged. This is coupled with low status of the aged relative to their children because of language barriers and codified discrimination against the immigrant generation that prevented citizenship and property ownership. The internment of Japanese in relocation camps during World War II, for example, transferred status and authority from the first generation (Issei) to the second generation (Nisei).

Generational conflict should not be overstated. Osako (1979) indicates that Japanese elderly do not suffer greatly from sudden status loss or isolation because Issei and Nisei continue to share their cultural heritage. But there is a reminder here that an understanding of the aging experience is further complicated by the unique experiences of particular cohorts.

American Indian Aged

American Indians constitute a rather young population—life expectancy is about 63, and only about 6 percent are 65 and over (Gelfand, 1982). However, the number of American Indian elderly has been increasing from 63,000 aged 60 and over in 1970 to 109,000 in 1980. A large majority of these are rural, living primarily on or near reservations in western states. This is the most economically disadvantaged group of the minority aged we have discussed (Block, 1979; Information on Aging, 1982). The American Indian population is characterized by very high unemployment and average income barely above the poverty level. A lifetime of deprivation—inadequate housing, extremely low education, irregular employment, poor medical care and nutrition—results in poor health and often grinding poverty in old age. Tuberculosis is five times more prevalent among them, and approximately three fourths of the elderly are mildly to totally impaired by health problems. A 1979–1980 survey found that 61 percent of the American Indian elderly have incomes of $5,000 or less; only 40 percent receive Social Security benefits, and SSI is the only source of income for one third of them (Information on Aging, 1982). Their isolation on reservations and status as wards of paternalistic federal agencies make aged American Indians an extremely vulnerable group.

Double Jeopardy or Leveling?

Not surprisingly, it is apparent that minority aged are disadvantaged in many ways. But another issue is whether minority disadvantages are greater or lesser in old age than earlier in the life cycle. This relates to an issue raised by Streib (1976): What is the relative importance of stratification by race, social class, age, and sex? The concept of *double jeopardy* (National Urban League, 1964) implies that the particular burdens of being black (or another minority) *and* old may widen racial differences in old age. On the other hand, *leveling* implies a narrowing of differences as "social class and race which seem important in youth evidently pass with time and fade when individuals are confronted with problems of survival" (Kent, 1971:26).

The evidence is mixed. Dowd and Bengtson (1978), in their study of blacks, Mexican-Americans, and whites in Los Angeles, found greater declines with age in income and subjective health for blacks and Mexican-Americans, indicating some double jeopardy, but mixed patterns, including some leveling, for various dimensions of life satisfaction and informal support. Pampel (1981) found some evidence of income leveling across age groups, with white males exhibiting the greatest income loss. He also found that inequality within the older population declined between 1947 and 1974, although substantial inequality remains. Ward (1983) used national survey data to compare the size of racial differences in income, subjective health, subjective well-being, and informal supports across age groups. Racial differences neither widened nor narrowed with age to any significant degree.

It appears questionable whether age stratification alters the consequences of other stratification systems. It also appears that social class may be the key differentiating factor within the older population. Henretta and Campbell (1976) indicate that the factors that determine income in old age are essentially the same as those earlier in life; the social class system persists in old age. Jackson (1980) has also noted that differences between black and white aged are largely attributable to socioeconomic status.

A fuller understanding of aging requires an appreciation of the interactions of age stratification with other stratification systems. Foner and Kertzer (1978) found age to be a "major organizing principle" in their study of preliterate African "age-set" societies. But there may be greater "interference" from other organizing principles (class, race, sex) in more complex modern societies. Whereas age is a universal stratifying criterion, its relative importance depends on other structural conditions in society.

SUMMARY

The relative position of the aged in any society depends on their particular physical and social environment. Older people were not necessarily better off in preindustrial society, but are in relatively better positions in stable societies characterized by cultural development, an extended family structure, and institutionalization of property. There are four prestige-generating components: advisory, contributory, control, and residual. Age itself is very seldom the source of prestige or power, but rather societal perceptions that presumably age-linked characteristics are worthy or useful. Some current preindustrial cultures may have unusual longevity because of dietary practices, continuity over the life cycle, and high social status for the aged, although claims of extreme longevity cannot be substantiated.

Modernization tends to be accompanied by declining status for older people. This can be linked to the combined impact of four accompaniments of modernization: more advanced health technology, economic change, urbanization, and mass education. Declining status for the aged may have begun prior to modernization, however, due to changing cultural ideals and values. Change in the position of older people in America from veneration during colonial times to lower status in modern society has involved a long, complex process of evolution in response to changes in social structure and values. The nature and consequences of modernization also depend on the cultural context in which they occur. Modernization in Japan and China, for example, does not appear to have undermined the status of old age within those cultures.

A model of age stratification provides a coherent framework for understanding the position of older people in any society because age is one criterion for allocating individuals into roles. This results in differential access by age to specific types of identities and rewards. If the aged are allocated into roles that are highly valued by the society, such as guardian of cultural traditions or family head, they will be accorded prestige and authority. If they are allocated into roles that are not highly valued, such as retiree, their relative position declines. Imbalance between role allocation and socialization for age-graded roles may create considerable difficulties for older people, and may also contribute to change in the age stratification system. Individuals also negotiate and shape their own life course, contributing to the complexity of aging.

Age stratification is also intertwined with other sources of role differentiation, such as social class, sex, and race. Ethnicity is an important source of variability within the older population, offering unique supports and difficulties associated with the collective experience of ethnic groups. Minority aged are clearly disadvantaged, but the nature of those disadvantages vary according to the unique histories and circumstances of particular minority groups. Research has failed to indicate any clear widening (double jeopardy) or narrowing (leveling) of racial differences in old age. Age stratification does not appear to alter the consequences of other stratification systems substantially, and social class may be the key differentiating factor within the older population.

chapter 4

The Psychological Experience of Aging

Up to this point we have largely taken a "macro" approach to aging, addressing the position of older people within the context of age stratification and the effects of aging on society. This chapter shifts to the "micro" approach of the individual as the unit of analysis in considering the psychological impact of aging on the older individual. Of course this concern cannot be divorced from the larger social context, which defines old age as a social experience and determines the accompaniments of aging and their social meanings.

The social psychology of aging has generated considerable debate, partly because of its implications for "successful" aging. There are a number of research traditions that focus on broad psychological theories of aging and developmental stages in the life cycle. Until recently developmental psychology was characterized by distinct, age-bracketed specialties with approaches emphasizing individual "maturation" through relatively universal stages (Baltes & Willis, 1979). It has become clear, however, that age-linked changes are multidimensional, multidirectional, and highly variable among individuals. A coherent, integrated understanding of the psychology of aging is far from complete, but a life course perspective offers a conceptual model for capturing the complexities of aging. Before discussing the implications of this perspective, two theories will be discussed that have framed much of the debate on the social psychology of aging—activity theory and disengagement theory.

ACTIVITY AND DISENGAGEMENT

Activity theory rests on the common-sense view that older people will be happier if they are active. Satisfaction is felt to depend on validation of self-concept through active participation in middle-aged roles, or substitutes for roles lost because of retirement, widowhood, and other age-related changes (Lemon et al., 1972; Longino and Kart, 1982). Role loss cuts the individual off from the supports necessary for reaffirming self-concept, thereby contributing to low morale and feelings of worthlessness.

> . . . older people are the same as middle-aged people, with essentially the same psychological and social needs. In this view, the decreased social interaction that characterizes old age results from the withdrawal by society from the aging person, and the decrease in interaction proceeds against the desires of most aging men and women. The older person who ages optimally is the person who stays active and who manages to resist the shrinkage of his social world. He maintains the activities of middle age as long as possible and then finds substitutes for those activities he is forced to relinquish. (Havighurst et al., 1968:161)

Although there are many ways in which roles and activities (work, marriage, social contacts, clubs) are related to morale, the picture is more complex than that painted by activity theory. Activity can decline without affecting morale (Maddox, 1970); indeed, a more leisurely life-style can be viewed as one of the rewards of old age. Lemon and associates (1972) and Longino and Kart (1982) have attempted to formalize and test the propositions of activity theory. This research has found that informal social activity has a modest association with indicators of well-being, but there was otherwise little support for the general propositions about the importance of role involvement and role support to self-concept and satisfaction. Indeed, Longino and Kart found a negative association between formal group activity and life satisfaction.

Activity theory is too facile a denial of differences between middle age and old age. It ignores qualitative changes accompanying retirement, declining health, or widowhood, and the variability of responses to such changes. Most older people remain active (see Chapters 7 and 9), but age-linked events may shift social and psychological orientations of individuals to different sources of satisfaction. Indeed, by suggesting that the aged "ought" to remain active to age successfully, it places people who are not or cannot remain active in an awkward position, implying that they are failures.

Disengagement theory represents an opposing view of aging, portraying the aging process as a mutual disengagement of the individual and society (Cumming & Henry, 1961; Cumming, 1963). The number of roles people play and the frequency of their interaction with others do tend to decline with age and there are some indications of a movement toward psychological disengagement. For example, there appears to be a greater *interiority* of personality—increased preoccupation with inner life as opposed to the outside world (Neugarten, 1969). These patterns themselves are not controversial, and disengagement theory served as a useful counterpoint to assumptions that older people *must* be active to age successfully. But debate quickly emerged over the reasons for disengagement and over its consequences.

According to the theory, disengagement has its ultimate basis in the probable decline with age in abilities and the universal expectation of death. The biology of aging presents the individual with an increasing inability to fulfill roles and maintain interpersonal contacts, which will be demoralizing and alienating unless shifts occur in roles and personality toward disengagement. Older people discard task-oriented interpersonal roles in favor of more peripheral roles. There is an overall decline in love-seeking and emotional ties, with the individual focusing increasingly on himself or herself. Disengagement may be initiated by either the individual or society, but becomes self-perpetuating.

Perhaps the most controversial aspects of the theory are its claims that this disengagement is universal and mutually satisfying for the aging individual and society. For the individual, disengagement presumably neutralizes the potential social trauma associated with biological decline and death and frees older people from behavioral norms and expectations, allowing them to be more "eccentric." As the death of persons occupying important roles and statuses is disruptive, disengagement is also felt to be "functional" for society by gradually removing those about to die from active involvement in the social structure. Finally, the theory suggests that disengagement is universal in two respects. First, aging individuals inevitably disengage from the social world, although the timing varies from individual to individual, depending on personality and social context. Second, it is argued that disengagement occurs in all cultures, although the particular form it takes may vary.

Disengagement theory generated immediate controversy. Some have criticized it on logical grounds. Hochschild (1975), for example, has suggested that debate and research bearing on disengagement theory have been inconclusive because of the nature of the theory itself, which provides an "escape clause." Counterevidence of engaged older persons, such as politicians, is refuted as examples of "unsuccessful disengagers," off in their timing, or truly exceptional individuals. Hochschild also suggests that disengagement is seen as a unitary process, when in fact there may be several types of disengagement, such as social disengagement and psychological disengagement, and one may occur without the other. Finally, Hochschild criticizes disengagement theory for ignoring the meanings held by the individual for aging and disengagement.

There is evidence that disengagement does occur with some older people. Indeed, in the restricted sense of relaxation and a leisurely, less competitive life, disengagement may be viewed as one of the rewards of aging. This, however, does not necessarily mean that disengagement is inevitable or satisfying. Longitudinal studies suggest that aging may have relatively little impact on activities (Palmore, 1970). Disengagement theory was originally based on the Kansas City Study of Adult Life, but other work from that study suggests that the typical pattern is actually high engagement-high satisfaction, rather than low engagement-high satisfaction (Havighurst et al., 1968).

Individuals may disengage socially but not psychologically, or selectively from certain areas of life, while continuing or even increasing their involvement in other activities. "*Extensive* social interaction may be gradually replaced by *intensive* local social interaction, involving fewer people. Loss of roles may heighten the subjective importance, and increase the effectiveness of those roles that remain" (Shanas et al., 1968:5). Loneliness, poor health, poverty, or self-derogation may prevent the enjoyment of a more relaxed life, making disengagement an unpleasant experience, and those who are disengaged in old age may have been so throughout their lives. Mass and Kuypers (1974), in a 40-year study of couples, found that disengaged older men showed some evidence of a disengaged life-style as young adults.

Disengagement also may not represent personal preference but the reaction of society and the failure to provide opportunities. Frances Carp (1978), for example, has compared persons moving into an apartment complex for older people with persons who were on the waiting list but did not move in. The complex offered regular responsibilities and activities for tenants. These heightened opportunities for involvement stimulated a latent demand for activity, and tenants exhibited wide-ranging increases in activity, whereas the others showed activity decline over time (disengagement). The research also indicates that increased activity was accompanied by higher morale and longevity. Such findings suggest that disengagement is not necessarily a natural preference of older people, but may instead be a response to the age stratification of roles and opportunities in modern societies. Disengagement may also reflect the diminished resources and status of the aged, who withdraw from interaction because they are in a weak negotiating position in interpersonal exchanges (Dowd, 1975).

This means that disengagement is best viewed as a reactive aging effect rather than as intrinsic. Once this is recognized, one can explore the complexities of engagement-disengagement. We need to investigate the different forms disengagement may take, variables that affect these forms and their timing, and the meaning for individuals of both engagement and disengagement (Hochschild, 1975). Distinctions must also be made between forced and freely chosen disengagement.

Opportunities for engagement exist in some societies but not others, as can be seen from the cross-cultural differences cited in Chapter 3. Disengagement may be a consequence of modernization, which restricts the range and importance of roles available to the aged. Similarly, the individual's location in the social structure will affect the extent and timing of disengagement. Retired college professors have opportunities for continued involvement that retired college janitors lack, and they may also differ in their desire for continued involvement.

Both activity theory and disengagement theory offer too simplistic a view of the aging process. They also have ideological overtones. Activity theory implies that one *ought* to remain active, whereas disengagement theory seems to justify withdrawal from the aged as being what they want. The evidence suggests, however, that there are a number of ways in which people can age successfully. To understand aging and its impact, one must also understand the life course experienced by particular individuals.

A LIFE COURSE PERSPECTIVE ON AGING

Disengagement theory ignores individual continuity over the life span and activity theory ignores the contingencies of present old age; but to understand the individual aging experience, we must view the aging person within the context of life-long development. Aging represents an interaction between the individual and previous patterns or styles of living, and constraints placed upon the ability to follow those patterns by the processes of aging. Throughout our lives we develop preferences, habits, and activity patterns, and we will tend to maintain those characteristics as we age. People are not reborn on their sixty-fifth birthday; the aging individual makes sense of the present and adapts to it in terms of his or her own past.

> . . . the individual seems to continue to make his own "impress" upon the wide range of social and biological changes. He continues to exercise choice and to select from the environment in accordance with his long established needs. He ages according to a pattern that has a long history, and that maintains itself, with adaptation, to the end of life. (Neugarten et al., 1968:176–177)

The ability to successfully exercise choice to achieve congruence between perceived needs and opportunities represents a better definition of successful aging than activity or disengagement.

However, aging represents more than simple personal continuity. There are many types of constraints on individuals' ability to maintain continuity. Biological decline and poor health affect capacities and activities. Changes in roles and relationships, such as those that accompany retirement and widowhood, will also limit continuity and require adaptation. Different societies provide varying opportunities for older people, and societal attitudes toward aging will affect the meanings attached to growing older by the individual because it is in terms of those meanings that the individual reacts to his or her increasing age and the changes that accompany it.

A life course perspective suggests an adaptive interaction between the individual and the accompaniments of aging. Aging is a dynamic, lifelong process, as individuals experience multiple sources of change throughout their lives. Baltes and Willis (1979) indicate three sources of development: (1) some experiences are age-linked, representing biological change and the age stratification of roles and socialization experiences; (2) other experiences are "history-graded," representing cohort and period effects; (3) other experiences reflect the idiosyncracies of individual biographies—some people marry early, some marry late, and some never marry; some have a stable job throughout their lives, some work sporadically in many jobs, and some never work. Complex combinations of these influences will yield variability in the nature of individual aging because individuals experience different events or the same events in different historical contexts or stages in the life cycle. Indeed, Baltes and Willis suggest that chronological age becomes less relevant in adulthood and old age as history-graded and idiosyncratic events gain in prominence and produce progressively larger individual variation. Other positions in the social structure, including social class and sex, are related to the nature and context of events experienced over the life course, contributing further to the multiplicity of the aging experience.

The combination of individual tendencies toward continuity and multiple sources of change makes an understanding of the aging process quite complicated. Every individual ages differently. But there may be certain patterns of stability and change.

Personality, Life-Style, and Psychological Orientation

There has been considerable research on the relationship between age and personality. A central issue in this work has concerned stability and consistency of personality characteristics, as opposed to change in personality across developmental stages of the life course (Brim and Kagan, 1980). McCrae and Costa (1982) describe four models of personality and aging which have guided this research. Early approaches portrayed a pattern of growth followed by decline later in adulthood. However, there appear to be few age-related changes in such personality traits as emotional stability, sociability, and imaginativeness. A second model focuses on qualitative personality shifts associated with life "stages." This approach, which is difficult to test, will be discussed later in this chapter. A third approach, which McCrae and Costa term the "typological model," will be reviewed in this section. This research has found a variety of personality "types" within the older population, but it is not clear that these are related to age. The fourth model, and the one receiving the greatest empirical support, emphasizes the considerable stability in personality as individuals age. Indeed, McCrae and Costa suggest that rather than viewing personality as being affected by age, personality can be viewed as a determinant of the life course through the choices made by individuals. This recognizes the negotiated nature of the life course discussed in Chapter 3.

These comments underscore the complexity of relationships between aging and personality. A life course perspective underlines the need to assess past, present, and future in attempting to understand aging as part of a lifelong process. One way in which the personal past is brought into present and future aging is through individual personality. Personality is a term we use to describe the behavioral and psychological approaches developed by individuals to meet the problems and tasks of everyday living. Over time, personality becomes a relatively stable characteristic of the self—a blueprint or recipe for living. But personality is also dynamic, continually evolving, and adapting to new demands faced by the individual. This means that although personality lends continuity to old age, personality change is also possible because aging brings new demands to be met.

We previously mentioned the "typological" approach to aging and personality. These approaches combine personality and lifestyle in seeking to describe typical *patterns of aging.* Some of the more noteworthy attempts to delineate these patterns are summarized in Table 4.1. Although drawn from different sources, these typologies have certain similarities. And they all point out the individual variability of reactions to aging—variability that is not captured by either activity or disengagement theory.

The Reichard et al. (1962) and Neugarten et al. (1968) typologies are empirical descriptions of general approaches to aging and display some basic similarities. Some people *(reorganizers)* substitute new activities for lost ones, corresponding rather closely to activity theory prescriptions for successful aging. Others (the *focused*) become selective in their activities, withdrawing from or losing some, but maintaining and perhaps increasing others. Both of these might be subsumed under the *mature* agers described by Reichard and associates. The

Table 4.1 PATTERNS OF AGING

Reichard et al. (1962)	Williams and Wirths (1965)	Neugarten et al. (1968)	Maas and Kuypers (1974)
Mature	World of work	Reorganizer	Family-centered fathers
Rocking-chair men	Familism	Focused	Hobbyist fathers
Armored	Living alone	Disengaged	Remotely sociable fathers
Angry men	Couplehood	Holding on	Unwell-disengaged fathers
Self-haters	Easing through life with minimal involvement	Constricted	Husband-centered wives
	Living fully	Succorance-seeker	Uncentered mothers
		Apathetic	Visiting mothers
		Disorganized	Employed (work-centered) mothers
			Disabled-disengaged mothers
			Group-centered mothers

disengaged and *rocking-chair men* correspond to the picture painted by diseng-agement theory of voluntary and contented withdrawal from responsibilities and involvements. All of these patterns seem to be associated with high satisfaction and "integrated" personalities.

Other older people appear to defend themselves from the perceived threats of aging by either clinging to middle-aged patterns *(holding on)* or erecting de-fenses against anxiety by closing in their world *(constricted)*. Both of these de-fenses are similar to an *armored* pattern, and such individuals seem to maintain satisfaction relatively successfully.

The *succorance-seekers* maintain themselves satisfactorily so long as their dependency needs are met by others they can lean on. The *apathetic* pattern refers to people who had perhaps been disengaged throughout their lives and for whom aging has reinforced long-standing patterns of passivity and low activity. Those who were *disorganized* showed low activity and poor psychological functioning. All three of these patterns appear to be accompanied by somewhat lower satisfac-tion and may correspond to the *self-haters* described by Reichard and associates.

The focus of the typology developed by Williams and Wirths (1965) differs from the others. Rather than describing reactions to aging per se, they are con-cerned with the main focus of an individual's style of life, which may be carried into old age. The *world of work* implies that the meaning for one's life is derived from work. It would be expected that retirement would be a particular problem for such persons. For others, life appears to revolve around the family—either the family as a whole *(familism)* or the marriage relationship *(couplehood)*. *Living alone* refers to persons who prefer a life-style of relative isolation. *Easing through life with minimal involvement* describes individuals with minimal commitment in all or most role areas: work, marriage, family. These people's activity level is rather low and they have had a long-standing pattern of disengagement from the world. *Living fully* refers to people who are involved in a variety of areas but do not focus on any one as the most important.

The typology offered by Maas and Kuypers (1974) combines elements of the other three, focusing on the patterns of *aging* and predominant *life-style.* Their approach is particularly noteworthy because it is based on longitudinal data. Couples who had first been interviewed as young parents in 1930 were rein-terviewed 40 years later. Despite a relatively small surviving sample (142), 10 different life-styles were found. Maas and Kuypers were interested in the relative stability of these life-styles. Maintenance of the *husband-centered wife* style was dependent upon a relatively advantaged social world: good health, stable resi-dence, retired husband. The *employed mothers* exhibited considerable change over earlier life-styles. In these cases, there was relief from an unsatisfactory mar-riage with its economic problems and entrance into a gratifying new life-style of independence and new friends. Except for the *family-centered fathers,* males showed considerable stability. Even the *unwell-disengaged fathers* had exhibited poor health, interpersonal conflict, and dissatisfaction earlier in life. Maas and Kuypers conclude that there is both stability and change in life-style, with women apparently being affected more than men by circumstances.

Studies such as these lend themselves to three general conclusions. First, people appear to exhibit many patterns of aging, even when samples are relatively small. Neither activity nor disengagement is a typical or normal reaction to growing old. Second, there appear to be many ways to age successfully, although some patterns are less successful than others. For example, Maas and Kuypers' *disabled-disengaged mothers* were more fearful and anxious, and Neugarten and associates found that *apathetic* and *disorganized* patterns were associated with relatively low satisfaction. Nonetheless, the other six patterns described by Neugarten and associates are associated with relatively high satisfaction.

As a third conclusion, the four studies in Table 4.1 found evidence of considerable stability of personality over the life cycle. Kuypers (1974) indicates that one's past affects coping and adaptation in old age and "persons are rooted in previous ways of being, perhaps prisoners to some aspects and beneficiaries of others" (p. 176). Longitudinal studies support a view of stability or constancy of personality during adulthood. One panel study found no significant changes on personality tests over a 25-year period (Woodruff & Birren, 1972). A more recent study of men aged 17 to 85 found very high levels of stability in a range of personality traits (e.g., sociability, emotional stability, friendliness) over a 6 to 12 year period (Costa et al., 1980); stability was evident for young, middle-aged, and older respondents. This research has also found that personality traits are good predictors of personal adjustment over extended periods of time (Costa et al., 1981).

Such findings appear to support the following conclusion:

> There is considerable evidence that, in normal men and women, there is no sharp discontinuity of personality with age, but instead an increasing consistency. Those characteristics that have been central to the personality seem to become even more clearly delineated, and those values the individual has been cherishing become even more salient. (Neugarten et al., 1968:177)

There is some evidence to support a general "aging-stability thesis" (Glenn, 1980), whereby early formative stages are followed by relative stability in attitudes and values. This may be attributable to a decline with age in inherent changeability, a wider spacing of significant events after young adulthood, or processes of choice and adjustment that resist change.

Personal stability is far from total, however, as events and social structure continue to influence the individual throughout adulthood. Work experiences, for example, appear to affect anxiety, alienation, self-esteem, and intellectual flexibility (Kohn & Schooler, 1973). While the dominant picture is one of stability in personality traits, there may be age differences in general psychological orientations (although it is unclear whether these reflect aging or cohort effects). Neugarten (1968, 1969) has suggested that there is an increase with age in *interiority* of personality—greater introspection and self-preoccupation as well as a shift in perception of the external environment.

> Forty-years-olds, for example, seem to see the environment as one that rewards boldness and risk-taking and to see themselves as possessing energy

congruent with the opportunities perceived in the outer world. Sixty-year-olds, however, perceive the world as complex and dangerous, no longer to be reformed in line with one's wishes. (Neugarten, 1968:140)

Neugarten's concept of interiority is echoed in other approaches to the psychology of aging, such as the disengagement theory, particularly subsequent revisions of the theory that placed greater emphasis on intrapsychic processes rather than societal pressures and functions (Cumming, 1963; Henry, 1965).

Kuhlen (1964) has described a similar shift in the nature of motivation. According to Kuhlen, there is a shift in late life from growth expansion to anxiety and threat as the sources of motivation. Earlier in life, one's basic motivation is toward achievement, status, self-actualization—to gain and maintain a position as a significant person in the world. The frustrations and limitations of old age result in constriction as an attempt to protect those resources that remain from the threats of aging. Thus there is a selective disengagement away from society-maintaining work and toward greater ego involvement. Like Neugarten, Kuhlen points to a shift from seeing the world as an opportunity for growth to viewing it as complex, dangerous, and not easily shaped to one's needs and demands.

Kuhlen's ideas receive some support from a study by Lowenthal and associates (1975) of people at "four stages of life": high school seniors, newlyweds, parents of the high school students, and older persons nearing retirement. Among their findings was an apparent shift in values with age. Persons in the earlier stages of the life cycle had an expansive orientation on achievement coupled with high expectations. Middle-aged and older persons, however, had more self-limiting orientations that stressed minimizing frustrations by coping with life's problems and not setting one's goals too high.

All these accounts suggest quite similar processes, whether described as interiority, disengagement, or anxiety-produced constriction. But the extent and sources of such changes remain unclear. Given the overall stability with age in personality traits found by most research, one must be cautious about age-related shifts in psychological orientation. Are such shifts natural and inevitable, the reflection of the modern context within which aging occurs or the product of a particular generation of older persons? What is needed is a more coherent developmental perspective on aging. The task of such an approach is to "investigate whether or not there are orderly and irreversible changes related to age that are significant in accounting for the differences between adults" (Neugarten, 1973:318). One also needs to study the variability of such processes in response to the experiences of individuals and cohorts.

It is beyond the scope of this book to present a full developmental theory of the life cycle. Nevertheless, we can look at some conceptual frameworks that help us understand the social-psychological experience of aging. First, each life stage may be thought of as having relatively unique developmental issues or crises that must be dealt with by the individual. Second, psychological functioning may be affected by age-linked stressful events. Finally, both of the above can be linked more generally to age-related changes in the roles and statuses occupied by individuals, thereby incorporating a developmental psychology of the life cycle within the model of age stratification.

DEVELOPMENTAL ISSUES AND AGING

A *developmental issue* may be defined as

> . . . a task which arises at or about a certain period in the life of the individual, successful achievement of which leads to his happiness and to success with later tasks, while failure leads to unhappiness in the individual, disapproval by the society, and difficulty with later tasks. (Havighurst, 1952:2)

The task of each life stage is presumably to integrate personal skills and needs with prescribed roles and expectations. The concepts of "tasks" or "stages" in the life cycle are useful in thinking about the ways in which individuals respond to aging, though their existence remains unclear.

Erik Erikson's (1950) theory of ego development is perhaps the most familiar approach in this area (Table 4.2). Erikson suggests that in middle adulthood one must develop a sense of establishing and guiding the next generation *(generativity),* thereby achieving a sense of contributing to the future. In late adulthood, the need is to develop a feeling of *ego integrity. Ego identity* in adolescence is the development of a self with a personal set of values. Ego integrity is the sense that one's life has been appropriate and meaningful—that the right choices were made. Erikson suggests that the failure to achieve ego integrity results in despair and a crippling fear of death.

Erikson's approach is typical in focusing on early stages in the life cycle. However, there has been growing interest in later adulthood, as exemplified by the popularity of works by Sheehy (1976) and Levinson (1978). Indeed, Smelser (1980) suggests that the adult years have become socially more problematic. Deaths of loved ones are more concentrated in middle adulthood rather than being lifelong and continuous; the empty nest and retirement occur earlier and last longer; the boundaries of midlife are sharper with expansion of roles expected to peak between ages 40 and 55. Let us turn to a more detailed look at the periods of interest to this book: middle age and old age.

Table 4.2   DEVELOPMENTAL ISSUES OVER THE LIFE CYCLE

Stage	Developmental issue
Early infancy	Trust vs. distrust
Later infancy	Autonomy vs. shame and doubt
Early childhood	Initiative vs. guilt
Middle childhood	Industry vs. inferiority
Adolescence	Ego identity vs. role confusion
Early adulthood	Intimacy vs. ego isolation
Middle adulthood	Generativity vs. ego stagnation
Late adulthood	Ego integrity vs. despair

Source: Adapted from Erik Erikson, *Childhood and Society,* 1950, New York: W. W. Norton.

Middle Age

Middle age might be thought of as a "confrontation between myth and reality" (Sarason, 1977:105). Middle age is often described as a time of culmination and introspective assessment of one's life (Gould, 1972; Kimmel, 1974; Sheehy, 1976; Levinson, 1978; Newman & Newman, 1979). Individuals assess their strengths and weaknesses and the accord between achievement and goals. They compare the "realities" of work and family with the "dreams" of youth: Is my work career going well? Have my children turned out the way I wished? Is my marriage fulfilling? Failure to match achievements and expectations may lead to feelings of depletion and failure, adjustment of aspirations to fit current realities, or one last effort to fulfill "the dream" (perhaps through career change or divorce).

Sheehy (1976) characterizes the ages 35 to 45 as the "deadline decade" when individuals assess whether they are "on schedule" personally and in terms of social expectations. Realization that one is halfway through the expected life cycle, so that one's own death is psychologically closer, may lead to a shift in perspective from "time since birth" to "time yet to live." This may contribute to reappraisal and intensified efforts to realize aspirations while there is still time.

The middle-aged also experience a variety of "partial deaths," such as physical attractiveness, physical strength, career opportunities (Kastenbaum, 1977). Because physical strength and attractiveness begin to decline, Peck (1956) argues that the middle-aged must come to value mental powers that withstand aging more successfully, and also that they must develop emotional flexibility:

> ... the capacity to shift emotional investments from one person to another, and from one activity to another ... this is the period, for most people, when their parents die, their children grow up and leave home, and their circle of friends and relatives of similar age begins to be broken by death. (Peck, 1956:45)

In their study, Lowenthal and her associates (1975) found that active reconstruction of the past peaked in middle age, revolving around past career choices and closing career options. For some this process is successful as they work through their doubts.

> One man, for example, not only had thought about the implications of past career choices but also was attempting to work through his doubts about the proper career path: "I think about what would have happened if I had gone into another business, if I had worked strictly as an accountant or if I had gone into the real estate business with a friend of mine. I knew a great deal about real estate and he had a great deal of money. I'm sure we would have made a successful venture. I may still do that, of course. But I keep wondering if I would have made more money at that type of work or been happier. I don't think I would have been as happy: accountants die young and real estate is dreary." (Lowenthal et al., 1975:131)

This study also indicates that middle age is not always seen as the prime of life. Many middle-aged men and women wished they were more imaginative in rechanneling their energies into new goals and activities. A critical issue of middle age seems to concern stagnation versus growth and the development of emotional and psychological flexibility that set the stage for successful adaptation to old age.

Old Age

The developmental issues of old age appear to be twofold. First, commentators on the psychology of old age often point to this as a time of "summing up" (Erikson, 1950; Butler, 1963; Gould, 1972; Newman & Newman, 1979). Erikson's concept of ego integrity implies that the aged need to review the appropriateness and meaningfulness of their lives the same as in middle age. However, review of the past during middle age seems to be more action-oriented, and discontent over the past may lead to behavioral change; on the other hand, the life review occurring in old age is a more passive attempt to make sense of one's life. Lowenthal and associates (1975) refer to older people as "reminiscing spectators." This introspection may serve to preserve identities no longer validated in current realities and remind individuals that their lives have been meaningful and worthwhile (Clausen, 1972).

> In age we have the privilege—which sometimes becomes a torture on sleepless nights—of passing judgement on our own performance . . . our efforts will not have been wasted if they help us to possess our own identities as an artist possesses his work. (Cowley, 1982:72–74)

The second developmental theme of old age is adjustment to new realities created by aging. One of these new realities is a changing perspective on time, which began in middle age. There is a realization that one's future is limited as death becomes a significant possibility. The feeling that time is running out may paradoxically have various effects, as is recognized by most students approaching a tough exam. Activity may be intensified to take advantage of what little time remains, but there may also be a feeling of impotence and inability to use what time is left, resulting in disengagement (e.g., going out drinking). Thus time can become an existential dilemma.

Altered time is not the only new reality of old age. In many ways the aged are cut off and set adrift from familiar roles, activities, relationships, and identities because of retirement, widowhood, the death of contemporaries, or their own physical limitations. We too often forget, in stereotypes of the serene "golden years," the enormous potential for change in the later years. The person who has worked 8 hours a day, 5 days a week, for 40 years, suddenly confronts a life without patterned work. The person who has been married for 50 years is suddenly widowed and alone. One's life long friends die or move away, leaving one stranded in an unfamiliar social world. Social losses and competence to deal with those losses represent critical social-psychological issues in later life (Bengtson, 1973b).

Peck (1956) has defined three developmental issues in old age that relate to a need for flexibility: (1) those who can find self-worth in a variety of activities and roles will be more successful than those whose sole basis of identity is the work role; (2) old age almost inevitably brings physical problems, which Peck suggests must be transcended or people will be overcome by their bodily "insults"; (3) the new prospect of personal death must be overcome. Peck is not suggesting passive resignation or denial, but rather the recognition of this possibility without letting it rule one's life.

These discussions of developmental issues in later life sensitize us to particular concerns associated with aging. Kimmel (1974), however, has rightly noted that for the most part they are rather general "armchair" theories that have not been rigorously tested and supported by empirical research. There are many remaining questions, the most central of which is whether these issues are universal. Aging is a very different experience in different cultures, and the ideas discussed here were developed in Western societies, in which loss is perhaps the primary accompaniment of aging. Would the same developmental tasks be found among the Abkhasians or the Japanese?

There are also likely to be differences in the timing and nature of developmental issues by social class, sex, and other sources of variation in the nature of aging. What happens to Erikson's *generativity* issue for those who do not have children? The danger is that these developmental issues are culture-bound and therefore reactive rather than intrinsic. The threat and anxiety described by Kuhlen (1964) may be attributable to the way society structures the situations of older people.

The housewife role offers an example of variation in the rhythm of events and associated issues in the life cycle. This role is characterized by an early peak of accomplishment and gratification, subsequent frustrations of repetitive and unconstructive work, and early "retirement" when children leave home (Lopata, 1966; Oakley, 1974). A recent study by the author compared the dimensions used to judge well-being by males, females in the labor force, and housewives in different age groups (Ward, 1980); such dimensions are likely to reflect salient developmental issues. Within each age group housewives proved to be distinct from the other groups. Among young adults the early peak of the housewife role resulted in greater salience of feelings of accomplishment and fulfillment. Throughout adulthood the "noncareer" nature of the housewife role, with its absence of explicit goals and timetables, was suggested by a lower salience of both life review and future orientation for housewives. The "middle crisis" is likely to carry a different meaning for such women. Whereas workers are assessing careers that are often at a peak of accomplishment and stature, Lowenthal and associates (1975) found that many middle-aged women displayed signs of desperation over the exit of children and limited possibilities for breaking out of the confines of the family to achieve personal growth. This indicates that developmental issues do not represent universal stages, but there is little understanding of the variation in the timing and nature of such issues.

There is also little understanding of the ways in which individuals deal with these issues. The timing and nature of age-related change will affect the aging experience of any individual. It should be remembered that aging can present the possibility of new goals and avenues of gratification as well as constriction and defensiveness. Which of these will occur depends on the meaning of change for the individual, the values attached to new opportunities, and the social supports enjoyed by the individual. We need to focus on the coping processes that mediate between personality types and the environment (Neugarten, 1973). How, for example, can individuals continue to function effectively if interiority increases with age and certain cognitive functions decline? Yet most older people do function effectively. We have also previously seen that there is little evidence of age-related changes in personality which might stem from developmental issues. Individuals are likely to cope with the concerns of old age in a manner consistent with their long-standing personalities.

We should not lose sight of the fact that the new realities that face aging individuals also offer important opportunities for positive and continuing personal growth. A magazine once published a series of vignettes on "ordinary" persons in their eighties who were living full, interesting lives: an 80-year-old college student who was elected Homecoming Queen, an 89-year-old woman with an active law practice, an 89-year-old woman who had made three trips to the Arctic Circle and two to the Antarctic in five years (Jones, 1978). These people have always led intriguing lives, and there are undoubtedly many others who are "liberated" in old age from confining middle-aged roles. Such older people have much to offer the young with a fascinating range of personal experiences, unique historical perspectives, and philosophies of life.

The fact that articles such as this exist suggests, however, that these older people are exceptional. It may be that fully lived, creative lives are exceptional among all age groups or that we consider such older people exceptional because they break our stereotypes about old age. Yet the evidence does suggest increased psychological restriction by many older people, whether we speak of disengagement or interiority. Lowenthal and her associates (1975) found that aging was accompanied by increased "blandness" with a decline in both positive and negative feelings. Older people in their study were less growth-oriented than younger people—less open, curious, and willing to experiment and change. They seemed to be seeking a relatively restricted life-style and viewed the world more pessimistically, as in the following example:

> One middle-aged man, acutely aware of eventual retirement, was very pessimistic and had no plans for it. His comments are typical of men and women at this stage of life: "It's just an unknown quantity. I can't see anything ahead. I suppose I could consider traveling, but that doesn't appeal to me too much now. More grandchildren? We have more than enough now. Just waiting to pass time before you die. Not knowing what to do. But age is the first thing against you in trying to do anything big or spectacular. Even if you decide on something, you may not have time to do it. I guess you have to be realistic about things. When you are young you have all of life ahead of you." (Lowenthal et al., 1975:110–111)

Rather than seeing these patterns as natural or inevitable aspects of the aging experience, we can more profitably view them as a response to the social context within which individuals attempt to grapple with aging. Specifically, we can look at the consequences of stressful life events and the role of age stratification in shaping the options and constraints of the aging experience.

STRESS AND AGING

The developmental crises and psychological changes linked to the aging process may represent attempts to cope with stressful age-related experiences. Stress is best viewed as a subjective transaction between an individual and his or her situation. It results from an imbalance between the perceived demand placed upon the individual (threat) and the perceived response capability (ability to cope with the threat) (Lazarus, 1966; McGrath, 1970). The greater the perceived imbalance, the greater the stress felt by the person. There is growing evidence that stress is linked to physical as well as psychological disorders (Dohrenwend & Dohrenwend, 1974; Eisdorfer & Wilkie, 1977).

In objective terms, old age might be viewed as less stressful than earlier adulthood because there is some evidence that older people experience fewer significant life events (George, 1980; Pearlin, 1980). Young adults are establishing occupational careers and marital relationships and are faced with responsibilities for young, dependent children. But it is the quality of events that is critical. Certainly older people potentially face several major transitions: retirement, widowhood, institutionalization. Even the prospect of these events may be stressful. Events in youth are more likely to represent gains and challenges ("entrance" events), whereas events in old age represent threats and losses ("exit" events) (McCrae, 1982). Pearlin (1980) also notes that the strains of young adulthood are often of the sort that dissipate with time, whereas those of old age are more irreversible and chronic (retirement, widowhood, illness).

There are a number of types of threats or situations that can be expected to be stressful (McGrath, 1970), each of which is evident in old age. There is the *physical threat* of injury, pain, or death. Older people encounter increasing health problems and the prospect of personal death. The poor health or death of one's contemporaries may add greatly to a personal feeling of anxiety among the aged. *Ego threat* involves injury or pain to the psychological self. The aged are vulnerable to losses of roles defining their identity (retirement, widowhood) and their general status may be devalued. Finally, there is *interpersonal threat*—the disruption of social relationships. The poor health or death of relatives and friends may constrict the social networks of older people as well as one's own limitations or residential mobility.

An illustration of the potential threat faced in old age can be found in the Social Readjustment Rating Scale developed by Holmes and Rahe (1967). People were asked to rate life events according to their intensity and the length of time required to adapt to them, regardless of their desirability. Table 4.3 shows the resulting ranking of the disruptiveness or threat inherent in various situations. Such rankings will vary across individuals and groups, but it is striking that many of the most disruptive events potentially accompany aging: death of spouse, family member, or close friend, personal illness, retirement, sex difficulties, change in financial state, and so on.

Such disruptive changes may additionally be more subjectively threatening for older than for younger people because there may be an emotional investment in familiar objects that provides a sense of continuity and security. Their loss represents a greater destruction of time and symbolic assets. For example, moving from a house in which one has lived for 40 years has a greater impact than moving from an apartment in which one has spent a much shorter time. A study of tornado victims found that the loss of houses and gardens had important symbolic meaning to older persons (Kilijanek & Drabek, 1979). Disruption of personal relationships through death, poor health, or residential change also becomes critical because the ties of older people may represent greater investment and commitment.

Older people may also have or perceive less ability to cope with disruptive life changes. A variety of personal resources mediate the effects of life events: finances, health, education, social supports, self-esteem, and perceived mastery and control over events (George, 1980; Pearlin et al., 1981). For example, older people may feel that there is less time available to cope with change and replace what may have been lost, particularly with a major loss such as a spouse. Physical limitations may also hinder adaptability and lead older people to feel that they have less energy to invest in adapting to changes. Individuals with such limitations may be able to adapt to a much narrower range of situations (Lawton & Nahemow, 1973). Most of us assume that we can handle most of the events we encounter. However, this taken-for-granted flexibility becomes suspect with the limitations of age, and a feeling of "precarious flexibility" may account for some of the cautiousness exhibited by older people (Gubrium, 1973).

Older people may feel a lack of control over events as fatalism and passivity are greater among the elderly. Such orientations limit the repertoire of coping strategies. Rodin (1980) conducted an experimental program in a nursing home to counteract such feelings by teaching coping skills and encouraging a perception

Table 4.3   THE SOCIAL READJUSTMENT RATING SCALE

Life event	Mean value
1. Death of spouse	100
2. Divorce	73
3. Marital separation from mate	65
4. Detention in jail or other institution	63
5. Death of a close family member	63
6. Major personal injury or illness	53
7. Marriage	50
8. Being fired at work	47
9. Marital reconciliation with mate	45
10. Retirement from work	45
11. Major change in the health or behavior of a family member	44
12. Pregnancy	40
13. Sexual difficulties	39
14. Gaining a new family member	39
15. Major business readjustment	39
16. Major change in financial state	38
17. Death of a close friend	37

Table 4.3 *(Continued)*

Life event	Mean value
18. Changing to a different line of work	36
19. Major change in the number of arguments with spouse	35
20. Taking on a mortgage greater than $10,000	31
21. Foreclosure on a mortgage or loan	30
22. Major change in responsibilities at work	29
23. Son or daughter leaving home	29
24. In-law troubles	29
25. Outstanding personal achievement	28
26. Wife beginning or ceasing work outside the home	26
27. Beginning or ceasing formal schooling	26
28. Major change in living conditions	25
29. Revision of personal habits	24
30. Troubles with the boss	23
31. Major change in working hours or conditions	20
32. Change in residence	20
33. Changing to a new school	20
34. Major change in usual type and/or amount of recreation	19
35. Major change in church activities	19
36. Major change in social activities	18
37. Taking on a mortgage or loan less than $10,000	17
38. Major change in sleeping habits	16
39. Major change in number of family get-togethers	15
40. Major change in eating habits	15
41. Vacation	13
42. Christmas	12
43. Minor violations of the law	11

Source: Thomas Holmes and Richard Rahe, "The Social Readjustment Rating Scale," *Journal of Psychosomatic Research* (1967), pp. 213–218. Reprinted by permission.

of personal control and responsibility. The treatment group exhibited less stress and fewer adjustment problems, illustrating the important role of psychological resources. Feelings of mastery and control are related to education, therefore coping difficulties may be partly attributable to the lower educational levels of current older cohorts.

Older people's ability to cope also may be reduced by the loss of social supports. Family and friends provide tangible assistance in times of need, but knowledge of their availability and caring may itself be enough to buffer the impact of events (Thoits, 1982). The difficulty for older people is that many of the stressful experiences they face (such as health problems, retirement, or widowhood) entail the disruption or loss of social supports. This is itself stressful and contributes to the stressfulness of other experiences.

Apart from the experience of actual physical or mental illness, stress may partly account for some of the observed psychological concomitants of aging. Disengagement, rigidity, and interiority may represent attempts to conserve what remains against the perceived threats of old age. Such social and psychological constriction may well result from a refocusing of motivation toward anxiety and threat, increasingly viewing the world as complex and dangerous. These processes can become a vicious cycle. Rigidity and cautiousness lead individuals to react passively and generally rather than adapting to the peculiar characteristics of specific situations, which further hinders their ability to cope. The sense of personal incompetence and threat increases, individuals become more cautious and anxious, and the cycle continues. To the extent that stress is internalized, generating self-blame, additional psychological problems may result.

> . . . the depressions of old age are primarily related to the loss of self-esteem which results from the aged individual's inability to supply his needs and drives (loss of narcissistic supplies) or to defend himself against threats to his security. (Busse, 1970:87)

Although events and transitions associated with aging may partly account for apparent changes in psychological orientation, feelings of threat and anxiety are neither inevitable nor universal among the aged. Indeed, there is some evidence that older people may use more mature and realistic coping mechanisms than younger people, having learned to eliminate those that are ineffective (McCrae, 1982). As suggested by the life course perspective, this depends on the earlier experiences of individuals. In a companion study to Elder's research on a sample of children during the Depression (discussed in Chapter 1), Elder and Liker (1982) studied the effects of deprivation on mothers of these children, who were reinterviewed in 1969. Although economic loss during the Depression diminished the emotional health of lower-status women in later life, Elder and Liker conclude that "the most vital, resourceful women from the middle class are those who were tested by the pressures of heavy income loss during the 1930s" (p. 259). Thus hardship earlier in life may test one's "mettle," resulting in better preparation for coping with losses associated with aging.

The threat associated with aging also depends partly on the position of older people in a system of age stratification—that is, the nature of role changes accompanying aging and the meanings of roles available to the aged. Social structure affects not only the occurrence of threatening events but also the availability of coping resources. The Abkhasian culture, for example, is characterized by a lack of stressful role transitions and cultural mechanisms to alleviate stress: stoicism and absence of competitiveness. To understand individual responses to aging, we must also look at the nature of age stratification because it determines the supports and options available to aging individuals. This requires that we first understand the relationship between aging and the *social self*.

AGING AND THE SELF

Questions of personal stability and change can be addressed within the perspective of *symbolic interactionism*. This perspective involves three premises.

> The first premise is that human beings act toward things on the basis of the meanings that the things have for them. . . . The second premise is that the meaning of such things is derived from, or arises out of, the social interaction that one has with one's fellows. The third premise is that these meanings are handled in, and modified through, an interpretive process used by the person in dealing with the things he encounters. (Blumer, 1969:2)

Thus we live in a symbolic environment in which meaning is not intrinsic to an object but is assigned to it through social interaction. We are active agents who construe the world and act in it on the basis of our interpretations. Language is perhaps the best example of shared symbols developed through interaction that give meaning to the objects around us.

This perspective has important implications for the study of aging. Objects or events must be assigned social meaning to make sense. The meaning of old age, retirement, widowhood, or leisure depends on the social and cultural context in which it occurs. Similarly, if the social context in which the individual interacts changes because of aging, the self will also change.

Symbolic interactionism suggests that humans have selves because they can take the attitude of others and see themselves as an object. The meaning of the self arises from social interaction and is determined by the symbolic meanings made available to the individual. This self cannot exist apart from society because individuals experience themselves through interaction with particular "significant others" and with the "generalized other" (society.)

Out of numerous interactions a more or less stabilized self-conception emerges. This self is a persistent core element around which other meanings and interpretations are organized. Because the self organizes and directs behavior, individuals become consistent in their actions.

> The crucial significance of the self as a social object is that it is the only object common to all the widely varied situations in which we participate. As such, it comes to serve as the anchoring point from which we make judgments and subsequent plans of action toward the many other objects in each specific situation. . . . We may think of it as consisting of all the answers the individual might make to the question "Who am I?" (Hickman & Kuhn, 1956:43)

The self is an identity commitment evolved from a long history of interactions and shaped by validation for particular views of the self found in role activities and symbolic interaction with others.

It is because of these considerations that the concept of *social roles* has come to occupy a place of importance in the study of aging. Social roles serve as links between structural and interactionist understandings of human behavior (Heiss, 1981). Persons come to occupy various positions in the social structure, and roles involve the expectations associated with particular positions. Roles "locate" individuals in social and symbolic worlds; because we play certain roles, we have access to certain interactions, meanings, and identities. As such, roles are the source of personal stability and personal change. Continuity in one's *role set* means continuity in social, interactional, and symbolic environments; discontinuity of roles means discontinuity in these environments.

On the one hand, stability of social roles will be accompanied by stability in self-concept. Particular identities continue to be validated because the individual interacts within relatively unchanging social worlds. Indeed, Neugarten suggests that an "institutionalized self" develops:

> In a sense, the self becomes institutionalized with the passage of time. Not only do certain personality processes become stabilized and provide continuity, but the individual builds around him a network of social relationships which he comes to depend on for emotional support and responsiveness and which maintain him in subtle ways. (Neugarten, 1964:198)

This applies as well to personality, the tendency of individuals to organize their behavior consistently in different situations and over a number of years (Kimmel, 1974). It represents a harmony between the individual and the environment, as unique adaptations to past experiences color present responses. Personality consistency evolves from the effects of memory, consistency in the situations one experiences, and habituated responses based on the accumulation of past experience (Kimmel, 1974).

The dependence of self and personality on social roles and interaction also implies the possibility of change in the self. Personality is an ongoing system that undergoes continuous change. "As the result of one's life history with its accumulating record of adaptations to both biological and social events, there is a continually changing basis within the individual for perceiving and responding to new events" (Neugarten, 1973:312). As there are changes in the social roles individuals occupy and the social situations they encounter, there will also be changes in the nature of the interactions they have with others and with the world. External consistencies that had previously reinforced internal consistencies break up; and as the self-concept changes, behavior directed by it will also change.

Aging may be accompanied by the disruption of long-term roles, which had previously lent consistency to the self, because of retirement, widowhood, health limitations, and so on. Thus there is considerable potential for personal change in response to age stratification. As interactions and group memberships change, the individual enters new roles and acquires new significant others and reference groups; former roles become less salient and the self-concept is changed. Cavan illustrates this with retirement:

> At the point of compulsory retirement . . . the means of carrying out the social role disappears: the man is a lawyer without a case, a bookkeeper without books, a machinist without tools. Second, he is excluded from his group of former co-workers: as an isolated person he may be completely unable to function in his former role. Third, as a retired person, he begins to find a different evaluation of himself in the minds of others from the evaluation he had as an employed person. He no longer sees respect in the eyes of former subordinates, praise in the faces of former superiors, and approval in the manner of former co-workers. The looking glass composed of his former important groups throws back a changed image: he is done for, an oldtimer, old-fashioned, on the shelf. (1962:527–528)

Personal change is more complex than this implies, however. Alteration of the "objective" social environment does not automatically alter self-perception, and former roles may still play a part. The retired sociologist, for example, may still define himself as a sociologist and derive esteem from that identity. Neugarten's (1969) notion of interiority implies that the self becomes less dependent on external factors for older people. The self is often more stable than one might expect. If an individual does not perceive circumstances as changed, his or her self will not be altered.

On the other hand, the considerable potential for change in personal circumstances may also make personal change highly likely. Bengtson (1973a) has suggested that older people may be more susceptible to social labeling because of the social reorganization they undergo. One study of older people concluded that because of the unusual amount of personal change and status ambiguity associated with aging, "life-after-sixty shares with adolescence an intensification of the intimate and self-reflexive. At both times of life, the question, Who am I? assumes poignant relevance" (Clark & Anderson, 1967:78).

The link between role change and personal change can be related to the developmental issues discussed earlier. The usefulness of a model of age stratification again becomes apparent. Shifts into and out of roles are age-graded with a typical sequencing of roles through the life cycle, disrupting the continuity of one's role set. Inasmuch as roles are associated with qualities, rewards, expectations, and evaluations, individuals of different ages encounter different social and symbolic worlds. Young adulthood is a time of expansion into new roles offering more rewards and responsibilities, therefore it is not surprising that a critical developmental issue at this stage is personal identity and the need for a stabilized sense of self. Kimmel (1974) argues that the role changes of youth propel individuals into the external social world because of the need to master new roles and develop new personal styles to deal with them. The middle years are a time of stability and balance, with relatively less personal change, when issues seem to involve looking at the self as it has become. Advancing years, at least in this society, may be accompanied by the loss of rewards, status, and long-term identities. Kimmel notes that this constriction of the social and symbolic environment is a "centripetal" force that makes internal processes more salient.

Furthermore, the *meanings* attached to age-related transitions are important. Retirement will have a very different impact depending on whether it is seen as a reward or as an implied rejection and failure. Thus it can be expected that the psychological issues that accompany aging will vary cross-culturally as age transitions and the meanings of those transitions also vary.

ROLE CHANGE AND SOCIALIZATION

There is a stereotyped notion that socialization and personality formation are confined to childhood, producing a relatively finished product. But socialization is a lifelong process as individuals move in and out of roles throughout adulthood (Bush & Simmons, 1981). Geographic and occupational mobility require adjustment to new situations. There may be mutual socialization by couples who have just married or have just become parents. Lamaze childbirth classes and the more recent "parenting" classes represent such adult-socialization experiences.

As noted in Chapter 3, socialization teaches individuals how to perform new roles, adjust to changing roles, and relinquish old ones. As such, socialization processes represent a cornerstone for the maintenance of society and for the well-being of individuals (Bush & Simmons, 1981). Because of role transitions experienced throughout life, socialization is a "continuous bilateral negotiation between the individual and the social system as he moves into new positions through time" (Bengtson, 1973a:19). Note the use of the term *negotiation*. Those being socialized are not passive in this process, but instead participate in the creation of their roles. Thus socialization perpetuates society and at the same time contains the seeds for change.

Socialization is not always successful, however. Individuals may be prepared for roles they will not play because of role-allocation barriers or enter roles for which they are not prepared. Riley (1976) indicates that role transitions are smoother when individuals are adequately prepared and there is continuity between old and new roles. *Anticipatory* socialization, occurring before the role transition, provides continuity for a smoother transition. Many childhood activities, for example, anticipate adult roles, either inculcating broad value orientations or legitimizing particular roles. This is the essence of early sex-role socialization. Similarly, during adulthood people are usually prepared for and looking forward to (even if with some apprehension) the new roles they will occupy—shifts from student to worker, single to married, couple to parent. On the other hand, *tenancy* socialization, occurring after entrance into the new role, does not smooth over the transition. The army draftee must be socialized into army life largely during basic training.

Society provides continuity for role transitions by making future roles visible and clear and by providing rites of passage, such as graduation and marriage ceremonies, which redefine the person and symbolize the transition. Irving Rosow (1974) has suggested that one of the basic problems of older people is that they are not socialized for an old-age role. Socialization properties operating throughout adulthood are felt to break down in old age. Rites of passage into old age are nonexistent or vague. Retirement dinners, for example, do not adequately serve this function and may instead "reflect the social judgment and policy of a collective that men or women beyond a certain age are not fit to work or that their services are no longer necessary" (Blau, 1973:214).

Adult role transitions typically involve a voluntary increase in responsibility and independence. Changes associated with aging, however, are more likely to be involuntary and to represent a loss of responsibility and increased dependence. Consequently, there is little motivation to prepare for the old-age role and much motivation to deny it. There is also little role continuity in the shifts associated with aging. For example, adults are socialized to value autonomy and productivity, but retirement is associated with dependence and an unproductive role.

The aged are left to make their own adaptations because modern cultures do little to prepare them for the positions occupied by older people. As we shall see later, for example, preretirement programs are infrequent and typically very limited. Rosow (1974) also suggests that socialization for old age is confined to informal situations and the aged have not made effective use of their age peers as role models. There is a tendency to maintain involvement with old groups and to continue acknowledging previous status characteristics. Additionally, there are few or no rewards for playing the new aged role.

This argument asserts that there is little motivation to enter old age, inadequate socialization experiences for the transitions of later life, and few expectations for guidance beyond simplistic "act your age" ideas.

> . . . the norms provide almost no expectations that effectively structure an older person's activities and general pattern of life. His adjustment in this respect results essentially from his individual decisions and choices, from *personal* definitions of what is appropriate and desirable. . . . In this sense, an old person's life is basically "roleless," unstructured by the society, and conspicuously lacking in norms, especially for nonfamilial relationships. (Rosow, 1974:69)

As was noted in Chapter 3, however, this argument may be overstated. Aging individuals may negotiate and create roles within their own particular social worlds, even in the absence of any formal or universal socialization for old age. Aging may represent ambiguity and loss, but it also presents opportunities for positive change and growth. Which of these occurs is partly dependent on the nature of allocation and socialization within a system of age stratification.

AGING, GROWTH, AND AGE STRATIFICATION

The individual aging experience is one of personal continuity confronted by age-related changes that can potentially uproot the aging person from his or her normal and familiar world and identities. Identity crisis is often not a bad thing, however. It is one way in which we grow, shedding identities that no longer fit and taking on those that do, and hopefully becoming better or more complete persons in the process. Yet the literature on the developmental psychology of aging is replete with descriptions of older persons who constrict and defend rather than grow.

Perhaps more important to the psychology of aging than lack of preparation for old-age roles is the actual content of those roles and options. Do the transitions of late life present aging individuals with opportunities for continued personal growth? The answer to this question offered by many commentators on the aging experience is no. In their study of stages in the life cycle, Lowenthal and associates (1975) point to the wasted potential of mature women and self-actualizing men who desire second careers but lack opportunities. Middle-aged women who seek meaningful involvement outside of the family seem especially thwarted. Lowenthal and associates suggest that psychologically "simplistic" women age more comfortably in the current society than complex women, who have not acquired protective, stress-avoiding life-styles.

There is growing recognition of the barriers created by modern age stratification to meaningful life experiences and options for personal change in both middle and old age. Sarason (1977) refers to the "one life-one career imperative," whereby career choices made in youth channel and "fill in" the rest of life, offering few opportunities for later change or growth. In middle age this contributes to an early sense of aging and feelings of being trapped. In old age one is limited to too narrow a range of options and role transitions in modern societies, which results largely in declining status and responsibility.

Despite lengthening of the expected life cycle to over 70 years, education and the major decisions about work and family careers are still confined to the first third of the life course, and major change, especially in work careers, becomes increasingly difficult with age. Sarason notes that it is far easier to change marriage partners than work careers. This situation represents a "disparity between society's rhetoric about growth and contemporary institutional realities" (Sarason, 1977:265). The age stratification system of modern societies faces the challenge of providing options for "loosening up life" (Butler, 1975) to make the later years of life more than simply playing out earlier decisions. This theme will be discussed again, particularly in relation to aging and the use of time.

SEX DIFFERENCES IN THE AGING EXPERIENCE

A life course perspective must recognize variability in the nature of aging. Age stratification is not isolated from other mechanisms for allocating roles. One of the most important of these is the system of sexual stratification, which is superimposed on the age-grading of roles and life events. Because of socialization, enticements, and barriers, men and women occupy different positions in society, and consequently their aging experiences differ. Unfortunately, our understanding in this area has been hindered by overblown stereotypes and myths about the differences between older men and women (Beeson, 1975; Payne & Whittington, 1976).

Diane Beeson has noted that "when women have been included as subjects their experience of aging has frequently been compared to that of men and evaluated as less problematic, less traumatic, and their difficulties seen as more easily resolved" (1975:52). To a large extent, this seems to be based on the assumption, exemplified in the following statement, that the life cycle is smoother for women:

> Disengagement from central life roles is basically different for women than for men, perhaps because women's roles are essentially unchanged from girlhood to death. In the course of their lives, women are asked to give up only pieces of their core socioemotional roles or to change their details. Their transitions are therefore easier. (Cumming, 1964:13)

This assumption of tranquillity is questionable. Indeed, it has been suggested that if women do adjust more easily to aging, it is because they are used to ill-defined, ambiguous roles and have already experienced impermanence in the form of role loss (Kline, 1975).

The more typical argument is that aging is a more difficult experience for women. Partly this refers to objective problems discussed in Chapter 2—women are more likely to be widowed, impoverished, and living alone. But sex differences have also been linked to the more general social positions of men and women. Susan Sontag suggests that there is a "double standard of aging":

> This society offers even fewer rewards for aging to women than it does to men. Being physically attractive counts much more in a woman's life than in a man's, but beauty, identified, as it is for women, with youthfulness, does not stand up well to age. Exceptional mental powers can increase with age, but women are rarely encouraged to develop their minds. . . . "Masculinity" is identified with competence, autonomy, self-control—qualities which the disappearance of youth does not threaten. . . . "Feminity" is identified with incompetence, help-lessness, passivity, noncompetitiveness, being nice. Age does not improve these qualities. (1975:32–33)

Thus, aging may be more difficult for women because they are more narrowly defined. Additionally, Sontag argues that there is a "humiliating process of gradual sexual disqualification" (p. 34), which perceives women as sexually "obsolete" earlier than men. There are few, if any, female counterparts to the Cary Grants of the male world.

An experimental study by Kogan (1979) provides an illustration of the "quickened aging" that may be perceived in women. Subjects were presented with photographs of men and women of different ages and asked to estimate the chronological age of persons in the photographs, place them in an age category (adolescent, young adult, middle-aged, elderly, or aged), and indicate three persons they would like to become acquainted with. Female photographs were placed in older age categories—that is, "middle-aged" and "elderly" having earlier onsets for females. Male subjects also showed a preference for meeting younger women and somewhat older men. However, this was only true for the male subjects, suggesting that age is more salient and value-laden for men than for women.

This last point suggests that a "double standard of aging" may have less personal impact on women than it seems. Indeed, there appear to be few sex differences in morale and self-esteem among older people (Turner, 1979; Liang, 1982). Turner indicates that although the onset of old age is perceived as earlier for women among adult respondents, older women typically have younger personal age identities than comparable men. Older women may be freed from earlier sex-role personality constraints, allowing for greater self-direction (Frieze et al., 1978). This possibility is echoed in the following statement by a 60-year-old woman.

> I feel that life under my own steam, in my own control is just beginning. It is exhilarating. I use my energies now for my own self-development and fulfill-ment. I am becoming a one-person do-it-myself authority on anything that concerns me—health, education, entertainment, adventure, relationships. . . . I feel liberated from a long, sticky period of role playing, stage-managed by everyone but myself, and am now moving into a period of being and becoming my-self—which is unfolding and surprising me at every turn: so far, pleasantly, although not without serious confrontations with my husband about my "right"

to do so. These confrontations have been to a large degree successful, although involving inevitable compromise on both sides . . . (Collins, 1976:6)

Neugarten (1968; 1969) suggests that older men become more receptive to affiliative and nurturant needs, whereas older women feel less guilty about aggressive and egocentric impulses; in short, a "feminization" of men and a "masculinization" of women seems to occur in late life. There is some empirical support for this idea. Lowenthal and associates (1975) found that men approaching retirement were more mellow and less ambitious and restless. Older women seemed to hit their stride, becoming less dependent and more assertive. Many confronted the empty nest with a sense of relief and changing patterns of dominance. These patterns are echoed in cross-cultural studies (Gutmann, 1977). Studies of Asian, Middle Eastern, African, and Amerindian cultures indicate that old men move from active to passive styles and women move from passive to active mastery, resulting in what Gutmann calls the "matriarchy of later life." Gutmann notes that this female dominance is largely exercised informally in family settings rather than in formal positions of power, and this often makes aged women vulnerable to charges of sorcery and witchcraft:

> The Moroccans capture the African consensus on the lethal nature of old women in this parable: each boy is born surrounded by a hundred devils and each girl is born surrounded by a hundred angels. However, with each passing year, a devil is exchanged for an angel; when a man reaches a hundred years of age, he is surrounded by angels, and the women by devils. (1977:311–312)

Gutmann further suggests that aged men and women are reverting to psychological needs that were suppressed early in life. Indeed, earlier sex-role differences would no longer seem functional in the context of the empty nest, retirement, and widowhood. We have noted that general flexibility contributes to successful aging, therefore successful agers may be those who combine the best of "male" and "female" traits.

The nature of the aging experience for women will be shaped by cohort succession. Present cohorts of older women were socialized to be passive and subordinate; it is only quite recently that women encounter several remaining decades of life after completing the traditional wife/mother role (Block et al., 1981). Future cohorts of older women will have been socialized into different attitudes and roles with greater education and more continuous occupational careers. As the baby-boom cohort ages, we seem to be seeing more favorable images at least of women in their thirties and forties—Jane Fonda, Mary Tyler Moore, Cheryl Tiegs. More egalitarian relations between men and women and strengthened inner resources of women may weaken the double standard of aging. Uhlenberg (1979) has pointed out, however, that most older women will continue to be widowed and have neither the responsibilities associated with the wife role nor the assistance of a spouse in arranging life activities so that society must meet the challenge of providing fulfilling roles for these women.

SUCCESSFUL AGING

A discussion of the social psychology of aging inevitably leads to the question: What constitutes successful aging? There is no shortage of conflicting prescriptions: be active, disengage; be future-oriented, review the past; conserve oneself, grow as a person. But if we have learned one thing from a developmental perspective on aging, it is that there are as many ways to age successfully as there are types of people. This challenges our own biases about what older people "ought" to be like. As one example, Lowenthal and associates (1975) found two quite different routes to equally high satisfaction in late life. Some were psychologically complex, taking a bouyant and expansive road to happiness. Others were psychologically simple, basing their satisfaction on constriction. Whereas this author prefers the former pattern of aging, all persons must approach old age in a manner that is right and consistent for themselves in order to feel satisfied.

Early approaches to successful aging took a prescriptive approach in defining "well-adjusted" old age. More recent approaches let aging individuals define for themselves the meaning of satisfaction. There are many measures and dimensions of this *subjective well-being* (Larson, 1978; George, 1979; George & Bearon, 1980). Sometimes this refers to satisfaction within domains—family, health, housing, and so on. More often it represents generalized assessments of one's life, including comparisons with the past, with goals and expectations, and with other older persons.

Within the older population, health and socioeconomic status are the most consistent predictors of perceived quality of life (Larson, 1978; George & Bearon, 1980). Other characteristics, including race, sex, retirement, widowhood, and social interaction, exhibit much less consistent patterns. This serves as a useful counterpoint to a crisis perspective on aging, whereby many of the processes discussed in this chapter might lead one to view old age as a time of great unhappiness.

This is further underscored by the fact that studies typically find no age differences in perceived quality of life, and in some cases find higher subjective well-being among older people (George & Bearon, 1980; Witt et al., 1980; Herzog & Rodgers, 1981). It is not clear what to make of this. Optimistically, it may mean that older people are able to respond effectively to the demands and challenges of aging. It probably also reflects adjustments made over time as aspirations become more realistic, unhappy marriages are dissolved, and people find better jobs or better housing. It may mean that older people are more accepting of familiar situations, are less willing to admit their problems, or even that unhappy people die earlier than happy people.

These patterns also reflect a tendency for older people to be more satisfied with their situations than seems warranted by objective reality. This is illustrated by the findings of a recent study of housing conditions of the elderly (Rabushka & Jacobs, 1980). Although objective ratings indicated that 50 percent of the houses occupied by older persons had a "critical defect," either a safety hazard or lack of required facilities, 77 percent of the respondents described their homes as trouble free and only 4 percent were dissatisfied with their housing. Figure

4.1 indicates the substantial gap between objectively defined and subjectively defined problems. Carp and Carp (1981) suggest that such gaps between objective and subjective realities reflect a defensive adaptation in the face of limited options and lack of control, similar to that found with other deprived groups. If you cannot change a situation, why not adjust to it and accept it?

This raises some complex issues. Although subjective well-being seems an unbiased measure of successful aging, do we wish to consider as successful aging satisfaction arrived at through defense and denial? We all have a feeling that certain lives *should not* be satisfying, even if they are; and if people understood the alternatives, they would be dissatisfied and press for change, thereby enriching their lives. This is a dilemma faced by any movement that seeks to liberate people (workers, housewives, old people) from the taken-for-granted realities that constrain their lives. The fact that these realities are taken for granted means that people do not appreciate how dissatisfied they "ought" to be with them.

This author does not wish to claim possession of "the answer" to how older people ought to live their lives, but it may be possible to define successful aging in terms of what old age might look like under a different set of circumstances, in a different social context. The current system of age stratification is only one among many possible systems. The present structure of the life course may be too confining, as suggested by the concept of the "one life-one career imperative," thereby robbing old age of certain potential satisfactions. The aged may well be unaware of missed options and opportunities because the age stratification system also shapes our expectations and perceptions of the life course.

One definition of successful aging involves meeting the developmental challenges presented to individuals by aging. The social structure could then also be

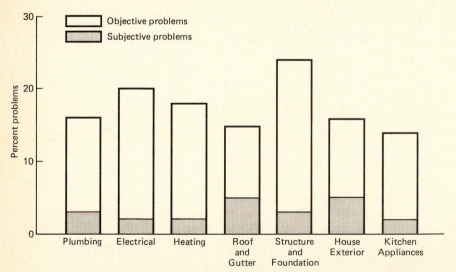

Figure 4.1 Subjective perceptions of housing problems compared with objective presence of housing problems in a sample of homeowners aged 60 and over. (*Source:* Reprinted with permission of Macmillan Publishing Co., Inc., from *Old Folks at Home* by Alvin Rabushka and Bruce Jacobs, p. 127. Copyright © 1980 by The Free Press, a Division of Macmillan Publishing Co., Inc.)

evaluated according to whether it hinders or facilitates the resolution of these challenges. A useful summary of the development issues posed by aging is provided by Clark and Anderson (1967), who outline five adaptive tasks to be accomplished in successful aging:

1. *Recognition of aging and definition of instrumental limitations:* an awareness and acceptance of the limits placed by age on one's health and energy.
2. *Redefinition of physical and social life space:* changing the boundaries of one's world to achieve an environment that can still be controlled; this may or may not require constriction (disengagement).
3. *Substitution of alternate sources of need-satisfaction:* as roles and relationships are lost, satisfaction must be found elsewhere.
4. *Reassessment of criteria for evaluation of self:* the older person must be able to find sources of self-worth that are not lost because of aging.
5. *Reintegration of values and life goals:* this implies that the above tasks must be accomplished and made coherent to give their "new" life meaning.

In their study Clark and Anderson found that most older people had handled these adaptive tasks successfully. Among those who were maladapted, the most frequent problem was the failure to achieve substitute sources of need-satisfaction. This suggests that major changes such as retirement and widowhood, which involve the loss of what may be central sources of need-satisfaction, would have particularly severe effects on older people. Problems in achieving meaningful substitutes may stem from the prevailing nature of age stratification in modern societies. These five tasks, however, should not be taken as the only ones possible. In some ways, they seem to suggest an acceptance and adaptation to biological and social aspects of old age as they are presented to the aging person. Again, we should not be afraid to consider alternative images of old age to those now available.

SUMMARY

There have been two general social-psychological theories of aging. Activity theory suggests that older people should remain active and involved, thus insuring stability of need-satisfaction and a positive self-image. Disengagement theory argues that social and emotional withdrawal from the world by aging individuals is mutually satisfying and functional for the individual and society. Both of these approaches have some supporting evidence, but both offer an oversimplified view of aging and its effects on the individual. A life course perspective is preferable, recognizing stability as well as change. Individuals seek to maintain previous patterns of living, but aging places constraints on the ability to maintain continuity. Aging patterns are complex and variable as each individual develops his or her own style of aging in light of personal history and current context.

Empirical investigations indicate a number of patterns of aging and apparently several ways to age successfully. Individuals exhibit considerable stability in personality throughout adulthood. There are some suggestions, however, of psychological changes associated with aging, including a tendency toward greater interiority. There are several possible reasons for age-related psychological change.

Developmental psychology offers several approaches to such change. Some approaches have focused on developmental issues unique to each life period. Middle age is characterized as a time of introspection and review, followed by a need for cognitive and emotional flexibility in adjusting to the new realities of old age. A process of life review also seems to be typical in old age. Such developmental sequences are likely to vary cross-culturally, depending on the nature of the age stratification system, and will also vary according to other social positions.

Stress may be another source of age-related psychological change. Old age may be a time of both heightened threat and declining response capability. While older people may experience fewer significant life events, the events of old age may be more irreversible and threatening. The social context is important here because it affects the meaning of age-linked events and the availability of resources for coping with threats. The experience of stress may be related to such psychological characteristics as disengagement and interiority.

Change may also be associated with alterations in the self. Identity and self emerge from interactions with others, as they validate particular identities, and the self lends consistency by directing behavior. Social roles provide access to particular social and symbolic worlds. To the extent that roles change with age, the self is vulnerable to change. Thus, age stratification in concert with symbolic interactions are the social sources of psychological change.

This emphasis on social roles implies that socialization is an important topic throughout the life cycle. Role transitions accompany aging, and it has been suggested that the failure of socialization to old age is a major problem for older people. The usual mechanisms and structures that facilitate adult socialization are felt to be lacking in old age, resulting in normlessness and a "roleless role." This may be overstated, however, as older people may be socialized within their own particularistic worlds.

The nature of personal change in late life offers opportunities for positive growth, but many older people are instead characterized by psychological constriction. This may be attributable to failures of socialization and the lack of structured options in middle and old age. The age stratification system may trap people in limited and limiting roles.

There are likely to be sex differences in the psychological impact of aging because men and women tend to occupy different positions in society. It may be that aging is more difficult for women because of a "double standard of aging." Alternatively, aging may free women from constraining sex roles. The future is likely to see changing images and capabilities of older women, presenting society with the challenge of providing significant roles for them.

Finally, there are many definitions and measures of successful aging. Age itself appears to have little association with subjective well-being. This may mean that most people cope quite effectively with aging, but there is also evidence that older people often accept substandard conditions. The social structure and systems of age stratification can be evaluated according to the degree to which they assist individuals in meeting the challenges posed by aging.

chapter 5

Images of Aging: Personal and Social

A number of topics covered in previous chapters touch on social and personal meanings of aging and old age. The model of age stratification recognizes that older people are evaluated according to their positions in the social structure. It has been suggested that modernization alters the meaning and value of aging and the aged. The personal consequences of transitions, such as retirement, depend on the meaning of aging for the individual. Indeed, coming to grips with the meaning of aging can be viewed as one of the developmental tasks of middle age and old age.

These considerations emphasize the importance of understanding the impact of aging on the individual's self-image and on his or her image to others. These issues are critical because of their relevance to self-esteem and overall satisfaction with life. Under what conditions do individuals come to see themselves as old? What is the personal significance of an "old" self-concept? This again brings us to a consideration of the place of the aged in any society—the relative status or stigma attributed to old age—and the psychological impact of the social context of aging.

AGING AND THE SOCIAL SELF

The *self* is a social object whose meaning is determined through an ongoing social and interpretive process (Rosenberg, 1981; Stryker, 1981). Self-perceptions are shaped by our perception of how others see us, as we "take the role of the other." Cooley describes his concept of the "looking-glass self" as follows:

A self-idea of this sort seems to have three principal elements: the imagination of our appearance to the other person, the imagination of his judgement of that appearance, and some sort of self-feeling, such as pride or mortification. . . . The thing that moves us to pride or shame is not the mere mechanical reflection of ourselves, but an imputed sentiment, the imagined effect of this reflection upon another's mind. (1902:184)

The self that emerges from these processes has two components. *Self-concept* refers to the set of traits we attribute to ourselves. We will be concerned in this chapter, for example, with such self-concepts as "middle-aged" and "elderly." Evaluations of the many self-concepts we all possess combine to form *self-esteem,* an overall judgment of our own value and worth. Not all self-concepts are equally important, of course, as self-esteem depends more closely on those roles and identities that are central. To the extent that old age is central to self-concept, the social and personal meaning of old age will also be central to self-esteem.

The social context of aging is important to these processes of self-perception. Individuals interpret their experiences in terms of the meanings available to them. If being retired is viewed as degrading and old age carries a stigma, individuals socialized in such a context face obvious problems in maintaining self-esteem. Even if individuals have not internalized such attitudes, stereotypes about old age shape the situations and opportunities they encounter.

The age stratification of roles and experiences will also affect the self-perceptions of individuals. Social roles contribute to definitions of self because they give us access to certain types of interactions (and therefore validation of certain identities) and because we have more generalized conceptions of the meaning and evaluation of different roles. Out of these roles and interactions a consistent sense of the self develops that directs behavior. Because the self is a social construct, however, role transitions may stimulate changes in self-concept and self-esteem, as individuals interact in different situations and encounter different meanings. The social self is both process and product, resulting in tension between the emerging self and the persisting, stable elements of the self. The reader has certainly experienced such changes in entering high school or college.

Aspects of the self persist, of course. The development of the self involves integration of newly acquired meanings with existing ones, rather than mere substitution of the new for the old. Even objective change in status or roles may not result in subjective changes in the self. Opposition to the perception of change comes from a sense of personal continuity. Because events must be ordered and given meaning to be comprehended, the failure to perceive change maintains stability of the self. Thus, "The awareness of constance in identity is, then, in the eye of the beholder rather than in the behavior itself" (Strauss, 1962:84). Nevertheless, it is clear that changes in roles, activities, and interpersonal relationships affect self-validation.

Some people have suggested that preoccupation with self-image diminishes with age so that older people are less concerned with reflections on the self. The concept of interiority, discussed in Chapter 4, suggests that the self-image of the aged depends less on external factors, and preoccupation with the inner aspects of experience will result in greater consistency in the self. It is true that retired physicians, carpenters, or teachers often still think of themselves as physicians, carpenters, or teachers.

But there is also a tremendous potential for change in one's roles and circumstances with age. Although the impact of these changes on self-image may be diminished in old age, it hardly seems likely that they will have no effects at all. When age-linked change accumulates—retirement, widowhood, gray hair, poor health—some consideration of self seems inevitable. This is created by the age stratification of roles and experiences. Considerations of self arise during periods of personal change or unstructured situations, such as adolescence and old age. Rosenberg (1965) states that there is a heightened awareness of the self during adolescence because (1) many major decisions are made during this period, (2) it is a time of unusual amounts of personal change, and (3) it is characterized by unusual status ambiguity. Similarly, aging involves an unusual amount of personal change and status ambiguity as well as a cluster of negative stereotypes in some societies. Thus, considerations of identity, including "age identity," are important in understanding the personal experience of aging.

SUBJECTIVE AGE IDENTITY

There appears to be relative agreement that people are "old" at around 60 or 65 (see Table 3.1 in Chapter 3), but substantial proportions of the older population consider themselves "young" or "middle-aged." Results from a study conducted by the author illustrate that substantial numbers of persons of even advanced age continue to resist such self-labels as "elderly" or "old" (Table 5.1). This is not surprising, given the general position of the aged in American society and the negative meanings attached to growing old. Asking people if they are elderly is not as bad as asking them if they abuse children, but it is certainly a potentially emotional question.

What is at issue here is the problematic shift in self-concept from middle-aged to old. Under what conditions do people come to conceive of themselves as old and what are the consequences of this new self-concept? Certainly age itself is a factor in age identification, but age alone is insufficient to explain shifts in age identification. Age is also partly a "proxy" for events that symbolize the onset of old age. For example, the employed 80-year-old may see himself or herself as

Table 5.1 SUBJECTIVE AGE IDENTITY ACROSS AGE GROUPS IN A SAMPLE OF PERSONS AGED 60 AND OVER

Subjective age identity	All respondents (60 and over)	Age		
		60–69	70–79	80 +
Young	22%	26%	16%	20%
Middle-aged	42%	54%	33%	19%
Elderly	21%	14%	30%	23%
Old	15%	6%	21%	38%
	100%	100%	100%	100%
Number interviewed	1134	587	387	160

Note: Responses to the question: "Do you think of yourself as young, middle-aged, elderly, or old?"

"middle-aged," whereas the retired 60-year-old has developed an "old" self-concept.

Table 5.2 lists the reasons given by one sample of older people for identifying themselves as either middle-aged or old. It is obvious that activity and health are among the most important determinants of age identity. Those who are in good health (or *feel* that they are in good health) continue to see themselves as middle-aged. Older persons can frequently pinpoint a particular incident (a heart attack, breaking a hip in a fall) that made them feel old. Health problems need not be this dramatic to cause a realization of personal aging, however. There are many nagging physical limitations that operate as daily reminders: tiring easily, having difficulty walking or driving, finding it harder to work around the house or yard.

There are two primary reasons why health is related to age identification. First, health reflects upon one's "body image," and this is closely linked symbolically to our images of "youth" and "old age." Appearance can be an important aspect of personal identity (Stone, 1962), and aging may first enter our awareness because of wrinkles or gray hair. The occurrence of certain health problems symbolically linked to aging (deafness, arthritis, heart problems) also triggers a change in self-concept.

The second reason for the importance of health is its effect on activity and life-style. The individual is no longer able to pursue normal activities and interests and, in this sense, a new "me" has developed. Thus it may not be health problems per se that result in awareness of personal aging, but rather health-related inability to maintain previous patterns of living.

Studies also indicate that shifts in age identification are linked to role change (Blau, 1956; Phillips, 1957). Retirement is clearly important, but it is unclear whether widowhood has much independent effect on age identification. A national survey indicated that widowhood and other family events are more important in defining women as "old," whereas retirement is more important for men (National Council on the Aging, 1975). These reflect existing sex-role stereotypes. For women who work, retirement may be as age symbolic as for men who work. There are a number of reasons retirement should define old age. It is a symbol of aging, a social event that serves as a rite of passage. There may also be an implied lack of fitness or decline, and retirement affects other aspects of one's pattern of living: income declines, work-related social interaction is disrupted, and so forth. Retirement is an event whose symbolic significance is difficult to ignore.

There are other sources of an identity as "old," such as low socioeconomic status and institutionalization (Peters, 1971). The results in Table 5.2 suggest that "state of mind" also defines age: "You're only as old as you feel." Such comments were most likely to be made by individuals who were in poor health or had retired, so these attitudes may reflect resistance to "objective" indicators of old age. It is interesting that, in the same study, age identification was not related to whether individuals had positive or negative attitudes about aging and old people. It is likely that persons identify themselves as middle-aged through continuity and habit until retirement or poor health disrupts that continuity and affects age identity regardless of attitudes toward growing old.

Table 5.2 REASONS GIVEN FOR PERSONAL AGE IDENTIFICATION

Identification as young or middle-aged (N = 148)	Number[a]	Percentage	Identification as elderly or old (N = 172)	Number[a]	Percentage
Still active and busy	85	59.8	Particular health problem (e.g., heart attack)	49	28.5
Good physical and/or mental health	84	59.1	Retirement	38	22.1
Positive mental attitude	41	28.9	Physical slowdown (e.g., tire easily)	35	20.3
Rapport with young people	20	14.1	Health restrictions	22	12.8
Youthful appearance	12	8.4	Just age (no other reason)	20	11.6
Mix with all ages	12	8.4	Change in social contacts	10	5.8
Can still handle own affairs	10	7.0	Illness or death of spouse	10	5.8
Other	10	7.0	Other	26	15.1

[a]Each respondent could give more than one response.

Source: Russell Ward, "Growing Old: Stigma, Identity, and subculture," Ph.D. Dissertation, Sociology, University of Wisconsin, 1974.

The key factor in the perception of aging and shifts in age identification appears to be the disruption of the individual's normal pattern of living—the extent to which aging brings change and the intrusiveness of that change. The primary element is the change created in activities and in the groups and individuals with whom the person interacts. Validation of particular aspects of the self occurs through interaction with others and the fulfillment of roles.

Friendship networks are important in validating self-images, and stable friendship cliques may operate as buffers against awareness of personal aging (Blau, 1956). The sense of continuity provided by a stable social network prevents mutual awareness of age changes; but associates may also be a source of altered age definition, particularly for those who are retired or have fewer friends. The self-image of older persons has greater autonomy if they can resist the isolating effects of role exit and conserve or rebuild social resources to be less vulnerable to any one set of influences (Blau, 1973).

Significant change must be symbolically perceived as such before changes occur in the self. For the aged, this symbolic change, which results in shifts in age identity, is represented in two forms of perceived deprivation. The first is *age-related deprivation,* whereby older people compare present situations with conditions earlier in life (Ward, 1977). Persons who are objectively deprived (for example, socially isolated) may have been so throughout their lives, and such deprivations will not affect age identity because they are not linked symbolically to the aging process. Poor health will not lead to an "old" self-concept for persons who have always been in poor health, but change and deprivation linked to aging (occuring after about 55) may trigger shifts in age identity. Age-related deprivations may include widowhood, retirement, and declines in health, activity, social contacts, and income. Ward (1977) found that a composite measure of such changes was a strong predictor of subjective age identity.

The second form of perceived deprivation is *peer-related deprivation,* whereby older people compare themselves with others their age. Such comparisons are an important source of feelings of well-being throughout life because individuals give meaning to their own situations by assessing them relative to others. Poor health may not trigger an "old" self-concept if the person still feels healthy for his or her age group. Bultena and Powers (1978) found that peer comparisons of health, finances, social contacts, and dependency are strongly linked to age identity; those who felt "better off" than others their age were much more likely to consider themselves middle-aged.

Subjective age identity represents an element of self-concept and tells us something about the symbolic meaning of aging. The impact of this self-concept on self-esteem, however, is likely to depend on the values and stereotypes attached to old age. The nature of social images of aging have been a topic of considerable interest in gerontology.

ATTITUDES TOWARD OLD PEOPLE

What are the consequences of viewing oneself as "old"? This brings us to a consideration of the evaluative dimension of age identity. If negative stereotypes stigmatize old age, there may be a number of negative consequences for older people.

Such stereotypes may lead to self-derogation or become self-fulfilling; stigma may be a source of isolation or disengagement; services may be shaped by negative images of old people. Stereotyping is a common means of dealing with an unfamiliar class of objects (Brubaker and Powers, 1976). Stereotypes shape the expectations and reactions of others and, ultimately, the social field within which the individual interacts. Regardless of their truth, they have important implications for the stereotyped person.

Old Age in Literature

Even in cultures that have venerated the aged, such as ancient Greece and the Puritan colonies of America, literary treatment of old age has been ambivalent, mixing respect with resentment, conflict, satire, and ridicule (de Beauvoir, 1972; Fischer, 1977). The Puritans, for example, referred to senility and the moral failings of the elderly, as in the character of the "old miser." In an analysis of Western drama beginning with the ancient Greeks and Romans, Banziger (1979) describes a common pattern portraying a romantic ideal of virtuous youth against obstructionist old age. He cites Shakespeare's *Romeo and Juliet* as an example.

There is evidence of a further decline in the status of old age in modern literature. Fischer (1977) notes four major motifs in modern literary treatment of old age. The least prevalent is the young spirit conquering age, as in Ernest Hemingway's *The Old Man and the Sea.* More common are themes involving the pathos of age, the emptiness of old age, and the use of old age as a revelation of the absurdity of life itself. That old age is seen as pathetic, rather than tragic, is important.

> Old age in modern American literature is not the stuff of tragedy. A truly tragic hero must have strength and dignity and purpose. But old age in twentieth-century fiction has been denied all of those qualities. When old age appears at all in a literary work, it is apt to be not tragic, but pathetic. The central theme is the weakness and dependence of age. (Fischer, 1977:124–125)

A study of popular magazine fiction from 1890 to 1955 concluded that there had been a "shift in the sociological prime-of-life from mature middle age (in 1890) to young adulthood (in 1955)" (Martel, 1968:56). In the more recent stories the post-40 years were seen as anticlimactic, with a greater emphasis on competition with youth. Perhaps the most striking trend seen in Martel's study is the relative disappearance of aged characters. Studies of children's books have found similar trends (Seltzer & Atchley, 1971; Ansello & Letzler, 1975; Peterson & Karnes, 1976). Older persons are either seldom portrayed or their roles in the stories are restricted and passive. We should be careful, however, about overemphasizing negative treatment of the aged. When they do appear, older characters are quite often positive. The issue is the relative invisibility of them and their real problems.

> What may be more important than the direct negative stereotyping, is the indirect picture of the older population that is shown. In an overwhelming number

of cases, older people were portrayed as only shadows who moved into and out of the major flow of the story at expeditious times. . . . Problems which face real older people each day were not recognized nor struggled with in the books. Older adults led a quiet, self-sufficient life, affecting few people and being seldom affected by others. In fact, the older persons seldom really existed in the eyes of others but quietly wandered through the pages, without trouble, gratification, or suffering. (Peterson & Karnes, 1976:230)

There are some hopeful signs, however. Banziger (1979) suggests that a new focus is emerging in modern drama—the desire of older people to reestablish autonomy in their lives. Loughman (1980) indicates that contemporary writers are challenging myths about the sexuality of older people. The success of such movies as *On Golden Pond* reflects a growing "marketability" of aging themes. A study of children's literature containing aging characters found that portrayals were not negative or stereotyped, reflecting instead a diversity of life-styles and circumstances (Blue, 1978). But the underrepresentation of older people in literature and drama continues to be a subtle form of stereotyping.

Aging and the Mass Media

The relative invisibility of old age in literature is echoed in network television programs. One analysis of programming from 1969 to 1971 found that older persons constituted less than 5 percent of the characters, and they were more likely to be portrayed as "bad guys" (Arnoff, 1974). Another study found that the aged appeared in only 1.5 percent of all portrayals, mostly in minor roles (Northcott, 1975). Although there was no particular emphasis on the problems encountered by older people, Northcott found a tendency to idealize vigor, attractiveness, and competence, and portray being "too young" or "too old" as undesirable.

Harris and Feinberg (1977) sampled daytime network programming. They found that although older people were proportionately represented, it was an unflattering portrayal, especially of older women, as being "unhealthy, unstylish, and uninteresting." Positive love relationships were largely confined to persons younger than 30, and there were no romantic involvements for characters over 60. Older characters also were less active and less healthy notably in commercials. Although the authority and esteem of males on television increased with age, largely reflecting prominent persons on news and talk shows, the status of women declined after age 40. Kubey (1980) found an underrepresentation of older people, especially of older women, in almost all forms of television fare. Portrayals were generally one-dimensional and rather negative, presenting older people as relatively ineffectual, unattractive, and unhappy.

Buchholz and Bynum (1982) analyzed newspaper stories involving older people and aging. They found that most of the stories were either positive (30 percent) or neutral (56 percent), with only 14 percent negative. But less than 3 percent of the stories covered such issues as health, retirement, and housing. The "event orientation" of newspapers meant that many of the stories involved obituaries, retirement notices, and the like, because the complicated long-range issues of aging were not seen as "newsworthy."

There are indications that aging is becoming a more viable subject for the mass media as greater interest is being shown in the realities and positive aspects of aging (Davis, 1975; Kubey, 1980). The television program "Over Easy" is a reflection of this trend. This is understandable, in light of the growing size of the older population and the increasing capabilities of older people. There is growing realization of the "aging market." But it appears that aging and the aged continue to be relatively invisible and/or negatively portrayed in the media. Hess (1974) suggests that the elderly represent "poor copy" because they are presumed to remind us of role loss, deprivation, and our own mortality.

Aging and Humor

Humor is another type of medium for cultural communication. Palmore's (1971) analysis of humor found that 56 percent of a sample of jokes about old age were negative, whereas 27 percent were positive, and 17 percent neutral. Jokes about women were more negative than about men and dealt with different subjects, such as age concealment and being an old maid—for example, comparing an "old maid" to "a lemon that has never been squeezed." Longevity, sex, retirement, and mental ability were the major topics about men, such as Oscar Wilde's comment that "Young men want to be faithful and are not; old men want to be faithless and cannot." It is interesting that portrayals of disengagement tended to be linked with negative jokes, whereas activity was seen in a more positive light.

Other studies of jokes (Davies, 1977; Richman, 1977), magazine cartoons (Smith, 1979), and humorous birthday cards (Demos & Jache, 1981) also found relatively negative themes that focused on loss of physical attractiveness, physical and sexual decline, ultraconservatism, and age concealment; whereas the most frequent positive themes involved sexual activity as an affirmation of life and the depiction of aging as a value in its own right. Richman found that 66 percent of a sample of jokes about older people were negative or critical, whereas 70 percent of jokes about children were positive.

Public Attitudes About Aging

Cross-cultural studies presented in Chapter 3 indicate that the position of the aged varies according to the nature of the society and its particular age stratification system. It is rarely age itself that yields respect, however. Ethnological and historical data seem to suggest that most societies view old age as tragic, ludicrous, revolting, or some combination of these (de Beauvoir, 1972). Our discussion of modernization certainly suggests that this is likely to be true of modern societies as well.

Numerous surveys have attempted to measure public attitudes toward aging and old people (McTavish, 1971; Bennett & Eckman, 1973; Branco & Williamson, 1982). These studies indicate that old age is a meaningful concept of which somewhat distinctive and largely negative perceptions are held. Stereotypes include

. . . views that old people are generally ill, tired, not sexually interested, mentally slower, forgetful, and less able to learn new things, grouchy, withdrawn, feeling

sorry for themselves, less likely to participate in activities (except, perhaps, religion), isolated, in the least happy or fortunate time of life, unproductive, and
defensive in various combinations and with varying emphases. (McTavish,
1971:97)

Older people themselves appear to possess such stereotypes. McTavish
notes that people in their sixties may have the most unfavorable attitudes toward
the elderly, whereas those in their thirties and forties are more positive.

To some extent these stereotypes represent lack of knowledge about older
people. The tendency to exaggerate problems experienced by the elderly was
noted in Chapter 2. Common misconceptions include overestimating institutionalization and poverty in the older population and believing that older people are
often bored, irritated, or angry (Palmore, 1980). Older people themselves attribute more problems to "most older people" than they encounter in their own
lives (National Council on the Aging, 1975).

But stereotyped views of older people may reflect more than just misinfor-
mation. Robert Butler has gone so far as to refer to *ageism:* "a deep and profound
prejudice against the elderly which is found to some degree in all of us" (1975:11).
He argues that ageism makes it easier to ignore the problems of the aged and
see them as different from ourselves, perhaps less than "human." This may be
true generally of people whom we stigmatize:

We believe the person with a stigma is *not quite human.* On this assumption
we exercise varieties of discrimination, through which we effectively, if often
unthinkingly, reduce his life chances. (Goffman, 1963:5, emphasis added)

The disengagement of older people, for whatever reason, and their invisibility in the media encourage such feelings. Butler sees ageism reflected in a wide
range of phenomena: stereotypes and myths, age discrimination, avoidance, epi-
thets and jokes.

More important, perhaps, than individual ageism is *institutional ageism,* the
extent to which institutional structures, including the age stratification system,
place the aged at a disadvantage, although possibly unintentionally. Retirement
is certainly not meant to create poverty, but it does so for some older people. Similarly, the ways in which educational, social, and religious institutions are structured
may unintentionally deny the aged access to meaningful roles and activities.

We must again be careful, however, about exaggerating negative images of
old age and old people. The danger of doing this can be seen in the results of
a poll commissioned by the National Council on the Aging (1975). Responses
to one set of questions concerning what people felt were the "best" and "worst"
years of a person's life show that the sixties and seventies were most often considered the worst life period and least often as the best (Table 5.3). This was as true
of older as of younger people. But the study also indicated that each part of the
life course carried its own blend of rewards and costs, and most people could
find good and bad aspects of every age period.

Youth (the teens and twenties) was valued as a time of few responsibilities
and pressures, allowing for more enjoyment of life, but was also seen as an unset-

Table 5.3 ATTITUDES IN A NATIONAL SAMPLE ABOUT THE
"BEST" AND "WORST" YEARS OF A PERSON'S LIFE
(PERCENTAGE OF POPULATION)

	"Best" years		"Worst" years	
	18–64	65+	18–64	65+
Teens	16	7	20	10
20s	33	17	5	7
30s	24	22	3	5
40s	13	17	3	3
50s	3	8	6	4
60s	1	6	12	14
70s	0	2	21	21
Other	1	2	6	7
Wouldn't choose any age	7	15	17	22
Not sure	2	4	7	7

Source: Myth and Reality of Aging in America, 1975, published by The National
Council on the Aging, Inc., a study prepared by Louis Harris and Associates, Inc., pp. 2, 12.
Reprinted by permission.

tled age, lacking maturity or wisdom. Middle age (the forties and fifties) was valued because of financial security, children being grown and on their own, and
the wisdom and experience of maturity, but its perceived costs included possible
illness and a sense of going downhill. The rewards attributed to the sixties and
seventies were surprisingly similar to those of youth: lack of responsibilities and
pressures, and greater freedom to enjoy life. But the perceptions of old age that
led people to define it as the worst period of life were illness, financial problems,
inability to get around, and loneliness.

Such perceptions may change over the life course. Chiriboga (1978) studied
the timing of "best" and "worst" ages with four groups: high school seniors, newlyweds, middle-aged parents, and persons nearing retirement. None of the respondents chose the sixties as the best age and one third mentioned old age as the
worst; but the choice of best age varied according to the age of the group—that
is, high school seniors chose the teens, newlyweds the twenties, middle-aged parents the thirties, and preretirees the forties. Although older groups were more
likely to see their best years as being in the past, evaluations of at least the
"young-old" period (sixties and seventies) seemed to improve with age. Younger
people downgraded all later decades, whereas middle-aged parents and preretirees drew distinctions between "young-old" and "old-old" (eighties and nine-
ties).

It appears that general attitudes toward old age and older people are somewhat negative but also mixed. The public often disagrees with positive statements
about older people and also often disagrees with negative statements (Branco &
Williamson, 1982). Images are certainly not overwhelmingly negative. The study
by the National Council on the Aging (1975) found that it was generally felt that
"most people over 65" are "very friendly and warm" and "wise from experience."
On the other hand, most older people were considered only "somewhat good at
getting things done," "bright and alert," or "open-minded and adaptable."

More negative attitudes appear to be expressed about older people *in gen-*

eral than about *particular* older people (Weinberger & Millham, 1975; Crockett et al., 1979). For example, Weinberger and Millham found that a representative 70-year-old was viewed unfavorably, but particular older persons (presented through pictures and autobiographies) were judged more self-accepting, satisfied, adjusted, and adaptable than 25-year-olds. Thus rejection of the aged as a group does not necessarily imply rejection of older people one has actually encountered. More positive responses to actual older people does not eliminate concern over negative general stereotypes, however. Branco and Williamson (1982) point out that there are a number of important settings (policymaking, for example) in which the elderly *as a group* are the object of discussion.

As noted in Chapter 3, modern societies may be moving toward more positive images of aging and older people. Succeeding cohorts of the aged are increasingly better off regarding health, education, and income, and the public views current older people as more "independent and resourceful" than older people 10 or 20 years ago (National Council on the Aging, 1975). Tibbitts (1979) suggests that over the past 30 years American society has developed more positive views of the roles and life-styles of older adults. He cites declining importance of the work ethic and growing awareness of the volunteer, educational, and political involvements of older people as contributing to this. In at least some segments of American society, the aged are becoming a visible and contented leisure class as our stress on productivity and the work ethic seems to be softening (Neugarten & Hagestad, 1976). Gerontology itself has helped to dispel some of the myths about aging.

Although accuracy demands a more balanced view than the earlier stress on negative stereotypes about aging, we must also avoid an overly optimistic stance. Although relative deprivation among the aged has declined, it still exists. Chapter 2 presents ample documentation of the problems that still face many older people, often to a greater extent than the young or middle-aged. And even if images of old age have been improving in recent years, there is still evidence that negative stereotypes about old age and old people continue to exist. Because this is an important aspect of the aging experience, we need to understand its sources and potential consequences.

SOURCES OF OLD-AGE ATTITUDES

There are two major sources of images concerning old age and old people. The first is the social structure within which aging occurs and the nature of the age stratification system. Societies value certain qualities and roles and reward those who possess them. As noted in Chapter 3, the status of the aged is undermined by modernization because of retirement systems, perceived obsolescence of older occupations, urbanization, and mass education. Any stigma attached to growing old must be seen in relation to what is valued in American society and presumed lost by the aged. This society emphasizes values of activity, personal productivity, and independence (self-reliance). These attitudes relate directly to loss of occupation, widowhood, poor health, and other changes that may accompany aging. The older person who has lost the major roles of productivity and independence is judged to be ineffective in contributing to the goals of society, and unique roles, such as guardian of the culture or family adviser, are no longer valued or available.

From a conflict perspective on age relations, ageism may be viewed as an "ideology" that legitimates the subordinate position of older people in the age stratification system (Dowd, 1980). Negative stereotypes held by young and old reduce resistance to retirement and more general disengagement. When such attitudes are internalized and accepted, even by the elderly, the nature of age stratification is not challenged.

The second source of negative images of old age and old people is our fear of old age and the problems we associate with it: low socioeconomic status, poor health, loneliness, senility, death. Although such fears are often exaggerated, they themselves contribute to the problem:

> Exaggerations of the problems of old age might instill in the young a deep-seated fear of growing old. They might force the young to struggle to look and act "young," thus inhibiting maturity and preventing the young from enjoying the natural and rewarding process of aging. They may cause fears of aging that inhibit normal, rational planning for their later years. (National Council on the Aging, 1975:39)

Those who are less knowledgeable about aging are more likely to have negative attitudes toward it and believe old age will cause them problems (Klemmack et al., 1980; Palmore, 1980).

Many of these fears relate to the value attached to independence. Self-reliance and autonomy are deeply engrained values, and we prize our independence very highly. We are socialized to see those who are dependent as inferior, as is reflected in the stigma attached to recipients of public welfare. The importance of independence is stressed in finances, housing, personal mobility, and family relationships. These attitudes affect not only our image of the aged but also the self-image and behavior of older persons themselves. One study found that:

> Some of the aged in our sample feel that, if help can be obtained only at the expense of institutionalization, if the small sphere of respectable autonomy that constitutes the aged person's shrunken life-space can be punctured like a child's balloon—then it may be best to gamble on one's own with survival. Such people will draw their curtains to avoid critical appraisals of their helplessness; they will not get enough to eat; they will stay away from the doctor and forgo even vital drugs; they will shiver with cold; they will live in filth and squalor—but pride they will relinquish only as a last resort. (Clark & Anderson, 1967:391)

It may seem ironic that negative stereotypes about the elderly persist, despite the growing disparity between stereotypes and reality and the findings of more positive attitudes toward particular older people. But older people who are well off continue to exaggerate the problems of other older people, viewing themselves as exceptions. Similarly, contact with older people who are active and healthy is not seen as disproving the stereotype; rather, such people are considered exceptions. This process of *pluralistic ignorance* (Hess, 1974), whereby one's own experiences are considered exceptional, allows stereotypes to continue in the face of seemingly contradictory evidence. You may view "most" older people negatively, even though all the older people you know do not fit these attitudes.

CONSEQUENCES OF OLD-AGE STEREOTYPES

That stereotypes about old age are important is reflected in debate over the "correct" label for older persons. The study conducted by the National Council on the Aging found considerable disagreement about such terms as *senior citizen, elderly,* and *old-timer* (Table 5.4). The obvious dislike of the term *old* certainly implies some stigma attached to the aging process. Goffman (1963) has described three basic types of stigma: abominations of the body (physical deformities), blemishes of individual character (weak will or laziness), and tribal stigma (race or religion). Old age can be viewed as a combination of abominations of the body (loss of physical attractiveness, crippling chronic diseases) and blemishes of individual character (dependency, diminishing intelligence). One might even entertain the notion of old age as a tribal stigma within the context of age stratification. Being labeled with a stigma, or labeling oneself, can critically affect self-identity and self-esteem (Schur, 1971).

Old age, as other types of stigma such as blindness or homosexuality, is viewed as a *master status trait,* defined by the fact that "Possession of one deviant trait may have a generalized symbolic value, so that people automatically assume that its bearer possesses other undesirable traits allegedly associated with it" (Becker, 1963:33). The master status trait is seen as the primary identifying char-

Table 5.4   TERMS BY WHICH PEOPLE 65 AND OVER LIKE TO BE REFERRED TO (PERCENTAGES)

	Like	Don't like	Doesn't matter	Not sure	Prefer
A senior citizen	50	15	34	1	33
A retired person	53	12	34	1	12
A mature American	55	13	30	2	13
An elderly person	38	30	31	1	6
A middle-aged person	37	25	34	4	3
An older American	37	28	33	2	3
A golden-ager	27	36	33	4	3
An old-timer	26	45	27	2	4
An aged person	19	50	30	1	1
An old man/old woman	8	67	24	1	1
None of these					3
Doesn't matter					12
Not sure					2

Source: Myth and Reality of Aging in America, 1975, published by The National Council on the Aging, Inc., a study prepared by Louis Harris and Associates, Inc., p. 228. Reprinted by permission.

acteristic of the individual. One is not a person who happens to be old, but an "old person," and assumed to have other attributes because of this.

This can affect the social and psychological world of the older person in a number of ways because of the impact on the perceptions and reactions of others. Older people may be excluded from various groups and activities because of their age, making them increasingly isolated. Societal reactions toward the aged may be a cause of disengagement. Old age becomes for many a time of potential embarrassment. Older people may become aware of carrying a stigma, and choose to withdraw from exchange relationships in which they have few resources and little power (Dowd, 1980). Goffman, in discussing the reaction of individuals to a "spoiled identity," notes that "shame becomes a central possibility" (1963:7), making stigmatized individuals hypersensitive to the reactions of others. Goffman further notes that "normals" may also be uneasy in such situations and attempt to avoid them. Persons who are crippled or blind often face this dilemma. Thus disengagement can be viewed as a mutual withdrawal from uneasy and potentially embarrassing situations by young and old.

Stereotypes about old age may affect the behavior of older people in a variety of other ways. Older persons may internalize and accept the negative meanings attached to aging and view age as a reasonable criterion for evaluating behavior. We develop images of old age during our youth, which haunt us when we carry them into our own old age. To the extent that the aged are expected to be different and act differently, they will be ostracized if they step out of the "role."

> If old people show the same desires, the same feelings and the same requirements as the young, the world looks upon them with disgust; in them love and jealousy seem revolting or absurd, sexuality repulsive and violence ludicrous. (de Beauvoir, 1972:3)

Negative stereotypes and images of older people in the media serve to maintain age norms and constraints, or at least do not counteract them.

Older people may accept the view of themselves as significantly different from "normal" persons—less vigorous and creative, less productive and efficient—and of old age as a time of decline in which they must forsake many normal pursuits and act in such a way as to make the stereotypes true. The stereotype of the "sexless older years" is a case in point (Rubin, 1968). Stereotypes that sexual intercourse is no longer possible and older people should not be interested in "such things," and the cultural link between youth and sexual attractiveness, all contribute to the decline of sexual activity. Older women may be particularly affected by such stereotypes.

> They are the neuters of our culture who have mysteriously metamorphosed from desirable young sex objects to mature, sexually "interesting" women, and finally, at about age 50, they descend in steady decline to sexual oblivion. This is the way society sees it. But this is not the way a lot of old women see it. They don't understand why older men can be considered "sexy" but never older

women. They are angered that old men can attract younger women and be commended for their prowess whereas older women are seen as "depraved" or "grasping for lost youth" when they show an interest in sex at all, let alone younger men. . . . Yet in spite of their capacities, older women have limited sexual outlets. They have been trained and locked in by the culture to accept the idea that they are no longer desirable sexual partners and that only younger women have sexual prerogatives. We are all familiar with the origins of this idea—namely that women are sexy as long as they are young and pretty and able to enhance a man's feelings of status and power. (Lewis & Butler, 1972:227)

Individuals who are "discreditable" may, of course, attempt to deny the personal appropriateness of the label, either by denying possession of the stigmatized attribute or by "reforming." Many stigmatized attributes, such as obesity, physical disability, and old age, cannot easily be denied once the label is applied, so denial typically occurs before the fact. For example, studies indicate that the mentally retarded (Edgerton, 1967) and the blind (Strauss, 1968) may resist identification with similar others in an attempt to evade negative self-definitions. Similarly, older people may try to "pass" as young with clothing, makeup, or mannerisms. As we have seen, there is also a tendency to deny such labels as "elderly" or "old." Denial of aging may create problems, however, if it means that older people refuse to perceive problems associated with aging and are therefore unwilling to seek needed assistance. And once the label "old" is applied to oneself, it appears to be irreversible. Bultena and Powers (1978) studied persons aged 60 and over in 1960 and reinterviewed them in 1970. In the initial survey only 25 percent considered themselves elderly or old, but this had increased to 63 percent 10 years later. Only 9 percent of those defining themselves as elderly in 1960, and none of those with an old identity, defined themselves as middle-aged in 1970; 57 percent of those with middle-aged identities in 1960 switched to elderly or old by 1970.

The psychological impact of age identity for persons who come to view themselves as elderly or old because of age and age-related deprivation will depend on the meanings held by them for growing old. The psychological tension resulting from stigma can be quite profound, as illustrated by the following passage written by a homosexual:

. . . the dominant fact in my life, towering in importance above all others, is a consciousness that I am different. . . . It is inescapable, not only this being different, but more than that, this constant awareness of dissimilarity. . . . It is not only shame at my own debasement that demoralizes me, but a great wave of self-doubt that is infinitely more difficult to cope with. Am I genuinely as "good" as the next fellow? . . . Because I am unable to stand up before the world and acknowledge that I am what I am, because I carry around with me a fear and a shame, I find that I endanger my confidence in myself and in my way of living, and that this confidence is required for the enjoyment of life. (Cory, 1951:7, 11)

A study several years ago by the author suggests that attitudes toward old age and old persons have considerable effects on the self-esteem of the aged

(Ward, 1977). Older respondents were presented with a series of stereotypes about old people, resulting in a score for negative attitudes toward old people. These attitudes toward old people in general were significantly related to self-esteem, and, indeed, were the strongest predictors of self-esteem in the study, accounting for an overall decline in self-esteem with age. It is interesting that attitudes toward old people were important even for those who considered themselves middle-aged, indicating that perhaps all persons over 60, for example, view themselves as "eligible" for the stigma they attach to being old.

The extent to which aging affects the overall self-image of individuals is still not clear, however. The National Council on the Aging (1975) survey found that most older people considered themselves very friendly and warm, wise from experience, bright and alert, open-minded and adaptable, and good at getting things done, exhibiting self-images similar to those of younger people; indeed, 40 percent of persons aged 65 and over considered themselves "very useful members of the community," compared with only 29 percent of those younger than 65. George (1980) suggests that the self-concept and self-esteem of older people remain remarkably stable over time because behavior and selective perception operate to maintain identity.

It is often assumed that people with lower status will have lower self-esteem because they are affected by the views of others and compare themselves with persons of higher status. But Rosenberg (1981) indicates that there is little evidence of this, partly because devalued persons typically interact and compare themselves with similar others. To the extent that older people interact largely with other older people, they will be insulated from stigma attached to old age. Additionally, studies finding more favorable attitudes toward particular older people than toward *most* older people suggest that the elderly encounter little stigma within their own circles of family and friends.

These patterns of self-esteem echo those for subjective well-being discussed in Chapter 4. Older people again seem better off than one might think. This indicates their resourcefulness, and the need to understand aging from the point of view of the individual. But it is not clear how to interpret the gap between objective and subjective reality. Although stable self-esteem seems a very welcome finding, it has been argued that the aged are unwilling to admit their position in modern society to others, and perhaps to themselves.

> The appearance of "mellowness" in many older people is a tactic to win acceptance and support. To protest their marginality would only alienate others, and this the person without any socially useful role cannot do because he lacks the opportunities for finding alternative social resources to replace his remaining social ties . . . so the old person will pretend obliviousness to younger people's indifference and neglect in order not to jeopardize his relations with them. (Blau, 1973:154)

Our knowledge and ideas about images of aging and their consequences remain highly speculative. There is a critical need to investigate the nature of old-age images *as they are encountered by the aging individual* among the peo-

ple and groups with whom he or she interacts. This is an integral part of socialization for old age and must be incorporated within life course perspectives on
aging and models of age stratification. As such, it is related to many other issues. How are age-related norms and expectations developed, translated, and
sanctioned in the experience of aging individuals? What role models are used
for successful aging? The studies we have cited about images of aging in literature and television suggest that there are relatively few positive models for older
people, but perhaps they turn to other sources for guidance (see Chapter 10).
To what extent is cultural imagery of aging incorporated into personal imagery,
and eventually into feelings about the aging self? These are important questions
that have too long been dealt with in a universalistic and speculative manner.
And there is an additional need to study changing images of aging because
more recent work suggests that modern views of old age are becoming less de-
rogatory and restrictive.

SUMMARY

The self is a social object whose meaning is derived from interactions with others.
This includes both self-concept and self-esteem. Changes in these aspects of self
may occur as the individual encounters and perceives change in his or her social
world. Although self-preoccupation may decline with age, adolescence and old
age are life periods in which major personal change makes considerations of the
self salient.

Substantial proportions of the older population resist such labels as "elderly" and "old." Shifts in age identity occur because of age-related deprivation—perceived personal change linked symbolically to the aging process.
Changes such as poor health and retirement disrupt life-style continuity and
change the individual's social world, resulting in awareness of a new "me."
Feelings of deprivation relative to age peers also contribute to older
self-concepts.

The impact of age identity depends on the meaning of growing old. Personal
attitudes toward aging are likely to reflect images in the larger social context.
The aged are underrepresented in literature and the media; and when they are
portrayed, it is often in negative, passive terms. Studies also indicate that negative
stereotypes are held about old age, although images of aging are not universally
negative. The sources of such stereotypes are twofold. The status of older people
is dependent on the positions they occupy in the social structure and the values
of modern societies imply devaluation of the roles of the aged. An additional
source of stereotypes are exaggerated fears about the problems of old age, particularly fear related to dependency. Attitudes toward older people may be softening,
however, and it appears that particular older people are responded to more favorably than older people in general.

Stereotypes about old people may be a cause of disengagement as the aged
withdraw from potentially embarrassing and discrediting social situations. They
may also result in self-fulfilling prophecies, as with the stereotype of the "sexless"
older years. Although stigma might be expected to lower the self-esteem of older

people, generally they seem to have favorable images of themselves. This may reflect interaction with other older people or the more favorable responses they encounter from family and friends. Additional research is needed to understand the nature and consequences of the social meanings for old age made available to the aging individual because this constitutes another way in which the social context affects the aging experience.

chapter 6

Work and Retirement

The twin issues of work and retirement have probably been the most studied aspects of aging, and with retirement have come a number of other issues: the meaningfulness of leisure, the adequacy of retirement income, declining status related to "nonproductive" roles. Whether a particular older person, or older people in general, works or retires is a major determinant of the aging experience. Retirement systems create new age strata, allocating the aged into new roles (and out of former roles). Retirement also creates new symbolic meanings for the aging process.

The attention given to retirement by social gerontologists is certainly warranted. Work and work-related values shape the life course in many ways, so retirement is a major transition. One cannot understand the developmental issues of old age without understanding the nature of work and retirement. Retirement is also a central component of the modern age stratification system. Many people have argued that, for better or worse, retirement defines the status of the aged in modern societies and sets off the modern aging experience from that of nonindustrial societies.

Until quite recently, retirement has been viewed as a crisis having profound social and psychological consequences in the lives of older persons. This stems from the assumption that work constitutes the central life interest at least for most men and that the work ethic requires one to work to be considered worthwhile. But the impact of retirement is often surprisingly benign, and many of our beliefs about work and retirement are facing serious challenges. Because of this, many of our traditional theories of aging are being exposed as myths that may have been true once but no longer fit current realities. Some of the issues that have been raised go to the very heart of the structure of the life course in modern societies and presage future changes in the nature of the aging experience. Before discussing retirement, however, we first need to look at the work experiences of older people.

WORK AND AGING

Although retirement has become the norm for persons over 65, approximately 20 percent of older males and 10 percent of older females continue to work. Employment is greater in some other countries; for example, over 30 percent of older males are employed in Yugoslavia and Portugal, and over 50 percent in Japan (Schulz, 1980). Older persons often work only part-time, however. Schulz indicates that approximately one half of employed older persons work part-time.

Occupations vary in their age structures, reflecting opportunities for self-employment or part-time work, the presence of mandatory retirement rules, physical and training requirements, and so on (Kaufman & Spilerman, 1982). Kaufman and Spilerman demonstrate that younger workers are overrepresented in occupations involving entry-level positions (bank teller), emergent technologies (computer programmer), and physical strength (warehouseman). The middle-aged are overrepresented in senior positions in a job sequence (school administrator). Older workers tend to be overrepresented in flexible (real-estate agent) or contracting (tailor) occupations. Free professional and craft occupations, such as physician or electrician, tend to have more uniform age distributions because they involve long-term affiliations. Finally, undesirable jobs with poor prospects for advancement (gardener, food-service worker) tend to overrepresent both young and old workers.

Work and the Life Course

Work represents a central involvement in the lives of most people, and "since occupation is such an important role in the life of an adult, it will have pervasive effects on personality and come to influence both work and nonwork spheres" (Mortimer & Simmons, 1978:440). Work is one dimension that structures the life course, thereby contributing to personal change during adulthood (Ward, 1982). The nature of work, for example, affects work-related attitudes and values. Although individuals choose occupations on the basis of their attitudes and values (occupational selection), their attitudes and values are also shaped by the quality of their work (occupational socialization), as workers adapt to situational contingencies and constraints (Mortimer & Lorence, 1979). The greater autonomy and challenge experienced by higher-status workers, for example, heightens the value they place on self-direction and encourages feelings of creativity and occupational command (Kohn & Schooler, 1982; Gecas, 1981). Noting that surprisingly high proportions of workers with menial routine jobs report being satisfied with their jobs, Gruenberg (1980) indicates that such workers come to upgrade the value of other rewards (money, job security) over time. Their "horizon of expectations" becomes limited as they become aware that the most important aspect of job satisfaction, meaningful use of skills and abilities, is not available to them. Thus workers adapt their work orientations to fit the quality of their jobs.

Work has more general effects on individual characteristics and life-styles, although there has been some debate about the nature of these effects (Wilson, 1980; Ward, 1982). One possibility, the *compensatory hypothesis,* is that people seek gratifications in nonwork areas to compensate for those that are not available in work. Workers with routine jobs involving little autonomy, for example, would seek creativity and self-direction in nonwork pursuits. There is greater support for the *spillover hypothesis,* however, whereby work and nonwork behaviors and attitudes are similar. It has been noted that alienating work creates more general feelings of self-estrangement (Blauner, 1964; Gruenberg, 1980; Gecas, 1981). Similarly, higher-status occupations foster self-esteem and intellectual flexibility, and such class differences are passed on to children through a heightened value placed on self-direction (Kohn & Schooler, 1982; House, 1981). Thus work experiences influence change and development throughout adulthood. They also serve as a source of variation in the nature and consequences of aging, as we shall see in discussing the effects of retirement.

Work careers also represent a context within which individuals confront the aging process (Karp & Yoels, 1981). Careers represent "the moving perspective in which the person sees his life as a whole and interprets the meaning of his various attributes, actions, and the things which happen to him" (Hughes, 1958:63). Workers assess whether they are "on time" concerning personal and social career schedules, and the timing of events and developmental issues is related to the rhythm of careers. Clausen (1972) suggests that the working class confronts an earlier "career ceiling" in the forties. This early closure of advancement opportunities may contribute to an early feeling of aging.

Aging and Work Performance

Although work clearly affects individuals throughout adulthood, it is also likely that aging affects work orientations and capabilities. One of the greatest difficulties older workers face is the stereotype of declining performance because of poor health or intellectual failings. Such stereotypes form implicit and explicit bases for age bias in hiring and compulsory retirement policies, but they have little basis in fact. Although there are numerous difficulties in measuring age differences in capacity or performance, and there is a lack of longitudinal studies, the accumulated evidence suggests that older workers perform as well as, if not better than, younger workers (Sheppard, 1976; Clark & Spengler, 1980a; Foner & Schwab, 1981). Physical and intellectual changes associated with aging are not great relative to job requirements, and "throughout most of work life, one's ability far exceeds the demands of one's job" (Clark & Spengler, 1980a:77). Even when age-related decrements may impair performance, individual variability among older workers is considerable. Indeed, greater experience may result in higher quality and more consistent work by older employees. In general there appear to be no appreciable differences between younger and older workers in productivity, accuracy, or even illness absenteeism. Work accidents preventable by good judgment appear to decline with age, although accidents preventable by a rapid response may increase with age and older workers tend to be disabled longer if they are injured.

Older workers also tend to be more attached to their work and express greater job satisfaction (Wright & Hamilton, 1978; Mortimer & Lorence, 1979). This reflects both occupational selection and occupational socialization, resulting in a closer match of individual values and work qualities. Younger workers are still searching for their "niche," whereas older workers have either found theirs or given up the hunt. Wright and Hamilton (1978) found that older workers expressed greater job satisfaction because they had "better" jobs according to the dimensions of work that were most important to them, including hours, job security, and fringe benefits. Older workers may also be unwilling to admit making the wrong decisions so late in their careers, or may simply recognize the tenuousness of their position, given the difficulties they would encounter in finding another job due to age biases in hiring practices.

One further indication of attachment to work is the fact that many persons continue to work following retirement from their primary occupation. One study found that about 20 percent of retirees continued working, usually part-time and about half of them in the same industry (Parnes, 1981). Such persons are more likely to have negative orientations toward retirement and have been involuntarily retired; they feel economically deprived and view work as a major source of satisfaction (Streib & Schneider, 1971; Fillenbaum & Madox, 1974). Streib and Schneider note that these motivating factors must be accompanied by certain enabling factors, primarily good health and white-collar occupation. The latter presumably provides certain job-seeking skills and a wider range of job opportunities in which physical strength is of little relevance.

Retraining and Job Redesign

Although older workers seem to perform well, problems associated with aging may drive them prematurely from the labor force. The likelihood of handicaps in health and physical strength increases with age. In addition, the work role may deteriorate around the individual as he or she ages with the infusion of newly trained workers and technical improvements, the creation of new occupations, or the reorganization of work roles (Riley, et al., 1972). The handicap to work created by these factors is often unnecessarily high, however. Standards of health and education set by employers are sometimes too high or irrelevant to the job, needlessly disqualifying many older workers. Society, rather than aging, creates obsolescence through the lack of retraining and an unwillingness to fit jobs to people rather than people to existing jobs.

As one solution to this problem, there has been considerable interest within industrial gerontology in *functional age* (Sheppard, 1976). This entails a close look at the particular abilities and experience of any older worker, which can then be used either to match the individual to an existing job or to redesign jobs to fit his or her capacities. Such approaches imply a recognition that chronological age tells us little about an individual and changes that occur with age need not be handicapping if there is a willingness to modify the work or the workplace.

Although some studies indicate that retraining may be more difficult for older workers, there is no doubt that it can be successful, perhaps as successful as for younger workers, and that occupational obsolescence is not inevitable or irremediable (Sheppard, 1976). Training programs for older workers must, however, be geared to their unique characteristics and capacities. Because of older workers' anxiety, lack of self-confidence, and tenuous learning skills related to low education and the length of time since their last educational experience, the techniques used for training younger people are often inappropriate. Tailoring approaches to the older worker may be more costly, though, as is job redesign, and this cost is itself a barrier to the employment of older workers. Failure to use such techniques, however, means that "continued reliance on the conventional methods of teaching and training older persons may only serve to perpetuate the stereotypes about 'old dogs not being able to learn new tricks' and thus compound the problems of older workers" (Sheppard, 1976:297).

Actually, workers of all ages would benefit from greater availability of retraining options. For the most part, all of our educational experience occurs early in life and is directed toward preparing us for a lifelong occupation, but "midcareer crises" and the desire for a second career seem to be increasing.

> Several societal developments seem to be at the heart of this phenomenon. The first of these is the increasing rate of change in our society—technological, economic, and cultural—that modern man finds so unsettling. Related to this "future shock" is the fact that commitment to one life-long occupation is no longer as feasible as it was in the past: "Once a coal miner, always a coal miner" is no longer a valid description in an age when the mine is quite likely to close down. A second factor is quite simply that workers are living longer; a forty-year working life is a great amount of time to devote to one career. Third, the general increase in expectations and in general education has left many workers with high aspirations in low-level jobs. For such workers a career change can be an avenue to mobility, self-actualization, and job satisfaction. (U.S. Department of Health, Education, and Welfare, 1973:123)

More flexible approaches to the allocation of work are being developed in many countries, including job sharing, extended leaves, and phased retirement (Morrison, 1979). This partly reflects a growing awareness of the value of experienced older workers and the invalidity of negative stereotypes about their capabilities. It also reflects the economic pressures from pension systems in an aging population, a topic we will discuss in greater detail later in this chapter. Although most of this century has seen a trend toward more and earlier retirement, mechanisms are now being explored for retaining older workers.

Barriers to Employment

There are a number of reasons for the employment difficulties of older workers aside from "natural" physical declines and skill obsolescence. Despite protection afforded by seniority, unemployment is higher among males over 55 than younger age groups (Sheppard, 1976), often because of shutdowns of plants and industries or mass layoffs that cost older workers their seniority. Once unemployed, the older worker tends to remain unemployed longer. One study found that unemployed older workers found work eventually, but it usually meant a significant loss of income and occupational status (Parnes, 1981).

Part of the problem, of course, is that older job seekers are often hampered by low education, poor health, or a lack of marketable skills. There are incentives against working, such as the Social Security ceiling on earnings, and many older persons are forced out of the labor force by mandatory retirement rules. There are also clear age biases that hinder older people in their attempts to gain employment.

Another problem is the unwillingness of employers to hire older persons, stemming from negative stereotypes about performance and skills and fear of the presumed costs (retraining, pension and insurance coverage, and so on). The Age Discrimination in Employment Act of 1967 was designed to protect workers between the ages of 40 and 65 against discrimination in hiring, termination, and compensation, and was amended in 1978 to include most workers up to age 70. The most blatant forms of age discrimination have declined since passage of this legislation, but discrimination has by no means been eliminated. In 1977, for example, age discrimination complaints were filed against more than 5,000 businesses (Soldo, 1980). One study of aerospace workers suggests that age discrimination may indeed be quite widespread (Kasschau, 1976). One half of the sample said they had personally experienced age discrimination in finding, holding, or advancing in a job. In a more general survey of persons aged 45 to 74 in Los Angeles County, Kasschau (1977) found that over 80 percent felt that age discrimination was "common" in this country; indeed, blacks and whites considered age discrimination to be at least as common as racial discrimination. Among whites, 26 percent said their friends had experienced it, and 13 percent felt they had personally been discriminated against because of age. The corresponding figures were even higher among blacks—38 percent and 23 percent, respectively.

Age biases are also apparent in public and private employment agencies. Studies of employment service applicants indicate that older job seekers receive fewer services; they are less likely to receive testing or counseling or to be referred to job interviews or retraining programs, and are less likely to be placed successfully (Schulz, 1980). On the other hand, older persons themselves may be less efficient or adaptive in their job-seeking efforts. One study found that older workers were less willing to change work methods or job-seeking techniques, to move to areas with better employment, to adjust salary expectations, or to engage in job retraining (Sobel & Wilcock, 1963). Older workers are apparently also handicapped by the fact that they use fewer job-seeking techniques and sources and contact fewer companies (Sheppard & Belitsky, 1966). Such differences may be related to lower achievement motivation and higher job interview anxiety among some older workers (Sheppard, 1976).

We noted in Chapter 2, however, that cognitive skills of older people can benefit from intervention. Gray (1983) reports on an evaluation of a "job club," through which older job-seekers received training in job search techniques and social support from group members. After 12 weeks, 83 percent of the persons in the study had been placed in a job, compared with only 26 percent of a control group who were referred to the usual job service. This offers a further example of the "plasticity" of aging.

However, the major sources of employment difficulties for older workers are structural, not social-psychological—primarily skill obsolescence (aggravated by insufficient retraining possibilities) and age bias in job allocation processes. Middle age is often a time of assessment and reappraisal, but society places many barriers in front of the person who wishes to reorient his or her life. Given the relative inflexibility of the existing work and job structure, midcareer adjustments of any sort are extremely difficult. Additionally, there are wasted talents and skills of older persons. Robert Butler (1975) has made an eloquent plea that society take advantage of capacities that may be particularly evident in the aged because of their accumulated experience and age: teaching, counseling, historical information, preservation of dying crafts, and so on. Butler cites the following example as an illustration of the talents that may be overlooked:

> Colonel Harlan Sanders, of Kentucky Fried Chicken fame, made his first million at age 73. A former gas station operator and restaurateur, Sanders was penniless when he retired at 65. With his first Social Security check for $105 he embarked on a promotion campaign for his recipe for fried chicken. Eight years later he sold the American and Canadian rights to the recipe for $4 million. "I went from rags to riches," he recalls. (Butler, 1975:84–85)

RETIREMENT ISSUES

Although many older persons continue to work, retirement is more typical in modern societies. Retirement is a social institution providing "orderly means of shifting older workers, or allowing them to shift, out of the labor force with a minimum of financial hardship in consideration of their past contributions" (Atchley, 1982:264). As straightforward as this statement seems, retirement and pension systems encompass many goals: reducing unemployment and creating opportunities for younger workers, stimulating and rewarding worker loyalty, reducing labor costs by replacing expensive older workers and deferring some wage increases until retirement, and allowing and supporting individuals' desire for retirement (Atchley, 1982). As we will see, each of these goals has shaped the current nature of retirement, and the goals underlying retirement policies have shifted over time in response to changing societal needs and perceptions. In addition to being a social institution, retirement is also an individual experience, involving an event, a role, and a process of adaptation. The societal and individual aspects of retirement combine to create a complex mix of interrelated issues.

Figure 6.1 presents a schematic view of the interrelated factors associated with retirement. Retirement decisions are shaped by the broader societal context, including mandatory retirement rules, patterns of age discrimination, availability of pensions, and levels of unemployment and inflation. Personal characteristics, including the value and quality of work, also affect decisions about whether and when to retire. The nature and context of the retirement decision combine with social and personality characteristics to shape the individual effects of retirement. For example, retirement may create problems when societies place a high value on work or retirees face high inflation. On the individual level, retirement may be more favorable if individuals are prepared financially and socially for the tran-

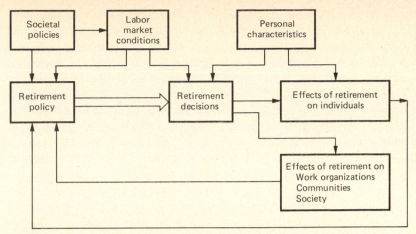

Figure 6.1 Factors in the retirement process. (*Source:* Robert Atchley, "Issues in Retirement Research," *The Gerontologist* 19 (1979), p. 45. Reprinted by permission.)

sition. Individual retirement decisions also accumulate to affect organizations, communities, and societies. Continued employment of older workers may reduce the promotion chances of younger workers, whereas increasing retirement dramatically heightens pension costs in an aging population. These individual and group effects of retirement will in turn affect retirement policy. If retirement is felt to cause poverty and demoralization, pressure builds to encourage work options. If an aging work force is felt to reduce corporate flexibility, retirement will be encouraged although rising pension costs create pressures to reduce or delay retirement.

Each of these aspects of retirement are discussed in the sections that follow. We will begin by discussing the emergence of retirement as a widespread institution during this century and the factors shaping individual retirement decisions. Following this is an investigation of the consequences of retirement and the factors that determine these consequences. Finally, retirement income and pension policy are discussed, as these are critical components of both the societal and individual context of retirement.

THE EMERGENCE OF RETIREMENT

Important changes have occurred during this century in the patterns of labor force participation by older men and women. There has been a steady decline in the proportion of males who work from over two thirds of all males 65 and older in 1900 to about one fifth currently. Table 2.11 (in Chapter 2) indicated that reduction in labor force participation has continued in recent decades for men aged 65 and over and aged 55 to 64. The pattern is different for women. Whereas the proportion of women aged 65 and over who work has remained stable at about 8 percent, there has been a substantial increase in the work force by women aged 55 to 64. As nearly one half of all women between 55 and 64 now work, retirement can no longer be considered a solely male phenomenon.

Retirement as a widespread institution is a product of twentieth-century industrialized societies. Retirement is not typical in less industrialized societies. The usual pattern is more gradual withdrawal, taking on tasks involving less physical effort or shorter hours (Foner & Schwab, 1981). A number of processes have contributed to declining involvement in work by older persons in modern societies, however.

One set of factors involves structural transformations in the economy: (1) declines in agricultural employment and the proportion of self-employed, (2) continual upgrading and changing of the work role through education, automation, and so on, (3) increases in large, bureaucratic firms, and (4) relative increases in white-collar occupations at the expense of blue-collar occupations (Foner & Schwab, 1981). These changes increase retirement rates for three reasons. First, they imply an accelerated obsolescence of the knowledge and skills of older workers. Emerging occupations requiring higher education and new technical skills are taken over by the young, whereas older workers tend to be concentrated in slow-growth industries with fewer available jobs. Retirement need not *necessarily* result from work changes. Automation, by lowering physical work demands, is often well-suited for older workers, but retraining opportunities are often quite limited. A lack of job opportunities pushes workers into retirement.

Second, these transformations increase retirement because they result in less individual control over the retirement decision. Those who are in agriculture or self-employed are still more likely to continue working, partly because they can withdraw gradually with more flexible schedules, but they are a smaller proportion of the work force. People increasingly work for larger, more bureaucratic organizations, which develop a set of policies applicable to all employees. This involves both a "push" and a "pull" to retirement. The push is the increase in mandatory retirement policies set at specific ages. The pull is the development of pension systems that make retirement more affordable and attractive.

This brings us to the third reason for increased retirement: changes in personnel policies. Mandatory retirement provisions have risen substantially in the past 30 years, often including options for early retirement. The rapid economic growth of this century provides an economic surplus to divert into pension systems, making retirement for older people who cannot or do not wish to work economically feasible (Schulz, 1980; Atchley, 1976a). For example, Social Security is now nearly universal in its coverage, but in 1948 only 13 percent of those over 65 were receiving payments. Viscusi (1979) indicates that rising Social Security benefits have had a substantial negative impact on the employment of older people. Similarly, private pensions cover an increasing proportion of workers. Social Security also discourages work through the retirement test of eligibility, which reduces willingness to work because Social Security benefits may be reduced (Schulz, 1980).

Another reason for the institutionalization of retirement is the aging of the population. Indeed, Graney and Cottam (1981) argue that rising retirement is primarily attributable to the dramatic growth of the older population rather than to structural changes in the economy. As noted in Chapter 3, this creates generational competition for jobs, particularly when rising worker productivity reduces the demand for labor. One result of the Depression was the development of Social Security to entice older workers out of the labor force and create jobs for younger workers, and this is still given as a primary justification for mandatory retirement policies.

These demographic trends combine with beliefs that older workers are inefficient and costly. Graebner (1980) argues that retirement and pension systems emerged because of the needs of capital, not because of humanitarian concerns. A rising concern over productive efficiency combined with a view that older workers are too inefficient and tradition-bound. Retirement was viewed as an impersonal mechanism to remove inefficient older workers and maintain promotion opportunities for younger workers (thereby increasing their productivity as well). Graebner notes that states began teacher retirement systems after 1910 because of the presumed backwardness of older teachers.

At the same time, however, older workers were viewed as more loyal and less mobile than young workers. Pension systems emerged as a mechanism to achieve efficiency and loyalty, retaining workers with the promise of a pension and using retirement to remove presumably inefficient older workers. Graebner notes that little thought was given to restructuring work to fit older workers; rather, pension systems represented a "tool of sloughing off traditional obligations to older workers" (p. 149). This occurred within a changing tone of employer-employee relations, attacking systems of seniority and personalism. It was also part of the larger history of government intervention in the economy. Social Security, for example, was viewed as a mechanism for dealing with unemployment and stimulating consumption.

This does not mean that retirement is necessarily forced on unwilling older workers. Retirement and pension systems also allow workers to leave burdensome jobs. We too often assume that work provides meaning and satisfaction to a worker's life when, in fact, the work may be boring or alienating. Braverman (1974) has argued that it has become increasingly true during this century. The craftsman who controls the production process from start to finish and can truly claim the product as *his* is replaced by the worker who does small, repetitive parts of some larger whole. Braverman relates this trend to monopoly capitalism, which seeks efficiency, simplicity, and routinization. This creates deadening and dead-end jobs, as illustrated by a study of automobile workers:

> Despite the claim by an automobile industry economist that "a constant upgrading of individuals is normal in the industry . . . limited only by the capacity and willingness of the individual," automobile workers cannot usually look forward to any substantial personal advancement through a series of progressively more skilled and better-paid jobs. Increasing mechanization, made profitable by the enormous volume of production, has left most automobile workers as semiskilled operatives. . . . As early as 1922, Henry Ford estimated that eighty-five per cent of the workers in his plants needed less than two weeks of training and that forty-three per cent could be working efficiently within one day. (Chinoy, 1965:19)

Braverman suggests that this "degradation of work" is characteristic of not only assembly-line workers but office workers as well. Thus more people may be willing to retire from repetitious work that involves little personal accomplishment or status.

This combines with the emergence of a "retirement ethic." At least since the 1940s retirement has increasingly been "sold" as a positive way of life with increasing opportunities for leisure involvement (Calhoun, 1978; Graebner, 1980). Pampel (1981), for example, argues that increasing retirement over the past 30 years is primarily due to the increased popularity of retirement and leisure. Thus the emergence of retirement reflects a great variety of structural and cultural changes that have taken place in modern societies.

THE DECISION TO RETIRE

It is clear that many factors have contributed to increasing retirement during this century. As reflected in Figure 6.1, individual retirement decisions are shaped by labor market conditions (unemployment, inflation), retirement policies (pensions, mandatory retirement rules), and personal characteristics (illness, desire for leisure). Decisions about whether to retire and the preferred timing of retirement are closely linked to the meanings attached to work and retirement as social roles, but the concern here is the immediate reason for retirement. Regardless of attitudes or desires, what in fact propels people into retirement?

Some older workers lack personal control over the retirement decision. This may involve loss of job because of poor health, plant shutdown, and so forth, but the greatest attention has been paid to mandatory retirement policies that prevent individuals from working beyond a certain age. This is often felt to be quite widespread, but the facts indicate otherwise. It appears that fewer than half of all workers are currently faced with even the possibility of mandatory retirement. A study made several years ago of workers 18 and above indicated that 36 percent were faced with a fixed age (National Council on the Aging, 1975).

It is difficult to determine how many workers retire because of mandatory policies. Some workers may be "nudged" into retirement by the realization that they will have to retire in a few years anyway. Also, not all those who retire at a mandatory age are unwilling to retire. Streib and Schneider (1971), in a longitudinal study of retirement, made a useful distinction between a worker's willingness to retire and whether the decision was voluntary or administrative. By combining the two issues, it becomes clear that mandatory is not necessarily the same as unwilling. Their sample was not representative of all workers, but the distribution is illuminating. About 30 percent were "truly" voluntary—willing—retirees. A second group (about 20 percent, slightly more women than men) made their own decision but were reluctant, probably retiring due to poor health. Some of those who were retired administratively were nonetheless willing to retire (about 20 percent), leaving approximately one third of men and women who were reluctant to retire and were forced to administratively. It is also instructive to note that the survey by the National Council on the Aging (1975) found that nearly one third of retirees indicated they would like to work, but only 11 percent said they would actually consider taking a job.

Schulz and associates (1974) found from a sample of Social Security beneficiaries that an even smaller proportion had been terminated because of mandatory retirement rules. They found that:(1) 46 percent had worked in firms without
mandatory policies, (2) 30 percent of the remainder retired before the fixed retirement age, (3) another 10 percent indicated they had been willing to retire anyway,
(4) 4 percent were unable to work in any case, and (5) another 3 percent were
able to find a new job following compulsory retirement. This left only 7 percent
of all the workers—whose retirement was attributable *purely* to administrative
rules—who were unwilling to retire, able to work, unable to find a new job, and
forced to retire by a mandatory policy. A more recent longitudinal study of older
workers found that only 3 percent of those who retired were unwilling, mandatory retirees (Parnes, 1981). Similarly, at General Motors in 1976 only 2 percent
of blue-collar workers stayed until the mandatory age of 68 (Schulz, 1980).

Control over the retirement decision varies by occupation, of course. Certainly the average physician has more control over work and retirement than the
average assembly-line worker. Also, the National Council on the Aging study
(1975) found that retirement was more likely to be forced for males, blacks, and
persons with low income or poor education. The basic policy issue is: Given the
many problems already faced by older workers, need we also force them to retire
simply because of age? Even if only a minority are directly affected by such policies, is not the position of all the aged altered by this type of age stratification
and its implications of unfitness?

Erdman Palmore (1972) has summarized the arguments that have been
made in support of compulsory retirement and indicated that each of them rests
on a shaky foundation. Compulsory retirement is often justified as being simple
and easy to administer and lending predictability to the retirement process. Inasmuch as most people are not directly affected by fixed-age policies, however, it
would seem that flexibility works reasonably well. Often the concern for predictability involves the presumed inferiority or poor health of older workers and the
consequent costs to the employer of either keeping them all on or trying to "weed
out" those who are unfit. Again, the problems seem greatly exaggerated. Age
alone is a very poor predictor of working ability. Techniques are being developed
to assess worker capabilities, and more could be done to redesign jobs to fit older
workers. It has also been argued that mandatory policies are easier on older workers—their impersonality prevents individual discrimination, saves face for the
worker, and gives retirement an inevitability. It seems rather odd to justify whole-
sale discrimination in order to protect individuals. It also seems that we have
reached a point where "People no longer need an excuse to retire. It is an accepted
part of life" (Atchley, 1976a:43). The argument that mandatory retirement does
not really hurt older persons because they have adequate retirement income and
can get another job if they desire also ignores the facts of the many barriers to
employment for older people. Although mandatory retirement is usually linked
to a pension plan, retirement income is far from adequate for many; indeed, mandatory retirement forces some people into poverty.

One of the reasons for the general institutionalization of retirement in this
century is that it opens up jobs for younger workers. But are not older people

as entitled as younger people to a decent income and whatever meanings are derived from work? And there are other ways to encourage older people to retire, including making retirement more attractive with activities and financial support. Palmore (1972) has suggested an interesting compromise, whereby workers would lose seniority rights at a certain age, no longer accumulate pension credits, and lose guaranteed continued employment, but would not be automatically retired and could continue to work up to their ability.

It seems clear that flexible policies are preferable to mandatory retirement. Robert Butler speaks eloquently of the waste of skills and experience caused by forced retirement, citing the following example:

> Sixty-nine-year-old philosopher Paul Weiss talked animatedly about his $1 million suit against Fordham University, charging age bias. This vital and vitalizing teacher had been offered the $100,000-per-year Albert Schweitzer chair . . . but then was denied it on the basis of age. . . .
>
> Weiss pointed out ironically that the chair was named for the famous Dr. Schweitzer, "many of whose major achievements came after he was older than the plaintiff." Schweitzer died at 90 in 1965. ". . . America will never be of age until it knows how to make most use of its people—no matter what their color, sex or years," wrote Weiss. In the complaint the professor was described as in "excellent" physical health. "He walks eight miles every day, swims and does various calisthenics. His mental condition is also beyond question excellent." (1975:65)

Professor Weiss lost his case, and court rulings have continued to uphold mandatory retirement policies. This does not mean, however, that there is public support for such measures. A poll commissioned by the National Council on the Aging (1981) investigated this issue. Only 37 percent of the public felt that older people should retire "to give younger people more of a chance on the job," and 90 percent agreed that "nobody should be forced to retire because of age if he wants to continue working and is still able to do a good job." Partly because of public pressure, the 1978 amendments to the Age Discrimination in Employment Act effectively eliminate mandatory retirement for federal employees, and increase the allowed limit from age 65 to 70 for most workers in private industry.

It is expected, however, that this legislation will have little impact on labor force participation by older people because so few are directly affected by mandatory retirement provisions. Parnes's (1981) longitudinal study found that 51 percent of retirees retired because of poor health, whereas 46 percent indicated they had retired voluntarily. The National Council on the Aging (1981) survey found that 62 percent of all retirees had retired by choice. But the term *voluntary* is somewhat misleading, as poor health may be a contributing factor. Although poor health has been declining as a reason for retirement as jobs have continued to be less physically demanding and the health of older people has improved (Atchley, 1976a), certain groups are more likely to cite poor health as a reason—blacks, agricultural and construction workers, and workers with lower education and income (Parnes, 1981).

Voluntary retirement may also be a euphemism for other reasons. For example, although women (particularly married women) retire voluntarily more often than men, this may not reflect less importance attached to work but rather to restricted job opportunities and the possibility that women are expected, encouraged, or even pressured to retire (Atchley, 1976a). Older persons also may say they retired by choice or because of poor health to avoid the implied rejection of retirement. There may be various pressures from younger coworkers and superiors, including exclusion and mockery. As an example, Blau cites the following incident from a newspaper article:

> And in South Chicago, a young mill hand described a birthday party that had been given one 67-year-old worker. "We painted up a big sign with 'Happy Birthday' on it . . . then on the other side we drew one of those old tire company ads showing a youngster holding a candle and saying 'time to re-tire.' We all thought it was funny. But the old man didn't see the joke." (1973:135)

White-collar workers may be more subtle, but personal coolness, failure to achieve status or salary promotions, or demotion following peak status may loosen one's work commitment and hasten retirement (Riley et al., 1972).

Although voluntary retirement may often result from limited job opportunities, poor health, and alienating job situations for older workers, there has also been an increase in leisure as an attraction to retirement. From 1951 to 1963, for example, there was an increase from 3 percent to 17 percent in those retiring because they prefer leisure (Palmore, 1964). Thus truly voluntary retirement may be on the increase, perhaps linked to declining importance attached to work.

Early retirement is one indication of willingness to retire. Since 1962, men and women have been able to retire at age 62 with reduced Social Security benefits. Private pension plans have also opened up possibilities for early retirement. Some union contracts, for example, include provisions for full pensions after 30 years of employment. There has clearly been a trend toward earlier retirement. The proportion of males aged 55 to 64 who were working declined from 90 percent in 1947 to 73 percent in 1979 (Soldo, 1980); 70 percent of new Social Security beneficiaries in 1978 were younger than 65 compared with 54 percent in 1968 (Foner & Schwab, 1981); and there was an increase from 1966 to 1976 in the proportion of older workers who expected to retire before 65 (Parnes, 1981). But even among early retirees health remains important. The Social Security Retirement History Survey found that poor health was the most common reason given for early retirement, and early retirement occurred disproportionately among those with poor health or long-term unemployment experience (Sheppard, 1976). Similarly, Parnes (1981) found that 90 percent of those who retired for health reasons did so before age 65. There appear to be two basic groups of early retirees: persons with good health and financial resources who desire additional leisure time, and persons with health problems who find work burdensome (Clark & Spengler, 1980a). Workers with high job commitment and satisfaction are less likely to retire early (Foner & Schwab, 1981), but the increased availability of pensions has facilitated exit from work for those who desire or need to.

In general it is clear that health limitations and the availability of pension income dominate the retirement decision. Clark and Spengler (1980a) note that the effect of pensions is particularly great for workers with health problems, determining their ability to leave work, but voluntary retirees are also more likely to have adequate pension income (Parnes, 1981). It is clear that increases in Social Security benefits have contributed to increased and earlier retirement (Munnell, 1977).

It may seem from this discussion that we know a great deal about retirement plans and decisions. This is not the case, however, Decisions to retire are shaped by complex combinations of period and cohort effects. Morgan (1979), for example, notes that recent cohorts of retirees have had relatively favorable historical experiences, including lower unemployment and inflation, which contribute to favorable orientations to retirement. Future cohorts will have had less favorable experiences of higher unemployment and inflation, therefore they may be more skeptical about retirement. Morgan cites the need for more information about individual plans and provisions for retirement to guide pension policy. It is not clear, for example, whether current debates about the financial solvency of Social Security will lead people to delay their retirement, or whether current tax incentives for Individual Retirement Accounts might lead people to save for retirement and perhaps retire earlier. As we shall see later, such questions are important in projecting pension costs and choosing among pension policy alternatives.

THE CONSEQUENCES OF RETIREMENT

Beyond decisions about whether and when to retire, there has been concern about the effects of retirement on the older worker. On the one hand, we have images of the "golden years" of retirement—travel, recreation, freedom. On the other hand, there are many gloomy portraits of the boredom and meaninglessness encountered by those who retire. This suggests that retirement constitutes a severe crisis, particularly for American males. Historically, work has been viewed as the central life task, integrating people, especially men, into the social structure by determining identity, patterns of participation, and life-style. A government report entitled *Work in America* asks:

> Why is a man a worker? First of all, of course, man works to sustain physical life—to provide food, clothing, and shelter. But clearly work is central to our lives for other reasons as well. According to Freud, work provides us with a sense of reality; to Elton Mayo, work is a bind to community; to Marx, its function is primarily economic. Theologians are interested in work's moral dimensions; sociologists see it as a determinant of status, and some contemporary critics say that it is simply the best way of filling up a lot of time. (U.S. Department of Health, Education, and Welfare, 1973:1)

Evidence indicates that unemployment is accompanied by low self-esteem and withdrawal from social interaction (Foner & Schwab, 1981). Similarly, retirement presumably undermines social supports and the bases of personal and social identity, taking on major social significance as a rite of passage. In light of the general work ethic, retirement is seen as "unproductive" and not "useful."

> It is a paradox of modern times that we expect to retire when we are old whereas all our lives great emphasis is placed upon work, achievement, production, efficiency, and self-development. (Taves & Hansen, 1963:105)

The question "Who are you?" is often answered: "I'm a carpenter" or "I'm a university professor," and through coworkers, with whom one shares experiences, information, and ideas, one gains identity and prestige as well as a feeling of "belonging." There is also the personal reassurance of worth associated with a meaningful job well done. According to this symbolic interactionist perspective, when work ceases certain identities and self-feelings also cease.

Combined with the centrality attached to work is a view that retirement is an ambiguous "roleless role" (Donahue et al., 1960; Rosow, 1974), involving few expectations about behavior and little socialization or preparation. A generally unpleasant evaluation of retirement as a useless role provides little incentive to prepare for or take the role. Thus, until meaningful social roles are created for retirement, the result will be normlessness, inactivity, depression, and disengagement.

This is certainly a gloomy portrait of retirement and the argument seems plausible. But how accurate is this picture? The "golden years" image of retirement certainly overlooks the complexity of the retirement experience, and retirement involves social and psychological trauma for some retirees. But studies of attitudes toward and adjustment to retirement indicate that its general consequences are relatively unremarkable and in many cases quite pleasant. In fact, the major determinants of retirement satisfaction appear to be health and financial security, not the identity crises stressed so often.

Attitudes Toward Retirement

Contrary to our often negative impressions, most people see retirement as "active, involved, expanding, full, and busy; as fair and good; as hopeful and meaningful; and as healthy, relaxed, mobile, able, and independent" (Atchley, 1976a:28). Most adults expect to retire by age 65, and indeed desire to do so, and only a very small minority actually seem to dread retirement. Opposition to retirement was fairly widespread before the 1950s, but the "selling" of retirement life-styles cited earlier and the expansion of pension coverage have contributed to an increase in activity options in retirement. Recent cohorts are more likely to intend to retire, have favorable attitudes toward retirement, and retire earlier. Such attitudes are important to retirement adjustment because favorable expectations often color perceptions of events. We all know that expecting (and wanting) to like something often leads us to like it more. On the other hand, if those expectations are based upon unrealistically rosy pictures of retirement, reality may prove an even more bitter pill to swallow.

Attitudes toward retirement are not uniform, of course; they vary according to a number of individual characteristics. For example, individuals at higher levels of income, education, and occupation tend to have more favorable attitudes toward retirement. This seemingly simple relationship obscures a number of processes. Anticipated financial problems are a major determinant of negative retirement attitudes. Unskilled and semiskilled workers have good reason to resist retirement because it will mean substantially lower income for most of them. Those who already have higher incomes realistically expect greater financial security in retirement. Atchley (1976a) also suggests that manual workers may perceive fewer alternatives to work so that the job becomes the lesser of two evils. Semiskilled and unskilled workers are likely to have developed fewer meaningful involvements outside of work, such as voluntary associations, reflecting the "spillover" hypothesis (Ward, 1982).

In other ways, however, social class is inversely related to willingness to retire. A survey of white males aged 50 and over found that 45 percent of blue-collar workers but only 24 percent of white-collar workers said they would not continue to work *if provided with an adequate income* (Sheppard, 1976). Willingness to retire is greater when work is of lower quality (less autonomy, variety, and responsibility). Thus,

> . . . retirement can be viewed frequently as an escape from an undesirable, unsatisfying work role, as a negative-type decision. The fact that most studies, if not all, of "retirement adjustment" reveal a high degree of satisfaction may partly be due to this "escape" function of retirement. . . . (Sheppard, 1976:303)

Workers at higher educational and occupational levels find their work more interesting, are more committed to it, and are therefore less inclined to retire. Thus they retire later even though their attitudes toward retirement may be more favorable (George, 1980; Ward, 1982).

The research cited above would lead one to expect that attitudes toward work and retirement are closely related. Paradoxically, this is not the case. Attitude toward work is at best a weak predictor of attitude toward retirement or feelings of job deprivation during retirement, even when work appears to occupy a central position in a person's life (Fillenbaum, 1971b; Goudy et al., 1975; George, 1980; Glamser, 1981a). Such attitudes do affect *whether* people retire and preferred age of retirement, but, again, this seems to be attributable to work as a plus, not retirement as a minus. Attitudes toward retirement appear to be determined more by such things as financial outlook, number of friends, social activities, and perceived preparation for the retirement role.

Studies have also found that older workers are often less accepting of retirement and prefer later retirement age (Atchley, 1976a; Ekerdt et al., 1980; Goudy et al., 1980). This appears to reflect a combination of age and cohort effects. In their longitudinal study, Ekerdt and associates found that preferred retirement age increased as workers neared retirement. This may reflect more realistic recognition of financial difficulties associated with retirement. Ekerdt and associates note, however, that this trend meant a convergence between preferred and expected retirement age, as workers came to conform to the social scheduling of the retirement event. The study also found that at comparable ages, younger cohorts expressed a preference to retire earlier than older cohorts. This cohort difference may reflect different orientations to work, retirement and leisure, as well as differential access to pension programs.

Adjustment to Retirement

Although attitudes toward retirement are rather favorable, this refers only to retirement as an abstract future possibility. What happens when workers confront their own retirement? The following is an example of what often seems to be expected of retirees:

> "Mr. Winter" single-handedly ran an operation that nobody else in his company fully understood, nor in fact cared to understand. As Mr. Winter reached his 64th birthday, a bright and talented younger man was assigned as an apprentice to learn the complex set of activities so that at the end of the year, he could take over the operation and the old master could benefit from a well deserved retirement. Mr. Winter objected, claiming that he did not want to retire, but the company had rules. Not long after retirement a substantial change in Mr. Winter took place. He began to withdraw from people and to lose his zest for life. Within a year after his retirement this once lively and productive businessman was hospitalized, diagnosed as having a senile psychosis. Friends from work and even family soon stopped coming to visit as they could evoke no response. Mr. Winter was a vegetable.
>
> About two years after the apprentice had stepped up to his new position of responsibility he suddenly died. The company found itself in a serious predicament. The function that was vacated was essential to company operations, but which no one else in the company could effectively perform. A decision was made to approach Mr. Winter and see if he could pull himself together enough to carry on the job and train somebody to take over. Four of his closest co-workers were sent to the hospital. After hours of trying, one of the men finally broke through. The idea of going back to work brought the first sparkle in Mr. Winter's eyes in 2 years. Within a few days, this "vegetable" was operating at full steam, interacting with people as he had years before. (U.S. Department of Health, Education, and Welfare, 1973:78–79)

This, however, is by no means a general phenomenon. Most persons appear to remain satisfied in retirement and cope quite satisfactorily with the social and psychological changes it entails.

Satisfaction is somewhat higher among the employed than among the retired, but this is largely attributable to differences in health and income, which are themselves the major determinants of retirement satisfaction (George, 1980; Foner & Schwab, 1981). Longitudinal studies have found little change in life satisfaction following or during retirement (Streib & Schneider, 1971; George & Maddox, 1977). Not only does retirement appear to have little impact on overall morale, but retirees express considerable satisfaction with retirement itself. Parnes (1981) found that four out of five retirees felt that retirement fulfilled or exceeded their expectations, and three out of four would retire at the same time or an earlier age if they had to do it over. In a control group for health and education, workers and retirees did not differ in overall morale or satisfaction with their housing, the area in which they lived, or their standard of living, and retirees were more satisfied with their leisure activities (Table 6.1). Another study found that 90 percent of retirees agreed that "things are as interesting as they ever were," and 55 percent that "these are the best years of my life" (Kimmel et al., 1978).

There may be some decline in feelings of involvement and usefulness (George, 1980), but such feelings are not necessarily eliminated by loss of the work role. Streib and Schneider (1971), for example, found a significant increase in feelings of uselessness following retirement, but only about 20 percent of their sample attributed such feelings to retirement. Loss of spouse or dependency because of illness are also likely to create feelings of uselessness. In addition, approximately three quarters of their sample reported at least some feelings of usefulness following retirement.

There is also little evidence that retirement causes poor health (Foner & Schwab, 1981; Minkler, 1981), although there are cases like that of "Mr. Winter." Remember that poor health is a major *cause* of retirement, and substantial numbers of people feel that their health improves following retirement, with the removal of the mental and physical strain of work (Streib & Schneider, 1971). This is particularly true for unskilled and semiskilled laborers, who have been doing heavy physical work.

Social participation is another area in which retirement might have an impact. Disengagement theory implies that retirement is the beginning of a more general process of social and emotional withdrawal from the world. Retirement may disrupt friendship and group ties to coworkers and work-based organizations (such as unions or chambers of commerce), but work is not *necessarily* a social experience; in any case, individuals often selectively disengage from some aspects of their life, expanding into other spheres of activity (leisure, citizenship service, and so on). Research indicates that there is continuity of activity following retirement with little or no change in social interaction or community activities, and few differences in the activities of retirees and workers of the same age (Streib

Table 6.1   SATISFACTION WITH VARIOUS ASPECTS OF LIFE AMONG RETIREES AND NONRETIREES WITH 12 YEARS OF EDUCATION (PERCENT "VERY HAPPY")

Percent "very happy" with:	Non retirees	Retirees	Healthy retirees[a]
Housing	70	67	72
Local area	68	64	66
Health condition	59	47	62
Standard of living	62	54	59
Leisure activities	54	57	65
Things overall	59	51	60
Number of respondents	503	299	185

[a]Includes all retirees except those classified as having retired for health reasons.

Source: Adapted from Herbert Parnes, *Work and Retirement: A Longitudinal Study of Men,* Cambridge, Mass.: MIT Press, p. 188. © 1981 by The Massachusetts Institute of Technology. Reprinted by permission.

& Schneider, 1971; Foner & Schwab, 1981; Mutran & Reitzes, 1981). In their longitudinal study Streib and Schneider found no change after retirement in seeing children and grandchildren, church attendance, having close friends, or taking part in associations and community activities.

But what about the retirement experience itself? What do people find satisfying and dissatisfying about being retired? Most of the research seems to be focused on sources of dissatisfaction, perhaps reflecting a cultural expectation that retirement "ought" to be dissatisfying. But retirement is unsatisfying because of difficult situations that accompany it rather than because of loss of the work role per se. Relatively few people seem to miss their jobs, as few retirees desire to return to work, and such return is usually due to financial reasons (George, 1980; Foner & Schwab, 1981). A National Council on the Aging (1981) survey asked persons over 65 who were retired or unemployed what they "missed about their jobs" (Table 6.2). The results indicate that it was often not the work itself that was most important, but the income, associations, and activity levels related to work. Thus retirees may lack alternatives for the activities and social contacts (with both the public and coworkers) provided by a job but not miss the job itself. Parnes (1981) found that four out of five retirees would not accept a job unconditionally if one was offered to them.

Some people do miss a feeling of being useful and the respect of others following retirement, but it is not clear how much impact this has. In a sample of retirees in Miami, 83 percent agreed that people treat a retired man with less respect, but only 15 percent felt that they *personally* were treated with less respect (Strauss et al., 1976). Many of them still identified with their former occupations as "retired lawyers" or "retired doctors." This sense of continued status was strongly related to education: over one third of those with less than a high school education felt status loss, compared with only 3 percent of the college-educated.

There are, moreover, pleasant aspects to not working as well as problems. The most frequently expressed reasons for satisfaction with retirement are the ability to enjoy leisure pursuits (such as travel and hobbies), the freedom to do

Table 6.2   THINGS RETIRED PEOPLE 65 AND OVER MISSED ABOUT THEIR JOBS
(PERCENTAGES)

	Missed	Did not miss	Not sure	One thing missed most
The money it brings in	71	28	2	30
The people at work	70	28	2	24
The work itself	57	41	2	12
The feeling of being useful	55	43	2	10
Things happening around me	51	46	3	4
The respect of others	48	49	3	2
Having a fixed schedule every day	44	54	3	5

Source: Aging in the Eighties: America in Transition, a study prepared for the National Council on the Aging, Inc. (NCOA), Washington, D.C. by Louis Harris and Associates, Inc., © 1981, p. 58. Reprinted by permission.

as one wishes, and a more relaxing life away from the tensions and responsibilities associated with work. The benefits of no morning alarm clock, no publication deadlines to meet, and no daily schedule to follow have occurred more than once to this author while writing this chapter.

As with any aspect of the aging experience, we need to keep in mind sources of variation in the nature and consequences of retirement. These include the current context of retirement as well as experiences and patterns over the life course that carry over into retirement. There is evidence that persons who retire early because of poor health are least satisfied with retirement, whereas those who retire willingly are more satisfied and adjust more quickly (Streib & Schneider, 1971; Parnes, 1981). It is less clear whether mandatory retirement itself results in low satisfaction. One study found that involuntary retirees were less satisfied with retirement, but this was largely attributable to poor health, lower income, and more negative preretirement attitudes (Kimmel et al., 1978).

Occupation appears to be an important determinant of retirement satisfaction. Although higher-level white-collar workers enjoy their work more and are more attached to it, they are also more satisfied with retirement (George & Maddox, 1977; George, 1980; Foner & Schwab, 1981). In their longitudinal study George and Maddox found that life satisfaction declined over time for lower-status retirees, but increased for middle- and upper-status retirees. This is partly due to greater health and financial problems among lower-status workers, but it also reflects differences in personal and social resources throughout the life course (Ward, 1982). Retirement is more likely to cause isolation for the working class than for the middle class, who typically develop broader ties outside of the work role (Simpson et al., 1966a; Rosenberg, 1970). This occurs partly because semiskilled workers are more likely to have disorderly work careers that prevent them from becoming fully integrated into their social surroundings, and new social involvements are difficult to establish following retirement. As noted in the earlier discussion of work, higher-status workers develop greater feelings of flexibility and self-confidence; and more meaningful work appears to "spill over" into a greater variety of meaningful nonwork pursuits throughout life, which are then available in retirement. Those who have worked with their "heads" are also better able to maintain continuity than those who have worked with their "hands." Structured opportunities for activities similar to work also vary by occupation. A study of retired academics found considerable opportunities to continue research activities (Rowe, 1976). Many took advantage of these opportunities, particularly those with high professional visibility. Thus, the retired sociologist may have access to libraries, professional meetings, and networks of colleagues that facilitate continued involvement. Analogous opportunities are not likely to be available to retired janitors, carpenters, or clerks.

Sex differences may also be a factor in retirement adjustment. Retirement has traditionally been assumed to be primarily a male problem, as exemplified in the following:

> Retirement is not an important problem for women because . . . working seems to make little difference to them. It is as though they add work to their lives the way they would add a club membership. (Cumming & Henry, 1961:144)

Family roles have been viewed as the primary sources of identity and self-worth for women, who are thought to work primarily because of economic necessity. Retirement represents a smoother transition due to continuity of the family "career" (housewife, mother, grandmother). But women have increasingly entered the labor force for longer stretches, seeking self-fulfillment and feelings of accomplishment. In 1900 the average woman could expect to spend only 6 of her 51 years of life expectancy working, compared with 23 of 75 years in 1970 (Fullerton & Byrne, 1976). Involvement in the labor force by women grew from 32 percent in 1947 to 45 percent in 1973, with the greatest increase occurring for women aged 55 to 64 (Sheppard, 1976).

There is still relatively little information on retirement among women. Virtually all of the studies reviewed earlier in this chapter were limited to male workers and retirees. Evidence suggests, however, that retirement is not necessarily smoother for women. Some studies indicate that retirement has less effect on satisfaction and self-esteem for women (Palmore et al., 1979) and that retired women may be happier than working women if income is adequate (Jaslow, 1976). Other studies have found that men and women attach equal importance to work, and more women than men miss people at work and the feeling of doing a good job (Streib & Schneider, 1971; Atchley, 1976b). Atchley's study of retired teachers and telephone company employees found that men liked retirement more and adjusted more quickly to it, whereas women were "more often lonely, anxious, unstable in self-concept, highly sensitive to criticism, and highly depressed" (1976b:208). This may reflect the fact that most of our cultural models for retirement pertain to men, because women are seen as retiring back to their "real domain," the home. If retirement is ambiguous for men, what must it be like for women? It may also be that women are more attached to work because they have had to overcome cultural barriers and sex discrimination. Finally, retired women are also more likely to face widowhood, disrupting both work and family careers. As work becomes an increasingly important part of the overall pattern of life for more women, more attention will have to be paid to their adjustment to retirement.

The overall impression to be gleaned from the many studies of retirement is that most people adjust favorably to it and find it a relatively satisfying experience. This conclusion deals a critical blow to gerontological approaches emphasizing the traumatic nature of the transition from work to retirement. Where did we go wrong? There are two answers to this question. First, social gerontologists have exaggerated the importance of work and work values in the lives of current cohorts, although they may have been accurate for earlier cohorts. Second, although the retirement transition may indeed be difficult and stressful, we too often overlook the capacity of people to come to grips with the most trying life events.

The Meaning of Work

The view that retirement will constitute a severe identity crisis stems from the assumption that work is a central life interest that defines one's "mission in life" and one's personal identity. But this assumption is questionable. The ancient Hebrews and Greeks saw work as a painful necessity that brutalized the mind (Parker & Smith, 1976). It was only later that work came to be viewed as a "calling." During the Renaissance, creative work was viewed as a joy in itself; and the "Protestant work ethic" of Martin Luther and John Calvin portrayed work as the path to salvation. Such work ethics no longer seem so widespread, however, and there is growing evidence of alienation and job dissatisfaction at virtually all occupational levels (Gecas, 1981).

In the first place, work means different things to different people. Work may be variously seen as a source of: (1) income, (2) something to do to pass the time, (3) self-respect and recognition from others, (4) friendship and collegial relationships, or (5) meaningful life experience through one's purpose in life, creativity and self-expression, novel experiences, or service to others (Friedmann & Havighurst, 1954). To say, then, that work may be missed in retirement says nothing about which of these aspects will be missed.

In addition to various meanings for work, there are many sources of satisfaction and dissatisfaction in any particular job. Attachment to and satisfaction with work depends on things such as relations with coworkers, financial rewards, convenience and "creature comforts," opportunities for career advancement, the provision of adequate resources to do a good job, and whether the work is interesting and meaningful (Kalleberg, 1977). *Work in America,* the report of a special task force of the Department of Health, Education, and Welfare (1973), concludes that "interesting work" is the most important aspect of a job, and the most oppressive aspects are constant supervision, lack of variety, isolation from others, and meaningless tasks. The study by Kalleberg found such intrinsic aspects of work as autonomy, participating in decision making, and being able to work on a "whole" job the most important determinants of job satisfaction. Studies indicate that blue-collar workers are less likely to see their jobs as intrinsically interesting or meaningful (Gruenberg, 1980). Retirement might be easier for such workers, as indicated in a study that asked workers in various occupations: "What type of work would you try to get into if you could start all over again?" The percentage who would voluntarily choose the same work again is indicated in Table 6.3. Clearly, the average blue-collar worker is less attached to his work than the average white-collar worker; but even more impressive is the fact that although occupations such as lawyer and professor appear to be satisfying, only 43 percent of the *white-*collar workers would choose the same job again, despite the fact that such jobs presumably offer more intrinsic satisfactions.

A number of writings have argued that both blue- and white-collar jobs are becoming less intrinsically meaningful, and more alienating and confining (U.S. Department of Health, Education, and Welfare, 1973; Braverman, 1974; Sarason, 1977). *Work in America* suggests that declining intrinsic satisfactions from work partly account for increasing absenteeism, sabotage, worker turnover, wildcat strikes, and similar problems for industry. For one thing, there is less opportunity to be one's own boss, as the work force has come to be dominated by large corporations and the government, which attempt to maximize control and predictability at the expense of worker independence. The goal of efficiency has often made tasks simplified, fragmented, compartmentalized, and under continuous supervision, which results in worker alienation.

**Table 6.3   PERCENTAGES IN OCCUPATIONAL GROUPS WHO
WOULD CHOOSE SIMILAR WORK AGAIN**

Professional and lower white-collar occupations	%	Working-class occupations	%
Urban university professors	93	Skilled printers	52
		Paper workers	42
Mathematicians	91	Skilled autoworkers	41
Physicists	89	Skilled steelworkers	41
Biologists	89	Textile workers	31
Chemists	86	*Blue-collar workers, cross section*	24
Firm lawyers	85		
Lawyers	83	Unskilled steelworkers	21
Journalists (Washington correspondents)	82	Unskilled autoworkers	16
Church university professors	77		
Solo lawyers	75		
White-collar workers, cross section	43		

Source: Reprinted from *Work in America,* by the U.S. Department of Health, Education and Welfare, 1973, p. 16, by permission of the MIT Press, Cambridge, Mass.

Alienation exists when workers are unable to control their immediate work processes, to develop a sense of purpose and function which connects their jobs to the over-all organization of production, to belong to integrated industrial communities, and when they fail to become involved in the activity of work as a mode of personal self-expression. (Blauner, 1964:15)

Attention is usually focused on blue-collar work in studies of such alienation, as workers feel that their careers are blocked and manual labor is denigrated. An auto worker explains:

"If you were in a plant you'd see—everybody thinks that General Motors workers have it easy, but it's not that easy. Some jobs you go home after eight hours and you're tired, your back is sore and you're sweatin'. All the jobs ain't that easy. We make good money; yeah, the money is real good out there, but that ain't all of it—cause there's really a lot of bad jobs out there." (U.S. Department of Health, Education, and Welfare, 1973:37)

Dissatisfaction with the meaning of work is not restricted to manual labor, however. Low-level white-collar jobs held by college graduates in factorylike offices, such newly created occupations as medical technicians and computer keypunch operators, and middle-level managers all often lack autonomy and participation in decision making and overall goals. A former corporation executive comments:

"You felt like a small cog. Working there was dehumanizing and the struggle to get to the top didn't seem worth it. They made no effort to encourage your participation. The decisions were made in those rooms with closed doors. . . . The serious error they made with me was not giving me a glimpse of the big picture from time to time, so I could go back to my little detail, understanding how it related to the whole." (U.S. Department of Health, Education, and Welfare, 1973:48)

Sarason (1977) has suggested that even highly educated professionals, such as physicians, lawyers, and university professors, are finding increasing dissatisfaction from work. Physicians, for example, confront growing independence of new health professionals, heavy paper work and regulations, large bureaucratic settings for medical practice, and a decline in the attribution of godlike qualities to them by patients. Many professionals lose their autonomy, becoming mere functionaries in bureaucratic organizations. As such trends continue at all occupational levels, work will decreasingly be *the* organizing center in life. Even almost 30 years ago a study found that work was not the central life interest for three out of four industrial workers (Dubin, 1956). This means that we must be careful about predicting retirement troubles linked to loss of the work role itself.

Retirement as a Process

Although the general consequences of retirement seem relatively benign, the retirement experience is not necessarily simple or unimportant, or adjustment to it easy. Retirement is a *process* that affects one's life in many ways (Atchley, 1976a). Unfortunately, we know very little about the complexity of the retirement transition as it is experienced by individuals.

Retirement as an event is a rite of passage from the world of work. Rites of passage, such as baptisms, weddings, or graduations, are designed to publicly redefine an individual by symbolizing status change, thereby facilitating role transition (Rosow, 1974). The retirement event, however, is very informal and seldom an adequate rite of passage (Rosow, 1974; Atchley, 1976a). Atchley points out, for example, that ceremonies such as retirement dinners tend to focus on past achievements and expressions of gratitude rather than on attractions in store, as do weddings and graduation ceremonies. This is no doubt a reflection of the uncertain status of retirement as a role, but the nature of retirement ceremonies is highly variable.

> The social position of the individual who is retiring probably influences the likelihood that a retirement ceremony will take place and what it will consist of. For example, retiring professors who are well known in their fields are often given an impressive send-off with speeches, academic papers, and perhaps even a book of tributes to the work of the Great Man. These ceremonies can take as much as two or three days and draw colleagues and friends from a great distance. For the lesser-known professors and administrators, a faculty tea will usually do, and it is not uncommon to see several people being dispatched at one of these affairs. Finally, Old Charlie in the maintenance department is made the subject of a special coffee break, at which all of his co-workers look at their shoes while the boss tries to remember exactly what it was that Charlie did around there for all those years. (Atchley, 1976a:55)

Very little is known about the nature of other aspects of the retirement event—what the last day of work is like or the symbolization and impact of retirement gifts (Atchley, 1976a).

Retirement can also be thought of as a role, presumably involving various norms and expectations, rights and duties. There is considerable debate about whether old age and retirement are normless or roleless (see Chapter 3), but some argue that there are certain expectations of the retired—they should manage without assistance (not become dependent), live within their incomes—as well as certain rights involving economic support, freedom of time, and so on (Atchley, 1976a). We need a better understanding of the expectations that really do face retirees as they interact with friends, family, or former coworkers and the impact this aspect of the retirement role might have.

In viewing reactions to retirement, bear in mind that it is not simply a question of being retired or not being retired. Atchley (1976a) notes that there are phases in the retirement experience.

1. *Preretirement* As retirement approaches, workers develop expectations and fantasies about what it will be like. Relatively few formally prepare for retirement, but realistic expectations can make the transition smoother, whereas unrealistic fantasies can create difficulties. Workers may adopt a "short-timer's attitude" toward the job as they prepare to leave it. In a study of older workers, Goudy (1981) found that two fifths of those who did not expect to retire had retired four years later. Such changes and the ability to retire without becoming demoralized may reflect a loosening of bonds between the worker and his or her job. Cohn (1979), for example, found that older workers were less likely to say they would continue working if it was not financially necessary, despite being as satisfied with their jobs as younger workers. This was possible because job satisfaction was less important to overall well-being among older workers, perhaps because of the "life review" discussed in Chapter 4.

2. *Honeymoon* A euphoric period may follow retirement in which

people try to "do all of the things I never had time for before." The honeymoon period tends to be a busy time, filled with hunting, fishing, card playing, sewing, seeing the grandchildren (or greatgrandchildren) and traveling, all at the same time. A typical person in this phase says: "What do I do with my time? Why, I've never been so busy!" The person in the honeymoon period of retirement is often like a child in a room full of new toys. He flits from this to that, trying to experience everything at once. (Atchley, 1976a:68)

Some individuals never experience this because they cannot afford it or because they have very negative attitudes toward retirement and the leisure role. The honeymoon period may be quite short or last a considerable time.

3. *Disenchantment* If the individual fails to develop a satisfying, stable routine, disenchantment may set in—activities are limited by low income or poor health, he or she cannot adjust to freedom from work or is inadequately prepared for the realities of retirement. Retirement, after all, is more than just a long vacation; it may last 20 years or more, and feelings of emptiness and boredom can occur.

4. *Reorientation* In this period the individual "takes stock," assesses the realistic choices available, and tries to develop a satisfying routine. He or she may receive help in this from family, friends, and community groups (such as senior citizen clubs). Mutran and Reitzes (1981) found that community involvement was an important predictor of well-being in retirement, and retirement affected identity and self-esteem only indirectly to the extent that it affected this involvement.

5. *Stability* In this phase individuals achieve the capacity to deal routinely with retirement living and the changes that accompany it. They are aware of abilities and limits and can live self-sufficiently. However, Atchley is careful to point out that "Many people pass into this phase directly from the honeymoon phase; others reach it only after a painful reassessment of personal goals; others never reach it" (1976a:70).

6. *Termination* People may reach a stage where retirement per se is no longer a relevant concern. Some return to work, but termination is more likely the result of illness and disability. Thus the person moves from the retirement role to the role of "dependent."

These retirement phases constitute an ideal type. For example, some individuals may never experience disenchantment, others may experience little else. However, these phases indicate the variety of experiences retirement may entail for any individual. Such phases probably characterize all major role transitions; certainly, similar phases can be identified for marriage. More research needs to be done on the factors that affect people's experience of any of these phases and the timing of progress through them. There have been many studies of retirement, but there is still much to be learned about the *process* of retirement *as it is experienced by the individual.*

It is often assumed that retirement creates a void requiring *substitutes* for the satisfactions derived from work, as illustrated in the following statement:

> In summary, it appears fairly clear that most do not want more work as such, but meaningful substitutes for work—activities that are interesting, challenging, and enduring enough so that the person can find himself in them without assuming a lot of responsibility or enduring undue stress. Most elderly people want to keep thinking, to do useful things, and to stay active, the achievement of which requires reasonably complex tasks or activities that stimulate and reward for long periods of time—not just occasional entertainment. (Taves & Hansen, 1963:116)

But how often does work "stimulate and reward for long periods of time"? The fact that money and health are the most important determinants of retirement satisfaction raises doubts about this type of "substitution theory." It is more appropriate to view retirement adjustment as an ongoing accommodation to changes in the scheduling of activities and personal contacts, which may affect one's entire pattern of behavior—leisure, level of living, physical functioning, and self-concept (Shanas, 1972).

Related to this concept of accommodation, Sussman (1972) has proposed an analytical model that focuses on options available to the retiree and the extent to which those options are limited by societal and individual attributes. There are many optional new "careers" available to retirees—another work career, leisure, education—however, they may be limited by society and the nature of age stratification. Sussman's approach reminds us that retirement is not really roleless; rather, the choices themselves are not clearly prescribed. It is perhaps like buying a new car. We lack total freedom because our range of choices is shaped by the auto manufacturers, but we do confront many options: rack-and-pinion steering, radial tires, stratified-charge engines, and so on. These things sound very nice, but those of us who are not mechanics often feel that we are groping in the dark in choosing one over another. So it is with the retiree, who is unfamiliar with the new options presented by retirement. Viewed in this light, retirement can be seen as an extremely complex transition that often requires hard work, wrenching reassessment of one's life, and considerable time to move through the phases of retirement. That most retirees adapt satisfactorily is a testament to the resilience of older persons.

This also reminds us that retirement frees older persons for meaningful activity patterns that provide opportunities for personal growth. Those opportunities depend on the social context. Barfield and Morgan (1978) cite evidence that retirement satisfaction may be declining. A national survey in 1968 found that 75 percent of retirees were satisfied with retirement, and only 10 percent were dissatisfied; a comparable survey in 1976 found only 56 percent satisfied, and 22 percent dissatisfied. This may reflect period effects, such as rising inflation that eats away at retirement income. It may also reflect succeeding cohorts of older persons who are better prepared to make retirement an enriching experience and less satisfied with the available opportunities for doing so (Foner & Schwab, 1981). In either case we are reminded that the quality of retirement, as aging in general, depends on the context in which it occurs.

RETIREMENT INCOME

In modern societies, which pressure and encourage older workers to retire, retirement income becomes a major social issue. It was noted in Chapter 2 that low income is a major problem for the aged, and retirement typically brings reduced income. Parnes (1981), for example, found an average income decline of about 40 percent in the year following retirement. Financial security is also a major determinant of retirement satisfaction.

The family has traditionally assumed a major responsibility in supporting the aged, but this expectation has declined. A national survey found that only 11 percent of adults between the ages of 18 and 64 felt that children should support their parents during retirement (National Council on the Aging, 1975). Retired people can also support themselves through accumulated savings. We still expect people to make some financial arrangements, but many do not or cannot do so adequately. Thus group pensions have become commonplace in modern societies, as a type of insurance, which spread out the risk and uncertainty associated with retirement through collective arrangements.

Social Security

Compulsory old-age insurance has a long history, dating back to 1889 in Germany, 1906 in Austria, 1908 in Great Britain, and 1913 in Sweden. More than 130 countries now have some type of old-age/disability/survivor's program, and these programs constitute the single most important source of income for older people in industrialized societies (Lowy, 1980).

The United States was a latecomer to the provision of such insurance. Early in this century Teddy Roosevelt called the lack of old-age insurance an "outrage" on the conscience of the American people (Fischer, 1977). But there was great resistance to the idea of compulsory old-age pensions because of the fear that it would destroy the spirit of individual enterprise and lead to socialism. During the 1920s and 1930s, however, there was rising support for a social security program because of growing recognition of poverty among the aged. The Depression was particularly hard on the aged as high unemployment, insufficient savings and pensions, and inability of the family to provide support helped convince people that it was hard to adequately prepare for old age (Achenbaum, 1978). Political movements, such as the Ham and Eggs movement and the Townsend plan, began to pressure for change, and in the early 1930s received support from the American Federation of Labor and the Democratic and Republican parties. Despite counterpressure from chambers of commerce and associations of manufacturers, most states had at least rudimentary old-age insurance programs by 1933 (Fischer, 1977).

With the Social Security Act of 1935 the United States became the last major industrial country to establish a public retirement pension. This legislation, intended to create jobs for younger workers, was only secondarily motivated by humanitarian concern for the aged. The program was weak and ineffectual in comparison with other Western nations, but it has been strengthened considerably since 1935, expanding to include such programs as survivor's benefits, disability insurance, and the Medicare health program—OASDHI (old-age, survivors, disability, and health insurance). The number of persons covered by the program has also expanded. By 1950 about 65 percent of workers were covered by Social Security; this has now risen to nearly 95 percent, excluding only federal employees and some state and local government employees with other pension coverage, some charitable, religious, and educational institutions, and some low-income farm and domestic employees (Lowy, 1980). The number of Social Security retirement beneficiaries has risen from 148,000 in 1940, to 10.6 million in 1960, to 23.3 million in 1980. Changes in the system were incorporated in the 1972 Social Security Amendments that increased benefit levels, set up automatic cost-of-living increases (tied to the Consumer Price Index), and established *Supplemental Security Income* (SSI) to replace aid to the indigent aged, blind, and disabled. SSI establishes an income "floor" below which no aged person should fall.

The old-age pension embodied in Social Security has achieved legitimacy, therefore policymakers are reluctant to make changes for fear of raising questions about the entire system. The national poll conducted for the National Council on the Aging (1975) found that 81 percent of the public felt that "the government should help support older people with the taxes collected from all Americans," 76 percent felt older people should be provided with enough to live on "comfortably," and 97 percent agreed that there should be cost-of-living increases for Social Security. A more recent poll conducted by the Social Security Administration (1980) found that three quarters of the public would voluntarily join Social Security, and about the same proportion would object strongly to its abolition. This strong public support has been accompanied by expansion of the financial importance of the system, making it the largest income maintenance program in this country. By 1981, OASDHI represented about one fourth of the total federal budget, and $12.1 billion in OASI benefits alone was being paid monthly to 36 million persons. About 90 percent of older people receive benefits, and it is the major source of income for two thirds (Marsh, 1981). Without Social Security, poverty would be substantially greater among the aged. In 1977, 60 percent of older people would have been below the poverty line without social insurance programs (primarily Social Security), whereas these programs alone reduced poverty to 21 percent (Lowy, 1980).

Certain basic principles have been built into Social Security legislation. Great pains have been taken to avoid a "welfare" stigma (with apparent success), so there is no means test. Participation is compulsory for workers in designated groups because of the difficulties and uncertainties faced by individuals in preparing for retirement, predicting future needs, inflation, retirement age, life expectancy, and so on (Schulz, 1980). As society will ultimately have to support those who do not or cannot provide adequate income in old age, the risk is shared through compulsory social insurance.

This insurance combines both equity and adequacy. Individual benefits are tied to prior earnings and length of coverage under the system. Social Security has represented a good "buy" because the typical retiree has received total benefits that far exceed accumulated contributions (Clark & Spengler, 1980a). Schulz (1980) has estimated that the average middle-income worker would have to save about 20 percent of annual earnings to achieve the retirement benefits provided by Social Security. Social Security also redistributes income in two ways: (1) from the young to the old as taxes paid by current workers subsidize the retired; (2) from higher-income to lower-income workers through a weighted benefit structure. Although financial adequacy is one aspect of the benefit structure, the level of adequacy is rather low because the intent has not been to provide comfortable incomes through Social Security alone. In 1982 average retirement benefits from Social Security were $8340 for married couples and $4872 for single persons, clearly low incomes by most standards.

The pension system provided by Social Security includes the following elements:

1. Benefits are financed by payroll taxes paid by employers and employees on income up to a certain level. In 1982 this tax was 13.4 percent (6.70 percent withheld from employees) on the first $32,400 of income.
2. If persons under 70 receive wage and salary income above a certain level ($6000 in 1982), benefits are reduced by $1 for each additional $2 earned.

The level of this retirement test increases automatically with increases in wage levels.

3. Benefits are paid to persons who have worked for a minimum period of time on a covered job. There is a maximum benefit limited by the ceiling placed on earnings on which the worker had made contributions.

4. Reduced early retirement benefits may be received beginning at age 62. This has proven to be a popular option; in 1978, 68 percent of all older workers chose to retire early. Of course, early retirement benefits are an economic necessity for persons who are in poor health or are unemployed and cannot find other work. Workers who delay receiving benefits after age 65 have an additional 3 percent added to their benefits for each year they do not receive Social Security from 65 to 72.

5. Dependents and survivors of beneficiaries are also entitled to benefits. Wives and children receive a dependent benefit of 50 percent of the worker's basic benefit. Widowed persons receive the full benefits to which the worker was entitled. Various other dependents and survivors are eligible for benefits under certain conditions.

A number of questions have been raised in recent years about the Social Security system. One issue is the equity of coverage for certain groups, notably females and blacks. As benefits are based on earnings history, they tend to be lower for women and blacks because of more erratic or marginal work careers with lower earnings, and blacks also receive fewer benefits because of lower life expectancy. Housewives are dependent on their husbands' benefits because housekeeping yields no credit as work, and women divorced before 10 years of marriage are not entitled to any of their husbands' benefits. Working women often lose their own Social Security benefits because the spouse benefit is greater and they cannot receive both. Indeed, the spouse benefit itself has been criticized, as single persons and two-earner households receive proportionately less of their tax contributions. Holden (1979) notes that the spouse benefit provides greater rewards for not working to wives of higher-income workers. Munnell (1977) has suggested that the *family* be used as the basis for taxation and benefits, converting to a strictly wage-related program that divides pension credits between husbands and wives.

The payroll tax has also been criticized for being a regressive tax. As only the first $32,400 (in 1982) of income is taxed, those with higher incomes pay a lower proportion of their overall income. For example, a janitor earning $10,000 in 1982 pays 6.70 percent of that to Social Security, whereas an executive earning $100,000 pays only about 2.2 percent of the total income. Although the weighted benefit structure means that lower-income workers can expect to receive proportionately higher benefits when they retire, their life expectancy is also likely to be shorter. Additionally, evidence indicates that much or all of the employer's tax is shifted to workers through lower wages and fringe benefits (Clark & Spengler, 1980a).

Financing questions also relate to the adequacy of Social Security benefits. Current levels clearly fail to provide truly adequate standards of living, in both an absolute and a relative sense. It has been estimated that in order to maintain the same living standard in retirement as existed just prior to retirement, pensions should replace 80 percent of gross income for low-income workers, 70 percent for middle-income workers, and 65 percent for high-income workers (Clark & Spengler, 1980a), recognizing that expenses and taxes will be lower in retirement. In 1981 Social Security benefits replaced an average of 55 percent of the last monthly paycheck. This replacement level requires significant lowering of the standard of living of the typical retiree.

Although these issues are important, the most basic question about Social Security has concerned the solvency of the system itself. As with all pension systems, Social Security has a *trust fund* to support payment of benefits. This trust fund was accumulated during the early years of Social Security when more revenue was taken in from taxes than was paid out in benefits. By 1976, however, Social Security was paying out $4.3 billion more than it was taking in. Although legislation enacted in 1977 was expected to stabilize the system into the next century, projections four years later indicated that the trust fund would be depleted by the mid-1980s. This growing deficit is a consequence of many factors. Population aging, combining increased life expectancy with declining fertility, increases the dependency ratio. There were 16.5 workers for every beneficiary in 1950, but this had declined to 3.2 by 1982, and is expected to be as low as 2 by 2030 when the baby-boom cohort is eligible for Social Security. In addition to the growing older population, more people are retiring and choosing early retirement, and people are living longer after retirement. Benefits have also been increasing; real benefits from Social Security (after inflation) rose almost 45 percent between 1970 and 1977 (Bridges & Packard, 1981). The fiscal problems have been compounded in recent years by the combination of inflation, which increases benefits, and recession, which reduces tax revenues because of unemployment and lower wages. Concerns about "bankruptcy" of Social Security have affected faith in the system. The Social Security Administration (1980) survey found that 61 percent of workers had little confidence that funds would be available for their own retirement benefits.

It is not a realistic possibility that Social Security will go bankrupt because the ultimate guarantee of the solvency of Social Security is the taxing power of the federal government. But guaranteeing its solvency requires some hard decisions. Many possibilities have been suggested (Munnell, 1977; Ball, 1978). Increased revenues could be generated by increasing taxes or incorporating groups not currently covered by the system, such as federal employees. Benefits could be reduced in some fashion or be taxed. Even very wealthy recipients pay no taxes on Social Security benefits, and this tax exemption cost the system an estimated $4.7 billion in 1978 (Ball, 1978). Other proposals would increase the eligibility age for benefits, further reduce benefits for early retirees, increase the delayed retirement credit, or liberalize the retirement test to encourage older workers to remain longer in the labor force.

Part or all of OASDHI could be funded through general revenues from the income tax. It has been noted that Social Security involves the somewhat contradictory goals of forced "insurance" (basing benefits on past contributions) and "welfare" (using weighted benefits to redistribute income) (Hollister, 1974). Are these goals better pursued through separate programs? Canada and Sweden, for example, combine a flat pension from general revenues with an earnings-related contributory benefit (Ball, 1978).

Virtually all reforms of Social Security encounter resistance. There is reluctance to finance all or part of Social Security through general tax revenues for fear it will come to be viewed as "just another welfare program," thereby jeopardizing the strong political support and public legitimacy it currently enjoys. Reducing benefits, increasing eligibility ages, or increasing penalties for early retirement will bring hardship to some workers, especially as poor health is a major reason for retirement, and such proposals are opposed by retirees and their advocates. Increasing payroll taxes might stretch our willingness to support the aged beyond the breaking point. It is already estimated that one fourth of American families pay more in Social Security taxes than they do in income taxes. It is instructive to note, however, that the Social Security Administration (1980) survey found that only one fourth of the public considers the payroll tax too high, expressing more objections to the income, gasoline, and sales taxes. Nearly two thirds would prefer to increase taxes rather than reduce benefits, and respondents preferred to increase payroll taxes instead of using general revenues.

These issues surrounding the solvency of Social Security were debated within a National Commission on Social Security Reform. After lengthy arguments on the proper mix of reforms, this Commission issued a report in January 1983 which became the basis of legislation enacted in April 1983. Through a mixture of increased revenues and reduced benefits, this legislation was expected to improve the financing of the Old-Age and Survivors and Disability Insurance trust funds by $165 billion during the 1980s, and to eliminate a projected $1.9 trillion deficit in the old age and disability programs over the next 75 years. The major provisions of this legislation included:

1. Previously enacted increases in the payroll tax were accelerated, so that employees and employers will each pay 7.65 percent by 1990. The tax for self-employed persons will also be increased to 100 percent of the combined employee/employer tax.
2. One-half of Social Security benefits is included as taxable income if that brings total income above $25,000 ($32,000 for married couples).
3. The July 1983 cost-of-living adjustment was delayed until January 1984, with such adjustments to be made each January thereafter.
4. The revenue base was broadened by requiring federal employees hired in 1984 and thereafter to be in the Social Security system. Employees of nonprofit organizations will also be required to be in the system, and state and local government employees now covered may no longer withdraw from the system.
5. The age of eligibility for full benefits will increase gradually from 65 to 66 between 2003 and 2009, and to 67 between 2021 and 2027. The reduction in benefits for persons retiring at 62 will also increase from 20 percent to 25 percent in 2009, and to 30 percent in 2027.
6. The incentive to delay retirement after 65 will gradually increase from 3 percent to 8 percent for each year prior to 70 between 1990 and 2008.

The "retirement test" reduction of benefits for outside earnings above a certain level will also be reduced from $1 for every $2 to $1 for every $3 after 1990.

These are not necessarily the final answers, of course. For example, they do not deal with the Medicare component of the system, which is likely to represent the next "fiscal crisis." The reforms also assume that Social Security will at best operate at current levels, but other suggestions would increase benefits, thereby exacerbating the financial problems of the system. If Social Security is to provide an adequate retirement life, benefits will obviously have to increase to higher levels of income replacement. Although benefits are now adjusted for inflation, some people have suggested that benefits should also be adjusted for economic growth to give the aged their fair share of more prosperous standards of living in the society as a whole.

Social Security is an essential program that must and will continue. Not only are the aged a disproportionately low-income group, but their ability to improve their own financial situation is also quite restricted. Personal savings are a difficult, risky, and uncertain method of providing for one's retirement, and private pensions are still inadequate. Barriers to older persons working further contribute to the need for Social Security. Rather than tinkering with this or that aspect of the Social Security system, we need to decide just what we wish to accomplish through it—welfare or insurance, adequate income or supplement? There is a need to carefully consider goals in supporting retirees, how those goals are best achieved and financed, and how a Social Security system fits within the overall social programs and policies for the aged, and indeed how programs for the aged relate to other policies directed at the well-being of the population.

Job-Related Pensions

Although Social Security provides nearly universal coverage and constitutes the most important source of income for retirees, many older persons receive pensions specifically linked to their jobs. Such pensions were slow to develop in the United States (Fischer, 1977). The first private pension plan was established in 1875 by the American Express Company and was followed by railroad pension plans. Industrial corporations were slower to act, and it was not until the period from 1900 to 1915 that corporations such as U.S. Steel, Standard Oil, DuPont, and Westinghouse instituted pensions for their employees. However, these plans protected only a small minority of long-term, loyal employees, were viewed as a favor rather than a right, and were small and easily lost.

Public employees were even worse off.

The United States government treated its animals better than its human work force. Four-legged federal workers retired on full rations, much to the fury of many employees. John W. Perry, a postal worker, was astonished to read in his union newspaper that an artillery horse named Rodney was retired from active duty with full support to the end of his days. "For the purpose of drawing a pension," Perry wrote, "it would have been better had I been born a horse than a human being. I have been a 'wheel horse' for the Government for the past fifty years and can not get a pension." (Fischer, 1977:167)

Few police, firemen, or teachers were covered. The first pension coverage for federal civilian employees was provided by the Civil Service Retirement Act of 1920.

Prior to the enactment of Social Security, only 3 to 4 million workers were covered by private pensions. There has been tremendous recent growth in such coverage, however, for a variety of reasons, including continued industrialization of the economy, periodic wage freezes encouraging growth in fringe benefits, tax inducements (for example, the Revenue Act of 1942 made employer pension contributions tax deductible), a Supreme Court decision in 1949 that pensions were a proper issue for collective bargaining, recognition by unions of the need to supplement Social Security, and the development of multiemployer pension plans (Schulz, 1980). Pension coverage increased from 12 percent of the labor force in 1940 to over 40 percent currently (Schulz, 1980), although only one in five retirees receives a job-related pension (Soldo, 1980). In 1978 pension funds had $500 billion in assets and owned approximately 20 percent of the country's financial securities (Graebner, 1980).

Still, most workers are not covered by such pensions, which are more prevalent in large firms with higher wages and higher rates of unionization, particularly in communications, public utilities, mining, and manufacturing (Schulz, 1980; Beller, 1981). Most state and local government employees are covered by job-related pensions. Pension coverage is relatively low for women, blacks, and lower-income workers in small, nonunion plants and low-wage industries such as retail sales and services.

Job-related pensions have generally been designed as supplements to Social Security, resulting in low average benefits. A recent survey of 977 pension plans found that the average annual pension for a worker with 30 years of service was $2720, which replaced an average 22 percent of working income (Schulz et al., 1979). Although pension coverage has increased and benefit levels should improve as the plans mature, the rate of growth in coverage has slowed. Expansion to areas not yet covered may be difficult as this typically involves smaller firms with higher worker turnover and less financial security (Schulz, 1980).

Schulz provides a good overview of private pension characteristics. Most covered workers are in noncontributory plans (financed solely by the employer) because only employer contributions are tax free. Multiemployer plans cover only one third of the workers but are more prevalent in certain industries (mining, construction, trade, transportation, and service). Benefits are generally based on earnings or a combination of earnings and years of service. Eligibility age is usually between 60 and 65, although it may be as low as 50 or as high as 70. Survivor's benefits have been a problem because most plans reduce benefits to those who elect to protect their spouses. This is a particular problem for women as they are less likely to have pensions of their own.

A number of problems have been associated with job-related pensions. Such plans face fiscal difficulties similar to those of Social Security (Sheppard & Rix, 1977). Large cities face particular problems with pension systems, given the combination of increasing numbers of retirees, a shrinking tax base, and growing demands for other services. In the District of Columbia in 1976, for example, pensions for police and firemen represented 43 percent of the entire payroll. Job-related pensions are based on reserve funding to insure payment of benefits, but many plans are inadequately funded. In 1977 unfunded pension liabilities represented 22 percent of the net worth of General Motors and 185 percent of the net worth of Lockheed (Greenough, 1980); the unfunded liability for New York City in the mid-1970s was $6 billion (Sheppard & Rix, 1977). Until recently, pensions were not insured against the organization or its pension fund going bankrupt. When Studebaker went out of business, workers under 65 lost all the money they had paid into the company's pension fund.

Vesting provisions have also typically been inadequate. If a person is vested, he or she can leave the company before retirement age and still be guaranteed benefits. For example, a person could work for Firm A for 10 years, move to firm B until retirement at age 65, and then receive pensions from both firms based on years of service. In the past workers were required to remain until retirement or work for a long time (20 or 30 years) before any benefits were vested. Another problem is a lack of *portability*—that is, pension contributions and rights with one organization are not transferrable to another. Take the case of a worker who spends 20 years with one company and 20 years with another. Assuming full vesting of benefits with both companies, the combination of two 20-year-service pensions would amount to less than one 40-year-service pension with portability of the 20 years of service in the first company to pension rights in the second company.

The Employee Retirement Income Security Act (ERISA) was enacted in 1974 to address some of these issues. For example, all private pension plans must vest benefits according to one of three options so that all covered workers would be guaranteed a full pension upon retirement after 10 or 15 years with the company, regardless of whether they stayed until retirement. Vesting increased for pension participants aged 50 and over from 42 percent in 1972 to 68 percent in 1979 (Rogers, 1981). The legislation also strengthens standards for financing and administering pension plans and has new requirements for disclosure to participants and the Social Security Administration. The Pension Benefit Guarantee Corporation offers insurance to workers whose pension plan collapses because of insufficient funds. Tax-exempt *individual retirement accounts* (IRAs) were also created for workers without pension coverage, and 1981 legislation extended these to virtually all workers.

Important gaps remain, however. Pension plans are still voluntary, leaving over half the private work force uncovered. Indeed, a number of small pension plans were terminated following passage of ERISA (Meier, 1979). State and local government plans are not covered by the law. Although these plans generally provide higher benefits than private pensions, they are also more seriously underfunded (King, 1978). Pension coverage remains low for women and low-income workers, and IRAs have been used primarily by workers earning $50,000 or more

(Schulz, 1981). Portability remains low, which penalizes worker mobility and career change. Access to survivor's benefits is also inadequate. Finally, few job-related pensions are protected against inflation. This is a major concern because persons can expect to be retired for 15 or 20 years. At a 10 percent inflation rate, for example, every $100 of pension income is worth only $39 after 10 years and $15 after 20 years (Clark & Spengler, 1980b).

Pension Policy

There are clearly many issues concerning retirement income support that must be addressed in the future. The financial problems we have discussed are common to the pension systems of all societies. Indeed, social insurance programs are generally more comprehensive in European countries, incorporating general programs such as unemployment compensation and national health insurance, so that taxes are often much higher than in the United States. In 1978, for example, payroll taxes in the Netherlands were 22.85 percent on employees and 26.51 percent on employers (Foner & Schwab, 1981).

The rising costs of pension systems are a natural accompaniment of the aging of populations with rising dependency ratios. Although there is concern over the short-term fiscal integrity of Social Security, much greater difficulties will occur around 2020 when the postwar baby-boom cohort becomes eligible for pension benefits. The twentieth century has seen the encouragement of more and earlier retirement. Indeed, retirement before the age of 65 is now the norm. Society may have to reverse itself, developing mechanisms that allow and encourage less and later retirement. Sheppard and Rix (1977) suggest that retirement *age* is the critical variable in pension policy. The age at which people retire is a major determinant of the overall cost of pension systems and is perhaps more amenable to manipulation. Later retirement can be encouraged by fostering greater job retraining and redesign as well as flexible work policies, such as job rotation or job sharing; by raising pension eligibility ages or increasing financial penalties for early retirement; by increasing financial incentives for delayed retirement; and so on. As an indication of the importance of retirement age, Sheppard and Rix (1977) indicate that the number of persons aged 62 to 64 will increase by 48 percent between 2000 and 2010. Will those persons be working and support pensions, or will they be retired and receive benefits?

Another basic issue in pension policy concerns the mix of income sources. The United States has a four-tiered system of retirement income: (1) needs-tested welfare programs, (2) contributory social insurance (OASI), (3) job-related pension plans, and (4) private savings (Greenough, 1980). People who are able to combine the latter three sources have comfortable retirement income, but each source separately is generally insufficient. Average income in 1978 was $9190 for persons receiving Social Security and a private pension, and such workers are able to achieve adequate income replacement (60 to 80 percent). But income was only $4210 for persons receiving only Social Security and income replacement was much lower (Marsh, 1981; Schulz, 1981). Approximately one third of persons receiving only Social Security have incomes below the poverty level (Soldo, 1980).

Nonpension sources generally contribute very little to retirement income.

What is the best mixture of public and private pensions? We have already seen some of the criticisms of Social Security. Private pensions do have certain advantages, notably their flexibility to the needs and desires of different worker groups and the investment of pension funds in the national economy, but numerous problems are associated with them: it is difficult to cover all workers, pensions are usually not inflation-proof, administrative costs are relatively high, and portability is difficult to achieve (Schulz, 1976). Social Security has the advantages of low costs—administrative expenses were only 1.5 percent of contributions in 1980—nearly universal coverage combined with cost-of-living adjustments, and guarantee of the financial integrity by the taxing power of the government that allows benefits to be provided without the large reserves needed to cover private pensions. Schulz (1981) has suggested that public and private programs could be better integrated, increasing Social Security benefits for lower- and middle-income workers who have less private coverage, and increasing income protection for those who are most disadvantaged under the present arrangements—single workers, widows, and two-worker couples.

Finally, it must be recognized that the current system of retirement income support is far from ideal, even with its financial problems. An ideal pension system might include the following: a guaranteed minimum income, higher levels of income replacement, universal coverage with immediate vesting and portability, full insurance of benefits, full survivor's benefits, and escalators tying benefits to the cost of living and general improvements in productivity and living standards (Schulz et al., 1974; Butler, 1975). Acceptance of such a plan, however, is clearly a long time in the future, if it ever occurs.

PREPARATION FOR RETIREMENT

It is clear that retirement generally represents a considerable change in patterns of living for most people. But older people usually adjust reasonably well to this change and ambiguity. Streib and Schneider (1971) suggest three reasons for this: (1) the roleless role actually has multiple role possibilities from which to choose, (2) ambiguity may itself be protective by reducing demands on the aged and making them more free, and (3) there is always the possibility for "reliving" past roles (reminiscing) or achieving vicarious gratification (through children or grandchildren). Thus,

A clearly defined role facilitates activity and gives a sense of security to a person involved in a network of impersonal universalistically oriented judgements and evaluations. This may not be the kind of world in which many older people live. In the later years of life, the *important* persons in one's life—friends and relatives—know who the older person is and, therefore, he moves in a world that is familiar to him, and with which he is familiar. He may not need a sharply defined extra-familial "role" to give him an identity or to facilitate his own activity in his everyday world. We suggest, therefore, that so far as the older person himself is concerned, his willingness to leave the work force and perhaps his satisfaction with other aspects of life are not dependent upon whether he has a clearly defined alternative role or not. (Schneider, 1964:56)

However, any role transition is facilitated by "anticipatory socialization," through which people learn what to expect as well as what to desire from a new role (Rosow, 1974), and lack of preparation or unrealistic expectations will certainly have an impact on the retirement experience. There are many aspects of retirement that can benefit from planning—financial, health, social, marital. Prospective retirees need to develop a greater understanding of the options available to them, as well as competence in selecting options and handling interactions with the many bureaucracies that affect retirement. A substantial minority of workers find retirement difficult, and others approach it with fear or resistance that, although it may later prove excessive, makes the transition more difficult.

The Prevalence of Preparation

Most people do little definite planning for retirement. The National Council on the Aging study (1975) compared what people 65 and over said were "very important" steps that ought to be taken to prepare for one's later years with those steps they had actually taken (Table 6.4). Some steps, particularly those involving health and income, had generally been taken, but this may not have occurred *before* retirement. Some things, such as building up savings, have to be started rather early in life. The study found that 35 percent had not prepared a will, 65 percent had not sought information from older people, and 92 percent had not participated in formal preparation programs. Older blacks and those with low incomes were least likely to have prepared.

When asked what they would have done differently to prepare for old age, people were most likely to indicate a need for more savings and investments (26 percent) and more or better education (14 percent) (National Council on the Aging, 1975). Finances should certainly be a focus for any planning effort. One study of a large manufacturing corporation found that most workers expected financial difficulties in retirement and were willing to save (Morrison, 1976). Few of them were able to save very much, however, and most had unrealistic expectations about postretirement earnings. There was a general lack of good information on which to base financial planning. The fact that education was mentioned second in the NCOA study suggests that the use of time and possession of skills and interests that withstand aging are important concerns.

There appear to be social class differences in retirement preparation (Simpson et al., 1966b; Atchley, 1976a). Upper-status workers, who are more reluctant to retire, see little need for formal preparation because they are used to manipulating their world. Semiskilled workers may be more fatalistic and in any case have less access to formal programs, but there is evidence that they are interested in preretirement programs (Fillenbaum, 1971b). Exposure to retirement information is greatest among middle-status workers, who tend to be favorably disposed to retirement and work in organizations with preretirement programs. Such workers may also give greater thought to retirement because they have greater

Table 6.4   PUBLIC 65 AND OVER WHO CONSIDER STEPS "VERY IMPORTANT" COMPARED WITH THOSE WHO HAVE ALREADY TAKEN STEPS

	Percentage who consider step "Very important"	Percentage who have already taken step
Make sure you'll have medical care available	88	88
Build up your savings	85	73
Learn about pensions and Social Security benefits	85	87
Prepare a will	79	65
Buy your own home	75	74
Develop hobbies and other leisure-time activities	61	62
Decide whether you want to move or continue to live where you are	53	72
Talk to older people about what it's like to grow old	27	35
Plan new part-time or full-time jobs	26	16
Enroll in retirement counseling or preparation programs	19	8
Move in with children or other relatives	7	9

Source: The Myth and Reality of Aging in America, 1975, published by The National Council on the Aging, Inc. a study prepared for The National Council on the Aging, Inc. (NCOA), Washington, D.C. by Louis Harris and Associates, Inc., © 1975, p. 120. Reprinted by permission.

flexibility in the timing of retirement and in the life-styles they will be able to lead (McPherson & Guppy, 1979). Those who do such planning and feel better prepared for retirement tend to have more favorable attitudes toward retirement while working and following retirement (Glamser, 1981a).

Preretirement Counseling

Preretirement counseling is a relatively new phenomenon that is still not very widespread. Glamser (1981b) indicates that only about 15 percent of even large companies have comprehensive preretirement programs, and less than half appear to have any form of preretirement program (Siegel & Rives, 1980). Most programs are limited, involving little more than information about retirement options and Social Security and pension benefits. Most are also geared for literate, middle-income workers, which may limit their usefulness (Atchley, 1976a). This is unfortunate, because Simpson and associates (1966b) found that exposure to information about retirement was particularly likely to encourage planning among semiskilled workers.

Obviously there are many things on which such programs could focus.

"Hard" information, particularly regarding finances and health, should always be a priority. Financial programs such as Social Security and job-related pensions, as well as health and social services for older people, can be very confusing. Ideally, such programs should also help ease the social and psychological transition from work to retirement and foster flexibility, as retirement is a varied and changing experience. Preretirement programs, especially those involving group discussions, offer an excellent opportunity to explore the individual's attitudes toward work and retirement and to help people deal more effectively with situations encountered following retirement. Peers in one's retiring cohort, and those who have retired earlier, can offer helpful suggestions and serve as role models and a particularly important source of anticipatory socialization.

There is evidence that preretirement counseling can be effective (Atchley, 1976a). Presumably, adjustment to retirement is enhanced by better preparation and more realistic expectations, resulting in higher postretirement involvement, lower job deprivation, better self-rated health, and greater satisfaction with retirement income.

Although preretirement programs seem to be helpful, little is known about the relative usefulness of different types. A study by Glamser and DeJong (1975) exemplifies the type of research needed. They randomly assigned older workers at six glass-manufacturing plants into three groups:

1. A control group with no preretirement counseling.
2. An individual briefing program involving booklets and an individual meeting with the personnel manager.
3. A group discussion program of eight sessions on the meaning of work and retirement, Social Security and Medicare, financial planning, health, leisure, family and friends, and living arrangements.

Participants in the group discussion program gained significantly more information about Social Security, Medicare, income, and health. Surprisingly, individual briefing was no more effective in teaching this information than no program at all. Workers in the group discussion program were more likely to feel prepared, and data in Table 6.5 indicate that they were more likely to plan and prepare for retirement (for example, make a will and talk over plans with spouse). Individual briefing was only slightly better than the control group in fostering such preparations. A similar study by Tiberi and associates (1978) also found that individual and "classroom" models of preretirement programs were less effective than group discussion.

Compared with control groups, preretirement programs do not appear to have much effect on overall morale or attitudes toward retirement (Glamser & DeJong, 1975; Tiberi et al., 1978). A six-year follow-up of the Glamser and De-Jong study also found no differences in length of time required to adjust to retirement, attitudes toward retirement, or life satisfaction (Glamser, 1981b). It may be unrealistic to expect short-term preretirement programs to contribute in a general way to long-term retirement adjustment. Such programs can help meet informational and emotional needs during the immediate transition from worker to retiree, however, by stimulating actual and perceived adequacy of preparation

Table 6.5 SELECTED RETIREMENT PREPARATION ACTIVITIES
UNDERTAKEN, BY TYPE OF PRERETIREMENT
PROGRAM (PERCENTAGE)

Activity	Group discussion	Individual briefing	Control group
Have figured out retirement income	63	55	35
Talked over retirement plans with spouse	90	35	55
Have made a will	63	35	30
Have reviewed insurance policies	52	22	30
Try to eat a well-balanced diet	79	65	50
Have arranged for health insurance	42	30	20
Have worked out ways to cut expenses	79	35	20
Have checked house for safety hazards	58	40	30
Have done some reading about retirement	79	70	35
Saving a little more money lately	79	52	50

Source: Francis Glamser and Gordon DeJong, "The Efficacy of Preretirement
Preparation Programs for Industrial Workers," *Journal of Gerontology* 30 (1975), p. 599.
Reprinted by permission.

for retirement (Morrow, 1981). Employers also cite such benefits as heightened
worker morale or loyalty and improved company image associated with preretirement programs (Siegel & Rives, 1980).

Some orientation to retirement should begin very early in life, when attitudes and expectations are first being formed, and formal programs concerned
with financial planning and the creative use of leisure time could begin at age
45. The transition into retirement could also be made more gradual through
shorter work weeks or longer vacations as workers near retirement.

This implies that preparation for, and adjustment to, retirement is the result
of lifelong patterns, and how to use time meaningfully cannot be taught suddenly.
Such capabilities must be carefully cultivated, but our age stratification system
has created a sudden transition into retirement and made available relatively few
options.

SUMMARY

Work is a central involvement shaping the life course. Work experiences affect
work values and attitudes, as persons select and are socialized by their occupations. Work experiences also affect nonwork attitudes and behaviors, and work
careers constitute an arena in which individuals confront their own aging. Thus
occupation is an important source of variation in the aging experience.

Many older people continue to work even after retiring from their primary occupation. The ability and desire to do so depends on occupation, family situation, health, and other considerations. In most respects older workers are as capable as younger workers and seem to be more committed to their work (for various reasons). Nevertheless, the potential for physical decline and job obsolescence create difficulties for older workers, and little has been done in this society to facilitate career changes at any age. High unemployment among older workers is partly due to their relatively low education, poor health, and inefficient job-seeking techniques, but it is also caused by age discrimination in hiring and employment services.

Retirement is a product of modern, industrialized societies. Structural transformations in the economy create skill obsolescence among older workers, remove individuals from the retirement decision, and result in new personnel policies that both "push" and "pull" toward retirement. The emergence of retirement and pension systems also represents efforts by industry to achieve efficiency and worker loyalty. It may also be that work is less meaningful than in the past, particularly when age no longer lends prestige to the older worker, creating less attachment to work and greater willingness to retire in the context of an emerging "retirement ethic."

Individual retirement decisions are shaped by many factors. Mandatory retirement directly affects relatively few workers. Poor health is a major reason for retirement, but there is also evidence of growing attractiveness of retirement and leisure. The availability of pension income is also a major factor in the retirement decision.

It has been suggested that retirement is a major crisis for social and personal identity, but most adults expect and desire to retire. Such attitudes are affected by occupational status and age. In addition, most retirees appear to adjust to retirement, with health and income being the primary determinants of retirement satisfaction. Relatively few people miss their jobs; but if they do, it is often because of a lack of alternative activities and associations. Retirement does offer rewards—leisure pursuits, independence, relaxation from responsibilities. Blue-collar workers have more problems adjusting to retirement because of financial difficulties and greater social disruption. The assumption that retirement is a male problem is unfounded, and women may actually have more difficulty adjusting to retirement than men.

One reason for the relatively unremarkable consequences of retirement is the fact that work is not necessarily a central life interest. There is growing evidence that blue-collar and white-collar work is becoming less meaningful and satisfying. Thus we must be careful in assessing the "loss" felt at retirement.

Retirement is a complex process. Individuals may face a variety of retirement phases—preretirement, honeymoon, disenchantment, reorientation, stability, and termination. The bonds between workers and jobs may loosen prior to retirement, and retirement adjustment is a matter of overall accommodation to changes in one's patterns of living.

Retirement income is a major concern because families and individuals often cannot or do not provide adequate finances. The Social Security Act of 1935 has been expanded to include nearly 95 percent of the aged. This program has strong public support and it has become the largest income maintenance program in the United States. Social Security is a contributory insurance program that also redistributes income, seeking to combine equity and adequacy. Questions have been raised about the equity of the system for various groups, particularly women and minorities. The major concerns have related to the fiscal integrity of the Social Security system. Financial problems have been created by the aging of the population, the growing prevalence of retirement, and recessionary economic trends. Legislation passed in 1983 combined revenue increases and benefit reductions designed to protect the solvency of the system.

Coverage from private pensions has grown considerably in recent years, although these pensions still involve only a minority of all workers and average benefits are rather low. The Employee Retirement Income Security Act of 1974 was enacted as a response to financial irregularities and problems of vesting and portability. This legislation outlines vesting requirements, strengthens requirements for managing pension plans, and provides pension insurance. Many problems remain with private pensions, however, such as expansion of coverage and portability.

Current pension policy contains four parts: welfare programs, social insurance, job-related pensions, and savings. Those who are able to combine income sources are generally comfortable, but Social Security alone is seldom adequate. There is clearly a need for improved integration of public and private pension programs.

Although the ambiguity of the retirement role may be overstated, preparation for any role change is advisable. Most people do little planning for retirement, however. Financial expectations seem to be a particular problem. Exposure to retirement information is greatest among middle-status workers. In general, preretirement counseling is relatively new and not widespread and is likely to be limited in scope, despite the need for social and psychological preparation as well as the provision of information on health and finances. Retirement preparation should be thought of as a lifelong process, and there are indications that preretirement counseling can produce a more positive transition into retirement.

chapter 7

The Use of Time: Opportunities and Constraints

This century has witnessed a steady growth in the amount of free time with shorter workweeks and longer vacations. The average workweek for males has declined from nearly 60 hours in 1900 to approximately 40 hours now. The emergence of retirement in particular has created a new "leisure class." This trend is reflected in Figure 7.1. The time of older persons is less structured by work and family roles, with a blurring of the distinction between *obligatory* (required) and *discretionary* (free) uses of time (Lawton, 1978). How this time is used is likely to have important consequences for overall enjoyment of life.

Aging and age stratification present critical challenges to the use of time (Ward, 1982a). Older people may be cast adrift from familiar worlds and identities by retirement, widowhood, declining health, residential change, and so on. How people use their time to accommodate to these disruptions of their normal styles of living will determine the nature of their aging experience. Release from normal, expected, or obligatory activity patterns may open new outlets for creativity, experimentation, self-expression, and personal growth, but we have already seen that the psychological consequences of old age are often constriction, disengagement, defensiveness, and passivity. The reasons for this involve limitations in options for using time as well as barriers and constraints in using those options.

The factors affecting the use of time correspond to some of the major themes and topics of this book. Aging frees time for new uses, but at the same time may create barriers of poor health or low income. Aging may also change the meaning and perception of time. We noted in Chapter 4 that there may be a changing time perspective, from "time since birth" to "time yet to live." The possibility of death

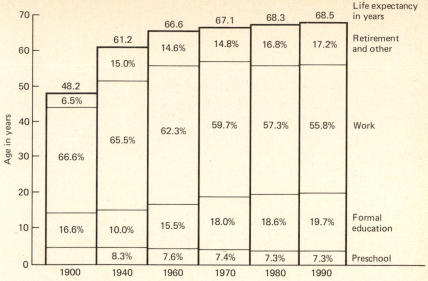

Figure 7.1 Lifetime distribution of education, work, and leisure for American men, from 1900 projected through 1990. (*Source:* "The Future of Retirement and Lifetime Distribution of Work," by Fred Best. Reprinted courtesy of *Aging and Work,* Summer 1979, Volume 2, Number 3, copyrighted and published by the National Council on the Aging, Inc., Washington, D.C.)

becomes an organizer of time, and Chapter 12 will discuss the sources and consequences of perceptions of limited remaining time associated with perceived nearness of death. Such orientations affect perceptions about the feasibility of available options for using time. There are some indications that the sense of time is speeded up for older people, perhaps reflecting a feeling that time is "running out." For example, experimental studies find that older persons underestimate time intervals (Wallach and Green, 1968; Levy, 1979).

Aging persons are also prisoners of their own pasts in at least two respects. First, each of us enters old age with particular personalities and styles of living through which we assess the appropriateness for ourselves of alternative roles and activities. Second, our membership in a specific cohort shapes our use of time through shared socialization and historical experiences. Whereas current cohorts of older people have relatively low levels of education, have been brought up on the work ethic, may have experienced greater religious socialization in childhood, and so on, the activity patterns of succeeding cohorts can be expected to change.

One of the most important factors affecting the use of time by older persons is the social context within which choices are made. Options are restricted by the prevailing age stratification system in modern societies. In the broadest sense this means that the choice between activity or disengagement is determined by the society, so that restricted role opportunities account for the social and psychological withdrawal of many older people. Age stratification also channels activities through the relative availability of leisure pursuits, voluntary associations, service roles, and the like in more subtle ways, however. Therefore the roles and activities of older people are a product of the complex interaction of personal history and preference, cohort differences, age-related opportunities and constraints, and the patterns facilitated or constrained by age stratification.

LEISURE

Leisure is a term that is recognizable and difficult to define. Clearly we view leisure as "nonwork," but not all such activity is truly leisure. There may be complex relationships between work and nonwork activities (Kelly, 1972). Some things are done as preparation for, or recuperation from, work, whereas others are engaged in as compensation for work (travel as an escape from factory work) or because it is expected of us (the businessman who belongs to Rotary). Still other pursuits are more freely chosen but still related to work (reading by college professors or the business golf game). *Unconditional leisure* refers to activities that are not escapes or work-related, but are engaged in as ends in themselves (Kelly, 1972). Thus leisure partly implies activity with a minimum of obligation. It is *expressive* activity, engaged in for its intrinsic satisfactions (Gordon et al., 1976). Leisure is also expected to be pleasant, although it may at times make us unhappy (when we lose a game or fail to master a musical instrument).

These meanings of leisure can be seen in the following definition:

> Leisure is an activity—apart from the obligations of work, family, and society—to which the individual turns at will, for either relaxation, diversion, or broadening his experiences and his spontaneous social participation, the free exercise of his creative capacities. (Dumazedier, 1967:16–17)

Thus leisure is defined by freedom of choice and intrinsic motivation (Kleiber & Kelly, 1980). The most desired activities are performed for their own sake, involving such inherent rewards as self-determination and feelings of competence (Iso-Ahola, 1980). Work is not the only source of creativity, sociability, or self-respect, and many people may be turning elsewhere for meaningful self-expression. The study of leisure therefore is important to an understanding of the meanings and satisfactions of life itself, particularly for the retired.

These definitions also indicate that leisure may have many functions. Pursuits such as meditation, hobbies, and spectator sports can provide relaxation, diversion, entertainment, or escape. Other activities provide opportunities for personal growth and development (cultural events, travel, artistic pursuits, education). Another form of leisure described by Kaplan (1975) is service to others, although we do not often think of volunteer roles as leisure. Finally, *sensual transcendence,* activities that provide an intense peak experience, such as highly competitive sports and sexual activity, may be an objective of some leisure activity (Gordon et al., 1976). What relationships do these options for meaning and satisfaction in leisure have to the aging experience?

Leisure and the Life Cycle

It would not be surprising to find that the use of time varies by age, if only because age is related to income, education, and other social characteristics. The quality of leisure time is also different for older people—the time available to them for leisure is greater and less fragmented (Kaplan, 1975). Leisure patterns are also related to age in that they may contribute to achievement of the developmental issues and tasks facing persons at different stages in the life cycle, and in any case will be shaped by the needs and preoccupations of each stage (Rapoport & Rapoport, 1975; Kelly, 1981). Kelly notes that leisure operates throughout the life course to assist in accommodating to changing personal investments, roles, and identities.

The relationship of leisure to developmental tasks can be seen in many ways. The play and games of childhood provide rehearsal for adult roles ("playing house"), opportunities to learn cooperation with others (think of the cooperation needed for a successful neighborhood football game), and reinforcement of personal competence and self-enterprise. Adolescents are concerned with developing personal identity, so their leisure pursuits involve exploration of the environment and sampling of new experiences. Young adults, on the other hand, leave age-graded groups to identify with more general social institutions. Leisure may be complementary to family and work, enriching these roles and relationships (Kelly, 1981). Interests may also come to focus more narrowly on occupation and family, rather than that broader interests are developed that can be sustained into middle age and retirement. During the thirties and forties, when one's life becomes structured by work and family, leisure patterns often become very home- and family-centered. People transfer habits from other contexts into their free time (work in another form, family activities, work-related citizenship roles) rather than developing new or creative patterns in the use of time. This may create problems in late middle age, leaving people unprepared for the new opportunities for expansion and enjoyment created by the empty nest and the winding down of the work career. This is illustrated by the following comment from a middle-aged housewife:

> You lose something of yourself by getting too involved in a house and children. The more you do, the more you want to do. My husband says I sound like I'm searching for something—well, there's so much to do, and you can waste it doing nothing. (Rapoport & Rapoport, 1975:257)

A study by Lowenthal and associates (1975) found middle-aged persons to be particularly concerned about channeling their energies into new goals and activities.

Leisure is also likely to play an important role in adjustment to old age. With retirement, for example, we have seen that accommodation to disrupted familiar patterns involves choosing among optional new "careers" in the use of time. Thus a major function of leisure in old age is the search for new sources of personal meaning and social integration to replace earlier sources that have been lost (Rapoport & Rapoport, 1975; Newman & Newman, 1979). A sense of "ego integrity" may require satisfaction in leisure roles, facilitating acceptance of a "nonproductive" role (Kleiber & Kelly, 1980). We need to look at the patterns older people use to achieve these goals and their relative success.

Patterns of Leisure in Old Age

The most obvious point to make is that older people have more potential nonwork time available to them. This time is not necessarily "free," however. Leisure is an element of life-style and as such is related to and constrained by social class, education, age, sex, and many other social characteristics (Zablocki & Kanter, 1976). Reflecting familiarity and lifelong preferences, leisure interests and activities are quite stable over time (Teague, 1980; Bossé & Ekerdt, 1981). Activity patterns found in one study (Table 7.1) indicate that there are many similarities between younger and older people in activities such as socializing, reading, gar-

Table 7.1 AGE DIFFERENCES IN PERSONALLY SPENDING "A LOT OF TIME" DOING VARIOUS ACTIVITIES, AND PUBLIC PERCEPTIONS THAT "MOST PEOPLE OVER 65" SPEND "A LOT OF TIME" DOING VARIOUS ACTIVITIES (PERCENTAGES)

	Personally spend a "lot of time"		Believe older people spend a "lot of time"
	18–64	**65 and over**	
Socializing with friends	55	47	52
Caring for younger or older members of the family	53	27	23
Working part-time or full-time	51	10	5
Reading	38	36	43
Sitting and thinking	37	31	62
Gardening or raising plants	34	39	45
Participating in recreational activities and hobbies	34	26	28
Watching television	23	36	67
Going for walks	22	25	34
Participating in sports, like golf, tennis or swimming	22	3	5
Sleeping	15	16	39
Participating in fraternal or community organizations or clubs	13	17	26
Just doing nothing	9	15	35
Doing volunteer work	8	8	15
Participating in political activities	5	6	9

Source: Adapted from *Myth and Reality of Aging in America,* copyright 1975, published by The National Council on the Aging, Inc. a study prepared by Louis Harris and Associates, Inc., pp. 57, 59. Reprinted by permission.

dening, and clubs. Table 7.1 also indicates a tendency by the public to exaggerate the passivity of older people (sleeping, just doing nothing, sitting and thinking).

There is evidence in Table 7.1, however, that some activities are related to age. Some differences, such as caring for family members and working, are quite natural accompaniments of role changes in later life. Other changes are more gradual throughout the life cycle. High leisure participations, particularly in activities outside the home or requiring exertion, tend to peak between 20 and 29, declining consistently thereafter (Gordon et al., 1976). But other differences represent limitations placed on the use of free time by older people. Indeed, a longitudinal study of retirees found that they overestimated the levels of activity they would have when retired (Bossé & Ekerdt, 1981). Although level of activity does not typically show significant decline until the seventies and eighties (Gordon et al., 1976), poor health, low income, and role loss may all disrupt activity patterns. And whereas the aged engage in a wide variety of leisure pursuits, some older people find that they have little to do.

Older persons are more likely to engage in solitary and sedentary pursuits (watching television, reading, sitting and thinking) and are less likely to engage in active and enriching behaviors (sports, cultural events) (Lawton, 1978; Kaplan, 1979; Bossé & Ekerdt, 1981; Moss & Lawton, 1982). In their study of time budgets, Moss and Lawton found that only 28 percent of the waking time of a community sample was spent in active interchange with other persons and an average of 7 hours a day was spent in relatively passive discretionary activities; watching television was the most engaged-in activity (3 hours), followed by relaxation (2 hours). A considerable amount of time was also spent on such obligatory activities as shopping, housework, and personal care. Moss and Lawton note that older persons with health impairments spend more time on these routine activities and also find them harder to perform; such persons are particularly in need of greater novelty in their lives.

It is clear that age-related decrements reduce the extent to which traditional leisure activities may be pursued, with "free" time often filled by obligatory and sedentary activities. Because of limitations on mobility, older people are inclined to feel that restaurants, theaters, parks, and libraries are inconvenient to get to and are less likely to utilize these community facilities (National Council on the Aging, 1975). There are undoubtedly also cohort differences in leisure preferences related to early socialization experiences, educational levels, and historical fads. Younger cohorts may view leisure in general as more meaningful and be receptive to a wider variety of pursuits. Lawton (1978) has suggested that more obligatory, less expressive orientations toward the use of time prevail among older cohorts.

As older people are heavy users of the mass media, particular attention has been given to this leisure activity (Atkins, 1976; Kubey, 1980). Although television represents the single most time-consuming leisure activity of older people, they watch television only slightly more often than younger groups. Preferences are also related to age, however. Older people are more likely than younger people to select programs with serious, informational content, including news programs, documentaries, and travelogues. In this respect television represents more than just a way to pass the time; perhaps it can partly compensate for a shrinking social world by providing electronic contact with the larger community. Older people also appear to prefer "personal" nonfiction programs (variety shows, quiz programs) rather than detective dramas or love stories. Their "captive" status is reflected in a generally enthusiastic and uncritical attitude toward television content (Kubey, 1980). But as noted in Chapter 5, television has not provided a particularly enlightened view of aging and older people.

Older people are not all alike, of course, so one would expect variations in activity according to such characteristics as sex, education, and ethnicity. Older men are more likely to participate in sports, fishing, travel, and gardening, whereas women more frequently favor "cultural production" (handiwork and crafts), television watching, socializing, and reading (Gordon et al., 1976; Payne & Whittington, 1976).

Socioeconomic status is another important determinant of overall life-style, including leisure pursuits. The activities of lower-status persons are more likely to include television watching, family socializing, hunting, fishing, and hobbies, often in same-sex groups, whereas higher-status people are more likely to prefer clubs and organizations, cultural events, travel, and parties (Havighurst, 1973; Gordon et al., 1976). These patterns are partly due to income differences, but they also reflect more basic differences in life-style. The life-styles of the middle class appear to be more community-oriented, whereas those of the working and lower classes are more home-centered (Havighurst & Feigenbaum, 1959).

This catalogue of activities engaged in by the elderly tells us only what they do, not what *satisfactions* are derived from leisure patterns or what *functions* they serve, nor what the elderly are *capable* of doing with a wider range of options. More important than the "what" of leisure is the "so what?" We need to consider the meanings of leisure patterns and their consequences for the aging experience.

The Functions of Leisure

We all have leisure pursuits we consider trivial and others we feel are as important as anything we do. For some of us, home repairs are just a chore; for others, they represent a creative outlet and a source of self-worth.

Characteristics of free-time activities vary widely. For example, they vary according to whether they involve the following: (1) autonomy (or are other-directed), (2) creativity, (3) enjoyment (or are simply time killers), (4) opportunities to develop talents, (5) instrumental ("productive") as opposed to expressive (emotional) outlets, (6) physical energy, (7) complementary or competitive relationships to work, (8) gregariousness, (9) service (as opposed to personal pleasure), (10) status or prestige, (11) relaxation from anxiety, and (12) ego-integration (as opposed to not fitting one's overall life-style) (Havighurst, 1961). Havighurst found that high personal adjustment was associated with activities characterized by autonomy, creativity, enjoyment, talent, instrumentality, physical energy, gregariousness, service to others, status, and ego-integration (compared with their opposites). Such findings suggest that not all leisure pursuits are equally meaningful and satisfying.

If inherent differences among leisure pursuits are so important, we need to know how specific activities are viewed by participants, but unfortunately there is little information to go on. An early study by Donald and Havighurst (1959) does shed some light on this matter. They asked respondents in Kansas City to indicate their reasons for engaging in various activities, and the following were those most frequently expressed: just for the pleasure of it (68 percent), welcome change from work (48 percent), new experience (42 percent), contact with friends (28 percent), chance to achieve something (23 percent), and makes the time pass (23 percent). Different activities served different typical functions. For example, fishing resulted in pleasure and a welcome change from work, but not new experiences, achievement, or creativity. Handicrafts yielded feelings of achievement and creativity, but were not typically a source of new experiences or contact with friends.

Older people derive satisfaction from a wide variety of activities, and the meanings of these activities are not entirely obvious. Lawton (1978) notes that although such obligatory activities as shopping and housework consume a greater share of the time of older people, these tasks may also be more meaningful through stimulating feelings of competence and self-continuity. A study of older participants at a legalized gambling (poker) club (Stone & Kalish, 1973) provides another example of the variability of functions of leisure. The average respondent made two or three visits to the club per week, with an average of 6 hours per visit; and despite expenses of about $30 (travel and table costs) and little expectation of winning, the respondents were enthusiastic about participating. Stone and Kalish offer some reasons for this. Gambling offers social life and at least a chance of winning, and one attraction may be that these clubs were *not* designed for "senior citizens." At a deeper level, older people lose many of their decision-making options and the excitement of facing personal success or failure (as they might on a job), which gambling changes by offering a real payoff and the opportunity to pit one's own skill and luck against others regardless of age (gambling is an age leveler). It also offers the possibility for social, emotional, and psychological engagement in an interesting activity, the opposite of disengagement.

The author does not wish to suggest that gambling is "the answer" for all older people. Many organizations, such as senior centers and nursing homes, attempt to develop activity programs for the aged (although activities are more likely to be successful when initiated by participants), however, we must pay attention to the participants' perceptions of activities. Lakin and Dray (1958) cite the example of a "hobby shop" set up in a nursing home. This provided an outlet in self-expression for some residents, but most of those who participated derogated the activities as "foolishness." A "sheltered workshop," through which people were paid for their work, proved to be a better source of positive self-images. It may be unfortunate that being paid is what makes an activity meaningful, but such perceptions must be carefully taken into account. This specific study offers an illustration of how values held by a particular cohort—in this case, seeming attachment to a relatively narrow work ethic—constrains the choice of activity options and determines whether particular uses of time are worthwhile for them.

This also reminds us that leisure orientations of older people are products of their experiences over the life course. As noted in Chapter 6, work experiences tend to "spill over" into nonwork pursuits (Ward, 1982b). Wilson (1980) indicates that work autonomy is associated with more "creative" leisure, and less social interaction on the job is associated with more "private" sources of leisure. More generally the effects of quality of work on self-direction and intellectual flexibility will be reflected in activity patterns. Havighurst (1961) found that older middle-class persons were more likely to engage in activities involving creativity, personal enjoyment, and development of talent. Thus stable class-based life-styles are maintained into later life.

Consequences of a Leisure Career

We have seen that leisure is potentially significant to adjustment in old age and that older people derive a variety of meanings from their leisure pursuits. It remains unclear, however, whether a leisure career, in which the absence of work makes leisure a more dominant source of meaning in a person's life, has primarily positive or negative consequences in old age. One of the reasons that retirement is often considered a difficult and even traumatizing role transition is the presumed meaninglessness of leisure pursuits, resulting in feelings of boredom or personal worthlessness. Stephen Miller (1965) has been the most eloquent spokesman for this point of view, referring to the "social dilemma" of the leisure participant. Miller argues that the leisure role has not achieved legitimacy as a replacement for work or as a source of identity and self-respect: it "only supports the position of the old as non-meaningful, non-functional or, at best, superannuated" (p. 81). There is an embarrassing stigma attached to leisure, which, Miller suggests, results in social withdrawal (disengagement) by the aged.

In a broader sense problems associated with leisure have been attributed to all members of modern society. The argument has been that the values associated with the work ethic inhibit our ability to take full advantage of free time, opening ourselves up to new experiences with a creative or playful attitude, by generating feelings of guilt and anxiety if we have "too much" leisure.

> One of our great hazards in considering leisure is that it is so commonly thought of as a residue, an empty category of experience that is "left over" when other life-sustaining activities have been accomplished. (Wilson, 1981:284)

Pfeiffer and Davis (1971) found that over half of a sample of middle-aged persons derived greater satisfaction from work than from leisure, whereas only about one in six derived greater satisfaction from leisure. They also found that dissatisfaction with leisure is apparently related to sex-linked transitions from work roles. Women were most dissatisfied from age 46 to 55, when family roles are being altered. Men, on the other hand, were least satisfied with leisure time from 66 to 71, the usual time for adjusting to retirement. Thus transitions from work to leisure are neither easy nor automatic for many, and some encounter boredom and identity crises.

Such arguments have important implications for all of us as available non-work time continues to expand in the future. But how much truth is there to this assessment? We have already seen that retirement is often not the crisis we assume it to be, and there is evidence that the same is true of the use of leisure time.

Arguments about leisure problems partly assume an overarching importance for the work role, but work is often not that important for individuals and its intrinsic satisfactions may be declining. Similarly, attachment to work does not necessarily lead to poor retirement adjustment. People derive self-conceptions from many roles and identities, and work-related identities often continue in retirement (Atchley, 1971). Even highly work-oriented people have been able to take up a satisfying leisure role. Thus,

> Each person generally has several roles that he stakes his identity on. Work may be at or near the top, but not necessarily so. There simply is not the kind of homogeneous consensus on the value of work that would keep it at the top for everyone. In fact, the many systems of competing values in a complex society insure that there will be a wide variety of self-values. Thus, the probability that retirement will lead to a complete identity breakdown is slight, and there may be just as many people who rely on leisure pursuits for self-respect as there are who rely on work, particularly among those with unsatisfying jobs. (Atchley, 1971:17)

The weight of the evidence suggests that leisure pursuits are neither traumatizing nor demoralizing for most older people. The rather unremarkable effects of retirement cited in Chapter 6 certainly support this conclusion. Embarrassment and identity loss associated with retirement are minimized by continuity in other activities (family, friends, church, and so on), creating retirement cohorts that may legitimize leisure. Generally, reluctance toward the leisure role is negligible when income is secure. The expansion of leisure time is not viewed negatively, and desired leisure pursuits are often a *cause* of retirement. There is a positive association between activity and feelings of well-being among retirees, as there is among older people in general (Foner & Schwab, 1981). A study by Peppers (1976) also found that those who increased their range of interests after retirement had higher morale than those whose activity levels remained constant or declined.

These patterns do not necessarily mean that activity itself creates well-being, because activity is also associated with better health and higher socio-economic status. That most people adapt relatively satisfactorily to the transition from work to leisure also does not necessarily mean that they are fully utilizing their capacities for self-expression, personal growth, or community involvement in a wide range of activity options. Many people may be responding to retirement by choosing a leisure pursuit that resembles work. The leisure pattern of other older people seems little more than the playing out of remaining middle-aged activities. One gets little sense from the literature that many older people use their increased free time to experiment with new sources and forms of self-expression, but this is less a result of what older people are capable of than of limited opportunities for cultivating more open approaches to the use of time earlier in life and the unavailability of wider options in old age.

VOLUNTARY ASSOCIATIONS

Group activities offer a variety of satisfactions for persons of any age, but membership in voluntary associations can offer important benefits for older people particularly. Such groups may be a source of social integration and diversion to fill the vacuum created by role losses such as retirement and widowhood. Voluntary associations may also provide services and information about services to older people, or serve as an arena for education or personal expression. In addition, groups may serve an advocacy function on behalf of older people.

The fact that older people are less likely to belong to voluntary associations than younger people has been taken as evidence of disengagement. More recent evidence suggests, however, that such age differences primarily reflect the lower average socioeconomic status of the aged (Cutler, 1977). Cutler's longitudinal studies indicate considerable stability in the general level of associational participation by older people, at least in their sixties. There is considerable *individual* change. Some people increase their participation in response to declining work and family responsibilities. Others report a decline with age because of poor health, transportation problems, residential change, or the loss of group-related roles (such as retirees who are no longer active in unions). But the overall picture is one of continued engagement with relatively widespread membership and participation in voluntary associations. Indeed, one study of older persons in a small midwestern city found that 80 percent (76 percent of those aged 80 and over) belonged to at least one voluntary association, and more than half of these belonged to more than one (Babchuk et al., 1979). Attendance was also quite regular, typically involving two to six meetings a month.

Age patterns of participation vary across types of associations. Data in Table 7.2 show these patterns for a representative sample of persons 18 and older in the United States (Cutler, 1976a). Older people (65+) are most likely to belong to church-affiliated groups and fraternal groups (e.g., lodges). There is a steady increase with age in membership in fraternal and church-related organizations, which Cutler suggests is due to generational differences in the types of groups that appeal to people. The functions performed by lodges and fraternal groups, for example, are now available elsewhere (Smith & Freedman, 1972). Greater membership in sports groups among the young is only partly due to the poorer health of older people (Cutler, 1976a). Membership in some groups reaches a peak in middle age and declines thereafter: labor unions, professional or academic societies, school service groups, youth groups, veterans' groups, service clubs (e.g., Rotary). Many of these memberships are related to work and family roles relinquished by older people. Thus, age stratification of roles affects patterns of group association. However, many groups exhibit no significant age differences: farm organizations, political clubs, hobby or garden clubs, school fraternities or sororities, and nationality groups (ethnic clubs).

Membership in voluntary associations is not evenly distributed among the older population. Older women are more likely than older men to belong to religious, volunteer, and cultural organizations, whereas older men are more likely to belong to unions, service clubs, and fraternal organizations (Cutler, 1976a;

Table 7.2 PERCENTAGE BELONGING TO 16 TYPES OF VOLUNTARY ASSOCIATIONS, BY AGE

Type of Association	Age						
	18–24	25–34	35–44	45–54	55–64	65–74	75+
Fraternal groups	3	9	14	15	15	17	23
Church-affiliated groups	27	34	46	45	48	48	52
Sports groups	26	23	23	19	12	8	5
Labor unions	13	16	17	21	22	11	7
Professional or academic societies	12	15	17	13	10	9	5
School service groups	8	22	31	18	8	5	1
Youth groups	13	11	19	10	5	4	1
Veterans' groups	2	4	9	14	13	8	11
Service clubs	4	8	11	13	9	8	8
Literary, art, discussion, or study groups	7	13	8	9	9	8	7
Farm organizations	3	3	4	6	6	4	4
Political clubs	2	5	6	4	4	4	7
Hobby or garden clubs	8	12	10	7	10	9	9
School fraternities or sororities	5	6	4	5	3	4	3
Nationality groups	3	3	3	4	2	3	3
Other groups	7	11	10	9	7	12	11

Source: Adapted from Stephen Cutler, "Age Profiles of Membership in Sixteen Types of Voluntary Associations." *Journal of Gerontology* 31 (1976), 464. Reprinted by permission.

Payne & Whittington, 1976; Babchuk et al., 1979). Men display a greater decline in overall group participation with age than do women. Blacks of all ages have higher rates of participation in voluntary associations than whites, perhaps as a compensation for racial discrimination (Clemente et al., 1975). Clemente and associates found that older blacks are particularly likely to belong to church-related groups and social or recreational clubs, whereas older whites are more likely to belong to ethnic organizations and senior citizen clubs. And group participation among the elderly is greater for those with better health, higher income, and greater education (Babchuk et al., 1979; Ward, 1979).

Participation in voluntary associations serves many functions and results in a variety of satisfactions; however, there has been little investigation of the perceptions of participants about their involvement. A study by the author suggests some ways in which the functions of group activities may differ (Ward, 1979). Group participants were asked to indicate three reasons they enjoyed the group activities in which they engaged (Table 7.3). Not surprisingly, socializing was the most frequent response. Other frequently mentioned reasons included opportunities for new experience, activities which are pleasurable in themselves, and helping society and others. Babchuk and associates (1979) indicate that older persons participate primarily for expressive reasons, involving the more immediate gratification from group activities. More instrumental objectives apart from the group itself, such as social influence, are less important.

Surprisingly, there is no evidence that membership in such groups contributes much to the psychological well-being of older people. Although older people who participate in voluntary associations have higher morale, such persons also have better health, higher income, and more education. When such individual characteristics are controlled, group membership is apparently unrelated to over-

Table 7.3 REASONS GIVEN BY A SAMPLE OF PERSONS 65 AND OVER FOR ENJOYING GROUP PARTICIPATION

Reason	Percentage[a]
(1) It brings me into contact with friends.	73
(2) It gives me new experience; I feel I learn something from it.	36
(3) I like it just for the pleasure of doing it.	35
(4) It makes the time pass.	34
(5) I like it because I like to do things that will be of benefit to society.	30
(6) I get to help other people.	23
(7) It gives me a chance to achieve something.	19
(8) It is a welcome change from my work.	12
(9) I feel I can respect myself for doing these things.	11
(10) It gives me more standing with other people.	8
(11) I feel that I am being creative.	6
(12) It makes me popular among other people.	6
(13) It helps me financially.	2

Number interviewed: 202
[a]Respondents were asked to indicate 3 reasons.
Source: Russell Ward. "The Meaning of Voluntary Association Participation to Older People," *Journal of Gerontology* 34 (1979), p. 441. Reprinted by permission.

all life satisfaction (Bull & Aucoin, 1975; Cutler, 1976b; Ward, 1979). Cutler did find a small effect of church-affiliated groups on satisfaction, but he noted that this could be due to various factors: a general effect of religiosity, intensity of involvement, or greater age homogeneity of such groups.

There are a number of possible reasons for the relative unimportance of group involvement. First, older people who belong to voluntary associations have typically been "joiners" throughout their lives; relatively few take them up in old age as compensation for other social losses (Lowenthal & Robinson, 1976). This suggests that we are prisoners of past activity patterns and there may be few new or attractive associational options available to older people. Many voluntary associations are linked to the roles and activities of young adulthood and middle age; relatively few are geared to the interests and needs of older people.

The lack of a relationship between voluntary association participation and overall morale may also reflect a general lack of "meaty" roles or personally meaningful involvement for all but a small leadership group within most associations. This may be particularly true of the aged who may be shunted aside by younger group members. For many, participation may yield little more than social interaction. In the study cited earlier (Ward, 1979), the third most frequent *first* reason for group participation was "It makes the time pass," which is hardly a glowing affirmation of the significance of their involvement. If voluntary associations offer little more than "lukewarm" social integration, they fail to serve as creative, self-expressive accommodations to new needs in the use of time.

Some types of group involvements seem to be more beneficial than others. Persons more satisfied with groups are inclined to stress such reasons for group involvement as new experiences, achieving something, being creative, and being helpful to others, and *active* participation through discussions, planning, and leadership involvement resulted in more novel experience and greater feelings of achievement and creativity (Ward, 1979). Participants in more social or recreational activities (such as cardplaying) tended to stress simply the pleasure involved and passing the time. These findings suggest that group participation by the elderly will be experienced as more meaningful and satisfying when it provides opportunities for active, intense involvement.

Age-Homogeneous Groups

The voluntary associations we have been discussing may include older people, but they are not organized *by* or *for* them. To the extent that the activity needs of older people are not adequately addressed in such groups or memberships are lost through moving or role change accompanying aging, groups that are more age-homogeneous should be encouraged.

There are costs and rewards involved in participating in more homogeneous old-age groups (Havighurst, 1949). One risks the possible stigma of associating with "old folks" and loses a sense of involvement in the larger community, but such groups can address the specific interests of older people and provide opportunities for prestige and leadership that may be limited in younger groups. These groups are likely to be most successful when they are run *by* older people, rather than *for* them, and when they allow for active participation—speakers, discussions, lobbying on older people's own behalf, and so on.

The increasing size of the older population and growing awareness of shared problems and interests heighten the likelihood that groups specifically designed for older people will be increasingly prevalent. This appears to have occurred in Japan, where "old people's clubs" have rapidly multiplied since the 1950s to include nearly half the older population in over 90,000 clubs throughout the country (Maeda, 1975). The emphases of these clubs, in order of importance, have been recreation, making crafts for money, learning (discussions, lectures, outings), health-related activities, and volunteer community service. In the United States, where senior citizen groups are usually sponsored by social service, recreation, and adult education agencies, a similarly wide range of programs may be found from purely social activities to social action and the provision of services. There are also various nationally organized associations for older persons, such as the American Association of Retired Persons/National Retired Teachers Association (AARP/NRTA). But participation in such organizations is much lower in the United States than in Japan. A recent national survey found that 23 percent of persons over 65 (and 8 percent of those between 55 and 64) had attended a "senior citizens center or golden age club" during the prior three months (National Council on the Aging, 1981).

Participation in old-age associations is relatively low partly because people are busy with other involvements, not interested in the activities that are offered, in poor health, or simply do not wish to associate with "old people." But there is also untapped interest in such groups. The National Council on the Aging study (1981) found that 27 percent of those over 55 (43 percent among blacks) would like to attend but were too busy, lacked convenient facilities, had inadequate transportation, or were in poor health.

Participation is also limited by the fact that senior citizen clubs tend to draw members from a narrow local area and include primarily higher-status older people who have had a "joining" life style (Trela, 1976; Ward, 1979). Hanssen and associates (1978) indicate that senior centers attract more active, capable older persons, who are drawn by recreational programming consistent with their life-styles. Tours, trips, and table games appear to be the most popular reasons for attending (Kaplan, 1979). Lack of participation by the poor and disadvantaged limits the use of such organizations as a type of social agency (Taietz, 1976). For those who do participate, however, old-age associations offer the potential for self-expressive uses of time that are more directly related to the aging experience.

EDUCATION AND AGING

Education is one use of time from which older people might clearly profit. It can assist in coping with the changes of later life, offer intellectual stimulation, and enhance performance in volunteer and advocacy roles. Unfortunately, education has not been an important activity for older people and society has done relatively little to encourage their participation, which has contributed to the distance between age groups and the difficulties accompanying the transitions from middle age to old age.

Modern societies have segregated education, work, and leisure into different parts of the life cycle, with important consequences for the age stratification system as a whole (Parelius, 1975). The tendency to think of education as something for the young creates more separated age strata in modern societies, such as adolescence. Because education is highly age-graded, new knowledge and socialization experiences produce social distance between generations. With education a major determinant of occupational placement, older people are at a disadvantage in occupational advancement or entering new occupations.

A more continuous integration of educational, work, and leisure opportunities would offer many potential benefits. There is a tendency for life in modern societies to become too programmed and rigid (Butler, 1975; Sarason, 1977). Education focuses too narrowly on preparation for careers that may become obsolete, rather than preparing young people to meet the opportunities and challenges of their whole life span. More flexible career counseling, as well as courses related to entrepreneurial skills, leisure-time preparation and usage, and aging and retirement may be needed (Peterson, 1975). Preparation (in the broadest sense) for retirement should be combined with educational opportunities throughout the life cycle as it is likely to be too late when one is 60. Older workers may face obsolescence or boredom because of a lack of opportunities for continual education and retraining. However, educational opportunities for older people should include more than work-related options; indeed, adult education has perhaps been oriented too much to work skills. One can also derive more intrinsic satisfactions from education, and educational experiences could be oriented toward the meaningful use of time and general preparation for retirement and postretirement.

Such proposals seem quite simple, but their effects could be quite far-reaching. Lifelong education has a tremendous potential for creating change in society, particularly in the blurring of age distinctions (Parelius, 1975). Adolescents would participate more widely in the adult world, perhaps through apprenticeship programs, and would experience less pressure to make so many important decisions early in life. As opportunities are opened for greater flexibility, there may be more identity crises during adulthood, which, Butler (1975) suggests, would help to "loosen up life". The "generation gap" between the young and middle-aged or older people would be narrowed, and continuous educational opportunities would provide new meaningful roles and activities in the later years.

There has been some movement toward opening up education for older people. This partly reflects declining college enrollments and that educational institutions recognize the need to recruit new types of students, including the aged. Nearly 3 million persons between ages 40–64 and some 400,000 aged 65 and over are enrolled in a wide range of courses (Tibbitts, 1979). A study by Covey (1980) found that older students wanted the same subjects available to the general college population. They also preferred age-integrated classes, although special educational opportunities for older persons, such as Elderhostel, have also been spreading. Rather than special age-related interests, however, older students stress learning new things, having new experiences, and being with other people (National Council on the Aging, 1975; Romaniuk & Romaniuk, 1982).

Progress has been limited, however. We have probably all read stories about 90-year-old high school or college graduates, but a recent survey found that only 5 percent of all persons over 65 are enrolled in some type of course (although this represents an increase from only 2 percent in 1974) (National Council on the Aging, 1981). This partly reflects the low educational background of current older cohorts. Older persons who are students have higher education, income, and occupational status; they meet the requirements for doing college-level work and are continuing a lifetime of educational activity (Covey, 1980).

Educational involvement in old age should rise in the future as older cohorts have higher levels of education. But despite recent growth, programs directed at the aged are still quite limited. Both formally and informally, our educational institutions remain "youth ghettos" with social and psychological barriers for older persons. The major reasons given by older people for not participating in educational courses are lack of interest (45 percent), being too old (27 percent), poor health (22 percent), and not having enough time (13 percent) (National Council on the Aging, 1975). The first two reasons indicate that your youthful orientation to education may discourage participation by the elderly, who come to view education as inappropriate for their age group.

There are additional barriers to involvement in education. Scheduling and location are critical because home responsibilities often make it difficult for older students to follow strict schedules, and physical restrictions, transportation problems, and fear of crime at night can limit mobility. Grading may often be inappropriate, given the different goals of older students and the likelihood (particularly for older men) that tests will be viewed as threatening to one's self-image (Goodrow, 1975). Involvement by older persons may also be resisted by younger students. One study of age-integrated classes at a university (Auerbach & Levenson, 1977) found increasingly negative attitudes by young students toward older students, who were viewed as unfair competition, because they could focus on just one course, and as "cluttering up" the classroom with irrelevant personal anecdotes. Students tended to segregate themselves from those of different ages.

Such problems do not mean that we should abandon efforts to achieve wider involvement by the aged in existing educational institutions, but these problems do suggest that we must be flexible and experiment with other forms and media of education. Television, for example, offers a particularly relevant tool for lifelong education (Kubey, 1980). Older people view television as a dependable, trusted medium of communication, and will therefore be more likely to accept information related to retirement preparation, health counseling, or the range of benefits and services available to them. Indeed, television offers largely untapped opportunities for influencing the entire population about aging and being old.

RELIGION AND AGING

We do not generally think of religion as a "use of time," but religious activities have long been considered important for the aged. Fear of death, for example, is often assumed to be a mainspring for religious commitment (Stark, 1968); as death presumably grows psychologically near in old age, people may turn to religion for personal solace. Inasmuch as religious affiliation represents the most widespread group involvement among older people, it may also represent their most important source of social integration. Religion is a very complex phenomenon, however. There are many religions and many denominations within them. There are also many dimensions of religiosity, including emotional experience, beliefs (e.g., belief in an afterlife), ritual practices, and personal knowledge and information (Moberg, 1965). Although most people identify themselves with some type of religion, this tells us very little about the nature and significance of their religious experience.

Religious involvement may become more important with age, or it may also decline. Disengagement theory would suggest a decline in religious participation, although perhaps not in the more personal aspects of religion. Religious activities may peak in early and middle adulthood because church membership is expected of persons in certain roles or the presence of children encourages attendance as a model for socialization (Bahr, 1970). Thus the relationship of religion to age is not likely to be a simple one, nor are its consequences for the aging experience likely to be clear-cut.

Church attendance apparently reaches a peak in middle and old age. The study conducted for the National Council on the Aging (1975) found that religious attendance was greatest among older people, and even 68 percent of those over 80 had attended a church or synagogue within the past year (76 percent of them had attended within the last week or two). Ritualistic practices outside the home may decline somewhat in very old age, primarily because of poor health, low income, or transportation difficulties, but they are at least partly compensated for by activities inside the home, such as reading the Bible, following religious broadcasts on television or radio, and personal prayer (Moberg, 1965; Mindel & Vaughan, 1978).

Older people also appear to attach greater importance to religion. The National Council on the Aging (1975) survey found that 71 percent of persons aged 65 and over considered religion "very important," compared with 49 percent of persons younger than 65. A similar study in a midwestern city found that three fourths of a sample of older people stated that God was very influential in their lives, whereas only 10 percent considered religion to be of little or no importance (Pieper, 1981). Older women are more likely than older men to participate in religious activities and to feel that religion is an important part of their lives, but their involvement also shows a greater decline with age than for men (Payne & Whittington, 1976). Religious involvement also appears to be greater for older blacks (National Council on the Aging, 1975). Religiosity is apparently quite stable. In a longitudinal study of older people lasting 17 years, Blazer and Palmore (1976) found gradual declines in religious *activity* but considerable stability in religious *attitudes*.

There is little evidence in these studies that people turn to religion as they age, although those who had been slightly religious may become more so. A study by Wingrove and Alston (1971) found that all cohorts displayed declines in church attendance after 1965. If this reflects a general secularization of American society, one would expect religion to be less important for older people in the future. A study by Wuthnow (1976) indicates that such predictions are risky, however. He notes that most evidence shows a religious revival during the 1950s, followed by declining religious commitment since the early 1960s. Using evidence from Gallup polls over this period, he shows that this declining religious participation is greatest among youth, resulting in much larger age differences than in the past (Figure 7.2). He attributes this to youthful involvement in the "counterculture," which has sought alternatives to established religions (Marxism, mysticism, and other philosophies). Thus each cohort develops its own patterns of religious involvement as a consequence of its unique history.

The consequences of religious involvement by older people are not entirely clear. Older people themselves cite many benefits: emotional support, giving meaning to life, social interaction (Pieper, 1981). Research also indicates positive associations between religious activities and religious attitudes and happiness, usefulness, and adjustment in old age, and the strength of these associations increased over time (Blazer & Palmore, 1976; Kivett, 1979). Consequences probably depend upon the meanings attached to religion. Moberg (1965) indicates that holding *conservative* religious beliefs is associated with greater serenity and less fear of death. Kivett (1979) makes a distinction between *extrinsic* religious motivation, involving self-protection and "comfort," and *intrinsic* motivation, whereby faith provides meaning and challenge. Her study found that intrinsic motivation was associated with greater feelings of internal control and a more positive self-concept.

But it is not clear from this research whether religiosity *itself* is beneficial because religious participation is related to other types of group involvement. Sat-

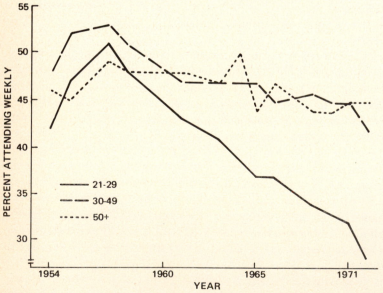

Figure 7.2 Weekly church attendance by age, 1954–1971. (*Source:* Robert Wuthnow, "Recent Patterns of Secularization: A Problem of Generations?" *American Sociological Review* 41 (1976), p. 857. Reprinted by permission.)

isfaction, serenity, or acceptance of death may result not from faith, but from participation in social networks and reference groups that offer support and security. This is not meant to deny the important role played by some churches in developing and providing services for the aged. Social groups for the elderly are often sponsored by churches and synagogues, and retirement housing, hospitals, and nursing homes are often run by religious institutions. Other services, such as Meals-on-Wheels, benefit from the cooperation of local churches. But the social and psychological importance of religion in the everyday lives of most older people remains unclear.

THE VOLUNTEER ROLE

Time spent in service to others is time well spent, regardless of one's age. Few other activities can rival volunteer work as a source of "good feelings" about oneself. For older people, the volunteer role is a potential source of meaningful activity and status that can counteract feelings of marginality associated with the completion or tapering off of parental and work roles. It may offer feelings of usefulness and self-respect, fill unused time, neutralize loneliness, and contribute to community well-being. A study comparing retirees who were volunteers at a VA hospital with retirees who were not volunteers found that volunteers had a greater "will to live" and higher life satisfaction as well as less anxiety and depression (Hunter & Linn, 1981). As we are becoming increasingly service-oriented, there are many public tasks that offer far more than just "make-work." Blau has even suggested a redefinition of citizenship to include obligatory public service, yielding benefits to not only participants but also society:

> The young need an opportunity to perform useful, socially relevant roles so as to establish a sense of efficacy; older people need productive roles for the same reason. The answer to both groups' needs, it seems to me, lies in the creation of new obligatory social roles in the public sector. Massive problems confront American society. Despite its enormous wealth, despite modest attempts to deal with our national problems in the areas of poverty, health care, and education, the ills of our society persist and proliferate. Much significant, essential work lies waiting while there are millions of young and old people eager to be useful. These human resources, now wasted, can and must be mobilized and organized to perform the work. (1973:204)

In other words, we and the aged will benefit from seeing the aged as *providers* of services, not just recipients.

Some service roles are already available to the elderly, such as Foster Grandparents, which recruits and trains older people to provide personalized care to institutionalized children; Retired Senior Volunteer Program (RSVP), which places volunteers in libraries, hospitals, schools, and other settings; and Service Corps of Retired Executives (SCORE), through which retirees help small businesses with their management problems. In addition to the benefits of volunteer work, programs such as Foster Grandparents provide supplementary income to low-income older people.

The elderly have proven to be effective in such service roles provided they are given adequate training, careful placement, and meaningful tasks. None of us enjoys trivial tasks or work that is frustrated by inadequate preparation. The elderly have shown a willingness to engage in such activities, even when pay is low or nonexistent, but we must be wary of exploiting them simply because their income is very low or they desire more meaningful community involvement. The programs mentioned above have been successful in this regard and have proven beneficial for older participants and the recipients of the services.

The Foster Grandparents program is an excellent example of how service roles for older people can be mutually beneficial. A small-scale evaluation of one program suggested the existence of a special compatibility of emotional needs between the older volunteers and institutionalized children (Saltz, 1971). They seemed to develop real family feelings, despite the relatively temporary nature of the relationship. The "grandparents" performed well, even when their health was poor. They displayed good job stability and attendance, had a beneficial impact on the children, and received favorable ratings from supervisors; and the volunteer experience was conducive to better health, vigor, and life satisfaction for them. They expressed satisfaction over having regular and purposive activity and the opportunity to be useful and appreciated.

Although volunteerism declines with age, approximately one in four persons 65 and over engages in some type of volunteer activity, and another 10 percent would like to do so (National Council on the Aging, 1981). This means that there is an available pool of nearly 8 million older volunteers. The most frequent activities of older people involve physical and mental health (hospitals and clinics), transportation (driving the handicapped), civic affairs (voter registration and lobbying), psychological and social support services (telephone reassurance for shut-ins), giveaway programs (thrift shops and emergency food), and family, youth, and children-oriented services (foster children and day care) (National Council on the Aging, 1975). The major barriers to such participation, as for almost all types of activity, were poor health and lack of transportation. Whereas poor health is perhaps difficult to deal with, service agencies could clearly increase their recruitment of older volunteers by providing transportation.

Volunteer participation is greater among older whites and those who are employed or have higher income (National Council on the Aging, 1981). A study by Monk and Cryns (1974) found that the volunteer role most attracted those who were young-old and better educated, had a broader range of social interests, and believed that they could make a valuable contribution. Other research indicates that volunteers are most likely to be female and widowed (Payne & Whittington, 1976). Men seem to view volunteer work as a substitute for the instrumental work role, whereas women view it as an expressive role ("doing good"). Payne and Whittington suggest, however, that women may increasingly be finding the values and status associated with work in the service role.

The service role offers meaningful activity for many older people and benefits to society. The elderly have not been effectively tapped as a resource, however. We need greater understanding of what makes different volunteer activities attractive and successful. There is also a need to develop ways of encouraging older people to participate, particularly those who have been relatively uninvolved. The results of the Monk and Cryns (1974) study suggest that we should encourage the feeling that older people's skills and contributions are valuable. This is hampered by societal stereotypes about the work deficiencies of the aged, but expanded service roles may help counteract many of the stigmatizing myths of old age.

SOCIAL CHANGE AND THE USE OF TIME

Old age and retirement, rather than being roleless, offer many possible roles, options, and careers. The difficulty is that there are little preparation and few guidelines for making choices, and whereas the options are numerous, their depth and quality are less certain. One wonders how socially and psychologically "meaty" these roles are for older people.

Many factors constrain the use of time. The middle-aged uncreative user of time is likely to remain the same in old age. The most important constraints, however, relate to how time and its uses are structured for us by the social structure and the age stratification system (Ward, 1982a).

The structured use of time has changed over the course of industrialization and modernization (Dumazedier, 1967; Kaplan, 1975). Preindustrial societies did not separate work and leisure into distinct worlds, and older people were encouraged and expected to work and rewarded for doing so. Thus the use of time was less of a problem. Industrial societies, however, have separated work from leisure, although still attaching great importance and status to productive work. The use of time is an issue particularly for older people, who leave the world of work, yet are still judged by the standards of that world.

We are now entering what some have referred to as the postindustrial society, however, which may reunite work and leisure, and leisure itself may be on the verge of being a dominant value. Kaplan (1975), for example, suggests that the fragmentation and routinization of work combines with the marketing of leisure goods and services to promote the value of leisure. Others point to a shift in cultural values toward self-actualization, self-expression, interdependence, and "capacity for joy" (Emery & Trist, 1973), which would "disinhibit" our free choice of options in the use of time.

This certainly paints a favorable future for leisure careers. Whether future cohorts of older people (or of all ages) actually achieve this Nirvana remains to be seen. The young may not be as guiltfree about leisure as they seem. More important, postindustrial values about the use of time must be expressed and realized within the structure of society, and here the age stratification system comes into play.

Our society has done relatively little to promote creative or self-expressive uses of time throughout the life cycle. The separation of leisure from the rest of life impairs "the application of imagination to ordinary life" (Rapoport & Rapoport, 1975:348) and prevents us from enriching all aspects of our lives through more creative uses of time. In addition, little is done to promote resourcefulness in using time. Education is geared toward vocational pursuits rather than "socialization for life," and leisure interests are subsidiary to work and family careers. Entering old age without sustainable leisure patterns, older people are unprepared to explore new options in using time.

Available activities may be shallow and unfulfilling because they are set up *for* older people or allow them few truly meaningful roles. Older people shy away from education because they are "too old" or from service roles because they question their own usefulness in a society that expects them to retire from "productive" roles, and few roles are available to them.

The author does not wish to overstate the case. Older people are relatively satisfied in their leisure pursuits, but in relation to what? That people can accommodate to reality does not justify that reality. In all respects, a satisfying old age is best built upon a satisfying youth and middle age. But we must also experiment with new options for older people, inventing and upgrading social roles for them. The freedom of time given to the aged by modern societies presents a challenge to use that time in mutually beneficial ways.

There is room for optimism. Future cohorts of older people will have more education, money, and better health, making them more capable and resourceful as well as more demanding of meaningful involvement in community life. They may be more concerned with the "higher-order" needs discussed at the end of Chapter 2: esteem, self-actualization, the desire to know and understand, and aesthetic needs. There already seems to be growing interest in opening up such involvement. As we have noted in earlier chapters, more positive roles are emerging for older people as modern soceities "mature" in the images and understandings of aging (Tibbitts, 1979). But much more exploration of new options in the use of time and the factors that facilitate and encourage participation by older people needs to be done. There is also a critical need to investigate the meanings and consequences for older people of the activities they pursue. The ways in which older people choose, and are constrained to choose, uses of time are major determinants of the aging experience.

SUMMARY

The use of time is an important issue for the aged in modern societies. Many options are available, but choice is constrained by the accompaniments of aging, past activity patterns, cohort experiences, and age stratification of opportunities.

Leisure activity is generally considered expressive, pleasant, and relatively nonobligatory. It is not simply amusement or escape, but rather covers a wide range of intensity and functions. Patterns of leisure are likely to vary over the life cycle in response to the developmental needs of each period. Although interests tend to narrow during adulthood, leisure in old age may focus more broadly on the search for new personally engaging involvements and social integration.

Although older people have more nonwork time, their freedom is often limited by poor health, low income, transportation difficulties, and so on. Their most frequent activities are socializing, television, and reading. Age differences are evident in such things as media preferences and attendance at cultural events, and older people are less active outside the home. The free time of older people often comes to be dominated by more obligatory and sedentary activities. Leisure pursuits vary widely in meaning, and individual variability in these meanings must be kept in mind, particularly when designing activity programs for the elderly.

It has been argued that leisure is considered degrading in industrial societies because of the importance attached to the work role. This argument overstates the importance of work. Although most people appear to derive greater satisfaction from work than leisure, most adjust satisfactorily to a leisure career, particularly when income is adequate and work styles can be transferred to leisure.

Voluntary associations offer a potentially important source of interesting activities, social integration, and social action on behalf of the elderly. There are a variety of barriers to participation, however, including poor health, inadequate transportation, residential mobility, and role loss. Age differences in membership patterns reflect such constraints, as well as cohort differences and the age-grading of social roles. Older people are most likely to belong to church-affiliated groups and fraternal groups. Formal associations vary by social class, sex, and race, and those who belong are likely to have been "joiners" throughout their lives.

There is little evidence that participation in voluntary associations *itself* contributes to morale. As with all uses of time, older people derive many meanings from group participation. Morale is higher for those who stress new experience, achievement, creativity, and service to others. These meanings are more likely to be derived from active than from passive participation.

Although age-homogeneous groups can specifically address the desires and needs of older people, relatively few participate in senior citizen clubs. Again, there are many barriers limiting involvement. Members tend to be "joiners," and there is little evidence that the poor and disadvantaged are drawn to such groups.

The age-grading of education has contributed to the social gaps between age strata and hindered the opportunity for midlife career change and general preparation for retirement and old age. If education, work, and leisure were integrated throughout the life cycle, life would be less rigidly programmed, with potentially far-reaching consequences for society. Although educational opportunities are opening up for them, relatively few older people are involved in educational pursuits. Greater care is needed in developing programs appropriate to their capacities, needs, and life-styles.

The link between religion and aging remains unclear. Religious activities outside the home tend to decline, but activities inside the home show some increase with age. Older people are more likely to express a variety of religious beliefs and to consider religion an important part of their lives, but there is no clear evidence that religion *itself* contributes to the psychological well-being of the aged. Of course, the activities of religious institutions are often beneficial to the elderly. Predictions about the future religiosity of older people are risky due to the mixture of general secularization and unique cohort experiences.

The volunteer role has been pointed to as a source of meaningful activities for the aged. A number of work and volunteer programs are available, and participation by older people has proven highly successful. There are barriers to involvement, however, and we know relatively little about what makes various service roles attractive.

The relationship between work and leisure has been altered in the transition to an industrial society. The postindustrial society may again achieve a convergence of work and play, supported by values stressing self-expression. However, realization of greater freedom in the use of time will require alterations in the age stratification of structured time.

chapter 8

The Family Life of Older People

The family is a major source of *primary* relationships that provides long-lasting, intimate, emotional ties with others. The marriage relationship is generally viewed as a keystone to the satisfaction of emotional needs, but interactions with other kin—offspring, parents, aunts, uncles, and so on—also offer a broad range of gratifications, from the purely social or emotional to financial support and other services. Thus the extent to which older people are embedded in a system of family relationships has a great potential impact on the aging experience. The 80-year-old widow with no living children and few contacts with relatives is in a very different position from the 65-year-old wife who lives near and interacts daily with her children and grandchildren.

Family relationships affect the aging experience in many ways. Family-based roles are an important part of the age stratification system. We saw in Chapter 3 that involvement of the aged in networks of kin often results in greater status and economic security, but industrialization and the democratization of family interaction in modern societies may have altered the nature of family ties. Age stratification also means an intermingling of conflict and affection within families (Foner, 1978). Reciprocal relationships and lifelong socialization build solidarity within families, whereas life stage inequalities of power and resources and cohort differences in attitudes and values breed conflict.

The family also relates to a life course perspective. The nature and timing of family transitions vary over time and across cohorts (Hareven, 1978). Prior to twentieth-century declines in fertility and mortality, for example, parenthood encompassed most of the adult life span. Now, with fewer children, earlier childbearing, closer spacing between children, and increased life expectancy, married couples can expect an extended postparental period. Families also merge the life course experiences of their members. Dual-career marriages in particular face problems of coordinating transitions during the life cycle.

In truth, we all belong to several families, each resulting in a different complex of roles. The *family of orientation* is the one into which we are born in the roles of daughter or son, sister or brother. The *family of procreation* is the one in which our own reproductive behavior occurs, making us a husband, wife, father, mother, grandparent, widower, or widow. From these basic families we also "inherit" an *extended family* of aunts, uncles, cousins, and in-laws. Kinship relations obviously offer broad possibilities for support or companionship in themselves or as compensation for other ties we have never made (because of singlehood) or have lost (because of widowhood). The effects and effectiveness of this broad network for the aged will be explored in this chapter; however, first we will look at the marriage relationship in old age and the consequences of its loss through widowhood.

THE AGING COUPLE

The marital relationship is potentially critical in later life. Very few older people (about 5 percent) have never been married. Because the spouse role implies intimacy and sharing, it may assume particular importance in fulfilling social and emotional needs in old age when other roles and associations may be lost through retirement, poor health, and other age-related changes. This is one reason for the possibility of important sex differences in the nature of aging, because most older men are married whereas most older women are widowed.

The increased longevity of modern society means that married couples have more time together as couples after the children have left and after retirement. Most people are still middle-aged by the time their children "move on," leaving the parents another 20, 30, or more years of living together. It is important to remember that marriage is not a static experience; the family has its own life cycle that involves a sequence of realignments in family structure and family relationships. Hill (1965) has suggested one sequence of stages representing this cycle:

1. *Establishment:* newly married, childless
2. *New parents:* oldest child under three
3. *Preschool family:* oldest child between three and six
4. *School-age family:* oldest child between six and 12
5. *Family with adolescent:* oldest child between 13 and 19
6. *Family with young adult:* oldest child 20 until first child leaves home
7. *Family as launching center:* from departure of first to departure of last child
8. *Postparental family:* after children have left home until retirement
9. *Aging family:* after retirement

Even a cursory consideration of these stages suggests differences in the marriage relationship. Becoming parents inevitably imposes some constraints on the freedom of a married couple and also affects residential choice, as space needs and other considerations are affected. Hill suggests that early stages are future oriented whereas later stages bring an easing in the pressure on resources.

The quality of the marriage relationship may itself vary among these stages. Many studies indicate a U-shaped pattern in which marital satisfaction is high among young couples, declines substantially in the thirties and forties when older children are present, and rises again to a peak in postparental and retirement stages (Rollins & Feldman, 1970; Gilford & Bengtson, 1979; George, 1980). Such patterns may reflect the pressures of child-care responsibilities and financial burdens in the middle stages of the family cycle.

Care should be taken in discussing family stages and their consequences, however. The U-shaped pattern of marital satisfaction, for example, is not consistently found, and there are many methodological problems associated with this research—not the least of which is use of a cross-sectional, rather than longitudinal, design (Schram, 1979). Any discussion of stages also overlooks the variability in family patterns (age at marriage, presence and timing of children, and so on), which make empirical use of family stages difficult (Nock, 1979). But it is useful to remember the changes in roles and relationships occurring over the family cycle. Let us turn to the stages most relevant to this book: the postparental family and the aging (retirement) family.

The Postparental Couple

The "empty nest" following the departure of children involves a major shift in the middle-aged family. As with most major role changes that accompany aging, this period brings problems and benefits.

The empty-nest period appears to be more problematic for women than for men. Deutscher (1964), for example, found that wives were more likely than their husbands to see this phase as either better or worse than previous phases. Similarly, Lowenthal and associates (1975) found the empty nest to be more salient for and more negatively viewed by women. Middle-aged women were more critical of their spouses, including a tendency to view husbands as overdependent on wives. Because of the sexual stratification of roles that encourages and restricts women, especially in current middle-aged and older cohorts, to take on primarily family roles, loss of the motherhood role may trigger a crisis of purposelessness that can result in depression (Bart, 1971).

The usual prescription for this empty-nest syndrome is to substitute new roles (hobby, school, work), but this may be quite difficult, especially for working- and lower-class women. Inability to fill this gap may be combined with other difficulties, including menopause or other physical changes and a feeling of failure in one's work career or in child raising, as when one's hopes and ambitions for children are not realized.

"Things hurt you a little deeper when you get older. (Q.: What kinds of things?) Oh, if you have real trouble, it hurts you worse. If your children have traits—(Q: What do you mean by traits?) Maybe you've been religious and gone to church and sent the kids to Sunday School regularly and, you know, put yourself out. Well, sometimes it ends up that the kids won't go near a church. They just say, 'I had all the church I need.' And education—well, you can't help but feel that they are foolish there. You have to know their personality. You can't make them over; you have to find out the hard way . . . (pause). . . . He had a voice like Nelson Eddy. Just beautiful. I tried to encourage him, but it didn't do any good. He would never do anything with it." (Deutscher, 1964:57)

A more general marital disenchantment may also occur at this stage, resulting in less marital satisfaction, loss of intimacy (confiding and kissing), and less sharing of activities (Pineo, 1961). Despite "efficient" selection of a spouse, unforeseen changes in situation, personality, or behavior or different roles and experiences as adults can lead people to drift apart. The marital relationship may also become subordinate to parental roles during child rearing, preventing cultivation of a relationship capable of standing on its own.

However, the evidence suggests that this disenchantment is not a widespread phenomenon. As noted earlier, most studies indicate that marital satisfaction is as high or higher among older couples as it is among child-rearing couples, and older couples typically report fewer problems and feelings of inadequacy (Troll et al., 1979; George, 1980; Glenn & McLanahan, 1981). It may simply be, of course, that those who are most dissatisfied have obtained a divorce, or there is a tendency to justify any situation that has lasted for 20 or 30 years to avoid appearing foolish. And although disenchantment is apparently not widespread, most people do not view this as the "best" time of marriage (Treas, 1975).

Nevertheless, the empty nest does offer rewarding possibilities to older couples. Many view this as a time of new freedom: freedom from financial responsibilities, freedom of movement, freedom from housework, freedom to be oneself. The following comment illustrates such feelings:

"There's not as much physical labor. There's not as much cooking and there's not as much mending and, well, I remarked not long ago that for the first time since I can remember my evenings are free. And we had to be very economical to get the three children through college. We're over the hurdle now; we've completed it. Last fall was the first time in 27 years that I haven't gotten a child ready to go to school. That was very relaxing." (Deutscher, 1964:55)

This sense of freedom may combine with feelings of accomplishment and satisfaction that adult children are now social resources (George, 1980). Lowenthal and associates (1975) found that most married people looked forward to the empty nest, and many experienced improved marital relationships based on greater closeness and companionship, increased mutual dependence, and the possibility for more undivided attention to each other. Nock (1979) found that older couples felt they understood each other better. This understanding and mutual dependence may be a key to marital quality in later life because, Feldman (1964) suggests, the qualities emphasized in older marriages shift from attraction and ardor to attachment and loyalty.

The Retirement Couple

The second major change in the later years of the family cycle occurs with retirement. Most research in this area has focused on the strains associated with a male retiree entering the wife's role sphere—the household. This domain has typically defined the wife's self-image, in which case the retiring husband may be seen as an "intruder" who is suddenly underfoot all the time and even threatens to encroach on her sphere of influence. We know however very little about the processes of how spouses adjust to this transition or about the nature of this transition for the increasing number of two-worker couples.

As indicated earlier, most retirement couples seem satisfied with the marital relationship and satisfaction may even reach its peak in this stage (Troll et al., 1979; Foner & Schwab, 1981). This does not mean that retirement marriages are devoid of adjustment problems. Retirement may disrupt familiar patterns of household division of labor. Marital satisfaction in retirement is generally related to greater equality and blurring of sex-role boundaries, as spouses emphasize expressive aspects of the relationship (shared activities and companionship, affection and understanding, communication) rather than instrumental roles as "good housekeeper" or "good provider" (Lipman, 1962; Thurnher, 1976; Troll et al., 1979). Some husbands may find this increased participation in household tasks demeaning. In a study of need-satisfaction in older marriages, Stinnett and associates (1972) found that men were most dissatisfied with lack of respect from their wives, whereas wives tended to be dissatisfied with poor communication. Nonetheless, it appears that sharing, companionship, and the ability to express feelings are the most rewarding aspects of older marriages.

The changing quality of roles and relationships in retirement marriages may alter the relative power of husbands and wives. Some observers have suggested that the husband's power declines when he loses the "leverage" provided by the breadwinner role. Blood and Wolfe (1960) found that the decision-making power of husbands declined with age, particularly after retirement, and Hill (1965) found a greater incidence of "wife-centered" families among retirement couples. Loss of authority for retired males may stem not only from their retirement but also from continued employment by wives and the higher occupational status often enjoyed by adult offspring. Adams (1975) has suggested that retired husbands might continue to control major decisions concerning finances or residence, whereas wives run the socioemotional aspects of the marriage. This interpretation is supported by the cross-cultural studies (cited in Chapter 4) showing that older women may exercise greater authority, but it is largely informal.

There may be social class differences in the role realignments of retirement marriages. Hochschild (1976) has suggested that the husband's power in working-class marriages may derive simply from being the *male,* which allows him to retire to the home without losing a sense of efficacy. Sharing and companionship, however, are viewed as more desirable by both spouses in the middle and upper strata (Kerckhoff, 1966a), reflecting a greater general acceptance of egalitarianism in such marriages. In working-class marriages, which tend to be more authoritarian and less companionate, activities and tasks are more likely to be segregated by sex. The wife expects more exclusive control over household affairs and the husband is less involved prior to retirement, therefore both may view increased involvement by the husband as undesirable, resulting in greater irritation for the wife and guilt for the husband.

It is clear, then, that retirement marriages may require difficult realignments, although most couples appear to be quite satisfied. A recent study of retired teachers and their wives illustrates the somewhat complex mixture of benefits and costs (Keating & Cole, 1980). The couples exhibited relatively high levels of marital satisfaction, with an increase in couple-oriented activities. Interestingly, however, only 12 percent of the wives felt there were no disadvantages. Most perceived a loss of personal freedom and privacy as husbands made more demands on their wives' time, and daily activities were generally determined by the husbands' needs. But wives were also more satisfied with this retirement stage. Whereas husbands were faced with feelings of being less useful, wives had renewed feelings of being needed.

We should remember, however, that this nurturing role may eventually represent a much greater cost to older women. The retirement marriage may evolve into a quite different pattern—the wife as care giver for a disabled husband. Older women often bear the burnt of support for their sick husbands, and these demands superimposed on their own needs may contribute to anger, frustration, guilt, and isolation (Fengler & Goodrich, 1979; Crossman et al., 1981). If formal and informal supports are lacking for those women, the retirement marriage has quite a different quality.

Despite these potential problems, the following summary statement remains true: "One may conclude that for the happily married older couple, marriage is central to the 'good life' " (Troll et al., 1979:53). Interdependence and companionship become important resources in adapting to the aging experience. This suggests that older unmarried people are at a disadvantage. Widowhood will be discussed later in the chapter. Let us now turn to divorce and singlehood, more unusual statuses in old age.

DIVORCE AND SINGLEHOOD

Among current older cohorts, divorce is a relatively unusual experience. Only about 10 percent of persons aged 65 and over have ever been divorced, and less than 5 percent report they are currently divorced (Uhlenberg & Myers, 1981). Uhlenberg and Myers note however that divorce among older people has more than doubled since 1960 and that divorce is much higher among younger cohorts. Divorce is inclined to be much more prevalent among future cohorts of older people. Uhlenberg and Myers estimate that slightly over one third of the 1945–1949 cohort will have their first marriages end in divorce, and remarriages are also more likely to end in divorce. In addition to the lack of marital support, divorce entails financial problems, especially for women, and disruption of kinship ties, which can be a particularly important source of support in later life.

Singlehood is also an unusual status in old age (only about 5 percent of older people have never married). Such persons are not necessarily "sentenced" to unhappiness. In a study of 22 never-married older persons, Gubrium (1975) found a preference for solitary pursuits and independence. For them, being single was "just another way of life"; they saw no stigma associated with it and could not understand why people would expect them to be lonely. But larger-scale surveys have found lower feelings of well-being among the never married than the married, and this appears to be more pronounced among older people (Ward, 1979). This partly reflects the gratifications of marriage and the difficulties of being single in a marriage-oriented culture. It is also likely that the variety and autonomy of single life-styles become more difficult to maintain in the face of health and financial problems in later life. Ward (1979) found that retirement was more demoralizing for never-married people. Their lower morale was also a function of lower satisfaction with family life. As with divorce, the more limited extended families of never-married persons may become a particular problem in old age. As we will see, the extended family is an important source of support for older persons.

SEXUALITY IN LATER LIFE

Although there is no physiological reason for most older people not to have an active and satisfying sex life, cultural norms and stereotypes often imply that sex is neither possible nor necessary in old age (Rubin, 1968; Lobsenz, 1974; Ludeman, 1981). Our youth-oriented culture reserves images of sexual interest and attractiveness for young people. The aged may be tragically cut off from legitimate feelings and gratifications by such stereotypes, shutting off normal sexual feelings because of shame, embarrassment, or fear of ridicule or censure. Partly because of this, and partly because current older cohorts were socialized to be less comfortable with their own sexuality, older people themselves often feel below average in sexual desire, skill, and capacity (Ludeman, 1981). Such feelings may be particularly difficult for older women, given the sexual double standard that reserves sexual initiative for men. As noted in Chapter 4, women may be considered sexually uninterested and uninteresting earlier than men, and menopause may be viewed as a decline or completion of sexual interest and activity (Block et al., 1981). Stereotypes of the "sexless older years" may affect the self-perceptions of older persons, as sexuality continues to be important to self-esteem in later life (Stimson et al., 1981). Stimson and associates found that whereas *amount* of sexual activity was important to younger men, *quality of performance* was more important to the self-esteem of older men. These factors were less important to older women, but loss of feelings of *attractiveness* had an affect on well-being.

Normal physiological aging brings changes that in themselves do not limit the ability to function sexually (Botwinick, 1978; Ludeman, 1981). There is some gradual decline with age in sexual responsiveness among males, whereas females exhibit smaller and later declines. But both cross-sectional and longitudinal studies show continuing sexual interest and capacity for most older people, and stable or even increasing activity is not unusual. The following anecdote captures the truth for both sexes:

An 84-year-old college professor was delivering a lecture on human sexuality at a well-known university. After the talk the professor asked if there were any questions.

"Yes," said one student from the rear of the lecture hall. "At what age do people lose interest in sex?"

The professor paused a moment, and then responded, "I'm not sure, but I know it's sometime after 84." (Branco & Williamson, 1982:388–390)

Pfeiffer and associates (1972) conducted a study of 261 male (98 percent were married) and 231 female (71 percent were married) volunteers aged 46 to 71 who were relatively healthy. The results, reported in Tables 8.1 and 8.2, do show declines with age for both sexes in current sexual interest and frequency of sexual intercourse, and there is also a widening gap with age between interest and activity. Nevertheless, sexuality is far from nonexistent, particularly for males: only 10 percent of the men 66 to 71 reported no sexual interest and 24 percent no sexual intercourse. It was a different story for women between 66 and 71: 50 percent reported no sexual interest and 73 percent no intercourse. Partly this reflects the fact that men report higher rates of sexual activity at all ages. But Pfeiffer and associates did find that sexuality continued to play an important role for the majority of both sexes.

Sex differences in such studies appear to indicate that in marriage it is the man who determines whether sexual activity will continue or cease. The most frequent reasons given by men for stopping were inability to perform, poor health, and loss of interest (Pfeiffer et al., 1972). Masters and Johnson (1966) report that the most important reasons for declining sexual performance in older males are sociopsychological, particularly a "fear of failure." Such feelings may create problems for older couples and lead a wife to feel rejected if she does not understand

Table 8.1 CURRENT LEVEL OF SEXUAL INTEREST FOR A GROUP OF OLDER SUBJECTS, BY AGE AND SEX

	Number	Level of sexual interest (percentage)			
		None	Mild	Moderate	Strong
Men					
46–50	43	0	9	63	28
51–55	41	0	19	71	10
56–60	61	5	26	57	12
61–65	54	11	37	48	4
66–71	62	10	32	48	10
Total	261	6	26	56	12
Women					
46–50	43	7	23	61	9
51–55	41	20	24	51	5
56–60	48	31	25	44	0
61–65	43	51	37	12	0
66–71	54	50	26	22	2
Total	229	33	27	37	3

Source: Eric Pfeiffer, Adriaan Verwoerdt, and Glenn Davis, "Sexual Behavior in Middle Life," *The American Journal of Psychiatry,* vol. 128:10, p. 1264, 1972. Copyright, 1972, the American Psychiatric Association. Reprinted by permission.

Table 8.2 CURRENT FREQUENCY OF SEXUAL INTERCOURSE FOR A GROUP OF OLDER SUBJECTS, BY AGE AND SEX

		Frequency of sexual intercourse (percentage)				
	Number	None	Once a month	Once a week	2–3 times a week	More than 3 times a week
Men						
46–50	43	0	5	62	26	7
51–55	41	5	29	49	17	0
56–60	61	7	38	44	11	0
61–65	54	20	43	30	7	0
66–71	62	24	48	26	2	0
Total	261	12	34	41	12	1
Women						
46–50	43	14	26	39	21	0
51–55	41	20	41	32	5	2
56–60	48	42	27	25	4	2
61–65	44	61	29	5	5	0
66–71	55	73	16	11	0	0
Total	231	44	27	22	6	1

Source: Eric Pfeiffer, Adriaan Verwoerdt, and Glenn Davis, "Sexual Behavior in Middle Life," *The American Journal of Psychiatry,* vol. 128:10, p. 1264, 1972. Copyright, 1972, the American Psychiatric Association. Reprinted by permission.

her husband's fear of impotence. Many older women experience heightened satisfaction following menopause because they are freed from the pressures of preventing pregnancy (Notman, 1980). Their greatest problem is the unavailability of socially sanctioned, capable partners, because of the sex ratio among the aged and because of social disapproval of sexuality in single or widowed older women. The sexual activity of older women is more completely determined by marital status, and their most frequent reasons for ceasing sexual activity involve the death, illness, or inability of their spouse (Pfeiffer & Davis, 1972; Pfeiffer et al., 1972).

There are other variables affecting sexuality among the aged. Sexual activity is greater among those with higher socioeconomic status or good health (Pfeiffer & Davis, 1972). More important, continued sexual activity and enjoyment depend on previous sexual behavior and experience, with much less decline among those who were sexually active in their middle years (Pfeiffer & Davis, 1972; Ludeman, 1981).

WIDOWHOOD

We have already seen evidence of the importance of marital relationships in later life. Marriage is a central social relationship because of its intrinsic importance and the links it provides to other social activities and social networks. The sense of desolation experienced with widowhood is caused by the severe changes in everyday life and other associated social roles it entails. The new widow can no longer play the role of confidant, lover, housekeeper, or "member of a couple," and these changes may have far-reaching effects on one's style of living and personal identity.

Many types of gratification accrue from our associations with others. Schutz (1966) has proposed three basic interpersonal needs for which we seek to establish and maintain satisfying social relationships:

1. *Inclusion:* the need to be recognized and to belong, to share experiences and ideas, to feel that the self is significant and worthwhile.
2. *Affection:* the need for intimate emotional attachments, to feel that the self is lovable, the need for nurturance and support
3. *Control:* the need for public esteem in order to feel that the self is competent and responsible

All three of these needs can be met in the marriage relationship. Certainly companionship and affection are major reasons for marrying, and interaction with one's husband or wife ideally engenders trust, emotional understanding, and ready access. Control needs can also find an outlet. For one thing, marriage involves a dyad in which one partner may exercise power over another. In a less Machiavellian sense, one can acquire feelings of competence and mutual respect from satisfactory role performance and mutual decision making.

Marriage may assume even more critical importance for older people. Because of commitments and emotional investments, some relationships come to be viewed as unique, fragile, irreplaceable, and nontransferable (McCall & Simmons, 1966). In addition, older people lose other roles and relationships when children leave home and with retirement, and limited physical mobility may restrict the range of relationships that provide fulfillment of their interpersonal needs. Widowhood is therefore a potentially critical aspect of the aging experience.

The Cultural Context of Widowhood

As with all aspects of the aging experience, the consequences of widowhood depend on its cultural context, particularly the extent to which being widowed disrupts one's wider social network and roles. The degree of disruption can be thought of as a continuum (Lopata, 1973). The Hindu *suttee* tradition, which involves the widow's self-immolation on the husband's funeral pyre, may be looked upon as the most "disruptive," and the cultural tradition of *widow inheritance,* in which the lost husband is soon replaced with another man from the same group, as the least disruptive. Other cultures, such as traditional India, have an intermediate *status role* of the widow, resulting in isolation reinforced by special clothing or physical characteristics. The tradition of widows wearing black or a veil for a period of time would fulfill this function. A variety of roles may be assigned to widows (Lopata, 1973). They may be expected to continue the role of wife by tending the grave or by remarrying. Societies in which a high "bride price" is paid may require widows to continue working for the husband's family, who invested so much in her.

Most societies incorporate widows into the extended family in some fashion, although status may be lost (Lopata, 1973). Lopata suggests that roles for widows are most restricted in patriarchal societies that institutionalize extensive rights of men over women. Modern societies exercise less control over widows because of the declining importance of the extended family, strong rights of property inheritance for widows, increased independence for women, and greater choice of marital partners and other social relationships; but this often means that widows are also more likely to be isolated, face economic problems, and lack a widow role to replace the wife identity (Lopata, 1979). The lack of expectations and institutionalized structures for widows creates greater freedom but there is also the possibility that many widows will be set adrift both psychologically and socially.

The Personal Consequences of Widowhood

As one might expect, widowhood often has negative consequences for older people. For example, those who are widowed exhibit higher rates of mortality and suicide and rate their health more negatively (Riley & Foner, 1968; Fenwick & Barresi, 1981; Helsing & Szklo, 1981). Because the spouse role is usually a pervasive aspect of identity, there is likely to be at least short-term stress as the widowed person negotiates new roles and identities (George, 1980). One's spouse is also lost as a source of interpersonal need-fulfillment.

We must be careful, however, about overstating the impact of widowhood. Former identities can be preserved through memory or children, just as status derived from work often continues in retirement, nor is "wife" a central role for all women. Lopata's (1973) study of widows aged 50 and over in Chicago indicated that lower-class and black women, compared with more highly educated and white widows, tended to downgrade the wife role. The hardships of lower-class life may result in anger directed at the husband, and such marriages tend to involve less communication and sharing of activities. It is also true that the lower morale experienced by widows may partly come from things that accompany widowhood (such as financial problems or poor health) rather than widowhood itself (Morgan, 1976).

Widowhood may also have its positive aspects. Relief may be the predominant feeling for those with unhappy marital histories.

One of the NORC interviewers was so struck by the vehemence of a widow's feelings that she explained in the margin: "This woman went on about how little she thinks of men. Let me tell you, she hates them!" This respondent had tried marriage twice and was miserable both times. "There is nothing good I can say about it. I would go to bed unhappy and cursing while my husband was alive. After he died, I could say my prayers and go to sleep in peace. Women in those days married a man and stuck it out, going about their routine of washing, ironing and cooking regardless of how miserable they were. But the Lord did me a favor and removed my husband, so I would live out the rest of my days in peace." (Lopata, 1973:83)

Another type of relief may follow the end of a long, lingering illness. In addition, many widows mention the independence and release from duties that accompany widowhood, as illustrated by the following comment: "You don't have to cook if you don't want to: your time is your own; you can come and go as you want; you don't have to be home if your husband isn't there" (Lopata, 1973:75–76). In fact, half the widows in Lopata's sample reported that they "like living alone."

None of this denies the very real problems associated with "grief work" and role-identity adjustments. Although most widowed persons attain acceptable and even satisfying levels of adjustment, the process may be quite difficult (George, 1980). Lopata (1979) found that 60 percent of her sample of widows required a year or more of getting over their grief, learning to be alone and independent, and to establish a new life. Interestingly, "husband sanctification" appears to play a role in this adjustment. Lopata (1981) found that husbands are often idealized as "extremely good, honest, kind, friendly and warm," particularly by older widows, whites, higher-educated persons, and widows who attached greater importance to the wife role. She suggests that husband sanctification not only serves to boost status and morale by keeping the husband's memory alive but also facilitates successful "grief work."

Obviously there are many other problems that may be associated with widowhood. Aged widows comprise a large percentage of the older poverty population; and taking on unfamiliar roles (such as financial manager for many women and housekeeper for many men) always requires adjustments. Many of the widows in Lopata's (1973, 1979) research were quite ignorant of financial matters, and their ability to work was restricted by age, poor health, and low marketable skills. Indeed, 78 percent experienced decreased income following widowhood and 35 percent were below the poverty level. Economic advice was a source of strain with family and friends. Many widows felt acutely vulnerable to bad financial advice or being cheated, and approximately one half felt that "people take advantage of you when they know you are a widow."

The Social Consequences of Widowhood

Widowhood inevitably results in at least a short-term social disruption and the need to fulfill many tasks during an often grief-stricken time. As we shall see in greater detail later, the family (adult offspring as well as the extended family) can be an important source of emotional, social, and financial support. Widows turn to relatives, especially children, more than to friends for assistance and support; Lopata (1979) found that 86 percent of the widows in her study considered children "very helpful" in establishing a new life. Assistance, particularly sharing a household, is more likely to involve unmarried children. Widows are also emotionally closer to daughters, and sons help primarily with financial matters, yard work, and car care. It is interesting that there was unwillingness on the part of the widows in Lopata's (1973, 1979) research to undertake too many obligations toward their adult children and some felt that children make unwarranted demands; for example, baby-sitting was often seen as an imposition. It appears that many widows have a keen sense of vulnerability to exploitation (financial, social, or otherwise) and are not desperate for just any kind of social contact.

Although children and perhaps other relatives can be important sources of support, widowed persons are increasingly inclined to live alone. The proportion of the widowed who live alone increased from less than 20 percent in 1940 to 50 percent in 1970 (Chevan & Korson, 1972). The widows in Lopata's (1973, 1979) research preferred "intimacy at a distance." Having been accustomed to running their own homes, they did not wish to become dependent subordinates in someone else's house. This was a particular concern with married children, where moving in might involve considerable role reversal, status loss, and competition. In addition, these widows did not wish to impinge on the right of their children to lead their own lives, free from "outside meddling." The likelihood of living with relatives does increase after age 80, however (due to physical and financial problems), and is greater among nonwhites, females, lower socioeconomic groups, and those with children (Chevan & Korson, 1972). Perhaps as a reflection of differences in cultural expectations, the widowed are less likely to live alone if they are foreign-born, live in a rural area, or come from a traditional Catholic background.

Whereas children represent a source of support, other social ties are often disrupted by widowhood. Lopata (1973, 1979) found little involvement with other relatives and reduced friendship ties, although widows made greater use of friends for emotional support than while they were married. Many widows had quite limited social activities and supports; more than half reported they never went to public places, 40 percent never entertained, and from 10 to 20 percent could name no one who made them feel "important," "secure," or "accepted." This disruption of social networks is quite unfortunate. Apart from providing the usual gratifications of friendships, friends can help recent widows by keeping them occupied, offering sympathy and understanding, helping with bereavement, and so on. In fact, at least one study suggests that contact with friends is a more important determinant of satisfaction than contact with family (Pihlblad & Adams, 1972). Social interaction does not decline for everyone, however. Those who experience less change are those who were immersed in family contacts, home-based housewives, highly isolated during marriage, or social activists while married (Lopata, 1973). Nonwhites and members of close-knit ethnic communities also experience fewer problems, apparently reflecting subcultural differences in orientation to marriage and social supports (George, 1980).

Why would widowhood disrupt social networks? One reason is that accompaniments of widowhood, such as poor health or poverty, have isolating effects. But it is also true that widowhood itself creates problems. Many social activities—visiting, attendance at public places—are engaged in as a couple with other couples. Widowhood threatens continuation in this "society of couples" (Blau, 1961; Lopata, 1973). The recent widow may feel like a "third wheel" or be viewed by wives as a potential rival. Interests and needs may change and the widow may feel dependent for transportation. The lack of a male escort in a "couple-companionate world" may engender a feeling of alienation because of status loss.

"I feel that. Well, how can I put it in words? Second class citizen, that's true, you do feel that way. Well, I think just the fact that you don't have an escort when you go places—I think that this is very pronounced and very evident if you go out to dinner. I don't like to go out to dinner alone, so consequently you try to get on the phone and call somebody else up and see if they're in the mood to go. This sets you apart, you see a couple of women . . . I can remember down in Miami, I hate Miami for that reason. When I was not a widow yet, you'd see groups of beautifully gowned, elegant looking elderly women, you knew they were all widows. Immediately they were an isolated segment of society in my mind at that time, and I'm sure when we go into a restaurant, maybe two or three or four of us, I'm sure that other people look at us the same way." (Lopata, 1973:191)

Lopata found that although few widows limited their contacts solely to other widows and most retained at least some of their former friends, most had experienced some strains in their friendships. Involvement in the larger community, through neighbors or voluntary association, may offer some compensation, but neighboring is largely sporadic as few are used to such visiting as a major source of social contacts, and few clubs actively encourage membership by widows. Lopata notes that current cohorts of older women have been socialized to be relatively passive outside of the home.

The disruptive effects of widowhood depend upon one's position in the social structure regarding age and sex peers and social class. For example, women over 65 may become involved in a "society of widows" because widowhood is actually the norm for them (Blau, 1961; Cumming & Henry, 1961), whereas younger widows may experience a greater decline in social position. Morgan (1976) found that widows had lower morale than married women, but *older* widows catch up with (and may even surpass) the morale of the married. Widowhood is also less prevalent among males, and may therefore be more socially disruptive because it places them in an "unusual" position. Pihlblad and Adams (1972), for example, found a greater disruption of friendships for widowers than for widows. As with women, being placed in an odd social category by widowhood declines with age.

There are also important, although in some ways contradictory, social-class differences in the disruptiveness of widowhood (Lopata, 1973, 1979). The greater sharing of activities and friendships in middle-class marriages would suggest greater problems for middle-class widows. But this is apparently more than counteracted by the greater social opportunities and social skills possessed by better-educated middle-class women. Although they have been more involved in the marital relationship, they have also developed a wider network of interpersonal relationships and a greater variety of social activities, and their greater education gives them more self-confidence and better skills in building social relations.

Loneliness

The social disruption that often accompanies widowhood implies that feelings of loneliness may be a particular problem. In Lopata's (1973) sample of widows,

48 percent said that loneliness was their greatest problem. Loneliness involves more than being alone; it involves "being without some definite needed relationship or set of relationships" (Weiss, 1973:17). Weiss suggests that two types of isolation may result in feelings of loneliness. *Emotional isolation* is the lack of a truly intimate tie. It involves separation anxiety and utter aloneness that cannot be alleviated by just any alternative social relationship. This is likely to accompany widowhood because of the intimacy and sense of uniqueness attached to the marital relationship, which make it very difficult to transfer the needs satisfied through marriage to other relationships. The widowed are also likely to experience *social isolation*—lack of a network of involvements with peers—which engenders feelings of boredom, aimlessness, and marginality. Social isolation is more easily dealt with than emotional isolation because a wider variety of social relationships is satisfactory.

There may be age differences in emotional and social isolation. Greater access to a "society of widows" may reduce social isolation for older widows, but there is no reason to expect that emotional isolation will lessen with age. Longer spouse relationships may be seen as more irreplaceable, and the loss (through death, poor health, or mobility) of other long-term intimates may have heightened the importance of the marital interaction.

Lopata (1969; 1973) indicates that there are many types of loneliness that may be experienced by widows. One can be lonely for an individual as a person, or miss having someone around, someone to share experiences with, or someone to care for and love. The loss of a companion is expressed by the following:

> I don't think anyone who hasn't experienced it can understand the void that is left after losing a companion for so many years—all the happy little things that come up and you think, 'Oh, I must share that'—and there isn't anyone there to share it with. . . ." (Lopata, 1969:251)

Lopata (1973) notes that widows are especially likely to feel lonely at dinnertime. Not only must they eat alone, but the entire rhythm of the housewife role is disrupted when there is no "object" for one's tasks. Widows may also feel lonely because they miss being the object of someone else's activities and love. Finally, there is the loneliness felt for life-style or set of activities engaged in as a couple.

There are a variety of ways to combat loneliness, of course. The usual prescription is to "keep busy," which may involve a self-conscious scheduling of activities, as engaged in by one widow:

> "I find that the lonesome part of the day is at dusk. I don't have my mail delivered and I usually go out and get my mail or do some shopping at this time—just to get away from the house then. People say they call me up at 6:00 and 'you're not home.'—I tell them it may be a good time for most people but it isn't a good time to get me because then I feel too lonesome. I just get out. I have a car so I drive around a little. I generally eat dinner late at night. . . . I have a little TV in the kitchen too so I can eat out there. I think it's kind of lonely to eat alone—that's why I watch TV or read the papers." (Lopata, 1969:256)

Many widows seek new roles and relationships through activities with family, friends, or voluntary associations, but success in this depends on the prevalence of widows among one's age sex peers and the prior development of social interests and skills.

Sex Differences

Most of this discussion has drawn on studies of widows, and relatively little research has included widowers. But the implications of widowhood are likely to differ for men and women. Bell (1971) has suggested that widowhood is more difficult for women because of traditional sex-role socialization and expectations, which make the marital role a more important part of the self for women. Their lesser social aggressiveness is combined with less opportunity and encouragement to remarry, and widows typically face a bleaker financial future. Atchley (1975), for example, found that widowers had greater social participation than widows because of the economic supports they possessed.

Some observers suggest that men have more difficulty adjusting to widowhood than women and encounter greater social isolation because of it (Blau, 1961; Berardo, 1970). Widowhood is more unusual for men, therefore a "society of widowers" is more difficult to achieve. Just as the wife may be relatively unprepared for certain tasks (financial management), the husband also may be unprepared for the daily tasks of running a household (cooking, cleaning, and so on). Widowhood may more often constitute a double blow for men, who are likely to have already experienced the social disruptions of retirement. Men also may experience greater difficulty satisfying emotional needs outside of marriage. Having typically cultivated fewer family ties, they may have more extensive friendship networks than women, who have more stable, long-lived, and intimate relations outside of marriage (with relatives and friends) (Hess, 1979). Table 8.3 presents results from a study investigating sex differences in the consequences of widowhood (Ward, 1981). Whereas widowed women have fewer confidants than their married counterparts, widowed men are more likely than married men to have *no* confidant; the study also found a stronger association between widowhood and lower morale among men. Lopata (1980) has noted that widowers have higher rates of mental illness, suicide, and mortality than widows.

Table 8.3   PRESENCE OF A CONFIDANT BY MARTIAL STATUS IN A SAMPLE
OF MEN AND WOMEN AGED 60 AND OVER

Confidants	Males		Females	
	Married	Widowed	Married	Widowed
None	8%	20%	5%	11%
1	68%	67%	61%	70%
2 or more	23%	12%	34%	19%
	100%	100%	100%	100%
Number of respondents	782	202	531	1,011

Source: Ward, 1981.

More important than whether widowhood is more difficult for men or women is the recognition that they are affected differently. In some ways widowhood is more difficult for women, in other ways for men, as both are placed at a disadvantage by prevailing sex roles. What these patterns suggest is that restricted roles and the failure to develop multidimensional social relationships will make any kind of role loss more traumatic. In any case, widowhood is clearly a difficult experience for most. Lopata (1973) has drawn certain conclusions from her study of widows in Chicago. First, the widowed need help with "grief work" because society largely leaves the individual to his or her own resources (see Chapter 12). A second pressing problem is companionship. Lopata observed an almost paranoic anxiety concerning social relationships. The larger community may be of assistance through widow-to-widow programs or adequate scheduling and transportation for social activities. Finally, Lopata suggests that what the widowed need is not a lot of advice, but rather confidence-building experiences that would encourage them to rebuild their patterns of living for themselves.

Remarriage

One course of action following widowhood is remarriage, although this is not a widespread phenomenon, and remarriage is less likely following widowhood than following divorce (Treas & Van Hilst, 1976). Lopata (1979) indicates that few widows expect to remarry. Many do not wish to lose their independence and are concerned about being taken advantage of or hurt again. Only 22 percent of the widows in her study had had a close relationship with a man since being widowed, and only 6 percent had remarried. Widowers are more likely to remarry. Whereas less than 20 percent of men widowed after 65 remarry, less than 5 percent of women widowed after 55 do so (George, 1980). This may reflect greater emotional dependence on marriage among men, but there are also simply more available older women than older men.

Remarriage does occur, of course. In 1970 there were approximately 60,000 marriages involving older people, almost all of which were remarriages (Treas & Van Hilst, 1976). These unions often involve people who have known each other for years, frequently as part of an earlier group of couples that included the former spouses (Lopata, 1979; Troll et al., 1979). The likelihood of remarriage is quite high for those widowed in their thirties or forties but declines rapidly with age. Remarriage is also more likely for whites, urban residents, widows with greater education and income, and younger widows with dependent children (Cleveland & Gianturco, 1976; Treas & Van Hilst, 1976; Lopata, 1979). Although some persons remarry because of anxieties about poor health or a wish to avoid becoming dependent on children, a desire for companionship and affection is the primary motivation (McKain, 1972; Troll et al., 1979). McKain found a high rate of success in a sample of 100 older newlyweds. He argues that success is more likely when the couple have known each other well for a long time, friends and relatives approve, and income is sufficient.

AGING AND THE EXTENDED FAMILY

Our discussion to this point has treated only one part of the family life of the aged—the marriage relationship. Obviously the family is a much broader social context that can affect the aging experience in many ways. As a source of social and emotional outlets and a variety of personal services, an older person's family can have tremendous benefits. On the other hand, the family can be a source of conflict and strain. For example, the aged are very reluctant to become dependent on their children because of the implications of role reversal and value conflict. In order to understand the impact of family ties on older people we first must understand their position in the larger family structure.

Modernization and the Family

The *classical extended family* of preindustrial societies has been described as a patriarchal organization of parents, unmarried children, married sons and their families, and occasionally brothers and their families, who lived together under the authority of the extended family (Sjoberg, 1956). Extended kin relationships were primary factors in determining occupational and political success. Beginning in the 1940s, articles appeared announcing the "death" of the extended family and its replacement by a more autonomous, even isolated *nuclear family* (parents and children) (Elder, 1981). This was attributed to the related processes of industrialization and urbanization. The new occupational system engendered by industrialization required greater mobility, thereby dispersing the family. New institutions emerged to take over functions formerly played by the extended family: economic production, education, financial support, health care. The more impersonal urban milieu fostered greater nonfamily involvement and smaller residences reduced the ability of families to live together. Finally, values stressing freedom of movement and democratic relationships were antithetical to the authority of the extended family.

This *structural-functionalist* argument asserted that as modernization reduced the functions of the family, its structure could be expected to change. The presumed remaining functions of the family—socialization of children and stabilization of adult personalities through the marital relationship—could best be performed in an autonomous nuclear family. If this shift from extended to nuclear family is real, the aged will be cut off from family supports they may have enjoyed in the past. But how much truth is there to this argument?

It should first be noted that the classic extended family has never been widespread. In the Plymouth colonies, for example, the nuclear family was typical (Demos, 1970). Lower life expectancy made the three-generational household unusual. Those who did survive to old age, however, were likely to live in a three-generational family because of values and norms and housing shortages. Older persons in the past also often controlled family property, but young people now are less dependent on family property, and values tend to support residential separation.

Nevertheless, empirical studies indicate that the demise of the extended family has been greatly exaggerated (Bengtson & DeTerre, 1980; Lee, 1980; Streib & Beck, 1980). Interaction among kin remains quite frequent, with affection and reciprocal provision of services, and people still consider their kinship ties important, even in the absence of residential proximity. It does not appear that urban life necessarily results in family deterioration or the replacement of kin ties by friends, neighbors, or voluntary associations.

What seems to have evolved is not an isolated nuclear family but rather a *modified extended family*. The extended family has become more geographically dispersed and exercises less authority. Kin relations have become more open and voluntaristic. But family ties remain important in fulfilling social and emotional needs and providing a wide range of services. An ideology of "taking care of one's own" persists among younger cohorts, although they allow other social institutions to take major responsibility (Sussman, 1976).

Why has the extended family continued to play an important role in modern society? Bengtson and DeTerre (1980) cite three sources of family solidarity: associational (frequent contact and exchange of support), consensual (norms of responsibility and reciprocity), and affectional. A combination of affection, general obligation, and long-term reciprocal commitments results in a "positive concern" for the well-being and activities of kin (Adams, 1967), because of which family ties tend to be more persistent than friendships, more narrowly based on sociability and similarity. How many of our friendships from college survive for 10 or 20 years? When we do develop positive concern about friends, we often say the person is "like a sister" or "like a father." This mutual interest keeps family ties alive over the years and across the distances that separate people. These family ties are sustained through ceremonies and holidays—weddings, funerals, christenings, Christmas.

Modernization has not stripped the extended family of its functions. Families remain the preferred source of help. Family assistance is not considered welfare, but stems instead from a long history of reciprocity. Mobility need not reduce family ties because a dispersed family can aid individuals who move, and modern communication and a monetary economy allow the family to communicate and exchange services without face-to-face interaction (Litwak & Szelenyi, 1969). Families also play an important mediating role between older persons and service bureaucracies (Bengtson & DeTerre, 1980). Indeed, intergenerational conflict may be reduced when families are less involved in direct provision of assistance. The extended family also offers a network of interpersonal relationships to compensate for or replace ties that are missing or lost for the single or widowed, for example. Thus, the aged can at least potentially be enmeshed in a complex family network of affectional ties and reciprocal assistance.

Family Involvement of Older People

One aspect of family involvement is living arrangements. Most older people prefer not to live with their children or other relatives. Shanas and associates (1968) found that only 8 percent of a national sample of older people said they preferred to live with children or other relatives whereas 83 percent preferred their own home. In recent decades the aged have increasingly lived in their own households (and more often with spouse) rather than with relatives. Between 1940 and 1975 the percentage living in a household of another relative declined from 15 to 4 percent for older men (65 +) and from 30 to 13 percent for older women (Mindel, 1979); even among older unmarried persons only about 20 to 25 percent reside in multigenerational households. These patterns do not mean that the elderly have been abandoned and forced to live alone because the family remains as a viable alternative for those who need it. Those who live with their children (or other relatives) are likely to be older, widowed, in worse health, and have lower income.

Probably a more important aspect of family involvement is the extent of actual interaction with kin. Approximately 80 percent of all older people have living children, and there is considerable interaction between older parents and their children (Bengtson & DeTerre, 1980; Lee, 1980; Streib & Beck, 1980). For one thing, they are likely to live in close proximity. A study conducted in the United States, Great Britain, and Denmark found that in all three countries over three quarters of older people with living children lived within 30 minutes of at least one child (Stehouwer, 1965). Interaction is frequent as well. Slightly over a half of older people see at least one of their children every day or two, and three fourths see one at least weekly (Shanas et al., 1968; National Council on the Aging, 1975; Shanas, 1979). Shanas found that only 11 percent of older people with living children had not seen at least one of them in the previous month. Contacts are also maintained with other family members. Between one third and one half of older people see a sibling every week or two (Shanas et al., 1968; National Council on the Aging, 1975; Shanas, 1979). Nearly three quarters of those with grandchildren see a grandchild on a weekly basis (National Council on the Aging, 1975). Shanas (1979) found that among older people with surviving children 87 percent had seen a child or some other relative within the past week. At the very least, it appears that most older people are not isolated from their children and other kin, and even those who do not live near their children compensate by telephoning and writing letters.

What needs does the family meet for the aged? There is the companionship and affection embodied in the "primary" nature of family ties, which make the extended family important in its own right and also as a wide-ranging network for compensation and replacement of interpersonal relationships. The aged are susceptible to social loss because of retirement, widowhood, illness or death of peers, and limited personal mobility. Relations with neighbors are typically restrained anyway, and older people may find it hard to make new friends because of poor health or low income (which restrict going out and entertaining). An English study found that the percentage who had been visited by a friend or neighbor during the previous week declined from 74 percent among respondents aged 50 to 59 to 53 percent among those 70 and over (Willmott & Young, 1960). The large number of relationships available in the extended family can compensate for such losses.

A reduced family network can create problems for older people. Although childlessness is not generally related to well-being in the older population, there are indications that it results in lower morale and greater loneliness for those who are widowed and for older women (75+) (Glenn & McLanahan, 1981; Singh & Williams, 1981; Beckman & Houser, 1982). This is also reflected in the lower family satisfaction of never-married older persons (Ward, 1979). Other family ties may partly compensate for those never established. Shanas (1979) found that 55 percent of childless older people had seen a sibling or other relative in the previous week. Similarly, Willmott and Young (1960) found that 43 percent of never-married older people had seen a sibling in the past 24 hours, compared with only 6 percent of those who had been married.

It is apparent that extended family ties are important to the aged, and aged family members may also play a key role in maintaining extended kin ties. Contacts with siblings, and particularly with more distant kin such as aunts, uncles, or cousins, may occur through intermediaries like older parents. If so, the death of this older intermediary may loosen or break up the extended family network.

In addition to the fulfillment of interpersonal needs, the extended family can provide more tangible help and services: help during illness, financial aid, child care, advice, gifts, and so on. Such mutual assistance is a widespread pattern. For example, Shanas and associates (1968) found that approximately two thirds of their respondents in the United States received help from children and a considerable minority relied on relatives as the sole source of assistance for everyday personal and household tasks. Shanas (1979) found that the immediate family (spouse and/or children) is the major and preferred source of assistance for bedfast older persons, and social services are used very rarely.

Assistance does not only flow *to* the aged; throughout the life cycle there are mutual and reciprocal patterns of aid. In the National Council on the Aging (1975) survey, older people reported giving considerable assistance to their children and grandchildren: 68 percent helped during illness, 42 percent gave financial assistance, 39 percent provided advice, 34 percent did shopping and ran errands, and 26 percent fixed things or helped with housekeeping. Even among persons 80 and over, 57 percent helped during illness and 38 percent helped financially. This pattern of mutual aid is illustrated in a study of three-generation families (Hill, 1965). Table 8.4 indicates the types of assistance given and received by each generation. No generation is entirely a giver or receiver, but giving is generally highest for parents and lowest for grandparents, although differentials are least in the economic sphere. Not surprisingly, married children received the greatest assistance with child care, whereas the grandparent generation was most likely to require help for illness and household management. Note, however, that 32 percent of the grandparents also provided illness assistance to younger generations, such as the grandmother who becomes a "live-in nurse" for a sick grandchild. Thus the aged are not simply reduced to "cashing in" the obligations accrued from their parental assistance.

Although the extended family can offer tremendous benefits to its aged members, a few words of caution are in order. The three- and four-generation family is no longer rare. Shanas and associates (1968) found that 44 percent of

Table 8.4 COMAPRISON OF HELP RECEIVED AND HELP GIVEN BY GENERATION FOR CHIEF PROBLEM AREAS (PERCENTAGES)

	Economic		Emotional gratification		Household management		Child care		Illness	
	Gave	Rec'd	Gave	Rec'd	Gave	Rec'd	Gave	Rec'd	Gave	Rec'd
Grandparents	26	34	23	42	21	52	16	0	32	61
Parents	41	17	47	37	47	23	50	23	21	21
Married children	34	49	31	21	33	25	34	78	47	18

Type of crisis (spanning header over Emotional gratification, Household management, Child care)

Source: Reuben Hill, "Decision Making and the Family Life Cycle," in *Social Structure and the Family: Generational Relations,* by Ethel Shanas and Gordon Streib (eds.), © 1965, p. 125. Reprinted by permission of Prentice-Hall, Inc., Englewood Cliffs, N.J.

their older sample were members of a three-generation family, and another 32 percent of four-generation families. Thus older persons may find themselves at the pinnacle of a vast network of literally hundreds of kin relationships. But there is great diversity in family structure, and many widowed or single older people find themselves completely isolated from social contacts. The extremes are illustrated by the following case histories:

> Mr. Fortune, aged seventy-six, lived alone in a two-room council flat . . . Mr. Fortune had been a cripple from birth and he was partly deaf. He was unmarried and his five siblings were dead. An older widowed sister-in-law lived about a mile away with an unmarried son and daughter. These three and two married nieces living in another borough were seen from once a month to a few times a year. . . . He spoke to one or two of the neighbors outside his flat but he had no regular contact with any of them. He had one regular friend, living a few blocks away, who came over to see him on a Sunday about once a month. (Townsend, 1957:171)

> A married woman of sixty-four lived with her husband, a single son, and a granddaughter. She had a part-time occupation as an office cleaner. Three married daughters lived nearby and she saw them and four of their children every day. She saw two of their husbands nearly every day and one once a week, her eldest son and his wife only once or twice a week. The surviving members of the husband's family were not seen, but two of the wife's nieces called every fortnight. She had a widowed friend living alone whom she visited once a fortnight but she took pride in not having any regular association with a neighbor. She went to the cinema once or twice a month. (Townsend, 1957:168)

Kerckhoff (1965) suggests that although we express norms that support a modified extended family, actual *behavior* is less likely to display this mutual support. Kinship relations have lost much of their obligatory nature and become more permissive and voluntary. Thus not all kin are truly "available." Distance divides children into intimates, weekenders, and holiday companions, and other family members are characterized as either "intimate" or "recognized" (seen only on ritual or holiday occasions) (Townsend, 1957). A study of working-class kinship in Philadelphia found that if the only proximate kin are *distant* relatives (aunts, uncles, cousins), contacts are likely to be only sporadic (Rosenberg & Anspach, 1973). Therefore the available extended family may be effectively limited to children and their spouses and siblings. Rosenberg and Anspach also found that the aged often experience an atrophy in their kin pool as relatives die and often have difficulty extending family relationships to compensate for losses.

The research on family involvement of the aged has largely focused on the frequency of family contacts, leading one to wonder about their quality and meaning. Irving Rosow (1965) points out that these studies do not necessarily indicate *emotional* closeness or warmth. Emergency aid is not the same as stable, continual interaction, and involvements may be largely ritualistic, as with holiday family gatherings. Older people value independence for their children and themselves, but there is also some ambivalence. They do not wish to impose or be dependent, but neither do they wish to be neglected or ignored: "They shouldn't have to visit me or take care of me, but it would be nice if they did."

Variations in Family Structure

The position of the aged in the family is affected by a number of factors. Studies indicate that the working class has stronger kinship ties, living closer and interacting more regularly with family than does the middle class (Troll et al., 1979; Lee, 1980). For example, studies of working-class areas around London suggest that most of the basic rights, obligations, and needs of individuals are expressed and satisfied within a three-generation extended family characterized by close residential proximity, daily interaction, and such reciprocal services as shopping, cleaning, and illness care (Townsend, 1957; Willmott & Young, 1960). Middle-class families partly compensate for greater geographic dispersion with the use of transportation and communication facilities, however, and are also involved in inter-family help networks. Lee (1980) suggests that the extended family may be particularly strong under conditions of extreme poverty, as family members seek to pool their resources, and under conditions of extreme wealth, as they seek to consolidate their resources (e.g., the Rockefellers and Kennedys).

Class differences in family interaction and assistance partly reflect differing proximity. Rural elderly also interact more frequently with relatives because there are more nearby. But these patterns may also reflect differences in family values. Kerckhoff (1966b), in a study in North Carolina, has found three conceptions that older people have of family norms:

1. *The extended family cluster:* parents live near children with considerable mutual aid and affection (expressed in 20 percent of the families)
2. *The modified extended family cluster:* mutual aid and affection, but no necessity for nearness (60 percent of the families)
3. *The nucleated family cluster:* expected to neither live near children nor engage in mutual assistance (20 percent of the families).

The modified extended family was clearly the modal category. Extended family values were most likely to be expressed by the rural working class with large families, whereas nuclear family values came largely from urban, well-educated, and mobile white-collar respondents with small families. Kerckhoff points out that older people with nuclear family values are likely to be pleasantly surprised by the extent to which mutual affection and aid continues in modern societies, whereas those holding extended family values may well be disappointed.

As noted in Chapter 3, minority aged are also embedded in extended family networks, and in some respects to a greater degree than older whites. For example, the National Council on the Aging (1975) survey found that older blacks were more likely to provide advice to children and grandchildren, suggesting that older blacks may play a more central role within the extended family. Extended family ties represent mutual support (material, social, and emotional) to assist survival in an environment hostile to a disadvantaged minority.

Finally, it appears that sex is the most important source of variation in family roles and involvements. Women tend to be closer to kin, to consider them more important, to interact more with family, and to be more active in kinship activities and obligations than men, who focus more exclusively on the marital relationship (Troll et al., 1979; Bengtson & DeTerre, 1980; Lee, 1980). This has a number of consequences. Older people are more likely to have contact with daughters than with sons and to live with the daughters' family, and older women are more likely to interact with and receive assistance from their children. However, these patterns may also represent considerable role overload for "women in the middle"—middle-aged working women who play the major role in assisting not only their children but also their parents (Brody, 1981).

THE GRANDPARENT ROLE

A final family role available to older people is that of grandparent. Actually, this is becoming a middle-aged role because it is increasingly common to have grandchildren in one's forties and fifties; and with widespread emergence of four-generation families, approximately 40 percent of the aged are great-grandparents. Grandparenting is a potentially important source of gratification and responsibility because it is one of the few new roles open to older people. We have already seen that the aged are involved in fairly regular interaction within the modified extended family, and grandparents can be an important source of assistance during family emergencies. Most of the research on grandparenthood however indicates that the role has limited significance for most older people and is often primarily symbolic and ritualistic with little meaningful involvement of grandparents in the lives of their grandchildren (Kahana & Kahana, 1971; Wood & Robertson, 1976; Troll, 1980).

Views of Grandparents

The most extensive study of the grandparent role was conducted by Neugarten and Weinstein (1964) through interviews conducted with 140 grandparents in Chicago. Although most grandparents expressed comfort and pleasure in the role, nearly one third mentioned some type of discomfort derived primarily from seeing the grandparent self-image as alien ("I'm too young to be a grandmother!"), conflict with parents over child rearing, or indifference (and occasional guilt because of it) to responsibilities for grandchildren.

The most prevalent meaning of the role was as "a source of *biological renewal* ('It's through my grandchildren that I feel young again') and/or *biological continuity* with the future ('It's through these children that I see my life going on into the future' or 'It's carrying on the family line')" (Neugarten & Weinstein, 1964:202). The next largest group felt remote from their grandchildren, expressing considerable psychological distance. Third in significance was emotional self-fulfillment through a new emotional role. Very few of these grandparents functioned as resource persons or achieved vicarious fulfillment. The overall pattern of these results suggests little authority over or involvement in the lives of grandchildren. Another study found that the grandparent role was limited to occasional baby-sitting, outings to the zoo or movies, and similar short-lived interactions (Wood & Robertson, 1976). Fewer than half reported ever telling grandchildren about family history and customs or teaching special skills (such as cooking or fishing).

Reported "styles" of grandparenting also reflect a relative lack of involvement (Neugarten & Weinstein, 1964). The most frequent style was a *formal* one, reflecting a "proper" role that clearly separated parental and grandparental functions. Although minor services and indulgences were allowed, care was taken not to interfere in child rearing. Two other roles were prevalent: (1) *fun-seeking,* emphasizing informality, playfulness, and mutual satisfaction, and (2) *distant figure,* largely confined to ritualized family gatherings. The *parent surrogate* was confined to grandmothers and very few functioned as a *reservoir of family wisdom.* Similarly, Robertson's (1976) study of 125 grandmothers found that over one half had *remote* or *symbolic* relations with grandchildren, attaching little personal significance to the role; less than one third attached personal and social significance to being a grandmother.

Variations in the grandparent role partly reflect the position of older people in the larger culture. Relationships between grandparents and grandchildren tend to be more formal and authoritarian when older people hold decision-making and economic power, but are warmer and more indulgent when grandparents are removed from authority (Kivnick, 1982). As noted in Chapter 3, grandparents are more likely to live in multigenerational households and participate in child care and housekeeping responsibilities in societies that have undergone rapid industrialization, such as Japan and China.

It also appears that maternal grandmothers and paternal grandfathers show the greatest closeness and warmth toward grandchildren (Kahana & Kahana, 1971). Apparently grandchildren are seen as more similar to one's own children through the father-son and mother-daughter relationships. We have also seen that family ties revolve around grandmother-daughter-granddaughter relationships. Because of the relative stability of the housewife role, grandmothers may have more relevant skills to offer granddaughters than grandfathers have for grandsons. Institutionalized older people have less interaction with grandchildren and the grandparent role has little significance for them (Kahana & Kahana, 1971). Their relationships with grandchildren tend to be extremely formalistic, perhaps reflecting the depersonalizing effects of institutional living. There are also indications that the grandparent role is more enjoyable and significant when interaction with grandchildren is frequent, involves trust and mutual respect, and is relatively free of interference from the parent generation (Kahana & Kahana, 1971; Lopata, 1973).

In a study of 68 black grandparents, Jackson (1971) found patterns similar to those indicated for whites. Interaction with grandchildren was relatively infrequent and grandparents did not play central roles within the black family. Interaction was more frequent for grandmothers and for those who were younger or lived alone. Although the majority expressed strong affectional closeness and provided a variety of supports, Jackson concluded that there was no support for the stereotyped view of black families as "powerful matriarchies" ruled by "black grannies."

Views of Grandchildren

There are few studies of grandparenting from the point of view of the grandchild, but two stand out. In a study of young children, Kahana (1970) links grandparenting to the changing needs of the developing grandchild. For children 4 or 5 years old, the grandparent is valued for his or her indulgent qualities—as someone who is "nice" and allowed to "spoil" the child. By age 8 or 9, the grandparent's active, fun-sharing role is stressed. But by the age of 11 or 12, there is a greater distance as the child grows away from the "doting grandparent." There is no indication here that the grandparent plays an authoritative role or a continuing significant part in the child's ongoing life.

Robertson (1976) studied 86 adult grandchildren (ages 18 to 24), who had quite favorable attitudes toward their grandparents. For example, they did not view them as too old-fashioned or likely to spoil children. They tended to view them as friends rather than "elders." Grandparents are sometimes notably lenient toward their grandchildren, engaging in a "privileged disrespect" between alternate generations (Townsend, 1957). The grandchildren in Robertson's study felt a responsibility to visit grandparents, provide emotional support, and give tangible help when needed. There were indications, however, that the grandparent role was not considered very significant. Grandchildren had few explicit behavioral expectations beyond gift giving and being the bearers of family history. Grandparents were not chosen as companions, advisers, liaisons with parents, role models, or financial supporters. The ideal grandparent was, first, "one who loves and enjoys grandchildren, visits with them, shows an interest in them," and, secondarily, one "who helps grandchildren out when they can, when asked or needed." The most important characteristics were being loving, helpful, understanding, a friend, and among the least important were their roles as mediators, companions, and teachers.

In general it appears that the grandparent role is largely informal. Although it may contribute to feelings of satisfaction, it is not typically significant or meaningful in the lives of either grandparents or grandchildren. Infrequent or sporadic social involvement is hardly a role to build one's identity around or to fill voids created by retirement and widowhood. Interaction is typically initiated by grandchildren or their parents rather than by grandparents (Robertson, 1977). Grandparents and grandchildren can have close emotional ties, but the grandparent role is more often one of diffuse nurturance or formal distance. Grandparents are "nice people" to whom we are tied by bonds of affection, but they seem to have little impact on our lives.

It must be recognized, however, that such conclusions are based on only a few small-scale studies. Troll (1980) suggests that there is recent evidence of reciprocal efforts to influence life-styles and values, therefore the role may have greater importance than has been thought. Grandchildren may also use their grandparents as role models when they eventually enter their own old age. Indeed, relationships with one's own grandparents are an important determinant of grandparent orientation and behavior (Kivnick, 1982). Kivnick found that persons who had positive grandchild experiences viewed grandparenthood as a more central and valued role.

AGING AND THE FAMILY: SOME CONCLUSIONS

Although the literature on the family is voluminous, there are critical gaps in our understanding. We know little about the *processes* of marital adjustment to the empty nest and retirement. The nature and quality of family interaction, including grandparenting, need much more investigation. There is little understanding of the implications of cohort-historical changes in the prevalence and timing of family transitions. What is the nature of retirement marriages for two-career couples? What are the effects of rising divorce rates on support from children and interaction with grandchildren? Such questions are important to a fuller understanding of the nature and variability of the life course.

Despite these uncertainties, we can draw some conclusions about the family life of older people. Although the extended family is an important source of support, there are limitations to this role (Ward, 1978). The extended family continues to be a viable institution for assisting with *acute* problems facing the aged—illness, financial help, support during bereavement. Every effort should be made to support the family's role in this regard, whether through financial assistance, counseling, home delivery of services, or some other mechanism. But the extended family now seems poorly suited to meeting the *chronic* material, social, and emotional needs of the aged. Assistance with such needs often represents a confining and stressful burden to children who had looked forward to freedom in middle age, and "children strive to delay the parents' institutionalization at considerable cost to themselves" (Robinson & Thurnher, 1979). The social and financial strains of caring for dependent older persons can contribute to lower family satisfaction (Mindel & Wright, 1982). Strain and resentment may have tragic consequences. It has been estimated that as many as 500,000 older people living with younger family members are physically abused (Wallace, 1980). A societal response is essential for problems of income, health care, housing, and transportation, which are too costly to be met by the family for more than a small minority of older persons. Families can then play an important role in mediating and coordinating formal services.

The effectiveness of the family as a helping institution may further decline in the future (Treas, 1977). Because of declining fertility rates, aging parents will have fewer descendants to call upon for assistance. There are also increasing numbers of "old-old" persons (75+), whose offspring are themselves elderly and less able to provide help. We have noted that women have been the mainstays of family networks, but Treas suggests that this involvement may be affected by the changing social roles (and interests, obligations, and constraints) of modern women.

Finally, one does not get a sense that family interaction is a major source of prestige, self-esteem, self-actualization, or meaningful uses of time. The family appears to have limited importance in the everyday lives of older people. Matthews (1979) notes that older people have lost their "significant place" in the family, which may force them to exchange compliance for support, use coercion and guilt to induce attention, or choose to be independent and do without. Meaningful roles and activities may be more available elsewhere, perhaps in the kinds of participations discussed in Chapter 7. Another possibility is involvement with friends and age peers, a topic of the next chapter.

SUMMARY

The family is a major source of primary social and emotional relationships. The family itself represents an arena of age stratification, and changing patterns of family structure reflect the variability of the life course. The marital relationship is particularly important because of the intimacy and sharing it implies.

In moving through the life cycle of the family, middle and old age bring two major transitions: the empty nest and retirement. The empty nest creates the potential for identity crises and disenchantment in the postparental marital relationship, but it also carries the possibility of greater freedom and independence and a renewal of couplehood. Retirement is a second transition requiring realignment of family roles. The key to retirement adjustment appears to be an emphasis on expressive qualities—companionship, sharing, and affection. Retirement marriages may eventually result in very difficult care-giving roles for older wives, but marriage represents a central source of well-being in later life. Divorced and never-married older persons are unusual and may be disadvantaged in fulfilling personal and interpersonal needs.

Although most older people are physiologically capable of active and satisfying sex lives, cultural stereotypes about "the sexless older years" may lead the aged to shut off normal sexual needs and gratifications. Sexual interest and activity tend to decline with age, but sexuality is far from nonexistent, particularly for males. The sexual performance of older males is often affected by sociopsychological factors, whereas older women are dependent on the availability of legitimized, capable partners. Sexual activity is also related to health, socioeconomic status, and previous sexual behavior.

The marriage relationship is important to older people because it is a focus for the fulfillment of all three interpersonal needs (inclusion, affection, and control) and because of a sense of uniqueness and irreplaceability attached to it. It is therefore not surprising that the widowed are less able to fill interpersonal needs, have higher rates of mortality and suicide, and are more likely to worry and be depressed. Although widowhood is not devastating for everyone, it can result in disrupted identity, poverty, and social and emotional isolation. One of the greatest problems is loneliness, as widows may experience various types of loneliness. The social disruptiveness of widowhood depends on one's social and cultural context. Unlike earlier societies, the modern role of widow is quite unstructured. Also, widowhood is more disruptive if it is unusual among one's age sex peers. For example, elderly widows may benefit from the availability of a "society of widows." Men appear to experience greater emotional and social disruption following widowhood, although they may be better off financially than widowed women. Remarriage following widowhood is unusual, particularly for women who are reluctant to give up their independence. Remarriage does occur, however, as older people seek companionship and support.

Some observers have suggested that modernization disrupts the extended family; however, a modified extended family has survived to provide tangible services and social and emotional support to older people. Older people prefer not to live with children, although poor health, low income, or widowhood may lead them to do so. But the aged tend to live near their children and to interact regularly with them, and many also interact with other relatives, such as siblings. The extended family provides a wide-ranging network of potential sources of interpersonal need-fulfillment. There is also considerable evidence of intergenerational exchange of services within the family. The extent to which older people are embedded in extended family relationships varies by social class and sex. Inasmuch as the extended family does retain importance for the aged in modern societies, more study is needed of the quality of these relationships.

The grandparent role does not appear to be a highly significant one for most older people. The primary styles are formal, fun seeking, or distant; few grandparents play authoritative or involved parts in the lives of their grandchildren. Grandparenting styles may be linked to the changing needs of the developing grandchild. Although attitudes of adult grandchildren are largely favorable, with feelings of responsibility and affection, expectations are few and grandparents are not seen as companions, advisers, or role models. Even their role as bearer of family tradition has been sharply reduced.

Many gaps remain in our understanding of the nature of family interaction and processes of adjustment to family transitions. The family is an important source of interaction and assistance in later life, but there are also limits to the ability of the family to provide assistance and to the quality of family involvements for older people.

chapter 9

Older People in the Community

We have been speaking of the aged as if they were displaced persons whose social ties are limited to work-related or family contacts. But older people are also residents of communities, living in neighborhoods and making friends. Too often we think of the elderly as not really part of their communities, as being helpless, dependent, and disengaged. Smith and Turk (1966) have pointed out that this stereotype fails to recognize that (1) older people are often important in keeping families together, (2) they often occupy positions of power in the community, (3) many prefer integration into the larger community to special age-homogeneous residences, and (4) they are likely to be the longest and most stable residents of a community. Thus older people *are* important members of their communities, and their position in the community is quite important to them. This does not mean that isolation is an unimportant concern. Indeed, there has been continuing gerontological interest in the social ties and supports of older people. As occupational and marital roles are lost, the neighborhood and surrounding community may assume heightened importance in the fulfillment of personal needs. Rosow (1967) has cited the importance of *social integration,* or social "belongingness," for the aged. We noted in Chapter 3 that some have argued that older people occupy a marginal social position in modern societies. Retirement, widowhood, health problems, and reduced finances create the possibility of weakened social integration. This suggests the importance of social involvement for older people.

More generally the social and physical environment may be particularly influential in the lives of the elderly. The *environmental docility hypothesis* asserts that reduced cognitive and physical competence (because of poor health, low education, and the like) means that older people may be affected more by their immediate environment and may be more passive in manipulating their surroundings to their own advantage (Lawton & Nahemow, 1973; Kahana, 1982; Lawton, 1980a). Related to this is the concept of *person-environment congruence,* underlining the importance of matching individual competence and preferences with environmental demands and opportunities. Proper matching will enhance well-being, whereas poor matching will be particularly problematic for the aged. This is reflected in social networks and housing situations.

SOCIAL NETWORKS

Social networks are important throughout the life course, offering both *instrumental* and *expressive* support (Fischer, 1977; Kahn, 1979). Instrumental support refers to more tangible assistance that includes advice, information, and services (loans, illness care, shopping, and the like). Expressive support refers to more intimate relationships that offer what Cobb (1976) refers to as "communicated sharing"—a feeling of being cared for and esteemed. Through the comparisons we make with others and our perceptions of their attitudes toward us, *significant others* and *reference groups* also become important determinants of self-concept and self-esteem (Rosenberg, 1981; Singer, 1981). Thus relationships with family, friends, and neighbors represent important sources of personal well-being, directly and indirectly, as protection against the effects of stressful life events (Pearlin & Schooler, 1978; Thoits, 1982).

Aging and Social Networks

The functions of social networks continue to be important in later life. Involvement with family and friends facilitates coping and adaptation through instrumental and expressive support. We saw widespread patterns of family assistance in Chapter 8, and similar patterns are evident with friends and neighbors. O'Brien and Wagner (1980) have noted that independent living is a myth, especially for older people who are physically frail. Rather, ability to remain independent often depends upon *interdependence,* as older people receive informal services that bolster their own sense of control. Regular social contacts provide an outlet to the outside world and at least an indirect check on the well-being of older persons. Social ties also play an important role in mediating between older people and formal service bureaucracies (Sussman, 1976).

Stable social networks lend a sense of continuity to the self (Lowenthal & Robinson, 1976). It should be remembered that older people are likely to have longer-lasting friendships, and old friends may indeed be the best friends. Not only do they share age-based similarities, but also their own relationship has a long history. As with work and marriage, increasing commitment is attached to friendships that persist, and such friendships can acquire the quality of "positive concern" more usually reserved for family relationships. These long-lasting friendships can be a tremendous source of social and emotional support during transitions associated with aging, particularly for those who lack institutional roles because they are retired, widowed, or single.

Friendships also play an important role in socialization, helping individuals to make smoother role transitions (Hess, 1972; George, 1980). Throughout our lives, as an integral part of the age stratification system, peers make many contributions to the socialization processes: emotional support during role transitions, provision of information about new and future roles, mutual opportunities for role rehearsal. Childhood play groups, for example, prepare children in many ways, both general and specific, for the adult roles they will play in the future with such seemingly simple things as "playing house," learning to abide by the rules of a game, and being able to cooperate in group efforts. Age peers can also be particularly helpful in preparing older persons for old age and assisting their adaptation to new situations and identities. Among the potential functions of age peer groups are the provision of emotional support, new group memberships and roles to replace those that are lost, norms and expectations to counteract the "normlessness" of old age, insulation from stigma, and real role models.

The value of a supportive peer group is illustrated in a study of older deaf persons (Becker, 1980). Early in life these persons had developed a strong sense of group identity with other deaf persons that helped them adapt to their social marginality and play down their disability. This shared social world continued into old age, helping forestall the impact of age-related losses. Becker suggests that the interdependence and mutuality exhibited in such "small societies" makes more general contributions to successful aging.

Social networks change over the life cycle, of course, Stueve and Gibson (1977) indicate that there is likely to be considerable social turnover early in adulthood when neighbors and coworkers substitute for childhood friends. This is generally followed by greater stability and long-term friendships. Old age may disrupt social networks, however. This is partly due to restrictions brought by illness, moving, and the death of friends. But disruption of social networks is also caused by the age stratification of roles (Hess, 1972). We typically make friends through the roles we play. Interaction with neighbors is greater when children are present in the home (Stueve and Gibson, 1977), and coworkers are often friends. Many friendships would not have been made except for the playing of certain roles, and older people, who are particularly likely to lose certain roles (through retirement, widowhood, and so on), are also vulnerable to losing the friendships associated with those roles. Loss of a role does not automatically sever friendships acquired through it, but friendships are highly voluntary and therefore quite fragile. They carry a connotation of "peership"—equality and similarity of status—that must be continually reaffirmed. A study by Lowenthal and associates (1975) found that similarity was the most important quality attributed to one's friends by people of varying ages. Role loss or role change removes this similarity, and if other bases of similarity are not present, the friendship will be lost.

Of course, the loss of one role often means taking on another, such as retiree or widow. Such roles may themselves be linked to friendships, as with the "society of widows" discussed in Chapter 8. But these roles do not usually open up opportunities for interaction the way work or marriage might. The role transitions of old age are largely role "exits" (Blau, 1973), involving a net loss of social opportunities. These role exits will be particularly disruptive of social participation when they set the aging individual apart from his or her age, sex, and social-class peers, differentiating the individual's interests and experiences from those of peers and reducing the mutuality upon which friendships are based (Blau, 1961, 1973). Thus the early retiree or the young widow often finds that role loss is particularly isolating. More generally the age stratification of roles narrows the social opportunities of many older people. Kahn (1979) notes that their "social convoy" is likely to become smaller and more unstable. And just as long-term friendships may be particularly important sources of support in old age, the loss of even one long-time friend (through death, illness, or residential move) can be especially devastating.

This does not mean that older people necessarily face social isolation. A significant minority are socially "impoverished," including long-term isolates and those who have experienced age-related losses (George, 1980). But most older people maintain meaningful social ties and possess a solid core of informal social supports.

Friends and Neighbors

Interaction with friends and neighbors is typical and often substantial. A national survey found that 60 percent of a sample of persons 65 and over had seen a close friend in the last day or so, and an additional 31 percent, within the last week or two (National Council on the Aging, 1975). Studies indicate that approximately two thirds of older people know at least one of their neighbors well and most are involved in mutual instrumental and expressive support with neighbors (Cantor, 1979; Ward et al., 1982). Most older people also have access to a *confidant,* an intimate relationship involving trust and expressive support (Babchuk, 1978; Cantor, 1979; Ward et al., 1982). However, this research also indicates that some older people are isolated: one third do not know any neighbors well, and from one sixth (Babchuk, 1978) to nearly one half (Cantor, 1979) have no confidant. Many older people report having fewer friends than in the past, although declines in social interaction are not likely to be pronounced until the midseventies and eighties.

The older population is not homogeneous in social participation, of course. Better health and high socioeconomic status are associated with having more friends and confidants and more frequent interaction with neighbors (Lowenthal & Robinson, 1976; Babchuk, 1978; Cantor, 1979; Ward et al., 1981). Length of residence in an area is also related to having more neighborhood friends, and city residents have less involvement with neighbors than suburban and rural older people (Ward et al., 1981). Lopata (1973) found that most of the widows she studied were quite restricted in the use of urban resources. These widows were not accustomed to using neighbors as a source of social contacts. Interaction was largely sporadic and "dropping over" was not a frequent occurrence.

There are consistent sex differences in the nature and quality of social networks (Lowenthal & Haven, 1968; Powers & Bultena, 1976; Babchuk, 1978; Hess, 1979). Older men typically have more friends, but older women have more intimate friends and a greater variety of confidants. Lowenthal and Haven (1968), for example, found that wives were the most likely confidants for men, but women were more likely than men to turn to children, other relatives, and friends. Women had greater flexibility in their intimate relationships, making them less dependent on the marriage relationship. Another study found that men are more likely to stress similarity in friendships whereas women place greater emphasis on reciprocity (support, understanding) (Lowenthal et al., 1975). To perhaps oversimplify, men seem to have "buddies" and women have "confidants" who can buffer social loss.

As noted earlier, social supports can be expected to make important contributions to the well-being of older persons. Surprisingly, however, evidence of a relationship between social activity and well-being is neither clear-cut nor consistent (Larson, 1978; Wood & Robertson, 1978; Conner et al., 1979). There has been a consistent failure to find a relationship with family contacts. A four-year longitudinal study found that declining social participation was generally accompanied by a decline in overall happiness (Graney, 1975); however, other research has found this to be true in only some cases.

There are several possible reasons for this inconsistent pattern. Social supports may be more important for certain subgroups of older people. Ward and associates (1982), for example, found stronger associations between morale and social involvement for older persons who were widowed or had health problems. Their vulnerability and relative isolation may make the interdependence of social networks particularly valuable. Lowenthal and Robinson (1976) distinguish between voluntary and involuntary social withdrawal, suggesting that declining social participation may be less important than whether it was chosen or forced on the individual. The *quantity* of interaction may also be less important than its *quality*. Lowenthal and Haven (1968) found that the presence of even one *intimate* friend serves as a buffer against age-linked social losses. Older people with this kind of confidant were able to experience declining social activity with considerably less depression. Finally, subjective feelings of social integration may be more important to morale than objective indicators. Liang and associates (1980) found that objective measures of social support (number and frequency of contacts) affected morale only to the extent that it determined *feelings* of loneliness and isolation. Similarly, another study found that whether children or neighbors were seen "enough" was more strongly related to morale than was actual contact (Ward et al., 1982).

The Relative Importance of Social Ties

Social networks are combinations of different types of social ties—family, friends, and neighbors. What are the relative functions and contributions of these different components? Two models have been suggested.

According to the *hierarchical-compensatory* model, kin (especially children) are preferred for social and emotional support, with friends and neighbors being used only to the extent that children are unavailable (because of distance, childlessness, and so on) (Cantor, 1979). This is attributed to the long-term bonds of affection and obligation noted in Chapter 8. Rules of reciprocity govern exchange relationships (Wentowski, 1981). Kin are expected to be the most consistent sources of help, as lifelong patterns of reciprocity and interdependence allow older people to receive assistance while maintaining self-esteem and feelings of independence.

Others have suggested that social ties are *task specific,* with each type of social tie best suited to particular functions (Litwak & Szelenyi, 1969; Dono et al., 1979). The more permanent, long-term commitments represented by family ties makes them most suitable for continuing assistance, but distance and limited face-to-face interaction makes them unsuited for quick emergency assistance. The proximity of neighbors makes them well suited for time emergencies and "watching over"; but because ties with neighbors are more short-lived, they are used less for continuing support. The particular value of friendships lies in their chosen quality and peership, compared with the more obligatory and ritualistic quality of kinship ties that may also involve generational conflict (Wood & Robertson, 1978). In a study of widows, for example, Arling (1976) found that family interaction, having a potential for conflict and unwanted dependency, was unrelated to morale, whereas involvement with friends and neighbors was associated with higher morale. He attributes this to greater equality, similarity, and mutuality in such relationships.

The truth is most likely some combination of the two models. Family ties are quite prominent in the social support networks of older people, being more frequently named for instrumental and expressive support (Babchuk, 1978; Cantor, 1979; Ward et al., 1982). Table 9.1 indicates the association between proximity of a child and type of person named as a confidant (Ward et al., 1982). The pattern indicates some preference for children, affected by their availability. But other social ties, including neighbors, are also chosen, even when children are nearby. Other relatives, and friends to a lesser extent, substitute as children are less accessible. This study found an even greater preference to use children for instrumental assistance, with neighbors (rather than kin) substituting when children are not available. Thus children are generally preferred sources of support, but this varies by type of support, and other relationships offer particular types of benefits.

The Role of Age Peers

Age peers may represent a particularly important component of the social networks of older people. For many reasons people tend to choose friends of their own age (Hess, 1972; Lowenthal et al., 1975; Powers & Bultena, 1976; Stueve & Gibson, 1977). The age stratification of roles results in relatively age-homogeneous settings for people to meet and become friends: the college populated by youth, the suburb in which young families reside, the work place of middle-aged persons, and so on. Age is also a measure of the type of *homophily,* or similarity, upon which friendships are based. There are two reasons that age yields similarity of experiences, interests, and activities. First, people of the same age come from the same birth cohort with common historical events and socializing experiences. Second, people of the same age are likely to share the same stage

Table 9.1 PERSON NAMED AS MOST IMPORTANT CONFIDANT, BY PROXIMITY OF NEAREST CHILD, IN A SAMPLE OF PERSONS AGED 60 AND OVER

	No children	Outside metropolitan area	Nearest child		
			Same metropolitan area	Same neighborhood	Same house or building[a]
Child	0%	25%	48%	50%	28%
Sibling	28%	19%	10%	10%	16%
Other relative	30%	13%	9%	9%	14%
Neighbor	28%	28%	23%	25%	28%
Friend	13%	15%	9%	7%	14%
	100%	100%	100%	100%	100%
Number of respondents	181	107	290	149	153

[a]Respondents named only confidants who were outside their own households.
Source: Ward et al., 1982.

in the life course—college, marriage, retirement. The shared interests and needs arising from this are the bases for friendships.

From an exchange perspective, reduced resource and authority of older people may place them at a disadvantage in their contacts with younger people (Dowd, 1980). Involvement with age peers may be more rewarding because they are on an equal-status footing, as familiarity and reciprocity minimize the costs of social exchange. Interaction with age peers may also represent attempts to select an "audience" that will help older people maintain their self-images (Matthews, 1979; George, 1980). Being in the company of others who are different, particularly when that difference places people at a disadvantage, can result in lower self-esteem because individuals are no longer able to have their own self-images validated (Rosenberg, 1981). Thus access to age peers may be an important aspect of person-environment congruence in later life.

The reduced mobility and associated environmental docility of older people also suggests that it may be important to have age peers nearby. Because the activities and interactions of the elderly are more localized, the similarity of neighbors represents a more prominent aspect of neighborhood quality (Kendig, 1976). One study of working-class older people found that three quarters of all those who had seen friends in the previous week said that *all* their friends lived on the same block (Rosenberg, 1970). Thus older people may be particularly vulnerable to the need to live immediately among people who can be their friends (peers) to avoid social isolation.

THE AGE MIX OF HOUSING FOR THE AGED

A question that arises is whether older people are better off in age-integrated settings, surrounded by a normal age mixture, or in age-segregated settings such as retirement communities or apartments for the aged. This question will not have a simple answer because the best living arrangement varies among individuals, but it would be useful to explore the relative advantages and disadvantages of the two types of housing arrangements. Age-segregated settings, be they retirement village or nursing homes, are sometimes seen as "dumping grounds" for the aged who are not wanted by their children or society. This impression is unfair and overlooks a variety of benefits to be gained from age concentration.

Resistance to age-segregated settings lies in the fact that only older people live there, as indicated in the following comments from a community sample of older people:

> "People in those places get to be chronic complainers and it's just because they are just with their own age groups and have no outside interests. . . . I don't think it's neighborly. I like to be with all ages and with children."
>
> "As far as I am concerned they are places you go to die. All you see is old age—very depressing. It is not conducive to an optimistic way of life. I like to look at the bright side of life."
>
> "Friends of mine that live in them tell me that they miss children and it seems like they are always going to funerals. You can't help wondering if yours will be the next one." (Sherman, 1971:131)

These respondents also disliked the loss of privacy, regimentation, and dependency implied by congregate living. They may simply not yet feel a need for the specialized services available in such housing. Those who have moved to old-age housing stress ease of maintenance and provision of services as their primary reasons (Sherman, 1971; Mangum, 1973; Heintz, 1976). They have found their homes too large and property taxes too high, and are seeking smaller, low-cost housing that still has certain amenities (particularly maintenance). Because of changes in physical strength and health, residents of old-age housing are also concerned that their health and personal needs can be cared for.

A second set of reasons stressed by movers to age-segregated settings is a desire for a better living environment. Climate is certainly one attraction of southern and western communities, and residents are attracted to the sociability and recreational facilities of retirement communities. People also move because they dislike their present neighborhoods. Heintz (1976) and Sherman (1971) found considerable antipathy to city life among the residents of retirement communities, including: bad neighbors (perhaps invasion of the neighborhood by "undesirables"), pollution, congestion, crime, too many children. These people were looking for a more relaxed, pleasant, and secure environment.

Interestingly, Sherman (1971), in her study of six different types of old-age housing, found that only one third of respondents expressed a desire to be with members of their own age group as an important factor in their decision to move. Although they were highly appreciative of the presence of friends, the decision to move into old-age housing was based primarily on a desire for various services and convenience.

There are many types of age-segregated housing. Some older people reside in retirement trailer parks, seeking ease of maintenance, controlled access, and sociability (Hoyt, 1954; Johnson, 1971). Communal living arrangements also exist for the aged (Streib & Streib, 1975; Sussman, 1976). Sussman notes that the Share-A-Home Association, consisting of a dozen older people living as a communal family in Florida, won a court ruling that the group was living as a "family" and therefore was not violating local zoning restrictions. These people jointly owned a 27-room mansion, shared expenses according to ability to pay, and hired a staff to run the house. The more common age-segregated settings, however, are old-age apartments and retirement communities.

Old-Age Apartments

Although retirement communities in Florida and Arizona have received much attention, the aged are more likely to live together within old-age housing developments in age-integrated communities. The most impressive early work on such settings was done by Irving Rosow (1967). Rosow recognized that age-integrated living arrangements could be successful, but only when certain conditions were met: (1) long-term residence in an area, (2) a relatively stable neighborhood that is socially homogeneous (in such things as class, race, or ethnicity), and (3) intact local primary groups (family and friends). Although these conditions are met for some, there are many older people who lack this social environment, such as the widow living in a fringe area of rapidly changing social composition, surrounded by people too different to be true friends. Rosow also argues that the stigma of aging and role losses experienced by the elderly results in a marginality best counteracted by age segregation. Thus the aged can achieve social integration within a segregated setting rather than being isolated in integrated settings.

Rosow (1967) tested his ideas in a study of apartment buildings in Cleveland, where he found that older people had more local friends and greater interaction with neighbors when there was a more dense concentration of age peers and, in any case, tended to choose friends from older residents. Put simply, older people had more friends (higher social integration) when surrounded by other older people. A study of six California retirement settings also found that residents reported more new friends and greater visiting with neighbors than matched controls living in integrated settings (Sherman, 1975a, 1975b). However, not all older people benefit from age concentration. Rosow found that the morale of isolates *declined* as age density increased because they did not wish to associate with neighbors, indicating the importance of person-environment congruence.

These studies also found networks of mutual assistance among the residents of age-concentrated housing, although there were limits to the utility of this support. Rosow found that the family was still the most important source of aid, and it did not appear that neighbors compensated for lack of family ties or could eliminate emotional dependence on children. Sherman also points out that not all of the sites she studied exhibited greater mutual assistance than the matched controls. Mutual dependency was greatest when the setting was isolated from the larger community and the residents were older, unmarried, and less mobile.

Illustrations of the type of social community that can arise in age-segregated settings are provided by two in-depth case studies of old-age apartment complexes: Merrill Court in San Francisco (Hochschild, 1973), and Les Floralies in France (Ross, 1977). In both cases there were already bases for the development of a sense of community among the residents. They were socially homogeneous to begin with: rural-born, working-class widows in Merrill Court, retired construction workers and their spouses in Les Floralies. Along with cohort similarities and shared problems of old age, this contributed to the feeling of being "all in the same boat." Residents were also faced with a "hostile" outside world that devalued and neglected the aged. Rather than seeing themselves as dependent because they lived in retirement housing, the residents viewed mutual assistance from age peers as making continued independence (from family and from society) possible. The importance of this background of shared experiences and problems is heightened by feelings that there is no place else to go. In the words of one Les Floralies resident: "After all, we are here for the rest of our lives" (Ross, 1977:85).

These background factors set the stage for the emergence of social communities, which was further facilitated by events and processes occurring within the residences. Community-wide interaction was centered at the Recreation Room in Merrill Court and at the communal noon meal at Les Floralies. Parties and elections (and resident decision making) were also focal points for community life. Interaction was initially fostered by formal activities and roles but soon spread to informal networks and loyalties on the living floors. Patterns of mutual assistance emerged that included exchange of goods and services (knitting, recipes, repairs) and help during illness. The residents of Merrill Court developed a systematic way of checking up on each other's well-being.

> Neighboring is also a way to detect sickness or death. As Ernestine related, "This morning I looked to see if Judson's curtains were open. That's how we do on this floor, when we get up we open our curtains just a bit, so others walking by outside know that everything's all right. And if the curtains aren't drawn by mid-morning, we knock to see." (Hochschild, 1973:53)

There are a number of indications of a true community in these residences. Residents had a keen sense of territory. Les Floralies residents, for example, defended an image of a residence, rather than a nursing home, and felt that "sick people should stay in their place" (Ross, 1977:89). A consensus emerged about "our way" of doing things that counteracted the usual ambiguity and normlessness of old age. Some activities were defined as *work*—making things for charity, playing in a five-piece band at nursing homes, working on the residents' committee—whereas others were *pure fun*—card parties, potluck dinners. Obligations were built up, such as the "Secret Pal" system at Merrill Court, whereby residents were anonymously paired to give $2 gifts on birthdays. Hochschild describes this as an "emotional insurance policy" to distribute a feeling of being remembered.

There was social pressure at Merrill Court to keep active and involved in the life of the community. Gossip was used as a means of social control and a way to relay information. This may seem oppressive, but all groups are oppressive in getting members to live up to the group's expectations. Les Floralies lacked this pressure to be active, but residents there had their own norms; conflict was disapproved, extreme flirtation was frowned upon, protection of individual privacy was stressed. Violation of norms was met with various sanctions, including "social quarantine" (e.g., no one would sit with the person at lunch).

A further indication of the true "groupness" of the setting was the emergence of an *internal* system of social status. Status was not determined by characteristics brought in by the residents, such as education or occupation, at least partly because there was such homogeneity. At Les Floralies, status was based on work roles in the residence and position within the two primary political factions (communist and noncommunist), which served as bases for interaction patterns and loyalties. Despite a norm against conflict, there was a considerable interpersonal gulf between these factions. Ross suggests that the very existence of political conflict shows that community life was important to residents. Status at Merrill Court had a different basis: the distribution of "luck" within a "poor dear" hierarchy.

> Those in politics and recreation referred to the passive card players and newspaper readers as "poor dears." Old people with passive life-styles in good health referred to those in poor health as "poor dears" and those in poor health but living in independent housing referred to those in nursing homes as "poor

dears." Within the nursing home there was a distinction between those who were ambulatory and those who were not. Among those who were not ambulatory there was a distinction between those who could enjoy food and those who could not. Almost everyone, it seemed, had a "poor dear." (Hochschild, 1973:60–61)

Thus members of a marginal, relatively disadvantaged group, which is often lumped together by society, were able to define their situation positively.

Because of reciprocity and similarity residents were much freer around each other. They could improvise new roles, act silly, reminisce, joke about old age, or discuss death—things they would do only in the presence of age peers. For example, they would rarely discuss death with kin or young people but needed to express their feelings somewhere. They also had access to role models of both successful and unsuccessful aging.

These peer relationships could not provide everything, however. Relationships with children constituted an emotional tie that peers could never be, and residents turned to kin in real emergencies. Hochschild notes:

In a deep sense and over the long run, the two kinds of relationships did not really compete; one could not replace the other even in the "time filling" sense. To the widows, children are a socio-emotional insurance policy that peers can never be. Kin ties run deeper and have a longer history than peer ties. When a grandmother is in deep trouble, she turns to blood ties first. When a widow needs a lot of money, she turns to kin; when she needs "something to tide her over till payday," she turns to a neighbor. When there was an accident or death in the building, peers were the first to find out, but kin were the first to be called. (1973:96)

Residents were also hesitant to incur too much obligation or more intimacy than was desired. Hochschild notes, for example, that they were more willing to invite someone in for a cup of coffee than for a meal, because a meal has deeper social implications. Nevertheless, the tit-for-tat quality of these peer relationships seem to offer benefits unattainable in more age-integrated housing arrangements.

Retirement Communities

With the possible exception of institutions for the aged, such as nursing homes, retirement communities represent the most age-segregated type of environment for older people. They are primarily a post-World War II phenomenon, apparently originating in Florida (Mangum, 1973). The earliest communities were run by nonprofit fraternal, church, and union groups to provide low-cost housing for their retired members, but private builders have become increasingly involved in planned communities. Such places have emerged to meet the need for smaller, cheaper, easily maintained housing, and to facilitate leisure life-styles for retirees.

There is tremendous variation among retirement communities. They are no longer confined to Sun Belt states like Florida and Arizona. Heintz (1976) has published a study of five retirement communities in the area between Philadelphia and New York City. Most retirement communities have age eligibility requirements (usually around 50 or 55) and planned services, housing design, land use, shared recreational facilities, and so on. They are usually relatively small, containing from 1500 to 7000 housing units (Heintz, 1976). Communities vary in the range of services and facilities offered to residents (hospital, buses, golf courses, and so on), the types of housing design (single-family dwellings, apartments, trailer parks), and therefore vary also in their costs. In her study Heintz found that the initial purchase price for a home varied from $16,407 to $30,996 among five communities, with a range from $9.82 to $77.80 for monthly maintenance. Retirement communities are generally beyond the means of most older people.

Various studies have found high morale among residents of retirement communities, in some cases higher than the morale of aged in integrated settings (Messer, 1967; Bultena & Wood, 1969; Heintz, 1976; Longino et al., 1980; Osgood, 1982). Longino and associates, for example, found that residents of midwestern retirement communities had greater social integration and more positive self-concepts than a national sample of older persons. Bultena and Wood (1969, 1970) have suggested three reasons for higher morale in retirement communities: (1) migrant retirees represent an elite in socioeconomic and health status; (2) such communities offer a pool of age peers as potential friends, yielding the benefits found in Rosow's research; (3) retirement communities facilitate a leisure life-style. Those who had moved to these communities are apparently already more oriented to leisure pursuits, and such settings provide facilities that include a wider range of specialized activities as well as a social environment and peer reference group supportive of leisure. Thus the residents are insulated from any stigma attached to leisure careers by the larger society. Messer (1967) also suggests that residents of age-segregated settings can become less active ("disengage") without feeling guilty. Interaction among age peers in an age-homogeneous setting encourages the development of their own values and norms, making them less dependent on the invidious judgments of society.

It appears, then, that age-segregated communities facilitate the social integration of their older residents. In a study of a retirement community, a mobile home park, and a condominium complex, Osgood (1982) found that each was a tightly integrated, close-knit community. Their residents were integrated through shared values, as the communities offered a variety of age-appropriate roles, activities, and norms. This counteracts the rolelessness and reduced social integration cited by Rosow (1967) as a problem of old age.

Residence in a retirement community does not necessarily imply isolation from family or the larger society. Heintz (1976) found that nearly half of the residents she studied participated in activities outside the retirement community. And Bultena and Wood (1969) found that migration to retirement communities did not precipitate separation or isolation from children. Nearly one fifth of the residents still had a child living within 20 miles. The presence of children does affect the decision to move; compared with nonmovers, residents of retirement communities had smaller families, were more likely to be childless, and were less likely to have had a child living in their community before the move. It is also true that one reason for moving to retirement communities is to avoid becoming dependent on children.

An additional issue concerning retirement communities is their impact on nearby or surrounding communities. There may be concern that a retirement community means a smaller tax base, greater service needs (particularly medical), and possible political dominance by conservative older voters, affecting such local issues as school budgets; but Heintz (1976), in a study of five eastern retirement communities, found these fears were groundless. All five generated a substantial revenue *surplus*. The property taxes they paid outweighed their use of local services; for example, they supported schools they did not use. There was no evidence that residence in retirement communities resulted in mobilization of an old-age political bloc. Analysis indicated that their voting turnout was not a significant factor in the approval or rejection of proposed school budgets.

The picture painted so far has been quite positive, but the reader should not be left with the impression that retirement communities are necessarily the best of all possible worlds. Although most published studies indicate considerable satisfaction by residents, they may miss such things as certain services (stores, restaurants), old friends and neighbors, and former houses. A study by Jacobs (1974) of a retirement community he calls Fun City offers ample evidence that such settings are not always what they seem. Although this was a planned community with many recreational facilities and social clubs, only about 500 of the 6000 residents participated in planned activities. An estimated 25 percent virtually never left their homes. The following illustrates a typical day in the passive way of life led by most residents:

MR. N.: Well, for me a typical day is—I get up at six a.m. in the morning generally, get the newspaper. I look at the financial statement and see what my stocks have done. I generally fix my own breakfast because my wife eats different than I do. So I have my own breakfast—maybe some cornflakes with soy milk in it—milk made out of soybeans that they sell in the health food store. And uh, then at eight a.m. my wife gets up. The dog sleeps with her all night. And uh, she feeds the dog. Then the dog wants me to go out and sit on the patio—get the sun and watch the birds and stuff in our backyard and we have quite a few rabbits back in there. And I finish my paper there. And then she sits and she looks at me. She'll bark a little bit. And uh, then she'll go to my wife, stand by my wife and bark at her. She wants me to go back to bed. So I have to go back to bed with her. So about eight-thirty a.m. I go back to bed again with my dog for about an hour. And then I get up and I read. And then I walk up around here and I go over to oh, the Mayfair [supermarket] and sit there and talk to people. We go over to the bank. They have a stockroom over there. For people that own stock. We discuss stocks and events of the day. And then I come home and maybe have lunch if I want to or not—it doesn't make any difference. *In fact, down here it doesn't make any difference when you eat or when you sleep. Because you're not going any place. You're not doing anything. And uh, if I'm up all night reading and sleep all day, what's the difference.* But then, I'll sit around and read and maybe a neighbor will come over or I'll go over to a neighbor's and sit down and talk about something. And lots of times, we go over to a neighbor's and we play cards 'til about five p.m. and then we come home and have our dinner. And the evening is . . . we are generally glued to the television until bedtime comes. And that's our day.

DR. J.: Is that more or less what your friends and neighbors do?

MR. N.: Some of them do. Some of them don't do that much. (1974:31)[1] [Emphasis added.]

Jacobs describes the community as an unnatural setting that fostered a blasé attitude and social isolation. Fun City was isolated from other communities and was not itself a true community—it lacked its own firemen, police, major medical facilities, public transportation, and adequate shopping. Despite being socially homogeneous to an extreme, residents tended to withdraw from all but casual and innocuous interactions to avoid giving or taking offense. Most of the residents had moved to Fun City from a large metropolitan area and experienced considerable "culture shock." All in all, Jacobs presents a rather dismal picture of what one resident called a "false paradise."

Age Segregation: Pros and Cons

Jacobs's study points out that age segregation can have negative consequences, but there are more general arguments that may be made against it. The most important is that integration—whether age, racial, religious, or any other—presumably promotes tolerance through a broadening exposure to people different from oneself. Lack of contact with the elderly may exacerbate negative stereotypes and fears concerning aging. In addition, the young themselves are deprived of the experience of their elders and of role models for the aging process. Perhaps housing integration could foster meaningful intergenerational contacts.

Unfortunately, housing heterogeneity appears to be a limited source of increased contact and tolerance. Increased tolerance is associated with equal-status, cooperative interactions (Seeman, 1981). Contacts with older people that lack such equality and similarity and involve dependence of older people may only confirm negative stereotypes. In order to be effective, age heterogeneity in housing

---

[1]From *Fun City: An Ethnographic Study of a Retirement Community* by Jerry Jacobs. Copyright © 1974 by Holt, Rinehart and Winston, Inc. Reprinted by permission of Holt, Rinehart and Winston, CBS College Publishing.

must be balanced by the similarity in interests and attitudes that leads to true friendships. Simply locating people near each other does not guarantee meaningful association—familiarity can breed contempt instead of tolerance.

Jacobs (1975) reports on a study of High Heaven, a high-rise retirement complex located on a university campus. It was hoped that shared facilities and activities (dining room, snack bar, films, volunteer programs) would foster interaction between residents and students. Indeed, the older residents liked to be around students, missed them when they were on vacation, and wanted to be involved, despite differences in their backgrounds. Unfortunately, Jacobs concludes:

> As things now stand there is little direct interaction between the residents of High Heaven and the university students. In fact, many students are literally unaware that retired persons live in High Heaven or that there is or ever was any affiliation between the residents and students. Most students are neutral to the presence of a limited number of residents in the student dining hall and some are puzzled; others are openly hostile. This is not to say that students do not from time to time help residents with their trays or show them other courtesies; they do, but the overall picture is one of indifference and clanishness, both on the part of students and residents. Each group stays very much to itself even when in the other's presence. (1975:24)

Differences between the groups were too great, and even when interaction developed, it was more along the lines of volunteer to dependent than young friend to old friend.

On the whole, though, age-segregated housing appears to offer some real potential benefits to older people: accessible peers for friendships, more similar others for comparison, a new normative reference group, and mutual assistance, which promote social integration and new bases of identity. Age-segregated settings can also promote leisure activities and offer more tangible benefits. Specialized housing may be more economical and can incorporate design features such as grab rails and low cupboards. Centralized services (personal maintenance, housekeeping, meal preparation, medical care) can be delivered more efficiently in group housing. But these residences are not nursing homes, objectively or in the minds of residents, and these services do not mean that residents are dependent. The combination of a supportive peer group and personal and health services provides an environment that facilitates continued independence.

Age-segregated housing is not a panacea for the problems experienced by older people, however. For one thing, older people often prefer contact with diverse age groups, including children, and do not desire association with "those old folks." Only a small minority of older people reside in old-age apartments and retirement communities, and a national survey found that only 23 percent prefer to spend most of their time with people of their own age (National Council on the Aging, 1975). Person-environment congruence underlines the importance of individual characteristics and preferences. Rosow's (1967) study suggests that age segregation has little effect for persons who desire isolation or are oriented toward broader community involvement. Another suggestion has been that older people with limited activity resources (health, income, social supports) will have higher morale in age-segregated settings where activity expectations are geared to older age groups (Gubrium, 1973).

Jacobs's (1974) study of Fun City also indicates that the structure of an age-segregated community affects its success. Fun City was too isolated and not a true community. Houses were laid out on a grid, like so many suburban tracts, providing no easy or common space for interaction. Merrill Court, on the other hand, had apartments opening onto a common area that facilitated interaction.

The variation among age-segregated settings is illustrated by Sherman's (1971, 1972, 1974, 1975c) comparisons of residents of six such settings—a retirement hotel, a rental village, an apartment tower, a purchase village, a cooperative village, and a life-care facility—with a matched group of community residents. Satisfaction with the retirement housing was approximately the same as the neighborhood satisfaction of the community sample. The greatest differences occurred among the age-segregated sites, and more urban (less isolated) sites seemed to work better. Dissatisfactions were site-specific, relating to meals, management, and proximity to community facilities. Residents of one site were particularly concerned about the lack of a hospital and sufficient doctors, which led them to worry more about their health, adversely affecting their overall morale. The primary reason for moving to group settings seems to be a desire for various services, therefore when such services are inadequate (as in Fun City), independent coping is not supported and satisfaction declines. This is exacerbated when residents are also isolated from the facilities of the larger community.

It was noted in Chapter 2 that older people tend to cluster in certain parts of cities, creating patterns of residential age segregation within a larger age-integrated context. This more normal form of age concentration may foster social supports and neighborhood satisfaction by offering access to age peers and involvement in the surrounding community (Ward, 1979). The evidence is mixed, however. Some studies have found that age concentration in apartment buildings and neighborhoods is associated with greater housing satisfaction, activity, and overall morale, attributable to increased feelings of personal security and the emergence of age-specific activity patterns and norms (Lawton & Nahemow, 1978; Teaff et al., 1978). But a recent study comparing age-segregated and age-integrated neighborhoods in a metropolitan area found little association between age concentration and involvement with neighbors, neighborhood satisfaction, or overall morale of older persons (Ward et al., 1981). It may be that specifically age-segregated settings, such as retirement communities, offer clearer benefits because they are chosen as such by residents, represent a larger concentration of age peers, and offer other amenities and services as part of a self-enclosed community.

Thus the impact of age-segregated housing may be limited. Nevertheless, age-segregated housing arrangements have a clear promise for at least some older people under favorable conditions. The lack of structure to old-age roles in modern societies provides freedom to "make" roles, but age stratification may set older people adrift socially and psychologically from familiar realities. However, the lack of macrostructure to old age may be compensated for by microstructures that provide norms, role models, interpersonal support, and socialization experiences. It is this microstructure that is represented by the emergence of community in some age-segregated settings.

THE IMPACT OF HOUSING

The concept of environmental docility reminds us that housing has a potentially decisive impact on the life-style and well-being of older people. By housing, we mean the total "context for living" in which the older individual is embedded, including physical characteristics, the interpersonal and social environment, characteristics of the surrounding neighborhood, and the availability and convenience of services (Carp, 1976; Lawton, 1980a). All of us are affected in many ways by where we live. Do we have pleasant neighbors? Is our housing in good physical condition? Do we feel safe on the streets? The answers to such questions affect feelings of happiness and security, which may be especially true for the aged.

Older people are found in many different housing arrangements: single-family houses, private apartments, and public housing, in rural, small-town, suburban, and city areas. Because of the tremendous heterogeneity in the older population, no one type of housing can be said to be the best. This is well illustrated by studies of older residents of skid row and "single room occupancy" (SRO) hotels (Stephens, 1975; Rooney, 1976; Eckert, 1979; Cohen & Sokolvsky, 1980). Such persons prefer relatively low social involvement and place a high value on autonomy and self-reliance. SROs represent an important "econiche" that provide support and semiinstitutional services (cheap restaurants, secondhand clothes, hotel housekeeping and security, street life) while maintaining independence.

Despite the fact that many older people have inadequate housing (see Chapter 2), and many are "overhoused" in terms of current needs (Lawton, 1980a), older people have very low rates of residential mobility. Residential relocation is potentially stressful, disrupting personal routines and social networks (George, 1980). Older people have a strong attachment to place because location represents an extension of self and a sense of "rootedness" (Rowles, 1980).

Nevertheless, improved housing can have important benefits. An excellent example is provided by research conducted in Victoria Plaza, a public housing complex for the elderly in San Antonio, Texas (Carp, 1975b, 1977; Carp & Carp, 1980). This complex included eight stories of apartments with a county Senior Center on the ground floor. Interviews were conducted with applicants who were then living in physically substandard housing or were socially isolated or in stressful situations (such as friction within a family). Those who eventually moved into the complex were compared with nonresidents in follow-up interviews conducted 12 to 15 months after the move. Whereas nonresidents exhibited little change, residents showed dramatic improvement in a wide variety of areas, including happiness, number of activities, number of friends, self-rated health, and optimism about the future. Residents felt the security of physical safety and having a nice place to live out the remainder of their lives. The effects were not simply short-lived "honeymoon reactions"—they were reflected in another follow-up after 8 years. Residents of Victoria Plaza even had better health and a lower mortality rate than nonresidents.

It is clear that housing for the aged can benefit enormously from proper planning. Such design features as grab rails, braces, higher wall outlets, and lower cabinets help achieve congruence between housing and the physical characteristics of older people. Housing design should involve older people themselves to maximize flexibility and choice. Hartman and associates (1976) used slides to illustrate housing options and small group discussions to determine the preferences of potential users. They found this type of "user needs survey" yielded quite satisfactory results. As examples of the kinds of preferences that may be expressed (and not realized by planners), they listed the following points:

1. Modern-looking buildings were preferred because they seemed cleaner and more prestigious.
2. Most wanted commercial use on the ground floor if it did not bring in undesirable outsiders.
3. Concern for street safety resulted in a desire for quick, secure entrances.
4. An aesthetically pleasing landscaped courtyard was overwhelmingly rejected as a "lovely place for a mugger to hide."
5. Most (and particularly men) wanted a lobby as a "hanging-out" place.

These older people were very conscious of territory, their own dignity, and personal safety. Rowles (1981) also indicates that housing should offer opportunities to overlook active outside scenes that provide a sense of ongoing, if vicarious, participation in events.

As a final note, specialized housing for the elderly should be designed to meet changing service needs as tenants age (Lawton et al., 1980). Under a *constant* housing model designed for a particular type of older person, disruptive relocations will be required when tenants no longer "fit." An *accommodating* model, offering a mix of services, provides environmental congruence for a wider range of needs by offering a continuum between independence and institutionalization. Lawton and associates describe a setting that involves independent living units but also meals, housekeeping, activity programs, and medical and social services as needed. "Life care" communities represent another accommodating approach. In one setting with which the author is familiar, residents pay a one-time membership fee (from $12,000 to $42,000) and monthly rental. They are then guaranteed use of an apartment, housekeeping and meal services, and a skilled nursing facility on the premises for the remainder of their lives. Although such living arrangements are largely restricted to the relatively affluent elderly, these settings contribute to important feelings of permanence and security.

NEIGHBORHOOD AND COMMUNITY CONTEXTS

In addition to housing features, the neighborhood and community have important effects on the well-being of older people, who are particularly dependent on the quality of their neighborhoods. The activities of many elderly are "block-bound," therefore they "must rely on the local area and its inhabitants to support their needs, while most of today's society reach far from home to meet the needs of everyday life" (Carp, 1976:249). The range of activity varies, depending on environmental factors (traffic, location of stores, and services), social factors (crime, ethnic mix), and personal factors (health, availability of an automobile). But it is clear that the neighborhood must be analyzed as an "environmental support system," whether assessing the quality of existing housing or designing new housing (Regnier, 1975; Kendig, 1976).

One aspect of this quality is proximity to community services and facilities. There appear to be "critical distances" beyond which older people will generally not travel for a particular service (Regnier, 1975; Newcomer, 1976). Table 9.2 indicates the nature of such distances and recommended locations to make facilities more accessible. These distances are often subjective, being affected by such things as hills, fear of crime, or climate. Distance barriers are more likely to be overcome for very significant purposes (medical care, seeing children), and less likely to be overcome when combined with economic barriers (barber/beauty shops, restaurants) (Lawton, 1980a). These barriers imply two needs in planning a livable neighborhood environment for older people (Regnier, 1975). First, there

Table 9.2 CRITICAL DISTANCES OF COMMUNITY SERVICES AND FACILITIES

Service	Critical distance	Maximum recommended distance
Bus stop	on-site to 3 blocks	1 block
Outdoor area	on-site to 3 blocks	3 blocks
Laundromat	on-site	on-site
Grocery store	1–10 blocks	6 blocks
Supermarket	1–10 blocks	6 blocks
Bank	1–10 blocks	6 blocks
Post office	1–3 blocks	3 blocks
Department store	1–3 blocks	3 blocks
Cleaners	1–11 blocks	6 blocks
Senior center	on-site	on-site
Beauty/barber shop	on-site to 10 blocks	10 blocks
Physician	1–10 blocks	10 blocks
Butcher shop	1–10 blocks	6 blocks
Snack bar	1–10 blocks	10 blocks
Public library	on-site to 10 blocks	10 blocks
Dentist	1–10 blocks	10 blocks
Eye doctor	1–10 blocks	10 blocks
Foot doctor	indeterminate	10 blocks
Center (for all ages)	used as a senior center	on-site
Movie	indeterminate	10 blocks
Church/synagogue	indeterminate	indeterminate
Bar	no importance	no importance

Source: From Newcomer, R., "An evaluation of neighborhood service convenience for elderly housing project residents." In P. Suedfeld and J. Russell (eds.), *The Behavioral Basis of Design,* Volume I, p. 304. Copyright © 1976 by Dowden, Hutchinson & Ross, Inc., Stroudsburg, Pa. Reprinted by permission of the publisher.

is a minimal core group of services that should be located within walking distance: bus stop, grocery store, drugstore, bank, post office, church. Second, there should be accessible (and inexpensive) transportation to reach other services, such as medical care, clubs, parks, libraries, luncheonettes, dry cleaners.

Transportation is an important consideration. Transportation difficulties are most likely to affect social and recreational activities, but they also affect access to virtually all services (Golant, 1976). This affects autonomy and quality of life, and Cutler (1975) found an association between adequacy of transportation and overall life satisfaction. The automobile is still the dominant form of transportation for older people, but physical changes increase reliance on public transportation and friends, particularly for older women. Public transportation presents many problems for the aged. Routes and schedules are often inconvenient for shopping or going to see physicians if such locations are distant or scattered. High steps, fast-moving doors, and exposed stops create additional problems. Consider using the New York City subway system with the physical limitations (not to mention fear of crime) of many older people; also, even a \$.50 bus fare can be a financial burden for the low-income older person.

Proximity to services and transportation are not the only, or even the most important, determinants of neighborhood satisfaction among the elderly. The most important sources of dissatisfaction appear to be crime, feelings of personal insecurity, and physical problems such as run-down housing, noise, and litter (Lawton, 1980b). The quality of relationships with neighbors is also an important dimension of neighborhood satisfaction (Toseland & Rasch, 1978; Bohland & Davis, 1979). Neighborhood satisfaction tends to be higher among homeowners and persons with higher socioeconomic status (Lawton, 1980a, 1980b).

The environmental issues we have discussed suggest that there are likely to be differences in the quality of city, suburban, and rural contexts for older people. Cities may offer benefits to older persons with limited mobility by providing a more accessible concentration of local services, essential to the daily needs of the aged, than the "sprawling" suburbs (Carp, 1975a; Cantor, 1975). Also, public transportation is more readily available in cities than in suburban and rural areas for nonlocal services, and the relative density of age peers within cities may provide greater possibilities for social interaction. Carp's (1975a) study of San Antonio, Texas, found that areas closer to the center of the city presented a more viable environment for older people—they experienced less lost time, got out into the community more often, and had better social networks.

Some aspects of urban life, however, constitute obstacles to mobility—crime and fear for personal safety, inconvenient bus stops and routes, and stairs. The physically handicapped of all ages are denied full use of the environment because urban design is based on the "mobility, size, strength, and capabilities of the average-sized, healthy, thirty-year-old male" (Bednar, 1977:1–2). There are many barriers—poor drainage, unsafe storm drains, irregular surfaces (bricks, cobblestones), long flights of stairs—that are invisible to the nonhandicapped, but limit the freedom of many older people, and "tell" them, through daily reminders, that they are less competent (Steinfeld, et al., 1977).

Other urban problems include lower-quality housing, neighborhood change and deterioration, crowding and traffic, and high costs of living. Housing and neighborhood satisfaction is typically higher for older people in suburban and nonmetropolitan areas (Golant, 1979; Lawton, 1980a). Social interaction with friends and neighbors is also greater in small communities (Lawton, 1980a). Cantor (1975) notes that the aged are often fearful of those who are different: different ethnic and racial groups, different life-styles, and so on. Thus the cultural diversity of cities that many people find attractive may prove to be unpleasant for some older persons. In addition, although some city services are readily accessible, others are widely scattered and fragmented, particularly medical care. The complexity, fragmentation, and depersonalization of urban health services often prove confusing and virtually impenetrable to many older persons (Cantor & Mayer, 1976). Public transportation is not well suited to going here for one doctor, there for another, and somewhere else to a hospital. Some elderly people just give up, with tragic results.

Urban renewal and redevelopment may also create problems for older people. Renewal of slum areas, for example, may disrupt the delicate balance of support provided by SROs (Eckert, 1979). "Gentrification," involving the upgrading of low-rent, deteriorated housing in the inner city into owner-occupied units such as condominiums, also may displace older people who are concentrated in such areas but cannot afford the renovated or converted housing (Henig, 1981).

Clearly city living offers advantages and disadvantages. The balance between the two depends on the desires and capabilities of each older individual and the nature of the community in which he or she lives.

CRIME AND THE ELDERLY

Considerable attention has been given by the media to crimes against the elderly. Older people are particularly vulnerable to many types of crimes. They are vulnerable to quackery and fraud for a number of reasons: social isolation, feelings of desperation and hopelessness concerning chronic illness, a desire for the "golden years" of retirement living, low levels of education, low and fixed incomes that make them susceptible to get-rich-quick schemes, and the mental confusion that may accompany age-related problems. Older people seeking a retirement home may succumb to high-pressure real estate schemes involving desert and swampland. Elderly women living alone may be targets of a "bank examiner" swindle. A widow receives a call from a "bank examiner," asking her to withdraw a large sum of money in order to trap a bank employee suspected of embezzlement. After handing over the money, receiving a receipt and a promise of a bonus for her assistance, the widow waits in vain for the return of her money. Variations on this theme involve impersonations of police or Social Security agents. The most tragic forms of fraud involve health quackery: worthless drugs and treatments that take advantage of the painful and progressive nature of such chronic conditions as cancer and arthritis. A startling figure is Butler's (1975) estimate that $25 is spent on fraudulent arthritis treatments for every $1 spent on arthritis research.

The fact that older people are often concentrated in high-crime inner-city areas, and may be sickly or weak, also makes them vulnerable to purse snatchings, muggings, and break-ins.

> The couple inched painfully from Fordham Road into a wasteland of the Bronx. Clinging to each other for support, the old man and woman mounted a curb and struggled for a moment while she regained her balance. Then, slowly, they went on. Watching them shuffle into the shadows of late afternoon, Detective Donald Gaffney sighed heavily and said, "There goes prime meat." (*Time,* 1976:21)

Young criminals refer to attacks on older people as "crib jobs" because it is as easy as taking candy from a baby (*Time,* 1976). The criminals may wait for Social Security checks to be left in mailboxes, or linger outside banks and stores to snatch purses, or follow the person to force their way in.

Actually fewer crimes are committed against older people than against other age groups. This is illustrated by the data in Table 9.3, drawn from victimization surveys in which respondents were asked about crimes committed against them (whether or not they had reported the incidents to the police). Studies indicate that the elderly are least likely to be victimized in many crime categories (rape, burglary, robbery, assault) and no more likely to be victimized in others (picked pockets, snatched purses) (Cook et al., 1978). The physical and economic consequences of crime are also not pronounced among older people who are victims of crime. Older victims generally suffer less absolute and relative economic loss than young adults, although their losses are the same or greater than those of middle-aged adults; and although older people are *one* of the groups most likely to be injured when victimized, they are not the most likely to be injured (Cook et al., 1978).

Lower rates of victimization among the elderly reflect an "opportunity model" of predatory crime (Cohen et al., 1981; Liang & Sengstock, 1981). Although older people may be more attractive victims because of reduced physical competence, their life-styles reduce exposure to risk. They are on the streets less often, and being home guards against crime. This also means that variations in life-style affect victimization risk. Victimization rates among older people are four times as high in cities as in rural areas, and rates are also higher for nonwhites, males, and unmarried older persons (Liang & Sengstock, 1981). A study of older public housing tenants found relatively high rates of victimization; 8 percent had been victims within the previous year and 14 percent within three years (Lawton & Yaffe, 1980). Thus victimization risk is much higher among certain segments of the older population. Liang and Sengstock (1981) estimate that the risk is 120 in 1000 for a 67-year-old black male who is divorced and living in a city of over 1 million, compared with only 7 in 1000 for a 67-year-old white female who is married and living in a suburb of 25,000 inhabitants.

Actual victimization may be less important than *fear of crime.* Older people express greater fear than other age groups despite their lower victimization rates, and their fears have increased in recent years (Cook et al., 1978). Such fears may have a chilling effect on life-style, limiting autonomy and feelings of control.

Table 9.3 VICTIMIZATION RATES (PER 1000 POPULATION) FOR SELECTED CRIMES BY AGE AND RACE, 1977

	Persons aged 12 and over			Persons aged 65 and over		
	Total	White	Black	Total	White	Black
Crimes of violence	33.9	33.0	41.9	7.5	7.0	13.4
Rape and attempted rape	0.9	0.9	1.0	0.1	0.1	—
Robbery and attempted robbery	6.2	5.4	13.0	3.4	3.0	7.9
With injury	2.2	1.9	5.2	1.9	1.8	3.4
Without injury	4.0	3.5	7.9	1.4	1.1	4.4
Assault	26.8	26.8	27.9	4.0	3.9	5.6
Aggravated	10.0	9.6	13.9	1.2	1.0	2.7
Simple	16.8	17.2	14.0	2.8	2.8	2.8
Personal larceny	97.3	98.2	90.0	23.6	23.1	26.9

Source: U.S. Bureau of the Census, 1979, p. 44.

Older people become afraid to go out, even for food, much less for such "luxuries" as church or social clubs. Traveling by bus becomes a major expedition into dangerous territory. These fears are not entirely unrealistic for those older persons who are already in poor health or quite frail—simply being knocked down can mean a long convalescence with a broken hip, or even death. In the words of a *Time* Magazine article, older people can become "prisoners of fear." The National Council on the Aging (1975) survey found that 23 percent of older people considered fear of crime a very serious personal problem and another 24 percent, as somewhat serious. This was indicated as a problem more often than poor health, low income, or loneliness. "Danger of being robbed or attacked" was the most frequently cited obstacle to getting around. Such fears affect housing and neighborhood satisfaction as well as overall morale (Lawton & Yaffe, 1980).

Fear of crime is particularly high in some segments of the older population. Size of the community is particularly important, as indicated in Table 9.4. Age differences in this study were virtually nonexistent in rural areas and small cities, but older residents of larger cities were quite likely to be fearful for their personal safety. Greater fear is also evident among older women, blacks, those living alone or having lower income, and persons living in high-crime areas (Lebowitz, 1975; National Council on the Aging, 1975; Clemente & Kleiman, 1976; Lawton & Yaffe, 1980; Yin, 1980). Thus low-income residents of inner-city areas, especially women and blacks, feel least secure because of the fear of crime.

There is some evidence that age-segregated housing arrangements may reduce fear of crime (Sherman et al., 1976; Lawton & Yaffe, 1980; Yin, 1980). Sherman and associates, for example, compared age-integrated, age-segregated, and mixed (an age-segregated high-rise in the midst of low-rise housing for younger families) housing projects. Older residents of age-integrated housing were more likely to have been victims of crime. The greatest differences were in *feelings* of safety, however—residents of some type of segregated arrangement (including mixed) felt substantially more secure. The authors suggest that this was not due to objectively greater security arrangements (such as patrolling); rather, informal groups fostered a sense of territory and provided natural surveillance, such as questioning strangers about their purposes. For example, interviewers in the study were much more likely to be questioned about their presence in the age-segregated buildings. More generally, social support and neighborhood familiarity are likely to affect fear of crime (Yin, 1980). Yin also notes that the attention given to crime by the mass media contributes to fear, particularly when older people have less perceived mastery over the environment.

There are a number of possible approaches to dealing with this crime problem. Programs in California, for example, have taken an informational approach, telling older people about security measures (locks, property identification), teaching them about confidence games and consumer fraud, and encouraging older women not to carry purses (Younger, 1976). A bimonthly information bulletin, "Senior Crime Preventer's Bulletin," was mailed out to older people. Other programs include increased surveillance and escort services (e.g., for going to the bank). Such policies should be aimed particularly at the high-risk groups noted earlier.

Table 9.4 PERCENTAGE FEARFUL[a] BY AGE AND PLACE OF RESIDENCE

	Place of residence[b]									
	Rural		Small city		Suburb		Medium city		Large city	
Age	%	N	%	N	%	N	%	N	%	N
Under 40	24	135	38	168	31	97	44	88	53	184
40–59	23	108	37	110	42	94	48	79	60	106
60 and over	19	101	39	66	50	34	63	35	71	78

[a]Respondents who said "yes" to the question: "Is there any area right around here—that is, within a mile—where you would be afraid to walk alone at night?"

[b]Rural: in open country, on a farm, or in a small town under 2,500; Small city: 2,500 to 50,000; Suburb: suburb near a large city; Medium city: 50,000 to 250,000; Large city: over 250,000.

Data are from a national survey conducted in 1973 by the National Opinion Research Center.

Source: Barry Lebowitz, "Age and Fearfulness: Personal and Situational Factors," *Journal of Gerontology* 30 (1975), p. 699. Reprinted by permission.

Policies should also focus on fear of crime. Whether programs directed at reducing crime against the aged are really effective is perhaps less important than their effects on *feelings* of safety. Indeed, efforts to educate older people about crime prevention may themselves heighten fear of crime among the elderly (Norton & Courlander, 1982). This fear contributes to a general perception of the world as complex and dangerous. It may be that such fear will decline because of cohort succession. Future older people will less frequently come from rural backgrounds, be immigrants, or have low educational and occupational status, and will therefore be less likely to possess the psychological characteristics (external locus of control, passivity, fatalism) which contribute to a fearful perception of the world.

SUMMARY

Social networks and living environments are particularly important to the well-being of older people because of their environmental docility, which means they are more dependent on the environment and less active in attempting to shape it. This also indicates the importance of congruence between individual and environmental characteristics.

Social networks offer many forms of instrumental and expressive support. Friendships also play an important role in socialization throughout life. Networks may become smaller and more unstable in old age. Most older people maintain involvement with friends and neighbors, although whether and how this affects overall well-being is not clear. The quality of interaction and subjective feelings of social integration appear to be more important than the number and frequency of social contacts. The relative importance of social ties may vary, as suggested by the hierarchical-compensatory and task-specific models of social networks. Family members, especially children, are generally preferred sources of social support, but friends and neighbors offer qualities that family ties may lack. Age peers may also make important contributions to identity maintenance and socialization for old age.

Age-segregated settings (apartments and retirement communities) offer potential benefits to the aged that include greater sociability, mutual assistance, group norms, and a positive reference group. There is considerable variation in types of retirement communities. Residents are drawn to them by their economy and the desire for a better living environment (climate, recreational facilities, security). Residents tend to have higher morale, partly due to self-selection, but also because of the availability of age peers and norms supporting leisure. Retirement communities apparently do not have detrimental financial or political effects on surrounding areas.

Age segregation can also have negative consequences. It may increase intergenerational intolerance and distrust, increasing the marginality of the aged. Housing is a limited source of such tolerance, however, and age integration may only heighten social isolation for some older people. Poorly planned retirement communities may create many problems, and many older people reject the idea of specialized housing. For those who are receptive, however, and may have limited activity resources, age-segregated settings appear to be beneficial.

Housing and neighborhood quality are important to the well-being of older people because they have strong attachments to a place. Although relocation can be stressful, improved housing offers clear benefits. Specialized housing for older people must be sensitive to their changing service needs, however.

Reduced mobility makes the local neighborhood particularly influential. The extent to which the neighborhood constitutes an environmental support system depends on the proximity of community facilities, transportation, physical quality, and social ties. City living offers both advantages and disadvantages for older people. Urban neighborhoods often have greater accessibility to a variety of local services, complemented by the availability of public transportation. Social integration may also be enhanced by the greater availability of age peers. Other aspects of cities create problems, however: poor housing, deteriorating neighborhoods, street crime. Health services are likely to be fragmented and confusing to the elderly. Urban renewal and redevelopment may also cause residential dislocation of older people.

Crime is one negative aspect of city living for the aged. Although fewer crimes are committed against the elderly than other age groups, fear of crime can severely restrict life-style. Such fears are most prevalent among older people living in cities, and among older women, blacks, and those with low income.

chapter *10*

The Politics of Age

Attention to the "politics of age" has focused largely on the politics of youth—youthful social movements concerning social issues and debates over a "generation gap." These issues themselves are important in understanding the nature of aging and its effects throughout the life cycle. Do they represent true social change and the emergence of cohorts with a new political consciousness and set of values or simply an eternal rebelliousness of youth that dissipates in middle age? The political arena exhibits complex combinations of aging, cohort, and period effects, as there is a continuing interplay between aging and social change.

There are also important issues related to the "politics of old age." We have seen that age groups differ in power, status, and authority. Dowd (1980) has noted from an exchange perspective that "age relations are power relations" (p. 39), as unequal access to power resources affects social status and chances in life. The position of the aged in American society raises the questions of whether they will develop activist political movements on their own behalf, and whether such movements imply increasing conflict among age groups in society. We have seen that the aged in modern societies suffer disproportionately from a number of material disadvantages, and they often face limited options in the meaningful use of time and some stigma attached to being old. We can expect that these problems would be reflected in a lack of political power and of resources by which to gain more power. But they could also lead to greater political activism by the aged on their own behalf as they attempt to improve their material and social standing.

AGE STRATIFICATION AND AGE CONFLICT

The model of age stratification suggests that some age conflict is inevitable. Because social positions are age-based, age becomes a basis for "structured social inequality" (Foner, 1974, 1979). Foner suggests that age inequality is as firmly entrenched as that based on class and sex. This inequality, combined with shared life-stage and cohort experiences, creates a potential for age group solidarity. Thus awareness of disadvantages caused by age stratification may create conflict and eventual change in the age stratification system. Although age conflict is always possible, there are factors that reduce it by forging ties across age strata and lessening age group solidarity (Foner, 1974). These factors warrant our attention because of their implications for future age conflict.

First, multiple group affiliations tend to reduce conflict in complex societies. Age-heterogeneous groups, such as the family or work groups, may reduce age conflict for a number of reasons. They foster common goals and interests—a sense of common fate—that override age differences. They also forge emotional ties and feelings of loyalty and responsibility across age boundaries, and people of different ages can socialize with each other. There is considerable evidence of cross-generational value transmission within families. This works in both directions, with children often affecting the attitudes and values of their parents, as well as vice versa. Foner suggests that a lack of age-heterogeneous affiliations may partly account for the rebelliousness of college students.

A second factor reducing age conflict is the inevitability of aging (age mobility). Younger people may anticipate their future age status, and older people can empathize with youth because they have been there themselves (although we often forget what it was like). This softens the perception of severe age differences.

Foner suggests that these conflict-reducing mechanisms are most effective with *material* issues concerning the distribution of economic resources. Such class-based issues tend to cut across age lines. *Ideal* issues, involving ethics and values, are much broader questions that may call forth generational differences. Ideal issues are more basic and deeply held, limiting compromise; they may also come to symbolize the status or power of specific age groups who believe that their values are "correct."

Using Foner's ideas, we can begin to question whether age conflict might not increase in the future. We have seen evidence of increased physical and social separation of the aged in modern societies with age-segregated residential settings and clubs and geographical dispersion of the extended family. As cross-age contacts diminish, the potential for age conflict increases. It is also possible that material issues are becoming more age-based as young and old people are increasingly in competition over support from general revenues. Social Security has implications for conflict over the old-age dependency ratio, with current workers subsidizing older nonworkers (a dependent population) and the ratio of nonworkers to workers rising, and along with it the tax burden for supporting Social Security. Kreps (1977) suggests that retirement and the concentration of work in the middle years has sharpened economic distinctions between generations and made clearer the flows of income between them. In discussing the possibility of a "backlash" against the elderly, Ragan (1976) quotes from an editorial appearing in the *Los Angeles Times:*

> The significant, semihidden story in the new federal budget is that America's public resources are increasingly being mortgaged for the use of a single group within our country: the elderly. . . . This is a ticklish subject to write about. No one wants to be accused of being niggardly toward his elders, and it is a matter of pride, not regret that in recent years this country has moved decisively to alleviate a long and shameful history of neglect. . . . But it is also a fact that the decision to meet those needs has been taken without a general awareness . . . of the tradeoffs involved. . . . As a result, there is a serious danger of a backlash against this belated policy of generosity toward the elderly, when today's wage earners begin to understand what has happened—and who is paying for it. . . . Clearly, this trend cannot continue for long without causing a bitter political struggle between the generations. (Broder, 1973)

This suggests that there is at least the potential for future conflict surrounding the problems of old age. The form that this might take depends partly on solidarity and activism within the older population. To more fully understand the future of age politics, however, we must first understand past and present political action and the effects of aging and cohort change as they relate to the age stratification of political activity and political conflict

AGE AND POLITICAL PARTICIPATION

Political participation refers to a number of distinct types of involvement, such as voting, interest in politics, formation of opinions, political leadership, party affiliation. Each of these appears to be related to age, but trends are by no means consistent. However, there is little evidence of any general disengagement by older people from the political arena, therefore the potential for activism on their own behalf does exist.

Voting

Studies of voting behavior have consistently shown the same age pattern: low voter participation among the youngest age groups (18–25), a steady increase to a peak in the early sixties, followed by a decline in the late sixties and beyond (Hudson & Binstock, 1976; Verba & Nie, 1972). This pattern is reflected in Figure 10.1. Note, however, that persons aged 75 and over continue to vote more than those in their twenties and early thirties. There are several possible reasons for the relatively low voter turnout among the young: lower partisanship (party identification), difficulties in registering for the first time, high rates of mobility, lack of full integration into the community (young people are still establishing their social positions), and less commitment to a society that has been structured *for* them by others (Foner, 1972; Verba and Nie, 1972). Part of the decline in voting by the aged is certainly attributable to health and transportation problems, which account for declines in many types of activities. Disengagement among some older people may also account for some of the decline, because there is evidence

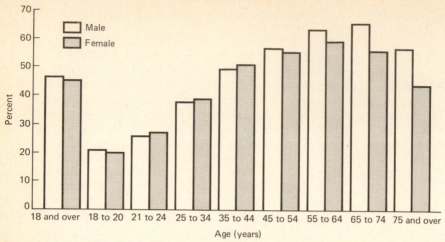

Figure 10.1 Voting in the United States, November 1978, by age and sex. (*Source:* U.S. Bureau of the Census, 1979, p. 17.)

that political activity by the aged depends on their objective and subjective involvement in the total life of the community (Turk et al., 1966). Socioeconomic factors are particularly important, however. Verba and Nie (1972) found no decline in voting with advanced age when socioeconomic status was controlled, indicating that the decline reflects a combination of aging (income) and cohort (education) effects.

Sex differences in voting are slight through most of the life cycle, but older women show a greater decline with age than older men. The reasons for this are not entirely clear, although Foner (1972) has offered some suggestions. Older women are likely to be widowed and may have formerly voted with their husbands; they are more likely to be in poor health; and women of this particular cohort may not be used to voting because many were socialized prior to women's suffrage.

Political Interest and Commitment

Voting is only one form of political participation and a weak one at that. Evidence suggests that, in a variety of additional ways, older people retain an interest in political affairs. Glenn (1969), for example, found that when the effects of education were controlled, older people were slightly *more* likely to hold political opinions than younger people. Older people display greater interest in political affairs (newspaper reading, television watching) (Williamson et al., 1982). Older people are also more attached to a particular party than younger people, apparently because of a sense of commitment built up over time (Campbell, 1971). Campbell indicates that although political activism, measured by such behaviors as party work and attendance at political meetings, is greatest in the thirties and forties and declines thereafter, older people still retain a greater level of activism than the young. In general the aged are actively engaged in moderate forms of political participation and are underrepresented only in more intensive forms (Hudson

& Binstock, 1976). There is no support for a view of the older voter as disinterested, disengaged, or misinformed, at least to any greater extent than the general electorate.

Political Leadership

Inasmuch as the status of the aged seems to fall in modern societies, one might expect to find few older persons occupying positions of political leadership. On the contrary, however, modern political leaders in the United States—senators, representatives, Supreme Court justices, presidents, and cabinet members—are older than their counterparts from the 1700s and 1800s (Lehman, 1953; Fischer, 1977). Even at the local community level, middle-aged and older people are overrepresented in such roles as community decision maker, museum leader, and trustee of an educational institution (Riley & Foner, 1968). We seem to be a society that celebrates youth but is controlled by the middle-aged and elderly.

How is it that so many individual older persons achieve status and power, despite the devalued status of the aged as a group? First, such positions typically require demonstrated excellence of achievement in other roles. To the extent that the structure of professions delays such achievement until at least middle age, the pool from which leaders are drawn will exclude the young. Supreme Court justices, for example, must work their way up various judicial and political ladders to achieve an attention-attracting prominence. Second, tenure is still an important correlate of political power. The concept of retirement without functional incapacities has been slow to reach the political arena. Political elites can retain power as long as they can exercise it, and power becomes stronger over the years. Also, trends toward "gerontocratic" leadership are more pronounced in stable, entrenched groups. Young elites emerge during periods of revolutionary change, such as the early history of the Nazi movement in Germany and communism in China (Hudson & Binstock, 1976).

The age pattern of political leadership appears to be changing, however, as legislators and cabinet members have been younger in recent years (Lammers & Nyomarkay, 1980). In their study of cabinet members in the United States, Canada, France, Germany, and the United Kingdom, Lammers and Nyomarkay found that older people have been underrepresented since the 1950s, and increasingly so in the 1960s and 1970s. They attribute this to a routinization and bureaucratization of recruitment that results in a narrower (middle-aged) age span. As a final note, the fact that political leaders are older does not necessarily mean that older people and their interests are being well represented. There is no evidence that such politicians vote on the basis of their age.

AGE AND POLITICAL ATTITUDES

There has been a tendency to stereotype the aged as conservative and rigidly opposed to change, leading some observers to suggest that the "graying of America" will cause cultural stagnation. Such views are unwarranted because of the complexity of the effects of both aging and cohort change on political attitudes. The aged of today are conservative in some ways, liberal in others, and the aged of tomorrow may well be a different breed of political cat.

Party Affiliation

One measure of political attitudes is party affiliation: Democrats are presumably more liberal, Republicans more conservative. Older voters are more likely than younger voters to identify themselves as Republicans (Campbell & Strate, 1981; Glenn, 1980). But people do not appear to shift from Democrat to Republican as they age, and younger voters can be expected to retain their current affiliations as they age. Indeed, since 1968 there has been greater growth of Democratic affiliation among the elderly than the middle-aged, and Democrats have outnumbered Republicans in the older population since about 1960 (Campbell & Strate, 1981).

Recent cohort phenomena suggest changing patterns of partisan loyalties (Abramson, 1975). The relationship between social class and party affiliation (working-class Democrats, middle-class Republicans), forged during the Depression, has been weakening in recent presidential elections, and there has been a rising proportion of voters who express no party affiliation. Both of these trends are most notable in cohorts that have entered the electorate since World War II, and the evidence suggests that they will continue over the life course of these cohorts. Inasmuch as this opens up the possibility of new coalitions based on factors other than party loyalty or social class, it removes one barrier to coalitions based on age. As these cohorts enter old age, they may be more willing to vote according to age interests rather than party affiliation. A similar conclusion is suggested by recent increases in "issue voting" (e.g., abortion) (Williamson et al., 1982).

Alienation

Many of our stereotypes about youth imply a sense of alienation. Young people's newness on the social scene, the fact that their values are still being formed, youthful identity crises, and the apparent rebelliousness reflected in youth movements imply the possibility of heightened alienation. But there are many meanings to the concept of alienation: powerlessness, meaninglessness, normlessness, cultural estrangement, self-estrangement, and social isolation (Seeman, 1975). Some of these notions may be heightened in old age. Disengagement and social isolation may cause feelings of cultural estrangement. If there is a lack of socialization to old age, feelings of normlessness or meaninglessness will also arise. This combined with changing bases of identity and a possible identity crisis in old age may create self-estrangement. Life cycle changes in alienation may be linked to the age stratification of roles and resources. Martin and associates (1974) suggest that the middle-aged are the "command" generation. They control many of the resources of the social system and participate most fully in that system. Older and younger people may have heightened feelings of alienation, but the psychological consequences may differ. Youthful alienation may result in attempts to forge a new political ideology, whereas alienation among older people may yield a sense of stagnation and despair.

Two recent studies indicate the complexity of the relationship between age and alienation. Cutler and Bengtson (1974) were concerned with political alienation—a sense of powerlessness and an inability to identify with the political system (estrangement). Using measures of political alienation (e.g., "People like me don't have any say about what the government does") from election surveys in 1952, 1960, and 1968, Cutler and Bengtson found that all cohorts showed essentially the same trends: a decline in alienation from 1952 to 1960, followed by an increase in 1968 to higher levels than in 1952. This indicates a period effect whereby all age groups are affected similarly by historical events. Cutler and Bengtson conclude, "There is no evidence of a process of aging which produces, or is in other ways related to, political alienation among adults during the period studied" (1974:174).

Martin and associates (1974) looked at more diverse dimensions of alienation: powerlessness, meaninglessness, normlessness, isolation, and self-estrangement. They expected alienation to vary with participation in the social structure, being lowest in middle age, highest in youth, and intermediate in old age. This expectation was largely confirmed, but the patterns were complex. The aged exhibited their greatest alienation in feelings of powerlessness and meaninglessness, even more so than the young, yet they were the lowest of the three age groups in social isolation and self-estrangement. This suggests that disengagement and identity crises may be less widespread than some studies have suggested. Older people were most alienated from political life and less alienated from family life.

Conservatism

To some degree older people are more likely to identify with conservative ideologies and take more conservative stands on social issues and policy priorities than younger age groups (Campbell & Strate, 1981; Glenn, 1980). In their analysis of national election studies from 1952 to 1980, Campbell and Strate found that older persons were more supportive of conservative law-and-order issues and school prayer, and were less supportive of liberal stands on such issues as abortion, marijuana, and women's rights. But their attitudes were generally in the same direction as the rest of the population, and the finding that conservatism is greater among the elderly must be tempered by other considerations. Certainly all older people are not more conservative than all younger people, nor are they monolithically conservative. Whereas the young are apparently more receptive to change in general, older people can be more liberal on policies that would benefit them as a group, such as governmental programs directed at medical care (Campbell & Strate, 1981). Young cohorts may in some cases be more conservative than older cohorts. The right-wing Nazi party in Germany received its major support from youth, and the youngest cohorts in Cuba tend to be less supportive of Fidel Castro's leftist revolution (Foner, 1974). Even a general conservatism may lead to positions that are considered liberal. The conservative isolationism on foreign policy that characterizes older people resulted in a more "dovish" stand on the Vietnam War than even the young (Campbell & Strate, 1981). Campbell and Strate also found that the attitudes of older people on social issues have been moving in a liberal direction, although more slowly than the rest of the population, and that small age differences in policy priorities are overshadowed by massive period effects. Similarly, a study of attitudes on abortion found increasing acceptance between 1965 and 1977 by all age groups, reflecting period effects rather than age or cohort effects (Cutler et al., 1980).

There are, of course, reasons to expect increasing conservatism with age. Foner (1972) has suggested that although cohorts follow general societal trends on *specific* issues, each cohort tends to change as it ages toward a more *general* conservative support for the existing system. Why might this general conservatism increase with age? Glenn (1974) notes that there are a number of meanings for conservatism: resistance to change, holding old attitudes, upholding the status quo or authority, unwillingness to take risks. Age might be related to such dimensions for a variety of reasons. Biological aging and social stresses may lead to rigidity and a fear of change. Position in the social structure (related to age stratification) also affects political attitudes. As individuals assume family responsibilities and reach higher socioeconomic levels, they may oppose liberal feelings of humanitarianism and egalitarianism in their own self-interest, although this does not explain the conservatism of older people who lose family responsibilities and often experience downward mobility. Glenn also suggests that attitudes may begin to stabilize as adult life "settles down," and new experiences have less effect as people accumulate them. Thus attitudes developed in middle age are more stable because they are based on a greater range of experiences, and the searching and experimentation of youth are left behind.

This "aging-stability thesis" suggests that the major impact of cultural and period shifts will be on younger cohorts (Glenn, 1974, 1980). Older people may follow societal trends (liberal *or* conservative) but to a lesser degree. Stability is likely to be greatest for fundamental orientations, especially values emphasized in childhood (religion, family, democracy), because their change requires more profound alterations in values (Foner, 1974; Glenn, 1980). Issues that are more specific and recent do not require such major shifts.

Perhaps the clearest implication of studies of political attitudes is that the relationship between age and political attitudes is highly complex, reflecting the interaction of aging, cohort, and period effects. They also reflect the age stratification of roles. Young and old people may be more alienated because their roles are marginal with little meaningful involvement in the social and political life of the community. It should be remembered that age is not the only factor affecting political attitudes and beliefs. Social class, race, ethnicity, and sex are but a few of the factors that cut across age groups. It is clear that the attitudes of older people can and do change, as they are influenced by developments affecting other age groups. Campbell and Strate conclude:

> The political orientations of older people are not peculiar. Knowing that someone is old will not help very much in predicting how conservative he or she is, in most important respects. The elderly are very much in the mainstream of American political opinions. (1981:590–591)

There are no simple age patterns, but one important conclusion is justified: *"Old age is not a period of political quiescence"* (Bengtson & Cutler, 1976: 153).

GENERATIONS AND SOCIAL CHANGE

Even when age differences in political orientation are evident, they may reflect cohort effects rather than age-related change. In this respect, cohort succession carries an important potential for social change. New cohorts, with different values, may build a world different from their parents. This depends on whether the "generation gap" is real or an illusion. During the 1960s there was much discussion of an apparent gap in values and attitudes between young people and their parents. Some argued that youth was antithetical to parental values, but others suggested this was simply a reflection of normal rebelliousness that would fade in mature adulthood. This relates to the distinction between *maturational* and *cohort-historical* processes as causes of a generation gap (Bengtson et al., 1974).

The maturational explanation attributes generation gaps to the sequence of biological, psychological, and social events in the life cycle. Intergenerational conflict results from the weak integration between age groups and society (Parsons, 1963; Eisenstadt, 1965). Because the middle-aged hold the major positions of responsibility, they are most attached to the status quo. In complex societies, other age groups (notably the young) become less integrated. Adolescence has become prolonged so that young people feel ready to assume adult positions before they are permitted to, resulting in skepticism and detachment and encouraging rebellion to take their rightful place in society (Braungart, 1974). Thus the generation gap is a natural conflict attributable to personality development and age-based social positions, which all cohorts undergo as they attempt to adapt to and prepare for adult roles.

This also suggests that the gap is more perceived than real. On the whole, adolescents and their parents appear to share similar values (Bengtson et al., 1974; Bengtson & Troll, 1978). In a study comparing young adults (16–26) and their parents (35–65), Acock and Bengtson (1980) found that attitudes of children showed greater differences from *perceived* parental attitudes than from *actual* parental attitudes. Similarly, a study of students and their parents found that parents minimized conflict as involving only personal habits and traits, whereas students saw friction in more basic issues of values, morality, politics, and life goals (Bengtson & Kuypers, 1971), and this may partly reflect lack of communication between generations. But Bengtson and Kuypers also suggest that these tendencies are related to *fear of loss* and a *developmental stake*. Each generation is afraid of losing something because of the other's behavior. Youth fear powerlessness and meaninglessness if their generation is not made distinctive from the parent generation. The desire to build their *own* world and establish their own identity, not simply carry out their parents', makes a perception of conflict essential. Parents, on the other hand, have a stake in having youth accept the parents' values and priorities. If the world they have constructed is rejected by the young, the parents' efforts have been meaningless. This approach suggests that perception of a generation gap reflects one's developmental stage in the life cycle.

Age differences in values and attitudes may also be due to cohort-historical processes, reflecting a true gap between generations that will persist. A "generational consciousness" may arise as successive cohorts experience unique historical events and socialization (Mannheim, 1952). Mannheim argues that not all cohorts become generations in the sense that they differ distinctively from other cohorts. New cohorts can take unique perspectives on the world because of their fresh contact with the social system; they can perceive the social structure in new ways because they lack previous experience with it. Additionally, social change means that new cohorts encounter a different social world and different social institutions from those encountered by their parents. When social change is sufficiently great, a truly new generation emerges. This cohort-as-generation is one factor that accounts for social change (Ryder, 1965).

Even in the absence of generational consciousness, the accumulation of individual decisions by cohort members may crystallize into new standards and norms that govern the decisions of future cohorts (Riley, 1978). As an example, Riley notes that cohorts experiencing reduced mortality also had lower fertility, resulting in a norm of smaller families. Similar developments may occur over time in patterns of education, work, and leisure.

One must be cautious in expecting cohort effects. Such effects assume that individuals experiencing the same event will be affected in similar ways, and that effects taking hold early in life will be carried forward and reflected in behavior throughout the life cycle (McQuaide & Sauer, 1979). McQuaide and Sauer suggest that these conditions are met only rarely. Events affect individuals with different social characteristics (class, sex, race) in different ways, as illustrated in Chapter 1 in the discussion of the effects of the Depression. Even when there is initial similarity, cohorts may be "pulled apart" by different subsequent experiences in the life course of individuals. Thus it is likely that very momentous historical experiences are required to create a true "generation."

It is also misleading to portray families and cohorts as competitors in value socialization. Bengtson (1975) suggests that families and age peers reinforce one another because families determine the social location and reference groups of children through decisions about residence, school, and the like. Indeed, Bengtson's study of three-generational families found that family and generation were both poor predictors of individual values. This suggests that core values are dependent on unique personal biographies rather than on general family and cohort influences.

The distinction between maturational and cohort-historical influences is an important one, however. If age differences reflect only maturation over the life cycle, there is little reason to expect change in the nature of youth, middle age, or old age. But if age differences reflect generational differences, the door is opened for many changes in the future. More work is clearly needed on the question of generational differences. If our youthful activists of the past two decades remain activist, for example, the politics of old age may be very different in 30 or 40 years. How much cohort homogeneity will be transferred into old age? This relates to potential change in the nature and meaning of political involvement in old age and leads us to a discussion of the past, present, and future of old-age activism.

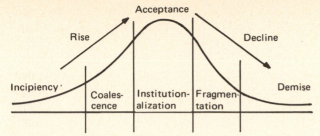

Figure 10.2 Normal pattern for the "natural history" of a social movement. (*Source:* Armond Mauss, *Social Problems as Social Movements,* Philadelphia: J. B. Lippincott, 1975, p. 66.)

THE SENIOR MOVEMENT: PAST, PRESENT, AND FUTURE

Our impressions of political movements tend to focus on youth, but there has actually been a long history of groups pushing for more favorable treatment of the elderly. Partly as a result of this activism, the needs of the aged currently enjoy considerable visibility, and although many problems still confront older people, a wide variety of programs have been directed at them. What does the future hold for the "senior movement"? If the aged grow increasingly activist in pushing for better material conditions and more meaningful involvement in modern society, will they encounter growing resistance from other groups, heightening the conflict among age groups or between the elderly and other disadvantaged groups over scarce resources? To answer such questions, we must understand the history and present status of old-age political activism and the processes through which social movements either progress or die away.

Mauss (1975) has described five stages in the "natural history" of social movements (Figure 10.2). Any particular social movement may vary from this ideal progression, depending on the response it receives from society, but this offers a very useful framework for looking at the past, present, and possible futures of the senior movement (Figure 10.3).[1]

Incipiency is the first stage of any social movement. This is a period of unorganized, uncoordinated efforts by a concerned public (the aged and their supporters) seeking an identity based on their perception of a threat to their interests. The basis of activism by the aged lies in the processes of modernization discussed in Chapter 3, which set them apart from society and create the kinds of shared problems and frustrations—inadequate pensions, poor housing, expensive medical care, devalued status—that can generate mass action. This incipiency stage lasted roughly from 1920 to 1950, as the few organizations that emerged were relatively short-lived and ineffectual.

The origins of the senior movement can be traced to a few individuals and groups campaigning for old-age pensions during the 1920s. Although these groups attracted relatively few adherents, pension experts had some influence on

---

[1]Material on the history of the senior movement is drawn from Henry Pratt's book, *The Gray Lobby* (1976).

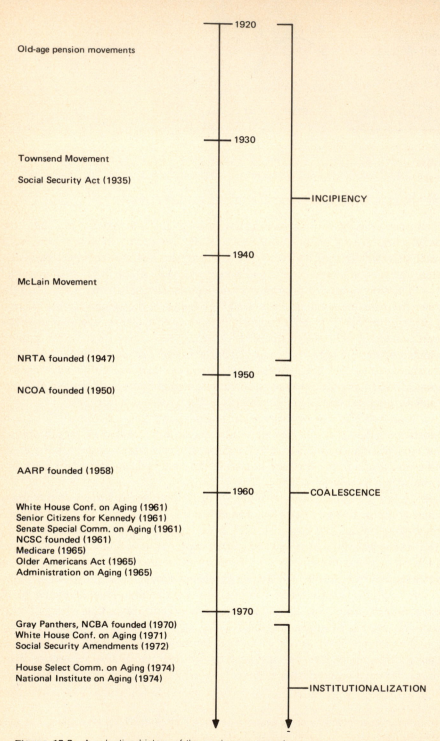

Figure 10.3 A selective history of the senior movement.

Franklin Roosevelt and policy groups that were shaping Social Security legislation. The Townsend Movement was the largest mass organization. Emerging in California during the 1930s, Dr. Francis Townsend eventually attracted over a million followers for his plan to provide a pension of $200 per month to those over 60 who would retire. The movement came too late to really influence Social Security policies, however, and eventually died out.

These early groups influenced the climate of public opinion but had no genuine direct political access or mass support. Their appeals ran counter to the values of thrift, self-reliance, and free enterprise preached by opponents. The early activity surrounding Social Security lapsed into what Pratt calls "the dismal years" of the 1940s. The only major old-age movement during these years was George McLain's "Citizens Committee for Old Age Pensions," which was supported by hundreds of thousands of older people in California and contributed to rising state expenditures on behalf of the aged. The national scene was relatively quiet, although the emergence of such groups as the National Retired Teachers Association (NRTA) and the Gerontological Society set the stage for later developments.

The second stage of social movements is *coalescence,* as formal and informal organizations emerge and begin to form common alliances, possibly in response to disappointment over the failure of society to adequately address their needs. Pratt notes that the aged have come to expect economic security and adequate health care, and their "revolution of rising expectations" made them increasingly restive over the pace of progress. Coalescence of the senior movement encompassed roughly the period from 1950 to 1970, culminating in the White House Conference on Aging of 1971.

Pratt attributes the true birth of the senior movement to trends in the 1950s. Efforts by public agencies to reach the aged and the growth of senior centers, combined with a growing sense of injustice, contributed to increased political consciousness among older people. Organized labor became interested in the needs of retirees, eventually helping in the push for Medicare. New leaders also emerged, such as Ethel Percy Andrus of the National Retired Teachers Association/American Association of Retired Persons (NRTA/AARP) and Charles Odell of the United Auto Workers retiree organization. However, two events were particularly critical to increasing the political access and effectiveness of old-age organizations: the involvement of older people in Kennedy's presidential campaign and the White House Conference on Aging of 1971.

The traditional association between older voters and the Republican party, partly due to Democrats being associated with inflation and high taxes, began to decline during the 1950s, and the Democratic party began to pay more attention to older voters. Although "Senior Citizens for Kennedy" did not convert many older voters, it did persuade party leaders to court older voters to a greater degree. State and local conferences related to the White House Conference on Aging of 1961 also enlarged the base of popular support for old-age issues. During the 1960s, legislation such as Medicare and the Older Americans Act, and the establishment of the federal Administration on Aging (AoA) and the Senate Special Committee on Aging, served as additional focal points for old-age activism.

It is the White House Conference on Aging of 1971, however, that Pratt cites as a watershed for old-age political influence. After initial resentment by such groups as the AARP and the National Council of Senior Citizens (NCSC) at being ignored in conference planning, steps were taken to involve national organizations in the conference, and they eventually came to play a major role. Thus the conference provided a forum for involvement and cooperation by old-age associations and forced them to clarify and relate their own goals to the broad needs of the elderly. The conferences also heightened the level of old-age awareness among government officials and increased the awareness among older people of the existence and potential benefits of national old-age organizations.

This points out that such gatherings are political events. Indeed, the 1981 White House conference also took place in a politicized climate. There were widespread charges that the Reagan administration "tampered" with delegates, through a preconference poll conducted by the Republican National Committee, manipulated committee assignments for political reasons, limited the access of delegates to documents, and prevented delegates from voting as a whole on committee recommendations. A report on the conference by the Leadership Council of Aging Organizations (1982) concludes that:

> To deny that the White House Conference on Aging is part of the political process is to show one's naivete. To permit partisan politics to taint the conference, however, is simply unacceptable, no matter which party or candidate tries it. The record of the Reagan Administration in the 1981 WHCoA is irrevocably tainted, and we can only hope that sufficient taint will attach that no future administration will be tempted to try a similar campaign. (p. A–5)

Pratt notes that the 1971 White House conference was more than just a "noble experiment" with few consequences. Recommendations were made in many areas—income, employment, health care, housing, nutrition, and so on. Many of the recommendations have been embodied in subsequent legislation, and old-age associations have achieved greater political visibility and access. For example, legislative lobbying has become an ongoing feature of the AARP, involving full-time staff members. Pratt cites evidence that the NCSC was instrumental in formulating and passing the 1972 Social Security Amendments, involving costly and inflationary measures benefitting the aged. Despite the conflict and drama surrounding the 1981 White House Conference, this has also been described as providing solid statements of need and policy (Leadership Council of Aging Organizations, 1982).

The senior movement now appears to be in the stage of *institutionalization,* characterized by society-wide organization and coordination, a large base of members and resources, regular political involvement, and growing respectability. Some old-age associations are now quite large. The NRTA/AARP has over 9 million members and offers a wide range of services to its members, including insurance, travel, prescription drugs, and lobbying. The NCSC has over 3 million members in some 3000 affiliated senior citizen clubs.

Other groups are smaller but nonetheless have considerable visibility. The

Gerontological Society of America has a membership of over 4000 professionals in the field and has become increasingly visible on the political scene. The National Council on the Aging (NCOA), established in 1950, is a group of subject-matter specialists for planning and consultation. The Gray Panthers, founded in 1970 by Margaret Kuhn, a retired church worker, is a loosely organized group of young and old that seeks to attack ageism in society.

> . . . a cabbie driving speaker Studs Terkel from the Washington, D.C., airport to their 1977 National Convention recognized the name Gray Panthers and asked "Aren't they violent?" "I answered, 'You bet they are'," Studs told the conventioneers. The 400 Panthers laughed with delight at the recognition of their refusal to accept the passivity usually identified with America's elderly. The Panthers are not self-effacing. Deeply angry, they rock boats, not chairs (Jacobs, 1980:93).

The National Caucus on the Black Aged (NCBA) emerged in 1970 to insure greater representation of the needs of elderly blacks at the 1971 White House Conference. It was composed of professionals in the field of aging who were concerned that the conference "would dilute the critical and special needs of the black and other minority aged, thereby weakening the effects of the total attack on the problems of the elderly of the nation" (Jackson, 1972:22). The NCBA has continued to hold annual conferences, establishing in 1973 the federally funded National Center on Black Aged for research and training.

These old-age organizations have become an established part of the political scene, with access to policy makers. They are more effective than earlier old-age associations. One important factor is greater public and official receptivity to the needs of the aged than in the 1930s and 1940s. Pratt (1976) suggests that the aged have become an "unrivaled minority"—no one wants to be against old people. In a sense, the problems of old age have become "fashionable." Nearly 80 percent of the adult population agree that "there is a real need for people to join together to work toward improving the conditions and social status of people over 65," and 37 percent say they would "certainly" or "probably" join such a group (National Council on the Aging, 1975). Talk about actually joining a movement should be viewed with some skepticism, but this does reflect a receptive attitude. Official receptivity is symbolized by the establishment of the federal Administration on Aging and the National Institute on Aging.

Old-age associations have also been more effective in taking advantage of this receptivity and access because they are stronger, more viable organizations (Pratt, 1976). For one thing, they have become bureaucratized, therefore less dependent for survival on a charismatic leader (as with the Townsend Movement) and they are less subject to internal divisiveness. This bureaucratization, combined with expanded membership and greater financial resources, makes them more effective in political lobbying. Twenty-five national organizations concerned with aging have combined to form the Leadership Council of Aging Organizations, which lobbies on behalf of older persons. These groups have also been more effective at manipulating symbols to appeal to the public and attract committed members, as can be seen in the growing support of the concept of "institutional ageism," analogous to institutional racism and sexism.

What will be the future of the senior movement? This brings us to the final two stages in Figure 10.2: *fragmentation* and *demise.* Ironically, the success of a movement in attaining official adoption of its goals may mean the death of the movement itself. Improvement, even if it is only a surface or symbolic success, leads to a bleeding off of mass support, as people feel that "something is being done" and move on to other concerns. This may lead to rivalry and conflict among the remaining segments of the movement. The demise of a movement may eventually occur either because it succeeds or because it loses support.

While there is no reason to expect fragmentation or demise of the senior movement in the near future, a number of issues have been raised concerning the extent to which older people can and do have political power (Estes, 1979; Williamson et al., 1982). Access does not guarantee success. Binstock (1974), for example, suggests that old-age organizations have focused primarily on adjustments to existing programs ("tinkering"), rather than putting forth strong proposals for major new policies and programs. The nature of compromise within "interest group politics" limits their ability to achieve more fundamental changes in the institutions affecting the lives of the aged.

It has also been suggested that the voting power of older people may be more perceived than real. The elderly constitute about 15 percent of eligible voters and tend to vote regularly, so they represent a potentially important swing vote in close elections. But this may largely be a bluff because "there is no evidence to indicate that aging-based interest appeals can swing a bloc of older persons' votes from one party or candidate to another" (Binstock, 1974:202–203). Binstock suggests that politicians are careful not to offend older voters, but make few major initiatives on their behalf. Indeed, a study of the Carter presidential campaign indicated that old-age issues were not given high priority, with little evidence that older people were viewed as an important constituency to either "hold onto" or "sway" (Riemer & Binstock, 1978).

There is also evidence that major legislation benefiting the elderly did not originally arise from a national thrust on their behalf or because of the efforts of age-based organizations. Rather, this legislation reflects the political popularity and legitimacy of older people and their usefulness to other political actors (Hudson, 1981). Harootyan (1981), for example, argues that enactment of Medicare represented the use of the aged as a "moral makeweight" to achieve some form of federally subsidized health care. The current environment of program reduction at the federal level, combined with rising costs of supporting an aging population, may weaken this legitimacy and usefulness.

The aging, long a favored social-welfare constituency in the United States, are in the early stages of being confronted with a series of obstacles which may put their favored status—and its concomitant material and symbolic benefits—in jeopardy. Rapidly rising public policy costs for meeting the needs of an aging population, a nascent but growing reassessment of policy benefits directed toward the elderly, and competitive pressures from other social-welfare

constituencies are now threatening two of the aging's longstanding political resources—their singular legitimacy as a policy constituency and their political
utility to other actors in the policy process. (Hudson, 1978:428)

Hudson suggests that the "graying" of the federal budget may cause older
people "to be viewed increasingly as a political *problem* and less as a source of
political *opportunity*" (p. 429).

If the legitimacy and utility of the elderly decline, the future vitality of the
senior movement will increasingly depend on support *by the aged* of old-age politics. Their participation depends upon emerging feelings of *aging group consciousness,* defined as:

> . . . elderly persons who become aware, not merely that they are old, but that
> they are subject to certain deprivations because they are old, and they react
> to these deprivations with resentment and with some positive effort to over-
> come the deprivation. Further, they are aware that most, or all, older persons
> are subject to these deprivations, and they feel a positive sense of identification
> with other elderly persons for this reason. For them, the elderly are a group,
> and not merely a category. (Rose, 1965b:19)

This consciousness contributes to feelings of belonging to a *subculture of
the aging.*

Does this kind of age consciousness exist? Arnold Rose (1965a, 1965b) has
argued that a subculture is already developing among older people in American
society, which he attributes to such recent trends as the growing number and
proportion of older persons in the population, better health and education among
the aged, the emergence of retirement communities, and unifying grievances, such
as the cost of health care. Others have argued, however, that the aged do not
constitute a true "minority group," partly because they lack widespread feelings
of group identity and readiness to organize on their own behalf (Streib, 1965;
Rosow, 1974).

There are understandable barriers to the feelings of group solidarity represented by aging group consciousness, not the least of which is resistance to the
perception of personal aging because of the stigma attached to old age. "But old
people are also mirrors for one another, mirrors in which they do not care to
see themselves—the marks of old age they behold vex them" (de Beauvoir,
1972:472). The aged are also not accustomed to thinking in terms of age identification. Other bases of differentiation have been salient throughout their lives:
race, sex, ethnicity, religion, social class. The older college-educated, middle-class
white may feel he or she has little in common with the older lower-class black.
Feelings of age solidarity are further minimized by contacts with other segments
of society through the family or the mass media and the use of them as reference
groups. Poor health and transportation problems accompanying old age may also
prevent older people from associating with one another.

There are conditions that might foster aging group consciousness, however.
What is required is a perception of similarity with age peers based on past experi-

ences and current common fate. Proximity in the form of some type of age-segregated situation would allow older people to develop a sense of the situation of age peers and of their similarities in interests, needs, and attitudes. Membership in age-segregated residential settings is still not widespread, however. Membership in old-age associations may also foster aging group consciousness. One study found that participation in age-graded groups fostered greater activist self-interest based on age: greater desire for political change, more receptivity to appeals for organized political activity, and an increased willingness to engage in activist political behavior (Trela, 1972). Groups like the NCSC and AARP can provide an opportunity for older people to more clearly define their interests and the political problems that confront them *collectively,* but membership in such groups still accounts for only a small minority of the older population.

Age segregation also does not necessarily result in political mobilization. A study of age-segregated residential settings, for example, found that they fostered social involvement and a preference for interaction with age peers, but little *politically* oriented consciousness (Longino et al., 1980). Longino and associates suggest that these subcultures are retreatist in content rather than activist. Similarly, Dowd (1980) suggests that age segregation may reduce age conflict by providing fairer (more satisfying) exchange relationships, thereby reducing discontent.

Even political age identification may be insufficient for political mobilization. Recent national election surveys asked people which of 16 social categories they felt "particularly close to" in "their ideas and interests and feelings" (Miller et al., 1980). Among older people in 1976, 28 percent felt "closest" to age peers and another 46 percent felt "close." But this group identification was related to *lower* voting because of lack of resources (income, education, health), feelings of personal powerlessness, and beliefs that the *group* could not increase its power.

As with class consciousness, aging group consciousness implies certain perceptions by the individual. There must be a recognition by the older person that his or her life chances depend on the group rather than on just personal resources. This implies an awareness of the age stratification system and the extent to which one's own relative position is determined by it. Thus the aging group conscious would attribute problems to the age-based system rather than to personal failure. There is little evidence of such feelings among the aged, and stigma combined with cross-generational associations will probably limit its emergence. There is also little evidence that the aged view age stratification as undesirable or changeable. Dowd (1980) describes ageism as an ideology that is internalized and legitimizes the existing system of age stratification.

The picture is not all one-sided, however. The aged are not quiet when it comes to voting, political interest, and the like, and they can be quite liberal about programs that would directly benefit them (Aren't we all?). The growing size of the older population, rising interest in gerontology, the visibility of old-age associations, and the ability of some older groups to coalesce despite their internal cleavages all indicate the possibility of continued or growing political activism by the aged. There is evidence that older people can mobilize around specific issues. Anderson and Anderson (1978) describe the recent "Adults Only Movement" in Arizona. The legality of adults-only (retirement) communities and sub-divisions was challenged in a court case. A political movement of older people emerged to protect what was felt to be a unique and desirable life-style and suc-cessfully lobbied for legislation to legalize such communities.

More importantly perhaps, the sources and facilitators of political activism still exist and may increase in the future. Social movements often arise from feel-ings of alienation, deprivation, and status inconsistency (Smelser & Smelser, 1981). Status inconsistency is the feeling that one's status in one area is out of line with one's status in another area, providing conflicting expectations, instabil-ity of the self, and a perception that rewards do not correspond with one's aspira-tions. Combined with feelings of deprivation compared to other groups or to one's expectations, this can create a preference for change in the political order. Feel-ings of status inconsistency and relative deprivation may occur in older people, particularly those who move from higher middle-aged status to a lower status in old age (loss of authority, financial problems). The Townsend Movement was a response to status loss caused by the Depression and consisted largely of profes-sionals, businessmen, and skilled workers who had been driven into the ranks of the deprived aged (Trela, 1976). We have also seen that the aged often experi-ence heightened alienation, particularly political powerlessness, which can lead to political activism.

Paradoxically, these feelings of status inconsistency and alienation may rise as we alleviate some of the most dire economic and medical problems of older people. Betterment of individual status may heighten feelings that the position of older people *as a group* is unjust. Thus institutional ageism may be more pro-nounced for older people who are better off individually but still treated as "just another old person." The "young-old" in particular can be expected to push for more meaningful involvement in community life (Neugarten, 1974).

It must be recognized, however, that status inconsistency and alienation present only a *potential* for political mobilization that may not be realized. Most older people do not see the political system as unresponsive or illegitimate, despite increases in alienation with age. Their relative satisfaction with political affairs, combined with well-established norms of self-reliance and a reluctance to burden other generations, limits the development of political activism. Additionally, downward mobility experienced by the aged does not necessarily result in general-ized alienation or distrust. Tissue (1970) found that older recipients of public as-sistance from middle-class backgrounds were dissatisfied with their own situa-tions but had not lost faith in the fairness of the larger social order. Thus, rather than political activism, status inconsistency and relative deprivation may result in stress-related psychological problems or social withdrawal (disengagement) (Trela, 1976).

Studies of student activism suggest that alienation in itself is also not enough to create political activism but that high perceived powerlessness in relation to the *system* must be combined with a low sense of *personal* powerlessness (Seeman, 1975). Older people tend to be more fatalistic than young people, however, and if aging results in lower self-esteem, this may also lessen feelings of personal effi-cacy (Ragan & Dowd, 1974). Other potential psychological accompaniments of aging, such as disengagement, conservatism, and interiority, would also limit activism, and the lack of political efficacy is compounded by low income and poor health.

But because many of these psychological traits represent cohort differences rather than the effects of aging, feelings of political efficacy may be higher among older people in the future. Future older people will be better equipped for effective political involvement, because of higher levels of education, and more accepting of protest politics (Table 10.1). If such attitudes reflect a political generation, they will be carried throughout the life cycle, and there is some indication that this may occur. A follow-up of former civil rights activists found that they had neither "matured out" of their activism nor "dropped out" because of disillusionment (Fendrich, 1974). They were concentrated in knowledge and human service industries and in change-oriented voluntary associations, and they were still committed to radical political and economic change.

Ragan and Dowd (1974) point to other developments that might enhance future political activism by the aged. Increased involvement in age-graded voluntary associations and lobbying groups, such as the AARP, may increase feelings of political efficacy to combine with subjective dissatisfaction and political distrust. Area Agencies on Aging are supposed to encourage political participation by older people in the development of services. Increased attention by the media to the problems of older people also contributes to an ideological basis for political movements. Therefore there is a *potential* for aging group consciousness and political activism. The fact that societies are age-stratified is an objective basis for age consciousness because the relative position and status of the aged are structurally determined.

There is no reason to believe that "senior power" can ever occupy a position of overriding political importance, that older voters will polarize around a few issues, or even that the aged can achieve the status of organized labor or organized business. The interests and needs of older people will continue to be seen as one set of problems among many others. Indeed, it may be advisable for old-age groups to broaden their appeal to other social-welfare constituencies on such is-

Table 10.1 PERCENT APPROVING
"NONCONVENTIONAL" POLITICAL
PARTICIPATION, BY AGE

	Age	
Percent approving of	18–35	60+
Protest politics	26.4	10.2
Civil disobedience	22.0	9.3
Sit-ins	10.8	3.2

Data are from the University of Michigan Center for Political Studies 1972 national presidential election survey.
Source: Neal Cutler and John Schmidhauser, "Age and Political Behavior," in Diana Woodruff and James Birren (eds.), *Aging: Scientific Perspectives and Social Issues,* New York: D. Van Nostrand Company, 1975, p. 402. Reprinted by permission.

sues as income maintenance and health insurance (this issue is discussed in Chapter 11). But there is also no reason to expect that old-age activism will fragment and die out in the foreseeable future. National old-age associations are now well established on the political scene and are visible and accessible. Support from older masses may well increase among future cohorts. Such potentially unifying issues as health care and retirement will remain, and the aged will continue to represent an important political force. Whether they will be effective in pursuing their goals and interests depends on many things, including receptivity from the larger society and competition with other groups making claims, and predictions are fraught with uncertainty.

THE CONSEQUENCES OF AGING GROUP CONSCIOUSNESS

One obvious potential consequence of aging group consciousness, and political activism based on it, is improvement of the position of older people in society. But even if this does not happen, there are benefits to be derived from age consciousness and involvement in what might be considered a subculture of the aging. Part of our self-image comes from the groups we identify with.

> The groups to which a person belongs serve as primary determiners of his self-esteem. To a considerable extent, *personal* feelings of worth depend on social evaluations of the groups with which a person is identified. Self-hatred and feelings of worthlessness tend to arise from membership in underprivileged or outcast groups. (Cartwright, 1950:440)

Given the devalued status of old age in modern societies, it is not surprising that the aged might resist identifying with other older people, in the same way that the mentally retarded (Edgerton, 1967) and the blind (Strauss, 1968) often resist identification with similar stigmatized others. Yet we have seen in earlier discussions (notably Chapters 4 and 5) some of the identity problems that may arise in old age, which association with age peers may help to handle.

Reference groups serve *comparative* and *normative* functions (Singer, 1981). Self-evaluations are derived from comparisons with persons we consider similar, and reference groups also provide expectations and standards that socialize individuals. Subcultures, such as a subculture of the aging, represent particularly salient and stable reference groups with cultural systems that are at least partially unique. They develop as a response to situations or problems shared by interacting persons. In this sense, subcultures may be defined as "a set of acquired patterns of conduct, a way of life that provides its participants with adaptive techniques to deal with a set of recurring problems" (Sarbin, 1970:31).

Stigmatization and isolation of the aged, as a reflection of their devalued status in the modern stratification system, creates shared problems of adjustment. It is the perception of these shared problems we have called aging group consciousness. In this sense, a subculture of the aging is conceptually similar to various deviant subcultures, such as the homosexual subculture (Hooker, 1966), which are attempts by stigmatized individuals to adjust to shared problems caused by conventional society's reaction to their activities or attributes. Such deviant subcultures fulfill three primary functions for their members, and a subculture for older people might serve similar functions.

First, deviant subcultures allow individuals to pursue deviant activities with less interference by providing "facilitating" places, hardware, and skills (Lofland, 1969). Although the aged are not usually thought of as "deviant" in this sense, we have seen in Chapter 9 that age-segregated settings may allow the aged to "let their hair down" more freely or to pursue a leisure career without guilt.

Reactions to deviants often result in their exclusion from normal roles and activities, perhaps because they are considered "tainted" or "unpleasant" in other ways (Goffman, 1963). Therefore, a second function of deviant subcultures is to reduce the marginality and isolation felt by those who are excluded from conventional groups. This will be important for the aged to the extent that society disengages *from* them.

The third function of deviant subcultures is perhaps most important because it relates to self-concept. Reference groups and subcultures act as mediators of culture, affecting our attitudes (including self-attitudes) through the evaluative information they provide about such cognitive categories as homosexual, blind person, or old person (Woelfel & Haller, 1971). Meanings available for stigmatized identities in the conventional culture are largely negative and can result in self-derogation. This is true for the aged, whose self-esteem may be lowered if they accept negative stereotypes about old age. A subculture of the aging might provide a more positive definition of "old person" and meaningful roles within which self-worth can be validated.

Old age can be a difficult turning point in personal identity because of the stigma attached to it and the disruptive changes in roles and relationships that may accompany it. According to Cavan (1962), satisfying adjustment in old age requires culturally approved positive values for old age, acceptance and respect of those values by society and the specific groups to which the aging individual belongs, and new roles for the expression of the new self-image. This could be provided by the age peer group in a subculture of the aging. Rosow (1974) points out that the peer group might simply allow collective denial of aging, but it can also be a major socializing influence because of the basic functions that peer groups can provide: group support, new memberships to replace those that have been lost, new roles and role models, a *positive* reference group, insulation from stigma, and new self-images. Role models like Albert Schweitzer and Bob Hope are too exceptional to be useful to the average older person, but one's peers can provide *real,* personal role models of successful aging.

A study by the author attempted to measure aging group consciousness and its consequences for self-esteem (Ward, 1977). Responses to several questions were combined to indicate the degree of aging group consciousness felt by the individual. Among those who considered themselves "elderly," aging group consciousness was related to significantly higher self-esteem, but not for those who considered themselves "middle-aged." This was apparently a reflection of reference group or comparison processes. Persons who lack aging group consciousness still view the middle-aged as their reference group, and this group is likely to be better off in health, income, and other aspects. When people compare themselves with others who are better off, feelings of deprivation and self-derogation are likely to result. With aging group consciousness, one's relative standing in a more similar comparison group appears more advantageous and self-esteem can be maintained.

SUMMARY

Age stratification creates the potential for age conflict by making age a basis for structured social inequality. This conflict may be reduced by age-heterogeneous group ties and the inevitability of "age mobility." Modern societies may heighten generational separation and create age-based material issues, however, which could exacerbate age conflict.

Old age is not a time of political quiescence. The aged continue to vote, are interested in politics, and often are part of the political leadership. The aged are more likely to be Republican, but this is a cohort phenomenon that has been changing in recent years. There are reasons to expect heightened feelings of alienation among the young and the old. The aged appear to feel greater powerlessness and meaninglessness, but less social isolation and self-estrangement. The political attitudes of older people do not fit simplistic stereotypes of conservatism. The aged are generally more conservative than younger people, but they can be liberal on policies that would benefit them and have followed recent societal trends toward liberalism (although at a slower rate). There are a number of reasons conservatism might increase with age (e.g., role change, accumulation of experience), but such age differences may also reflect cohort effects.

Cohort succession may be a source of social change, but one must be cautious in expecting such effects. Generation gaps may reflect either the generational consciousness of cohorts experiencing unique events or the natural rebelliousness of maturing youth. Cohort effects assume similar historical influences that are carried throughout the life course, but events are often experienced in different ways and individuals have unique personal biographies.

The senior movement has gone through a long history of incipiency and coalescence, culminating in the White House Conference on Aging of 1971. Since then old-age associations have enjoyed a good deal of political visibility and access. But their success has depended on the perceived political legitimacy and utility of the elderly, and these may be weakening. Political consciousness within the older population has an uncertain future. Barriers such as the perceived stigma of old age, the diversity within the older population, continuing contacts with other segments of society, and limited mobility will continue to exist, and alienation and status inconsistency do not inevitably result in political activism. But future cohorts of older people are likely to have greater feelings of political efficacy because of their greater education and history of activism. Thus the aged represent a potentially important political force.

To the extent that it represents a subculture of the aging, aging group consciousness may yield psychological benefits for the aged. Age peers represent an important reference group, providing age-appropriate norms, role models, social supports, and more favorable images of aging. Thus other older persons represent a positive factor in shaping self-esteem.

chapter 11

Services for Older People

Throughout this book we have tried to strike a balance between recognizing the problems experienced by the aging and avoiding a stereotyped exaggeration of those problems. This chapter will necessarily focus more heavily on the former, discussing service needs, delivery, and utilization. But many older people have no need, or minimal need, for these services. Some older people are overserviced, that is, institutionalized because of a lack of sufficient alternatives in the community. With this note of caution, this chapter will cover two broad areas of concern. First, what institutional services are required by the aged, how are they organized, and what are the effects of institutionalization on the older individual? Second, what community-based services are available (or should be available), and what factors affect their development, delivery, and use?

The most basic theme of this book has been that the nature of aging is shaped by its social context. The concepts of environmental docility and person-environment congruence, introduced in Chapter 9, stress the importance of physical and social environment in the lives of older people, and the services to be discussed in this chapter are potentially critical features of that environment. Inadequate or inappropriate services are likely to be particularly detrimental to the quality of life of the aged. On the other hand, appropriate services may be particularly beneficial. This is recognized in the *social reconstruction model* diagrammed in Figure 11.1. Recognizing the susceptibility of the aged to social labeling and other environmental factors, Kuypers and Bengtson (1973) suggest three types of inputs to bolster coping ability.

First, the aged need to be liberated from the "functionalist ethic," which stigmatizes them for not playing productive roles. Second, there is a need for ser-

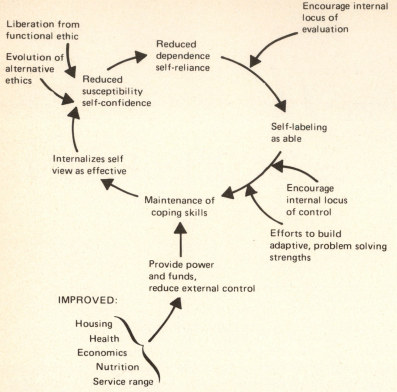

Figure 11.1 The social reconstruction model. (*Source:* Joseph Kuypers and Vern Bengtson, "Social Breakdown and Competence," *Human Development* 16 (1973), p. 197. Reprinted by permission of S. Karger AG, Basel, Switzerland.)

vices that enhance adaptive capacities and a lessening of debilitating environmental conditions. Too often, living environments set up barriers that penalize the elderly, continually calling into question their competence and attacking self-esteem.

> . . . those who choose furniture utilized in settings for older persons tend to ignore the penalties imposed by chairs or sofas too low or too soft or without arms on those who by virtue of arthritis or restricted mobility or stiffness or other deficits find it enormously difficult to get in and out of such chairs. The same criteria can readily be applied to other aspects of the environment which presume to serve the aged: poorly designed beds; storage space so low or so high as to be virtually inaccessible to the elderly; tables of unsuitable height or dimensions; visual and other orienting cues virtually indistinguishable or nonexistent; windows, elevators, water faucets, and heat controls almost impossible to manipulate by stiff fingers or aged joints; wheelchairs which are unstable or allow discomforting and even unsafe slumping by the elderly occupant; heavy doors and "blind" entry and exit portals; eating and cooking utensils and stoves, medicine cabinets, storage bottles and stairs which often range from

the inconvenient and unsuitable for the aged to the unsafe and positively dangerous. (Schwartz, 1975:290)

Finally, internal locus of control should be encouraged. The environment should facilitate actual and perceived self-determination and responsibility. The ability of older people to solve their *own* problems should be supported rather than simply doing things *for* them. Such social reconstruction can be fostered by a wide range of community and institutional programs, but it can also be undermined by lack of appropriate services.

Older people's needs for services also relate to many of the issues discussed in earlier chapters. The longevity characteristic of modern societies means that a greater part of the resources must be allocated to support an older population. This increase in the old-age dependency ratio may then become a political issue. The perceived needs of the elderly also affect their relative status by shaping stereotypes and fears attached to aging. It is probably true, for example, that most people exaggerate the need for nursing homes, and this colors their overall image of the aged.

INSTITUTIONALIZATION OF THE AGED

The likelihood of living in an institutional setting increases with age, as indicated in Table 11.1. Only about 5 percent of persons aged 65 and over reside in nursing homes, however. This increases to nearly 22 percent for those 85 and over, but this is still clearly a minority. As noted in Chapter 2, such statistics underestimate the likelihood that an older person will *at some time* be institutionalized. Vicente and associates (1979) followed up a sample of older community residents studied in 1965. Of those who had died by 1975, 39 percent had been in a convalescent hospital or nursing home at least once and 16 percent had a stay of 6 months or more, with the most common pattern being a continuous stay ending in death. But the fact remains that it is unusual, even rare, for an older person to be in an institution such as a nursing home. At all ages, women are more likely than men to be institutionalized, and women constitute 71 percent of the nursing-home population. Older whites are more likely to reside in nursing homes, whereas nonwhites are more likely to be in mental hospitals (Kart & Beckham, 1976). Low utilization of nursing homes by nonwhites is a reflection of many factors, includ-

Table 11.1   NURSING HOME RESIDENTS PER 1000 POPULATION, BY AGE, SEX, AND RACE, 1977

	Total	Male	Female	White	Nonwhite
Under 65	0.9	0.9	1.0	0.9	0.8
Age 65 and over	47.9	30.7	59.7	49.7	30.4
65–74	14.5	12.7	15.9	14.2	16.8
75–84	68.0	47.4	80.6	70.6	38.6
85 and over	216.4	140.0	251.5	229.0	102.0

Source: Hing, 1981, p. 4.

ing discrimination, lack of access, and preferences by nursing homes for persons who are relatively healthy and financially secure.

The institutionalized population is relatively old. The average age of nursing-home residents is 78, with an average age at admission of 75.4 (Hing, 1981). Virtually all nursing-home residents have some chronic condition or impairment, with an average of 3.9 impairments per patient. Approximately one sixth have some mental disorder—most often chronic OBS (organic brain syndrome)—as the primary diagnosis. Functional status is also lower: 33 percent have some vision impairment, 25 percent some speech impairment, and 45 percent are incontinent at least some of the time; 86 percent need at least some assistance with bathing, 69 percent with dressing, and 66 percent with walking; 32 percent are confined to wheelchairs and 5 percent are bedfast. The median stay in a nursing home is about a year and a half. The typical pattern is for the nursing home to be a "last home"; however, some 20 percent return to the community at some point (Gelfand & Olsen, 1980).

Processes Leading to Institutionalization

One obvious reason for entering a nursing home is the presence of physical problems that make living in the community impossible. But many nursing-home residents could benefit from supportive services in the community and are in institutions because of the lack of such alternatives. There are many older people whose physical or psychological problems are equal to or worse than those of institutional residents, but who are nevertheless able to remain in the community. In his discussion of mental hospitals, Goffman (1961) has suggested that mental patients suffer from "contingencies" as much as from mental illness. Persons may enter or leave mental hospitals not because they are necessarily sicker than those on the outside or are cured, but because of their social class, marital status, family ties, and other nonmedical factors. Similar processes operate with the elderly. Older persons who enter institutions are more likely to have no or few children, were never married or are widowed, have low income, and were living alone or with nonrelatives prior to entry (Vladeck, 1980; Hing, 1981). Gelfand and Olsen (1980) indicate that over a half of all nursing-home residents have no living close relatives.

In their 10-year follow-up study of community residents, Vicente and associates (1979) found that the best predictors of being institutionalized were being unmarried, living alone, and being 75 or older at the time of the original survey. Having longer stays in institutions was associated with being unmarried, aged 75 and over, living alone, being white, with low income, and having health problems. Note that poor health at the time of the original survey was related to length of stay but *not* to whether people entered an institution. Vicente and associates conclude that "medical need may not be the sole or even major determinant of entry or length of stay in nursing homes" (p. 367).

What these findings suggest is the necessity of a balance between need for support and available networks *in the community* that can provide support. As losses occur, the aged try a variety of alternatives, including living with family, and typically display high residential mobility prior to entrance into a nursing home. Thus the institution is often a last resort after other avenues have been exhausted or when they are not available. Premature admission to an institution results from a lack of social or financial supports in the community. In effect, socioeconomic needs are met with a health-care "solution."

The stereotype that older people are in nursing homes because they have been rejected or forgotten by their families has little basis in fact. Many lack such support because they have never married, have no children, or have few children nearby. For some, loss of a supportive relationship may trigger entry into a nursing home:

> In many personal accounts the sudden loss of a supporting relative was plainly critical. A wife died or went into a hospital. A son was killed in an accident. A daughter emigrated to Canada with her husband and family. A widowed sister became more infirm and moved to live with her married children. A niece was no longer able to live with her aunt because she took a residential nursing appointment. The death or the sudden illness of close relatives were the most common events precipitating admission. (Townsend, 1965:176)

Support in the community may also eventually prove too burdensome. Indeed, institutionalization may improve family relations. In a study of nursing-home residents and the children with whom they were most involved, Smith and Bengtson (1979) found evidence of continuation or improvement of family ties following institutionalization: 45 percent exhibited renewed or discovered close ties and 25 percent had continued closeness, whereas 20 percent showed continued separateness and only 10 percent a reduction or abdication of family ties. Smith and Bengtson note that institutionalization reduces the strain of care giving and allows family members to focus on socioemotional interaction. Institutionalization is also a way for older persons to maintain their independence from family, thereby avoiding conflict, and physical and mental functioning may be improved by services available in nursing homes.

THE POLITICAL ECONOMY OF OLD-AGE INSTITUTIONS

Many types of institutions house the aged, including chronic disease hospitals (e.g., tuberculosis hospitals) and mental hospitals. Institutions for the aged date back at least to the Gerontochia established by the Christian church in the third and fourth centuries, but the more typical pattern was to house them in poorhouses or workhouses, along with the sick, mentally ill, destitute, and criminal. Because of this, institutionalization of the aged came to be viewed as the penalty for "improvident or dissolute life" (Townsend, 1964:15). Such attitudes linger on, contributing to a stigma attached to nursing-home residence. Another alternative was private homes run by ethnic-based organizations. Nursing homes run for profit began to be more prevalent by the 1940s. For the most part these were relatively small "mom and pop" operations, but their number and size began to increase by the early 1960s because of the availability of construction loans and low-cost mortgages (Vladeck, 1980).

The past 20 years have seen a virtual explosion in the nursing-home industry. In 1900 2 percent of the aged (80,000 residents) 65 and over were institutionalized. By 1963 2.5 percent were institutionalized, with approximately 500,000 residents in 11,000 nursing homes. By 1977, however, 4.8 percent of the older population resided in nursing homes, involving 1.1 million persons in nearly 18,000 homes (Vladeck, 1980; Hing, 1981).

This increase in the nursing-home population partly reflects increases in the older population, particularly the old-old (75+), and changes in family living arrangements. It also reflects a changing pattern of psychiatric care. The share of the institutionalized older population residing in mental hospitals declined from 24 percent to 10 percent between 1940 and 1970. To a great extent this is a result of the revolution in psychiatric care accompanying the use of tranquilizing drugs, which has produced a general deemphasis of hospitalization for mental disorders. This was supposed to bring more humane and accessible treatment to the mentally impaired while maintaining their community ties, but for the aged it has often meant substitution of a nursing home for a mental hospital. It has been estimated that since 1967 there have been more mentally ill elderly in nursing homes than in all other types of psychiatric facilities (Shanas & Maddox, 1976). Kahn (1975) notes that the aged have dropped out of the psychiatric-care system into the "custodialism" of nursing homes. The deinstitutionalization of mental illness provides an instructive example of a potentially useful program which has been poorly implemented, leading to neglect of vulnerable subgroups. The needs of the aged with mental disorders may be ignored and neglected because the facilities and staff of nursing homes are ill equipped to meet them.

However, the watershed event for the nursing-home industry was the enactment of *Medicare* and *Medicaid* in 1965, which essentially provided a government subsidy of nursing-home care and profits.

Medicare provides national health insurance for the elderly through the Social Security program and finances up to 100 days in a "skilled nursing facility" for posthospitalization care. Medicaid, which is financed jointly by federal and state governments, provides medical insurance for the indigent (of all ages), including unlimited nursing-home benefits for those who qualify (eligibility rules vary by state). By 1977 two thirds of the $12 billion annual income of the nursing-home industry came from government sources. Medicare represents limited nursing-home coverage, therefore it provides only about 7 percent of nursing-home income and is the primary source of payment for only 2 percent of nursing-home residents (Lowy, 1980; Soldo, 1980). Thus Medicaid is the major source of support for nursing-home care: over 60 percent of nursing-home income comes from Medicaid, it is the primary source of payment for nearly a half of nursing-home residents, and nursing-home costs account for about 40 percent of Medicaid expenditures. Indeed, many nursing-home residents are forced to "spend down" to Medicaid because eligibility rules essentially require them to exhaust their personal resources.

The United States is one of the few countries in which institutional care has any significant component in the profit-making sector. In 1977 77 percent of all nursing homes were *proprietary* (private commercial ownership), involving

68 percent of all residents; 18 percent of homes (21 percent of residents) had voluntary nonprofit ownership, generally with some religious affiliation, and 6 percent of homes (10 percent of residents) were government-run (U.S. Public Health Service, 1979). The average home had 83 beds. Proprietary homes are typically smaller than voluntary nonprofit homes, whereas government-run homes are typically much larger. Occupancy is generally high, as nearly three quarters of the homes report having a waiting list for new residents (Vladeck, 1980).

There are various types of nursing homes, related to level of care provided and certification under Medicare and Medicaid. *Skilled nursing facilities* (SNF), certified for Medicare and Medicaid, provide intensive nursing care on a 24-hour-a-day basis. *Intermediate care facilities* (ICF) certified only for Medicaid, provide supportive care and less intensive nursing care. Among nursing homes in 1977, 19 percent were certified as SNF (21 percent of residents), 24 percent were both SNF and ICF (41 percent of residents), 32 percent were ICF only (28 percent of residents), and 25 percent were certified for neither level of care (11 percent of residents) (U.S. Public Health Service, 1979). These levels are somewhat ambiguous and the needs of residents change. Vladeck (1980) suggests that from 10 to 40 percent of nursing-home residents are at the wrong level (generally too high). Other semiinstitutional settings are variously referred to as *personal care, board and care,* or *domiciliary care* homes. These provide a protective environment with meals and some personal care services.

Government financing in nursing-home care is essential, given the often low income of older persons and the often catastrophic expenses related to such care. The average monthly charge for nursing-home care in 1977 was $689, including $1167 for Medicare SNF, $873 for Medicaid SNF, and $610 for Medicaid ICF (U.S. Public Health Service, 1979).

Nursing Home Exposés

This section is not meant to imply that all nursing homes, or perhaps even most, are bad places. Institutions can have a beneficial impact, and many useful studies and programs have emerged from nursing homes. Nevertheless, there is sufficient evidence from various exposés of the nursing-home industry to indicate the existence of a number of "horror stories" connected with nursing-home care. Townsend's (1964) review of institutional care in Great Britain was one of the first of these, citing many inequities and shortcomings among residential facilities for the aged. Later studies in the United States echoed these problems (in particular, see Townsend, 1971; Mendelson, 1975; Vladeck, 1980). Vladeck, for example, notes that government reports have estimated that half of all nursing homes are substandard in some respect. Some of the practices found in nursing homes represent abuse of the public through fraud and corruption. More serious and tragic, however, are the frauds and abuses perpetrated on residents of nursing homes.

Most of the nursing home scandals involved financial chicanery and political influence. But the indifference, neglect, and physical abuse of patients continues: infirm old people are left lying for hours in their own excrement; severely scalded or even drowned in presumably attended bathtubs; illegally restrained in "geriatric chairs"; or attacked, sometimes suffering broken limbs, by nursing home employees. Although the overall quality of nursing homes improved substantially in the preceding decade, there were still, in the United States in 1978, nursing homes with green meat and maggots in the kitchen, narcotics in unlocked cabinets, and disconnected sprinklers in nonfire-resistant structures. (Vladeck, 1980:4)

Vladeck indicates that there is a high level of criminal activity in the nursing-home industry that includes embezzlement and extortion from residents and their families, padding of costs or receiving government reimbursement for services not given, and tax fraud. Studies have reported kickback arrangements between nursing homes and pharmacists or laboratories to increase profits.

Sometimes the kickback is paid in cash, other times in more unusual ways: buying a car for the nursing home operator or paying his way on his vacation. One pharmacy paid two nursing homes $4,400 a year supposedly to maintain "drug supply rooms": the rooms turned out to be broom closets. The presence of those closets permitted the homes to obtain a higher rate from Medicare on the grounds that they were offering an extra service. (Mendelson, 1975:178)

Studies have also reported the occurrence of "gang visits" to nursing homes by physicians who "cruise" quickly through the home and charge each patient for an individual visit.

The GAO, in its Ohio investigation, found not a few examples of such gang visits. One doctor billed the government for 71 patient visits in a single day and 56 on another; he charged the taxpayers for a total of 960 patient visits in one three-month period. Another doctor billed for 487 visits to patients in a sixteen-day period, including 90 on one day and 86 on another. A podiatrist put in for 750 visits, including 32 on one Sunday. All these doctors were also handling their usual load of non-Medicaid patients. (Mendelson, 1975:44)

The most serious abuses, however, are those that directly affect quality of care and the safety of residents. Nursing homes may be deficient in many ways: poor hygiene, inadequate food, poorly coordinated medical services and records. One problem that has captured periodic public attention is nursing-home fires. In January of 1970, 32 patients died in a fire at an Ohio nursing home.

Harmar House was a classic example of the breakdown in standard enforcement. From 1967 to 1969, the home was listed as deficient in "specifications of alarm signals, frequency of fire drills, and assignment of personnel responsibility in a crisis." In April, 1969, the county health department nurse surveying the facility reported that the deficiencies had been removed; apparently they had not been. At the time of the fire, Harmar House had had no fire drill in ten months, although Medicare standards require a drill at least three times a year. Employees testified that they had no idea what their duties were in case of an emergency. The aid who rescued the patient in room 104 had been working at the home for several months but had never been told that one of the first principles of confining fire is to close the door of the room where the fire starts. The four-minute delay in notifying the fire department was due in part to her mistaken belief that the room sensor automatically signaled the fire department. (Townsend, 1971:63–64)

Despite tragedies such as this, in 1974 59 percent of all SNFs had "serious fire safety violations" (U.S. Senate Special Committee on Aging, 1974); yet *all* of these homes were *still licensed and certified by the federal government.*

Inadequate medical care is also a prevalent problem. Glasscote and associates (1976) found that a "distressing" number of nursing homes could not get a physician to come for periodic visits or when there was a change in the condition of a patient the physician had placed in the home. Glasscote and associates also found a lack of familiarity with the special needs of older patients, as there was little difference in the handling of residents with different diagnoses. Nationally, only about a third of nursing-home residents receive any type of therapy (physical, speech, recreational, and so on).

Inadequate medical care may also involve carelessness in the prescription and administration of drugs and possible overdrugging for "ease of maintenance." A retired nursing-home administrator comments:

> A layman doesn't know what to look for in a nursing home. He walks in and sees a patient is nice and quiet and he thinks this guy is happy. And the nurse tells him: "This is John. John is one of our best patients. He sits here and watches television."
> But you just take a look at John's pupils, and you'll see what condition John is in. John is so full of thorazine that it's coming out his ears. Thorazine—that's a tranquilizer they use. It's a brown pill. It looks like an M&M candy.
> The nursing home where I worked kept at least 90 percent of the patients on thorazine all the time. They do it for the money. If they can keep John a vegetable, then they don't have to bother with him. They never have to spend anything to rehabilitate him. (Townsend, 1971:114)

Nursing-home residents take an average of 3.2 medications and 48 percent receive tranquilizers (Hing, 1981). One survey found an average of 6.1 prescriptions per patient; and 15 percent of patients were taking 10 prescriptions or more (Vladeck, 1980). Glasscote and associates (1976) found enough medication mistakes to "cause concern."

These inadequacies partly reflect the fact that staffing is a continual problem. Geriatric medicine has traditionally had low status, the combined result of ageism, stereotypes that the elderly are untreatable, feelings that resources should go to younger patients, and the often demoralized and depressed state of nursing-home patients. Thus, there has been a chronic shortage of physicians, nurses, therapists, and other professional staff. Vladeck (1980) estimates that there are only 1.5 nursing personnel per 100 nursing-home residents and that 90 percent of direct patient care is delivered by aides. Aides receive very low pay; Glasscote and associates (1976) note that supermarket checkers may earn more than nursing-home aides. The aides are also largely unskilled and untrained, as few nursing homes have well-developed in-service training programs. In this respect, profit concerns mean that "the minimum state requirement becomes automatically translated into the maximum" (Glasscote et al., 1976:82). Low pay and inadequate training, combined with the often depressing nature of the work in some nursing homes, results in an estimated annual turnover among aides of 75 percent. The situation may in some cases lead to patient abuse. Stannard (1973) cites the case of a confused nursing-home resident who was left unattended in a bath; he was later found sitting in a tub of scalding water, and eventually died from the burns. Stannard suggests that patient abuse can occur with relative impunity because aide-patient interaction is largely invisible and hostility and suspicion separate aides and other staff (particularly nurses), which limits control. Abuse often represents discipline of "troublesome" patients who wander or are incontinent.

If problems like these can occur in nursing homes, for which many regulations have been enacted, it may be that abuses are even more widespread in other settings that receive less scrutiny. Roberts (1974) reports on a survey of boarding homes, which are essentially unregulated and receive the most impoverished elderly. Approximately half of the homes were rated good to excellent, but the rest were little better than "human warehouses." For example, 38 of the 81 homes had "emergency" or "major" structural violations of building codes. Although medical problems were prevalent among residents, many of the homes lacked individualized care, dietary programs, or trained medical personnel.

THE IMPACT OF INSTITUTIONALIZATION

The problems we have discussed certainly represent important determinants of the consequences of being institutionalized. But more generally nursing homes also represent an environmental setting. The concept of environmental docility reminds us that because nursing-home residents are likely to have reduced competence, the nature of the nursing home as a living environment is critically important. The institutional world can have a tremendous impact on residents, for better or worse.

Relocation Studies

Institutionalization may literally be a life-or-death issue. In an early study Aldritch and Mendkoff (1963) studied residents who had to be relocated after their nursing home closed. Comparing mortality rates in the year following the move with expected rates (based on the previous 10 years at the home), they found that actual mortality rates were higher than expected (32 percent versus 19 percent), primarily within the first 3 months. The following case is an example:

> Miss E. W., aged 85, had been in the Home for twenty-four years following a back injury. She walked with a cane and had been an active and alert participant, requiring no nursing supervision. She was anxious about the Home's closing, expressed fear of any change in her situation, and became depressed and

withdrawn. After arranging her belongings and taking care of her personal affairs, she withdrew further and lost all interest in the daily activities of the Home. She frequently spoke of death and stated that she had no reason to live. While efforts were being made for transfer, she died, apparently of arteriosclerosis. (Aldritch & Mendkoff, 1963:190)

A number of other studies have also found that relocation, from home to institution or from one institution to another, can sometimes result in physical, psychological, and social deterioration, and even death (Schulz & Brenner, 1977; Coffman, 1981; Kowalski, 1981). Such effects tend to be greater for patients who are most vulnerable—those older and in poorer physical and mental health. This research indicates, however, that such consequences are not attributable to relocation per se, but to circumstances that may surround relocation. The effects are evident when relocation is disruptive, involving uncertainty, confusion, and deterioration of social supports. Coffman (1981) suggests that there are fewer problems when residents move together, keeping their relationships with each other and with staff intact, or move from one stable population to another. Increasing predictability, achieved by involving patients in decisions, trial visits, and making the new environment as similar as possible to the old one, lessens the need for wrenching adjustments. And the impact of relocation is less when residents can exercise greater control—when the move is voluntary or the new environment encourages autonomy, interaction, and integration in the outside community. As noted in Chapter 9, relocation to an *improved* environment can also have a decidedly *beneficial* result. Borup (1982) suggests that moderate institutional change can have positive effects when accompanied by individualized assessment of need and adequate preparation for relocation. Such patterns indicate that the quality of the institutional environment is critical to the well-being of residents.

The Consequences of Being Institutionalized

Compared with community residents, institutionalized older people exhibit an *institutional syndrome* of low morale, negative self-image, preoccupation with the past, feelings of personal insignificance, intellectual ineffectiveness, docility and withdrawal, anxiety and fear of death (Tobin & Lieberman, 1976). Many have taken this as an indication that nursing homes create more problems than they cure. Scott, in a thought-provoking study, argues that agencies for the blind often make the blind more dependent—more "blind"—than they need to be.

The disability of blindness is a learned social role. The various attitudes and patterns of behavior that characterize people who are blind are not inherent in their condition but, rather, are acquired through ordinary processes of social learning. Thus, there is nothing inherent in the condition of blindness that requires a person to be docile, dependent, melancholy, or helpless; nor is there anything about it that should lead him to become independent or assertive. Blind men are made, and by the same processes of socialization that have made us all. (1969:14)

Similar processes may operate within nursing homes.

Goffman (1961) used the term *total institution* to refer to places (such as mental hospitals, prisons, or army barracks) that are cut off from the surrounding world and impose regimented schedules on "inmates," presumably to achieve some overall goal—treatment, rehabilitation, conversion. Goffman is concerned with the effects of such institutions on residents, particularly in creating social and psychological disabilities. Inmates experience a *curtailment of self* as they lose control of many seemingly trivial things that define their individuality (institutional uniforms, furniture, haircuts, and so on), and they lose their autonomy and spontaneity in regimentation of eating, sleeping, and play. A gulf of suspicion, hostility, and derogation separates staff and residents, limiting meaningful interaction. There is a loss of privacy, further limiting personal autonomy and opportunities for emotional release and self-evaluation. In all of these ways "total institutions disrupt or defile precisely those actions that in civil society have the role of attesting to the actor and those in his presence that he has some command over his world" (Goffman, 1961:43).

The concern is that residents may eventually lose the capacity to *be an individual*—to act in a self-directed, autonomous fashion—as decisions are constantly made for them. Rather than social reconstruction, institutions may create social breakdown. The individual becomes increasingly oriented to the world of the institution and isolated from the outside world, thereby losing the capacity to exist independent of the institution.

Institutions vary in their degrees of totality. A "shopping list" of sorts can be used to determine the totality of any nursing home (Bennett & Nahemow, 1965; Kiyak et al., 1975). Some criteria relate to life inside the home: sequential scheduling of activities, few provisions for personal property, involuntary recruitment, dormitory-style living, formalized rules and sanctions, little resident involvement in governance; others relate to access to the outside world: availability of private phones, proximity and ease of travel to the community, allowances for leaving during the day or for a weekend, scheduled activities outside the institution. A total nursing home is one that provides a custodial, protected environment for its residents, severing ties to the community. It is oriented toward an orderly routine, rewarding residents who perform the "proper" role of dependency and passivity. This may involve an aspect of infantilism, where first names or a patronizing "dear" are always used for residents, who are stereotypically perceived as having little capacity for autonomy or personal growth.

Nursing-home residents may encounter the loss of autonomy and privacy that contribute to social breakdown, as illustrated in the following example:

> The staff took the attitude that the old people had surrendered any claims to privacy. The residents were washed and dressed and conveniently arranged in chairs and beds—almost as if they were made ready for a daily inspection. An attendant was always present in the bathroom, irrespective of old people's capacity to bathe themselves. The lavatories could not be locked and there were large spaces at the top and bottom of the doors. The matron swung open one door and unfortunately revealed a blind old woman installed on the w.c.

She made no apology. In a dormitory she turned back the sheets covering one woman to show a deformed leg—again without apology or explanation. (Townsend, 1964:5)

Residents may also encounter loss of the aspects of self associated with personal possessions. Institutional coldness combined with hospitallike smells and routine imply a loss of "home" and the little details associated with it.

"It isn't home here. I woulda' liked to have stayed with the children. We had a cat and I miss that cat quite a bit. I miss my little radio and the window I had where you could see the dog in the yard next door. Sometimes I really miss that nice little carpet I had next to my bed. I was used to that." (Gubrium, 1975:87)

These problems are compounded by the disruption of social interaction. Those who enter nursing homes have already experienced disruption of daily habits and routines. Loss of access to old friends combines with difficulty adjusting to new ones. Social and psychological withdrawal may substitute for the lack of physical privacy. In addition, residents are restricted in doing things for each other: cooking, caring during illness, and so on.

The residents of Weldon Manor are actively discouraged from helping one another, as I saw for myself during the two days I was there. One of the women said, "We are not supposed to help. It does seem short-sighted to a good few of us here. I think it's made me rather unkind." Another added to this, "I'm not supposed to lift a finger for anybody and I'm not even allowed to wash up. I'd like to. . . . We're not always good-tempered with each other. It's a lonely life, you know, with nothing to do and plenty of time to do it in." (Townsend, 1964:82)

Although these restrictions are no doubt motivated by concern for the safety and well-being of the residents and the liability of the institution, they nevertheless prevent the development of reciprocal relationships on which friendships can be built.

Gottesman and Bourestom (1974) conducted an observational study of 1144 residents in 169 Detroit nursing homes. They found that 56 percent of the residents' time during the day was spent doing *nothing;* only 17 percent of the time were they observed in contact with any other person; and only 7.5 percent of the time were they in contact with nonstaff. The residents typically developed few close friends within the institution. An observational study by Fontana (1977) also found little interaction among residents. Residents did not want to admit they "belonged" there nor associate with other residents, who they viewed as inferior. Tesch and Whitbourne (1981) found that involvement with fellow residents was seen as undesirable because residents valued privacy and independence more than contact with others.

Low interaction within nursing homes may combine with few outside social contacts. A 1977 survey of nursing-home residents found that 69 percent had not participated in any event outside their homes within the past month, and only

11 percent had an overnight leave within the past year (Markson, 1980). Disruption of familiar social networks may be particularly demoralizing because, as studies indicate, social continuity makes important contributions to the well-being of nursing-home residents (Harel, 1981; Tesch & Whitbourne, 1981).

Interaction may also be minimal with staff. Fontana (1977) found that aides were very busy and had little time for social interaction. Residents were viewed as work objects rather than human beings and were classified on the basis of work routines (e.g., "nonfeeders" versus "feeders," who need to be hand-fed).

This does not mean that nursing homes do not develop their own social systems. For example, Gubrium's (1975) study of "Murray Manor" found a complex social environment. Friendship was important to residents, and cliques developed along lines similar to the "poor dear" hierarchy discussed in Chapter 9. There was a keen sense of territoriality concerning room assignments, seating in the dining room, and the use of lounges. But social relationships were not encouraged by staff and were even hindered by staff orientations. Gubrium notes, for example, that although administrative ("top") staff gave lip service to social and emotional needs as part of total care, because they really only checked on physical care, the floor staff did little else too. Their concern was with meeting routine schedules, and residents were considered unrealistic or irrational when the residents' demands could not be met within the normal routine. Although dignity and respectful care were important to residents, such concerns as well as the social relationships among residents were largely ignored by staff.

Some studies suggest that totality and length of residence in such nursing homes are related to declines in physical, psychological, and social capabilities (Dick & Friedsam, 1963; Coe, 1965; Lawton & Nahemow, 1973; Elwell, 1981). Elwell, using a sample of nursing-home residents in New York, found that totality and custodialism were related to greater declines in physical and mental functioning and that the apparent effects of totality increased over time.

These studies imply that nursing homes, at least partly because of their characteristics as total institutions, create demoralized, depersonalized, passive, and withdrawn residents. They do not "nurse," but rather foster dependency and an incapacity to function in the community. These studies are suggestive, however, rather than conclusive, because of the difficulties in separating the effects of the institution from the other explanations for the characteristics of institutional populations.

Tobin and Lieberman (1976) note that there are three alternative explanations of the institutional syndrome exhibited by nursing-home residents. First, nursing-home residents are not a random sample of the older population. Their psychological states may simply reflect the physical and mental problems that led them to the institution. Second, there may be "preadmission effects," linked to feelings of separation or rejection and negative attitudes toward entering an institution. Finally, relocation research suggests that environmental discontinuity may account for the impact of institutionalization. These explanations refer to the stress imposed by losses that create dependency and a need for institutional services, loss of familiar supports, entrance into a strange environment, and labeling effects of being in a nursing home.

Certainly there are many aspects of the preadmission period that might have detrimental effects on older people. The aged have negative views of institutions and prefer to live in their own homes. There are many negative symbols attached to nursing homes: the lingering image from earlier times of the poorhouse, a sacrifice of highly valued independence, an underlining of the losses associated with aging and the nearness of death, feelings of being cast aside by family and society. In addition, there may be inadequate preparation for entrance into the nursing home, which heightens feelings of confusion and personal distress. These reactions to institutions may lead those who enter to dwell on the past or withdraw socially and psychologically from an unpleasant reality.

Tobin and Lieberman (1976) have conducted one of the few studies that attempt to assess the relative importance of these effects. They interviewed 100 persons on a waiting list for admission to three nursing homes; then reinterviewed those who entered (85 persons) 2 months after admission and again 1 year later. Two groups were used for comparison: a sample of community residents and a sample of relatively healthy persons who had lived in these homes for 1 to 3 years. From the initial interviews, it was apparent that "most of the psychological qualities attributed to the adverse effects of entering and living in an institution *were already present in people on the waiting list*" (p. 77, emphasis added). Persons on the waiting list were more like the institutional than the community sample, and in some ways were worse than those already in the institution.

In their follow-up conducted one year after admission, Tobin and Lieberman found that among those who had not died or shown extreme deterioration there was no evidence of psychological deterioration. Problems of adjusting to the institution were most acute during the first few months, as people felt resentment toward family, left behind prized possessions, experienced a sometimes overwhelming sense of institutionalization (e.g., group bathrooms, large dining halls), and had low status in the resident social system. But as residents began to establish their own slot in the world of the home, they became more satisfied and less anxious. Tobin and Lieberman conclude that "the status of the 'old-timer' appears to be largely a function of his status just before admission" (p. 198), and the most significant transition may be from community to waiting list rather than waiting list to institution. This is a time of accumulating losses, dependency, and deterioration in social networks, colored by feelings of separation and abandonment.

Another study by Myles (1978) suggests that institutionalization may also have beneficial effects. Comparing community and nursing-home residents at comparable levels of illness and disability, he found that nursing-home residents had higher *subjective* ratings of their health. He attributes this to protective aspects of institutions that minimize the disruptive effects of physical disabilities on everyday life. As subjective health was the most important determinant of morale for both groups, this indicates that institutionalization may indirectly contribute to morale.

These studies raise doubts about the impact of institutional life, but they do not disprove the potentially harmful consequences of nursing homes. The samples were small, with limited comparability and representativeness, and the nursing homes studied were apparently of high quality and relatively nontotal. There is a great need for comparative research among different types of nursing homes. These studies do caution us, however, that the creation of passive, withdrawn, dependent institutional populations is not an inevitable effect of nursing homes. Nursing homes should strive to have beneficial impacts on the social and psychological functioning of residents; at the very least, they should be structured to prevent further decline among persons who have already experienced deterioration of psychological and social skills.

QUALITY OF INSTITUTIONAL CARE

There is ample evidence that nursing homes *can* benefit residents. It is clear, for example, that older people can make effective use of the entire range of mental-health services (Butler & Lewis, 1981). In an 11-year study of over 1000 patients discharged from one skilled nursing home, Kaplan and Ford (1975) found that 61 percent were discharged to independent living in their own households. Kaplan and Ford attribute this to the effective use of a multidisciplinary team: physicians, nurses, physical therapists, occupational therapists, speech therapists, social workers.

What approaches need to be taken? Tobin and Lieberman (1976) point out that there are four distinct phases connected with institutionalization: (1) predecision (leading to the need for institutional services), (2) anticipatory (being on the waiting list), (3) initial adjustment to the institution, and (4) longer-term adaptation. Their study suggests that phases 2 and 3 may be most critical. Support can be provided through realistic familiarization with the new environment and humanization of the institution, perhaps providing objects from the resident's former world as anchors. Because interaction is critical to self-concept and adaptation, efforts should be directed at facilitating social involvement.

The social reconstruction model (see Figure 11.1) also emphasizes self-determination and responsibility. Nursing-home residents may be overprotected. Bennett and Nahemow (1965) have noted that nursing homes and mental hospitals often have virtually no social adjustment criteria; nothing is expected, so nothing is rewarded. Without the opportunity to succeed (or fail) on their own, residents become dependent, apathetic, and withdrawn. In an experimental study Langer and Rodin (1976) found that when decision making, personal responsibility, and freedom were encouraged among nursing-home residents, they were happier and received more favorable nurses' ratings on alertness, general improvement, sociability, and activity.

Nursing-home environments need to be richer, more complex, and more challenging to residents while keeping in mind their existing limitations. As stressed by the concept of person-environment congruence, institutions should strive for a match between residents' competence (both cognitive and physical) and environmental demands (Lawton and Nahemow, 1973). When environmental challenge is too low, people experience either deprivation or complacency; when it is too high, they experience overload. Lawton and Nahemow suggest the need for "minimal goals" rehabilitation, where environmental demands are slightly above the person's accustomed level of performance. This encourages increased feelings of competence and personal power, without putting people out on a limb. There are many ways to encourage initiative and responsibility within nursing homes, from room decoration to resident governance.

Factors Affecting Quality of Care

It is apparent that nursing homes can contribute to either social reconstruction or breakdown of their residents. It is also evident that nursing homes vary greatly in quality. Quality of care is difficult to define, however. On the one hand, it refers to the availability of treatment resources—professional staff, records and facilities, therapeutic programs, and so on. But quality of care also involves the social and psychological milieu of the nursing home, which is more difficult to assess. Lemke and Moos (1980) have described a Multiphasic Environmental Assessment Procedure for rating institutional settings along three dimensions: (1) physical and architectural resources, (2) resident and staff resources, and (3) social-environmental resources. Based on such dimensions, a number of studies have attempted to determine the characteristics of high- and low-quality nursing homes. Nursing homes that are certified for Medicare, conform to licensing standards, and are accredited (by such organizations as the Joint Committee on Hospital Accreditation) tend to offer more treatment resources (Kosberg & Tobin, 1972; Kosberg, 1973; Levey et al., 1973; Kart & Manard, 1976). Larger nursing homes that are more expensive and have more professional staff have more treatment resources. In a study of SNFs in New York, Ullmann (1981) found that size was related to better building quality (because larger homes were generally newer), better rehabilitation services, and greater use of in-house staff.

Quality of the social environment is much more difficult to assess, and findings are conflicting. Curry and Ratliff (1973) found that larger homes were more likely to isolate residents from the community and from interactions with other residents and staff; Kart and Manard (1976) indicate that smaller nursing homes appear to be more homelike. As is so often true in medical settings, greater size may bring better technical care, but at the cost of a more impersonal, bureaucratic environment. But Lemke and Moos (1980) found that larger settings provided more social activities and greater resident involvement in decision making. Lemke and Moos also found that a higher level of care (e.g., SNF versus ICF) was associated with less choice and control (greater totality) for residents.

Variations among nursing homes partly reflect variations in their residents. To the extent they are able, nursing homes will prefer healthier residents who are better off financially. Lemke and Moos (1980) found that larger settings and those with lower staffing levels were more selective and less tolerant of low levels of functioning. As in so many other ways, the poor are disadvantaged in nursing-home care. Blacks and persons supported by public aid (Medicaid) reside in poorer-quality nursing homes, whereas homes located in higher-income, suburban areas have more treatment resources (Kosberg & Tobin, 1972; Kosberg, 1973). Kosberg also found that poor residents are more likely to receive only custodial care from staff, and Elwell (1981) found that nursing homes with more Medicaid patients had more custodial environments (greater totality).

The potential tension between profits and quality and the proprietary nature of the nursing-home industry have long been issues. A study of SNFs in California found that higher quality of care was associated with lower profitability (Fottler et al., 1981). But studies have indicated that there are few major differences in treatment resources based on type of ownership (Kosberg & Tobin, 1972; Kosberg, 1973; Levey et al., 1973; Kart & Manard, 1976). Vladeck (1980) suggests that the best voluntary homes are the best there are, whereas the worst nursing homes are almost exclusively proprietary, but that there is substantial overlap between proprietary and voluntary homes. Kart and Manard (1976) indicate that voluntary nonprofit homes have better staff attitudes and social milieu; public homes, the worst; and proprietary homes, intermediate. But Vladeck (1980) suggests that voluntary homes may be more discriminatory and more reluctant to accept Medicaid patients and persons with greater disabilities, and Elwell (1981) found that voluntary homes had more custodial environments. Thus there is no simple or clear relationship between nursing-home quality and type of ownership.

How can the quality of nursing homes be improved? Average quality no doubt has improved. Levey and associates (1973) found an increase in the quality of Massachusetts nursing homes between 1965 and 1969. There is certainly room for additional improvement, however. The nursing-home industry is closely regulated in theory with many standards set by federal and state agencies and inspections by states. And regulation does seem to help because certification and licensing are related to higher-quality care.

Existing regulations have however been inadequate and ineffective in many ways. Agencies that inspect nursing homes are typically understaffed and underfinanced, and regulation of nursing homes is so fragmented that no single agency has clear authority. The apparent shortage of nursing-home beds also means that a substandard home is better than none at all; and agencies often have few weapons against noncompliance except license revocation. The criteria of quality also represent quantifiable, health-related measures of "inputs" and "process" (staffing and facilities) rather than "outcome" measures of the physical, psychological, and social health of residents or quality of life in the institution (Vladeck, 1980; Spilerman & Litwak, 1982).

Spilerman and Litwak (1982) suggest that "reward structures" are a key to shaping quality of care in nursing homes. Reimbursement policies under Medicare and Medicaid represent one type of reward. Current policies, which essentially pass costs on to the government, provide little incentive to control costs, and may result in reduced services or less acceptance of unprofitable patients who require more services. There is also no incentive to go beyond minimum requirements. Lawton (1980) suggests that financial incentives could be provided to nursing homes that *demonstrate* innovative and high-quality care. He also notes that there is a need to subsidize staff training at all levels.

Spilerman and Litwak (1982) indicate that current reward structures neither motivate nor control staff behavior. They suggest, for example, that the residents' ratings of staff performance might be linked to personnel decisions and that residents' associations with hired representatives might have some oversight functions. It has also been suggested that nursing-home residents fare best when many outside groups (government agencies, charitable organizations, other community groups, families) monitor the operation of nursing homes to enhance their responsiveness (Vladeck, 1980; Spilerman & Litwak, 1982). One study found that better care was given to those who received visitors from the community (family, friends, personal physicians), implying the existence of someone in the community who might hold the nursing home accountable (Gottesman & Bourestom, 1974). Families are often not very thorough or sophisticated in placing their aged members in nursing homes. According to one study, 51 percent of a sample of families had not even visited the nursing home before placement (York & Calsyn, 1977). The major reasons for selecting a nursing home were availability of a bed and location—hardly the best indicators of quality. Such factors as quality of staff, physical care, activity programs, and cleanliness were much less influential in family decisions.

Perhaps the essential problem is the failure of the public to pay sufficient attention to the nursing-home industry and the treatment received by the elderly. Kart and Manard conclude that *"lack of continued effective public pressure is the most basic reason for the failure of nursing home regulation"* (1976:255).

COMMUNITY-BASED SERVICES FOR THE AGED

Although institutions can have beneficial effects, it seems generally preferable to keep the aged in the community whenever possible. Some type of institution will always be necessary, but there have been many complaints that some residents of nursing homes are there needlessly. In 1977 only 43.8 percent of nursing-home residents required intensive nursing care (intravenous injection, oxygen therapy), full bed bath, or less intensive nursing care (application of sterile bandages or dressings) (Hing, 1981). Lawton (1980) conservatively estimates that from 10 to 18 percent of nursing-home residents, or as many as 200,000 persons, could be maintained in the community. This again points out that medical need is not the sole determinant of institutionalization. Indeed, it has been estimated that older people in the community with extreme physical limitations outnumber those in institutions by 2 to 1 (Soldo, 1980). Thus many institutionalized older people might remain in the community were sufficient services available, and others are handicapped by the lack of a full range of services, although they manage to remain in the community.

The older population would clearly benefit from a wider range of community-based services. Apart from the potentially negative effects of institutionalization, *home* is an important idea for all of us, and particularly for the elderly. Home is part of their identity, lends a sense of familiarity, and helps the aged maintain personal autonomy and control. Congregate living of any type is often seen as a loss of personal liberty and dignity.

Types of Community Services

There are no set answers for the provision of services to older people in the community. Each individual's own living situation must be assessed for its match to his or her competence. Many things are involved, among them: functional health, psychological well-being, and potential support from family and friends. Butler and Lewis (1981) note that many skills are required for independent community living: orientation to time, place, and person; cooking and feeding oneself; bathing, dressing, grooming, toileting, continence; transferring from bed to chair; standing and walking; climbing stairs; fire and accident security; shopping, money management; ability to follow instructions (medication); ability to seek assistance when needed; social participation. Community services should be designed to further and protect the dignity, independence, and integration of the individual. The concept of social reconstruction is important in this regard (see Figure 11.1).

The answer is not simply deinstitutionalization, but rather the provision of a *continuum of care* to meet the changing needs of aging individuals. Coward (1979) has described a useful framework of five types of services related to "developmental phases" of aging.

1. *Adjustive and integrative services:* Such programs, aimed primarily at the "young-old," will enhance their social integration and adjustment to new roles and situations. Included are employment and volunteer programs, counseling concerning retirement, income, and bereavement, and social and recreational programs.
2. *Supportive services:* Aimed at the somewhat older elderly, these programs will help them remain in their usual and preferred living arrangement. Included are visiting homemaker and health services, delivery of meals, friendly visiting and telephone reassurance programs, escort services, and day care or geriatric day hospitals.
3. *Congregate and shelter-care services:* Day care and specialized housing alternatives can protect the more frail "old-old" from the hazards of community living.
4. *Protective services:* Advanced aged with deteriorated functioning may require services that protect their rights and welfare. This includes legal services, help with managing financial affairs, and oversight and coordination of the multiple services that a particular individual may require.
5. *Specialized terminal-care facilities and services:* These involve programs to assist dying persons and their families in meeting medical, psychological, and social needs.

There are a number of general concerns that cut across the five service areas. These services imply a continuum of housing, offering a variety of living arrangements from independent community living to dependent institutional care. Many older people can live in their own homes with supportive services, including household repairs, to prevent disruptive relocation, but many elderly homeowners find it too difficult to maintain their homes. So-called *reverse annuity mortgages* can provide homeowners with income from their housing assets without having to sell and move out. For more impaired older persons, *congregate housing* can provide shelter, nutrition, housekeeping, and some personal-care assistance. Foster family care provides another quasi-familial living arrangement (Newman & Sherman, 1980).

The housing continuum may be provided in a single location. As noted in Chapter 9, this accommodating model reduces relocation stress and is more flexi-

ble in meeting changing needs. Gutman (1978) describes a multilevel housing arrangement that includes self-contained suites, congregate housing, and intermediate and skilled nursing care. Some observers have felt that this mixing might undermine the morale of healthy older persons, but Gutman found that residents
of the multilevel housing had higher morale and greater interaction with neighbors than older people in the community or in more traditional retirement housing.

As noted in Chapters 8 and 9, networks of family, friends, and neighbors
are also important aspects of maintenance in the community. It has been estimated that 60 to 80 percent of long-term care needs, other than nursing-home
care, are met informally by family and friends. Services should support these informal efforts. This may mean counseling or financial assistance. *Respite* services,
which temporarily take over care from families, can also ease the burdens of care
giving.

Another critical need is for programs that provide information and referral
as well as coordination of services. Such programs should not be considered subsidiary to "real" services. Older persons too often lack knowledge of or access
to available alternatives, and inadequate assistance can often be traced to inappropriate placement. Mentally impaired older people face particular problems.
Frankfather (1977), in a study of one community, found that the "confused elderly" were bounced around from one agency to another. Because their "senility"
was regarded as irreversible, handling them was considered a waste of resources.
Defined as inappropriate cases ("dump jobs"), the confused elderly were quickly
referred elsewhere in a perpetual cycling through the service system.

> Old people are just moved around like so much rotten fruit. (administrator,
> Thompson Nursing Home Corporation) It's just like dropping a hot potato.
> Maybe someone will stop and pick it up. (psychiatric nurse, emergency room,
> PH) They ship them out of here as if they were a side of beef. (social worker
> 1, CH) (Frankfather, 1977:156)

Particularly necessary is oversight of a specific individual's service needs.
Many older people have multiple problems (physical, mental, economic, social)
that must be dealt with through many programs and service providers. Too often
there is no coherence to the provision of these services—the left hand rarely
knows what the right is doing. ACCESS, developed in Rochester, N.Y., provides
an excellent example of a program that evaluates needs of older persons, recom-
mends community and institutional placement alternatives, and provides case
management to assure continuity of care (Eggert et al., 1980). A similar program
in Connecticut found that more services could be provided at the same cost, and
there was evidence of increased morale and feelings of control among participants
(Hodgson & Quinn, 1980).

Estimating Need and Cost

One reason for the recent increased interest in community services is the belief
that they are less costly than institutional approaches. This is true only up to

a point. One must consider many types of costs connected with maintaining the aged in the community, among them: housing, nutrition, personal care, and volunteer expenses. When the intent is to support family-based care, one must also assess economic, social, and psychological costs to the family. Community alternatives are not necessarily inexpensive. Vladeck (1980), for example, indicates that congregate housing may cost from $600 to $1000 per month.

The comparative costs of community and institutional care depend on the impairment level of the elderly. When impairment is low, home care is more economical than nursing-home care. Beyond a certain level of impairment, however, it becomes more costly to support community living because too many costly services are required. This is illustrated in Figure 11.2. For extremely disabled older persons, institutions are less expensive because of the centralization of services. Figure 11.2 also indicates that community services are likely to be cost efficient for all but the most disabled persons. Such services remain inadequate, however, and we lack sufficient information about the extent of need for services in any community and the factors that insure suitable placement.

FACTORS AFFECTING DELIVERY AND USE OF SERVICES

It has been pointed out for many years that certain community or institutional services would be helpful to older people, yet services for the aged are still woefully inadequate in many respects. Services that are *ideally* needed may never be *actually* implemented, and even when services are developed there is no guarantee that older people can, or will, use them. There are three types of factors

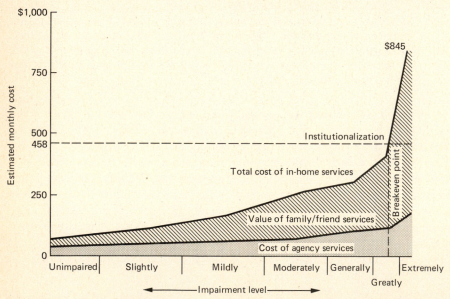

Figure 11.2 Estimated monthly costs of home services and institutionalization for people 65 and over at varying levels of impairment, 1977. (*Source:* Beth J. Soldo, "America's Elderly in the 1980s," *Population Bulletin* 35, no. 4 (1980), Washington, D.C.: Population Reference Bureau, Inc., p. 27.)

that affect the delivery and use of services: (1) *predisposing* factors, (2) *enabling* factors, and (3) *illness level* factors (Ward, 1977).

Predisposing Factors

Predisposing factors are characteristics that affect the likelihood that individuals will need services and seek assistance. Increased age is itself associated with greater need for a variety of services. Within the older population, there are also certain subgroups, such as widows and minority aged, with greater service needs. Thus when communities assess the likely demand for future medical and social services, with an eye toward rational planning, they should begin by looking at the demographics: the future proportions of old-old (75+) persons, widowed people, low-income aged, and so on. Current "retirement states," such as Florida and Arizona, will have to give some thought to the aging of their retirement populations over the next 20 years as this affects the dependency ratio and the demand for services.

Other predisposing characteristics affect service use through their association with values, attitudes, beliefs, and behavior patterns. For example, low education is related to less use of preventive services (Ward, 1977). Such facts must be kept in mind when targeting services for particular subgroups of the aged.

Willingness to use services is often affected by attitudes and beliefs. In a study of rural elderly Moen (1978) found that a "nonaccepter syndrome" was associated with denial of need, refusal to seek help even when need was expressed, and refusal to accept help when offered. She attributed this to a striving for independence and hostility toward welfare compounded by lack of knowledge and confusion over eligibility and costs. Such attitudes may be partly a cohort phenomenon, because current older cohorts stress individualism and the work ethic. Government social welfare programs are relatively recent and may be viewed as more legitimate by future cohorts.

A welfare stigma varies among services. One study of attitudes toward 13 social programs (such as Aid to Families with Dependent Children and unemployment compensation) found that Social Security was the least stigmatized (Williamson, 1974). But other programs for the aged may not fare as well; for example, Williamson found that public housing was a relatively stigmatized program.

Enabling Factors

Assuming that people are willing to use a service, they must also have access to it. This access is affected by a number of enabling factors: (1) the service must exist, (2) delivery of the service must be structured in such a way that people actually receive assistance, (3) people must know that the service exists, (4) the service must be accessible to people, and (5) the service must be affordable. The failure of any one of these means that even the most brilliantly conceived program will fail. It has been estimated, for example, that only 55 percent of older persons eligible for Supplemental Security Income actually participate in the program; this represents a combination of lack of knowledge and reluctance to accept "welfare."

The federal government has played a major enabling role (discussed in a later section) through its policies and programs directed at the aged. The structure of services and related financial arrangements represent only one set of enabling factors, however. Information and transportation are also important enabling variables. Unfortunately, those at whom services are most clearly aimed (with poor health, low income, over 75) are often least knowledgeable about what services are available. A Canadian study of older people in Edmonton, Alberta, found that awareness of services was only slightly better than chance; only one fourth could correctly indicate the services provided by merely half of 35 health-related agencies (Snider, 1980). Awareness was the strongest predictor of service use, even greater than health or income. This again points out the critical importance of information and referral services. Unfortunately we know very little about the sources of information and referral used by the aged. They probably depend on the community setting. Taietz (1975) indicates that direct knowledge and word of mouth are effective in rural areas, but the aged must rely on mass communication in more complex urban areas.

As noted in Chapter 9, adequate transportation is also important. A number of programs that attempt to alleviate transportation problems have been developed (Golant, 1976). Reduced-fare programs have consistently resulted in increased use of mass transit, particularly during off-peak periods. West Virginia has experimented with transportation stamps for low-income and handicapped older people. Some newer systems, such as San Francisco's Bay Area Rapid Transit (BART), have incorporated special design features, including wider doors and extended handrails. So-called *demand responsive* services, such as dial-a-ride or special bus routes, have proven reasonably efficient, especially when computerized. But transportation continues to be a critical need for many older people, particularly for those who live in rural and suburban areas where public transportation is least developed and special programs are usually very costly.

The rural elderly are especially at risk regarding access to social services. Although the urban-rural gap has been narrowing, services continue to be less available and accessible in rural areas (Taietz & Milton, 1979; Nelson, 1980). This is partly because of the reduced resources (budgets, staffing) of rural agencies and local governments, making it difficult to mobilize additional efforts.

Minority aged are at risk as well. They may encounter a number of objective and subjective barriers: distance to services, lack of minority staffing, barriers of language and culture, or mistrust of government programs. A study of a sample of counties found that minority aged were served fairly by most agencies; but minorities were most often overlooked in sparsely populated areas and when they were a small share of the population (Holmes et al., 1979). Use of community services by minority older persons was related to the presence of minority staff and location of offices in minority neighborhoods.

Illness Level Factors

Even though people may be predisposed to use a service and have access to that service, they may fail to use it. Many social and psychological factors affect decisions to seek help. The tendency of people to deny aging may translate into a reluctance to admit age-related difficulties, whether medical, psychological, or social. As noted in Chapter 4, the aged may also shift their frame of reference for evaluating need from *objective* to *subjective* indicators, which change less with age. This reflects people's ability to settle for what they have, yet it constitutes a potential barrier to the provision of services that are objectively needed.

It is also true that the *evaluation* of need by service providers, or by those who might refer older people to services, is a vital link in the processes by which services are delivered. There is evidence of at least some age biases among the various helping professions, which historically have dealt with the needs of younger people for acute problems (Beattie, 1976). There has long been a serious shortage of staff for services directed at the aged; for example, there are only about 10 percent of the number of homemakers and home health aides needed (Butler, 1975). Butler (1976) also notes that medical schools have paid scant attention to geriatric medicine—few students are exposed to the problems of older patients (through courses or clinical experience, as in nursing homes) and few faculty have geriatric expertise. Many physicians have been unwilling to accept Medicare and Medicaid patients, particularly those in nursing homes, because of red tape, inadequate reimbursement, lack of back-up staff, and feelings that nursing homes are unpleasant to visit (Kart et al., 1978).

The lack of receptivity toward dependent or impaired older persons extends beyond service providers and includes the larger community. Frankfather (1977), for example, found senior citizen centers to be closed societies of middle-class women who were intolerant of deviance and forced "outsiders" to withdraw from involvement. Nursing-home residents in particular were stereotyped as "mumblers and droolers" and made to feel unwelcome at the center. This lack of tolerance and general support for the impaired elderly is a significant barrier to their maintenance in the community. Those who do manage to remain in the community may become the sort of wandering street characters found in any community.

> . . . Coughin' Annie (chef, Main Street Luncheonette). . . . the Cryer—She spends all day feeding pigeons and crying (chef, luncheonette). . . . the Picker—The old guy comes in here every day. He spends about an hour going through the barrels. If he finds anything of obvious value, he returns it to us. I guess he's just looking for something to do, and it's safer and warmer in here than out on the street (clerk, post office). . . . the Night Watchman—He walks the streets all night. About two A.M. he's at the fire station getting coffee, then at four he's over at the post office, and by six the luncheonette is open so he goes there (policeman 1). (Frankfather, 1977:28)

Even when the aged reach treatment, they may still encounter age bias. Aged patients are often stereotyped as bothersome and complaining and treated with avoidance, paternalism, and infantilism (Butler, 1975). The complaints may be written off as "just old age," and most older persons are not as forthright as the following gentleman in challenging such assertions:

> Mr. Morris was one of the volunteers for study at the National Institute of Health at the age of 92. He lived to be 102 years old. Near the end of his life he was having pain in his left leg and went to see his doctor. The doctor declared, "Sam, for Pete's sake, what do you expect at 102?" Sam retorted, "Look, my right leg is also 102 but it doesn't hurt a bit. Now explain that!" (Butler, 1975:182)

The stereotyped reaction that the aged cannot benefit from therapy and services should go to more "hopeful" (youthful) clients persists. The aged may not be referred to needed services or are sent too late in the course of their problem for services to be effective. Kucharski and associates (1979), for example, presented a sample of physicians with case vignettes of persons having obvious psychiatric symptoms, varying the age of the person described. The physicians recommended referral for psychological assistance for two thirds of the younger (under 40) cases, but for less than one half of the older (over 60) cases. A similar study with nurses found that they were much more likely to diagnose older cases as OBS with institutionalization recommended, and these cases were much less likely to be seen as having a chance of at least partial recovery (Ciliberton et al., 1981).

"Senility" presents a particular problem, as indicated in Frankfather's (1977) study of service providers in one community. He found that *senile* had become a catchall phrase for dependent or deviant behavior by confused older persons. Such persons were then labeled as irreversible and therefore hopeless; worse yet, perhaps, these cases were not even interesting. Almost universally, professionals (physicians, social workers, psychiatrists) considered handling mentally impaired older people to be "dirty work" that wasted their skills.

> The labels "senile dementia" and "organic brain" syndrome are the only diagnostic categories that define the deviant as totally beyond rehabilitation. Only for such elderly is an assumption of therapeutic failure incorporated into the agents' perspective. Senility is like no other deviant label, and its unique quality serves an explicit social function: the diagnosis legitimizes, with the authority invested in the scientist, the exclusion and removal of old people who constitute a social problem. The empirical pattern is clear: those labeled senile presumably cannot be rehabilitated and therefore need only be maintained, generally in nursing homes. While society hopes that confused elderly are not ill-treated under maintenance strategies, it demands that they are efficiently and economically removed. If they are "senile," it does not matter where they go. (Frankfather, 1977:190)

The nature of service organizations may constitute yet another barrier to the utilization of services. Older clients may be discouraged or antagonized by the impersonality of bureaucratic agencies—long waits, inattention to psychological or social needs, failure to understand what is expected of clients. It is too easy to blame older clients for inability to communicate their needs or follow instructions when providers are at least equally to blame for communication breakdowns (McKinlay, 1975). The cautiousness and fatalism felt by many older people may lead them to withdraw rather than actively challenge and pursue what they need. Older people, for example, are less likely to challenge the authority of physicians, which reflects less sophisticated health knowledge and a greater general acceptance of authority (Haug & Lavin, 1981). Because they are more likely to have serious and disabling conditions, and because current older cohorts have been socialized to accept the goodwill and authority of physicians, Haug and Lavin note that older people are more likely to take a "sick" role than a "consumer" role.

THE GOVERNMENT AND SERVICES FOR THE AGED

For most of human history, support of the aged has been a private concern, shouldered by the family, ethnic and religious groups, and other voluntary and charitable sources. The late nineteenth century represented a major turning point, however, as problems of the aged became a public concern (Hudson & Binstock, 1976). Because of the dislocations created by industrialization, and ideological changes concerning the role of government, industrial societies began to undertake major social programs as part of the birth of the modern welfare state. Germany led the way during the 1880s, enacting a series of health, accident, and old age/invalidity programs, followed over the next 25 years by emerging policies in countries such as Denmark, New Zealand, Great Britain, and Sweden. As noted earlier, the United States was a comparative latecomer, enacting the Social Security Act in 1935.

The need for a range of core social services is generally recognized in industrial societies (Beattie, 1976). Some form of income maintenance is virtually universal, and most industrialized countries supplement this with comprehensive health insurance and services. Beyond these similarities, however, there are important variations in the emphases of national programs. Some countries (e.g., Canada and Yugoslavia) are still expanding their long-term care facilities. Swedish policy, on the other hand, is directed at supporting family care. The greatest emphasis on home medical care appears to occur in Great Britain and the Soviet Union. Approximately 20 countries have developed home-help services (both personal and health care). These are most advanced in countries such as Sweden, Norway, and Great Britain, and least developed in the United States, France, Japan, and Italy.

The locus of responsibility for services to the aged also varies cross-culturally. In socialist societies the government plays an overriding role. The United States, on the other hand, has less government coordination and delivery of services. In Great Britain 90 percent of all long-term care facilities are publicly run, compared with only 23 percent in the United States. The tendency in the United States has been for the government to financially back services delivered by private agencies. This is particularly evident with home-help services and the nursing-home industry.

The United States still lags behind many European countries in support of services for the aged. The percentage of the total gross national product spent on social security programs is generally much greater in Europe, as are the taxes to support such programs (Williamson et al., 1982). Services are often more comprehensive compared with the piecemeal approach to government programs in the United States. Williamson and his associates cite Sweden as an example of providing comprehensive societal guarantees of a satisfactory standard of living to which citizens have a *right*.

The Depression of the 1930s, however, made clear the inadequacy of charity, local relief, and family support in the United States, and the widespread deprivation could no longer be attributed simply to moral failure or laziness. It became clear that poverty was a product of the social structure, and the federal government has since become increasingly involved in social welfare programs. Programs and services for the aged have acquired strong legitimacy and grown enormously over the years. Some 48 major federal programs are directed specifically at older persons, and perhaps as many as 200 affect them in some way (Soldo, 1980). There has been a general increase in federal spending for social welfare, but the greatest growth has been for services benefitting older people the most. For example, Medicare has increased nearly tenfold since 1965, and OASI tripled between 1970 and 1979. This growth is reflected in Table 11.2. Total expenditures for the aged have increased dramatically since 1960 (even adjusting for inflation), representing an increasing share of the federal budget. By 1981 such spending represented 26.4 percent of federal expenditures, involving $195.2 billion; OASDI represents the largest component (14.8 percent of federal expenditures in 1981), followed by Medicare (5.4 percent). Although part of this increase is because of growth in the older population, Clark and Menefee (1981) indicate that it primarily reflects *real* growth in programs for the elderly. Such growth also means that older people are better off, especially in income, than they were 10 or 20 years ago.

The proliferation of programs for the aged stems from many sources. Governmental involvement is essential because of the inability of normal market

Table 11.2 FEDERAL EXPENDITURES FOR PERSONS AGED 65 AND OVER, 1960–1978

Year	Total expenditures (billions)	Expenditure per aged individual	Total expenditures in 1978 dollars (billions)	Percent of federal budget
1960	$ 12.8	$ 768	$ 27.3	13
1965	$ 18.8	$1,019	$ 38.1	16
1970	$ 38.2	$1,902	$ 62.6	19
1975	$ 75.7	$3,379	$ 88.4	23
1978	$112	$4,678	$112	24

Source: Robert Clark and John Menefee, "Federal Expenditures for the Elderly: Past and Future," *The Gerontologist* 21 (1981), p. 134. Reprinted by permission.

mechanisms to meet the needs of the aged, given their disproportionately low incomes and difficulties to improve their financial position, and the often catastrophic expenses associated with aging (particularly chronic health care). Such programs have also achieved very strong legitimacy as rewards for past contributions to society and investment by the young for their own old age. For example, one study found that public support of programs for older people ranks second only to national defense and ahead of programs for the disabled, aid to schools, and benefits for the poor (Klemmack & Roff, 1981). As noted in Chapter 10, this public sympathy has made the elderly a politically convenient group for the passage of such otherwise unpopular programs as national health insurance (Medicare) and guaranteed income (SSI).

A considerable variety of programs address the needs of older people (Gelfand & Olsen, 1980; Lowy, 1980; Kutza, 1981) that include income maintenance (OASHDI, SSI), health care (Medicare, Medicaid), housing (low-rent public housing, construction and rehabilitation loans), and social services (multipurpose senior centers, homemaker and home health services, day care). Some of these programs are directly aimed at improving the lives of older people by mandating and funding services. Others seek to encourage various benefits and safeguard the elderly, such as legislation regulating private pensions. Still others have supported the training of professionals in the field of aging and research in gerontology.

The centerpiece of federal legislation on behalf of the older population is the Older Americans Act (OAA) of 1965, and its subsequent amendments. This legislation created the Administration on Aging and has funded training, research, and program evaluation. OAA also funds and seeks to stimulate a broad spectrum of social services, designating the general services that are to be provided and the priorities to be followed. Coordination of the delivery of services within communities is sought by channeling them through an "aging network" of State and Area Agencies on Aging (usually encompassing one or a few counties).

Government programs clearly benefit older people in a variety of ways. *Age-entitlement* programs are specifically *for* the elderly, either virtually all older people (OASI, Medicare) or low-income older people (SSI). But *need-entitlement* programs, based more generally on financial need, benefit the aged disproportionately because of their low income; for example, about 40 percent of all Medicaid benefits go to the aged. Older people also benefit from various housing subsidies and food stamps. In avoiding cuts to "legitimate" programs for older people, such as Social Security, we often overlook the disproportionate hardships caused older people by cuts to "welfare" programs.

Two general delivery strategies have been employed in addressing the needs of older people: (1) direct provision of income, so that the aged can buy necessary goods and services, and (2) provision of "income-in-kind" (housing, food stamps, medical care). Both approaches have advantages and disadvantages (Williamson, 1975). Income strategies, such as Social Security and SSI, are simple and have low administrative costs, but they assume that the market is capable of meeting the needs of older people if they have money. Strategies that directly provide goods and services can meet immediate needs and are a corrective for faulty markets or poor consumer choice, but disadvantages include high administrative costs, local inequities because of eligibility rules and quality control, the stigma that is often attached to such programs as food stamps, restricted freedom of choice, and the inferiority of services that can result from having a "guaranteed" market. These disadvantages are quite evident with Medicaid: enormous amounts of red tape, public subsidization of inferior nursing homes, the unwillingness of many physicians to accept Medicaid patients, local differences in eligibility, and so on. Thus, Medicaid subsidizes inadequate care for the elderly poor, supporting class bias in medical services. Yet direct income strategies may result in no health care at all.

We have painted what seems a very rosy picture of government efforts on behalf of older people. But although a great deal of money has been spent on myriad programs, many gaps remain. There is duplication and fragmentation of services, and the United States still lacks a coherent, comprehensive social policy toward the aged. The vast bulk of federal expenditures involve income maintenance and health services; less than 1 percent is spent on social services representing the continuum of care discussed earlier in the chapter (Soldo, 1980). Lowy (1980) notes that current programs are biased against home-based services, presenting financial barriers to community living. For example, older people appear to receive a fair share of subsidized public housing, but there is little commitment to upgrading the housing *currently* occupied by older persons, with homeowners and rural elderly in greatest need (Struyk & Soldo, 1980). Benefits are not well targeted toward the most vulnerable groups—the widowed, the old-old, the minority aged. Hudson (1980) indicates, for example, that 80 percent of health-care benefits for older people go to those who are not poor, compared with 51 percent to nonpoor younger people.

What accounts for this incoherence? One problem is that programs reflect short-term, limited responses that in turn reflect the short time cycles of political life (Estes, 1979; Vladeck, 1980). To the extent that politicians are primarily concerned with reelection and passage of legislation that will have quick, tangible results, there is less rational consideration for long-term needs and consequences. The financing problems of Social Security certainly illustrate lack of a farsighted orientation.

The lack of coherent old-age policy has also been attributed to the nature of "interest group liberalism" (Binstock & Levin, 1976; Estes, 1979; Hudson, 1981). Caught in the middle of competing interests and a system of fragmented power, programs are compromised in adoption and implementation to secure support and neutralize opposition. This limits the effectiveness of social intervention through compromise and resistance to real innovation by existing organizations because agencies seek the path of least resistance. Estes (1979) suggests that existing policies serve the interests of the "aging enterprise" (agencies and professionals) rather than those of the older population. She argues that more advantaged older people are co-opted by largely symbolic recreational and social programming, whereas little is done to address the economic and social conditions of the most disadvantaged and vulnerable. Focusing on smaller-scale benefits to individuals, little attention is given to broader structural reforms (in income, housing, health care) that would address the sources of problems.

The Administration on Aging has a legislative mandate to be an advocate on behalf of the aged, coordinating existing programs and stimulating new ones. But this advocacy function has never been clearly defined, and the agency has had insufficient authority and resources to pursue it (Estes, 1979; Fritz, 1979). Estes argues that the "new federalism," increasing state and local determination of problems and solutions, will only aggravate matters. She suggests that withdrawal from *national* priorities and standards will only reduce accountability and the likelihood of innovative or structural change and that the most vulnerable aged will not fare well in the competition for limited program dollars.

Estes also argues that separate, age-segregated policies that focus on the "special" needs of older people reinforce their isolation and dependency.

> In using the term *aging enterprise,* I hope to call particular attention to how the aged are often processed and treated as a commodity in our society and to the fact that the age-segregated policies that fuel the aging enterprise are socially divisive "solutions" that single out, stigmatize, and isolate the aged from the rest of society. (Estes, 1979:2)

This is not to say that older people have entirely suffered from a view that they have special needs. As noted in Chapter 10, they have benefited from a rather unique political legitimacy and utility. But that support may decline. Hudson (1978) suggests that the favored status of older people is in jeopardy because of three factors: (1) rising costs and the "graying of the federal budget," reflected in Table 11.2; (2) public perceptions that the well-being of the elderly has improved (as indeed it has in many ways); (3) competitive spending pressures. Separate (age-entitlement) programs may reach their limit with little possibility for further improvement and perhaps difficulty in maintaining what has been achieved. The most vulnerable elderly, who have not received high priority, may suffer further gaps. Middle-class programs, such as OASI and Medicare, have greater support from the public and organized interest groups, whereas those that serve primarily the poor elderly (SSI, Medicaid, Food Stamps) are less visible and receive less public support (Klemmack & Roff, 1981; Nelson, 1982).

It may become increasingly difficult in the future to justify special programs for the aged, although they suffer disproportionately. It can be argued that people should be helped because they are *in need,* not because they are *old* and in need or simply *old.* Estes (1979) and Neugarten (1982) have argued that we need "universalist" policies, such as national health insurance or income maintenance, rather than separate programs for older people. Older people are more likely to be poor and/or sick, but they have no monopoly on these conditions. Unfortunately such general programs have even less political support so that the needs of not only the aged but also the nonaged may be lost in the shuffle. Perhaps the only clear conclusion is that we appear to be at a critical point in the development of policies that adequately address the needs of older people. Williamson and associates (1982) suggest that the primary concern in the short run will involve resisting substantial reductions in existing programs, whereas long-term prospects will depend on the health of the general economy, as this affects ability and willingness to support comprehensive programs.

Medicare

The Medicare program is a good example of the potentials and the limitations of social policies directed at older people. Older people have disproportionate health-related expenses, and health costs have had a high rate of inflation. Given their disproportionately low income, it is clear that the aged need assistance if they are to get the health care they require.

Enacted in 1965, Medicare was designed to eliminate at least some of the financial barriers to health care for the older population. It has two parts. Hospital insurance (Part A), financed through the Social Security payroll tax, covers 90 days of inpatient hospital care, 100 days of posthospital care in an SNF, and up to 100 home health visits connected with the hospitalization for persons eligible for Social Security and certain other groups (such as those with severe kidney disease). Supplemental medical insurance (Part B), participation in which is voluntary, covers physician services, home health services not linked to prior hospitalization, and various other medical services, such as laboratory fees and ambulance service. Part B is jointly financed from general tax revenues and premiums paid by enrollees ($12.20 per month in 1982).

Medicare has clearly been beneficial. Expenditures under Medicare have risen from $7.1 billion in 1970 to $47.8 billion in 1982, with virtually universal coverage of the older population (99 percent in Part A, 96 percent in Part B). In 1982 Medicare paid 44 percent of the health-care expenses of older people, compared to 35 percent in 1970. But there are also many health costs not borne by Medicare. Figure 11.3 indicates trends in sources of payment of health-care expenses. Although Medicare and other public programs (including Medicaid) have paid increasing amounts of money, inflation has meant that the average older person now has more out-of-pocket expenses. Older people spend nearly 20 percent of their income on health costs, which is nearly the same as before Medicare (U.S. Senate Special Committee on Aging, 1981). More than half of the older population has private health insurance, but this covers only about 7 percent of their health-care bill. Too often such coverage is expensive and duplicative, and does not adequately protect against extraordinary expenses.

Medicare financing has increased access to health care. Davis and Schoen (1978) note that there are probably fewer older people with excessively high out-of-pocket expenses because a major portion of Medicare expenditures goes to a relative few with very large medical bills. Inequality in access to health care has also probably been reduced. But there are gaps in coverage, as can be seen in Table 11.3. Medicare focuses rather narrowly on acute care rather than chronic health needs characteristic of aging. It covers a substantial share of hospital and physician costs, but pays little for nursing-home care, and nothing for dentists, drugs, and appliances (eyeglasses, hearing aids).

Although the most basic goal of Medicare was to increase access to health services, it was also hoped that Medicare would encourage greater coordination

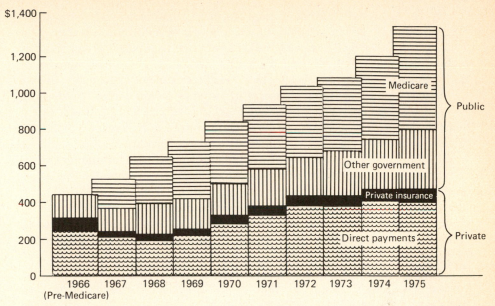

Figure 11.3 Per capita personal health care expenditures for the aged, by source of funds: 1966–1975. (*Source:* Marian Gornick, "Ten Years of Medicare: Impact on the Covered Population," *Social Security Bulletin* 39, no. 7 (1976), p. 19).

and comprehensiveness of health care for the aged and facilitate more diversity (preventive care, home health services, extended care). But this has not occurred. For example, only 2.5 percent of Medicare expenditures go to home health care. A longitudinal study of the impact of Medicare in five midwestern communities found: (1) physicians were not making more home visits or nursing-home calls, (2) there was no decline in the use of traditional nursing homes, (3) care for the

Table 11.3 HEALTH CARE EXPENDITURES FOR PERSONS 65 AND OVER, BY SOURCE OF FUNDS, 1975

| | | | Source | |
| | | | Public | |
	Total[a]	Private (%)	Medicare (%)	Other (%)
Total health expenses	$30,383	34.4	42.0	23.5
Hospital care	$13,467	10.2	72.2	17.6
Physician services	$ 4,862	40.9	54.1	5.1
Dentist services	$ 540	92.9	–	7.1
Other professional services	$ 441	49.8	38.0	12.2
Drugs and drug sundries	$ 2,629	86.9	–	13.1
Eyeglasses and appliances	$ 506	98.4	–	1.6
Nursing-home care	$ 7,650	46.7	3.1	50.3
Other health services	$ 288	8.2	–	91.8

[a]Millions of dollars.

Source: Marjorie Mueller and Robert Gibson, "Age Differences in Health Care Spending, Fiscal Year 1975," *Social Security Bulletin* 39 (1976), p. 25.

elderly was not better coordinated, and (4) sharp initial increases in home-care programs during the late sixties had been followed by a decline thereafter (Coe et al., 1974). Other than increased institutional staffs to process Medicare information, expansion of traditional acute-care capacities, and some increase in SNFs, Coe and associates conclude that "Medicare has not appreciably altered the organization of health care services in our study communities" (p. 260).

In a general analysis of the effectiveness of Medicare and Medicaid, Davis and Schoen (1978) conclude that neither has attempted to change the health-care system or improve its efficiency. Indeed, both have contributed to spiraling health-care costs. This partly illustrates the problems of implementation within the context of "interest group liberalism." Feder (1977) indicates that the Social Security Administration, which was charged with implementing Medicare, was unwilling to take on the medical establishment because the agency was more concerned with building a consensus behind the program. Thus there was insufficient concern about cost escalation and a policy of nonintervention regarding the structure and quality of care.

Davis and Schoen (1978) also indicate that Medicare has failed to guarantee equal access to health care for all older people. It neglects the problems of those in areas with few health-care resources and poor transportation. Provisions under Medicare also require recipients to share some of the costs of even covered services, reinforcing a tendency for services to be used according to income rather than health-care needs. This discourages the low-income elderly, who are disproportionately black, rural, or reside in the South.

Older people are better off with Medicare than without, but substantial gaps and inequities still exist. Medicare costs have also been escalating, rising at an average annual rate of 18.8 percent since 1972. This is partly attributable to aging of the population, but spiraling health care costs are the primary cause; for example, hospital costs rose at an average annual rate of 15 percent from 1968 to 1978. The gaps, inequities, and cost of Medicare, combined with debates about the appropriateness of age-entitlement programs, have led to suggestions that Medicare be replaced with a more general system of health-care financing that would control costs, protect individuals against catastrophic expenses, and provide equitable access for all members of the population.

SUMMARY

Services represent a critical dimension of the environmental context of aging, potentially helping or harming the aged. A social reconstruction model recognizes the value of appropriate services in bolstering independence and coping.

Only about 5 percent of the older population resides in institutions, although the chances are higher that any individual will be institutionalized at some time. Although nursing-home residents exhibit many functional disabilities, institutionalization is not solely attributable to medical need. The processes leading to institutionalization are best viewed as a deteriorating balance between need and available support, the institution being a last resort when other alternatives have failed.

There has been tremendous growth in the nursing-home industry, reflecting the aging of the population, changing patterns of psychiatric care, and government subsidy through Medicare and Medicaid. Most nursing homes are run for profit and can be classified according to the level of care provided. Regulation of nursing homes has been lax, and many abuses still exist. The most tragic abuses have involved safety and quality of care for patients. Inadequate staffing has been a continuing problem.

The impact of institutionalization is an important issue. Relocation can literally be lethal when it involves considerable environmental discontinuity. Institutionalized older people share many negative social and psychological traits, arising from various sources: the type of people who enter institutions, reaction to the losses that create a need for institutional services, the stigma attached to nursing homes, and the impact of the nursing home as a total institution. Nursing-home residents may encounter depersonalization and restricted social interaction. Although institutional life may contribute to an "institutional syndrome" among nursing-home residents, this is neither a necessary nor an inevitable consequence, and improved environments can have beneficial effects.

There is ample evidence that nursing-home residents can benefit from counseling and rehabilitation services, particularly if these are closely tied to individual needs and competence. Better quality care is apparently available in larger, more expensive homes that are certified and conform to licensing standards, whereas smaller homes are more likely to foster sociability. The poor in particular are consigned to the worst institutions. Poor quality care is a consequence of understaffed regulatory agencies, fragmented responsibility, lack of alternatives, and inadequate reward structures.

The aged can benefit from a wide range of community services, representing a continuum of care to meet changing needs. These need to be linked together through adequate programs of information and referral. Community alternatives help older persons avoid institutionalization and are likely to be less expensive, although not for the extremely disabled.

Three factors affect the delivery and use of services. Predisposing factors, including demographic characteristics and service-related attitudes, affect the likelihood of older people seeking assistance. Older people, for example, will seek to avoid a welfare stigma. Enabling factors, including income, knowledge, and transportation, affect access to services. Rural and minority aged are particularly at risk with regard to access to services. Illness level factors, such as denial of age-related problems and age biases among helping professionals, affect the likelihood that older people will actually come in contact with services.

Organized social programs for the aged first emerged with the birth of the modern welfare state in the 1880s. There continue to be important cross-national differences in these programs, with the United States lagging behind some European countries. The federal government has played an increasingly prominent role in the United States, however. Many age-entitlement and need-entitlement programs address the needs of older people, with the Older Americans Act of 1965 being the centerpiece of federal legislation on aging. Programs are often less effective than they might be, however, because of compromise, fragmented responsibility, and the short-term perspective taken on problems. Programs are biased against home-based services, and are not well targeted toward the most vulnerable elderly.

The unique legitimacy of programs for older people may be lessening as costs rise and competing spending pressures develop. This may create particular problems for the most vulnerable segments of the older population. Difficult choices may have to be made between separate programs for the aged and more general policies addressing needs in the entire population.

The Medicare program exemplifies the potentials and limitations of social policy. Although it has increased access to needed health services, many gaps and inequities remain, and Medicare has had little impact on the ways in which services are organized and delivered.

chapter 12

Death and Dying

By coincidence and design, death and dying are the subjects of the final substantive chapter of this book. Discussion of these issues in connection with social gerontology is appropriate from a number of points of view. Death is, after all, the inevitable final act in the aging experience. We need to understand how the aged confront their own finitude and how the social context affects this confrontation. In modern societies, death has also been increasingly confined to the end of the natural life span; simply put, it is increasingly the old who die. This link between old age and death may thus contribute to our fears and stereotypes about aging and old age, and attempts to deny our own finitude through "distancing" behaviors may also lead us to withdraw from the aged, who mirror our mortality. This link also gives special relevance for the aged to many current public issues surrounding dying and death, such as euthanasia and debates over "appropriate death."

The fact that death becomes a more salient experience in old age may affect the aging experience in many ways. As the deaths of friends and family occur with greater frequency, older people may experience what Kastenbaum and Aisenberg (1976) call "bereavement overload." Psychological correlates of old age, such as rigidity, cautiousness, or fatalism, may be linked to the perception of impending death. Disengagement theory attributes basic social, psychological, and emotional changes to individual and societal preparation for death.

A discussion of death is also relevant to the study of aging because it is relevant to the human condition in general. Many human activities and institutions are shaped by inevitable mortality. Some have even suggested that death

319

is a primary motivating force—that one can interpret human existence in terms of anticipation of death.

> . . . the idea of death, the fear of it, haunts the human animal like nothing else; it is a mainspring of human activity—activity designed largely to avoid the fatality of death, to overcome it by denying in some way that it is the final destiny for man. (Becker, 1973:ix)

DEATH AND SOCIAL STRUCTURE

Society structures the nature of death. Because it is a universal and recurring event, which in many ways threatens to disrupt the social order, all cultures develop values, beliefs, and practices concerning death (Volkhart & Michael, 1957; Blauner, 1966). These cultural practices shape individual orientations and reactions to death, one's own and the deaths of others. It is also true that death affects the social structure and thereby the lives of the living.

Although the inevitability of death has not altered, other aspects of death have changed over the centuries, particularly as a consequence of the "mortality revolution" that has accompanied modernization (Goldscheider, 1971). In pre-industrial societies, death rates were very high (and life expectancy low) and fluctuated widely with time and location in response to the largely uncontrolled effects of climate, epidemics, war, and famine. Compared with today, death was particularly high in the early years of the life course. For example: (1) life expectancy in Europe between the thirteenth and the seventeenth centuries ranged between 20 and 40 years; (2) even among the British aristocracy of the sixteenth and seventeenth centuries, approximately 20 percent of all infants failed to survive; (3) during the fourteenth century, an estimated one fourth to one third of the entire population of Europe died of plague; and (4) 44 percent of the population of Marseilles, France, died during an epidemic in 1720–1722 (Goldscheider, 1971).

Exposure to death in these high-mortality societies was considerable for all members of society, and there seemed to be little control over the "mysterious" forces of nature. The nature of death may account for some of the structural aspects of these societies (Goldscheider, 1971; Kastenbaum & Aisenberg, 1976; Marshall, 1980). Because death disrupted family life in almost random, unplanned ways, there was an emphasis on the extended family as a more permanent and less precarious structure than the nuclear family. Because of high rates of infant mortality, high fertility was encouraged. Romantic love was downplayed in favor of arranged marriages; there was little time to dawdle through time-consuming, haphazard searches for "true love." Another mechanism for reducing the disruptiveness of death was to reduce the importance of those who died. Thus in high-mortality societies there were reduced emotional attachments within the nuclear family. As parents could expect that one third to one half of their children would die before the age of 10 (Marshall, 1980), infants especially were unlikely to be viewed as "real people." The following advice from a Puritan writer illustrates this emotional distancing.

Remember that although, Parents and Children, Husbands and Wives, Friends and Acquaintance are pleasant, yet they are but uncertain, withering and dying Enjoyments. You are favoured with them around you to Day, but to morrow they may expire and give up the Ghost, and leave you sighing and disconsolate. . . . In short, The more immoderately you love them, the less Satisfaction, (in all Probability) will they yield you, and the greater will your Smart and Vexation be in parting with them. When a Friend or Relative is taken away, upon whom the Heart and Affections are too eagerly set, how terribly does it disquiet and rack the Man? In a Word, Overmuch to love a Relative is the Way to increase, if not double the Anguish of parting with him. (Stannard, 1977:58–59)

With the regular presence of uncontrolled death, there was a pressure for religious and magical explanations and the development of elaborate rituals and procedures to manage the disruptiveness of death, which was likely to occur to those in the prime of life who were still vital to society's business. Blauner (1966) suggests that ghosts are reifications of these people who die with "unfinished business," and elaborate rituals evolve to appease the dead. In the Middle Ages in Europe, with no technological defenses against death and religious imagery of eternal torture and damnation, a preoccupation with death developed, perhaps as a way of controlling fear, which was reflected in art, children's death games ("ashes, ashes, all fall down"), dancing manias, and witchcraft.

By the nineteenth century, however, the mortality revolution in Europe was lowering mortality rates and reducing the wide fluctuations (except for those due to warfare). This was a consequence of medical advances, improved sanitation and public health measures, and a general rise in living standards. Although Europe and the United States led the way in these advances, developing countries have shown very swift recent changes, as seen in some examples cited by Goldscheider (1971). From 1921 to 1951, Jamaica showed reductions in mortality that required 130 years in Sweden. Infant mortality in Singapore declined from 168 to 28 per 1000 births between 1930 and 1960. In Mauritius, deaths because of malaria declined from 3534 in 1945 to only 3 in 1955. As we have seen in Chapter 2, death has increasingly become the province of the old.

The location of death has also changed in modern societies. Two or three generations ago, most people died at home, surrounded by family and friends in a familiar environment. Now perhaps two thirds of all deaths occur in institutions, primarily general hospitals (Lerner, 1970). The proportion of all deaths that occurred in nursing homes also doubled from 1962 to 1972, and approximately one fifth of the deaths to persons 55 and over now occur in nursing homes (Ingram & Barry, 1977).

Thus the nature of death is very different in modern societies, and in some ways we are insulated from it. Members of preliterate societies might spend as much as 100 days per year participating in funerals (Kalish, 1981). Uhlenberg (1978) indicates that among persons born in 1870 only about half would have both parents alive by age 15 and less than 10 percent would not experience the death of a parent or sibling by that age (compared with over 90 percent and 80 percent, respectively, for the 1950 birth cohort). Those who die have lost social importance and visibility. The aged, who are most likely to die, are often already socially disengaged and therefore "less important" to society, and the young can maintain a social and psychological distance from death, which is not a real prospect for them. Dying and death are segregated from our worlds through bureaucratization—special dying institutions (hospitals, nursing homes) and death specialists (the mortuary industry). We have also achieved a type of technological mastery over death, enormously reducing the capriciousness of it and the possibility of premature death. Illich (1976) suggests that death has been transformed from a natural to an unnatural event that must be fought rather than accepted. Medical technology has created new moral and legal questions about the prolongation of life in institutional settings and stimulated the development of a "death and dying movement" that surrounds concern over achieving a "good death" and the "right to die" (Charmaz, 1980).

Death has also become "privatized" in modern societies, involving small groups of kin and friends rather than the larger community (Marshall, 1980). Because death is not as real or as uncontrollable, and the dead are seen as less powerful, there is less social disruption and therefore less need for elaborate traditions and rituals. Funerals are criticized as irrelevant and exploitative and, at the very least, are less important to the group as a whole.

> The social substructure of the funeral is weakened when those who die tend to be irrelevant for the ongoing social life of the community and when the disruptive potentials of death are already controlled by compartmentalization into isolated spheres where bureaucratic routinization is the rule. Thus participation and interest in funerals are restricted to family members and friends rather than involving the larger community, unless an important leader has died. Since only individuals and families are affected, adaptation and bereavement have become their private responsibility, and there is little need for a transition period to permit society as a whole to adjust to the fact of a single death. (Blauner, 1966:386)

Whereas the bureaucratization and privatization of death reflect the lessened social disruptiveness of death in modern societies, it has been suggested that they may make death more disruptive for the individual (Marshall, 1980; Kalish, 1981). Individuals lack broader cultural frameworks for understanding and accepting the possibility of their own deaths. Feeling ignorant in the face of death, people feel awkward and withdraw, thereby isolating those who are dying. The deritualization of death means that individuals are left on their own to handle bereavement and grief. This brings us to a consideration of attitudes and values concerning death and of the problems faced by those who are dying, those who care for the dying, and those who are bereaved.

ORIENTATIONS TOWARD DEATH

Death has many meanings: punishment or reward; validation of worth or purpose; various forms of loss and separation; reunion with those who have died before; a "great leveler" of class differences; an organizer of time, representing the boundary to life (Kastenbaum, 1977a; Kalish, 1981). Death is obviously a very personal issue, but meanings of death and attitudes toward death are also a product of collective experience (Bengtson et al., 1977). Thus orientations toward death vary by position in the social structure, including age, sex, and social class. The larger culture is also a source of our views of "death as a thought," to use Kastenbaum and Aisenberg's (1976) phrase.

Ariés (1981) has outlined five models of death that trace changing imagery and rituals associated with death in Western societies.

1. *Tame death,* characteristic of the early Middle Ages, represented a simple and dignified preparation for death. The individual was subordinated to the good of the group. There was acceptance of the naturalness of death, with regret but not rebellion.
2. *Death of the self,* evident from the eleventh to the seventeenth century, reflected individualism and importance of the immortal soul. Individuals sought to perpetuate their memories through visible monuments and the use of wills as literary documents.
3. *Remote and imminent death,* in the seventeenth and eighteenth centuries, reflected disruption of the traditional order by science and rationalism. Rituals and cemeteries became more simple and austere, and individuals were advised to achieve an edifying death by thinking about death throughout life. Some traditional barriers were breached, as, for example, in images linking death and sexuality.
4. *Death of the other,* emerging in the nineteenth century, represented the age of the "beautiful" death. Death was viewed as a comforting and exalted form of salvation and reunion. Stannard (1977) refers to the sentimentalization of death in children's books and pastoral cemeteries.
5. Ariés describes the twentieth-century model as the *invisible death,* as death is banished into institutions and private experiences rather than communal rituals. Thus the bureaucratization and privatization of death in modern societies represents a compartmentalized and trivialized approach to death.

A heavy silence has fallen over the subject. When this silence is broken, as it sometimes is in America today, it is to reduce death to the insignificance of an ordinary event that is mentioned with feigned indifference. Either way, the result is the same: neither the individual nor the community is strong enough to recognize the existence of death. (Ariés, 1981:614)

The nature of meanings of death in a society will be reflected in individual orientations to death. Kastenbaum and his associates (1976) have investigated personifications of death by asking: "If death were a person, what sort of a person would Death be?" One image, the *macabre,* presents death as a repulsive, overpowering person, as in the following quote from a male undergraduate:

Physically, Death is a walking death. He is a male, about 89 years old, and is very bent over. His hair is scraggly, his face is wrinkled, almost not recognizable as human flesh.

His eyes are sunken, his teeth are rotting (the ones left). As noted above, he is bent, if not a hunchback, and can hardly move. His hands and other append-ages are also in terrible shape. Personality-wise, he's grouchy, cranky, sullen, sarcastic, cynical, mean, evil, disgusting, obnoxious, and nauseating—most of the time—only, very, very seldom does his good side show through. (Kasten-baum & Aisenberg, 1976:128)

This image seems a legacy of the Middle Ages, when death was omnipresent and often horrible. A more modern image is the *automaton*—death as an objec-tive, unfeeling instrument, lacking human qualities.

He would never speak. He would be void of all emotions. He would exist under a superhuman type of energy. He would move slowly as if remorsefully, but he would not be so in the slightest. He would never tire, nor would he ever become energetic. He would just go about his business in a matter-of-fact way. (Kasten-baum & Aisenberg, 1976:132)

Kastenbaum and Aisenberg suggest that the automaton represents a reac-tion to modern science and technology, where death has become sterile and mean-ingless.

Attitudes Toward Death

Attitudes toward death are extremely complex and changeable, shifting with situ-ation, mood, and cultural surroundings, and they vary by age, sex, education, religiosity, and so on. Such complexity is understandable, given the multifaceted nature of death attitudes. For example, an analysis of scales measuring death atti-tudes found that five different dimensions were included in the scales: negative evaluation of one's own death, reluctance to interact with the dying, negative re-actions to pain, avoidance of reminders of death, and preoccupation with thoughts of death (Durlak & Kass, 1981). Thus, there is no reason to believe that attitudes toward death can be characterized in any simple or straightforward way. Death-related attitudes are also very difficult to study because of their sensitive emotional quality. Until recently there was relatively little work in this area, and the vast majority of studies have been conducted with highly specialized popula-tions: college students, medical staff, terminal patients, and so on. The validity of responses to questions about death is also difficult to ascertain. Suppose some-one tells you that he or she has little fear of death, and seldom thinks about his or her own death. On the surface, this might seem to indicate acceptance of death, but this acceptance may instead be a type of denial.

One continuing argument has revolved around whether our attitudes and behaviors concerning death constitute acceptance or denial (Dumont & Foss, 1972). Denial implies that we refuse to truly believe or recognize death as a per-sonal possibility. Acceptance, on the other hand, means personal awareness of our own finitude, planning for death, and perhaps even approving of it.

One can find various types of evidence for the denial of death. At the very least, death symbols are emotion-laden, and some have argued that death has become the great taboo of modern societies, perhaps replacing sex as the "new pornography" (Gorer, 1965). Dumont and Foss (1972) point to funeral customs that mask the reality of death (cosmetic embalming, cushioned caskets) and the many euphemisms that soften death (pass away, cross over the bar, kick the bucket). There may also be the feeling that *they* will die, not *me,* or that if I don't go to the doctor, my symptoms can't be serious, a type of magical immortality (Kastenbaum, 1977a).

Humans have many strategies for circumventing the finality of death, thereby achieving a "symbolic immortality" that transcends physical death (Toynbee et al., 1968; Lifton, 1977). This may occur biologically, by living through our descendants, or it may involve a merging or oneness with nature. We achieve immortality through our works or fame that lives on. This book may give the author some small sense of immortality. The famous among us are often concerned about their "place in history," and write memoirs to assure it. The immortality of the soul, perhaps dwelling in an afterlife, also denies the finality of death.

Why should we fear or deny death? It is, after all, as natural as life itself, and some would argue that denial of death is morbid and a sign of psychological maladjustment. Others suggest, however, that fear of death and denial are natural responses to the dilemma of knowing that *people* die, yet being unable to really comprehend our *own* death or nonexistence (Becker, 1973; Hinton, 1972). We gain comfort by denying the death of ourselves and our loved ones, except as very distant possibilities. The inability to comprehend and face death may be greater in modern societies than in the past because death is more removed from our experience.

There are many aspects that contribute to fear of death: pain and bodily degeneration, loss of control and humiliation, interruption of goals, the impact on survivors, fear of punishment, and simple fear of *not being* (Kastenbaum & Aisenberg, 1976; Schulz, 1978). The uncertainty of death is unsettling, and fear of dying may be greater than fear of death. There is a common desire to die relatively quickly (once dying begins) with little suffering and with honor or dignity.

Diggory and Rothman (1961) investigated the relative importance for an adult sample of seven values destroyed by death. These values (or reasons for fearing death), in decreasing order of importance, were:

1. My death would cause grief to my relatives and friends.
2. All my plans and projects would come to an end.
3. The process of dying might be painful.
4. I could no longer have any experiences.
5. I would no longer be able to care for my dependents.
6. I am afraid of what might happen to me if there is a life after death.
7. I am afraid of what might happen to my body after death.

The ranking of these values varies according to the sample used. Shneidman (1971), using a sample that was primarily young, female, single, and of high socioeconomic status, found that the loss of experiences was most important, followed by the pain of dying and concern for dependents, with the cessation of plans and grief to others falling in importance. Kalish and Reynolds (1976), with a somewhat older sample of lower socioeconomic status, found that grief to others was most important, followed by concern for dependents and the pain of dying. Thus there is no universality to the values threatened by death.

There are indications that women are more concerned with the grief of others, effects on the body, and the pain of dying, whereas men are more disturbed by the ending of plans and projects (Diggory & Rothman, 1961; Kastenbaum, 1977a). Married persons are more concerned than the unmarried about inability to care for dependents (Diggory & Rothman, 1961). Many of these differences reflect the fact that social roles (and their age stratification) influence what is important to us—personal experience for the young, care of dependents for older, married persons, and so on—thereby determining the values threatened by death (Kastenbaum & Aisenberg, 1976).

Kalish and Reynolds (1976) investigated age differences in these fears or concerns. They found that the middle-aged (40 to 59) were most likely to stress the grief to others and the end of their plans and prospects. Older respondents (60+) were more likely to be concerned with what would happen to their bodies (perhaps reflecting greater body preoccupation in old age), but were less concerned with grief to others, inability to care for dependents, and the ending of experiences. However, another study of older persons found a somewhat different ranking (Wass et al., 1979). The "most distasteful" aspects of death were perceived to be the pain of dying and grief to relatives and friends, but concern over what happened to their bodies was rarely expressed.

There is clearly no straightforward way to characterize death attitudes. Just as fears are quite variable, individuals accept death for many reasons. American society in particular tends toward rationality, and with medical advances, death is increasingly viewed as the natural completion of the life cycle in old age. Death may also be perceived as acceptable because it represents release from misery and suffering or a reunion with loved ones (Kastenbaum & Aisenberg, 1976).

Surveys indicate that when asked directly, relatively few adults consider fear of death important compared with other concerns, and their attitudes about death primarily reflect acceptance (Kastenbaum & Aisenberg, 1976; Kalish, 1976). Riley's (1970) survey of a national sample offers good examples of this. His findings included the following:

1. 89 percent agreed that death can "sometimes be a blessing," 82 percent agreed that it is "tragic only for the survivors," whereas only 53 percent felt that death "always comes too soon," and 14 percent said that "to die is to suffer."
2. Approximately one third of the respondents often thought about death; such thoughts were frequently triggered by illness, the death of others, and accidents or "near misses."

3. 80 percent felt that it was better to make plans concerning death than to ignore or deny it.
4. Many had made preparations regarding death: 70 percent had bought life insurance, 50 percent had talked about death with others, 25 percent had made funeral arrangements and drawn up a will.

Bengtson and associates (1977) asked a sample of persons aged 45 to 74: "How afraid are you of death?" Nearly two thirds replied "not at all," one third replied "somewhat," and only 4 percent said "very." Kalish and Reynolds (1976) also found that most of their respondents appeared unafraid of death and would accept it peacefully. They found that although death may be less intrusive in modern societies, their respondents were not isolated from death experiences. Within the previous 2 years, over 80 percent knew someone who had died, two thirds had gone to a funeral, and over one third had visited or talked with a dying person.

There is evidence, then, that we deny and accept the reality of death. Such conflicting attitudes may be inevitable, given what Weisman (1972) terms the *primary paradox* surrounding death: although we can recognize the universality of death, we cannot imagine or comprehend our own death. Other factors contribute to rational, intellectual acceptance of death, coupled with emotional, psychological denial (Dumont & Foss, 1972). Kalish and Reynolds (1976) found that their younger respondents expected not to die until they were 75. Although the decline of religious and ritualistic practices surrounding death may indicate greater acceptance, loss of these reassuring supports may also create greater apprehensiveness. Thus our death-related experiences are never totally positive or negative, leaving a complex mixture of feelings and emotions. Kalish and Reynolds conclude from their study that "The overall impression is one of a practical and reasonable approach to the handling of death with perhaps a dash of avoidance when personal-emotional aspects are touched upon" (1976:49).

Fear and denial of death vary among individuals, of course. Some studies have found women to be more fearful and anxious, but others have found no difference (Schulz, 1978; Kalish, 1981). Persons with less education tend to think more about death and feel more threatened by death (e.g., they say that death always comes too soon or that to die is to suffer) (Riley, 1970). Interestingly, courses on death seem to have little effect on fear of it, although they seem to make discussion less taboo and may facilitate the development of personal philosophies concerning death (Bell, 1975; Leviton, 1977). Religiosity has complex relationships with death attitudes. Those who are most religious tend to display lower death anxiety, but this may also be true of those who are most confirmed in their lack of religious beliefs (Kalish, 1976, 1981). Marshall (1980) notes that religion can either comfort or create anxiety about the afterlife, but religion does represent one way individuals may attempt to make sense of death.

Death and the Life Cycle

It is reasonable to expect that changes in conceptions of death and attitudes toward death will occur over the life cycle, at least partly in response to developmental processes. This can be seen in Maria Nagy's (1948) classic study describing these stages in the child's developing conception of death:

1. **Ages 3 to 5:** Death is viewed as reduced life and as temporary, with predominant themes of departure and separation.
2. **Ages 5 to 9:** Children recognize the finality of death, but personify a Death-man as an outside agent who might still be eluded.
3. **Ages 9 and above:** Death is recognized as personal, universal, and inevitable.

Death is an abstract concept whose full understanding requires intellectual maturity and acquisition of death-relevant information (Kastenbaum & Aisenberg, 1976; Charmaz, 1980). For example, young children have little understanding of *future,* therefore will have difficulty comprehending the end of their future.

One must be careful, however, about exaggerating the inability of even very young children to develop perceptions and feelings about death. Children are exposed to many types of death, such as the death of flowers, pets, or family members, death images on television, and they often display considerable curiosity about death (Kastenbaum & Aisenberg, 1976). Children's conceptions of death depend on many things: developmental level, inquisitiveness, types of experiences with death, communication and support from others (Kastenbaum, 1977a, 1977b; Charmaz, 1980). The sociocultural context affects death experience, therefore one could expect different conceptions of death from children in the Middle Ages or during wartime (as in Lebanon). Adult ambiguities, evasions, or myths about death may only confuse children. Kalish (1981) notes that children *learn* to fear death, perhaps because it is spoken of in hushed tones tinged with dread. The best approach seems to be not to treat discussions of death with children as taboo, but rather to be open, direct, and accurate, and to use the many childhood encounters with death to recognize natural feelings and questions, creating an open environment for the expression of feelings (Kastenbaum, 1977b; Bluebond-Langner, 1977).

Young adults appear to take a stance toward death that sets them apart from other age groups. Kalish and Reynolds (1976) suggest that younger persons may be more introspective, enabling them to conceptualize better their own "nonexistence." It is also true that they are only beginning to develop the emotional ties with others that make their grief and the inability to care for dependents more important in later adulthood. Other results from Kalish and Reynolds's study indicate that whereas the young are more open about death in some ways (they are more likely to advocate that a dying person should be told that he or she is dying), they are also more fearful of death and would fight against their own death more actively. This anxiety is partly alleviated by seeing death as only a distant possibility.

Middle age is another stage of the life cycle that affects our relationship with death (Kastenbaum, 1977b). This may be the time when we encounter our first personally relevant or disturbing death, such as the death of our parents. Kastenbaum notes that we develop a "pecking order of death"—we expect certain people to die before we do. When parents die, this brings one's own death psychologically closer. Middle age is also a time when death is less uncommon among peers, and the middle-aged may experience "partial deaths" of attractiveness, physical strength, career opportunities. Kalish and Reynolds (1976) found that their middle-aged respondents expressed the most anxiety about the interview itself, perhaps because of some realization that youthful postponement of the possibility of death can be maintained for only a short time more. Awareness of the possibility of one's own death represents one feature of the midlife transition, and the developmental tasks discussed in Chapter 4 partly reflect attempts to adjust to and make sense of this new fact (Marshall, 1980). Indeed, coming to terms with one's own mortality represents a developmental task that begins in middle age and continues into later life.

A sense of impending death has long been considered important in the psychology of old age. Presumed consequences include social and emotional disengagement, the need for a sense of ego integrity, and the tendency to engage in a life review. Marshall (1980) refers to an *awareness of finitude,* or perceived distance from death, which is not simply a function of chronological age; it is affected by things such as parents' age at death, number of living siblings, deaths of friends (particularly age peers), self-perceived health, subjective age identity, and reduced obligations in work and family roles (Marshall, 1975a; Bengtson et al., 1977; Keith, 1982).

The awareness of finitude and a perception of limited remaining time have a number of consequences. Marshall (1980) suggests that they stimulate a need for "legitimation of biography" to make sense of one's life and of one's death, echoing the concepts of ego integrity and life review discussed in Chapter 4. If successfully achieved, this leads to new freedom; one has achieved a meaningful life and can view the future in a more relaxed way.

Death is also an organizer of time, and awareness of finitude triggers different perceptions and uses of time. Just as fears of death vary, however, responses to the proximity of death also differ.

Kalish and Reynolds (1976) have found that older people appear to react differently from younger people to the possibility of their own death (Table 12.1). There was a decline with age in the likelihood of altering life-style or attempting to complete projects and an increase in a more contemplative approach to impending death. Interestingly, older respondents were also more likely to consider sudden death more tragic than slow death. Apparently they wanted more time to see loved ones one last time, bring their affairs together, and reminisce.

These patterns reflect an acceptance of death among older persons found in many studies. Older people are more likely than younger people to think about death and talk about it with others, and they express less fear and anxiety about death (Kalish, 1976, 1981; Marshall, 1980). Kalish and Reynolds (1976), for example, found that older respondents (60+) thought more about death, had made more preparations (funeral arrangements, writing a will), were less afraid of death, felt better able to face dying, and would accept death more peacefully than younger and middle-aged persons. Kalish (1981) suggests a number of reasons for this apparent greater acceptance of death. Having reached their expected age,

Table 12.1 RESPONSES (PERCENTAGE) OF 434 RESPONDENTS TO
THE QUESTION: "IF YOU WERE TOLD THAT YOU HAD A
TERMINAL DISEASE AND SIX MONTHS TO LIVE, HOW
WOULD YOU WANT TO SPEND YOUR TIME UNTIL YOU
DIED?"

	Age		
Use of time	20–39	40–59	60+
Marked change in life style, self-related (travel, sex, experiences, etc.)	24	15	9
Inner-life centered (read, contemplate, pray)	14	14	37
Focus concern on others, be with loved ones	29	25	12
Attempt to complete projects, tie up loose ends	11	10	3
No change in life style	17	29	31
Other	5	6	8

Source: Richard Kalish and David Reynolds, *Death and Ethnicity: A Psychocultural Study,* p. 68, © 1976 by The Ethel Percy Andrus Gerontology Center, University of Southern California. Reprinted by permission.

older people may feel that they are living on borrowed time, making death seem less unfair. Kalish and Reynolds found that the death of an elderly person was almost universally considered the least tragic type of death. Legitimation of biography and feelings of ego integrity contribute to an acceptance of death as fair, as older persons have worked through their fears and anxieties.

Problems associated with aging, such as poor health or low income, and processes of disengagement may also diminish the value of life and the threat of death. Disengagement (for whatever reason) reduces concern over grief to others and inability to care for dependents. Death may be viewed as preferable to inactivity, uselessness, or physical and mental deterioration, reflecting values of independence and self-control. Marshall (1980) reports on a study asking a sample of older persons if they would like to live to be 100. Most said they would not, and none gave an unqualified yes. Charmaz (1980) notes that older people often take a "participating" stance toward death, viewing it as an honor, fulfillment, or reunion. Control over their own death is important. A 93-year-old man, discussing the prospect of death, stated, "It's mine . . . Don't belong to nobody else" (Kastenbaum & Aisenberg, 1976: 103). Fear of losing control and becoming a burden may outweigh fear of death, as reflected in the following statement by an older woman:

I don't know what I will do when I can no longer take care of myself. I just hope I go quickly—I don't want to be a burden to my children. I don't want them to have to take care of me. There's no room in their lives to take care of an elderly person and besides, I've been around long enough and seen enough to know what that's like. . . . I certainly don't want to become one of these mindless old souls who don't know sic'em from come here. There's nothing sadder than those poor things out at X (a local convalescent hospital). Some of those old people don't even know their relatives. As far as I am concerned, I'd rather be dead than be like that. (Charmaz, 1980:77)

Finally, acceptance of death by older persons also reflects processes of socialization. Other older people can be an invaluable source of support. Studies of age-segregated settings indicate that they facilitate discussion of death, allowing the aged to come to grips with their own feelings and achieve an acceptance of death that does not require denial (Hochschild, 1973; Marshall, 1975b). Age peers serve as role models of how to face up to death, how to react appropriately to the death of others, and how to die in a "good," or dignified, way. This is not a morbid preoccupation with death. Marshall, in his study of one retirement village, found that death was managed in a low-key manner: funerals were held elsewhere, grief was restrained, obituaries were discreet. But through interaction with other older people, discussing feelings that could not be discussed as easily with family or younger people, residents were able to view death as an appropriate completion of the life cycle. An 88-year-old woman commented that "it's time people shuffled off by 90." An 81-year-old widow remarked:

"Heavens! I've lived my life. I'd be delighted to have it end. The sooner the better. I nearly went with a heart attack. It would have been more convenient to go when my daughter was in _____ rather than in _____. I feel I've lived my life, and I don't want to be a care to anybody. That's why I'm glad to be here [in Glen Brae]. No, I don't want to mourn when I go. I've had a good life. It's time." (Marshall, 1975b:1127)

Comparing some attitudes toward death among the residents of this retirement village with those from Riley's (1970) national sample, Marshall found greater acceptance of death, as "sometimes a blessing," "tragic only for the survivors," and not "always coming too soon."

Not everyone has access to such socialization experiences, of course, and orientations toward death vary within the older population. Preoccupation with death appears to be greater among those who live alone or have worse self-rated health (Bengtson et al., 1977; Wass et al., 1979). Keith (1979) found that older women were more "positivist," with favorable orientations toward life and death, whereas older men were more "negativist," having less favorable orientations toward both.

It does appear, however, that older people generally have more open and accepting orientations toward death, despite, or perhaps because of, its objective and subjective nearness. But only scattered studies have included age as a factor in death-related attitudes. This is an area that needs much more investigating, particularly in explaining why such age trends occur. Are these differences truly consequences of age, or do they reflect cohort phenomena instead? Current cohorts of older people are more religious and have less education, for example, and these variables themselves seem to have important effects on attitudes about death. Until recently, death and dying have been neglected topics in social gerontology. This neglect is unfortunate and overlooks the relevance of thanatology (the study of death) to the aging experience.

REACTIONS TO THE DYING

To this point, we have discussed attitudes toward death as an abstract possibility. What happens when death is a real possibility? How do others react to the dying? And how do the dying themselves react to the process?

There are many indications of a social and psychological withdrawal from the dying by those around them. Families may use pretense to stave off the reality of dying, or visit less frequently. Hospital staff find ways to avoid contact with death.

> Nurses can also find ways to delegate the death watch, usually to someone who is not quite aware of the task he is being asked to perform (another use of "role switching"). If the dying patient is in a room with an alert patient, the nurse may leave the room with a "pressing work" excuse, asking the alert patient to call her immediately if he notices a change in the other patient. Nurses will also ask an ever-present family member, or perhaps a chaplain, to sit with the patient. If no one is available, a patient may be left to die alone, between periodic checks, though nurses find this outcome most disturbing unless he is already comatose. (Glaser & Strauss, 1966:247)

There are many reasons for this distancing from the dying: the implied failure associated with death, particularly for health professionals, our own fears and insecurities concerning death, and feelings of inadequacy about how to respond ("What do I say?") (Kastenbaum & Aisenberg, 1976).

Death in modern societies is increasingly likely to be a frequent occurrence in nursing homes and on some wards of general hospitals. Sudnow (1967), in a study of a county hospital, notes that it was a mark of sophistication for staff that they could no longer count the number of deaths they had witnessed except for unusual types of death. To lessen the social and emotional disruptiveness of death, such institutions "bureaucratize" it by isolating death from other aspects of the setting and developing predictable, routinized procedures for managing it.

One way to manage death is to contain and isolate it from the normal social world. Sudnow (1967) describes some of the strategies designed to isolate death. Dying patients are typically moved to private rooms or curtains are drawn around their beds. When patients die, their bodies may be removed under pretense of going for an X ray, and they are never moved during visiting hours. Similar processes seem to go on in nursing homes: closing doors, pulling curtains, removing bodies during meal times, handling the dead as if they were still alive (Gubrium, 1975). In Sudnow's study, the hospital morgue was located in an inaccessible part of the basement, and the morgue attendant made every effort to avoid others when carrying out his duties. For example, he would carry a logbook and keep looking downward to avoid interactions while going to get a body or transporting one.

Another way of managing death is through predictability, which allows staff to handle death through routine procedures, coordinate their treatment of the individual, and avoid disruptive scenes that arise from unexpected death. This implies that the determination that someone is *dying* is as much a socially created prediction as a medical fact.

> "Dying" becomes an important, noticeable "process" insofar as it serves to provide others, as well as the patient, with a way to orient to the future, to organize activities around the expectability of death, to "prepare for it." The notion of "dying" appears to be a distinctly social one, for its central relevance is provided for by the fact that it establishes a way of attending a person. In the hospital, as elsewhere, what the notion of "dying" does, as a predictive characterization, is place a frame of interpretation around a person. (Sudnow, 1967:68–69)

Glaser and Strauss (1968) refer to staff conceptions of a *dying trajectory*—the expected shape and duration of the dying process for the patient—which affects their attitudes toward and treatment of the individual. There are four types of death expectations based on its certainty and time remaining (Glaser & Strauss, 1968):

1. Death is certain and will occur at a known time.
2. Death is certain, but the time is unknown.
3. Death is uncertain, but there is a known time when certainty will be established (e.g., following a series of tests).
4. Death is uncertain, and it is not known when this uncertainty will be resolved.

Staff members experience greater stress and disorganization when these expectations are not clearly communicated or when death occurs unexpectedly, too slowly, or too quickly. It is better for the staff when death occurs "on schedule," permitting normal procedures for handling it. All of this relates to an attempt to rationalize death.

Predictions are based on many things other than the illness. The timetable of the "dying career" in a nursing home, for example, may be based on social activity, mobility, functional control (continence), and mental capacity (Gustafson, 1972). In another study Marshall (1976) found that the perceived dying trajectory in a nursing home was related to successive residential transitions from a private or dormitory room to the infirmary, and finally to "dying rooms."

One important implication of the dying trajectory is that it affects the attitudes and behaviors of others toward the dying person. With expected, lingering dying, for example, active diagnosis and treatment may be suspended, and dramatic rescue scenes in the final hours are unlikely. The focus of treatment shifts from cure to comfort and attempts to relieve suffering. A more unfortunate possibility is that *social* death will precede *biological* death, involving withdrawal and treating the person as if he or she were already dead.

> *Social death* must be defined situationally. In particular, it is a situation in which there is absence of those behaviors we would expect to be directed toward

a living person, and the presence of behaviors we would expect when dealing with a deceased or nonexistent person. Social death is read by observing how others treat and fail to treat the person with whom we are concerned. The individual himself may be animated enough and potentially responsive. As a matter of fact, the individual may be desperately seeking recognition, attention, interaction. The concept of social death recognizes that a significant aspect of being a person is being a person in the eyes of others. In other words, this concept calls attention to the basic status of being a person in society. We may appreciate more keenly how contingent and even precarious being a person in society can be when we are alert to the possibility of a living human being treated as though dead or nonexistent. (Kastenbaum, 1977a:31)

Social death may involve a declining frequency of visits, the tendency of staff to discuss their case as if the individual were not present, and similar withdrawal from the individual as a social being. Nursing-home residents may engage in a frantic struggle against this dying timetable, as in the hoarding of greeting cards to signify that one is still socially alive (Gustafson, 1972).

All of these reactions to death represent institutional responses. Dying threatens the normal routinization of emergencies in hospitals. But reactions to the dying are more than just institutional responses; they are also attempts by individual staff members to deal with their own feelings.

Although health professionals, such as nurses and physicians, may encounter death frequently, particularly within certain specialties, they are largely left on their own in handling the dying and bereaved. They carry their own fears and insecurities into medical situations. It has been suggested that physicians are even more fearful of death than the average person, and that becoming a physician may represent an attempt to master those fears (Schulz & Aderman, 1976).

Fear of death, and attempts to avoid contact with it, may be further reinforced by the nature of medical education. Although it appears that physicians who have received some formal instruction concerning death and dying relate better with dying patients, most medical students receive very limited death education (Dickinson & Pearson, 1980). However, their education does result in certain stances regarding death (Kastenbaum & Aisenberg, 1976; Coombs & Powers, 1976). Early contact with cadavers and autopsies desensitizes them to death stimuli, teaching a scientific approach to death. They are taught to maintain a "detached concern" for patients, emphasizing objectivity and lack of emotional involvement. The physician is idealized as the bulwark against death; stress placed on saving lives makes death a sign of failure, ineptitude, and lack of mastery. Helping people die runs counter to this perception of the healing role. It is not a task to which physicians can apply their costly skills and training.

The nature of modern death may also contribute to professional unease over dying (Thomas, 1980). The normal inevitability of death was clearer in the past with higher mortality throughout the life cycle and greater firsthand experience with death. Dying occurred more typically at the end of short struggles against infections rather than at the end of prolonged chronic illness. Now dying seems more "unnatural" and occurs in situations where medicine may comfort but not cure.

Various strategies, which may be maladaptive to the interactional needs of the dying patient, are used to deal with this stress. Physicians may avoid the dying; when cure is impossible, the task of comforting is left to other staff. Patients and their families may be dealt with impersonally, as cases ("the kidney in 307"), rather than as whole persons with social, psychological, and emotional needs. Failure to keep this emotional distance may make death very disturbing, as illustrated in the following statement by a staff member on an intensive care unit:

> We found Richard to be a very interesting, intelligent, and likeable person. He had worked in a hospital previously and therefore understood much of what was happening to him and what his prognosis was. His attitude was one of kindness, concern, and warmth, all of which was easy to return. He had a wife and family that were very concerned about him and were equally considerate and kind to the staff. Because of these qualities in Richard and his family, it became very easy to become involved in them. Richard became not just a patient but also a person. His care was made more emotionally difficult by the fact that, unlike most patients, everything he asked for was preceded and followed by "please" and "thank you." He sincerely appreciated everything that we did for him. We found it difficult to care for him because we knew he was going to die. We tried to be cheerful to him, despite the fact that most of us felt quite depressed concerning him and his condition. Many of us who took care of him often wished he would stop being so nice, so considerate, and be the opposite—almost as though it would be easier for us to adjust to his death if we could be angry at him. (Swanson & Swanson, 1977:248)

Swanson and Swanson refer to a "death saturation" experienced by staff under such conditions and the need to provide emotional support for staff as well as patients. Failure to do so will only heighten emotional withdrawal or exhaustion.

In some ways, nurses may have greater difficulty handling death and dying than physicians because nurses have the most intimate daily contact with dying patients, particularly in emergency and intensive care settings, where there is a constant state of readiness and tension (Benoliel, 1977). Nurses are often the first to discover death and bear the major emotional burden of lengthy terminal care, which lacks the tangible satisfaction of nursing someone back to health. This intimate contact with death is compounded by the responsibility vacuum created by their subordinate status to the physician; for example, it is not the nurses' decision when or whether to tell a patient of his or her status, or to inform the family of a death (Kastenbaum & Aisenberg, 1976). As with physicians, there is little educational preparation for handling death. Studies cited by Kastenbaum and Aisenberg indicate that nurses tend to cling to a model of efficient, impersonal care in which they should avoid making mistakes or giving in and letting their feelings show. When a sample of nurses was asked how they would react to a patient saying, "I think I'm going to die soon" or "I wish I could just end it all," the most likely response was to "turn off" the patient by changing the subject, engaging in denial, or taking a fatalistic approach. Only 18 percent said they would be willing to discuss the patient's feelings. Yet such discussions are often very important and beneficial for the dying.

Reflecting the processes discussed in this section, the deaths of older people appear to be less disturbing (Marshall, 1980; Kalish, 1981). As noted earlier, their deaths are generally viewed as less tragic because death is anticipated and the elderly have less "social value." In a study of health-care personnel in hospitals and nursing homes, Lerea and LiMauro (1982) found greater grief expressed by hospital staff. Expectations of death and beliefs that it was a "blessing" may soften the effects of death, as in this comment by a SNF nurse:

> Mr. L. lived at _____ convalescent center for more than 7 years. He was such a kind, dignified man. I watched him go downhill all the time . . . unable to feed himself, incontinent, confused. When he died, it was like I lost my own father. I grieved but I was also relieved. (Lerea & LiMauro, 1982:607)

Staff are also protected from feelings of failure by beliefs that rehabilitative efforts are less effective with the aged and that they will die soon anyway, if not from this illness then from some other. Emotional involvement is also reduced because older persons who are dying are more often confused or comatose.

REACTIONS OF THE DYING

Although the organizational and staff responses to death we have discussed are understandable, they also create a difficult environment for the dying patient. One increasing concern is that modern societies create a "crisis in dying." As people increasingly die in unfamiliar, depersonalized institutions, an acceptable, dignified, or appropriate death becomes more difficult to achieve. Weisman (1972) notes that common misconceptions about the terminally ill (they do not want to know what the future holds, reconciliation and preparation for death are impossible to achieve, only the suicidal or psychotic are willing to die) become rationalizations for withdrawal or ignoring their human needs. The dying process is usually relatively short (75 to 80 percent of the mortally ill die within three months of their last hospital admission) and only a minority experience unrelieved pain (Hinton, 1972). Even among terminal geriatric patients, most are able to communicate and are conscious of their surroundings up to the very end (Weisman & Kastenbaum, 1968). Yet institutional staff too often pay little attention to the psychological well-being and needs of the dying.

Awareness of Dying

How aware are the terminally ill of their condition, and how much should they be told? Glaser and Strauss (1966) have found four types of *awareness contexts:* (1) *closed awareness,* where the patient is unaware of his or her condition, (2) *suspected awareness,* in which the patient is suspicious but not sure, (3) *mutual pretense,* where patient and staff know but deny knowledge to each other, and (4) *open awareness,* when patient and staff acknowledge the reality of the situation. It appears that most terminally ill patients have at least some awareness of their condition because they receive many clues: direct and overheard statements, bodily symptoms, changes in the behavior of others or in treatment routines, changes in physical location (Kalish, 1970; Hinton, 1972). Even terminally ill children seem to be usually aware that they are dying, despite efforts by staff and parents to shield them, and may experience feelings of isolation or anger concerning the overprotectiveness of others (Binger et al., 1969; Waechter, 1971). This awareness is often what Weisman (1972) calls *middle knowledge,* between open acknowledgment and total denial. The terminally ill may fluctuate between open and closed awareness in response to changes in the course of the illness or equivocation by others. Weisman also notes that they may display an awareness of the diagnosis, but not of its implications.

In mutual pretense, denial is typically shared by avoiding dangerous topics (death itself, future plans) and maintaining little fictions (Glaser & Strauss, 1966). Family and staff are unlikely to initiate discussions of death, often because they feel this is best for the patient, and the patient picks up these signals. To protect their feelings and avoid jeopardizing what few social relationships remain, the patient plays along. Although this lends a certain amount of privacy and minimizes embarrassment, mutual pretense creates very strained, unreal interactions and prevents the patient from expressing feelings and concerns within close personal relationships. There may be a severe sense of isolation, as shown in the following statement by a cancer patient:

> I began to realize I desperately needed to talk to someone. But there was no one. The nurses at the hospital were friendly but cautious about answering my questions. The doctors were efficient but very busy. I couldn't talk to my wife because I didn't want to upset her. I tried to talk to some of my friends, but I saw it was bothering them. Some told me not to worry because everything was going to be all right. The doctors certainly knew more about my prognosis than they indicated, so I knew they were just trying to evade the issue. Some of my other friends were affected emotionally by what had happened to me, and they didn't make very good listeners. They were concerned but couldn't bear to discuss anything with me. (Kelly, 1977:185–86)

There may eventually be a break to open awareness when suffering and the need to talk make the pretense too difficult to maintain, but the convenient fictions are not always easy to break through.

Since most terminally ill people sense their predicament anyway, the ability to talk about it usually brings a feeling of relief. At the very least, they should be granted real opportunities to express their feelings. Although this is somewhat less true for older people, studies indicate that most persons (usually about 90 percent) would prefer to be told if they were terminally ill (Kalish, 1976; Blumenfield et al., 1979; Wass et al., 1979; Veatch & Tai, 1980).

The dying may give off many cues, verbal and nonverbal, of their willingness to engage in open awareness. It appears that doctors are increasingly inclined to inform terminal patients of their condition, particularly specialists who are most likely to see the terminally ill (Veatch & Tai, 1980). Veatch and Tai suggest that this reflects changing beliefs about harm caused by disclosure and the increased value of patient autonomy and self-determination. An increasingly sophisticated public is viewed as part of the medical team, rather than emphasizing medical paternalism, and chronic patients are often better able to participate in their own care than acutely ill patients who are incapacitated.

Reactions to Dying

In many ways the terminally ill show few emotional differences from the seriously ill or even the healthy (Kalish, 1976). They are, however, more likely to exhibit anxiety (Hinton, 1972; Kastenbaum & Aisenberg, 1976). There are, after all, many naturally fearful aspects to dying: physical distress, strange tests and treatments, loneliness and separation, loss of control and personal identity, and so on. Nevertheless, the dying do not appear to be overwhelmed by fear. Lieberman (1965) found little fearfulness or preoccupation with death among a sample of terminal geriatric patients. Kalish (1969), in a study of persons who had been "reprieved" from a close call with death (automobile accidents, near-drownings), found that only 23 percent had been fearful or in panic; the most frequent first reaction had been concern for family and other survivors.

Anxiety may be linked to dying, but depression seems to be a more frequent response (Hinton, 1972). This includes depression about one's own loss of health and control and reactions to impending death. It also involves concern for others—their grief, and the extent to which the dying patient is a burden to them.

Some persons react more favorably to the dying process than others. Hinton (1975) found better adjustment to terminal illness among those who had coped well with problems throughout their lives and viewed their lives as more satisfying or fulfilling. These personal differences may actually affect longevity. In a study of cancer patients, Weisman and Worden (1975) found greater than expected longevity among those who were assertive and had established cooperative, mutually responsive relationships with others. Because of their positively expressed assertiveness, they received more attention and better care. On the other hand, those who were apathetic, had death wishes, or had a long-standing pattern of mutually destructive relationships survived a shorter time. They possessed traits that created alienation in their personal lives and in encounters with staff.

In her groundbreaking work with the terminally ill, Elisabeth Kübler-Ross (1969) suggests that the dying may experience five stages in their reactions to impending death:

1. Denial. According to Kübler-Ross, nearly all patients initially react with denial, which is a healthy buffer. Unfortunately, this may continue if others are not open to dealing with the person's fears and concerns. She notes that most patients are eventually willing to talk about dying, but have little opportunity to do so.

2. Anger. The second stage involves a "why me?" reaction, and anger may be displaced on family or staff. The following statement by a leukemia patient reflects the mixture of anger and guilt that may be felt by dying patients over the behavior of others and loss of personal control.

> Often when Art and the children came, I was too drained and sick to do much talking. I felt guilty about Art having to drive back and forth, handle the children, our home, and his business as well. So, at times, I would urge him to remain at home. At other times, when I was feeling more energized, I would become resentful that he couldn't spend more time with me. I was angry, too, that no one was around to give him the support I felt he needed.
>
> The bulk of my anger became displaced on my hospital environment, particularly those aspects that threatened my own sense of control. These aspects included having to endure endless waiting in the x-ray department when I was racked with chills and fever; experiencing the traumatic loss of my hair that became symbolic for all my potential losses; seeing my body waste away and having no appetite to combat it; vomiting perpetually and continually; feeling trapped in a bleak, grey room that overlooked the barren rooftops of the city. (Jaffe & Jaffe, 1977:200–01)

Such feelings need to be respected and understood, but they often lead instead to withdrawal and avoidance.

3. Bargaining.   In the third stage, the patient may bargain, often with God, to live long enough to reach some deadline, or to postpone death as a prize for good behavior. This may reflect a partially successful "will to live." There is some evidence of an "anniversary reaction" where mortality rates are lower before special dates such as birthdays, holidays, and awaited reunions (Kalish, 1981); for example, John Adams and Thomas Jefferson both died on the Fourth of July, a date of obvious significance to them.

4. Depression.   The fourth stage represents a natural grief over the final separation of death—grief for oneself and also for those who will be left behind. As with anger, others must "open the door" for the expression of such feelings.

5. Acceptance.   The final stage is achieved only if the dying person is able, or allowed, to express and deal with earlier feelings, such as anger and depression. This is not a happy stage, but is rather almost void of feelings. There is a sense that one's tasks have been accomplished, the struggle is over. It is, in the words of one patient, "the final rest before the long journey" (Kübler-Ross, 1969:113).

Kübler-Ross suggests that those around the dying person should not force the stages, but should be open to the individual moving through the stages as he or she is ready to do so. Withdrawal and denial only make a final acceptance more difficult to achieve. Kübler-Ross also notes that some feelings of hope usually persist through all stages, and conveyed hopelessness by others makes the dying process extremely difficult.

The work of Kübler-Ross indicates the importance of allowing the dying to express their feelings, however uncomfortable this may be for us. It is not easy for the family to encounter anger and depression, but such feelings may be necessary for the dying person. However, her scheme is best thought of as an inventory of possible moods or orientations. There is no evidence that the dying experience a universal or invariant sequence of stages (Schulz & Aderman, 1974; Kastenbaum, 1977a). The person may shift back and forth between denial and acceptance, or follow apparent acceptance with more anger or depression. There is a danger that these five stages could become a self-fulfilling prophecy, as patients are forced to follow the expectations. Weisman and Kastenbaum (1968) note from their studies of the terminally ill that, although acceptance of death seemed to be the most frequent response, there were other reactions: apathy, apprehension, anticipation.

> Acceptance refers to patients who spoke about death in a dispassionate and realistic way; apathy describes patients who seemed indifferent to almost any event, including death; apprehension refers to patients who openly voiced fear and alarm about death; and anticipation applies to patients who showed acceptance plus an explicit wish for death. (Weisman & Kastenbaum, 1968:22)

There is no "typical" way to die. The dying process is shaped by an individual's own personality and life-style, the specific illness, and by the context within which it occurs. Charmaz (1980) points out that emotional reactions by the dying may be created by the environment—patient denial as a response to staff denial, or anger as a fitting response to staff attitudes and behavior. The openness stressed by Kübler-Ross is an important aspect of this environment and leads to a discussion of caring for the dying.

CARING FOR THE DYING

It is obviously difficult to present any "manual" for caring for the dying. Many of the responses to the dying person we have discussed—dying trajectories, limiting the obtrusiveness of death—are best seen as natural responses by individuals and organizations to exceptionally difficult social and emotional situations. And in some cases they represent commendable sensitivity, as in the unobtrusive removal of dead bodies from nursing homes. But organizational and staff responses to death and dying can also create a wall of denial and social distance around dying patients, meeting organizational needs at the expense of the needs of the dying.

In many ways the needs of the dying are not unique. Kalish (1981), for example, notes that the dying are as concerned as the living with Maslow's hierarchy of needs (which we discussed in Chapter 2). The ability of the dying to meet those needs will be limited by physical pain, feelings of abandonment, and contexts that limit autonomy and personal growth. But just as they have throughout their lives, individuals seek to maintain as much control over their dying as possible and to render it meaningful (Marshall, 1980). The goal of those who care for the dying should be to help them achieve an *appropriate death.*

> The concept of an appropriate death is based upon the view that dying can be a positive act, not just a calamity that overtakes a person. In appropriate death, the patient is helped to resolve conflict within the limits of his personality and in accordance with the aspirations of his ego ideal. Admittedly, an appropriate death is usually only partially attained, but it is a feasible goal to work toward. An appropriate death is, essentially, one that the patient might have chosen for himself, had he a choice. Conversely, whatever is done to impoverish, demean, or reduce a patient's autonomy and self-esteem will necessarily be a defeat for those who look after him. (Weisman & Kastenbaum, 1968:43)

Achieving a death appropriate to the individual requires a number of things (Kalish, 1976, 1981; Kastenbaum, 1977a; Schulz, 1978). Relief from physical suffering should be a high priority of treatment. The individual's preferences and life-style should also be respected and opportunities to exercise control and responsibility provided. Charmaz (1980) notes that the social experience of dying (deterioration of body and self-image, institutional treatment as an object, isolation) frequently results in a "diminished self," attacking the person's viability as a competent, responsible actor. Those who care for the dying must support the dying individual's decision-making options, paying attention to privacy and individuality and supporting the individual's role as a knowledgeable participant. Issues discussed in Chapter 11, person-environment congruence and social reconstruction, should not be discarded simply because someone is dying. Hope for the dying does not depend solely on survival or absolute control, but rather on what Weisman (1972) calls "significant survival," "the belief that we do something worth doing, and that others think so too" (p. 21).

Achieving an appropriate death also requires an open awareness context, combined with warm and intimate personal relationships that provide encouragement and reassurance. Patients, family, and staff all need opportunities to vent their feelings. Sometimes this means nothing more than good listening. There is also a need for privacy and personal leave-taking, which require respect for the dignity of the individual. An open context does not mean that dying persons should be forced to be open about their feelings. There is tremendous individual variability in reactions and preferences concerning dying, and we should be wary about any list of rules. But the context must allow for the expression of individual needs and preferences.

Contexts for Dying

As with the aging experience as a whole, it is clear that the nature and meaning of dying depend on the context in which it takes place. Studies of dying persons indicate that most prefer to die at home, and indeed most receive considerable physical and emotional support from family during early stages of dying (Marshall, 1980; Kalish, 1981). This can prove quite burdensome to family members, however, particularly when the course of dying is unpredictable and prolonged. At least the later stages of dying are increasingly likely to occur in an institutional context in modern societies.

Unfortunately, dying is more likely to be a "managed" process in an institutional setting so that individuals lose control over their own dying. Dying is a total experience, involving the total person, which runs counter to the hospital's fragmented emphasis on "the disease" (Mauksch, 1975), and expression of anger or depression violates the "culture" of the hospital. The dying face a "death valley" atmosphere of isolation, little communication, and hushed tones (Weisman & Kastenbaum, 1968). They experience perhaps the most *total* of institutions, with constricting rules and regulations that yield no autonomy.

Problems in caring for the dying may be especially acute in nursing homes, where death is prevalent. One study found that the average nursing home experienced nearly two deaths every month (Ingram & Barry, 1977). Nursing-home personnel are too seldom prepared for care of the dying, and the frequency of death may be one reason for the high turnover among workers in nursing homes.

The difficulties associated with dying in the institutional atmosphere of hospitals and nursing homes represent one impetus for the emergence of the *hospice* model of caring for the terminally ill (Stoddard, 1978; Osterweis & Champagne, 1979; Holden, 1980). As much a philosophy as a place, a hospice is oriented to providing a "caring community" for the dying. The first, St. Christopher's Hospice, opened in 1967 in Great Britain by Cicely Saunders, is literally geared toward providing hospitality to the dying.

> Those who welcome each patient to St. Christopher's do so with the conviction that he or she is an important person and that hospitality to a stranger is a prime necessity. Those concerned take care to know the name of newcomers before they arrive, and a senior nurse joins the stewards at the ambulance to welcome them personally. The patient is lifted directly into a warm bed, and his family travels in the lift with him to the ward. It is impossible to overemphasize what such a welcome means to a mortally sick person who has so often felt alien and rejected. He has been the "failure" who cannot get better in the acute ward, feeling obscurely that it is his own fault, or he has suffered long pain at home which has led to despair of ever finding peace. (Saunders, 1977:163)

The first hospice in the United States was developed in New Haven in 1974, and nearly 200 existed by 1978.

The hospice is designed for supportive care after reasonable efforts to cure have been exhausted. Its philosophy combines inpatient and home care. It seeks to support home care as long as possible through consultation and the efforts of an interdisciplinary professional staff and volunteers. Short-term residential care may be available for management of symptoms, respite for family, or the final stages of dying if home care is not possible. Hospice efforts may also be directed at counseling for bereaved persons and community education about dying.

Emphasis on a personal touch, rather than technology, is found throughout the program of the hospice. Communication and family involvement are stressed. Reduction of anxiety through control of symptoms and chronic pain is emphasized. This contributes to the overall goal of preserving dignity and personal control over the dying process. Coordination of inpatient and home care provides continuity between home and the hospice. This approach seems to be effective. Saunders (1977) notes that 8 to 10 percent of those who enter St. Christopher's return home, and some have achieved unexpected remissions of up to 5 years. In a comparison with matched patients who were dying in more traditional settings, residents of St. Christopher's had greater mobility, rated their pain as less severe, and were less likely to view the staff as "busy" (Saunders, 1977). In addition, 78 percent felt that "the hospital is like a family," compared with only 11 percent of the comparison group.

Hospices take a number of forms. St. Christopher's is a free-standing facility with its own home-residential care. However, most are home care and counseling services with loose links to existing inpatient services (Holden, 1980). Still others are primarily inpatient programs within hospitals. Although the availability of hospices has grown, they are still not available to most terminally ill persons. Osterweis and Champagne (1979) also note that unresolved issues remain: lack of integration with existing services (including hospitals), inadequate sources of funding for their creation and operation, and inconsistent reimbursement by medical insurance for the costs of individual care. But such settings are clearly useful for the achievement of an "appropriate" death. They also serve to sensitize institutions and professionals to the social and emotional needs of dying persons for whom a hospice is either inaccessible or inappropriate.

Munley and associates (1983) suggest that hospice principles could help counteract the dehumanizing aspects of nursing-home life for residents and staff. It may be difficult to transfer the hospice model to nursing homes, given their high staff turnover, longer stays for residents, and emphasis on profit and efficiency. But Munley and associates note that such constraints must be confronted if the hospice movement is to expand beyond its present small scale.

BEREAVEMENT

Death is never truly an isolated, individual event. There are always survivors who themselves have social, psychological, and emotional needs related to the death experience. Survivors need not have an intimate relationship with the deceased to have severe reactions. Disaster victims often display feelings of guilt ("Why did *I* live?") or depression. For example, Lifton (1967) found feelings of profound guilt and a "psychic numbing" that made the resumption of meaningful activity nearly impossible among the survivors of the atomic bomb dropped on Hiroshima.

Bereavement is associated with higher rates of suicide, mental hospitalization, and even higher mortality during the first year (Schulz, 1978; Marshall, 1980; Kalish, 1981). Higher mortality may reflect a number of processes: fatigue, self-neglect, a common environment with the deceased, or stress and a "broken heart." Thus, just as the dying need supportive assistance in handling death, so also do the survivors of death need help in managing their "grief work." Kübler-Ross (1969) suggests, for example, that her "stages" of dying also apply to the dying patient's family.

A few definitions are in order before we proceed. *Bereavement* refers to the status of being deprived—one occupies a new social role—and the process of reacting to this loss; *grief* is the response made to this bereavement; and *mourning* signifies culturally patterned expectations about the expression of grief. Although the nature of grief seems to have certain universal qualities, the definition of who is bereaved varies among cultures, as does the content of the prescribed mourning role.

> In cross-cultural terms, the specific content of the role varies widely: weeping; personal preparation of the corpse for burial, gashing one's own body with knives or sharp sticks, protracted seclusion; fasting, wreaking vengeance on those responsible for the death, special religious obligations of prayer or sacrifice, sharp and humiliating alterations in dress and appearance, and so on. (Volkhart & Michael, 1957:297)

How do people respond to the death of others? Lindemann (1944) argues that acute grief constitutes a distinct syndrome.

> The picture shown by persons in acute grief is remarkably uniform. Common to all is the following syndrome: sensations of somatic distress occurring in waves lasting from twenty minutes to an hour at a time, a feeling of tightness in the throat, choking with shortness of breath, need for sighing, and an empty feeling in the abdomen, lack of muscular power, and an intense subjective distress described as tension or mental pain. (Lindemann, 1944:142)

Morbid grief reactions do not appear to be qualitatively different from normal ones; they differ only in intensity and duration (Schulz, 1978). Common reactions include: shock and disbelief, psychological numbness, depression, loneliness, fatigue, loss of appetite, sleeplessness, and anxiety about one's ability to reorganize and carry on (Glick et al., 1974; Kalish, 1976, 1981; Schulz, 1978). There may be self-questioning and guilt—"Could I have done more?"—that may be linked to anger and resentment. Restlessness may combine with an inability to initiate activity; routines related to the deceased have now lost their significance, and new patterns have not emerged as replacements.

Schulz (1978) indicates that the initial response of shock and disbelief followed by all-encompassing sorrow typically lasts for the first few weeks. This is followed by an intermediate phase of confronting daily life without the deceased, often involving a pining and searching for the presence of the deceased and an obsessional review seeking meaning for the death. Gradually, however, the bereaved person is likely to readjust to his or her "new" world and begins to focus on new activities and relationships. Individual emotional adjustment and adjustment in social roles is required.

As with dying, however, bereavement does not exhibit a fixed sequence of stages but is characterized instead by overlapping responses and individual variability (Marshall, 1980). In a longitudinal study of widows and widowers under 45, Glick and associates (1974) found that although grief and its associated reactions were most severe during the first few weeks, the impact of bereavement persisted and recurred throughout the first year. After the first year, most felt in control of their lives; grief had faded, although feelings of loneliness continued. Even this was not universally true, however; at the end of the year, 28 percent of the widows still agreed that they "would not care if I died tomorrow."

Studies indicate that the bereaved receive support from many sources—the immediate atmosphere of warmth and concern constitute "society at its best" (Glick et al., 1974; Lopata, 1979). Kin are particularly helpful, especially children and their spouses. In her study of older widows, Lopata (1979) found that daughters were more important providers of emotional support, whereas sons were more likely to provide practical assistance (such as yard work). Friends may also provide important social support.

Glick and associates (1974) found that reactions to loss often intensified following the funeral when the prescribed mourning period was over, others returned to their own lives, and the bereaved were left to face their new life on their own. There was often uncertainty about the type and length of appropriate mourning, and some were defensive about returning to normality. This bereavement period was managed by strenuous efforts to carry on, particularly controlling feelings around others to avoid losing their respect. Lopata (1979) found that this early period involved a mixture of emotional problems (especially loneliness) and practical difficulties (especially financial matters).

Glick and associates (1974) indicate a gradual acknowledgement of reality and reconstruction of patterns of living during the first year, although there were still intermingled periods of grief and despair. By the end of the year, most had acquired a sense of competence in managing their new lives, as reflected in the following statement:

> I never thought I could take what I have had to take. I thought I would fall apart. But I fought my way back. So maybe I'm stronger than I ever realized. I always leaned on Phil. I always felt that I leaned on him. But now I've got to stand on my own two feet. I just never thought I could do it, but I have. I found out I was a bit stronger than I thought I was. (Glick et al., 1974:215)

The older widows in Lopata's (1979) study appeared to require more time to establish a new life, equated with getting over much of the grief and learning to be alone and independent. Nearly 40 percent required more than a year to do so, and 16 percent needed more than two years.

Adjustment to bereavement appears to be less successful when death is sudden or unexpected (Glick et al., 1974; Schulz, 1978; Kalish, 1981). Glick and associates found that expected death did not reduce subsequent grief, but there was better eventual adjustment, apparently because of emotional and psychological preparation for the changes to come. This "anticipatory grief" allows an earlier return to normal functioning. Sudden death seems to constitute a shock that overwhelms coping capacities, and the reality of death is much more difficult to accept. This is one reason death of the aged is less disruptive; in a sense, their death is always expected, even when sudden.

The benefits of anticipatory grief should not be overstated, however. Interaction during a terminal period is very intense, an emotional pressure cooker. This may be a particular problem for women, who typically bear the most responsibility in caring for the dying (Kalish, 1977). As a reflection of the strains involved in waiting for death to occur, a study of aged widows and widowers found that adjustment to widowhood was less satisfactory when there had been an extended period of anticipatory grief (Gerber et al., 1975). Kalish (1981) also suggests that anticipatory grief may lead to withdrawal from dying persons, such as the elderly, once grieving has been completed.

Social and Cultural Context of Bereavement

The social and cultural context can either facilitate or inhibit successful adjustment to grief and bereavement. Mourning involves cultural assumptions about bereavement behavior, which are intended to assist individuals in their "grief work." Mourning rituals serve to channel and legitimate the normal expression of grief, defining the appropriate timing of bereavement, and also rally support for the bereaved from family and friends, publicize the new status and roles, and assist individuals in accepting the reality of death. But it has been argued that this assistance has broken down in modern societies as bereavement has been deritualized, leaving the survivors on their own to handle grief privately (Volkhart & Michael, 1957; Hinton, 1972; Kastenbaum, 1977a; Charmaz, 1980). Continued grief is seen as deviant, and there are few socially appropriate channels for the expression of natural grief reactions. The bereaved are therefore likely to view their feelings as abnormal and are unable to resolve feelings of guilt, anger, or depression. This may be exacerbated by other types of roles; for example, men seem to have more difficulty expressing grief (Glick et al. 1974; Kalish & Reynolds, 1976). There are other barriers to expression of grief. Kalish and Reynolds found that emotional expression was considered appropriate in private but not in public, and older people were less willing to express their grief through tears, perhaps as a way of protecting themselves from bereavement overload.

Lopata (1979) suggests that widowhood is particularly disorganizing in modern urban society. The wife identity is shattered without a comfortable widow role as substitute. Widows must change from dependent to independent persons when they are separated from support by the modified extended family. Charmaz (1980) also notes that emphasis on the nuclear family causes grief to be handled alone. Common problems of the widows in Lopata's study included lack of opportunity to grieve, lack of emotional support and daily services after a short "official" mourning period, and lack of self-help support groups.

This is not to say that no rituals surround death in modern societies. Although there has been a certain deritualization of death, all cultures still develop values, beliefs, and practices related to death. This cultural system, which Kastenbaum (1977a) has called the *death system*, has many components: people (funeral directors, florists, life-insurance agents), places (funeral homes, hospitals, historic battlefields), times (Memorial Day, Good Friday), objects (tombstones, skull and crossbones), and symbols (black armbands, funereal music). The death system serves many functions, including prediction and prevention of death, care of the dying, disposal of the dead, and lending meanings to death. The greatest focus, however, has been on the sociological and psychological functions of the death system in helping society and the individual to deal with the problems created by death. Funerals, for example, are felt to fulfill important functions for the living—for the immediately bereaved and the larger social group (Mandelbaum, 1959; Pine et al., 1976). In this sense "a funeral ceremony is personal in its focus and is societal in its consequences" (Mandelbaum, 1959:189). All cultures have developed such rituals and ceremonies, although their form varies considerably.

One function of the funeral is to serve as a *rite of passage* for the deceased, an appropriate and fitting conclusion to the person's life. Eulogies and a respectful gathering pay tribute to the deceased, emphasizing his or her worth and helping us put the person's life and significance for us into perspective.

Funerals and related ceremonies also provide important functions for the bereaved by serving as a focal point for expressing grief, accepting the reality of death, and accomplishing the transition back into the normal social world. Prescribed mourning behavior provides a legitimized outlet for grief in a situation in which the support of others is made available. Tasks and rituals bring home the reality of death. These rituals also help the bereaved determine when they have grieved enough.

Finally, funerals are important for the social group as a whole by providing an opportunity to display solidarity and reaffirm the values of the group. The funeral demonstrates family cohesion and shows that the social order goes on despite the disruptiveness of individual death. Funerals also remind those present of their own finitude, and perhaps underline the meaning of death in that culture.

The importance of funerals and associated customs is related to the precariousness of society (Marshall, 1980) and is likely to be heightened in the high-mortality societies discussed earlier in the chapter. Modern societies, in which death is controlled, isolated, and largely confined to the old, have less need for funeral rituals. This does not mean that individuals no longer require their supportive functions; however, the modern funeral has been challenged as being irrelevant to the needs of the bereaved.

> . . . contemporary practices do little more than ceremonially announce the death and the corresponding changed status of the survivors. Since no guidelines are constructed for the future statuses of the bereaved, any grief that is experienced later by that person becomes a private burden for which neither the funeral industry nor the community takes responsibility. (Charmaz, 1980: 203–204)

There may also be inadequate support from professionals, such as funeral directors and clergy, whose task it is to counsel and comfort the bereaved. Funeral directors have come to emphasize their status as *professionals,* based on underlying theory and knowledge, ethics, and service to others (Pine, 1975). In recent years, they have particularly advanced a view of themselves as professionals who "serve the living" as "grief specialists." But Pine indicates that one third of the funeral directors in the United States have only a high-school education or less. He also notes that in terms of specialized training, 12 percent have no training, 62 percent have one year or less, and only 26 percent have college-level training in "mortuary science."

The most ancient and traditional "grief specialists" have been the clergy. Kastenbaum and Aisenberg (1976) suggest that clergy can be helpful precisely because they serve no medical or technological function, but that they are most useful when they simply offer comfort rather than theological lectures. Clergy, however, may have their own difficulties dealing with death, including the expectations of others that clergy will naturally know how to handle death and dying. Too often this leads to defensive styles: ritualized religiosity, a businesslike manner, denial of death (Wood, 1976). The counseling role of the clergy may also be on the decline. Kalish and Reynolds (1976) found that younger people were much less likely than those over 60 to turn to religion or the clergy for comfort during bereavement.

The evidence on support for the bereaved is not clear-cut, however. Few of the widows in Lopata's (1979) study indicated receiving much support from professionals or agencies. A study of a sample of older persons found that 44 percent considered funerals "not very important" or "not important at all," and 78 percent felt funerals were "very much overpriced" (Wass et al., 1979). But Fulton (1976) notes that most people approve of traditional funerals and that such funerals may result in fewer adjustment problems. He also suggests that national funerals—John and Robert Kennedy, Martin Luther King—have fulfilled important social functions. Glick and associates (1974) found that widows were aware of who had attended funerals, and attendance *itself* was seen as a tribute as well as offering support and reaffirmation.

> He had a very large funeral and of course when you're young you have not only your own friends, but your family and your family's friends, and he had thought a great deal of many of the people who came. It was very dignified and very simple. It was the way he lived, in a very dignified and simple manner. This meant a lot to me, that so many people would pay him such a great tribute. It was a tremendous funeral procession and the church was packed. I think he would have been kind of proud to have known this. (Glick et al., 1974:116)

Nearly all the bereaved expressed gratitude to funeral directors for their comfort and support and for their professionalism, whereas clergy, interestingly, were seen as providing little personal solace or counsel.

The funeral will undoubtedly continue as a response to death, and some type of group ritual appears to be beneficial. But it also seems clear that many of the trappings of modern funerals, including cosmetic restoration of the body, are unnecessary. Kastenbaum and Aisenberg (1976) suggest that funerals should be less expensive and take more sensible physical approaches, focusing instead on the psychological and social needs of the survivors. Kastenbaum and Aisenberg also point out, however, that the problems of funerals are often simply reflections of a general lack of clear cultural norms to meet the needs of the bereaved.

EUTHANASIA AND THE RIGHT TO DIE

We have noted many times that the changing nature of death in modern societies has altered the ways we deal with it, in some cases creating problems for the dying and bereaved. Complex philosophical, social, and legal issues have also resulted, to a great extent from advances in medical technology that blur the distinction between life and death and create a mechanized atmosphere that threatens "death with dignity." These issues are not unique to aging but have a special relevance for the aged.

Concern over the quality and meaningfulness of human life is reflected in debates over issues such as abortion and genetic engineering. More relevant to this discussion is debate over the "right to die" and the right of others to help people die through *euthanasia,* sometimes called "mercy killing." Interest in this issue focused on the case of Karen Quinlan, who was hospitalized in April of 1975 with a diagnosis of drug-induced coma (Kastenbaum, 1977a). Suffering from severe and irreversible brain damage, she has never regained consciousness, and her breathing was maintained by a respirator. When physicians refused to remove her from the respirator, Karen Quinlan's parents asked the courts to name them legal guardians so that she could be allowed to die. The New Jersey Supreme Court ruled in their favor, stating that the respirator could be turned off if physicians agreed that there was no chance of her regaining consciousness. Fourteen months after lapsing into a coma, Karen Quinlan was removed from the respirator. At the time of this writing, Karen Quinlan is still alive in a nursing home and still in a coma.

This case illustrates some of the exceedingly complex medical, legal, social, and ethical issues surrounding the question of euthanasia. Under what conditions should people be "allowed" or "helped" to die, and who should make the decision? Kastenbaum (1977a) notes that "death with dignity" is an empty phrase in this case; the special poignancy arises from the suffering of those around Karen Quinlan. But her case is not unique; what is unique is that it surfaced to public attention.

Debate over euthanasia has a long history. In the first century A.D., the Roman philosopher Seneca stated:

> If I can choose between a death of torture and one that is simple and easy, why should I not select the latter?—Why should I endure the agonies of disease—when I can emancipate myself from all my torture?—I will not depart by death from disease as long as it may be healed and leaves my mind unimpaired—but if I know that I will suffer forever, I will depart, not through fear of pain itself, but because it prevents all for which I live. (Russell, 1975:54)

Some form of euthanasia has been advocated by such persons as Sir Thomas More, Francis Bacon, and Benjamin Franklin, and condemned by such others as St. Augustine and St. Thomas Aquinas (Mannes, 1973; Russell, 1975). Something of a social movement has arisen around euthanasia since the 1930s, when the Voluntary Euthanasia Legalization Society was formed in England, followed by the Euthanasia Society of America. The Euthanasia Education Council was founded in 1972 (Heffernan & Maynard, 1977). But attempts to legalize euthanasia have been defeated in Great Britain (in 1936, 1950, and 1969) and New York State (in 1947) and have languished in the legislative committees of a number of states for decades.

Euthanasia involves two issues: an appeal to mercy for the dying and the *right* of the dying to die (Bok, 1975). These issues revolve around three distinctly different types of patients: the terminally ill who are conscious, the irreversibly comatose (such as Karen Quinlan), and brain-damaged or severely debilitated patients with good chances for survival but at a low level of existence (severely deformed newborns, senile aged) (Crane, 1975).

Different meanings and types of patients make euthanasia a very tangled issue. In an attempt to bring some order to the discussion, Fletcher (1968) has defined four types of *elective death.* The first is *voluntary and direct,* where death is chosen and carried out by the patient, in effect, a form of suicide. Patients do have a right to refuse treatment, but family and staff may incur legal liabilities if they help someone commit suicide. Physicians may administer pain-relieving drugs that have the additional effect of hastening death, as causing death is not the primary motive in such cases, but it is not legally clear whether physicians have a duty to prevent suicide, given the nature of the doctor-patient relationship (Cantor, 1975; Meyers, 1975).

The second form of elective death is *voluntary and indirect,* where the patient, although no longer conscious, has granted discretion to others to cease "heroic" or "extraordinary" treatment. This type is embodied in the "Living Will," an example of which is shown in Figure 12.1. In 1977 California passed a "right to die" law, allowing physicians to disconnect life-support equipment when the patient has signed a Living Will. It must be signed at least 72 hours before the act, witnessed by two unrelated persons who are not included in the estate, and renewed every 5 years. Variations of this law now exist in several other states.

A third elective death is *indirect and involuntary,* where treatment is ceased and the patient is allowed to die, sometimes called *passive* or *negative* euthanasia. Such actions have a very uncertain legal status. Meyers (1975) and Cantor (1975) note that the special nature of the doctor-patient relationship probably imposes a duty to continue "ordinary" treatment, but that there are no clear legal or medical standards about what constitutes "extraordinary" treatment, or whether treatment must be continued in hopeless cases. Physicians may potentially be liable to prosecution for murder or manslaughter, although such cases are almost never prosecuted.

The fourth type of elective death is *direct and involuntary,* where an affirmative action, such as a lethal injection, is taken to end life although the patient is not capable of giving consent. This *active* or *positive* euthanasia is closest to the idea of mercy killing.

The moral distinction between passive euthanasia (allowing death) and active euthanasia (causing death) seems rather fuzzy, especially as causing death by withholding treatment may be more drawn out and painful than doing something to bring about death. But active euthanasia is a form of criminal homicide, as the law gives life a preeminent value, and neither good motives nor consent are legal defenses (Meyer, 1975; Cantor, 1975). However, few cases are prosecuted and juries are often unwilling to convict.

Many arguments have been made for and against the concept and practice of euthanasia (Behnke and Bok, 1975; Russell, 1975; Charmaz, 1980). Proponents emphasize compassion for the suffering of the dying and a concern for human

TO MY FAMILY, MY PHYSICIAN, MY CLERGYMAN, MY ATTORNEY:

If the time comes when I can no longer take part in decisions for my own future, let this statement stand as testament of my wishes:

If there is no reasonable expectation of my recovery from physical or mental disability, I, _____ , request that I be allowed to die and not be kept alive by artificial means or heroic measures. Death is as much a reality as birth, growth, maturity and old age—it is the one certainty. I do not fear death as much as I fear the indignity of deterioration, dependence, and hopeless pain. I ask that drugs be mercifully administered to me for terminal suffering even if they hasten the moment of death.

This request is made after careful consideration. Although this document is not legally binding, you who care for me will, I hope, feel morally bound to follow its mandates. I recognize that it places a heavy burden of responsibility upon you, and it is with the intention of sharing that responsibility and of mitigating any feelings of guilt that this statement is made.

Figure 12.1 Sample of a "Living Will." (*Source:* The above form is based on "A Living Will," developed by the Euthanasia Educational Council, 250 West 57th Street, New York, New York 10019.)

dignity and choice in achieving a "good death." They argue that life is not an *absolute* good, but its quality and meaningfulness should be considered.

An increasing number of vital functions can be maintained by mechanical respirators, artificial kidneys, cardiac stimulators and other ingenious devices. No one will doubt their importance when used for an acutely ill patient, who may thereby survive a crisis and return to reasonable health. Nevertheless, the use of such mechanical aids to prolong a very limited form of life in an incurably ill person remains debatable. If such measures can be continued to bring some useful, enjoyable life, most would wish to use them. If they can only maintain a truncated semblance of life, as in a permanently unconscious being, there is little justification. They can easily cause distress to the living—the fully living. (Hinton, 1972:141)

Treatment in such cases really prolongs dying, not living, and remote chances for recovery are not felt to justify prolonged suffering. Proponents of euthanasia typically point out that most religious teachings do not require maintenance of life as a supreme obligation. Pope Pius XII, for example, stated in 1957 that termination of extraordinary measures in certain circumstances and relief of pain with drugs that also hasten death were acceptable. It is also argued that physicians are not obligated to continue heroic measures in hopeless cases. Fletcher (1968), for example, refers to the "vitalistic error," which places biological life above all other considerations.

Opponents of euthanasia have focused on a number of issues. One argument is that medical diagnosis and prognosis are not infallible and in some "hopeless" cases the patients have survived to lead meaningful lives. The possibility of new medical discoveries is also held out. Patients are often unable to communicate their own feelings about whether their lives are worth saving, and decisions about newborns are particularly wrenching. There is the additional fear that euthanasia will be based not on the best interests of the *patient,* but on such considerations as the emotional or financial burden for others, the need for organs to transplant, or the "social worth" of the patient. Sudnow (1967) cites cases of a child and an elderly person who entered an emergency room with virtually identical symptoms; the elderly person was almost immediately pronounced dead, whereas the child received strenuous and prolonged treatment from a large team of professionals. Even when consciously made, there is some question about whether patient requests for euthanasia are truly voluntary or a product of temporary pain and depression, lack of full awareness about their condition, or concern about being a burden to others. From this perspective, the hospice seems an alternative approach to achieving "death with dignity."

Probably the most basic objection raised to euthanasia is that it cheapens life and may be too tempting a solution for those considered too burdensome or unproductive by society; that it will dull our sensitivities to the helpless and "defective." In other words, where will we draw the line on who is *worth* saving? Concern is raised that euthanasia, or even the concept of a natural death, may lead us to prematurely reject the will to live of the "useless" elderly and become tantamount to a form of "gerontocide" (Kastenbaum & Aisenberg, 1976).

Decisions concerning euthanasia have largely been confined to physicians, with relatively little visibility. The traditional stress on saving lives as an absolute medical ethic seems to allow little room for positive definitions of death, but this view conflicts with the other task of the physician—to alleviate suffering. Indeed, despite its uncertain legal status, passive euthanasia appears to be a widely accepted part of medical practice. Williams (1973) found that 87 percent of a sample of physicians approved of passive euthanasia in principle, and *81 percent had practiced it.* Duff and Campbell (1973) found, in a study of 299 consecutive deaths in a special-care nursery, that 43 (14 percent) involved withholding of treatment when there was a hopeless prognosis for "meaningful life," as with multiple deformities. They noted that this is accepted medical practice, although it receives little publicity.

In a study of attitudes among a national sample of physicians, Crane found ample evidence that nonmedical, social criteria—notably, expected quality of life—were used in determining how actively to treat patients.

Evidence from the present study suggests that physicians respond to the chronically ill or terminally ill patient not simply in terms of physiological definitions of illness but also in terms of the extent to which he is capable of interacting with others. The treatable patient is one who can interact or who has the potential to interact in a meaningful way with others in his environment. (1975:61)

The emphasis was on social capacity rather than social *value,* and the priority for active treatment was: (1) salvageable with physical damage, (2) salvageable with mental damage and unsalvageable with physical damage, and (3) unsalvageable with mental damage. Physicians were highly critical of "unnecessary" resuscitations, and a study of hospital records showed that patients with brain damage were less likely to be resuscitated. Under various conditions, decisions about treatment were affected by such other nonmedical criteria as patient attitudes, financial burdens, and age. For example, hospital records indicated that 73 percent of the deaths involving patients 10 to 39 years of age involved resuscitation attempts, compared with only 33 percent for those 80 and over.

These studies all indicate that physicians consider expected quality of life in deciding whether to continue treatment. Crane (1975) found, however, that physicians were generally reluctant to withdraw all treatment on their own initiative. There was much less acceptance of positive euthanasia, reflecting a strong norm against direct killing. In the study referred to earlier, Williams (1973) found that only 18 percent of a sample of physicians approved of positive euthanasia.

The public appears to be moving toward greater acceptance of the concept of euthanasia. In 1950, 1973, and 1977 national samples were asked: "When a person has a disease that cannot be cured, do you think doctors should be allowed by law to end the patient's life by some painless means if the patient and his family request it?" Acceptance of this voluntary elective death was 36 percent in 1950, 53 percent in 1973, and 63 percent in 1977 (Ostheimer & Ritt, 1976; Ward, 1980). As are physicians, the public is more accepting of passive than active euthanasia: a 1973 Harris poll found that 62 percent thought physicians should "let him die," but only 37 percent agreed that they should "put him out of his misery" (Ostheimer & Ritt, 1976).

Clergy also exhibit acceptance of the concept of euthanasia. In one study of Catholic and Protestant clergy, 60 percent approved of passive euthanasia, reflecting a consensus that there is no moral obligation to employ "extraordinary" treatment (Nagi et al., 1977). But only 12 percent approved of active euthanasia, and Catholic clergy were less accepting of both active and passive euthanasia.

Issues surrounding euthanasia may have particular poignancy for the aged. We have already seen that older people are less fearful and anxious about death. Having reached the end of a natural life span, many older people may find the dying process, with its attendant possibilities of pain, dwindling personal competence, and isolation, more fearful than death itself. The following comments of an 88-year-old psychologist, who has himself researched the aging experience, are illustrative:

At the age of 88, crippled by rheumatism, plagued by insomnia, of failing vision, must I wait out a "natural" death—perhaps becoming mindless, incontinent, locked in a back ward of a nursing "home"? Do I have any rights as to the time and nature of my dying? (Pressey, 1977:296)

One study of older persons found that only 11 percent wanted all possible means, including transplants and kidney machines, to be used to keep them alive (Wass et al., 1979).

Research indicates, however, that older people are less likely to agree than younger people that patients should be allowed to die, even if they or their families request it (Kalish & Reynolds, 1976; Ostheimer & Ritt, 1976; Haug, 1978; Ward, 1980). Table 12.2, for example, indicates a steady decline with age in acceptance of voluntary euthanasia. This seems to partly reflect a more general stance about patient-physician interaction. Haug (1978) found that the best predictor of favorable attitudes toward elective death was the general belief that people have a right to make their own health decisions without relying on a physician's advice. Such beliefs may well reflect cohort differences in the godlike qualities attributed to physicians.

Indeed, whereas age differences in general attitudes about death appear to reflect aging effects, age differences in attitudes toward euthanasia appear to reflect cohort effects. Ward (1980) found that less acceptance of euthanasia was attributable to less education and greater religiosity among older cohorts. On the other hand, greater acceptance of euthanasia was exhibited by older people with low income, low self-rated health, and low life satisfaction. As there is greater perceived closeness to death in old age, making euthanasia a less abstract and more salient *personal* issue, the acceptability of euthanasia appears to become linked to the quality of one's own life.

There are many unresolved issues surrounding elective death and euthanasia. How much suffering legitimates euthanasia? Must the patient be terminal, and if so, how close to death? The problems are less severe when the individual is conscious and competent to make his or her own decisions, although every care should be taken to insure that the decision is not based on emotional or financial burdens to others, the person is fully informed and provided with options, and elective death is not the only alternative to dehumanized suffering. The most difficult decisions involve those who have no voice: deformed newborns, the senile aged, and the comatose. And who makes those decisions? Duff and Campbell (1973) suggest that it is difficult for families to understand what faces them in such situations, making it difficult to grant truly "informed consent" for either

Table 12.2   AGE DIFFERENCES IN A NATIONAL SAMPLE IN ACCEPTANCE OF EUTHANASIA[a]

	Age				
	18–29	30–44	45–59	60–69	70+
Agree	73%	61%	60%	58%	49%
Disagree	27%	39%	40%	42%	51%
	100%	100%	100%	100%	100%
Number of respondents	354	418	372	175	128

[a]"When a person has a disease that cannot be cured, do you think doctors should be allowed by law to end the patient's life by some painless means if the patient and his family request it?"

Source: Russell Ward, "Age and Acceptance of Euthanasia," *Journal of Gerontology* 35 (1980), p. 424. Reprinted by permission.

giving or withholding treatment. But Duff and Campbell also suggest that it is dangerous to go beyond family members and staff who are most familiar with a particular situation.

Decisions must inevitably be based on the individual case. There is, however, also a need to more generally define and limit the criteria to be used in supporting or ending lives. Legislators are naturally reluctant to take a firm stand on as complicated a moral issue as euthanasia; but legislation could be directed toward defining the situations in which it might be permissible and procedures for determining and carrying out actions, and could provide legal protection for the persons involved, especially patients and physicians.

The intrusion of social criteria into medical decision making is in part a function of the fact that *resources are limited*—we cannot do everything for everyone. The unfortunate truth is that the huge expenses incurred in keeping some people alive takes resources away from such things as medical research and preventive medicine and may indirectly contribute to the death of others (Fuchs, 1974). This problem is well illustrated in the excruciating decisions involved in organ transplants (Fox & Swazey, 1974). Organs for transplant are scarce. How do we decide who receives a heart or a kidney, and what are our priorities? Do we spend money on organ transplants and kidney dialysis to benefit a relative few, or consign these people to death and spend our health resources on prevention and outreach? How many visiting nurses are not funded for the sake of one heart transplant? These life-and-death issues, including but not limited to elective death and euthanasia, are exceedingly difficult, and in some ways distasteful, but they cannot be ignored.

SUMMARY

The "mortality revolution" accompanying modernization has brought increased life expectancy and shifts in the major causes of death, and death is increasingly confined to the aged. The typical location of death has also shifted from home to institutions. These changes affect the social structure. High-mortality societies are characterized by stress on the extended family, reduced importance of children, high fertility, and an emphasis on religion. Modern people are more insulated from death, as the aged die in special institutions. There is less need for elaborate cultural rituals, and funerals are criticized as being irrelevant. But the bureaucratization and privatization of death may have made it more disruptive for individuals.

There are many meanings for death, and imagery and rituals surrounding death in Western societies have changed over the centuries. Cultural meanings are reflected in individual values and attitudes. In some ways we deny death, attempting to achieve some magical or symbolic feeling of immortality. Many fears may be attached to death, although the greatest concerns appear to be the grief of others, the pain of dying, and the ending of projects and experiences. Other evidence suggests a relative acceptance of death. Probably both denial and acceptance exist, reflecting the naturalness of death and an inability to truly comprehend our own nonexistence.

Death conceptions change over the life cycle. Children only gradually perceive the finality and inevitability of death, although even very young children have perceptions of death. Middle age is often a time of personally relevant deaths which may heighten death anxiety, and awareness of finitude is considered a key feature of the psychology of old age. This may trigger a life review, seeking to make sense of one's life. The aged think more about death, but their attitudes appear to be more accepting than those of younger people. They also appear less likely to reorganize their lives in the face of death. Legitimation of biography, the perceived fairness of death in old age, problems associated with aging, fear of dependency, and processes of socialization for death may all contribute to greater acceptance of death in later life.

The dying often face withdrawal by others, sometimes amounting to "social death." Hospitals and other "dying institutions" seek to minimize the disruptiveness of death through isolation and routinization, which is reflected in staff predictions of the dying trajectory. Medical staff receive little preparation for caring for the dying, and their responses may reflect their own fears and insecurities. Death implies failure and may be dealt with by avoidance or detachment. Staff need emotional support in the face of possible "death saturation." There is evidence, however, that the deaths of older people are experienced as less tragic and disruptive.

The dying often have some awareness of their condition, but may engage in mutual pretense to protect others. Unfortunately, because it is difficult to break through this shared denial, the social and emotional needs of the dying are too often unmet. The dying tend to exhibit many reactions—anxiety, depression, anger—but they are not typically overwhelmed by fear. There do not appear to be universal stages to the dying process, and, although many achieve acceptance, there are a variety of reactions to impending death.

In caring for the dying it must be recognized that the needs of the terminally ill are in many ways not unique. In particular, a dying individual needs to maintain some control over the dying process. Those who care for the dying should strive for an "appropriate death." sensitive to the needs and preferences of the individual. This may be difficult to achieve in institutions such as hospitals and nursing homes, where dying is a managed process. This is one reason for the emergence of the hospice model, emphasizing personal dignity, autonomy, and control of pain. Hospices take many forms, from counseling and home care to inpatient facilities. Hospice principles can also be applied to more traditional settings such as nursing homes.

The bereaved also have important needs that must be met. There are many complex reactions to bereavement, and adjustment problems may continue for a year or more following the loss. Bereavement appears to be much more difficult when death is sudden or unexpected. The sociocultural context can either facilitate or inhibit successful adjustment. The "death system" is designed to assist both society and the individual. It has been argued that the bereaved receive little support from funerals and "grief specialists" in modern societies, however, making "grief work" more difficult. But most people seem to approve of traditional funerals, and some type of ceremony appears to be beneficial to the bereaved.

Changes in the nature and location of death, and in medical technology for "combating" death, have created new issues and given increased relevance to a concern over "death with dignity." These issues are reflected in debates about elective death and euthanasia. Proponents of euthanasia stress relief of suffering, human dignity, and the importance of quality of life. Opponents cite the uncertainty of medical knowledge and the danger of cheapening life. Passive euthanasia has been an accepted part of medical practice for some time, and the public is increasingly supportive. But active euthanasia has little support among physicians or lay persons. Despite more accepting general attitudes toward death, older people are less accepting of euthanasia. This reflects less education and greater religiosity of current older cohorts.

chapter 13

The Future of the Aging Experience

We have seen many examples of the complexity of the aging experience for those undergoing it and for those who wish to study it. We need to avoid seemingly simple explanations and assessments of the nature of aging and of the aged. Such issues as retirement, widowhood, and political activism require a certain tolerance of ambiguity on the part of social gerontologists. Rather than encountering a "typical old person," we find many different old persons of different ages, generations, sexes, and races. Instead of either "the golden years" or "gloom and misfortune," we find that aging entails a complicated mix of pleasure and pain. Recognition of this variability and complexity is absolutely essential to an accurate portrayal of the aging experience. This is true if our goal is the scientific study of aging and its effects or to develop expectations of what our own old age will be like.

The necessity of an accurate portrayal of the aging experience leads us to a consideration of what aging will be like in the future. We have seen that the nature of aging is shaped in important ways by the context within which it occurs. To the extent that the future world differs from present and past worlds, the aging experience will also be different. In addition, the aged of the future will literally be different people with different historical and cohort backgrounds. Before proceeding to the future, however, let us return briefly to some key concepts and themes of this book.

THE NATURE OF AGE DIFFERENCES

There has never been any doubt that age differences exist in behaviors, attitudes, values, and other personal characteristics, although we should be wary of exaggerating those differences. Age differences reflect aging effects, cohort effects, period effects, and their complex interactions.

As individuals move through the life cycle they encounter events and changes in social situations as well as the biological effects of aging. Thus it may be true that political attitudes, such as conservatism or alienation, are affected by age, as age determines other positions and needs. Similarly, length of commitment to various roles, including work career and marriage roles, is likely to affect attitudes and behaviors concerning those roles. Other studies suggest that perceived closeness to death has psychological consequences. These aging effects may be either intrinsic, giving them a certain universality and inevitability, or reactive, meaning that they are shaped by their context. It appears, for example, that disengagement by the elderly may be a response to their position in modern societies.

Individuals and the cohorts they comprise also move through history, experiencing broader events and social changes that affect the quality and rhythm of the life cycle. As cohorts vary in work experiences, socialization regarding family and religion, or experiences with political activism, to name but a few examples, age differences will arise. Historical events have complex effects. Many cohorts may react differently to the same historical events because of their different positions in the life cycle, or there may be variations in response within a single cohort.

Intrinsic aging effects lend continuity to the aging experience. But reactive aging effects and cohort effects imply that aging may be quite different in the future as new cohorts of older people encounter new social contexts for aging. Thus general social change creates new problems and issues for aging individuals.

CONCEPTUAL FRAMEWORKS

The most basic theme of this book is that the nature and meaning of the aging experience depends on the social context in which it occurs. This is underlined in the three conceptual frameworks introduced in Chapter 1: age stratification, symbolic interactionism, and the life course perspective.

Societies structure the positions and roles of individuals according to their age, thereby creating a variety of age differences and age inequalities. Allocation according to age occurs formally and informally and is evident in the timing of marriage and family decisions, work career events, education, and so on. A model of age stratification helps us understand cross-cultural differences in the relative position of age groups and suggests the possibility of age conflict over the allocation of roles and their associated rewards. This model also helps us understand the types of developmental issues that may arise as people age and the difficulties they may encounter in transferring into expected old-age roles.

The age stratification system for any society is neither unchanging nor simple, however. As changes occur in the encompassing social structure, age stratification will also be modified, and with it the nature of the aging experience. Nor does the age stratification system exist in isolation. Roles are stratified according to criteria other than age, including sex, race, and social class. Although age stratification implies that age has a leveling effect, it is clear that the aging experience differs for men and women, blacks and whites, middle class and working class.

Symbolic interactionism, however, reminds us that individuals are also conscious actors in their worlds, who behave and adapt to situations and events on the basis of their own perceptions and meanings for these situations and events, which arise from social interactions with others. The symbolic interactionist perspective has important implications for the study of aging. Most basically, it means that the aging experience is shaped by the *meanings* individuals attach to old age: their expectations, stereotypes, fears, desires. This provides a link to the larger culture and age stratification, as these meanings define old age in a particular society. The age stratification of roles and experiences shapes individuals' perceptions of the world, but each individual also encounters a unique blend of experiences and interactions, which further shape the meanings of aging and old age. This is one reason for variation in the aging experience by sex, race, ethnicity, social class, religion, and place of residence. In order to truly understand the aging experience, we must be able to take the point of view of the person who is aging. We have long since passed the point where we can accept simple conclusions about the nature of aging in any society.

The importance of a symbolic interactionist perspective also becomes apparent when we recognize the tremendous potential for change in the social and symbolic worlds of the aging. Role losses, residential mobility, health problems, and other age-related changes pull the elderly from familiar groups. They are alienated from past worlds and identities and at the same time granted the potential for new worlds and new identities, which creates the possibility of satisfying personal change and growth, but also may result in stress, marginality, and unhappiness.

The complexity and variability of the aging experience is captured in the life course perspective. On the one hand, individuals age according to their own personal histories and desires for continuity. On the other hand, the life course is structured by social forces and historical changes. This reminds us that old age cannot be understood in isolation from earlier parts of the life course of individuals. It also reminds us that a search for "universals" in the aging experience is likely to be fruitless. Age itself tells us very little about a person. The biological, psychological, and social aspects of aging exhibit "plasticity;" they are not fixed, inevitable, or unchangeable. This should lead us to expect a very different aging experience in the future.

AGING IN THE FUTURE

Social forecasting, based on extrapolation from current trends, is always a risky business because we cannot be sure that such trends will not be stopped or accelerated by unforeseen future events. Even more difficult are attempts to predict major alterations in the structure of society in 50 or 100 years. Nevertheless, forecasting must take place if we are to rationally and self-consciously set policies affecting future generations. Decisions made now, however gropingly, will affect the world of the future, and the failure to make decisions, to set long-term policies, is itself a decision, probably carrying even greater risks.

Forecasting the future may also help us to shape and choose from alternative futures. The alternatives we are presented with often seem highly conflicting.

Some futurists paint a glowing portrait of Utopia with glistening new technologies and an end to poverty and scarcity. An optimistic belief in the inevitability of progress has declined in recent years, however, as each day seems to heighten our awareness of a new crisis. Some paint a doomsday portrait of the future, in which energy and food sources are depleted and rich and poor nations are locked in mortal struggle.

The inevitability of progress is suspect, but so is the inevitability of global chaos. Beyond that, all predictions are speculative and debatable. Perhaps the best we can do is assess the "normal, expectable future" (Neugarten, 1975b), and on that basis attempt to shape the future in beneficial ways.

Pampel (1981) notes that changes in the position of older people may arise because of either "compositional" change, involving cohort replacement, or "processual" change, involving environmental and period changes. Thus, to understand something of aging in the future, we must look at those who will be old and the social context in which they will age.

The Future Aged

The sheer size of the future older population, in number and proportion, will certainly rise in the future. This trend will be most evident between 2010 and 2020, when most members of the post-World War II "baby boom" enter old age.

But the dimensions of this population aging are uncertain because of the indeterminacy of future fertility and mortality rates. The social problems created by rapid growth of the older population may subside after about 2020 if low fertility, limited impact of further mortality changes, and low levels of immigration bring little additional growth in the relative size of the older population (Uhlenberg, 1977). The financing of Social Security, for example, may stabilize by about 2050 with the passing of the baby-boom cohort. Some demographers foresee continuing low fertility; however, others forecast a rise, and perhaps a cycle of booms and busts in the birth rate (Treas, 1981). Such a fertility "roller coaster" would make planning difficult because fertility affects the future size of the old-age dependency ratio. Treas (1981), for example, projects the following population characteristics in 2050 under different fertility conditions: (1) if fertility is 1.7 births per female, 22.6 percent of the population will be aged 65 and over with an old-age dependency ratio of 38.8; (2) if fertility is 2.1, the comparable figures will be 17.6 percent and 30.2; (3) if fertility rises to 2.7, the figures will be 12.3 percent and 22.0.

Even more dramatic differences will be related to changes in mortality and life expectancy. Longevity is extended in two ways (Hayflick, 1977; Gordon, 1979; Fries & Crapo, 1981). The first is through the reduction or elimination of major causes of death, so-called "curve squaring" (referring to the survival curve that was illustrated in Figure 2.1). As we noted in Chapter 2, this reduction in "premature death" accounts for the increased life expectancy in modern societies. Medical advances and changing life-styles may reduce deaths due to heart disease or cancer as well as postpone death and invalidism until ages closer to the limit of the life span. Such changes could yield significant increases in life expectancy. One scenario of curve-squaring technological advances presented by Gordon

(1979) projects an older population of 74 million older persons (23 percent of the population) and a life expectancy of 86 years in 2025, compared with 46 million older persons (14 percent of the population) without the technological advances. Although it is risky to predict major advances in disease elimination, it was the consensus of a panel of specialists in biological and medical aspects of aging that life expectancy would increase by 5 to 10 years by the year 2000, primarily through advances in disease control (Neugarten & Havighurst, 1977).

The second mechanism for extending longevity is alteration of the biological "clock" that results in physiological decline and increased vulnerability to disease as organisms age. The upper limit of the human life span has apparently not changed over the course of recorded history, although increasing numbers survive toward this upper limit. The panel of experts mentioned above could reach no consensus that the "essential mechanisms of the biology of aging" were likely to be well understood by the year 2000, but a sizable group did consider this likely (Neugarten and Havighurst, 1977). It is possible that the future will bring extensions to the life span itself, in addition to greater average life expectancy. The dramatic consequences of such a breakthrough are illustrated by the hypothetical survival curves in Figure 13.1.

It is not entirely clear whether dramatic increases in longevity, resulting in life expectancy of 90, 100, or 110 years, should be welcomed or avoided. It may mean a much longer period of healthy and rigorous life with much shorter periods of reduced functioning before death. But it may also mean keeping mar-

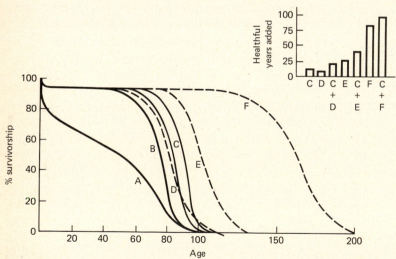

Figure 13.1 Past, present, and potential future human survivorship curves: (A) ancient times to early nineteenth century, (B) present survivorship curve, (C) range of curves to be expected if the "major killers" were conquered (circulatory and neoplastic diseases), (D) survivorship that would derive from an 8–12 percent decrement in rate of aging, (E) hypothetical survivorship produced by a 20–30 percent decrease in rate of aging, (F) longer-range hypothetical survivorship potentially derivable from a combination of factors in curves D and E plus genetic intervention. (*Source:* Bernard Strehler, "Implications of Aging Research for Society," *Federation Proceedings* 34 (1975), p. 7, © by the Federation of American Societies for Experimental Biology. Reprinted by permission.)

ginally functional individuals alive for extended periods of time, constituting a growing burden on society. In either case, society and its institutions will face some critical issues. This is a topic we will return to shortly.

Although the precise dimensions of future aging are difficult to predict, it is nonetheless clear that the size and proportion of the older population will continue to increase as part of a worldwide phenomenon. The more developed countries will continue to have proportionately older populations, but similar trends will be evident in less developed countries.

A number of predictions can be made about the characteristics of future older cohorts (e.g., see Neugarten, 1975a; Palmore, 1976). They will be better educated, with higher occupational status and income than present older people. Although mortality rates are likely to show only slow declines, with no dramatic changes in life expectancy, older people in the future will probably be in better health, assuming there will be more effective forms of public-health and health-care systems. We saw in Chapter 3 that recent decades have seen improvement in the relative status of older people, and such trends are likely to continue.

Cohort change may mean that some of the difficulties now associated with aging will decline. For example, the proportion of the aged who are foreign-born or rural-born has been declining rapidly (Uhlenberg, 1977). Thus older cohorts of the future are much less likely to encounter the additional culture shock of moving from one society to another or from rural to urban residence. The effects of cohort succession may be particularly evident for certain subgroups of the older population. Future cohorts of older women, for example, will have experienced quite different roles and expectations during their lives, so that the aging experience for women may be quite different. Uhlenberg (1977) also notes that in the future, successive cohorts of the aged will be more similar to each other than they presently are, so that we can direct our attention to developing more *stable* mechanisms for enhancing the quality of their lives.

These changes in the status of older people suggest some possible changes in the activities and life-styles of future aged. They indicate a lessening of the minority-group status of the aged as the extent of age differences declines. Perhaps this also means that age stratification will become less important as a differentiating principle in future societies. More affluent older people, faced with increased free time, will engage in a greater variety of leisure life-styles, perhaps with greater emphasis on service roles (Havighurst, 1975). Their higher status, combined with a greater history of activism, have led many to expect greater political awareness and activism by future older cohorts. Neugarten (1975b) suggests this is most likely for the young-old (ages 55 to 75), who are retiring earlier, are relatively healthy and affluent, and seek a wider range of options for community involvement.

This reminds us that the age structure of a population and the characteristics of the older people also have consequences for the society itself. The most obvious of these concerns the cost of services for increasing numbers of the aged. The sheer size of the older population and growth in the old-age dependency ratio will increase the costs of pensions, health care, housing, and other programs for older people. Greater political sophistication and expectations of government assistance among future cohorts of older people may heighten the demands placed on government. Lowy (1980) also notes that growth is likely to be greatest for subgroups of the older population that are most needy: women, the old-old (aged 75 and above), and nonwhite aged. But there is no reason to expect that an older population will necessarily create vast crises in financing services. There will be declining pressure to support children and adolescents, as their share of the population declines. In the next century, the *old-age* dependency ratio will continue to rise, but the *overall* dependency ratio will decline. In addition, because future older people are likely to be more affluent and healthy, they may have less need for services.

The effects of an aging population on society extend beyond the cost of services, particularly if life expectancy increases by another 20 years or more. Strehler (1975) suggests that the presence of proportionately fewer young adults will result in less social upheaval and a greater sense of continuity in society. He notes, however, that society needs to avoid smothering the innovativeness of youth because tenure and seniority may lead to a monopolization of power by older persons. Population aging could potentially result in age conflict and antagonism toward the aged because of their power and seniority and the growing cost of programs directed at them (Neugarten, 1972).

Extension of the life span might disrupt the equilibrium of society and its institutions (such as work and family), with potentially far-reaching implications (Neugarten, 1972; Zeckhauser, 1974; Gordon, 1979). To take but one example, retirement at 60 or 65 would seem anachronistic if life expectancy is 100 years and vigorous health is maintained until 90. Work, leisure, and education would need to be integrated throughout the life cycle to meet individual and societal needs. Rather than the model of a single lifelong career, we may see multiple and successive careers as well as greater use of job sharing and part-time work.

This recognition of the effects of aging on society combines with a recognition of the importance of the social context in shaping the aging experience and leads us to think about the nature of society in the future.

The Postindustrial Society

Bell (1973) has presented a view of the future of modern societies he refers to as the *postindustrial society.* Bell predicts a shift from a goods-producing to a service economy, with rising preeminence of the professional and technical occupational classes. The professional and technical class is expected to be the largest occupational group in the United States by the year 2000. They will be working in an economy based on services and information, continuing the recent tremendous growth in government employment. Modern societies are characterized by enormously rapid change, altering the complexity and scale of the problems that confront us. Bell expects that those who control knowledge will be the new elites of the postindustrial society. Scientists will play enhanced roles as advisers and advocates within an increasingly centralized system of decision making and policy formulation. Policy making will increasingly stress logical, rational, and technical assessment of choices and their consequences.

Some of Bell's ideas are relevant to the concerns of this book. Dowd (1980), for example, suggests that the technocracy of postindustrial society will further reduce the control that the aged and other relatively powerless groups have over their own lives. Similarly, Karp and Yoels (1982) argue that the emerging postindustrial society has brought the intrusion of professionals into all parts of the life cycle—birth, puberty, midlife, old age, and death. We are taught to rely on "experts" to achieve "natural" childbirth, resolution of the "midlife crisis," and finally a "good" death. The individual has been removed from control over his or her own life transitions. Aging itself, Karp and Yoels argue, has come to be viewed as a social problem.

Two aspects of postindustrial society have particular relevance for the future of the aging experience. The first concerns the values of postindustrial society and their effects on the nature of the life cycle and the status of older people. The second concerns the nature of policy making and the setting of goals and priorities in the postindustrial society.

One reason suggested for the apparent decline in status for the aged in modern industrial societies concerns the dominant values of such societies (achievement, productivity, independence) and the inability of the elderly to fulfill these values in the roles available to them. Some analysts of the postindustrial society have suggested, however, that there will be a greater questioning of the key values of industrial society, particularly the work ethic and the emphasis on economic growth. Bell (1973) points to a growing contradiction between the social structure with its emphasis on rationalization, progress, and mastery of nature, and the culture with its growing emphasis on consumption and the quality of life. Values of frugality, dedication to work, and delayed gratification are being challenged by emerging cultural values of personal liberation and the acting out of impulses and desires. It is argued that postindustrial society will see greater emphasis on the quality and meaning of life, human relationships, and a cultivation of satisfying social experiences (Rapoport & Rapoport, 1975). Trist (1976) suggests that the following shifts in cultural values will occur in postindustrial society: from achievement to self-actualization, from self-control to self-expression, from independence to interdependence, and from endurance of distress to capacity for joy.

Such value shifts may already be underway. There appears to be increased questioning of traditional forms of work, education, and family and sex roles, as in the loss of the central importance of work in the lives of many people, making retirement and leisure less of an identity crisis than many thought they would be. If these value shifts do occur, they have important implications for the future of the aging experience. The postindustrial society may offer positive rewards for disengagement for young and old as an emphasis on leisure and self-actualization grows stronger. Thus, as values of achievement and independence become less important, the relative status of the aged should improve. Indeed, as the group with the greatest freedom of time and action, future older people, particularly the young-old, may be best able to take advantage of an emerging emphasis on self-expression and self-actualization.

The aged—indeed, all of us—could benefit from a "loosening up" of life (Butler, 1975), so that we are no longer locked into lifelong careers by decisions made early in life. In the postindustrial society we may see new, more flexible approaches to the life course. New concepts of work may emerge that include redistribution of the workweek, opportunities for periodic sabbaticals, and career change at all occupational levels (Neugarten, 1975b; Butler, 1975). Butler also suggests that we may see institutionalization of the concept of *education for life* throughout the life cycle. Although these changes point to identity crises throughout the life cycle because major decisions and changes are no longer confined to adolescence and old age, Butler suggests that this is healthy, unfreezing roles and allowing us to rebel against aspects of our lives that no longer fit. These changes would also bring a blurring of age distinctions. As change is built into all parts of the life course, the aging in particular will be faced with less discontinuity compared with other groups. As was true of the rising relative status of the aged in the future, this means that age stratification assumes less importance and the aged become less distinct from other age groups.

Many of the current concepts and debates within social gerontology center on discontinuity and failure of socialization for the "roleless role" of old age. Changes in cultural values and the flexibility of life-styles in postindustrial society would force us to rethink many of our approaches to the problems of aging. And current older people may represent a unique sociological group. After all, a life *expectancy* of 80 years is a comparatively new phenomenon. Shanas (1975) points out that recent cohorts of older people have, in a sense, been pioneers in the unexplored territory of widespread advanced age. They have perhaps failed to make intelligent use of extended life expectancy, still patterning their life careers (work, education, family, leisure) on the basis of decisions made in the teens and twenties.

> One would think that a man who had little chance of living beyond thirty-five would want to cram all the important stages of his life into a brief period. Conversely, one might expect that if given twice the time in which to live out his life cycle, an individual might plan and space out the major events in his life, such as education, marriage, birth of his children, beginning of his work career, and so on—to gain the optimal advantage of all this additional time. But, in reality, little intelligent use is being made of the extension of life expectancy in terms of the spacing of key events in the life cycle. (Browning, 1969:22)

We are now encountering cohorts of people who expect to live to an advanced age and who may have a greater sensitivity to the life cycle and the nature of aging. Rising interest in courses in social gerontology itself suggests that the problems of socialization to old age may be less pronounced in the future as people prepare their life-styles for an expanded life course.

Flexible life-styles and age sensitivity are not inevitable, however. Current trends represent only a very tentative beginning. These visions of postindustrial culture imply major restructuring and redirection of social institutions as well as of individual character and motivation. Their realization requires opportunities provided by the social structure in the form of flexible work arrangements, encouragement of life-cycle education, and expansion of alternative community roles. If these opportunities lag behind shifts in cultural values, as Bell (1973) implies they currently do, dislocations and dissatisfaction will emerge throughout the life cycle. And our options and resources in the future will also necessarily be constrained. Heilbroner (1974) has argued that our mounting environmental and energy problems create a necessity to limit growth, rather than optimistically seeking as much economic and technological progress as possible. This may prove costly for life-style and the quality of life. Bell (1973) agrees that future growth may have to be limited, as we increasingly question our ability to master nature. Limited resources will make relative scarcity and the relative costs of alternative policies critical political issues in the postindustrial society. This suggests that options for loosening up life may not always be available and leads us to a consideration of policymaking in the future.

The future postindustrial society will be faced with even more rapid change and complex issues than now. The diffusion of innovations throughout the society and increasing interdependency of all segments of society alter the *scale* of policy issues. Few issues are still local, whether concerning the economy, crime, the environment, or energy, and decentralized political structures are increasingly inadequate for confronting these issues. Bell (1973) argues that problems are increasingly *communal* rather than individual or interest group concerns. In addition, decisions made about one aspect of society, such as the economy, have complex effects on other aspects, such as the environment.

All of these trends argue for greater societal guidance based on technical knowledge and analysis to outline constraints, detail procedures, and assess the consequences of choices (Bell, 1973; Lakoff, 1976). For example, Bell notes the increased reliance on such techniques as systems analysis and cost effectiveness. He argues that the government will play an increased role in setting policy, based on centralized, rational planning and conscious definition of goals and priorities. There will be less emphasis on government's role as simply the arbiter among competing interest groups, and less reliance on the private, unregulated market.

If this view of the future is correct, it bodes well for the elderly. Those of us who are "scientific types" place great value on rationality and are always frustrated by the failure of policymakers to pursue carefully analyzed objectives. Programs for the aged have consistently suffered from fragmentation and lack of long-term objectives. Centralized policy, informed by technical knowledge, implies greater comprehensiveness and accuracy in meeting the needs of older people. Lakoff (1976) also notes the rise in collectivist ideologies—socialism or social liberalism—in which the state plays a greater role in insuring social justice for disadvantaged groups, including the aged.

And yet doubts linger. Can the future really be so promisingly rational? This question arose in an exchange between Peterson and associates (1976) and Cohen (1976). The former foresee a shift in political philosophy in postindustrial society, toward more liberal policies, protection of individual rights, and improvement in the quality of life and social justice. They expect a clear national policy for aging to be developed. Cohen, however, suggests that existing power relationships and the national style of piecemeal policy formulation are not easily changed and there is little evidence that future policies will be more comprehensive or coordinated. Indeed, he argues that we already have a national policy on aging, embodied in Title I of the Older Americans Act of 1965, but it has never been implemented. Finally, it must be noted that we presently seem to be in a period of reduced federal involvement in generating and supporting policies to address needs at the national level.

We are faced therefore with alternative futures: one of rational, comprehensive policies or one of more interest-group competition and "irrationality" in response to problems. A mixture of the two futures is likely to be found in post-industrial society. Policies must increasingly be centralized, with greater long-term planning informed by available knowledge, if society is to avoid chaos. But the world can never be this rational and conflicts will inevitably arise. Scientists and technicians may play expanded roles, but their power and control will remain limited and incomplete. Interest groups will still compete for resources in the political arena, and the aged are likely to continue to be disadvantaged in this competition. Although they may be more activist on their own behalf in the future, other groups will also make demands on the system. Resources are always limited, and will perhaps be especially so in the future, and we are already encountering a fiscal crisis in the ability of government to meet social needs. One must question the extent of continuing commitment to meeting the needs of the elderly, as there is a growing contradiction between expanding demand for governmental services and rising rebellion over the costs and centralized control associated with those services. It is noteworthy in this regard that Social Security, historically a political "sacred cow," is coming under increasing criticism.

As always, we are faced with complicated prospects for the future. The claims of the aged are not based on a special status conferred by age, as in many primitive societies, but on the general ethical ideal of social justice (Lakoff, 1976). Many other groups are making claims on the basis of social justice, and there is little reason to expect major improvement in the political position of the aged. The welfare of older people should improve, at least in the sense of eliminating their gravest problems: lessening of dire poverty, greater availability of basic medical care, expanded low-income housing, and the like. It is unlikely, however, that future social policy will assure them of a comfortable or prosperous life. This will still be determined by individual resources and the ability of the aged to benefit from programs designed for the *general* welfare of the population.

POLICY AND PLANNING FOR THE AGED

It is not especially difficult to outline policy needs for the older population. Indeed, the United States has already outlined the basic requirements of policy for the aged in the Older Americans Act of 1965, which listed the following 10 "Objectives for Older Americans":

1. An adequate income
2. The best possible physical and mental health
3. Suitable housing

4. Full restorative services
5. Opportunity for employment without age discrimination
6. Retirement in health, honor, and dignity
7. Pursuit of meaningful activity
8. Efficient community services when needed
9. Immediate benefit from proven research knowledge
10. Freedom, independence, and the free exercise of individual initiative

No one could argue with these laudable goals; yet we have seen ample evidence of failure to meet them. Despite the multiplicity of government efforts, Estes (1979) and others have argued that the United States still lacks a coherent national aging policy. And too many older people continue to suffer from inadequate income, substandard housing, job discrimination, lack of medical care, and restricted opportunities to exercise personal choice in life-styles.

Clearly, much remains to be done. The 1981 White House Conference on Aging developed nearly 700 recommendations, representing one agenda for the 1980s. Several foci are apparent in these recommendations (Leadership Council of Aging Organizations, 1982). There was overwhelming support for preserving and improving programs related to income security. Social Security was viewed as the cornerstone in this effort, as well as the need to insure adequate income through expansion of employment opportunities and private pensions. Recommendations also emphasized the need for a comprehensive health care system, particularly a community-based continuum of services. The need to assist families and other informal caregivers was also recognized, partly reflecting a desire to maintain "maximum independence in the least restrictive setting." Recommendations concerning social services addressed the need for improved access and coordination, as well as more specific needs relating to transportation, housing alternatives, and crime prevention. Special concerns of subgroups of the older population were also emphasized, including older women, rural elderly, and minority aged.

Two aspects of the recommendations of the conference warrant special note. First, the recommendations explicitly support categorical programs for older people (such as the Older Americans Act). In light of the discussion of age-entitlement programs in Chapter 11, this emphasis may be shortsighted. It is related, however, to a second thrust of the recommendations—the essential responsibility of the federal government for protecting the rights and well-being of older people. For example, one recommendation states that "any lessening of this commitment would be an abdication of the Federal Government's responsibility toward its older citizens." Unfortunately, as we noted in Chapter 11, it is difficult to be optimistic about preserving existing government efforts in aging, much less expanding and improving those efforts. Estes (1979) notes that the major issues affecting the aged are national, not local (income maintenance, health insurance, retirement policy), yet this seems a time of retreat from the setting of national priorities and commitments.

The task before us is to implement programs that truly address the needs of older people. To do so, such programs should reflect the "3 C's" underlined by Lowy (1975): continuity, comprehensiveness, and coordination. There is a need for wide-ranging programs, from community support to institutional care, to address changing needs without requiring wrenching changes in personal life-styles.

Policy directed at the aged should also encourage and support flexibility and the exercise of personal options, recognizing the hierarchy of needs present throughout life. Age stratification in modern societies often restricts the roles and opportunities of older persons. A postindustrial society would best benefit the aging experience by loosening restrictions through support of increased options in work, leisure, service roles, and other aspects of life-style. Specific services and programs should avoid the specter of a "therapeutic state" that structures people's lives for them. Rather, we should structure programs to support people of all ages in their efforts to adapt to their situations in their own chosen ways. In other words, we should support the "right to be different" (Kittrie, 1971). Kahn recognizes this need in his call for future policies of minimal intervention:

> Intervention can be harmful as well as helpful. Although resources for intervention should be available when needed, it is best to follow a policy of *minimal intervention;* that is, intervention that is least disruptive of usual functioning in the usual setting. Thus, it would be more sensible to provide care in the home or day-care center than in the hospital; in the storefront rather than in the clinic; in the neighborhood rather than downtown; for brief rather than for long periods; with neighborhood personnel rather than with explicit medical or social agency professionals. Minimal intervention as a positive concept must be differentiated from neglect. It must also be differentiated from "maximal-minimal" intervention, in which the person is removed from his community, then placed in an institution that provides no psychological or social compensatory measures. (1975:29)

One aspect of Bell's vision of postindustrial society is particularly relevant for policy directed at the aged: the need for rational, informed approaches to increasingly complex problems. Intervention must be based on carefully evaluated knowledge. This knowledge must begin with the causes of the problems to be addressed by policies and the recognition that there may be multiple causes. Some of these causes cannot be easily manipulated through conscious policies; thus we must address ourselves to those areas in which intervention can have some impact. When intervention does occur, it should involve conscious outlining of the *theory* upon which it is based, the *objectives* we hope to achieve, and the *particular population* for whom it is relevant, and there should be careful assessment of both the *implementation* of programs (the processes by which they operate) and their *impact* (Estes & Freeman, 1976).

Unfortunately, knowledge about how to best address the problems encountered by individuals as they age is not advanced. Because of this, Lakoff (1976) has suggested that we need to encourage a variety of social experiments rather than prematurely settling on any single set of policies. We have noted that it is a matter of debate whether policy formulation in the future will be any more rational or informed than it has been in the past. One can only hope that policymakers choose intelligently among the alternative futures that face us.

THE FUTURE OF SOCIAL GERONTOLOGY

The portrait painted of a scientific-technical meritocracy in postindustrial society implies an expanded importance of social gerontology and social gerontologists in shaping the aging experience. How well will this role be filled? The scientific study of aging has made enormous progress during the past 30 years, and yet as a field it is still in its infancy. This is frustrating in some respects, as there are many gaps in our understanding of this part of the life cycle, but there is also something exciting about a field undergoing intellectual ferment.

Many of the older paradigms of social gerontology (disengagement theory, notions about the retirement crisis) are being replaced by frameworks emphasizing age stratification and approaches to the life course. These newer approaches are far from complete; at this point they constitute *sensitizing perspectives* rather than coherent, testable theories.

Two gaps in our understanding of aging are particularly evident. The first concerns the influence of social structure and the cultural and historical contexts in which the aging process occurs. Estes (1979) notes that gerontological theories have tended to "focus on what old people do rather than on the social conditions and policies that cause them to act as they do" (p. 11). She further argues that this focus on the aging individual is reflected in individualistic policies and programs that pay insufficient attention to the structural sources of problems of the aged. The role of the social context in shaping the aging experience is recognized in the model of age stratification, but much more work is needed to flesh out all the ramifications of this model. How do age norms and expectations develop and change? How do these norms differ within subgroups of the population or across cultures, and how are they translated or internalized by individuals? How, and under what conditions, are individuals socialized for their positions in the age stratification system? Through what mechanisms does age stratification facilitate or hinder the options of individuals? How aware are individuals of the nature of age stratification, and how does this awareness affect activism and consciousness based on age? These are just some of the questions that need to be explored.

The second gap concerns our understanding of the *processes* by which people adapt to their own aging experience. Age stratification and other approaches to the social context of aging inform us of the likely problems and tasks in the transitions to old age. And we have many studies of the consequences of these transitions for older individuals. But we have little understanding of the processes by which these consequences are arrived at—of the adaptations made over time by individuals within social contexts. What are the first few days, months, or years of retirement (or widowhood, leisure, grandparenting) like? Suppose the aged disengage from their social surroundings. How does this occur? What influences their choices? How do their views of themselves and the world change over time?

We have seen that the roles of modern older people are quite vague compared with older people in earlier societies. But discussions of rolelessness and alienation notwithstanding, the ability to "make" one's own roles is not such a bad thing because it implies less social "oppression," and although little *formal* socialization occurs, this does not mean that no socialization occurs.

At the most basic level, we need to understand how the aged come to view their own old age in particular ways, and knowledge about the general status of the aged in society or public stereotypes of aging are of limited utility. There is ample evidence that attitudes toward particular types of people are often poor predictors of actual behavior toward them (Deutscher, 1973). What are the real sources of older people's images of aging? How do these sources relate to the general context of their aging? How do these images lead the aged to choose their own patterns of aging? These are questions that remain to be addressed. They constitute the marriage of age stratification and symbolic interactionism, pointing to a more complete *understanding* of the aging experience.

We have seen throughout this book that many questions remain unanswered. We have just begun to tap the depth and variety of the aging experience. Tremendous changes are occurring in the study of specific substantive areas, such as retirement, widowhood, death and dying, housing, and politics, and many new middle-range theories are emerging to help understand these aspects of the aging experience. In addition, there is increasing recognition that the study of aging in any society must be informed by broader frameworks; one cannot understand aging as a developmental period without looking at the whole of the life cycle, retirement without looking at work, widowhood without looking at marriage. Events affecting society also affect the nature of the aging experience in that society. Thus social gerontology must continue to look to many disciplines (such as sociology, psychology, economics, political science) to accomplish a true understanding of the processes of social and psychological aging. And as societies change in the future, as we perhaps enter a postindustrial society, many of our present concepts and theories about aging will have to be reevaluated, and in some cases discarded, as we try to understand the aging experience for different types of people in a different type of society.

There are some clear general research needs. In an assessment of articles on psychological gerontology, Seltzer (1975) notes that there has been little attention paid to problems of reliability and validity of measurement. Although findings are often repetitious, there is little cumulative impact, and studies are often not comparable because of differences in sampling and measurement. An assessment of work in social gerontology would undoubtedly find the same problems. More attention needs to be paid to coherent lines of research that conform to rigorous requirements of scientific research. The study of aging also requires its own particular research strategies. Most notably, there is a need for greater emphasis on longitudinal and cohort studies of the life cycle and comparative cross-national research to investigate continuities and variations in the aging experience in different cohorts and cultures.

Sampling has been a particular problem in social gerontology. It is admittedly difficult—costly and time-consuming—to get a truly representative sample of the older population. Researchers must often settle for available samples from nursing homes or senior centers, which obviously present biased views of the aging experience, and there is a tremendous gap in knowledge about racial and ethnic subgroups of the aged. Even sex differences have often been ignored. For example, we know relatively little about the reactions of older women to retirement, or of older men to widowhood.

Valid study of the aging experience and effective comprehensive programs to meet the needs of the aged require accurate information. Hopefully, research will better provide this in the future. There are some hopeful signs. Recognizing that one general census cannot adequately fill information needs, an increasing number of special censuses are being undertaken to provide data about such areas as housing, crime victimization, and health. This coincides with rising interest in the development of *social indicators* to inform decision makers about policy needs and provide one way to measure progress in dealing with social problems.

> Social indicators—statistics, statistical series, and all other forms of evidence—are summary measures that enable policy and decision makers to assess various social aspects of an ongoing society and to evaluate specific programs and determine their impact. Social indicators help experts and lay persons alike to better understand their own and other societies with respect to values and goals and the nature of social change. (Miller, 1977:267)

Indicators are currently being refined to measure such diverse characteristics of the society as crime, health, privacy, and even the "quality of life" (Campbell, 1981).

There is a particular necessity to develop adequate indicators of the need for various programs and the efficiency and effectiveness of those programs. The fragmented nature of services for the aged, and of responsibility for those services, makes coherent evaluation difficult. It also appears that localities have inadequate information for planning and evaluating their efforts. A recent study of techniques used for "needs assessment" by state and local agencies responsible for services for older people concluded, "The overall quality of the majority of needs assessments was so low as to provide little meaningful input to the planning process" (Lareau & Heumann, 1982: 324).

Social gerontology has enjoyed relatively favorable funding support. In 1975 the National Institute on Aging (NIA) was established within the National Institutes of Health with a mandate "to conduct and support biomedical, social, and behavioral research and training related to the aging process and the diseases and other special problems and needs of the aged" (Murphy, 1976:696). Funding support has also come from other governmental agencies, such as the Administration on Aging, the National Institute of Mental Health, and the Veteran's Administration, and from private sources, such as the Russell Sage Foundation and the NRTA-AARP Andrus Foundation.

Continuation and expansion of support for research and training in gerontology remains essential, especially in light of the aging of the population. For example, programs for the aged require many types of personnel: administrative and managerial, professional staff, direct service delivery. Too often, however, such personnel have little training in geriatrics or gerontology. And the continuing level of commitment to research and training in gerontology and to programs directed at the aged is uncertain. Funding for federal social programs has been under attack in recent years, and support for gerontological efforts have been no exception. Without continuing federal support, however, the needs we have been discussing cannot be met.

It has been suggested that the postindustrial society will be faced with problems of increasing complexity and scale and that there will be a greater need for *informed* policy formulation. This has important implications for the future of social gerontology. The complexity of issues in the study of aging require interdisciplinary approaches, and this will be even more true in the future. That is why the emergence of interdisciplinary programs for research and training in gerontology at many universities is a very encouraging trend.

The complexity of aging and the explosion of interest in this area are creating their own problems of information coordination. There is a growing necessity for comprehensive information systems to meet the needs of researchers and policymakers (Miller & Cutler, 1976). The need for policies based on the best available knowledge also requires a continuing dialogue among researchers, planners, and practitioners. Such dialogues encounter difficulties in any area, and gerontology is no exception. Research may lack relevance for policy needs and programs, and discipline boundaries and language barriers further hinder the translation of research into practice (Urban & Watson, 1974). Such barriers must be overcome, however, if we are to achieve rational, comprehensive programs to meet the needs of older people.

SOME FINAL COMMENTS

The aging experience is neither "good" nor "bad." As with all aspects of life, old age is a complicated mix of benefits and costs, problems and potentialities. This book has attempted to provide an appreciation of this complexity. Those who study aging and all of us who age can better accomplish both tasks when we have an accurate picture of what can be expected. Accuracy is the goal of all scientific endeavor because it is the root of understanding.

The reader will have an opportunity to shape the aging experience in three ways. Some who read this book may choose a career in social gerontology. There is a tremendous need for researchers, social workers, planners, housing managers, physicians, nurses, teachers, program directors, and other professionals in the various fields associated with aging. As citizens, our impact on society and its future affects the context within which the aging experience takes place. Finally, all of us will shape our own aging experiences, in light of our own life-styles and patterns of living. It is hoped that this book has contributed in some way to all three of these endeavors.

References

CHAPTER 1

Bengtson, Vern
    1973   *The Social Psychology of Aging.* Indianapolis: Bobbs-Merrill.
Bengtson, Vern, Patricia Kasschau, and Pauline Ragan
    1977   "The impact of social structure on aging individuals." In James Birren and K. Warner Schaie (eds.). *Handbook of the Psychology of Aging.* New York: Van Nostrand Reinhold.
Binstock, Robert and Ethel Shanas (eds.)
    1976   *Handbook of Aging and the Social Sciences.* New York: Van Nostrand Reinhold.
Birren, James and Vivian Clayton
    1975   "History of gerontology." In Diana Woodruff and James Birren (eds.). *Aging: Scientific Perspectives and Social Issues.* New York: D. Van Nostrand.
Birren, James and K. Warner Schaie (eds.)
    1977   *Handbook of the Psychology of Aging.* New York: Van Nostrand Reinhold.
Cain, Leonard D., Jr.
    1967   "Age status and generational phenomena: The new old people in contemporary America." *The Gerontologist* 7:83–92.
Calhoun, Richard
    1978   *In Search of the New Old: Redefining Old Age in America, 1945–1970.* New York: Elsevier.
Carp, Frances and Abraham Carp
    1981   "It may not be the answer, it may be the question." *Research on Aging* 3:85–100.
Clausen, John
    1972   "The life course of individuals." In Matilda Riley, Marilyn Johnson, and Anne Foner (eds.). *Aging and Society.* Vol. 3: *A Sociology of Age Stratification.* New York: Russell Sage.

de Beauvoir, Simone
  1972 *The Coming of Age.* New York: Putnam's Sons.
Elder, Glen, Jr.
  1974 *Children of the Great Depression.* Chicago: University of Chicago Press.
  1981 "History and the life course." In Daniel Bertaux (ed.). *Biography and Society: The Life History Approach in the Social Sciences.* Beverly Hills: Sage.
Finch, Caleb and Leonard Hayflick (eds.)
  1977 *Handbook of the Biology of Aging.* New York: Van Nostrand Reinhold.
Fischer, David
  1977 *Growing Old in America.* New York: Oxford University Press.
Glenn, Norval
  1974 "Aging and conservatism." In Frederick Eisele (ed.). *Political Consequences of Aging.* The Annals of the American Academy of Political and Social Science 415 (September):176–186.
  1977 *Cohort Analysis.* Beverly Hills: Sage.
  1980 "Values, attitudes, and beliefs." In Orville Brim, Jr. and Jerome Kagan (eds.). *Constancy and Change in Human Development.* Cambridge, Mass.: Harvard University Press.
Hall, G. Stanley
  1922 *Senescence, the Second Half of Life.* New York: Appleton.
Hareven, Tamara
  1978 "Introduction: The historical study of the life course." In Tamara Hareven (ed.). *Transitions: The Family and the Life Course in Historical Perspective.* New York: Academic Press.
  1980 "The life course and aging in historical perspective." In Kurt Back (ed.). *Life Course: Integrative Theories and Exemplary Populations.* Boulder: Westview Press.
Hogan, Dennis
  1981 *Transitions and Social Change: The Early Lives of American Men.* New York: Academic Press.
Johnson, Harold, Joseph Britton, Calvin Lang, Mildred Seltzer, E. Percil Stanford, Rosemary Yancik, Claire Maklan, and Anne Middleswarth
  1980 "Foundations for gerontological education." *The Gerontologist* 20 (3—Part II): 1–61.
Maddox, George and James Wiley
  1976 "Scope, concepts and methods in the study of aging." In Robert Binstock and Ethel Shanas (eds.). *Handbook of Aging and the Social Sciences.* New York: Van Nostrand Reinhold.
Mannheim, Karl
  1952 "The problem of generations." In Karl Mannheim (ed.). *Essays on the Sociology of Knowledge.* New York: Oxford University Press.
Marshall, Victor
  1978 "No exit: A symbolic interactionist perspective on aging." *Aging and Human Development* 9:345–358.
McQuaide, Michael and William Sauer
  1979 "The concept of cohort: Its utility for social gerontology." *Sociological Symposium* 26:28–41.
Medvedev, Zhores
  1974 "Caucasus and Altay longevity: A biological or social problem?" *The Gerontologist* 14:381–87.

Mills, C. Wright
  1959   *The Sociological Imagination.* New York: Oxford University Press.
Neugarten, Bernice
  1974   "Age groups in American society and the rise of the young-old." In Frederick
         Eisele (ed.). *Political Consequences of Aging.* The Annals of the American Acad-
         emy of Political and Social Science 415 (September):187–198.
Neugarten, Bernice and Joan Moore
  1968   "The changing age-status system." In Bernice Neugarten (ed.). *Middle Age and
         Aging.* Chicago: University of Chicago Press.
Neugarten, Bernice, Joan Moore, and John Lowe
  1968   "Age norms, age constraints, and adult socialization." In Bernice Neugarten
         (ed.). *Middle Age and Aging.* Chicago: University of Chicago Press.
Palmore, Erdman
  1978   "When can age, period, and cohort be separated?" *Social Forces* 57:282–295.
Pampel, Fred
  1981   *Social Change and the Aged: Recent Trends in the United States.* Lexington: Lex-
         ington Books.
Peterson, David and Christopher Bolton
  1980   *Gerontology Instruction in Higher Education.* New York: Springer.
Pollak, Otto
  1948   *Social Adjustment in Old Age: A Research Planning Report.* Bulletin 59. New
         York: Social Science Research Council.
Poon, Leonard and Alan Welford
  1980   "Prologue: A historical perspective." In Leonard Poon (ed.). *Aging in the
         1980s: Psychological Issues.* Washington, D.C.: American Psychological Associ-
         ation.
Reich, Warren
  1978   "Ethical issues related to research involving elderly subjects." *The Gerontologist*
         18:326–337.
Riley, Matilda
  1971   "Social gerontology and the age stratification of society." *The Gerontologist*
         11:79–87.
  1978   "Aging, social change, and the power of ideas." *Daedalus* 107 (4):39–52.
Riley, Matilda and Anne Foner
  1968   *Aging and Society.* Volume 1: *An Inventory of Research Findings.* New York:
         Russell Sage.
Riley, Matilda, Marilyn Johnson, and Anne Foner (eds.)
  1972   *Aging and Society.* Volume 3: *A Sociology of Age Stratification.* New York: Rus-
         sell Sage.
Roth, J.
  1963   *Timetables.* Indianapolis: Bobbs-Merrill.
Ryder, Norman
  1965   "The cohort as a concept in the study of social change." *American Sociological
         Review* 30: 843–61.
Smelser, Neil and Sydney Halpern
  1978   "The historical triangulation of family, economy, and education." In John
         Demos and Sarane Spence Boocock (eds.). *Turning Points: Historical and Socio-
         logical Essays on the Family.* Chicago: University of Chicago Press.
Streib, Gordon and Clement Schneider
  1972   *Retirement in American Society.* Ithaca, N.Y.: Cornell University Press.

Stryker, Sheldon
  1981   "Symbolic interactionism: Themes and variations." In Morris Rosenberg and
        Ralph Turner (eds.). *Social Psychology: Sociological Perspectives.* New York:
        Basic Books.
Uhlenberg, Peter
  1979   "Demographic change and problems of the aged." In Matilda Riley (ed.). *Aging
        from Birth to Death: Interdisciplinary Perspectives.* Boulder: Westview Press.
Winsborough, Halliman
  1979   "Changes in the transition to adulthood." In Matilda Riley (ed.), *Aging from
        Birth to Death: Interdisciplinary Perspectives.* Boulder: Westview Press.
Woodruff, Diana
  1975   "Introduction: Multidisciplinary perspectives of aging." In Diana Woodruff and
        James Birren (eds.). *Aging: Scientific Perspectives and Social Issues.* New York:
        D. Van Nostrand.

CHAPTER 2

Atkinson, Joseph and Marc Schuckit
  1981   "Alcoholism and over-the-counter and prescription drug misuse in the elderly."
        In Carl Eisdorfer (ed.). *Annual Review of Gerontology and Geriatrics.* Volume
        2. New York: Springer.
Baltes, Margret and Paul Baltes
  1982   "Microanalytical research on environmental factors and plasticity in psychologi-
        cal aging." In Tiffany Field, Aletha Huston, Herbert Quay, Lillian Troll, and
        Gordon Finley (eds.). *Review of Human Development.* New York: John Wiley
        & Sons.
Barrows, C. and L. Roeder
  1977   "Nutrition." In C. Finch and L. Hayflick (eds.), *Handbook of the Biology of
        Aging.* New York: Van Nostrand Reinhold.
Biggar, Jeanne
  1980a   "Who moved among the elderly, 1965 to 1970: A comparison of types of older
        movers." *Research on Aging* 2:73–92.
  1980b   "Reassessing elderly Sunbelt migration." *Research on Aging* 2:177–190.
Bock, E. Wilbur
  1972   "Aging and suicide: The significance of marital, kinship, and alternative rela-
        tions." *Family Coordinator* 21:71–79.
Botwinick, Jack
  1977   "Intellectual abilities." In James Birren and K. Warner Schaie (eds.). *Handbook
        of the Psychology of Aging.* New York: Van Nostrand Reinhold.
  1978   *Aging and Behavior.* New York: Springer.
Branco, Kenneth and John Williamson
  1982   "Stereotyping and the life cycle: Views of aging and the aged." In Arthur Miller
        (ed.). *In the Eye of the Beholder: Contemporary Issues in Stereotyping.* New York:
        Praeger.
Butler, Robert and Myrna Lewis
  1982   *Aging and Mental Health: Positive Psychosocial Approaches.* St. Louis: C. V.
        Mosby.
Carp, Frances
  1976   "Housing and living environments of older people." In Robert Binstock and

Ethel Shanas (eds.). *Handbook of Aging and the Social Sciences.* New York: Van Nostrand Reinhold.

Cerella, John, Leonard Poon, and Diane Williams
1980 "Age and the complexity hypothesis." In Leonard Poon (ed.). *Aging in the 1980s: Psychological Issues.* Washington, D.C.: American Psychological Association.

Chevan, Albert
1982 "Age, housing choice, and neighborhood age structure." *American Journal of Sociology* 87:1133–1149.

Cockerham, William, Kimberly Sharp, and Julie Wilcox
1983 "Aging and perceived health status." *Journal of Gerontology* 38:349–355.

Cole, Stephen
1979 "Age and scientific performance." *American Journal of Sociology* 84:958–977.

Cowgill, Donald
1974 "The aging of populations and societies." In Frederick Eisele (ed.). *Political Consequences of Aging.* The Annals of the American Academy of Political and Social Science 415 (September): 1–18.
1978 "Residential segregation by age in American metropolitan areas." *Journal of Gerontology* 33:446–453.

Dennis, Wayne
1966 "Creative productivity between the ages of 20 and 80 years." *Journal of Gerontology* 21:1–8.

Eisdorfer, Carl and Bernard Stotsky
1977 "Intervention, treatment, and rehabilitation of psychiatric disorders." In James Birren and K. Warner Schaie (eds.). *Handbook of the Psychology of Aging.* New York: Van Nostrand Reinhold.

Fernandes, Judy
1981 "Undernutrition among the elderly." *Journal of Nutrition for the Elderly* 1 (¾):79–81.

Ferraro, Kenneth
1980 "Self-ratings of health among the old and the old-old." *Journal of Health and Social Behavior* 21:377–382.

Fozard, James
1980 "The time for remembering." In Leonard Poon (ed.). *Aging in the 1980s: Psychological Issues.* Washington, D.C.: American Psychological Association.

Friedman, Joseph and Jane Sjogren
1981 "Assets of the elderly as they retire." *Social Security Bulletin* 44 (1):16–31.

Fries, James and Lawrence Crapo
1981 *Vitality and Aging.* San Francisco: W. H. Freeman.

Gatz, Margaret, Michael Smyer, and M. Powell Lawton
1980 "The mental health system and the older adult." In Leonard Poon (ed.). *Aging in the 1980s: Psychological Issues.* Washington, D.C.: American Psychological Association.

George, Linda and Lucille Bearon
1980 *Quality of Life in Older Persons: Meaning and Measurement.* New York: Human Sciences Press.

Hickey, Tom
1980 *Health and Aging.* Monterey, Calif.: Brooks/Cole.

Horn, John and Gary Donaldson
1980 "Cognitive development in adulthood." In Orville Brim, Jr. and Jerome Kagan

(eds.). *Constancy and Change in Human Development.* Cambridge, Mass.: Harvard University Press.

Hoyer, William and Dana Plude
1980 "Attentional and perceptual processes in the study of cognitive aging." In Leonard Poon (ed.). *Aging in the 1980s: Psychological Issues.* Washington, D.C.: American Psychological Association.

Kart, Cary, Eileen Metress, and James Metress
1978 *Aging and Health: Biologic and Social Perspectives.* Menlo Park, Calif.: Addison-Wesley.

Kurtzman, Joel and Phillip Gordon
1976 *No More Dying: The Conquest of Aging and the Extension of Human Life.* Los Angeles: J. P. Tarcher.

LaGory, Mark, Russell Ward, and Thomas Juravich
1980 "The age segregation process: Explanation for American cities." *Urban Affairs Quarterly* 16:59–80.

Lawton, M. Powell
1980 "Housing the elderly: Residential quality and residential satisfaction." *Research on Aging* 2:309–328.

Leaf, Alexander
1973 "Getting old." *Scientific American* 229(3):44–52.

Lesnoff-Caravaglia, Gari
1978 "The five percent fallacy." *Aging and Human Development* 9:187–192.

Lichter, Daniel, Glenn Fuguitt, Tim Heaton, and William Clifford
1981 "Components of change in the residential concentration of the elderly population: 1950–1975." *Journal of Gerontology* 36:480–489.

Liska, Allen
1981 *Perspectives on Deviance.* Englewood Cliffs, N.J.: Prentice-Hall.

Longino, Charles, Jr.
1979 "Going home: Aged return migration in the United States 1965–1970." *Journal of Gerontology* 34:736–745.

Longino, Charles, Jr., and Jeanne Biggar
1982 "The impact of population redistribution on service delivery." *The Gerontologist* 22:153–159.

Longino, Charles, Jr., and David Jackson (eds.)
1980 "Migration and the aged." *Research on Aging* 2:131–280.

Lowenthal, Marjorie
1964 "Social isolation and mental illness in old age." *American Sociological Review* 29:54–70.

Manton, Kenneth, Sharon Poss, and Steven Wing
1979 "Black/white mortality crossover: Investigation from the perspective of the components of aging." *The Gerontologist* 19:291–300.

Markides, Kyriakos and Charisse Pappas
1982 "Subjective age, health, and survivorship in old age." *Research on Aging* 4:87–96.

Marsh, Robert
1981 "The income and resources of the elderly in 1978." *Social Security Bulletin* 44(12):3–11.

Marshall, James
1978 "Changes in aged white male suicide: 1948–1972." *Journal of Gerontology* 33:763–768.

Maslow, Abraham
  1954   *Motivation and Personality.* New York: Harper & Row.
Miller, Marv
  1979   *Suicide After Sixty: The Final Alternative.* New York: Springer.
Myers, George
  1978   "Cross-national trends in mortality rates among the elderly." *The Gerontologist*
         18:441–448.
National Council on the Aging
  1975   *The Myth and Reality of Aging in America.* Washington, D.C.
Palmore, Erdman and William Cleveland
  1976   "Aging, terminal decline and terminal drop." *Journal of Gerontology* 31:76–81.
Petersen, David, Frank Whittington, and Elizabeth Beer
  1979   "Drug use and misuse among the elderly." *Journal of Drug Issues* 9:5–26.
Pfeiffer, Eric
  1977   "Psychopathology and social pathology." In James Birren and K. Warner Schaie
         (eds.). *Handbook of the Psychology of Aging.* New York: Van Nostrand Rein-
         hold.
Rabushka, Alvin and Bruce Jacobs
  1980   *Old Folks at Home.* New York: Free Press.
Rubenstein, Laurence, Lois Rhee, and Robert Kane
  1982   "The role of geriatric assessment units in caring for the elderly: An analytic re-
         view." *Journal of Gerontology* 37:513–521.
Schaie, K. Warner
  1975   "Age changes in adult intelligence." In Diana Woodruff and James Birren (eds.).
         Aging: Scientific Perspectives and Social Issues. New York: D. Van Nostrand.
Schuckit, Marc
  1977   "Geriatric alcoholism and drug abuse." *The Gerontologist* 17: 168–74.
Schulz, James
  1980   *The Economics of Aging.* Belmont, Calif.: Wadsworth.
Schulz, Richard
  1978   *The Psychology of Death, Dying, and Bereavement.* Reading, Mass.: Addison-
         Wesley.
Seiden, Richard
  1981   "Mellowing with age: Factors influencing the nonwhite suicide rate." *Aging and
         Human Development* 13:265–284.
Shore, Herbert
  1976   "Designing a training program for understanding sensory losses in aging." *The
         Gerontologist* 16: 157–165.
Siegel, Jacob
  1981   "Demographic background for international gerontological studies." *Journal of
         Gerontology* 36:93–102.
Snyder, Phyllis and Ann Way
  1979   "Alcoholism and the elderly." *Aging* January/February.
Soldo, Beth
  1980   "America's elderly in the 1980s." *Population Bulletin* 35 (4):1–47.
Strauss, Anselm
  1975   *Chronic Illness and the Quality of Life.* St. Louis: C.V. Mosby.
Strehler, Bernard
  1975   "Implications of aging research for society." *Federation Proceedings* 34:5–8.

Struyk, Raymond and Beth Soldo
  1980   *Improving the Elderly's Housing: A Key to Preserving the Nation's Housing Stock and Neighborhoods.* Cambridge, Mass: Ballinger.
Uhlenberg, Peter
  1977   "Changing structure of the older population of the USA during the twentieth century." *The Gerontologist* 17: 197–202.
United States Bureau of the Census
  1940   *Comparative Occupation Statistics for the United States: 1870–1940.* Washington, D.C.: U.S. Government Printing Office.
  1975   *Historical Statistics of the United States, Colonial Times to 1970,* Bicentennial Edition, Part 1. Washington, D.C.: U.S. Government Printing Office.
  1976   "Demographic aspects of aging and the older population in the United States." *Current Population Reports,* Series P–23, No. 59. Washington, D.C.: U.S. Government Printing Office.
  1979   "Social and economic characteristics of the older population: 1978." *Current Population Reports,* Series P–23, No. 85. Washington, D.C.: U.S. Government Printing Office.
  1981a "Population profile of the United States: 1980." *Current Population Reports,* Series P–20, no. 363. Washington, D.C.: U.S. Government Printing Office.
  1981b "Marital status and living arrangements: March 1980." *Current Population Reports,* Series P–20, No. 365. Washington, D.C.: U.S. Government Printing Office.
  1981c "Characteristics of the population below the poverty level: 1979." *Current Population Reports,* Series P–60, No. 130. Washington, D.C.: U.S. Government Printing Office.
United States Public Health Service
  1981a *Vital Statistics of the United States: 1977.* Volume II—*Mortality,* Part A. National Center for Health Statistics. Washington, D.C.: U.S. Government Printing Office.
  1981b "Current estimates from the National Health Interview Survey: United States, 1980." *Vital and Health Statistics,* Series 10, No. 139. National Center for Health Statistics. Washington, D.C.: U.S. Government Printing Office.
Walmsley, Sean and Richard Allington
  1982   "Reading abilities of elderly persons in relation to the difficulty of essential documents." *The Gerontologist* 22:36–38.
Willis, Sherry and Paul Baltes
  1980   "Intelligence in adulthood and aging: Contemporary issues." In Leonard Poon (ed.). *Aging in the 1980s: Psychological Issues.* Washington, D.C.: American Psychological Association.

CHAPTER 3

Achenbaum, W. Andrew
  1978   *Old Age in the New Land: The American Experience since 1790.* Baltimore: The Johns Hopkins Press.
Achenbaum, W. Andrew and Peter Stearns
  1978   "Old age and modernization." *The Gerontologist* 18:307–312.
Atchley, Robert
  1975   "The life course, age grading, and age-linked demands for decision-making." In

Nancy Datan and Leon Ginsberg (eds.). *Life-Span Developmental Psychology: Normative Life Crises.* New York: Academic Press.

Beller, Suha and Erdman Palmore
1974   "Longevity in Turkey." *The Gerontologist* 14:373–376.

Benet, Sula
1974   *Abkhasians: The Long-Living People of the Caucasus.* New York: Holt, Rinehart and Winston.

Bengtson, Vern
1973   *The Social Psychology of Aging.* Indianapolis: Bobbs-Merrill.
1979   "Ethnicity and aging: Problems and issues in current social science inquiry." In Donald Gelfand and Alfred Kutzik (eds.). *Ethnicity and Aging: Theory, Research, and Policy.* New York: Springer.

Bengtson, Vern, Linda Burton, and David Mangen
1981   "Family support systems and attribution of responsibility: Contrasts among elderly blacks, Mexican-Americans, and whites." Paper presented at the annual meeting of the Gerontological Society of America, Boston.

Bergman, Shimon
1980   "Israel." In Erdman Palmore (ed.). *International Handbook on Aging: Contemporary Developments and Research.* Westport, Conn.: Greenwood Press.

Bloch, Herbert and Arthur Niederhoffer
1958   *The Gang.* New York: Philosophical Library.

Block, Marilyn
1979   "Exiled Americans: The plight of Indian aged in the United States." In Donald Gelfand and Alfred Kutzik (eds.). *Ethnicity and Aging: Theory, Research, and Policy.* New York: Springer.

Calhoun, Richard
1978   *In Search of the New Old: Redefining Old Age in America, 1945–1970.* New York: Elsevier.

Cantor, Marjorie
1979   "The informal support system of New York's inner city elderly: Is ethnicity a factor?" In Donald Gelfand and Alfred Kutzik (eds.). *Ethnicity and Aging: Theory, Research, and Policy.* New York: Springer.

Carp, Frances and Eunice Kataoka
1976   "Health care problems of the elderly of San Francisco's Chinatown." *The Gerontologist* 16:30–38.

Chadwick, Terry
1976   "Review of The Honorable Elders." *The Gerontologist* 16:560–561.

Cherry, Ralph and Scott Magnuson-Martinson
1981   "Modernization and the status of the aged in China: Decline or equalization?" *Sociological Quarterly* 22:253–261.

Clark, Margaret
1967   "The anthropology of aging: A new area for studies of culture and personality." *The Gerontologist* 7:55–64.

Clemente, Frank, Patricia Rexroad, and Carl Hirsch
1975   "The participation of the black aged in voluntary associations." *Journal of Gerontology* 30:469–472.

Cohn, Richard
1982   "Economic development and status change of the aged." *American Journal of Sociology* 87:1150–1161.

Cowgill, Donald

1974a "The aging of populations and societies." In Frederick Eisele (ed.). *Political Consequences of Aging. The Annals of the American Academy of Political and Social Science* 415 (September):1–18.

1974b "Aging and modernization: A revision of the theory." In Jaber Gubrium (ed.). *Late Life: Communities and Environmental Policies.* Springfield, Ill.: Charles C. Thomas.

Davis, Donald

1971 "Growing old black." In U.S. Senate Special Committee on Aging, *The Multiple Hazards of Age and Race: The Situation of Aged Blacks in the United States.* Washington D.C.: U.S. Government Printing Office.

de Beauvoir, Simone

1972 *The Coming of Age.* New York: Putnam's Sons.

Demos, John

1978 "Old age in early New England." In John Demos and Sarane Boocock (eds.). *Turning Points: Historical and Sociological Essays on the Family.* Chicago: University of Chicago Press.

Dowd, James

1980 *Stratification Among the Aged.* Monterey, Calif.: Brooks/Cole.

Dowd, James and Vern Bengtson

1978 "Aging in minority populations: An examination of the double jeopardy hypothesis." *Journal of Gerontology* 33:427–436.

Elder, Glen, Jr.

1981 "History and the life course." In Daniel Bertaux (ed.). *Biography and Society: The Life History Approach in the Social Sciences.* Beverly Hills: Sage.

Elliott, H. W.

1886 *Our Arctic Province: Alaska and the Seal Islands.* New York: Scribner's.

Fischer, David

1977 *Growing Old in America.* New York: Oxford University Press.

Foner, Anne and David Kertzer

1978 "Transitions over the life course: Lessons from age-set societies." *American Journal of Sociology* 83:1081–1104.

Gelfand, Donald

1982 *Aging: The Ethnic Factor.* Boston: Little, Brown.

Goody, Jack

1976 "Aging in nonindustrial societies." In Robert Binstock and Ethel Shanas (eds.). *Handbook of Aging and the Social Sciences.* New York: Van Nostrand Reinhold.

Greer, Colin (ed.)

1974 *Divided Society: The Ethnic Experience in America.* New York: Basic Books.

Henretta, John and Richard Campbell

1976 "Status attainment and status maintenance: A study of stratification in old age." *American Sociological Review* 41:981–992.

Hogan, Dennis

1978 "The variable order of events in the life course." *American Sociological Review* 43:573–586.

1980 "The transition to adulthood as a career contingency." *American Sociological Review* 45:261–276.

Holmberg, A. R.

1969 *Nomads of the Long Bow.* Garden City, N.Y.: Natural History Press.

Holzberg, Carol
  1982   "Ethnicity and aging: Anthropological perspectives on more than just the minority elderly." *The Gerontologist* 22:249–257.
House, James
  1981   "Social structure and personality." In Morris Rosenberg and Ralph Turner (eds.). *Social Psychology: Sociological Perspectives.* New York: Basic Books.
Information on Aging
  1982   "Native American elderly." *Information on Aging,* no. 27 (October). Institute of Gerontology, The University of Michigan—Wayne State University.
Jackson, Jacquelyne
  1980   *Minorities and Aging.* Belmont, Calif.: Wadsworth.
Jackson, Jacquelyne and Bertram Walls
  1978   "Myths and realities about aged blacks." In Mollie Brown (ed.). *Readings in Gerontology.* St. Louis: C. V. Mosby.
Kalish, Richard and Sharon Moriwaki
  1973   "The world of the elderly Asian American." *Journal of Social Issues* 29:187–209.
Kent, Donald
  1971   "Changing welfare to serve minority aged." In *Minority Aged in America.* Institute of Gerontology, The University of Michigan—Wayne State University.
Krause, C.
  1978   *Grandmothers, Mothers and Daughters.* New York: Institute on Pluralism and Group Identity.
Kutzik, Alfred
  1979   "American social provision for the aged: An historical perspective." In Donald Gelfand and Alfred Kutzik (eds.). *Ethnicity and Aging: Theory, Research, and Policy.* New York: Springer.
Laslett, Peter
  1976   "Societal development and aging." In Robert Binstock and Ethel Shanas (eds.). *Handbook of Aging and the Social Sciences.* New York: Van Nostrand Reinhold.
Leaf, A.
  1973   "Every day is a gift when you are over 100." *National Geographic* 143 (1):93–118.
Lennon, Mary
  1982   "The psychological consequences of menopause: The importance of timing of a life stage event." *Journal of Health and Social Behavior* 23:353–365.
Lozier, John
  1975   "Accommodating old people in society: Examples from Appalachia and New Orleans." In Nancy Datan and Leon Ginsberg (eds.). *Life-Span Developmental Psychology: Normative Life Crises.* New York: Academic Press.
Maeda, Daisaku
  1980   "Japan." In Erdman Palmore (ed.). *International Handbook on Aging: Contemporary Developments and Research.* Westport, Conn.: Greenwood Press.
Maldonado, David, Jr.
  1975   "The Chicano aged." *Social Work* 20:213–216.
Marshall, Victor
  1978   "No exit: A symbolic interactionist perspective on aging." *Aging and Human Development* 9:345–358.
Mazess, Richard and Sylvia Forman
  1979   "Longevity and age by exaggeration in Vilcabamba, Ecuador." *Journal of Gerontology* 34:94–98.

Mirowsky, John and Catherine Ross
  1980 "Minority status, ethnic culture, and distress: A comparison of blacks, whites, Mexicans, and Mexican Americans." *American Journal of Sociology* 86:479–495.
Myerhoff, Barbara
  1978 *Number Our Days.* New York: Simon and Schuster.
National Urban League
  1964 *Double Jeopardy, the Older Negro in America Today.* New York.
Neugarten, Bernice and Gunhild Hagestad
  1976 "Age and the life course." In Robert Binstock and Ethel Shanas (eds.). *Handbook of Aging and the Social Sciences.* New York: Van Nostrand Reinhold.
Neugarten, Bernice and Joan Moore
  1968 "The changing age-status system." In Bernice Neugarten (ed.). *Middle Age and Aging.* Chicago: University of Chicago Press.
Neugarten, Bernice, Joan Moore, and John Lowe
  1965 "Age norms, age constraints, and adult socialization." *American Journal of Sociology* 70:710–717.
Osako, Masako
  1979 "Aging and family among Japanese Americans: The role of ethnic tradition in the adjustment to old age." *The Gerontologist* 19:448–455.
Palmore, Erdman
  1975a "The status and integration of the aged in Japanese society." *Journal of Gerontology* 30:199–208.
  1975b *The Honorable Elders.* Durham, N.C.: Duke University Press.
  1976 "The future status of the aged." *The Gerontologist* 16:297–302.
Palmore, Erdman and Kenneth Manton
  1974 "Modernization and the status of the aged: International comparisons." *Journal of Gerontology* 29:205–210.
Palmore, Erdman and Frank Whittington
  1971 "Trends in the relative status of the aged." *Social Forces* 50:84–91.
Pampel, Fred
  1981 *Social Change and the Aged: Recent Trends in the United States.* Lexington, Mass.: Lexington Books.
Piovesana, Gino
  1974 "The aged in Chinese and Japanese cultures." In William Bier (ed.). *Aging: Its Challenge to the Individual and to Society.* New York: Fordham University Press.
Press, Irwin and Mike McKool Jr.
  1972 "Social structure and status of the aged: Toward some valid cross-cultural generalizations." *Aging and Human Development* 3:297–306.
Riley, Matilda
  1976 "Age strata in social systems." In Robert Binstock and Ethel Shanas (eds.). *Handbook of Aging and the Social Sciences.* New York: Van Nostrand Reinhold.
Riley, Matilda, Marilyn Johnson, and Anne Foner
  1972 *Aging and Society.* Vol. 3: *A Sociology of Age Stratification.* New York: Russell Sage.
Rosow, Irving
  1965 "And then we were old." *Trans-Action* 2:20–26.
  1974 *Socialization to Old Age.* Berkeley: University of California Press.
Shanas, Ethel, Peter Townsend, Dorothy Wedderbum, Henning Friis, Paul Milhoj, and Jan Stehouwer
  1968 *Old People in Three Industrial Societies.* New York: Atherton Press.

Simmons, Leo
1945   *The Role of the Aged in Primitive Society.* New Haven, Conn.: Yale University Press.
1960   "Aging in preindustrial societies." In Clark Tibbitts (ed.). *Handbook of Social Gerontology.* Chicago: University of Chicago Press.
Soldo, Beth
1980   "America's elderly in the 1980's." *Population Bulletin* 35 (4): 1–47.
Stearns, Peter
1976   *Old Age in European Society: The Case of France.* New York: Holmes & Meier.
Streib, Gordon
1976   "Social stratification and aging." In Robert Binstock and Ethel Shanas (eds.). *Handbook of Aging and the Social Sciences.* New York: Van Nostrand Reinhold.
Treas, Judith
1979   "Socialist organization and economic development in China: Latent consequences for the aged." *The Gerontologist* 19:34–43.
Trinidad, Luisa
1977   "The Spanish-speaking elderly." In Barbara Newsome (ed.). *Insights on the Minority Elderly.* Washington, D.C.: The National Center on Black Aged.
Uhlenberg, Peter
1979   "Demographic change and problems of the aged." In Matilda Riley (ed.). *Aging from Birth to Death: Interdisciplinary Perspectives.* Boulder, Col.: Westview Press.
United States Bureau of the Census
1973   *Census of Population, 1970: Detailed Characteristics.* Final Report PC (1)–D 1, United States Summary. Washington, D.C.: U.S. Government Printing Office.
Valle, R. and L. Mendoza
1978   *The Elder Latino.* San Diego, CA: San Diego State University.
Ward, Russell
1983   "The stability of racial differences across age strata." *Sociology and Social Research* 67:312–323.
Waring, Joan
1975   "Social replenishment and social change: The problem of disordered cohort flow." *American Behavioral Scientist* 19:237–256.
Wood, Vivian
1971   "Age-appropriate behavior for older people." *The Gerontologist* 11:74–78.
Wylie, Floyd
1971   "Attitudes toward aging and the aged among black Americans: Some historical perspectives." *Aging and Human Development* 2:66–70.

CHAPTER 4

Baltes, Paul and Sherry Willis
1979   "Life-span developmental psychology, cognitive functioning and social policy." In Matilda Riley (ed.). *Aging from Birth to Death: Interdisciplinary Perspectives.* Boulder, Col.: Westview Press.
Beeson, Diane
1975   "Women in aging studies: A critique and suggestions." *Social Problems* 23:52–59.
Bengtson, Vern
1973a *The Social Psychology of Aging.* Indianapolis: Bobbs-Merrill.

1973b "Self-determination: A social-psychological perspective on helping the aged." *Geriatrics* 28:118–130.

Blau, Zena
1973 *Old Age in a Changing Society.* New York: New Viewpoints.

Block, Marilyn, Janice Davidson, and Jean Grambs
1981 *Women Over Forty: Visions and Realities.* New York: Springer.

Blumer, Herbert
1969 *Symbolic Interactionism: Perspective and Method.* Englewood Cliffs, N.J.: Prentice-Hall.

Brim, Orville, Jr., and Jerome Kagan
1980 *Constancy and Change in Human Development.* Cambridge, Mass.: Harvard University Press.

Bush, Diane and Roberta Simmons
1981 "Socialization processes over the life course." In Morris Rosenberg and Ralph Turner (eds.). *Social Psychology: Sociological Perspectives.* New York: Basic Books.

Busse, Ewald
1970 "Psychoneurotic reactions and defense mechanisms in the aged." In Erdman Palmore (ed.). *Normal Aging.* Durham, N.C.: Duke University Press.

Butler, Robert
1963 "The life review: An interpretation of reminiscence in the aged." *Psychiatry* 26 (1):65–76.
1975 *Why Survive?: Being Old in America.* New York: Harper & Row.

Carp, Frances
1978 "Effects of the living environment on activity and use of time." *Aging and Human Development* 9:75–91.

Carp, Frances and Abraham Carp
1981 "Age, deprivation, and personal competence: Effects on satisfaction." *Research on Aging* 3:279–298.

Cavan, Ruth
1962 "Self and role in adjustment during old age." In Arnold Rose (ed.). *Human Behavior and Social Processes.* Boston: Houghton Mifflin.

Clark, Margaret and Barbara Anderson
1967 *Culture and Aging.* Springfield, Ill.: Charles C. Thomas.

Clausen, John
1972 "The life course of individuals." In Matilda Riley, Marilyn Johnson, and Anne Foner (eds.). *Aging and Society.* Vol. 3: *A Sociology of Age Stratification.* New York: Russell Sage.

Collins, M.
1976 "Pioneering the future." *Prime Time* 5(6):4–7.

Costa, Paul, Jr., Robert McCrae, and David Arenberg
1980 "Enduring dispositions in adult males." *Journal of Personality and Social Psychology* 38:793–800.

Costa, Paul, Jr., Robert McCrae, and Arthur Norris
1981 "Personal adjustment to aging: Longitudinal prediction from neuroticism and extraversion." *Journal of Gerontology* 36:78–85.

Cowley, Malcolm
1982 *The View from 80.* New York: Penguin Books.

Cumming, Elaine
1963 "Further thoughts on the theory of disengagement." *International Social Science Journal* 15:377–393.

1964　"New thoughts on the theory of disengagement." In Robert Kastenbaum (ed.). *New Thoughts on Old Age.* New York: Springer.

Cumming, Elaine and William Henry
1961　*Growing Old: The Process of Disengagement.* New York: Basic Books.

Dohrenwend, Barbara and Bruce Dohrenwend (eds.)
1974　*Stressful Life Events: Their Nature and Effects.* New York: John Wiley.

Dowd, James
1975　"Aging as exchange: A preface to theory." *Journal of Gerontology* 30:584–594.

Eisdorfer, Carl and Frances Wilkie
1977　"Stress, disease, aging and behavior." In James Birren and K. Warner Schaie (eds.). *Handbook of the Psychology of Aging.* New York: Van Nostrand Reinhold.

Elder, Glen, Jr., and Jeffrey Liker
1982　"Hard times in women's lives: Historical influences across forty years." *American Journal of Sociology* 88:241–269.

Erikson, Erik
1950　*Childhood and Society.* New York: W. W. Norton.

Frieze, I., J. Parsons, P. Johnson, D. Ruble, and G. Zellman
1978　*Women and Sex Roles: A Social Psychological Perspective.* New York: W. W. Norton.

George, Linda
1979　"The happiness syndrome: Methodological and substantive issues in the study of social psychological well-being in adulthood." *The Gerontologist* 19:210–216.
1980　*Role Transitions in Later Life.* Monterey, Calif.: Brooks/Cole.

George, Linda and Lucille Bearon
1980　*Quality of Life in Older Persons: Meaning and Measurement.* New York: Human Sciences Press.

Glenn, Norval
1980　"Values, attitudes, and beliefs." In Orville Brim, Jr., and Jerome Kagan (eds.). *Constancy and Change in Human Development.* Cambridge, Mass.: Harvard University Press.

Gould, Roger
1972　"The phases of adult life: A study in developmental psychology." *American Journal of Psychiatry* 129:521–531.

Gubrium, Jaber
1973　*The Myth of the Golden Years: A Socio-Environmental Theory of Aging.* Springfield, Ill.: Charles C. Thomas.

Gutmann, David
1977　"The cross-cultural perspective: Notes toward a comparative psychology of aging." In James Birren and K. Warner Schaie (eds.). *Handbook of the Psychology of Aging.* New York: Van Nostrand Reinhold.

Havighurst, Robert
1952　*Developmental Tasks and Education.* New York: Longmans, Green.

Havighurst, Robert, Bernice Neugarten, and Sheldon Tobin
1968　"Disengagement and patterns of aging." In Bernice Neugarten (ed.). *Middle Age and Aging.* Chicago: University of Chicago Press.

Heiss, Jerold
1981　"Social roles." In Morris Rosenberg and Ralph Turner (eds.). *Social Psychology: Sociological Perspectives.* New York: Basic Books.

Henry, William
1965　"Engagement and disengagement: Toward a theory of adult development." In

Robert Kastenbaum (ed.). *Contributions to the Psychobiology of Aging.* New York: Springer.

Herzog, A. Regula and Willard Rodgers
1981 "Age and satisfaction: Data from several large surveys." *Research on Aging* 3:142–165.

Hickman, C. Addison and Manford Kuhn
1956 *Individuals, Groups, and Economic Behavior.* New York: Dryden Press.

Hochschild, Arlie
1975 "Disengagement theory: A critique and proposal." *American Sociological Review* 40:553–569.

Holmes, Thomas and Richard Rahe
1967 "The Social Readjustment Rating Scale." *Journal of Psychosomatic Research* 11:213–218.

Jones, Tony (ed.)
1978 "Going strong in your 80s." *Quest/78* 2 (2):113–128.

Kastenbaum, Robert
1977 *Death, Society, and Human Experience.* St. Louis: C. V. Mosby.

Kilijanek, Thomas and Thomas Drabek
1979 "Assessing long-term impacts of a natural disaster: A focus on the elderly." *The Gerontologist* 19:555–566.

Kimmel, Douglas
1974 *Adulthood and Aging.* New York: John Wiley.

Kline, Chrysee
1975 "The socialization process of women: Implications for a theory of successful aging." *The Gerontologist* 15:486–492.

Kogan, Nathan
1979 "A study of age categorization." *Journal of Gerontology* 34:358–367.

Kohn, Melvin and Carmi Schooler
1973 "Occupational experience and psychological functioning: An assessment of reciprocal effects." *American Sociological Review* 38:97–118.

Kuhlen, Raymond
1964 "Developmental changes in motivation during the adult years." In James Birren (ed.). *Relations of Development and Aging.* Springfield, Ill.: Charles C. Thomas.

Kuypers, Joseph
1974 "Ego functioning in old age: Early adult life antecedents." *Aging and Human Development* 5:157–179.

Larson, Reed
1978 "Thirty years of research on the subjective well-being of older Americans." *Journal of Gerontology* 33:109–125.

Lawton, M. Powell and Lucille Nahemow
1973 "Ecology and the aging process." In Carl Eisdorfer and M. Powell Lawton (eds.). *The Psychology of Adult Development and Aging.* Washington, D.C.: American Psychological Association.

Lazarus, Richard
1966 *Psychological Stress and the Coping Process.* New York: McGraw-Hill.

Lemon, Bruce, Vern Bengtson, and James Peterson
1972 "An exploration of the activity theory of aging: Activity types and life satisfaction among in-movers to a retirement community." *Journal of Gerontology* 27:511–523.

Levinson, D.
  1978   *The Seasons of a Man's Life.* New York: Alfred A. Knopf.
Liang, Jersey
  1982   "Sex differences in life satisfaction among the elderly." *Journal of Gerontology*
         37:100–108.
Longino, Charles, Jr., and Cary Kart
  1982   "Explicating activity theory: A formal replication." *Journal of Gerontology*
         37:713–722.
Lopata, Helena
  1966   "The life cycle of the social role of the housewife." *Sociology and Social Research*
         51:5–22.
Lowenthal, Marjorie, Majda Thurnher, and David Chiriboga
  1975   *Four Stages of Life.* San Francisco: Jossey-Bass.
Maas, Henry and Joseph Kuypers
  1974   *From 30 to 70.* San Francisco: Jossey-Bass.
McGrath, Joseph (ed.)
  1970   *Social and Psychological Factors in Stress.* New York: Holt, Rinehart and Wins-
         ton.
McCrae, Robert
  1982   "Age differences in the use of coping mechanisms." *Journal of Gerontology*
         37:454–459.
McCrae, Robert and Paul Costa, Jr.
  1982   "Aging, the life course, and models of personality." In Tiffany Field, Aletha Hus-
         ton, Herbert Quay, Lillian Troll, and Gordon Finley (eds.), *Review of Human
         Development.* New York: John Wiley & Sons.
Maddox, George
  1970   "Fact and artifact: Evidence bearing on disengagement theory." In Erdman Pal-
         more (ed.). *Normal Aging.* Durham, N.C.: Duke University Press.
Neugarten, Bernice
  1964   *Personality in Middle and Late Life.* New York: Atherton Press.
  1968   "Adult personality: Toward a psychology of the life cycle." In Bernice Neugar-
         ten (ed.). *Middle Age and Aging.* Chicago: University of Chicago Press.
  1969   "Continuities and discontinuities of psychological issues into adult life." *Human
         Development* 12 (2):121–130.
  1973   "Personality change in late life: A developmental perspective." In Carl Eisdorfer
         and M. Powell Lawton (eds.). *The Psychology of Adult Development and Aging.*
         Washington, D.C.: American Psychological Association.
Neugarten, Bernice, Robert Havighurst, and Sheldon Tobin
  1968   "Personality and patterns of aging." In Bernice Neugarten (ed.). *Middle Age and
         Aging.* Chicago: University of Chicago Press.
Newman, B. and P. Newman
  1979   *Development Through Life: A Psychosocial Approach.* Homewood, Ill.: Dorsey.
Oakley, A.
  1974   *The Sociology of Housework.* New York: Pantheon Books.
Palmore, Erdman
  1970   "The effects of aging on activities and attitudes." In Erdman Palmore (ed.). *Nor-
         mal Aging.* Durham, N.C.: Duke University Press.
Payne, Barbara and Frank Whittington
  1976   "Older women: An examination of popular stereotypes and research evidence."
         Social Problems 23:489–504.

Pearlin, Leonard
   1980   "Life strains and psychological distress among adults." In Neil Smelser and Erik
           Erikson (eds.). *Themes of Work and Love in Adulthood.* Cambridge, Mass.: Har-
           vard University Press.
Pearlin, Leonard, Morton Lieberman, Elizabeth Menaghan, and Joseph Mullan
   1981   "The stress process." *Journal of Health and Social Behavior* 22:337–356.
Peck, Robert
   1956   "Psychological developments in the second half of life." In John Anderson (ed.).
           Psychological Aspects of Aging. Washington, D.C.: American Psychological As-
           sociation.
Rabushka, Alvin and Bruce Jacobs
   1980   *Old Folks at Home.* New York: The Free Press.
Reichard, Suzanne, Florine Livson, and Paul Peterson
   1962   *Aging and Personality.* New York: John Wiley.
Riley, Matilda
   1976   "Age strata in social systems." In Robert Binstock and Ethel Shanas (eds.).
           Handbook of Aging and the Social Sciences. New York: Van Nostrand Reinhold.
Rodin, Judith
   1980   "Managing the stress of aging: The role of control and coping." In Seymour Le-
           vine and Holgar Ursin (eds.). *Coping and Health.* New York: Plenum Press.
Rosow, Irving
   1974   *Socialization to Old Age.* Berkeley: University of California Press.
Sarason, Seymour
   1977   *Work, Aging, and Social Change.* New York: The Free Press.
Shanas, Ethel, Peter Townsend, Dorothy Wedderbum, Henning Friis, Paul Milhoj, and
Jan Stehouwer
   1968   *Old People in Three Industrial Societies.* New York: Atherton Press.
Sheehy, Gail
   1976   *Passages: Predictable Crises of Adult Life.* New York: E. P. Dutton.
Smelser, Neil
   1980   "Issues in the study of work and love in adulthood." In Neil Smelser and Erik
           Erikson (eds.). *Themes of Work and Love in Adulthood.* Cambridge, Mass.: Har-
           vard University Press.
Sontag, Susan
   1975   "The double standard of aging." In *No Longer Young: The Older Woman in
           America.* Occasional Papers in Gerontology no. 11. Institute of Gerontology,
           The University of Michigan—Wayne State University.
Thoits, Peggy
   1982   "Conceptual, methodological, and theoretical problems in studying social sup-
           port as a buffer against life stress." *Journal of Health and Social Behavior*
           23:145–158.
Turner, Barbara
   1979   "The self-concepts of older women." *Research on Aging* 1:464–480.
Uhlenberg, Peter
   1979   "Older women: The growing challenge to design constructive roles." *The Geron-
           tologist* 19:236–241.
Ward, Russell
   1980   "Sex differences in adult development and well-being." Paper presented at the
           annual meeting of the Gerontological Society of America, San Diego.
Williams, Richard and Claudine Wirths
   1965   *Lives Through the Years.* New York: Atherton Press.

Witt, David, George Lowe, Charles Peek, and Evans Curry
  1980   "The changing association between age and happiness: Emerging trend or meth-
         odological artifact?" *Social Forces* 58:1302–1307.
Woodruff, Diane and James Birren
  1972   "Age changes and cohort differences in personality." *Developmental Psychology*
         6 (2):252–259.

CHAPTER 5

Ansello, E. F. and J. S. Letzler
  1975   "The depiction of the elderly in early childhood literature." Paper presented at
         the Annual Meeting of the Gerontological Society, Louisville, Kentucky.
Arnoff, C.
  1974   "Old age in prime time." *Journal of Communication* 24:4.
Banziger, George
  1979   "Intergenerational communication in prominent Western drama." *The Gerontol-
         ogist* 19:471–480.
Becker, Howard
  1963   *Outsiders: Studies in the Sociology of Deviance.* New York: The Free Press.
Bennett, Ruth and Judith Eckman
  1973   "Attitudes toward aging: A critical examination of recent literature and implica-
         tions for future research." In Carl Eisdorfer and M. Powell Lawton (eds.). *The
         Psychology of Adult Development and Aging.* Washington, D.C.: American Psy-
         chological Association.
Blau, Zena
  1956   "Changes in status and age identification." *American Sociological Review*
         21:198–203.
  1973   *Old Age in a Changing Society.* New York: New Viewpoints.
Blue, Gladys
  1978   "The aging as portrayed in realistic fiction for children 1945–1975." *The Geron-
         tologist* 18:187–192.
Branco, Kenneth and John Williamson
  1982   "Stereotyping and the life cycle: Views of aging and the aged." In Arthur Miller
         (ed.). *In the Eye of the Beholder: Contemporary Issues in Stereotyping.* New York:
         Praeger.
Brubaker, Timothy and Edward Powers
  1976   "The stereotype of 'old'—A review and alternative approach." *Journal of Geron-
         tology* 31:441–447.
Buchholz, Michael and Jack Bynum
  1982   "Newspaper presentation of America's aged: A content analysis of image and
         role." *The Gerontologist* 22:83–88.
Bultena, Gordon and Edward Powers
  1978   "Denial of aging: Age identification and reference group orientations." *Journal
         of Gerontology* 33:748–754.
Butler, Robert
  1975   *Why Survive? Being Old in America.* New York: Harper & Row.
Chiriboga, David
  1978   "Evaluated time: A life course perspective." *Journal of Gerontology* 33:388–
         393.
Clark, Margaret and Barbara Anderson
  1967   *Culture and Aging.* Springfield, Ill.: Charles C. Thomas.

Cooley, Charles Horton
  1902   *Human Nature and the Social Order.* New York: Scribner's.
Cory, Donald
  1951   *The Homosexual in America: A Subjective Approach.* New York: Greenberg.
Crockett, Walter, Allen Press, and Marilyn Osterkamp
  1979   "The effect of deviations from stereotyped expectations upon attitudes toward
         older persons." *Journal of Gerontology* 34:368–374.
Davies, Leland
  1977   "Attitudes toward old age and aging, as shown by humor." *The Gerontologist*
         17:220–226.
Davis, Richard
  1975   "Television communication and the elderly." In Diana Woodruff and James Bir-
         ren (eds.). *Aging: Scientific Perspectives and Social Issues.* New York: D. Van
         Nostrand.
de Beauvoir, Simone
  1972   *The Coming of Age.* New York: Putnam's Sons.
Demos, Vasilikie and Ann Jache
  1981   "When you care enough: An analysis of attitudes toward aging in humorous
         birthday cards." *The Gerontologist* 21:209–215.
Dowd, James
  1980   *Stratification Among the Aged.* Monterey, Calif.: Brooks/Cole.
Edgerton, Robert
  1967   *The Cloak of Competence.* Berkeley: University of California Press.
Fischer, David
  1977   *Growing Old in America.* New York: Oxford University Press.
George, Linda
  1980   *Role Transitions in Later Life.* Monterey, Calif.: Brooks/Cole.
Goffman, Erving
  1963   *Stigma: Notes on the Management of Spoiled Identity.* Englewood Cliffs, N.J.:
         Prentice-Hall.
Harris, Adella and Jonathan Feinberg
  1977   "Television and aging: Is what you see what you get?" *The Gerontologist*
         17:464–468.
Hess, Beth
  1974   "Stereotypes of the aged." *Journal of Communication* 24:76–85.
Klemmack, David, Lucinda Roff, and Richard Durand
  1980   "Who knows how much about aging?" *Research on Aging* 2:432–444.
Kubey, Robert
  1980   "Television and aging: Past, present, and future." *The Gerontologist* 20:16–35.
Lewis, Myrna and Robert Butler
  1972   "Why is women's lib ignoring old women?" *Aging and Human Development*
         3:223–231.
Loughman, Celeste
  1980   "Eros and the elderly: A literary view." *The Gerontologist* 20:182–187.
McTavish, Donald
  1971   "Perceptions of old people: A review of research methodologies and findings."
         The Gerontologist 11:90–101.
Martel, Martin
  1968   "Age-sex roles in American magazine fiction (1890–1955)." In Bernice Neugar-
         ten (ed.). *Middle Age and Aging.* Chicago: University of Chicago Press.

National Council on the Aging
   1975   *The Myth and Reality of Aging in America.* Washington, D.C.
Neugarten, Bernice and Gunhild Hagestad
   1976   "Age and the life course." In Robert Binstock and Ethel Shanas (eds.). *Handbook of Aging and the Social Sciences.* New York: Van Nostrand Reinhold.
Northcott, Herbert
   1975   "Too young, too old—Age in the world of television." *The Gerontologist* 15:184–186.
Palmore, Erdman
   1971   "Attitudes toward aging as shown by humor." *The Gerontologist* 3:181–186.
   1980   "The Facts on Aging Quiz: A review of findings." *The Gerontologist* 20:669–672.
Peters, George
   1971   "Self-conceptions of the aged, age identification, and aging." *The Gerontologist* 11:69–73.
Peterson, David and Elizabeth Karnes
   1976   "Older people in adolescent literature." *The Gerontologist* 16:225–231.
Phillips, Bernard
   1957   "A role theory approach to adjustment in old age." *American Sociological Review* 22:212–217.
Richman, Joseph
   1977   "The foolishness and wisdom of age: Attitudes toward the elderly as reflected in jokes." *The Gerontologist* 17:210–219.
Rosenberg, Morris
   1965   *Society and the Adolescent Self-Image.* Princeton, N.J.: Princeton University Press.
   1981   "The self-concept: Social product and social force." In Morris Rosenberg and Ralph Turner (eds.). *Social Psychology: Sociological Perspectives.* New York: Basic Books.
Rubin, Isadore
   1968   "The 'sexless older years'—A socially harmful stereotype." *The Annals of the American Academy of Political and Social Sciences* 376:86–95.
Schur, Edwin
   1971   *Labeling Deviant Behavior: Its Sociological Implications.* New York: Harper & Row.
Seltzer, Mildred and Robert Atchley
   1971   "The concept of old: Changing attitudes and stereotypes." *The Gerontologist* 11:226–230.
Smith, M. Dwayne
   1979   "The portrayal of elders in magazine cartoons." *The Gerontologist* 19:408–412.
Stone, Gregory
   1962   "Appearance and the self." In Arnold Rose (ed.). *Human Behavior and Social Processes.* Boston: Houghton Mifflin.
Strauss, Anselm
   1962   "Transformations of identity." In Arnold Rose (ed.). *Human Behavior and Social Processes.* Boston: Houghton Mifflin.
Strauss, Helen
   1968   "Reference group and social comparison processes among the totally blind." In Herbert Hyman and Eleanor Singer (eds.). *Readings in Reference Group Theory and Research.* New York: The Free Press.
Stryker, Sheldon
   1981   "Symbolic interactionism: Themes and variations." In Morris Rosenberg and

Ralph Turner (eds.). *Social Psychology: Sociological Perspectives.* New York: Basic Books.

Tibbitts, Clark
1979 "Can we invalidate negative stereotypes of aging?" *The Gerontologist* 19:10–20.

Ward, Russell
1974 "Growing old: Stigma, identity, and subculture." Ph.D. Dissertation, Sociology. University of Wisconsin.
1977 "The impact of subjective age and stigma on older persons." *Journal of Gerontology* 32:227–232.

Weinberger, Linda and Jim Millham
1975 "A multi-dimensional, multiple method analysis of attitudes toward the elderly." *Journal of Gerontology* 30:343–348.

CHAPTER 6

Achenbaum, W. Andrew
1978 *Old Age in the New Land: The American Experience since 1790.* Baltimore: The Johns Hopkins Press.

Atchley, Robert
1976a *The Sociology of Retirement.* New York: Schenkman.
1976b "Selected social and psychological differences between men and women in later life." *Journal of Gerontology* 31:204–211.
1979 "Issues in retirement research." *The Gerontologist* 19:44–54.
1982 "Retirement as a social institution." In Ralph Turner and James Short, Jr. (eds.). *Annual Review of Sociology.* Vol. 8. Palo Alto, Calif.: Annual Reviews.

Ball, Robert
1978 *Social Security Today and Tomorrow.* New York: Columbia University Press.

Barfield, Richard and James Morgan
1978 "Trends in satisfaction with retirement." *The Gerontologist* 18:19–23.

Beller, Daniel
1981 "Coverage patterns of full-time employees under private retirement plans." *Social Security Bulletin* 44 (7):3–11.

Blau, Zena
1973 *Old Age in a Changing Society.* New York: New Viewpoints.

Blauner, Robert
1964 *Alienation and Freedom.* Chicago: University of Chicago Press.

Braverman, Harry
1974 *Labor and Monopoly Capital: The Degradation of Work in the Twentieth Century.* New York: Monthly Review Press.

Bridges, Benjamin and Michael Packard
1981 "Price and income changes for the elderly." *Social Security Bulletin* 44 (1):3–15.

Butler, Robert
1975 *Why Survive? Being Old in America.* New York: Harper & Row.

Calhoun, Richard
1978 *In Search of the New Old: Redefining Old Age in America, 1945–1970.* New York: Elsevier.

Chinoy, Ely
1965 *Automobile Workers and the American Dream.* Boston: Beacon Press.

Clark, Robert and Joseph Spengler
1980a *The Economics of Individual and Population Aging.* Cambridge, Mass.: Cambridge University Press.

1980b "Economic responses to population aging with special emphasis on retirement policy." In Robert Clark (ed.). *Retirement Policy in an Aging Society*. Durham, N.C.: Duke University Press.

Clausen, John
1972   "The life course of individuals." In Matilda Riley, Marilyn Johnson, and Anne Foner (eds.). *Aging and Society*. Vol. 3: *A Sociology of Age Stratification*. New York: Russell Sage.

Cohn, Richard
1979   "Age and the satisfactions from work." *Journal of Gerontology* 34:264–272.

Cumming, Elaine and William Henry
1961   *Growing Old: The Process of Disengagement*. New York: Basic Books.

Donahue, Wilma, Harold Orbach, and Otto Pollak
1960   "Retirement: The emerging social pattern." In Clark Tibbitts (ed.). *Handbook of Social Gerontology: Societal Aspects of Aging*. Chicago: University of Chicago Press.

Dubin, Robert
1956   "Industrial workers' worlds." *Social Problems* 3:131–142.

Ekerdt, David, Raymond Bossé, and John Mogey
1980   "Concurrent change in planned and preferred age for retirement." *Journal of Gerontology* 35:232–240.

Fillenbaum, Gerda
1971a   "Retirement planning programs—at what age, and for whom?" *The Gerontologist* 11:33–36.
1971b   "On the relation between attitude to work and attitude to retirement." *Journal of Gerontology* 26:244–248.

Fillenbaum, Gerda and George Maddox
1974   "Work after retirement: An investigation into some psychologically relevant variables." *The Gerontologist* 14:418–424.

Fischer, David
1977   *Growing Old in America*. New York: Oxford University Press.

Foner, Anne and Karen Schwab
1981   *Aging and Retirement*. Monterey, Calif.: Brooks/Cole.

Friedmann, Eugene and Robert Havighurst
1954   *The Meaning of Work and Retirement*. Chicago: University of Chicago Press.

Fullerton, Howard and James Byrne
1976   "Length of working life for men and women, 1970." *Monthly Labor Review* (February):31–35.

Gecas, Viktor
1981   "Contexts of socialization." In Morris Rosenberg and Ralph Turner (eds.). *Social Psychology: Sociological Perspectives*. New York: Basic Books.

George, Linda
1980   *Role Transitions in Later Life*. Monterey, Calif.: Brooks/Cole.

George, Linda and George Maddox
1977   "Subjective adaptation to loss of the work role: A longitudinal study." *Journal of Gerontology* 32:456–462.

Glamser, Francis
1981a   "Predictors of retirement attitudes." *Aging and Work* 4:23–29.
1981b   "The impact of preretirement programs on the retirement experience." *Journal of Gerontology* 36:244–250.

Glamser, Francis and Gordon DeJong
   1975   "The efficacy of preretirement preparation programs for industrial workers."
          Journal of Gerontology 30:595–600.
Goudy, Willis
   1981   "Changing work expectations: Findings from the Retirement History Study."
          The Gerontologist 21:644–649.
Goudy, Willis, Edward Powers, and Patricia Keith
   1975   "Work and retirement: A test of attitudinal relationships." *Journal of Gerontol-
          ogy* 30:193–198.
Goudy, Willis, Edward Powers, Patricia Keith, and Richard Reger
   1980   "Changes in attitudes toward retirement: Evidence from a panel study of older
          males." *Journal of Gerontology* 35:942–948.
Graebner, William
   1980   *A History of Retirement: The Meaning and Function of an American Institution,
          1885–1978.* New Haven: Yale University Press.
Graney, Marshall and Doris Cottam
   1981   "Labor force nonparticipation of older people: United States, 1890–1970." *The
          Gerontologist* 21:138–141.
Gray, Denis
   1983   "A job club for older job seekers: An experimental evaluation." *Journal of Geron-
          tology* 38:363–368.
Greenough, William
   1980   "The future of employer pensions." In Robert Clark (ed.). *Retirement Policy in
          an Aging Society.* Durham, N.C.: Duke University Press.
Gruenberg, Barry
   1980   "The happy worker: An analysis of educational and occupational differences in
          determinants of job satisfaction." *American Journal of Sociology* 86:247–
          271.
Holden, Karen
   1979   "The inequitable distribution of OASDI benefits among homemakers." *The Ger-
          ontologist* 19:250–256.
Hollister, Robinson
   1974   "Social mythology and reform: Income maintenance for the aged." In Frederick
          Eisele (ed.). *Political Consequences of Aging. The Annals of the American Acad-
          emy of Political and Social Science* 415 (September):19–40.
House, James
   1981   "Social structure and personality." In Morris Rosenberg and Ralph Turner
          (eds.). *Social Psychology: Sociological Perspectives.* New York: Basic Books.
Hughes, Everett
   1958   *Men and Their Work.* New York: The Free Press.
Jaslow, Philip
   1976   "Employment, retirement, and morale among older women." *Journal of Geron-
          tology* 31:212–218.
Karp, David and William Yoels
   1981   "Work, careers, and aging." *Qualitative Sociology* 4:145–166.
Kasschau, Patricia
   1976   "Perceived age discrimination in a sample of aerospace employees." *The Geron-
          tologist* 16:166–173.
   1977   "Age and race discrimination reported by middle-aged and older persons." *So-
          cial Forces* 55:728–742.

Kalleberg, Arne
1977   "Work values and job rewards: A theory of job satisfaction." *American Sociological Review* 42:124–143.

Kaufman, Robert and Seymour Spilerman
1982   "The age structures of occupations and jobs." *American Journal of Sociology* 87:827–851.

Kimmel, Douglas, Karl Price, and James Walker
1978   "Retirement choice and retirement satisfaction." *Journal of Gerontology* 33:575–585.

King, Francis
1978   "The future of private and public employee pensions." In Barbara Herzog (ed.). *Aging and Income: Programs and Prospects for the Elderly.* New York: Human Sciences Press.

Kohn, Melvin and Carmi Schooler
1982   "Job conditions and personality: A longitudinal assessment of their reciprocal effects." *American Journal of Sociology* 87:1257–1286.

Lowy, Louis
1980   *Social Policies and Programs on Aging.* Lexington, Mass.: Lexington Books.

McPherson, Barry and Neil Guppy
1979   "Pre-retirement life-style and the degree of planning for retirement." *Journal of Gerontology* 34:254–263.

Marsh, Robert
1981   "The income and resources of the elderly in 1978." *Social Security Bulletin* **44** (12):3–11.

Meier, Elizabeth
1979   "Developments and trends in the private pension plan sector." *Aging and Work* 2:129–132.

Minkler, Meredith
1981   "Research on the health effects of retirement: An uncertain legacy." *Journal of Health and Social Behavior* 22:117–129.

Morgan, James
1979   "What with inflation and unemployment, who can afford to retire?" In Matilda Riley (ed.). *Aging from Birth to Death: Interdisciplinary Perspectives.* Boulder, Col.: Westview Press.

Morrison, Malcolm
1976   "Planning for income adequacy in retirement: The expectations of current workers." *The Gerontologist* 16:538–543.
1979   "International developments in retirement flexibility." *Aging and Work* 2:221–234.

Morrow, Paula
1981   "Retirement planning programs: Assessing their attendance and efficacy." *Aging and Work* 4:244–252.

Mortimer, Jeylan and Jon Lorence
1979   "Work experiences and occupational value socialization: A longitudinal study." *American Journal of Sociology* 84:1361–1385.

Mortimer, Jeylan and Roberta Simmons
1978   "Adult socialization." In Ralph Turner, James Coleman, and Renée Fox (eds.). *Annual Review of Sociology.* Vol. 4. Palo Alto, Calif.: Annual Reviews.

Munnell, Alicia
1977   *The Future of Social Security.* Washington, D.C.: The Brookings Institution.

Mutran, Elizabeth and Donald Reitzes
  1981 "Retirement, identity and well-being: Realignment of role relationships." *Journal of Gerontology* 36:733–740.
National Council on the Aging
  1975 *The Myth and Reality of Aging in America.* Washington, D.C.
  1981 *Aging in the Eighties: America in Transition.* Washington, D.C.
Palmore, Erdman
  1964 "Retirement patterns among aged men: Findings of the 1963 Survey of the Aged." *Social Security Bulletin* 27: 3–10.
  1972 "Compulsory versus flexible retirement: Issues and facts." *The Gerontologist* 12:343–348.
Palmore, Erdman, William Cleveland, John Nowlin, Dietolf Ramm, and Alene Siegler
  1979 "Stress and adaptation in later life." *Journal of Gerontology* 34:841–851.
Pampel, Fred
  1981 *Social Change and the Aged: Recent Trends in the United States.* Lexington, Mass.: Lexington Books.
Parker, Stanley and Michael Smith
  1976 "Work and leisure." In Robert Dubin (ed.). *Handbook of Work, Organization, and Society.* Chicago. Rand McNally.
Parnes, Herbert
  1981 *Work and Retirement: A Longitudinal Study of Men.* Cambridge, Mass.: MIT Press.
Riley, Matilda, Marilyn Johnson, and Anne Foner
  1972 *Aging and Society.* Vol. 3: *A Sociology of Age Stratification.* New York: Russell Sage.
Rogers, Gayle
  1981 "Vesting of private pension benefits in 1979 and change from 1972." *Social Security Bulletin* 44 (7):13–29.
Rosenberg, George
  1970 *The Worker Grows Old.* San Francisco: Jossey-Bass.
Rosow, Irving
  1974 *Socialization to Old Age.* Berkeley: University of California Press.
Rowe, Alan
  1976 "Retired academics and research activity." *Journal of Gerontology* 31:456–461.
Sarason, Seymour
  1977 *Work, Aging, and Social Change.* New York: The Free Press.
Schneider, Clement
  1964 "Adjustment of employed women to retirement." Unpublished doctoral dissertation, Cornell University, Ithaca, New York.
Schulz, James
  1976 "Income distribution and the aging." In Robert Binstock and Ethel Shanas (eds.). *Handbook of Aging and the Social Sciences.* New York: Van Nostrand Reinhold.
  1980 *The Economics of Aging,* 2nd ed. Belmont, Calif.: Wadsworth.
  1981 "Pension policy at the crossroads: What should be the pension mix?" *The Gerontologist* 21:46–53.
Schulz, James, Guy Carrin, Hans Krupp, Manfred Peschke, Elliott Sclar, and J. Van Steeberge
  1974 *Providing Adequate Retirement Income—Pension Reform in the United States and Abroad.* Hanover, N.H.: New England Press for Brandeis University Press.

Schulz, James, T. Leavitt, and L. Kelly
    1979 "Private pensions fall far short of preretirement income levels." *Monthly Labor Review* 102 (February):28–32.
Shanas, Ethel
    1972 "Adjustment to retirement: Substitution or accommodation?" In Frances Carp (ed.). *Retirement.* New York: Behavioral Publications.
Sheppard, Harold
    1976 "Work and retirement." In Robert Binstock and Ethel Shanas (eds.). *Handbook of Aging and the Social Sciences.* New York: Van Nostrand Reinhold.
Sheppard, Harold and A. Harvey Belitsky
    1966 *The Job Hunt.* Baltimore: Johns Hopkins Press.
Sheppard, Harold and Sara Rix
    1977 *The Graying of Working America: The Coming Crisis in Retirement-Age Policy.* New York: The Free Press.
Siegel, Sidney and Janet Rives
    1980 "Preretirement programs within service firms: Existing and planned programs." *Aging and Work* 3:183–191.
Simpson, Ida, Kurt Back, and John McKinney
    1966a "Attributes of work, involvement in society, and self-evaluation in retirement." In Ida Simpson and John McKinney (eds.). *Social Aspects of Aging.* Durham, N.C.: Duke University Press.
    1966b "Exposure to information on, preparation for, and self-evaluation in retirement." In Ida Simpson and John McKinney (eds.). *Social Aspects of Aging.* Durham, N.C.: Duke University Press.
Sobel, Irvin and Richard Wilcock
    1963 "Job placement services for older workers in the United States." *International Labor Review* 88:129–156.
Social Security Administration
    1980 *Social Security Bulletin* 43 (8).
Soldo, Beth
    1980 "America's Elderly in the 1980s." *Population Bulletin* 35 (4):1–47.
Strauss, Harold, Bruce Aldrich, and Aaron Lipman
    1976 "Retirement and perceived status loss." In Jaber Gubrium (ed.). *Time, Roles, and Self in Old Age.* New York: Human Sciences Press.
Streib, Gordon and Clement Schneider
    1971 *Retirement in American Society.* Ithaca, N.Y.: Cornell University Press.
Sussman, Marvin
    1972 "An analytic model for the sociological study of retirement." In Frances Carp (ed.). *Retirement.* New York: Behavioral Publications.
Taves, Marvin and Gary Hansen
    1963 "Seventeen hundred elderly citizens." In Arnold Rose (ed.). *Aging in Minnesota.* Minneapolis: University of Minnesota Press.
Tiberi, Daniel, Virginia Boyack, and Paul Kerschner
    1978 "A comparative analysis of four preretirement education models." *Educational Gerontology* 3:355–374.
U.S. Department of Health, Education, and Welfare
    1973 *Work in America.* Cambridge, Mass.: MIT Press.
Viscusi, W. Kip
    1979 *Welfare of the Elderly: An Economic Analysis and Policy Prescription.* New York: Wiley-Interscience.

Ward, Russell
  1982   "Occupational variation in the life course: Implications for later life." In Nancy
          Osgood (ed.). *Life After Work: Retirement, Leisure, Recreation and the Elderly.*
          New York: Praeger.
Wilson, J.
  1980   "Sociology of Leisure." In Alex Inkeles, Neil Smelser, and Ralph Turner (eds.).
          Annual Review of Sociology. Vol. 6. Palo Alto, Calif.: Annual Reviews.
Wright, James and Richard Hamilton
  1978   "Work satisfaction and age: Some evidence for the 'job change' hypothesis." *So-
          cial Forces* 56:1140–1158.

CHAPTER 7

Atchley, Robert
  1971   "Retirement and leisure participation: Continuity or crisis?" *The Gerontologist*
          11:13–17.
Atkins, Charles
  1976   "Mass media and the aging." In Herbert Oyer and E. Jane Oyer (eds.). *Aging
          and Communication.* Baltimore: University Park Press.
Auerbach, Doris and Richard Levenson, Jr.
  1977   "Second impressions: Attitude change in college students toward the elderly."
          The Gerontologist 17:362–366.
Babchuk, Nicholas, George Peters, Danny Hoyt, and Marvin Kaiser
  1979   "The voluntary associations of the aged." *Journal of Gerontology* 34:579–587.
Bahr, Howard
  1970   "Aging and religious disaffiliation." *Social Forces* 46:60–71.
Best, Fred
  1979   "The future of retirement and lifetime distribution of work." *Aging and Work*
          2:173–181.
Blau, Zena
  1973   *Old Age in a Changing Society.* New York: New Viewpoints.
Blazer, Dan and Erdman Palmore
  1976   "Religion and aging in a longitudinal panel." *The Gerontologist* 16:82–85.
Bossé, Raymond and David Ekerdt
  1981   "Change in self-perception of leisure activities with retirement." *The Gerontolo-
          gist* 21:650–654.
Bull, C. Neil and Jackie Aucoin
  1975   "Voluntary association participation and life satisfaction." *Journal of Gerontol-
          ogy* 30:73–76.
Butler, Robert
  1975   *Why Survive? Being Old in America.* New York: Harper & Row.
Clemente, Frank, Patricia Rexroad, and Carl Hirsch
  1975   "The participation of the black aged in voluntary associations." *Journal of Ger-
          ontology* 30:469–472.
Covey, Herbert
  1980   "An exploratory study of the acquisition of a college student role by older peo-
          ple." *The Gerontologist* 20:173–181.
Cutler, Stephen
  1976a   "Age profiles of membership in sixteen types of voluntary associations." *Journal
          of Gerontology* 31:462–470.

1976b "Membership in different types of voluntary associations and psychological well-being." *The Gerontologist* 16:335–339.

1977 "Aging and voluntary association participation." *Journal of Gerontology* 32:470–479.

Donald, Marjorie and Robert Havighurst
1959 "The meanings of leisure." *Social Forces* 37:355–360.

Dumazedier, Joffre
1967 *Toward a Society of Leisure.* New York: The Free Press.

Emery, F. and E. Trist
1973 *Towards a Social Ecology.* London: Plenum.

Foner, Anne and Karen Schwab
1981 *Aging and Retirement.* Monterey, Calif.: Brooks/Cole.

Goodrow, Bruce
1975 "Limiting factors in reducing participation in older adult learning opportunities." *The Gerontologist* 15:418–422.

Gordon, Chad, Charles Gaitz, and Judith Scott
1976 "Leisure and lives: Personal expressivity across the life span." In Robert Binstock and Ethel Shanas (eds.). *Handbook of Aging and the Social Sciences.* New York: Van Nostrand Reinhold.

Hanssen, Anne, Nicholas Meima, Linda Buckspan, Barbara Henderson, Thea Helbig, and Steven Zarit
1978 "Correlates of senior center participation." *The Gerontologist* 18:193–200.

Havighurst, Robert
1949 "Old age—an American problem." *Journal of Gerontology* 4:298–304.

1961 "The nature and values of meaningful free-time activity." In Robert Kleemeier (ed.). *Aging and Leisure.* New York: Oxford University Press.

1973 "Social roles, work, leisure, and education." In Carl Eisdorfer and M. Powell Lawton (eds.). *The Psychology of Adult Development and Aging.* Washington, D.C.: American Psychological Association.

Havighurst, Robert and Kenneth Feigenbaum
1959 "Leisure and life style." *American Journal of Sociology* 64:396–404.

Hunter, K. and Margaret Linn
1981 "Psychosocial differences between elderly volunteers and non-volunteers." *Aging and Human Development* 12:205–213.

Iso-Ahola, Sappo
1980 "Toward a dialectical social psychology of leisure and recreation." In Seppo Iso-Ahola (ed.). *Social Psychological Perspectives on Leisure and Recreation.* Springfield, Ill.: Charles C. Thomas.

Kaplan, Max
1975 *Leisure: Theory and Policy.* New York: John Wiley.
1979 *Leisure: Lifestyle and Lifespan.* Philadelphia: W. B. Saunders.

Kelly, John
1972 "Work and leisure: A simplified paradigm." *Journal of Leisure Research* 4:50–62.

1981 "Leisure interaction and the social dialectic." *Social Forces* 60:304–322.

Kivett, Vira
1979 "Religious motivation in middle age: Correlates and implications." *Journal of Gerontology* 34:106–115.

Kleiber, Douglas and John Kelly
1980 "Leisure, socialization, and the life cycle." In Seppo Iso-Ahola (ed.). *Social Psy-*

chological Perspectives on Leisure and Recreation. Springfield, Ill.: Charles C.
Thomas.

Kubey, Robert
  1980   "Television and aging: Past, present, and future." *The Gerontologist* 20:16–35.
Lakin, Martin and Melvin Dray
  1958   "Psychological aspects of activity for the aged." *American Journal of Occupational Therapy* 12:172–175.
Lawton, M. Powell
  1978   "Leisure activities for the aged." In Marvin Wolfgang (ed.). *Planning for the Elderly. Annals of the American Academy of Political and Social Sciences* 438 (July):71–80.
Levy, S.M.
  1979   "Temporal experience in the aged: Body integrity and the social milieu." *Aging and Human Development* 9:313–344.
Lowenthal, Marjorie and Betsy Robinson
  1976   "Social networks and isolation." In Robert Binstock and Ethel Shanas (eds.). *Handbook of Aging and the Social Sciences.* New York: Van Nostrand Reinhold.
Lowenthal, Marjorie, Majda Thurnker, and David Chiriboga
  1975   *Four Stages of Life.* San Francisco: Jossey-Bass.
Maeda, Daisaku
  1975   "Growth of old people's clubs in Japan." *The Gerontologist* 15:254–256.
Miller, Stephen
  1965   "The social dilemma of the aging leisure participant." In Arnold Rose and Warren Peterson (eds.). *Older People and Their Social Worlds.* Philadelphia: F. A. Davis.
Mindel, Charles and C. Edwin Vaughan
  1978   "A multidimensional approach to religiosity and disengagement." *Journal of Gerontology* 33:103–108.
Moberg, David
  1965   "Religiosity in old age." *The Gerontologist* 5:78–87.
Monk, Abraham and Arthur Cryns
  1974   "Predictors of voluntaristic intent among the aged: An area study." *The Gerontologist* 14:425–429.
Moss, Miriam and M. Powell Lawton
  1982   "Time budgets of older people: A window on four lifestyles." *Journal of Gerontology* 37:115–123.
National Council on the Aging
  1975   *The Myth and Reality of Aging in America.* Washington, D.C.
  1981   *Aging in the Eighties: America in Transition.* Washington, D.C.
Newman, B. and P. Newman
  1979   *Development Through Life: A Psycho-Social Approach.* Homewood, Ill.: Dorsey.
Parelius, Ann
  1975   "Lifelong education and age stratification." *American Behavioral Scientist* 19:206–223.
Payne, Barbara and Frank Whittington
  1976   "Older women: An examination of popular stereotypes and research evidence." *Social Problems* 23:488–504.
Peppers, Larry
  1976   "Patterns of leisure and adjustment to retirement." *The Gerontologist* 16:441–446.

Peterson, David
    1975   "Life-span education and gerontology." *The Gerontologist* 15:436–441.
Pfeiffer, Eric and Glenn Davis
    1971   "The use of leisure time in middle life." *The Gerontologist* 11:187–195.
Pieper, Hanns
    1981   "Church membership and participation in church activities among the elderly."
           Activities, Adaptation and Aging 1 (3):23–29.
Romaniuk, Jean and Michael Romaniuk
    1982   "Participation motives of older adults in higher education: The Elderhostel expe-
           rience." *The Gerontologist* 22:364–368.
Rapoport, Rhona and Robert Rapoport
    1975   *Leisure in the Family Life Cycle.* London: Routledge and Kegan Paul.
Saltz, Rosalyn
    1971   "Aging persons as child-care workers in a Foster-Grandparent program: Psycho-
           social effects and work performance." *Aging and Human Development*
           2:314–340.
Sarason, Seymour
    1977   *Work, Aging and Social Change.* New York: The Free Press.
Smith, Constance and A. Freedman
    1972   *Voluntary Associations.* Cambridge, Mass.: Harvard University Press.
Stark, Rodney
    1968   "Age and faith: A changing outlook or an old process?" *Sociological Analysis*
           29:1–10.
Stone, Ken and Richard Kalish
    1973   "Of poker, roles, and aging: Description, discussion, and data." *Aging and
           Human Development* 4:1–13.
Taietz, Philip
    1976   "Two conceptual models of the senior center." *Journal of Gerontology*
           31:219–222.
Teague, Michael
    1980   "Aging and leisure: A social psychological perspective." In Seppo Iso-Ahola
           (ed.). *Social Psychological Perspectives on Leisure and Recreation.* Springfield,
           Ill.: Charles C. Thomas.
Tibbitts, Clark
    1979   "Can we invalidate negative stereotypes of aging?" *The Gerontologist* 19:
           10–20.
Trela, James
    1976   "Social class and association membership: An analysis of age-graded and
           non-age-graded voluntary participation." *Journal of Gerontology* 31:198–203.
Wallach, M. and L. Green
    1968   "On age and the subjective speed of time." In Bernice Neugarten (ed.), *Middle
           Age and Aging.* Chicago: University of Chicago Press.
Ward, Russell
    1979   "The meaning of voluntary association participation to older people." *Journal
           of Gerontology* 34:438–445.
    1982a "Aging, the use of time, and social change." *Aging and Human Development*
           14:177–187.
    1982b "Occupational variation in the life course: Implications for later life." In Nancy
           Osgood (ed.). *Life After Work: Retirement, Leisure, Recreation and the Elderly.*
           New York: Praeger.

Wilson, J.
1980   "Sociology of leisure." In Alex Inkeles, Neil Smelser, and Ralph Turner (eds.).
        Annual Review of Sociology. Vol. 6. Palo Alto, Calif.: Annual Reviews.
Wilson, Robert
1981   "The courage to be leisured." *Social Forces* 60:282–303.
Wingrove, C. Ray and Jon Alston
1971   "Age, aging, and church attendance." *The Gerontologist* 11:356–358.
Wuthnow, Robert
1976   "Recent patterns of secularization: A problem of generations?" *American Socio-
        logical Review* 41:850–867.
Zablocki, Benjamin and Rosabeth Kanter
1976   "The differentiation of life styles." *Annual Review of Sociology.* Vol. 2. Palo Alto,
        Calif.: Annual Reviews.

CHAPTER 8

Adams, Bert
1967   "Interaction theory and the social network." *Sociometry* 30:64–78.
1975   *The Family: A Sociological Interpretation.* Chicago: Rand McNally.
Atchley, Robert
1975   "Dimensions of widowhood in later life." *The Gerontologist* 15:176–178.
Bart, Pauline
1971   "Depression in middle-aged women." In Vivian Gornick and Barbara Moran
        (eds.). *Women in Sexist Society.* New York: New American Library.
Beckman, Linda and Betsy Houser
1982   "The consequences of childlessness on the social-psychological well-being of
        older women." *Journal of Gerontology* 37:243–250.
Bell, Robert
1971   *Marriage and Family Interaction.* Homewood, Ill.: Dorsey.
Bengtson, Vern and Edythe DeTerre
1980   "Aging and family relations." *Marriage and Family Review* 3 (½):51–76.
Berardo, Felix
1970   "Survivorship and social isolation: The case of the aged widower." *Family Coor-
        dinator* 19:11–15.
Blau, Zena
1961   "Structural constraints on friendship in old age." *American Sociological Review*
        26:429–439.
Block, Marilyn, Janice Davidson and Jean Grambs
1981   *Women Over Forty: Visions and Realities.* New York: Springer.
Blood, Robert and Donald Wolfe
1960   *Husbands and Wives.* New York: The Free Press.
Botwinick, Jack
1978   *Aging and Behavior.* New York: Springer.
Branco, Kenneth and John Williamson
1982   "Stereotyping and the life cycle: Views of aging and the aged." In Arthur Miller
        (ed.). *In the Eye of the Beholder: Contemporary Issues in Stereotyping.* New York:
        Praeger.
Brody, Elaine
1981   " 'Women in the middle' and family help to older people." *The Gerontologist*
        21:471–480.

Chevan, Albert and J. Henry Korson
  1972 "The widowed who live alone: An examination of social and demographic factors." *Social Forces* 51:45–53.
Cleveland, William and Daniel Gianturco
  1976 "Remarriage probability after widowhood: A retrospective method." *Journal of Gerontology* 31:99–103.
Crossman, Linda, Cecilia London, and Clemmie Barry
  1981 "Older women caring for disabled spouses: A model for supportive services." *The Gerontologist* 21:464–470.
Cumming, Elaine and William Henry
  1961 *Growing Old: The Process of Disengagement.* New York: Basic Books.
Demos, John
  1970 *A Little Commonwealth: Family Life in Plymouth Colony.* New York: Oxford University Press.
Deutscher, Irwin
  1964 "The quality of postparental life." *Journal of Marriage and the Family* 26:52–59.
Elder, Glen, Jr.
  1981 "History and the family: The discovery of complexity." *Journal of Marriage and the Family* 43:489–519.
Feldman, Harold
  1964 "Development of the husband-wife relationship." *Preliminary report, Cornell Studies of Marital Development: Study in the Transition to Parenthood.* Department of Child Development and Family Relationships, New York State College of Home Economics, Cornell University.
Fengler, Alfred and Nancy Goodrich
  1979 "Wives of elderly disabled men: The hidden patients." *The Gerontologist* 19:175–183.
Fenwick, Rudy and Charles Barresi
  1981 "Health consequences of marital-status change among the elderly: A comparison of cross-sectional and longitudinal analyses." *Journal of Health and Social Behavior* 22:106–116.
Foner, Anne
  1978 "Age stratification and the changing family." In John Demos and Sarane Boocock (eds.). *Turning Points: Historical and Sociological Essays on the Family.* Chicago: University of Chicago Press.
Foner, Anne and Karen Schwab
  1981 *Aging and Retirement.* Monterey, Calif.: Brooks/Cole.
George, Linda
  1980 *Role Transitions in Later Life.* Monterey, Calif.: Brooks/Cole.
Gilford, Rosalie and Vern Bengtson
  1979 "Measuring marital satisfaction in three generations: Positive and negative dimensions." *Journal of Marriage and the Family* 41:387–398.
Glenn, Norval and Sara McLanahan
  1981 "The effects of offspring on the psychological well-being of older adults." *Journal of Marriage and the Family* 43:409–421.
Gubrium, Jaber
  1975 "Being single in old age." *Aging and Human Development* 6:29–41.
Hareven, Tamara
  1978 "Introduction: The historical study of the life cycle." In Tamara Hareven (ed.). *Transitions: The Family and the Life Course in Historical Perspective.* New York: Academic Press.

Helsing, Knud and Moyses Szklo
  1981   "Mortality after bereavement." *American Journal of Epidemiology.* 114:41–52.
Hess, Beth
  1979   "Sex roles, friendship, and the life course." *Research on Aging* 1:494–515.
Hill, Reuben
  1965   "Decision making and the family life cycle." In Ethel Shanas and Gordon Streib (eds.). *Social Structure and the Family: Generational Relations.* Englewood Cliffs, N.J.: Prentice-Hall.
Hochschild, Arlie
  1976   "Disengagement theory: A logical, empirical, and phenomenological critique." In Jaber Gubrium (ed.). *Time, Roles, and Self in Old Age.* New York: Human Sciences Press.
Jackson, Jacquelyne
  1971   "Aged blacks: A potpourri towards the reduction of racial inequalities." *Phylon* 32:260–280.
Kahana, Eva
  1970   "Grandparenthood from the perspective of the developing grandchild." *Developmental Psychology* 3:98–105.
Kahana, Eva and Boaz Kahana
  1971   "Theoretical and research perspectives on grandparenthood." *Aging and Human Development* 2:261–268.
Keating, Norah and Priscilla Cole
  1980   "What do I do with him 24 hours a day? Changes in the housewife role after retirement." *The Gerontologist* 20:84–89
Kerckhoff, Alan
  1965   "Nuclear and extended family relationships: A normative and behavioral analysis." In Ethel Shanas and Gordon Streib (eds.). *Social Structure and the Family: Generational Relations.* Englewood Cliffs, N.J.: Prentice-Hall.
  1966a "Family patterns and morale in retirement." In Ida Simpson and John McKinney (eds.). *Social Aspects of Aging.* Durham, N.C.: Duke University Press.
  1966b "Norm-value clusters and the strain toward consistency among older married couples." In Ida Simpson and John McKinney (eds.). *Social Aspects of Aging.* Durham, N.C.: Duke University Press.
Kivnick, Helen
  1982   "Grandparenthood: An overview of meaning and mental health." *The Gerontologist* 22:59–66.
Lee, Gary
  1980   "Kinship in the seventies: A decade review of research and theory." *Journal of Marriage and the Family* 42:923–934.
Lipman, Aaron
  1962   "Role conceptions of couples in retirement." In Clark Tibbits and Wilma Donahue (eds.). *Social and Psychological Aspects of Aging.* New York: Columbia University Press.
Litwak, Eugene and Ivan Szelenyi
  1969   "Primary group structures and their functions: Kin, neighbors, and friends." *American Sociological Review* 34:465–481.
Lobsenz, Norman
  1974   "Sex and the senior citizen." *New York Times* Magazine, 20 January.
Lopata, Helena
  1969   "Loneliness: Forms and components." *Social Problems* 17:248–261.
  1973   *Widowhood in an American City.* Cambridge, Mass.: Schenkman.

1979   *Women as Widows: Support Systems.* New York: Elsevier.
1980   "The widowed family member." In Nancy Datan and Nancy Lohmann (eds.).
        Transitions of Aging. New York: Academic Press.
1981   "Widowhood and husband sanctification." *Journal of Marriage and the Family*
        43:439–450.
Lowenthal, Marjorie, Majda Thurnher, and David Chiriboga
1975   *Four Stages of Life.* San Francisco: Jossey-Bass.
Ludeman, Kate
1981   "The sexuality of the older person: Review of the literature." *The Gerontologist*
        21:203–208.
Masters, William and Virginia Johnson
1966   *Human Sexual Response.* Boston: Little, Brown.
McCall, George and J. L. Simmons
1966   *Identities and Interactions.* New York: The Free Press.
McKain, Walter
1972   "A new look at older marriages." *Family Coordinator* 21:61–69.
Matthews, Sarah
1979   *The Social World of Old Women: Management of Self-Identity.* Beverly Hills:
        Sage.
Mindel, Charles
1979   "Multigenerational family households: Recent trends and implications for the
        future." *The Gerontologist* 19:456–463.
Mindel, Charles and Roosevelt Wright, Jr.
1982   "Satisfaction in multigenerational households." *Journal of Gerontology*
        37:483–489.
Morgan, Leslie
1976   "A re-examination of widowhood and morale." *Journal of Gerontology*
        31:687–695.
National Council on the Aging
1975   *The Myth and Reality of Aging in America.* Washington, D.C.
Neugarten, Bernice and Karol Weinstein
1964   "The changing American grandparent." *Journal of Marriage and the Family*
        26:199–204.
Nock, Steven
1979   "The family life cycle: Empirical or conceptual tool?" *Journal of Marriage and
        the Family* 41:15–26.
Notman, M.
1980   "Adult life cycles: Changing roles and changing hormones." In J. Parsons (ed.).
        The Psychobiology of Sex Differences and Sex Roles. Washington, D.C.: Hemi-
        sphere.
Pfeiffer, Eric and Glenn Davis
1972   "Determinants of sexual behavior in middle and old age." *Journal of the Ameri-
        can Geriatrics Society* 20:151–158.
Pfeiffer, Eric, Adriaan Verwoerdt, and Glenn Davis
1972   "Sexual behavior in middle life." *American Journal of Psychiatry* 128:1262–1267.
Pihlblad, C. T. and David Adams
1972   "Widowhood, social participation and life satisfaction." *Aging and Human De-
        velopment* 3:323–330.
Pineo, Peter
1961   "Disenchantment in the later years of marriage." *Marriage and Family Living*
        23:3–11.

Riley, Matilda and Anne Foner
  1968   *Aging and Society.* Vol. 1: *An Inventory of Research Findings.* New York: Russell
          Sage.
Robertson, Joan
  1976   "Significance of grandparents: Perceptions of young adult grandchildren." *The
          Gerontologist* 16:137–140.
  1977   "Grandmotherhood: A study of role conceptions." *Journal of Marriage and the
          Family* 38:165–174.
Robinson, Betsy and Majda Thurnher
  1979   "Taking care of aged parents: A family cycle transition." *The Gerontologist*
          19:586–593.
Rollins, Boyd and Harold Feldman
  1970   "Marital satisfaction over the family life cycle." *Journal of Marriage and The
          Family* 32:20–28.
Rosenberg, George and Donald Anspach
  1973   *Working Class Kinship.* Lexington, Mass.: Lexington Books.
Rosow, Irving
  1965   "Intergenerational relationships: Problems and proposals." In Ethel Shanas and
          Gordon Streib (eds.). *Social Structure and the Family: Generational Relations.*
          Englewood Cliffs, N.J.: Prentice-Hall.
Rubin, Isadore
  1968   "The 'sexless older years'—a socially harmful stereotype." *Annals of the Ameri-
          can Academy of Political and Social Science* 376:86–95.
Schram, Rosalyn
  1979   "Marital satisfaction over the family life cycle: A critique and proposal." *Journal
          of Marriage and the Family* 41:7–12.
Schutz, William
  1966   *The Interpersonal Underworld.* Palo Alto, Calif.: Science and Behavior Books.
Shanas, Ethel
  1979   "The family as a support system in old age." *The Gerontologist* 19:169–174.
Shanas, Ethel, Peter Townsend, Dorothy Wedderbum, Henning Friis, Paul Milhoj, and
Jan Stehouwer
  1968   *Old People in Three Industrial Societies.* New York: Atherton Press.
Singh, B. Krishna and J. Sherwood Williams
  1981   "Childlessness and family satisfaction." *Research on Aging* 3:218–227.
Sjoberg, Gideon
  1956   "Familial organization in the pre-industrial city." *Marriage and Family Living*
          18:30–36.
Stehouwer, Jan
  1965   "Relations between generations and the three-generation household in Den-
          mark." In Ethel Shanas and Gordon Streib (eds.). *Social Structure and the Fami-
          ly: Generational Relations.* Englewood Cliffs, N.J.: Prentice-Hall.
Stimson, Ardyth, Jane Wase, and John Stimson
  1981   "Sexuality and self-esteem among the aged." *Research on Aging* 3:228–239.
Stinnett, N., Linda Carter, and J. E. Montgomery
  1972   "Older persons' perceptions of their marriages." *Journal of Marriage and the
          Family* 34:665–670.
Streib, Gordon and Rubye Beck
  1980   "Older families: A decade review." *Journal of Marriage and the Family*
          42:937–956.

Sussman, Marvin
  1976 "The family life of old people." In Robert Binstock and Ethel Shanas (eds.). *Handbook of Aging and the Social Sciences.* New York: Van Nostrand Reinhold.

Thurnher, Majda
  1976 "Midlife marriage: Sex differences in evaluation and perspectives." *Aging and Human Development* 7:129–135.

Townsend, Peter
  1957 *The Family Life of Old People.* London: Routledge and Kegan Paul.

Treas, Judith
  1975 "Aging and the family." In Diana Woodruff and James Birren (eds.). *Aging: Scientific Perspectives and Social Issues.* New York: D. Van Nostrand.
  1977 "Family support systems for the aged: Some social and demographic considerations." *The Gerontologist* 17:486–491.

Treas, Judith and Anke Van Hilst
  1976 "Marriage and remarriage rates among older Americans." *The Gerontologist* 16:132–136.

Troll, Lillian
  1980 "Grandparenting." In Leonard Poon (ed.). *Aging in the 1980s: Psychological Issues.* Washington, D.C.: American Psychological Association.

Troll, Lillian, Sheila Miller, and Robert Atchley
  1979 *Families in Later Life.* Belmont, Calif.: Wadsworth.

Uhlenberg, Peter and Mary Anne Myers
  1981 "Divorce and the elderly." *The Gerontologist* 21:276–282.

Wallace, Carol
  1980 "Granny bashing: When adults abuse their elderly parents." *Daily News,* New York (February 7): C 10.

Ward, Russell
  1978 "Limitations of the family as a supportive institution in the lives of the aged." *Family Coordinator* 27:365–373.
  1979 "The never-married in later life." *Journal of Gerontology* 34:861–869.
  1981 "Sex differences in the impact of widowhood: Social supports and life satisfaction." Paper presented at the annual meeting of the Society for the Study of Social Problems, Toronto.

Weiss, Robert
  1973 *Loneliness: The Experience of Emotional and Social Isolation.* Cambridge, Mass.: MIT Press.

Willmott, Peter and Michael Young
  1960 *Family and Class in a London Suburb.* London: Routledge and Kegan Paul.

Wood, Vivian and Joan Robertson
  1976 "The significance of grandparenthood." In Jaber Gubrium (ed.). *Time, Roles, and Self in Old Age.* New York: Human Sciences Press.

CHAPTER 9

Arling, Greg
  1976 "The elderly widow and her family, neighbors and friends." *Journal of Marriage and the Family* 38:757–768.

Babchuk, Nicholas
  1978 "Aging and primary relations." *Aging and Human Development* 9:137–151.

Becker, Gaylene
1980 *Growing Old in Silence.* Berkeley: University of California Press.
Bednar, Michael (ed.)
1977 *Barrier-Free Environments.* Stroudsburg, Pa.: Dowden, Hutchinson and Ross.
Blau, Zena
1961 "Structural constraints on friendship in old age." *American Sociological Review* 26:429–439.
1973 *Old Age in a Changing Society.* New York: New Viewpoints.
Bohland, James and Lexa Davis
1979 "Sources of residential satisfaction among the elderly: An age comparative analysis." In Stephen Golant (ed.). *Location and Environment of Elderly Population.* Washington, D.C.: V. H. Winston & Sons.
Bultena, Gordon and Vivian Wood
1969 "The American retirement community: Bane or blessing?" *Journal of Gerontology* 24:209–217.
1970 "Leisure orientation and recreational activities of retirement community residents." *Journal of Leisure Research* 2:3–15.
Butler, Robert
1975 *Why Survive? Being Old in America.* New York: Harper & Row.
Cantor, Marjorie
1975 "Life space and the social support system of the inner city elderly of New York." *The Gerontologist* 15:23–26.
1979 "Neighbors and friends: An overlooked resource in the informal support system." *Research on Aging* 1:434–463.
Cantor, Marjorie and Mary Mayer
1976 "Health and the inner city elderly." *The Gerontologist* 16:17–24.
Carp, Frances
1975a "Life-style and location within the city." *The Gerontologist* 15:27–34.
1975b "Impact of improved housing on morale and life satisfaction." *The Gerontologist* 15:511–515.
1976 "Housing and living environments of older people." In Robert Binstock and Ethel Shanas (eds.). *Handbook of Aging and the Social Sciences.* New York: Van Nostrand Reinhold.
1977 "Impact of improved living environment on health and life expectancy." *The Gerontologist* 17:242–249.
Carp, Frances and Abraham Carp
1980 "Person-environment congruence and sociability." *Research on Aging* 2:395–415.
Clemente, Frank and Michael Kleiman
1976 "Fear of crime among the aged." *The Gerontologist* 16:207–210.
Cobb, Sidney
1976 "Social support as a moderator of life stress." *Psychosomatic Medicine* 38:300–314.
Cohen, Carl and Jay Sokolvsky
1980 "Social engagement versus isolation: The case of the aged in SRO hotels." *The Gerontologist* 20:36–44.
Cohen, Lawrence, James Kluegel, and Kenneth Land
1981 "Social inequality and predatory criminal victimization: An exposition and test of a formal theory." *American Sociological Review* 46:505–524.

Conner, Karen, Edward Powers, and Gordon Bultena
   1979   "Social interaction and life satisfaction: An empirical assessment of late-life pat-
           terns." *Journal of Gerontology* 34:116–121.
Cook, Fay, Wesley Skogan, Thomas Cook, and George Antunes
   1978   "Criminal victimization of the elderly: The physical and economic conse-
           quences." *The Gerontologist* 18:338–349.
Cutler, Stephen
   1975   "Transportation and changes in life satisfaction." *The Gerontologist* 15:155–
           159.
Dono, John, Cecilia Falbe, Barbara Kail, Eugene Litwak, Roger Sherman, and David Siegel
   1979   "Primary groups in old age: Structure and function." *Research on Aging*
           1:403–433.
Dowd, James
   1980   *Stratification Among the Aged.* Monterey, Calif.: Brooks/Cole.
Eckert, J. Kevin
   1979   "Urban renewal and redevelopment: High risk for the marginally subsistent el-
           derly." *The Gerontologist* 19:496–502.
Fischer, Claude (ed.)
   1977   *Networks and Places: Social Relations in the Urban Setting.* New York: The Free
           Press.
George, Linda
   1980   *Role Transitions in Later Life.* Monterey, Calif.: Brooks/Cole.
Golant, Stephen
   1976   "Intraurban transportation needs and problems of the elderly." In M. Powell
           Lawton, Robert Newcomer, and Thomas Byerts (eds.). *Community Planning for
           an Aging Society: Designing Services and Facilities.* Stroudsburg, Pa.: Dowden,
           Hutchinson & Ross.
   1979   "Central City, suburban, and nonmetropolitan area migration patterns of the
           elderly." In Stephen Golant (ed.). *Location and Environment of Elderly Popula-
           tion.* Washington, D.C.: V. H. Winston & Sons.
Graney, Marshall
   1975   "Happiness and social participation in aging." *Journal of Gerontology*
           30:701–706.
Gubrium, Jaber
   1973   *The Myth of the Golden Years: A Socio-Environmental Theory of Aging.* Spring-
           field, Ill.: Charles C. Thomas.
Hartman, Chester, Jerry Horovitz, and Robert Herman
   1976   "Designing with the elderly: A user needs survey for housing low-income senior
           citizens." *The Gerontologist* 16:303–311.
Heintz, Katherine
   1976   *Retirement Communities: For Adults Only.* New Brunswick, N.J.: Center for
           Urban Policy Research, Rutgers—The State University of New Jersey.
Henig, Jeffrey
   1981   "Gentrification and displacement of the elderly: An empirical analysis." *The
           Gerontologist* 21:67–75.
Hess, Beth
   1972   "Friendship." In Matilda Riley, Marilyn Johnson, and Anne Foner (eds.). *Aging
           and Society.* Vol. 3: *A Sociology of Age Stratification.* New York: Russell Sage.
   1979   "Sex roles, friendship, and the life course." *Research on Aging* 1:494–515.

Hochschild, Arlie
  1973   *The Unexpected Community.* Englewood Cliffs, N.J.: Prentice-Hall.
Hoyt, G. C.
  1954   "The life of the retired in a trailer park." *American Journal of Sociology*
          59:361–370.
Jacobs, Jerry
  1974   *Fun City: An Ethnographic Study of a Retirement Community.* New York: Holt,
          Rinehart and Winston.
  1975   *Older Persons and Retirement Communities: Case Studies in Social Gerontology.*
          Springfield, Ill.: Charles C. Thomas.
Johnson, Sheila
  1971   *Idle Haven: Community Building Among the Working-Class Retired.* Berkeley:
          University of California Press.
Kahana, Eva
  1982   "A congruence model of person-environment interaction." In M. Powell Law-
          ton, P. G. Windley, and Thomas Byerts (eds.), *Aging and the Environment: Theo-
          retical Approaches.* New York: Springer.
Kahn, Robert
  1979   "Aging and social support." In Matilda Riley (ed.). *Aging from Birth to Death:
          Interdisciplinary Perspectives.* Boulder, Col.: Westview Press.
Kendig, H.
  1976   "Neighborhood conditions of the aged and local government." *The Gerontologist*
          16:148–156.
Larson, Reed
  1978   "Thirty years of research on the subjective well-being of older Americans." *Jour-
          nal of Gerontology* 33:109–125.
Lawton, M. Powell
  1980a   *Environment and Aging.* Monterey, Calif.: Brooks/Cole.
  1980b   "Housing the elderly: Residential quality and residential satisfaction." *Research
          on Aging* 2:309–328.
Lawton, M. Powell, Maurice Greenbaum, and Bernard Liebowitz
  1980   "The lifespan of housing environments for the aging." *The Gerontologist*
          20:56–64.
Lawton, M. Powell and Lucille Nahemow
  1973   "Ecology and the aging process." In Carl Eisdorfer and M. Powell Lawton (eds.).
          The Psychology of Adult Development and Aging. Washington, D.C.: American
          Psychological Association.
  1978   "Social areas and the well-being of tenants in housing for the elderly." Paper
          presented at meetings of the Gerontological Society, Dallas.
Lawton, M. Powell and Silvia Yaffe
  1980   "Victimization and fear of crime in elderly public housing tenants." *Journal of
          Gerontology* 35:768–779.
Lebowitz, Barry
  1975   "Age and fearfulness: Personal and situational factors." *Journal of Gerontology*
          30:696–700.
Liang, Jersey, Louis Dvorkin, Eva Kahana, and Florence Mazian
  1980   "Social integration and morale: A re-examination." *Journal of Gerontology*
          35:746–757.
Liang, Jersey and Mary Sengstock
  1981   "The risk of personal victimization among the aged." *Journal of Gerontology*
          36:463–471.

Litwak, Eugene and Ivan Szelenyi
1969 "Primary group structures and their functions: Kin, neighbors, and friends." *American Sociological Review* 34:465–481.

Longino, Charles, Kent McClelland, and Warren Peterson
1980 "The aged subculture hypothesis: Social integration, gerontophilia and self-conception." *Journal of Gerontology* 35:758–767.

Lopata, Helena
1973 *Widowhood in an American City.* Cambridge, Mass.: Schenkman.

Lowenthal, Marjorie and Clayton Haven
1968 "Interaction and adaptation: Intimacy as a critical variable." *American Sociological Review* 33:20–31.

Lowenthal, Marjorie and Betsy Robinson
1976 "Social networks and isolation." In Robert Binstock and Ethel Shanas (eds.). *Handbook of Aging and the Social Sciences.* New York: Van Nostrand Reinhold.

Lowenthal, Marjorie, Majda Thurnher, and David Chiriboga
1975 *Four Stages of Life.* San Francisco: Jossey-Bass.

Mangum, Wiley
1973 "Retirement villages." In Rosamonde Boyd and Charles Oakes (eds.). *Foundations of Practical Gerontology.* Columbia: University of South Carolina Press.

Matthews, Sarah
1979 *The Social World of Old Women: Management of Self-Identity.* Beverly Hills: Sage.

Messer, Mark
1967 "The possibility of an age-concentrated environment becoming a normative system." *The Gerontologist* 7:247–250.

National Council on the Aging
1975 *The Myth and Reality of Aging in America.* Washington, D.C.

Newcomer, Robert
1976 "An evaluation of neighborhood service convenience for elderly housing project residents." In P. Suedfeld and J. Russell (eds.). *The Behavioral Basis of Design.* Vol. I. Stroudsburg, Pa.: Dowden, Hutchinson & Ross.

Norton, Lee and Michael Courlander
1982 "Fear of crime among the elderly: The role of crime prevention programs." *The Gerontologist* 22:388–393.

O'Brien, John and Donna Wagner
1980 "Help seeking by the frail elderly: Problems in network analysis." *The Gerontologist* 20:78–83.

Osgood, Nancy
1982 *Senior Settlers: Social Integration in Retirement Communities.* New York: Praeger.

Pearlin, Leonard and Carmi Schooler
1978 "The structure of coping." *Journal of Health and Social Behavior* 19:2–21.

Powers, Edward and Gordon Bultena
1976 "Sex differences in intimate friendships in old age." *Journal of Marriage and the Family* 38:739–747.

Regnier, Victor
1975 "Neighborhood planning for the urban elderly." In Diana Woodruff and James Birren (eds.). *Aging: Scientific Perspectives and Social Issues.* New York: D. Van Nostrand.

Rooney, James
1976 "Friendship and disaffiliation among the skid row population." *Journal of Geronotology* 31:82–88.
Rosenberg, George
1970 *The Worker Grows Old.* San Francisco: Jossey-Bass.
Rosenberg, Morris
1981 "The self-concept: Social product and social force." In Morris Rosenberg and Ralph Turner (eds.). *Social Psychology: Sociological Perspectives.* New York: Basic Books.
Rosow, Irving
1967 *Social Integration of the Aged.* New York: The Free Press.
Ross, Jennie-Keith
1977 *Old People, New Lives.* Chicago: University of Chicago Press.
Rowles, Graham
1980 "Growing old 'inside': Aging and attachment to place in an Appalachian community." In Nancy Datan and Nancy Lohmann (eds.). *Transitions of Aging.* New York: Academic Press.
1981 "The surveillance zone as meaningful space for the aged." *The Gerontologist* 21:304–311.
Seeman, Melvin
1981 "Intergroup relations." In Morris Rosenberg and Ralph Turner (eds.). *Social Psychology: Sociological Perspectives.* New York: Basic Books.
Sherman, Edmund, Evelyn Newman, and Anne Nelson
1976 "Patterns of age integration in public housing and the incidence and fears of crime among elderly tenants." In Jack Goldsmith and Sharon Goldsmith (eds.). *Crime and the Elderly: Challenge and Response.* Lexington, Mass.: Lexington Books.
Sherman, Susan
1971 "The choice of retirement housing among the well-elderly." *Aging and Human Development* 2:118–238.
1972 "Satisfaction with retirement housing: Attitudes, recommendations and moves." *Aging and Human Development* 3:339–366.
1974 "Leisure activities in retirement housing." *Journal of Gerontology* 29:325–335.
1975a "Patterns of contacts for residents of age-segregated and age-integrated housing." *Journal of Gerontology* 30:103–107.
1975b "Mutual assistance and support in retirement housing." *Journal of Gerontology* 30:479–483.
1975c "Provision of on-site services in retirement housing." *Aging and Human Development* 6:229–247.
Singer, Eleanor
1981 "Reference groups and social evaluations." In Morris Rosenberg and Ralph Turner (eds.). *Social Psychology: Sociological Perspectives.* New York: Basic Books.
Smith, Joel and Herman Turk
1966 "Considerations bearing on a study of the role of the aged in community integration." In Ida Simpson and John McKinney (eds.). *Social Aspects of Aging.* Durham, N.C.: Duke University Press.
Steinfeld, Edward, James Duncan, and Paul Cardell
1977 "Toward a responsive environment: The psychosocial effects of inaccessibility." In Michael Bednar (ed.). *Barrier-Free Environments.* Stroudsburg, Pa.: Dowden, Hutchinson & Ross.

Stephens, Joyce
  1975   "Society of the alone: Freedom, privacy, and ultilitarianism as dominant norms in the SRO." *Journal of Gerontology* 30:230–235.
Streib, Gordon and Ruth Streib
  1975   "Communes and the aging: Utopian dream and gerontological reality." *American Behavioral Scientist* 19:176–189.
Stueve, Anne and Kathleen Gibson
  1977   "Personal relations across the life-cycle." In Claude Fischer (ed.). *Networks and Places: Social Relations in the Urban Setting.* New York: The Free Press.
Sussman, Marvin
  1976   "The family life of old people." In Robert Binstock and Ethel Shanas (eds.). *Handbook of Aging and the Social Sciences.* New York: Van Nostrand Reinhold.
Teaff, Joseph, M. Powell Lawton, Lucille Nahemow, and Diane Carlson
  1978   "Impact of age integration on the well-being of elderly tenants in public housing." *Journal of Gerontology* 33:126–133.
Thoits, Peggy
  1982   "Conceptual, methodological, and theoretical problems in studying social support as a buffer against life stress." *Journal of Health and Social Behavior* 23:145–158.
Time
  1976   "The elderly: Prisoners of fear." New York (November 29): 21–22.
Toseland, R. and J. Rasch
  1978   "Factors contributing to older persons' satisfaction with their communities." *The Gerontologist* 18:395–402.
U.S. Bureau of the Census
  1979   "Social and economic characteristics of the older population: 1978." *Current Population Reports,* Series P–23, No. 85. Washington, D.C.: U.S. Government Printing Office.
Ward, Russell
  1979   "The implications of neighborhood age structure for older people." *Sociological Symposium* 26:42–63.
Ward, Russell, Mark LaGory, and Susan Sherman
  1982   "The relative importance of social ties." Paper presented at meetings of the Gerontological Society of America, Boston.
Ward, Russell, Mark LaGory, Susan Sherman, and Deborah Traynor
  1981   "Neighborhood age structure and support networks." Paper presented at meetings of the Gerontological Society of America, Toronto.
Wentowski, Gloria
  1981   "Reciprocity and the coping strategies of older people: Cultural dimensions of network building." *The Gerontologist* 21:600–609.
Wood, Vivian and Joan Robertson
  1978   "Friendship and kinship interaction: Differential effect on the morale of the elderly." *Journal of Marriage and the Family* 40:367–375.
Yin, Peter
  1980   "Fear of crime among the elderly: Some issues and suggestions." *Social Problems* 27:492–504.
Younger, Evelle
  1976   "The California experience in crime prevention programs with senior citizens." In Jack Goldsmith and Sharon Goldsmith (eds.). *Crime and the Elderly: Challenge and Response.* Lexington, Mass.: Lexington Books.

CHAPTER 10

Abramson, Paul
1975 *Generational Change in American Politics.* Lexington, Mass.: Lexington Books.
Acock, Alan and Vern Bengtson
1980 "Socialization and attribution processes: Actual versus perceived similarity among parents and youth." *Journal of Marriage and the Family* 42:501–515.
Anderson, William and Norma Anderson
1978 "The politics of age exclusion: The Adults Only Movement in Arizona." *The Gerontologist* 18:6–12.
Bengtson, Vern
1975 "Generation and family effects in value socialization." *American Sociological Review* 40:358–371.
Bengtson, Vern and Neal Cutler
1976 "Generations and intergenerational relations: Perspectives on age groups and social change." In Ethel Shanas and Robert Binstock (eds.). *Handbook of Aging and the Social Sciences.* New York: Van Nostrand Reinhold.
Bengtson, Vern, Michael Furlong, and Robert Laufer
1974 "Time, aging, and the continuity of social structure: Themes and issues in generational analyses." *Journal of Social Issues* 30:1–30.
Bengtson, Vern and Joseph Kuypers
1971 "Generational difference and the developmental stake." *Aging and Human Development* 2:249–260.
Bengtson, Vern and Lillian Troll
1978 "Youth and their parents: Feedback and intergenerational influence in socialization." In Richard Lerner and Graham Spanier (eds.). *Child Influences on Marital and Family Interaction: A Life-Span Perspective.* New York: Academic Press.
Binstock, Robert
1974 "Aging and the future of American politics." In Frederick Eisele (ed.). *Political Consequences of Aging. Annals of the American Academy of Political and Social Science* 415:199–212.
Braungart, Richard
1974 "The sociology of generations and student politics: A comparison of the functionalist and generational unit models." *Journal of Social Issues* 30:31–54.
Broder, David
1973 "The old: Benefits put a dangerous drain on U.S. funds." *Los Angeles Times,* February 1.
Campbell, Angus
1971 "Politics through the life cycle." *The Gerontologist* 11:112–117.
Campbell, John and John Strate
1981 "Are old people conservative?" *The Gerontologist* 21:580–591.
Cartwright, Dorwin
1950 "Emotional dimensions of group life." In Martin Reymart (ed.). *Feelings and Emotions.* New York: McGraw-Hill.
Cavan, Ruth
1962 "Self and role in adjustment during old age." In Arnold Rose (ed.). *Human Behavior and Social Processes.* Boston: Houghton Mifflin.
Cutler, Neal and Vern Bengtson
1974 "Age and political alienation: Maturation, generation, and period effects." In Frederick Eisele (ed.). *Political Consequences of Aging. Annals of the American Academy of Political and Social Science* 415:160–175.

Cutler, Neal and John Schmidhauser
  1975   "Age and political behavior." In Diana Woodruff and James Birren (eds.). *Aging: Scientific Perspectives and Social Issues.* New York: D. Van Nostrand.
Cutler, Stephen, Sally Lentz, Michael Muha, and Robert Riter
  1980   "Aging and conservatism: Cohort changes in attitudes about legalized abortion." *Journal of Gerontology* 35:115–123.
de Beauvoir, Simone
  1972   *The Coming of Age.* New York: Putnam's Sons.
Dowd, James
  1980   *Stratification Among the Aged.* Monterey, Calif.: Brooks/Cole.
Edgerton, Robert
  1967   *The Cloak of Competence.* Berkeley: University of California Press.
Eisenstadt, S. N.
  1965   *From Generation to Generation.* New York: The Free Press.
Estes, Carroll
  1979   "Toward a sociology of political gerontology." *Sociological Symposium* 26: 1–27.
Fendrich, James
  1974   "Activists ten years later: A test of generational unit continuity." *Journal of Social Issues* 30:95–118.
Fischer, David
  1977   *Growing Old in America.* New York: Oxford University Press.
Foner, Anne
  1972   "The polity." In Matilda Riley, Marilyn Johnson, and Anne Foner (eds.). *Aging and Society.* Vol. 3: *A Sociology of Age Stratification.* New York: Russell Sage.
  1974   "Age stratification and age conflict in political life." *American Sociological Review* 39:187–196.
  1979   "Ascribed and achieved bases of stratification." In Alex Inkeles, James Coleman, and Ralph Turner (eds.). *Annual Review of Sociology.* Vol. 5. Palo Alto, Calif.: Annual Reviews.
Glenn, Norval
  1969   "Aging, disengagement, and opinionation." *Public Opinion Quarterly* 33:17–33.
  1974   "Aging and conservatism." In Frederick Eisele (ed.). *Annals of the American Academy of Political and Social Science* 415:176–186.
  1980   "Values, attitudes, and beliefs." In Orville Brim, Jr. and Jerome Kagan (eds.). *Constancy and Change in Human Development.* Cambridge, Mass.: Harvard University Press.
Goffman, Erving
  1963   *Stigma: Notes on the Management of Spoiled Identity.* Englewood Cliffs, N.J.: Prentice-Hall.
Harootyan, Robert
  1981   "Interest groups and aging policy: Interest groups and the development of federal legislation affecting older Americans." In Robert Hudson (ed.). *The Aging in Politics: Process and Policy.* Springfield, Ill.: Charles C. Thomas.
Hooker, Evelyn
  1966   "The homosexual community." In James Palmer and Michael Goldstein (eds.). *Perspectives in Psycho-Pathology.* New York: Oxford University Press.
Hudson, Robert
  1978   "The 'graying' of the federal budget and its consequences for old-age policy." *The Gerontologist* 18:428–440.
  1981   *The Aging in Politics: Process and Policy.* Springfield, Ill.: Charles C. Thomas.

Hudson, Robert and Robert Binstock
   1976   "Political systems and aging." In Robert Binstock and Ethel Shanas (eds.). *Handbook of Aging and the Social Sciences.* New York: Van Nostrand Reinhold.
Jackson, Hobart
   1972   "The White House Conference on Aging and black aged." In Jacquelyne Jackson (ed.). *Proceedings of Research Conference on Minority Group Aged in the South.* Durham, N.C.: Duke University Center for the Study of Aging.
Jacobs, Ruth
   1980   "Portrait of a phenomenon—the Gray Panthers: Do they have a long-run future?" In Elizabeth Markson and Gretchen Batra (eds.). *Public Policies for an Aging Population.* Lexington, Mass.: Lexington Books.
Kreps, Juanita
   1977   "Intergenerational transfers and the bureaucracy." In Ethel Shanas and Marvin Sussman (eds.). *Family, Bureaucracy and the Elderly.* Durham, N.C.: Duke University Press.
Lammers, William and Joseph Nyomarkay
   1980   "The disappearing senior leaders: Cabinet member age structures in five Western nations, 1868–1978." *Research on Aging* 2:329–350.
Leadership Council of Aging Organizations
   1982   *Shaping America's Aging Agenda for the 80's: A Report on the 1981 White House Conference on Aging.* Washington, D.C.
Lehman, H. C.
   1953   *Age and Achievement.* Princeton, N.J.: Princeton University Press.
Lofland, John
   1969   *Deviance and Identity.* Englewood Cliffs, N.J.: Prentice-Hall.
Longino, Charles, Kent McClelland, and Warren Peterson
   1980   "The aged subculture hypothesis: Social integration, gerontophilia and self-conception." *Journal of Gerontology* 35:758–767.
McQuaide, Michael and William Sauer
   1979   "The concept of cohort: Its utility for social gerontology." *Sociological Symposium* 26:28–41.
Mannheim, Karl
   1952   "The problem of generations." In Karl Mannheim (ed.). *Essays on the Sociology of Knowledge.* New York: Oxford University Press.
Martin, William, Vern Bengtson, and Alan Acock
   1974   "Alienation and age: A context-specific approach." *Social Forces* 53:266–274.
Mauss, Armand
   1975   *Social Problems as Social Movements.* Philadelphia: J. B. Lippincott.
Miller, Arthur, Patricia Gurin, and Gerald Gurin
   1980   "Age consciousness and political mobilization of older Americans." *The Gerontologist* 20:691–700.
National Council on the Aging
   1975   *The Myth and Reality of Aging in America.* Washington, D.C.
Neugarten, Bernice
   1974   "Age groups in American society and the rise of the young-old." In Frederick Eisele (ed.). *Political Consequences of Aging. Annals of the American Academy of Political and Social Science* 415:187–198.
Parsons, Talcott
   1963   "Youth in the context of American society." In Erik Erikson (ed.). *Youth: Change and Challenge.* New York: Basic Books.

Pratt, Henry
  1976   *The Gray Lobby.* Chicago: University of Chicago Press.
Ragan, Pauline
  1976   "Another look at the politicizing of old age: Can we expect a backlash effect?"
          Paper presented at the Annual Meeting of the Society for the Study of Social
          Problems, New York.
Ragan, Pauline and James Dowd
  1974   "The emerging political consciousness of the aged: A generational interpreta-
          tion." *Journal of Social Issues* 30:137–158.
Riemer, Yosef and Robert Binstock
  1978   "Campaigning for the 'senior vote': A case study of Carter's 1976 campaign."
          The Gerontologist 18:517–524.
Riley, Matilda
  1978   "Aging, social change, and the power of ideas." *Daedalus* 107 (4):39–52.
Riley, Matilda and Anne Foner
  1968   *Aging and Society.* Vol. 1: *An Inventory of Research Findings.* New York: Russell
          Sage.
Rose, Arnold
  1965a "The subculture of aging: A framework for research in social gerontology." In
          Arnold Rose and Warren Peterson (eds.). *Older People and Their Social World.*
          Philadelphia: F. A. Davis.
  1965b "Group consciousness among the aging." In Arnold Rose and Warren Peterson
          (eds.). *Older People and Their Social World.* Philadelphia: F. A. Davis.
Rosow, Irving
  1974   *Socialization to Old Age.* Berkeley: University of California Press.
Ryder, Norman
  1965   "The cohort as a concept in the study of social change." *American Sociological
          Review* 30:843–861.
Sarbin, Theodore
  1970   "The culture of poverty, social identity, and cognitive outcomes." In Vernon
          Allen (ed.). *Psychological Factors in Poverty.* Chicago: Markham.
Seeman, Melvin
  1975   "Alienation studies." *Annual Review of Sociology.* Vol. 1. Palo Alto, Calif.: An-
          nual Reviews.
Singer, Eleanor
  1981   "Reference groups and social evaluations." In Morris Rosenberg and Ralph Tur-
          ner (eds.). *Social Psychology: Sociological Perspectives.* New York: Basic Books.
Smelser, William and Neil Smelser
  1981   "Group movements, sociocultural change, and personality." In Morris Rosen-
          berg and Ralph Turner (eds.). *Social Psychology: Sociological Perspectives.* New
          York: Basic Books.
Strauss, Helen
  1968   "Reference group and social comparison processes among the totally blind." In
          Herbert Hyman and Eleanor Singer (eds.). *Readings in Reference Group Theory
          and Research.* New York: The Free Press.
Streib, Gordon
  1965   "Are the aged a minority group?" In Alvin Gouldner and S. M. Miller (eds.).
          Applied Sociology. New York: The Free Press.
Tissue, Thomas
  1970   "Downward mobility in old age." *Social Problems* 18:67–77.

Trela, James
  1972 "Age structure of voluntary associations and political self-interest among the aged." *Sociological Quarterly* 13:244–252.
  1976 "Status inconsistency and political action in old age." In Jaber Gubrium (ed.). *Time, Roles, and Self in Old Age.* New York: Human Sciences Press.
Turk, Herman, Joel Smith, and Howard Myers
  1966 "Understanding local political behavior: The role of the older citizen." In Ida Simpson and John McKinney (eds.). *Social Aspects of Aging.* Durham, N.C.: Duke University Press.
U.S. Bureau of the Census
  1979 "Social and economic characteristics of the older population." *Current Population Reports,* Series P–23, No. 85. Washington, D.C.: U.S. Government Printing Office.
Verba, Sidney and Norman Nie
  1972 *Participation in America.* New York: Harper & Row.
Ward, Russell
  1977 "Aging group consciousness: Implications in an older sample." *Sociology and Social Research* 61:496–519.
Williamson, John, Linda Evans, Lawrence Powell, and Sharlene Hesse-Biber
  1982 *The Politics of Aging: Power and Policy.* Springfield, Ill.: Charles C. Thomas.
Woelfel, Joseph and Archibald Haller
  1971 "Significant others, the self-reflexive act and the attitude formation process." *American Sociological Review* 36:74–87.

CHAPTER 11

Aldritch, C. Knight and Ethel Mendkoff
  1963 "Relocation of the aged and disabled: A mortality study." *Journal of the American Geriatrics Society* 11:185–194.
Beattie, Walter
  1976 "Aging and the social services." In Robert Binstock and Ethel Shanas (eds.). *Handbook of Aging and the Social Sciences.* New York: Van Nostrand Reinhold.
Bennett, Ruth and Lucille Nahemow
  1965 "Institutional totality and criteria of social adjustment in residences for the aged." *Journal of Social Issues* 21:44–76.
Binstock, Robert and Martin Levin
  1976 "The political dilemmas of intervention policies." In Robert Binstock and Ethel Shanas (eds.). *Handbook of Aging and the Social Sciences.* New York: Van Nostrand Reinhold.
Borup, Jerry
  1982 "The effects of varying degrees of interinstitutional environmental change on long-term care patients." *The Gerontologist* 22:409–417.
Butler, Robert
  1975 *Why Survive? Being Old in America.* New York: Harper & Row.
  1976 "Medicine and aging: An assessment of opportunities and neglect." Testimony before the U.S. Senate Special Committee on Aging.

Butler, Robert and Myrna Lewis
  1981   *Aging and Mental Health.* St. Louis: C. V. Mosby.
Ciliberton, David, Jack Levin, and Arnold Arluke
  1981   "Nurses' diagnostic sterotyping of the elderly: The case of organic brain syndrome." *Research on Aging* 3:299–310.
Clark, Robert and John Menefee
  1981   "Federal expenditures for the elderly: Past and future." *The Gerontologist* 21:132–137.
Coe, Rodney
  1965   "Self-conception and institutionalization." In Arnold Rose and Warren Peterson (eds.). *Older People and Their Social World.* Philadelphia: F. A. Davis.
Coe, Rodney, Henry Brehm, and Warren Peterson
  1974   "Impact of Medicare on the organization of community health resources." *Milbank Memorial Fund Quarterly* 52:231–264.
Coffman, Thomas
  1981   "Relocation and survival of institutionalized aged: A re-examination of the evidence." *The Gerontologist* 21:483–500.
Coward, Raymond
  1979   "Planning community services for the rural elderly: Implications from research." *The Gerontologist* 19:275–282.
Curry, Timothy and Bascom Ratliff
  1973   "The effects of nursing home size on resident isolation and life satisfaction." *The Gerontologist* 13:295–298.
Davis, Karen and Cathy Schoen
  1978   *Health and the War on Poverty: A Ten-Year Appraisal.* Washington, D.C.: The Brookings Institution.
Dick, Harry and Hiram Friedsam
  1963   "Adjustment of residents of two homes for the aged." *Social Problems* 11:282–290.
Eggert, Gerald, Joyce Bowlyow, and Carol Nichols
  1980   "Gaining control of the long-term care system: First returns from the Access experiment." *The Gerontologist* 20:356–363.
Elwell, Frank
  1981   "Old-age institutions: A study in social stress." Unpublished doctoral dissertation, Department of Sociology, State University of New York at Albany.
Estes, Carroll
  1979   *The Aging Enterprise: A Critical Examination of Social Policies and Services for the Aged.* San Francisco: Jossey-Bass.
Feder, Judith
  1977   *Medicare: The Politics of Federal Hospital Insurance.* Lexington, Mass.: Lexington Books.
Fontana, Andrea
  1977   *The Last Frontier.* Beverly Hills: Sage.
Fottler, Myron, Howard Smith, and William James
  1981   "Profits and patient care quality in nursing homes: Are they compatible?" *The Gerontologist* 21:532–538.
Frankfather, Dwight
  1977   *The Aged in the Community.* New York: Praeger.

Fritz, Dan
   1979   "The Administration on Aging as an advocate: Progress, problems and perspectives." *The Gerontologist* 19:141–150.
Gelfand, Donald and Jody Olsen
   1980   *The Aging Network: Programs and Services.* New York: Springer.
Glasscote, Raymond and Associates
   1976   *Old Folks at Homes: A Field Study of Nursing and Board-and-Care Homes.* Washington, D.C.: Joint Information Service of the American Psychiatric Association and the National Association for Mental Health.
Goffman, Erving
   1961   *Asylums.* Garden City, N.Y.: Anchor Books.
Golant, Stephen
   1976   "Intraurban transportation needs and problems of the elderly." In M. Powell Lawton, Robert Newcomer, and Thomas Byerts (eds.). *Community Planning for an Aging Society: Designing Services and Facilities.* Stroudsburg, Pa.: Dowden, Hutchinson and Ross.
Gornick, Marian
   1976   "Ten years of Medicare: Impact on the covered population." *Social Security Bulletin* 39 (7):3–21.
Gottesman, Leonard and Norman Bourestom
   1974   "Why nursing homes do what they do." *The Gerontologist* 14:501–506.
Gubrium, Jaber
   1975   *Living and Dying at Murray Manor.* New York: St. Martin's.
Gutman, Gloria
   1978   "Issues and findings relating to multilevel accommodation for seniors." *Journal of Gerontology* 33:592–600.
Harel, Zev
   1981   "Quality of care, congruence and well-being among institutionalized aged." *The Gerontologist* 21:523–531.
Haug, Marie and Bebe Lavin
   1981   "Practitioner or patient—Who's in charge?" *Journal of Health and Social Behavior* 22:212–228.
Hing, Esther
   1981   "Characteristics of nursing home residents, health status, and care received: National Nursing Home Survey United States, May–December 1977." *Vital and Health Statistics,* Series 13, No. 51. National Center for Health Statistics. Washington, D.C.: U.S. Government Printing Office.
Hodgson, Joseph and Joan Quinn
   1980   "The impact of the triage health care delivery system on client morale, independent living and the cost of care." *The Gerontologist* 20:364–371.
Holmes, Douglas, Monica Holmes, Leonard Steinbach, Thomas Hausner, and Bruce Rocheleau
   1979   "The use of community-based services in long-term care by older minority persons." *The Gerontologist* 19:389–397.
Hudson, Robert
   1978   "The 'graying' of the federal budget and its consequences for old-age policy." *The Gerontologist* 18:428–440.
   1980   "Old-age politics in a period of change." In Edgar Borgatta and Neil McCluskey (eds.). *Aging and Society: Current Research and Policy Perspectives.* Beverly Hills: Sage.

1981 (ed.). *The Aging in Politics: Process and Policy.* Springfield, Ill.: Charles C. Thomas.

Hudson, Robert and Robert Binstock
1976 "Political systems and aging." In Robert Binstock and Ethel Shanas (eds.). *Handbook of Aging and the Social Sciences.* New York: Van Nostrand Reinhold.

Kahn, Robert
1975 "The mental health system and the future aged." *The Gerontologist* 15:24–31.

Kaplan, Jerome and Caroline Ford
1975 "Rehabilitation for the elderly: An eleven-year assessment." *The Gerontologist* 15:393–397.

Kart, Cary and Barry Beckham
1976 "Black-white differentials in the institutionalization of the elderly: A temporal analysis." *Social Forces* 54:901–910.

Kart, Cary and Barbara Manard
1976 "Quality of care in old age institutions." *The Gerontologist* 16:250–256.

Kart, Cary, Eileen Metress, and James Metress
1978 *Aging and Health: Biologic and Social Perspectives.* Menlo Park, Calif.: Addison-Wesley.

Kiyak, Asuman, Eva Kahana, and Nira Lev
1975 "The role of informal norms in determining institutional totality in residences for the aged." Paper presented at the Annual Meeting of the Gerontological Society, Louisville, Ky.

Klemmack, David and Lucinda Roff
1981 "Predicting general and comparative support for government's providing benefits to older persons." *The Gerontologist* 21:592–599.

Kosberg, Jordan
1973 "Differences in proprietary institutions caring for affluent and nonaffluent elderly." *The Gerontologist* 13:299–304.

Kosberg, Jordan and Sheldon Tobin
1972 "Variability among nursing homes." *The Gerontologist* 12:214–219.

Kowalski, N. Claire
1981 "Institutional relocation: Current programs and applied approaches." *The Gerontologist* 21:512–519.

Kucharski, L. Thomas, Royce White, Jr., and Marjorie Schratz
1979 "Age bias, referral for psychological assistance and the private physician." *Journal of Gerontology* 34:423–428.

Kutza, Elizabeth
1981 *The Benefits of Old Age: Social-Welfare Policy for the Elderly.* Chicago: University of Chicago Press.

Kuypers, Joseph and Vern Bengtson
1973 "Social breakdown and competence: A model of normal aging." *Human Development* 16:181–201.

Langer, Ellen and Judith Rodin
1976 "The effects of choice and enhanced personal responsibility for the aged: A field experiment in an institutional setting." *Journal of Personality and Social Psychology* 34:191–198.

Lawton, M. Powell
1980 *Environment and Aging.* Monterey, Calif.: Brooks/Cole.

Lawton, M. Powell and Lucille Nahemow
1973 "Ecology and the aging process." In Carl Eisdorfer and M. Powell Lawton (eds.).

The Psychology of Adult Development and Aging. Washington, D.C.: American Psychological Association.

Lemke, Sonne and Rudolf Moos
  1980   "Assessing the institutional policies of sheltered care settings." *Journal of Gerontology* 35:96–107.

Levey, Samuel, Hirsch Ruchlin, Bernard Stotsky, David Kinloch, and William Oppenheim
  1973   "An appraisal of nursing home care." *Journal of Gerontology* 28:222–228.

Lowy, Louis
  1980   *Social Policies and Programs on Aging: What Is and What Should Be in the Later Years.* Lexington, Mass.: Lexington Books.

McKinlay, John
  1975   "Who is really ignorant—physician or patient?" *Journal of Health and Social Behavior* 16:3–11.

Markson, Elizabeth
  1980   "Institutionalization: Sin, cure, or sinecure for the impaired elderly." In Elizabeth Markson and Gretchen Batra (eds.). *Public Policies for an Aging Population.* Lexington, Mass.: Lexington Books.

Mendelson, Mary
  1975   *Tender Loving Greed.* New York: Vintage Books.

Moen, Elizabeth
  1978   "The reluctance of the elderly to accept help." *Social Problems* 25:293–303.

Mueller, Marjorie and Robert Gibson
  1976   "Age differences in health care spending, fiscal year 1975." *Social Security Bulletin* 39 (6):18–31.

Myles, John
  1978   "Institutionalization and sick role identification among the elderly." *American Sociological Review* 43:508–520.

Nelson, Gary
  1980   "Social services to the urban and rural aged: The experience of Area Agencies on Aging." *The Gerontologist* 20:200–207.
  1982   "A role for Title XX in the aging network." *The Gerontologist* 22:18–25.

Neugarten, Bernice
  1982   *Age or Need? Public Policies for Older People.* Beverly Hills, Calif.: Sage.

Newman, Evelyn and Susan Sherman
  1980   "Foster-family care for the elderly: Surrogate family or mini-institution?" *Aging and Human Development* 10:165–176.

Roberts, Pearl
  1974   "Human warehouses: A boarding home study." *American Journal of Public Health* 64:269–276.

Schulz, Richard and Gail Brenner
  1977   "Relocation of the aged: A review and theoretical analysis." *Journal of Gerontology* 32:323–333.

Schwartz, Arthur
  1975   "Planning micro-environments for the aged." In Diana Woodruff and James Birren (eds.).*Aging: Scientific Perspectives and Social Issues.* New York: D. Van Nostrand.

Scott, Robert
  1969   *The Making of Blind Men.* New York: Russell Sage.

Shanas, Ethel and George Maddox
  1976   "Aging, health, and the organization of health resources." In Robert Binstock

and Ethel Shanas (eds.). *Handbook of Aging and the Social Sciences.* New York: Van Nostrand Reinhold.

Smith, Kristen and Vern Bengtson
  1979 "Positive consequences of institutionalization: Solidarity between elderly parents and their middle-aged children." *The Gerontologist* 19:438–447.

Snider, Earle
  1980 "Awareness and use of health services by the elderly: A Canadian study." *Medical Care* 18:1177–1182.

Soldo, Beth
  1980 "America's elderly in the 1980s." *Population Bulletin* 35 (4):1–47.

Spilerman, Seymour and Eugene Litwak
  1982 "Reward structures and organizational design: An analysis of institutions for the elderly." *Research on Aging* 4:43–70.

Stannard, Charles
  1973 "Old folks and dirty work: The social conditions for patient abuse in a nursing home." *Social Problems* 20:329–342.

Struyk, Raymond and Beth Soldo
  1980 *Improving the Elderly's Housing: A Key to Preserving the Nation's Housing Stock and Neighborhoods.* Cambridge, Mass.: Ballinger.

Taietz, Philip
  1975 "Community complexity and knowledge of facilities." *Journal of Gerontology* 30:357–362.

Taietz, Philip and Sande Milton
  1979 "Rural-urban differences in the structure of services for the elderly in upstate New York counties." *Journal of Gerontology* 34:429–437.

Tesch, Stephanie and Susan Whitbourne
  1981 "Friendship, social interaction and subjective well-being of older men in an institutional setting." *Aging and Human Development* 13:317–327.

Tobin, Sheldon and Morton Lieberman
  1976 *Last Home for the Aged.* San Francisco: Jossey-Bass.

Townsend, Claire
  1971 *Old Age: The Last Segregation.* New York: Bantam Books.

Townsend, Peter
  1964 *The Last Refuge.* London: Routledge and Kegan Paul.
  1965 "The effects of family structure on the likelihood of admission to an institution in old age." In Ethel Shanas and Gordon Streib (eds.). *Social Structure and the Family: Generational Relations.* Englewood Cliffs, N.J.: Prentice-Hall.

Ullmann, Steven
  1981 "Assessment of facility quality and its relationship to facility size in the long-term care industry." *The Gerontologist* 21:91–97.

U.S. Public Health Service
  1979 "The National Nursing Home Survey: 1977. Summary for the United States." *Vital and Health Statistics,* Series 13, No. 43. National Center for Health Statistics. Washington, D.C.: U.S. Government Printing Office.

U.S. Senate Special Committee on Aging
  1974 *Developments in Aging: 1973 and January-March 1974.* Washington, D.C.: U.S. Government Printing Office.
  1978 *Medi-gap: Private Health Insurance Supplement to Medicare.* Washington, D.C.: U.S. Government Printing Office.

1981   *Health Care Expenditures for the Elderly: How Much Protection Does Medicare Provide?* Washington, D.C.: U.S. Government Printing Office.

Vicente, Leticia, James Wiley, and Allen Carrington
1979   "The risk of institutionalization before death." *The Gerontologist* 19: 361–367.

Vladeck, Bruce
1980   *Unloving Care: The Nursing Home Tragedy.* New York: Basic Books.

Ward, Russell
1977   "Services for older people: An integrated framework for research." *Journal of Health and Social Behavior* 18:61–70.

Williamson, John
1974   "The stigma of public dependency: A comparison of alternative forms of public aid to the poor." *Social Problems* 22:213–228.
1975   *Strategies Against Poverty in America.* New York: Schenkman.

Williamson, John, Linda Evans, Lawrence Powell, and Sharlene Hesse-Biber
1982   *The Politics of Aging: Power and Policy.* Springfield, Ill.: Charles C. Thomas.

York, Jonathan and Robert Calsyn
1977   "Family involvement in nursing homes." *The Gerontologist* 17:500–505.

CHAPTER 12

Ariés, Philippe
1981   *The Hour of Our Death.* Translated by Helen Weaver. New York: Alfred A. Knopf.

Becker, Ernest
1973   *The Denial of Death.* New York: The Free Press.

Behnke, John and Sissela Bok (eds.)
1975   *The Dilemmas of Euthanasia.* Garden City, N.Y.: Anchor Books.

Bell, Bill
1975   "The experimental manipulation of death attitudes: A preliminary investigation." *Omega* 6:199–205.

Bengtson, Vern, José Cuellar, and Pauline Ragan
1977   "Stratum contrasts and similarities in attitudes toward death." *Journal of Gerontology* 32:76–88.

Benoliel, Jeanne
1977   "Nurses and the human experience of dying." In Herman Feifel (ed.). *New Meanings of Death.* New York: McGraw-Hill.

Binger, C. M., A. R. Albin, R. C. Feuerstein, J. H. Kushner, S. Zager, and Cynthia Mikkelsen
1969   "Childhood leukemia: Emotional impact on patient and family." *New England Journal of Medicine* 280:414–418.

Blauner, Robert
1966   "Death and social structure." *Psychiatry* 29:378–394.

Bluebond-Langner, Myra
1977   "Meanings of death to children." In Herman Feifel (ed.). *New Meanings of Death.* New York: McGraw-Hill.

Blumenfield, Michael, Norman Levy, and Diane Kaufman
1979   "The wish to be informed of a fatal illness." *Omega* 9:323–326.

Bok, Sissela
1975 "Euthanasia and the care of the dying." In John Behnke and Sissela Bok (eds.). *The Dilemmas of Euthanasia.* Garden City, N.Y.: Anchor Books.

Cantor, Norman
1975 "Law and the termination of an incompetent patient's life-preserving care." In John Behnke and Sissela Bok (eds.). *The Dilemmas of Euthanasia.* Garden City, N.Y.: Anchor Books.

Charmaz, Kathy
1980 *The Social Reality of Death: Death in Contemporary America.* Reading, Mass.: Addison-Wesley.

Coombs, Robert and Pauline Powers
1976 "Socialization for death: The physician's role." In Lyn Lofland (ed.). *Toward a Sociology of Death and Dying.* Beverly Hills: Sage.

Crane, Diana
1975 *The Sanctity of Social Life: Physicians' Treatment of Critically Ill Patients.* New York: Russell Sage.

Dickinson, George and Algene Pearson
1980 "Death education and physicians' attitudes toward dying patients." *Omega* 11:167–174.

Diggory, James and Doreen Rothman
1961 "Values destroyed by death." *Journal of Abnormal and Social Psychology* 63:205–210.

Duff, Raymond and A. G. M. Campbell
1973 "Moral and ethical dilemmas in the special-care nursery." *New England Journal of Medicine* 289:890–894.

Dumont, Richard and Dennis Foss
1972 *The American View of Death: Acceptance or Denial?* New York: Schenkman.

Durlak, Joseph and Richard Kass
1981 "Clarifying the measurement of death attitudes: A factor analytic evaluation of fifteen self-report death scales." *Omega* 12:129–141.

Fletcher, Joseph
1968 "Elective death." In E. Fuller Torrey (ed.). *Ethical Issues in Medicine.* Boston: Little, Brown.

Fox, Renée and Judith Swazey
1974 *The Courage to Fail: A Social View of Organ Transplants and Dialysis.* Chicago: University of Chicago Press.

Fuchs, Victor
1974 *Who Shall Live? Health, Economics, and Social Choice.* New York: Basic Books.

Fulton, Robert
1976 "The traditional funeral and contemporary society." In Vanderlyn Pine et al. (eds.). *Acute Grief and the Funeral.* Springfield, Ill.: Charles C. Thomas.

Gerber, Irwin, Roslyn Rusalem, Natalie Hannon, Delia Battin, and Arthur Arkin
1975 "Anticipatory grief and aged widows and widowers." *Journal of Gerontology* 30:225–229.

Glaser, Barney and Anselm Strauss
1966 *Awareness of Dying.* Chicago: Aldine.
1968 *Time for Dying.* Chicago: Aldine.

Glick, Ira, Robert Weiss, and C. Murray Parkes
1974 *The First Year of Bereavement.* New York: Wiley-Interscience.

Goldscheider, Calvin
  1971 *Population, Modernization, and Social Structure.* Boston: Little, Brown.
Gorer, Geoffrey
  1965 *Death, Grief and Mourning.* Garden City, N.Y.: Doubleday.
Gubrium, Jaber
  1975 *Living and Dying at Murray Manor.* New York: St. Martin's.
Gustafson, Elizabeth
  1972 "Dying: The career of the nursing home patient." *Journal of Health and Social Behavior* 13:226–235.
Haug, Marie
  1978 "Aging and the right to terminate medical treatment." *Journal of Gerontology* 33:586–591.
Heffernan, Robert and Charles Maynard
  1977 "Living and dying with dignity: The rise of old age and dying as social problems." In Armand Mauss and Julie Wolfe (eds.). *This Land of Promises: The Rise and Fall of Social Problems in America.* Philadelphia: J. B. Lippincott.
Hinton, John
  1972 *Dying.* Baltimore: Penguin Books.
  1975 "The influence of previous personality on reactions to having terminal cancer." *Omega* 6:95–112.
Hochschild, Arlie
  1973 *The Unexpected Community.* Englewood Cliffs, N.J.: Prentice-Hall.
Holden, Constance
  1980 "The hospice movement and its implications." In Renée Fox (ed.). *The Social Meaning of Death. Annals of the American Academy of Political and Social Science* 447:59–63.
Illich, Ivan
  1976 *Medical Nemesis.* New York: Pantheon Books.
Ingram, Donald and John Barry
  1977 "National statistics on deaths in nursing homes: Interpretations and implications." *The Gerontologist* 17:303–308.
Jaffe, Lois and Arthur Jaffe
  1977 "Terminal candor and the coda syndrome: A tandem view of fatal illness." In Herman Feifel (ed.). *New Meanings of Death.* New York: McGraw-Hill.
Kalish, Richard
  1969 "Experiences of persons reprieved from death." In A. Kutscher (ed.). *Death and Bereavement.* Springfield, Ill.: Charles C. Thomas.
  1970 "The onset of the dying process." *Omega* 1:57–69.
  1976 "Death and dying in a social context." In Robert Binstock and Ethel Shanas (eds.). *Handbook of Aging and the Social Sciences.* New York: Van Nostrand Reinhold.
  1977 "Dying and preparation for death: A view of families." In Herman Feifel (ed.). *New Meanings of Death.* New York: McGraw-Hill.
  1981 *Death, Grief, and Caring Relationships.* Monterey, Calif.: Brooks/Cole.
Kalish, Richard and David Reynolds
  1976 *Death and Ethnicity: A Psychocultural Study.* Los Angeles: University of Southern California Press.
Kastenbaum, Robert
  1977a *Death, Society, and Human Experience.* St. Louis: C. V. Mosby.
  1977b "Death and development through the life span." In Herman Feifel (ed.). *New Meanings of Death.* New York: McGraw-Hill.

Kastenbaum, Robert and Ruth Aisenberg
  1976 *The Psychology of Death: Concise Edition.* New York: Springer.
Keith, Pat
  1979 "Life changes and perceptions of life and death among older men and women." *Journal of Gerontology* 34:870–878.
  1982 "Perceptions of time remaining and distance from death." *Omega* 12:307–318.
Kelly, Orville
  1977 "Make today count." In Herman Feifel (ed.). *New Meanings of Death.* New York: McGraw-Hill.
Kübler-Ross, Elisabeth
  1969 *On Death and Dying.* New York: Macmillan.
Lerea, L. Eliezer and Barbara LiMauro
  1982 "Grief among health care workers: A comparative study." *Journal of Gerontology* 37:604–608.
Lerner, Monroe
  1970 "When, why, and where people die." In Orville Brim et al. (eds.). *The Dying Patient.* New York: Russell Sage.
Leviton, Daniel
  1977 "Death education." In Herman Feifel (ed.). *New Meanings of Death.* New York: McGraw-Hill.
Lieberman, Morton
  1965 "Psychological correlates of impending death: Some preliminary observations." *Journal of Gerontology* 20:181–190.
Lifton, Robert
  1967 *Death in Life: Survivors of Hiroshima.* New York: Random House.
  1977 "The sense of immortality: On death and the continuity of life." In Herman Feifel (ed.). *New Meanings of Death.* New York: McGraw-Hill.
Lindemann, Erich
  1944 "Symptomatology and management of acute grief." *American Journal of Psychiatry* 101:141–148.
Lopata, Helena
  1979 *Women as Widows: Support Systems.* New York: Elsevier.
Mandelbaum, David
  1959 "Social uses of funeral rites." In Herman Feifel (ed.). *The Meaning of Death.* New York: McGraw-Hill.
Mannes, Marya
  1973 *Last Rights.* New York: William Morrow.
Marshall, Victor
  1975a "Age and awareness of finitude in developmental gerontology." *Omega* 6:113–129.
  1975b "Socialization for impending death in a retirement village." *American Journal of Sociology* 80:1124–1144.
  1980 *Last Chapters: A Sociology of Aging and Dying.* Monterey, Calif.: Brooks/Cole.
Mauksch, Hans
  1975 "The organizational context of dying." In Elisabeth Kübler-Ross (ed.). *Death: The Final Stage of Growth.* Englewood Cliffs, N.J.: Prentice-Hall.
Meyers, David
  1975 "The legal aspects of voluntary medical euthanasia." In John Behnke and Sissela Bok (eds.). *The Dilemmas of Euthanasia.* Garden City, N.Y.: Anchor Books.
Munley, Anne, Cynthia Powers, and John Williamson
  1983 "Humanizing nursing home environments: The relevance of hospice principles." *International Journal of Aging and Human Development,* in press.

Nagi, Mostafa, M.D. Pugh, and Neil Lazerine
   1977   "Attitudes of Catholic and Protestant clergy toward euthanasia." *Omega*
          8:153–164.
Nagy, Maria
   1948   "The child's theories concerning death." *Journal of Genetic Psychology* 73:
          3–27.
Osterweis, Marian and Daphne Champagne
   1979   "The U.S. hospice movement: Issues in development." *American Journal of Public
          Health* 69:492–496.
Ostheimer, John and Leonard Ritt
   1976   "Life and death: Current public attitudes." In Nancy Ostheimer and John Os-
          theimer (eds.). *Life or Death—Who Controls?* New York: Springer.
Pine, Vanderlyn
   1975   *Caretaker of the Dead: The American Funeral Director.* New York: Irvington.
Pine, Vanderlyn, et al.
   1976   *Acute Grief and the Funeral.* Springfield, Ill.: Charles C. Thomas.
Pressey, Sidney
   1977   "Any rights as to my dying?" *The Gerontologist* 17:296.
Riley, John
   1970   "What people think about death." In Orville Brim et al. (eds.). *The Dying Pa-
          tient.* New York: Russell Sage.
Russell, O. Ruth
   1975   *Freedom to Die: Moral and Legal Aspects of Euthanasia.* New York: Human Sci-
          ences Press.
Saunders, Cicely
   1977   "Dying they live: St. Christopher's Hospice." In Herman Feifel (ed.). *New Mean-
          ings of Death.* New York: McGraw-Hill.
Shneidman, Edwin
   1971   "You and death." *Psychology Today* 5 (6):43.
Schulz, Richard
   1978   *The Psychology of Death, Dying, and Bereavement.* Reading, Mass.: Addi-
          son-Wesley.
Schulz, Richard and David Aderman
   1974   "Clinical research and the stages of dying." *Omega* 5:137–143.
   1976   "How the medical staff copes with dying patients: A critical review." *Omega*
          7:11–21.
Stannard, David
   1977   *The Puritan Way of Death.* New York: Oxford University Press.
Stoddard, Sandol
   1978   *The Hospice Movement: A Better Way of Caring for the Dying.* New York: Vin-
          tage Books.
Sudnow, David
   1967   *Passing On: The Social Organization of Dying.* Englewood Cliffs, N.J.: Pren-
          tice-Hall.
Swanson, Thomas and Marcia Swanson
   1977   "Acute uncertainty: The intensive care unit." In E. Mansell Pattison (ed.). *The
          Experience of Dying.* Englewood Cliffs, N.J.: Prentice-Hall.
Thomas, Lewis
   1980   "Dying as failure." In Renée Fox (ed.). *The Social Meaning of Death. Annals
          of the American Academy of Political and Social Science* 447:1–4.

Toynbee, Arnold, A. Keith Mant, Ninian Smart, John Hinton, Cicely Yudkin, Eric
Rhode, Rosalind Heywood, and H. H. Price
   1968   *Man's Concern with Death.* New York: McGraw-Hill.
Uhlenberg, Peter
   1978   "Changing configurations of the life course." In Tamara Hareven (ed.). *Transi-*
          tions: The Family and the Life Course in Historical Perspective. New York: Aca-
          demic Press.
Veatch, Robert and Ernest Tai
   1980   "Talking about death: Patterns of lay and professional change." In Renée Fox
          (ed.). *The Social Meaning of Death. Annals of the American Academy of Political*
          and Social Science 447:29–45.
Volkhart, Edmund and Stanley Michael
   1957   "Bereavement and mental health." In A. Leighton, J. Clausen,
          and R. Wilson (eds.). *Explorations in Social Psychiatry.* New York: Basic
          Books.
Waechter, Eugenia
   1971   "Children's awareness of fatal illness." *American Journal of Nursing*
          71:1168–1172.
Ward, Russell
   1980   "Age and acceptance of euthanasia." *Journal of Gerontology* 35:421–431.
Wass, Hannelore, Milton Christian, Jane Myers, and Milledge Murphy, Jr.
   1979   "Similarities and dissimilarities in attitudes toward death in a population of older
          persons." *Omega* 9:337–354.
Weisman, Avery
   1972   *On Dying and Denying.* New York: Behavioral Publications.
Weisman, Avery and Robert Kastenbaum
   1968   "The psychological autopsy: A study of the terminal phase of life." *Community*
          Mental Health Journal. Monograph no. 4.
Weisman, Avery and J. William Worden
   1975   "Psychosocial analysis of cancer deaths." *Omega* 6:61–75.
Williams, Robert
   1973   "Propagation, modification, and termination of life: Contraception, abortion,
          suicide, euthanasia." In Robert Williams (ed.). *To Live and to Die: When, Why,*
          and How. New York: Springer.
Wood, Juanita
   1976   "Control by definition: The minister as death worker." Paper presented at An-
          nual Meeting of the Pacific Sociological Association,

CHAPTER 13

Bell, Daniel
   1973   *The Coming of Post-Industrial Society.* New York: Basic Books.
Browning, Harvey
   1969   "The timing of our lives." *Transaction/Society* 6:22–27.
Butler, Robert
   1975   *Why Survive? Being Old in America.* New York: Harper & Row.
Campbell, Angus
   1981   *The Sense of Well-Being in America: Recent Patterns and Trends.* New York:
          McGraw-Hill.

Cohen, Elias
  1976 "Comment: Editor's Note." *The Gerontologist* 16:270–275.
Deutscher, Irwin
  1973 *What We Say/What We Do.* Glenview, Ill.: Scott, Foresman.
Dowd, James
  1980 *Stratification Among the Aged.* Monterey, Calif.: Brooks/Cole.
Estes, Carroll
  1979 *The Aging Enterprise.* San Fransisco: Jossey-Bass.
Estes, C. L. and Howard Freeman
  1976 "Strategies of design and research for intervention." In Robert Bistock and Ethel Shanas (eds.). *Handbook of Aging and the Social Sciences.* New York: Van Nostrand Reinhold.
Fries, James and Lawrence Crapo
  1981 *Vitality and Aging.* San Francisco: W. H. Freeman.
Gordon, Theodore
  1979 "Prospects for aging in America." In Matilda Riley (ed.). *Aging from Birth to Death: Interdisciplinary Perspectives.* Boulder, Col.: Westview Press.
Havighurst, Robert
  1975 "The future aged. The use of time and money." In Bernice Neugarten (ed.). *Aging in the Year 2000: A Look at the Future. The Gerontologist* 15 (1–Part II):10–15.
Hayflick, Leonard
  1977 "Perspectives on human longevity." In Bernice Neugarten and Robert Havighurst (eds.). *Extending the Human Life Span: Social Policy and Social Ethics.* Washington, D.C.: U.S. Government Printing Office.
Heilbroner, Robert
  1974 *An Inquiry into the Human Prospect.* New York: W. W. Norton.
Kahn, Robert
  1975 "The mental health system and the future aged." In Bernice Neugarten (ed.). *Aging in the Year 2000: A Look at the Future. The Gerontologist* 15 (1–Part II):24–31.
Karp, David and William Yoels
  1982 "Experts and aging: The life cycle as a social problem." Paper presented at the Annual Meeting of the Society for the Study of Social Problems, San Francisco.
Kittrie, Nicholas
  1971 *The Right to Be Different.* Baltimore: Johns Hopkins Press.
Lakoff, Sanford
  1976 "The future of social intervention." In Robert Binstock and Ethel Shanas (eds.). *Handbook of Aging and the Social Sciences.* New York: Van Nostrand Reinhold.
Lareau, Leslie and Leonard Heumann
  1982 "The inadequacy of needs assessment of the elderly." *The Gerontologist* 22:324–330.
Leadership Council of Aging Organizations
  1982 *Shaping America's Aging Agenda for the 80's: A Report on the 1981 White House Conference on Aging.* Washington, D.C.
Lowy, Louis
  1975 "Social welfare and the aging." In Marian Spencer and Caroline Dorr (eds.). *Understanding Aging.* New York: Appleton-Century-Crofts.
  1980 *Social Policies and Programs on Aging.* Lexington, Mass.: Lexington Books.

Miller, Delbert
  1977 *Handbook of Research Design and Social Measurement.* New York: David
        McKay.
Miller, Emily and Neal Cutler
  1976 "Toward a comprehensive information system in gerontology: A survey of prob-
        lems, resources, and potential solutions." *The Gerontologist* 16:198–206.
Murphy, Donald
  1976 "Report from the National Institute on Aging: The research grant support mech-
        anism." *Journal of Gerontology* 31:696–704.
Neugarten, Bernice
  1972 "Social implications of a prolonged life-span." *The Gerontologist* 12:323,
        438–440.
  1975a (ed.) *Aging in the Year 2000: A Look at the Future. The Gerontologist* 15 (1–Part
        II).
  1975b "The future and the young-old." In Bernice Neugarten (ed.). *Aging in the Year
        2000: A Look at the Future. The Gerontologist* 15 (1–Part II):4–9.
Neugarten, Bernice and Robert Havighurst (eds.)
  1977 *Extending the Human Life Span: Social Policy and Social Ethics.* Washington,
        D.C.: U.S. Government Printing Office.
Palmore, Erdman
  1976 "The future status of the aged." *The Gerontologist* 16:297–302.
Pampel, Fred
  1981 *Social Change and the Aged: Recent Trends in the United States.* Lexington,
        Mass.: Lexington Books.
Peterson, David, Chuck Powell, and Lawrie Robertson
  1976 "Aging in America: Toward the year 2000." *The Gerontologist* 16:264–270.
Rapoport, Rhona and Robert Rapoport
  1975 *Leisure and the Family Life Cycle.* London: Routledge and Kegan Paul.
Seltzer, Mildred
  1975 "The quality of research is strained." *The Gerontologist* 15:503–507.
Shanas, Ethel
  1975 "Discussion." In Bernice Neugarten (ed.). *Aging in the Year 2000: A Look at
        the Future. The Gerontologist* 15 (1–Part II):38.
Strehler, Bernard
  1975 "Implications of aging research for society." *Federation Proceedings* 34:5–8.
Treas, Judith
  1981 "The great American fertility debate: Generational balance and support of the
        aged." *The Gerontologist* 21:98–103.
Trist, Eric
  1976 "Toward a postindustrial culture." In Robert Dubin (ed.). *Handbook of Work,
        Organization, and Society.* Chicago: Rand McNally.
Uhlenberg, Peter
  1977 "Changing structure of the older population of the USA during the twentieth
        century." *The Gerontologist* 17:197–202.
Urban, Hugh and Wayne Watson
  1974 "Response to bridging the gap: Alternative approaches." *The Gerontologist*
        14:530–533.
Zeckhauser, Richard
  1974 "The welfare implications of the extension of life." *The Gerontologist* 14:2–3,
        93, 95.

Index

Abkhasians
  status of aged among, 57–59
  stressless role transitions among, 100
Acceptance
  or denial of death, 324–327
  of impending death, 339–340
Activity theory of aging, 82–83
Age. *See also* Aged; Age stratification;
    Aging; Old age; Older people;
    Socialization
  and alienation, 264–265
  categories, 9
  and conservatism, 265–266
  differences of, 9
  and political attitudes, 264–266
  and political participation, 261–263
Age conflict, and age stratification,
    260–261
Aged. *See also* Age
  age mix of housing for, 238–240
  in America, 63–66
  attitudes toward, 118–119

crimes against, 253–257
of future, 361–364
prestige components of, 57
social movements of, 269–279
status among Abkhasians, 57–59
Age differences
  aging effects, 10–11
  cohort effects, 11–13
  nature of, 358–359
Age Discrimination in Employment Act
    (1967), 139
Age entitlement programs, government,
    311
Age-grading of roles, 68–72
Age-homogeneous groups, 189–190
Age identity, subjective, 115–118
Ageism, 39, 122
Age mix of housing for aged, 238–
    248
Age norms, and socialization, 72–75
Age-related deprivation, 118
Age segregation

Age segregation (*Continued*)
  in cities, 28
  in housing, pro and con, 245–248
Age strata, 68
Age stratification, 18. *See also* Age
  and age conflict, 260–261
  and aging, 105–106
  development, aging, and, 105–106
  model of, 66
Aging. *See also* Age
  and age stratification, 105–106
  and biological change, 30–32
  classical pattern, 35–36
  development, age stratification, and,
      105–106
  and developmental issues, 92–97
  developmental perspective on, 85–92
  development of science of, 2–4
  effects of, 10–11
  and education, 190–192
  and employment barriers, 136–138
  and extended family, 218–225
  and friendship, 118, 233
  in future, 358–374
  and health conditions, 32–35
  and humor, 121
  in literature, 2, 119–120
  and mass media, 120–121
  model of, 66–67
  and modernization, 59–63
  in modern societies, 62–63
  and politics, 259–282
  and postindustrial society, 364–370
  reasons for studying, 6–7
  and religion, 192–195
  and self, 100–103
  sex differences in experience of,
      106–108
  and social networks, 232–238
  and social self, 113
  and stereotypes, 126–130
  and stress, 97–100
  successful, 109–111
  and symbolic interactionism, 18
  and television, 120–121
  and work, 133–138
  and work performance, 134–135
Aging couple, 202–203
  post-parental, 203–204
  retirement, 205–206
Aging effects, 10–11
Alcoholism, 41
Alienation, and age, 264–265
American Association of Retired
      Persons/National Retired Teachers
      Association (AARP/NRTA), 190
American Indian aged, 79–80
Andrus, Ethel Percy, 271
Anger, at impending death, 338–339
Anticipatory grief, 345
Anticipatory socialization, 104
Apartments, old age, 239–242
Ariés, Philippe, 323
Aristotle, 2
Asian-American aged, 78–79
Attitudes
  toward aged, 121–124
  toward death, 324–327
  sources of, 124–126
Automaton, personification of death,
      324

Bargaining, and impending death, 339
Bell, Daniel, 364–365
Bereavement, 343–348
Blacks
  aged, 77–78
  family life, 224
  grandparent role, 226

China, aging in, 62–63
Chronic illness, implications of, 33–35
Chronic organic brain syndrome, 37–40
Citizens Committee for Old Age
      Pensions, 271
City, age segregation in, 28
Cohort Analysis (Glenn), 15
Cohort effects, aging, 11–13

Cohort flow, 68
Community-based services for aged, 249–252, 301–309
Conservatism, 265–266
Cooley, Charles Horton, 113
Counseling, preretirement, 171–173
Cowgill, Donald, 59–61
Creativity, in older people, 38
Crimes against elderly in city, 252–257
Crisis of middle age, 93–94
Cross-sectional study, 14
Cult of old age, 63–64

Death, 319–357
    attitudes toward, 324–327
    bereavement, 343–348
    denial or acceptance of, 324–327
    and life cycle, 327–332
    meanings of, 322–324
    and right to die, 348–355
    and social structure, 324–327
Death system, and funeral, 346–348
de Beauvoir, Simone, 2, 54
Demographic characteristics, 21–52
    life expectancy, 23–25
    older population, 21–23
    place of residence, 27–29
    sex ratio, 25–27
Demographic transition, and life expectancy, 23–25
Denial
    or acceptance of death, 324–327
    of impending death, 338
Denmark, aging in, 63
Dependency ratio, 22
Depression, 40
    and impending death, 339
Depression, Great, 11–12, 141, 310
Deprivation, age-related, 118
Development, aging, and age stratification, 105–106
Developmental issues and successful aging, 92–97

Developmental perspective on aging, 85–92
Disenchantment, retirement phase, 157
Divorce, 206–207
Double jeopardy, 80
Double standard of aging, 107
Drug abuse, 41
Dying
    awareness of, 336–338
    caring for the, 340–343
    reactions of the, 336–340
    reactions to, 338–340
    reactions to the, 332–336
Dying trajectory, 333

Economic status of older people, 42–48
Education
    and aging, 190–192
    of older people, 42–43
Ego development, 92
Ego threat, and stress, 97
Elder, Glen, Jr., 11–12
Elective death, 350
Emotional isolation, and widowhood, 215
Employee Retirement Income Security Act (1974), 167
Employment, barriers to, 136–138
Empty nest syndrome, 203–204
Erikson, Erik, 94
Euthanasia, 348–355
    opposition to, 352–353
    public acceptance of, 353–355
Euthanasia Education Council, 349
Euthanasia Society of America, 349
Extended family, 218–225
    and aging, 228
    older people in, 56–57

Family
    involvement of older people in, 219–224

Family (*Continued*)
  and modernization, 218–219
  variations in structure, 224–225
Family life, 201–230
  aging couple, 202–203
  grandparent role, 225–227
  sexuality in old age, 207–209
  widowhood, 209–217
Fear, and crimes against elderly,
    253–257
Forced retirement, 142–146
Foster Grandparents program, 196
Franklin, Benjamin, 2, 349
Friendship
  and aging, 118
  functions of, 232–234
  and interactions with friends and
    neighbors, 234–235
Friendship networks, and age identity,
    234–238
Functional psychological disorders, 40

Galton, Sir Francis, 3
"Gang visits" of doctors to nursing
    homes, 290
Generations, and social change,
    267–268
Gerontological Society, 4
Gerontology, development of, 4–6
Glenn, Norval, 15
Goffman, Erving, 126
Government, and services for aged,
    309–316
Grandchildren, view of grandparent
    role, 227–228
Grandparent role, 225–227
Great Depression, 11–12, 141
Grief, 343–344
Grief specialists, 347–348
Group consciousness, aging,
    consequences of, 279–281

Hall, G. Stanley, 3
Ham and Eggs Movement, 160

Health, 29–35
  chronic illness, 33–35
  conditions, 32–33
  disability, 33
  older population, 30
Health conditions, older people, 32–35
Herodotus, 6
Hispanic aged, 78
Homophily, 236
Honeymoon, retirement phase, 157
Hospices, 342–343
Housing for aged
  age mix of, 238–248
  age segregation, pro and con,
    245–248
  impact of, 248–249
  old age apartments, 239–242
  retirement communities, 242–245
Humor and aging, 121
Hypochondriasis, 40

Income, and retirement, 159
Indirect and involuntary elective death,
    350
Individual retirement account (IRA),
    167
Industrial society, aging in, 59–66
Infant mortality, and life expectancy,
    24–25
Institutionalization
  of aged, 285–287
  consequences of, 293–298
  impact of, 292–298
  processes leading to, 286–287
  quality of care, 298–301
Intellectual abilities, older people,
    36–38
Interiority of personality, 90–91
International Association of
    Gerontology, 3
Interpersonal threat, and stress, 97
Intrinsic aging effects, 10
Irreversible organic brain syndrome, 40
Israel, aging in, 63

Japan, aging in, 62
Job design and retraining, 135–136
Job-related pensions, 165–160
John XXIII, Pope, 38
Journal of Gerontology, 3

King Lear (Shakespeare), 2
Knowledge, strategic, and status of
    older people, 55
Kübler-Ross, Elisabeth, 338

Labor force participation, 45
Learning capacity versus performance,
    37–38
Leisure, 178–185
    consequences of career, 184–185
    functions of, 182–184
    and life cycle, 178–179
    patterns in old age, 180–182
Leveling, 80
Life cycle, 87–92
    and leisure, 178–179
    and work, 133–134
Life expectancy, and demographic
    transition, 23–25
Life style, and aging, 87–92
Literature
    aging themes in, 2
    old age in, 119–120
Living arrangements, and housing
    quality, 44–45
Loneliness, and widowhood, 214–216
Long-distance migration, 28–29
Longitudinal study, 14
"Looking-glass self," 113

Macabre, personification of death, 323
McLain, George, 271
McLain Movement, 271
Manic reactions, 40
Marital status, older people, 43
Master status trait, old age as, 126

Medicaid, and nursing homes, 288
Medicare, 314–316
    and nursing homes, 288
Meir, Golda, 38
Memory, in older people, 37
Men. *See* Sex differences
Mercy killing, 349
Middle age
    and developmental issues, 93–94
    and relationship to death, 329
Middle knowledge of dying, 337
Minority aged, 75–80
Modernity versus modernization, 59
Modernization
    and aging, 59–63
    and family, 218–219
    model of (Cowgill), 59–61
Mortality revolution, 321
Mourning, 343

National Institute on Aging, 3
Needs hierarchy, 49
NRTA/AARP, 190
Nursing homes
    exposés of, 289–292
    factors affecting quality of care,
        298–301
    and institutionalization of aged,
        285–287
    political economy of, 287–289

Old age. *See also* Age
    defined, 7–9
    developmental issues, 92–97
    in literature, 2, 119–120
    patterns of leisure in, 180–182
    sexuality in, 207–209
    sources of attitudes on, 124–126
    stereotypes of, 126–130
Older Americans Act (1965), 368
Older people. *See also* Age
    alcoholism and drug abuse, 41
    chronic illness implications, 33–35

Older people (*Continued*)
  disability, 33
  education, 42–43
  family involvement of, 219–224
  health, 29–35
  health conditions, 32–33
  intellectual abilities, 36–38
  marital status, 43
  minority, 75–80
  personal experience versus public
    expectations of problems, 50–51
  population of, 21–23
  psychological disorders, 40
  psychological functioning, 35–38
  residence, 27–29
  social and economic characteristics,
    42–48
  suicide, 41–42
Organic brain syndrome (OBS), 40–41
Organic psychological disorders, 40–41

Panel study, 14–15
Paranoid reactions, 40
Party affiliation, 264
Peership, and friendship, 236–238
Pension
  job-related, 165–168
  policy on, 168–169
Performance
  versus learning capacity, 37–38
  work, 134–135
Period effects, aging, 13–14
Personality and aging, 87–92
Physical threat and stress, 97
Picasso, Pablo, 38
Pius XII, Pope, 351
Place of residence, older population,
  27–29
Plato, 2
Policy, and planning for aged, 368–370
Political attitudes
  alienation, 264–265
  conservatism, 265–266
  party affiliation, 264

Political economy of nursing homes,
  287–289
Political interest and commitment,
  262–263
Political leadership, 263
Political participation and aging,
  261–263
Ponce de León, Juan, 2
Population of older people, 21–23
Postindustrial society, 364–370
  policy formulation in, 368–370
Postindustrial values and aging,
  365–368
Poverty, older people and, 46–48
Preindustrial societies, aging in, 53–59
Preparation for retirement, 169–173
Preretirement, 157
Preretirement counseling, 171–173
Property, and status of older people,
  56–57
Psychological disorders, 38–42
Psychological functioning, older people,
  35–38
Psychological orientation and aging,
  87–92

Quételet, 3
Quinlan, Karen, 349

Reactive aging effect, 10–11
Religion and aging, 192–195
Relocation, and institutionalization,
  292–293
Remarriage, 217
Reorientation, retirement phase, 158
Research, methodological issues, 14–17
Retired Senior Volunteer Program
  (RSVP), 195
Retirement, 138–175
  adjustment to, 149–153
  attitudes toward, 147–149
  consequences of, 146–147
  emergence of, 139–142

forced, 142–146
preparation for, 169–173
as process, 156–159
and social role, 156–159
voluntary, 142–146
versus widowhood, 153
Retirement communities, 242–245
Retirement couple, 205–206
Retirement income, 159
and job-related pensions, 165–168
and pension policy, 168–169
and Social Security, 160–165
Retraining and job design, 135–136
Reversible organic brain syndrome,
40–41
Right to die, 348–355
Role, age-grading of, 68–72
Role change, and socialization, 74–75,
103–105

St. Christopher's Hospice, 342
Saunders, Cicely, 342
Self, and aging, 100–103
Self-concept, 114
Self-esteem, and age, 114
Senescence, the Second Half of Life
(Hall), 3
Senior movements, 269
Service Corps of Retired Executives
(SCORE), 195
Services for aged, 283–318
and government, 309–316
Medicare, 314–316
Sex, stratification by, 106
Sex differences
and aging experience, 106–108
and retirement, 152
and widowhood, 216–217
Sex ratio, older people, 25
Sexuality, in old age, 207–209
Singlehood, 206–207
Social change, and use of time, 197–198
and generations, 267–268
Social death, 333–334

Social gerontology, 4–6
future of, 371–374
Socialization. *See also* Age
and age norms, 72–75
and role change, 74–75, 103–105
Social movements of aged, 269–279
Social networks, 232–238
Social Security, 160–165
and retirement, 142–146
Social Security Act (1935), 3, 160
Social time, 8
"Society of widows," 215
Sontag, Susan, 107
Stability, retirement phase, 158
Stereotypes, old age, consequences of,
126–130
Strategic knowledge, and status of aged,
55
Stress, and aging, 97–100
Subculture of aging, 275
Suicide, in older population, 41–42
Symbolic interactionism, and aging, 18,
100

Television
and aging, 120–121
and leisure, 181–182
Terminal drop, theory of, 37
Termination, retirement phase, 158
Time, 176–200
and social change, 197–198
Townsend, Francis, 271
Townsend Movement, 160, 271
Trust fund, Social Security, 163

Voluntary and direct elective death,
350
Voluntary and indirect elective death,
350
Voluntary associations, 186–190
age-homogeneous groups, 189–190
Volunteer role, 195–197
Voting, and age, 261–262

White House Conferences on
    Aging, 3, 272, 369
Widowhood, 209–217
    cultural context, 210–211
    loneliness, 214–216
    personal consequences, 211–212
    and remarriage, 217
    versus retirement, 153
    sex differences, 216–217
    social consequences, 212–214

Women. *See* Sex differences
Work, 132–175
    and aging, 133–138
    degradation, and retirement, 141–
        142
    meaning of, 153–156
Work performance, and aging, 134–
    135
Wright, Frank Lloyd, 38

84 85 86 9 8 7 6 5 4 3 2